Doors
TO THE
Sacred

Newly revised and expanded in light of the *Catechism of the Catholic Church*, and with an expanded resource section, *Doors to the Sacred* remains a detailed account of the historical and cultural evolution of the sacraments—and the rituals and practices associated with them. Since its initial publication, the book has garnered widespread critical acclaim:

"This is an admirably ambitious effort to achieve a summary description of sacramental ritual for a nonspecialized audience."

—America

"The author's extensive research is evident in this valuable reference… written in easy-to-understand language and designed to increase the knowledge of any reader concerned with religious topics. Martos first traces the many kinds of sacraments operative in various religions and shows the differences between Catholic and Protestant observances today….He shows how the sacraments developed and have been adapted to changing circumstances while preserving their innate religious meanings."

—Los Angeles Times

"[Martos] gives an amazing amount of detail and yet never confuses the reader. He even manages to translate the philosophical terminology of medieval sacramental theory into understandable language…."

—National Catholic Reporter

"[A]n important and accessible contribution to modern religious thought."

—The Booklist

"Joseph Martos has produced the first credible comprehensive textbook of sacramental theology in this country since Vatican II….His *Doors to the Sacred* looks like a solid theoretical and historical treatment of the sacraments. Professors of liturgy and religious education will rejoice to see this text."

—Commonweal

DOORS
TO THE
SACRED

A HISTORICAL INTRODUCTION
TO SACRAMENTS
IN THE CATHOLIC CHURCH

VATICAN II GOLDEN ANNIVERSARY EDITION
UPDATED AND ENLARGED WITH CHARTS AND GLOSSARY

Joseph Martos

Liguori
LIGUORI, MISSOURI

Imprimi Potest: Harry Grile, CSsR, Provincial,Denver Province, The Redemptorists

Published by Liguori Publications, Liguori, Missouri 63057.
To order, call 800-325-9521 or visit Liguori.org

Library of Congress Cataloging-in-Publication Data
Martos, Joseph, 1943-
  Doors to the sacred : a historical introduction to sacraments in the Catholic Church : updated and expanded with charts and glossary / Joseph Martos. — Vatican II Golden Anniversary Edition.
    pages cm
  Includes index.
  1. Sacraments—Catholic Church. 2. Catholic Church—Doctrines. I. Title.
  BX2200.M355 2014
  234'.16088282--dc23
                          2014004117

p ISBN: 978-0-7648-2451-7
e ISBN: 978-0-7648-6961-7

Liguori Publications, a nonprofit corporation, is an apostolate of The Redemptorists. To learn more about The Redemptorists, visit Redemptorists.com.

Printed in the United States of America
18 17 16 15 14 / 5 4 3 2 1

To my students past and present,
and to my friends in Barrington,
who taught me the importance of
meeting people where they are.

And to Bernard Lonergan,
who helped me to see
how they get there.

CONTENTS

FOLDOUT: TIMELINE OF CHURCH HISTORY

PREFACE

It has been over thirty years since I began doing the research that led to the writing of the first edition of this book. At that time, I made a decision not to include footnotes to the sources of my information because I was writing the book primarily for students, and I knew that students usually don't take the time to read footnotes. In subsequent editions, I followed the same practice, but readers who are interested in learning where the historical information in these pages comes from can find it in the books listed under the heading, "For Further Study," in the annotated bibliographies, especially under the subheading, "History," if there is one. As a young writer, one of my greatest worries was that critics would find errors of fact and misinterpretations of theology in what I had written, but to my great relief, the initial book reviews were laudatory, as have been the reviews of the subsequent editions. Looking back, I have come to realize that the difference between plagiarism and research is that plagiarism means stealing information from just one source, and that research means stealing from many sources.

In the subsequent editions, spaced roughly ten years apart, I added information about developments in sacramental practice and theology during the previous decade. The 1991 edition included information about the Rite of Christian Initiation of Adults and the permanent diaconate, for example, which were implemented in the United States in the 1980s, and the 2001 edition included what the *Catechism of the Catholic Church* (published in English in 1994) says about sacraments. On the theological side, postmodern approaches and liturgical theology were not in the first edition but were added when they became part of the academic scene. In this edition, I have paid more attention to the concerns of Pope John Paul II and Pope Benedict XVI in reining in what they perceived as excesses in liturgical creativity and aberrations in sacramental theology. Recent developments such as the introduction of the third edition of *The Roman Missal*

(© 2010 International Commission on English in the Liturgy Corporation) have been applauded by conservatives and lamented by liberals, but it is still too soon to tell how church rituals and their interpretation will be affected under Pope Francis and subsequent pontiffs.

The initial audience for this book was students who had grown up as Catholics before Vatican II and who were therefore curious to know how the church's sacraments could change so drastically in a few decades after having remained stable for centuries. As one religious educator noted shortly after the council, if a sailor on one of Columbus' ships had gone to confession before leaving land, and if an astronaut in the space program had gone to confession before leaving earth, they both would have used the same rite of penance. The world had changed and so the church was going through some updating, but Catholics at the time needed assurance that change is acceptable because it had happened many times prior to the sacramental stability imposed by the Council of Trent in the sixteenth century.

The audience for this latest edition, published fifty years after the Second Vatican Council, is still largely students, but now they are mostly people who have grown up in the post-Vatican II church. As a result, they lack some of the background knowledge that an earlier generation of readers brought to the book. Maps of the ancient and medieval worlds were included in the second edition, and this edition goes further to include a historical timeline foldout and a glossary of philosophical and theological terms to make for easier reading and better comprehension of a subject that covers continents and spans millennia. If you are unfamiliar with church history, it would be helpful for you to look over the timeline foldout that appears between pages 316 and 317 to get a sense of the major periods (e.g., patristic era, Middle Ages, modern era) through which the Catholic sacraments and their theology developed. If you are unfamiliar with Catholic theology, you would benefit from looking at the glossary on page 547, not to memorize these terms in advance, but to see which words can be looked up if necessary when you come across them while doing the reading. For an overview of each chapter, you can listen to my lectures at TheSacraments.org (click on "Related works available online") or at Liguori.org/doorstothesacred.

In scholarly publications, the purpose of bibliographies is to document the sources of information presented, but in this book the purpose is educational and suggestive. Because it is now quite easy, using online booksellers and databases such as WorldCat, to find complete bibliographical data about any book, the bibliographies found at the end of each chapter provide titles but not subtitles, and they name the publisher but not the place of publication. When feasible, titles have been grouped under subheadings to help readers pursue further research in specific areas of interest, and the one-sentence description of each book is meant to help them get a sense of what various authors are saying. You will notice that the authors are not listed in alphabetical order, but in one of two ways: either the most important books to read are listed first regardless of date of publication, or the books are listed according to the date of publication to give a sense of how the treatment of topics has evolved over the past five decades. You could say that the annotated bibliographies are meant to be read as a supplement to what is found in the chapters as well as to be a guide For Further Reading and study.

JOSEPH MARTOS
LOUISVILLE, KENTUCKY

HISTORY AND SACRAMENTS

*Theology and other branches of knowledge, especially those of a historical
nature, must be taught with due regard for the ecumenical point of view,
so that they may correspond more exactly with the facts.*
—Second Vatican Council

All history involves interpretation. There was a time when historians believed that their task was simply to discover the past and to put it down on paper the way it really happened. This is still the idea of history that many people have. Historians themselves, however, have come to the conclusion that written history is never that simple. The history that is found in books (including this one) always involves selection and interpretation: selection because no book can record the past in all its minute detail, and interpretation because no historian can avoid trying to explain why things happened the way they did. History as written is always an attempt to interpret and explain the past, as well as record it.

This does not mean that written history is not objective. Objectivity in history means trying to find an interpretation that really fits the facts, and so a lot depends on the number and kind of facts that are available. When new facts are brought to light by the uncovering of ancient ruins or the recovery of lost manuscripts, sometimes history has to be rewritten. The natural sciences follow the same procedure: when scientific research results in new discoveries, sometime the old theories have to be revised or replaced by new ones that fit the facts that are now available. For in the long run, the objectivity of history and science depends on the objectivity of historians and scientists, that is, upon their ability to discover the relevant facts and to develop an explanation of how they fit together.

Until the mid-twentieth century, the Roman Catholic Church's understanding of its seven sacraments was largely independent of historical facts. According to one definition, sacraments were "signs instituted by Christ to give grace," even though there was little evidence in the scriptures that Jesus of Nazareth actually instructed his followers to perform some of these rituals. And the sacramental rituals themselves were assumed to have remained substantially unchanged for nineteen hundred years, even though there was no direct evidence that this was actually so. Yet it is not as though Catholic theologians intentionally decided to ignore historical facts in developing their explanations of the sacraments. Many of the facts were simply unknown, buried in the archives of the Vatican and other old libraries. More importantly, though, the reason they did not bother to dig through these documents was that they believed that the truths of faith were changeless and unaffected by history.

But historical research in the nineteenth century made Catholics begin to reevaluate this position, and by the early twentieth century it was generally accepted that many of the Roman church's beliefs and practices had indeed changed through the years. Changed practices presented little difficulty. Catholics believed that the church was entitled to modify its ecclesiastical regulations and adapt its forms of worship to the customs of different peoples, provided of course that nothing essential was altered. And changed teachings could be understood as doctrinal development. Catholics believed that the church, under the guidance of the Holy Spirit, was becoming more aware of the fullness of divine revelation. Thus, what was perhaps only implicit in scripture could in the course of time become an explicit part of the church's doctrines. Likewise, anything that was tacitly accepted throughout the church's history could, if need be, become an explicitly proclaimed doctrine. In short, Catholics admitted a certain amount of doctrinal development, but this development was considered to be an evolution from less perfect to more perfect formulations of Christian doctrines.

During this period, then, historical differences in the theology of the sacraments were usually regarded as stages in the evolution of the church's understanding of its sacramental rituals, with the doctrinal pronouncements of the Council of Trent in the sixteenth century being considered final and normative for all subsequent centuries. Historical accounts of the sacraments were accordingly written from a terminal point of view: the Catholic Church has finally arrived at the best understanding of the sacraments, but we can go back in history to discover how it came to these truths. Moreover, this terminal point of view often led to the assumption that the most recent customs in sacramental practice were likewise the best since they too were the result of a long evolution under the guidance of the Holy Spirit.

As historical studies continued into the twentieth century, however, they began to suggest that this model for interpreting changes in the Catholic Church's beliefs and practices was inadequate. Scripture scholars began to regard many of the things that previous theologians had found implicit in scripture as the reading of later ideas into earlier texts. Historians began to discover that some of the perennial practices of the church were not nearly as ancient as they were once thought to be. And liturgical experts began to awaken suspicions that the latest sacramental rituals were not always the best for the contemporary church, especially since they had undergone little change since the Renaissance.

The Second Vatican Council in the mid-1960s and the liturgical reforms of the subsequent decade did much to revise the Catholic Church's sacramental practices, immediately by allowing them to be performed in other languages besides Latin, and later by redesigning the sacramental rituals themselves. A real effort was made both to update the sacraments and to incorporate the insights of biblical, historical, and liturgical research into the new rites. And at the same time, Catholic theologians were concerned about showing that the revised rites represented not a break from tradition but a recovery of older traditions.

But if the previous model for explaining the historical changes in the sacraments has been found inadequate—the developmental model of moving continuously from the less perfect to the more perfect—what other model can be adopted? It must be one that can account for the historical facts that we have now come to know. For Catholics it must be one that both acknowledges the validity of previous traditions and allows for the possibility of growing beyond those traditions. For ecumenists it must be one that looks at the past with a critical eye, simply trying to understand why things happened the way they did and not always trying to justify the Roman Catholic position. And for humanists it must be one that is open to both a theistic and a natural explanation of the sacraments without demanding acceptance of any theological justification for them. In a word, the model must account for the internal evolution of sacramental theory and practice without appealing to external causes such as divine providence, and yet it must remain open to that further interpretation by believers and theologians.

That such a model is available can be learned from looking at books and articles that have been written about the history or theology of the sacraments in Catholicism. Many of the authors utilize this model without expressly adverting to it, particularly in their studies of individual sacraments. And it has become so commonplace that in one form or another it can be found even in textbooks and audiovisual materials produced for religious education. Basically the model is an application of the notion that experience gives rise to ideas which bring about changes in behavior and experience, which in turn suggest new ideas that lead to new experiences, and so on. To say it more simply, the things that people do influence what they think, and what they think influences what they do.

Applying this basic notion now to the history of theology we can say very broadly that the religious experience of the early Christian community gave rise to theological ideas which influenced the religious experiences of Christians in the Roman Empire, and that those experiences in turn generated ideas which affected the religious experiences of Christians in medieval Europe, and so forth. More specifically with regard to the sacraments, we shall see that the sacramental experiences of Christians in one period of history generated a sacramental theology which in turn influenced the sacramental experiences of Christians in a later period, when the process repeated itself.

Needless to say, the actual historical process of sacramental experience affecting sacramental theology affecting sacramental experience (and so forth) was hardly ever as neat and simple as this basic notion. Above all, it has not been a straight-line development. There have been dead ends and untried paths. There have been radical turning points and there have been places where no turns were possible. There has been some backtracking, and even some going around in circles. Nor is it true that the sacraments were immune from political and cultural influences. But these generalizations will have to suffice until we examine the history of sacramental practice and theory more closely.

The single thread, then, which runs through this book and ties all the chapters together is this notion that ideas and experiences, thinking and doing, theory and practice, mutually influence each other over the course of time. This is the principle that we shall be using to develop an interpretation of the Catholic sacraments, which I believe is both true to the facts of history and faithful to the basic teachings of Christianity.

There are also some fundamental assumptions on which this book is based, and it might be good to mention them in this introduction.

One is that religious experience, and specifically sacramental religious experience, is a genuine human experience. It is not an aberration or distortion of consciousness which somehow removes one from reality. For those who have had it, it is as real as fear and as important as love. It is also a common (although perhaps not universal) human experience. It is not restricted to primitive peoples and it is not exclusive to religious fanatics. And though there are a variety of such experiences and an even greater diversity in the descriptions of them, there is a sameness that often pervades these descriptions and makes it possible to recognize one's own experience in the words of another person. Whether one ascribes these experiences to God or to a god or to some natural cause is a matter of further interpretation. But religious experience, or the experience of the sacred, is as transpersonal and as transcultural as the experience of joy or of sorrow. In other words, sacramental experiences are things that happen to people, and so they have a place in a work of history; they can be historical facts.

The second assumption is that the Catholic understanding of the word "sacrament" can be broadened, and it has to be broadened if we are going to use the model mentioned earlier to explain the history of the sacraments. Not long ago the term "sacrament" in Catholic theology referred exclusively to seven liturgical rites. Since the Second Vatican Council, Catholic theologians have expanded the meaning of the term so that it can be applied to Christ and to the church as well. But before the Middle Ages it had an even broader meaning, and it is this meaning of "sacrament" that we shall have to use if we are to develop an understanding of the sacraments that can cover the past twenty centuries and be open to developments in future centuries. By doing so we shall be able to regard the narrower theological definitions of the term "sacrament" as authentic Catholic applications of this broader meaning, while retaining the broader meaning when talking about sacraments in other religions and about other "unofficial" sacraments in Christianity.

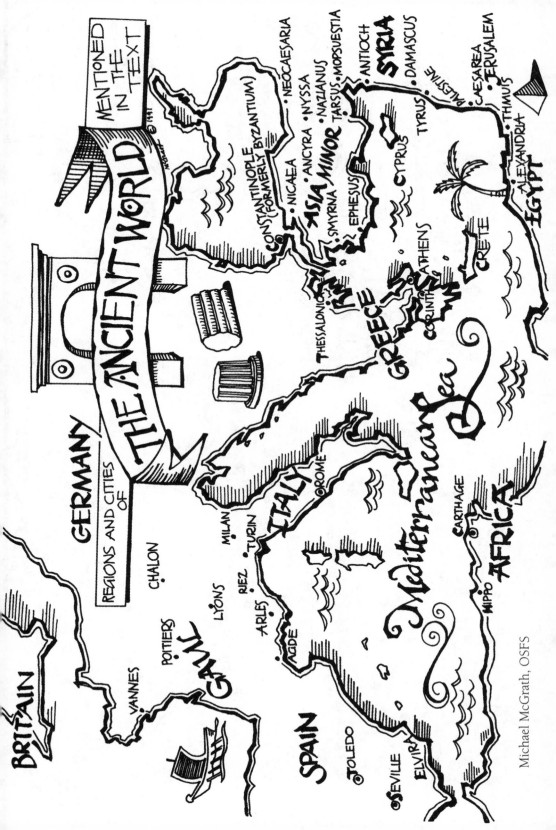

Michael McGrath, OSFS

Part One

A HISTORY OF SACRAMENTS

CHAPTER I

SACRAMENTS IN ALL RELIGIONS

People cannot be united in any religion, whether it be true or false, unless they are brought together through a common sharing of some visible signs or sacraments; and the power of these sacraments is so effective that scorning them is considered sacrilegious.

—Saint Augustine

Any object or event is sacramental in which the transcendent is perceived to be present. Sacramental objects are holy objects, laden with divine power.

—Paul Tillich

Surprising as it may seem to Roman Catholics, every religion in the world makes use of sacraments. No other religion calls them sacraments, but this is because no other religion has borrowed its theological words from classical and medieval Latin.

1. The Meaning of Sacrament

The term "sacrament" comes from the Latin word *sacramentum*. In pre-Christian times a *sacramentum* was a pledge of money or property that was deposited in a temple by parties to a lawsuit or contract, and that was forfeited by the one who lost the suit or broke the contract. It later came to mean an oath of allegiance made by soldiers to their commander and the gods of Rome. In either case, the *sacramentum* involved a religious ceremony in a sacred place.

3

Christian writers in the second century AD borrowed the term and used it to talk to their Roman contemporaries about the ceremony of Christian initiation. They explained that baptism was something like the *sacramentum* administered to new recruits—it was a ritual through which people began a new life of service to God. Then as Christianity replaced polytheism in the empire, the original Roman usage of the word disappeared and the Christian usage expanded. By the time of St. Augustine in the fifth century, any sacred symbol or ceremony could be called a *sacramentum*. Although the word was still used primarily in regard to the ceremony of initiation, it could also be applied to blessings, liturgical feasts, and holy objects. Indeed Augustine once defined *sacramentum* as "a sign of a sacred reality," and he noted that according to this general definition anything in the world could be considered a sacrament since all of creation was a sign of God. Christian usage in later centuries became more restricted, however, and by the twelfth century the word was applied only to the seven church rituals known to Catholics as *the* sacraments. And after the sixteenth century the usage of the word was restricted still further by those Protestants who limited the number of sacraments to fewer than seven.

Nevertheless, the term has not been the exclusive property of the Christian churches. "Sacrament" has been used in fiction and poetry, meaning a sign or symbol, and "sacramental" has been used with the meaning of symbolic or sacred. And in the field of religious studies the word is sometimes used as a general term for anything that represents a hidden reality that is sacred or mysterious. Understood in this sense, "sacrament" has a very Augustinian, almost universal applicability. Any ritual or object, person or place, can be considered sacramental if it is taken to be a symbol of something that is sacred or mysterious. And there is nothing in the universe that cannot be taken as a symbol of something else.

Moreover, what is sacred and mysterious does not have to be supernatural or divine, even though it might be. What a sacrament symbolizes is always sacred in the sense that it is precious or important, and it is always mysterious in the sense that it is not fully understood. But whether or not a sacrament symbolizes something that is beyond the human realm is an open question. Those who prefer a natural explanation tend to reduce what is symbolized to something that is purely human (for example, it is something valuable to society). Those who prefer a supernatural explanation tend to ascribe what is symbolized to a transcendent order (for example, it is something revealed by God).

Whichever explanation is preferred, "sacrament" can still be broadly defined as a sign or symbol of something that is sacred and mysterious. And if sacraments are understood in this broader sense, then the religions of the world are full of sacraments. Every religion has places and actions, objects, and even persons which are symbolic of some mysterious realities that are sacred to that religion. Sacred places may be temples or churches, mountains or rivers, shrines or cities. Sacred actions may be praying or singing, eating or fasting, dancing or meditating, stylized rituals or spontaneous gestures. Sacred objects may be pictures or statues, vestments or vessels, tools or writings, food or drink, crafted or natural. Sacred persons may be priests or victims, kings or saints, shamans or virgins, gurus or prophets.

So it is that Christians assemble in churches, that Hindus bathe in the Ganges, that Muslims make pilgrimages to Mecca. So it is that monks kneel and chant, that Jews eat a Passover meal, that Polynesians dance, and Quakers sit still. So it is that Catholics kneel before a crucifix, that tribal shamans wear special clothing, that Protestants cherish the Bible, that Buddhists abstain from meat. But none of these places are visited, none of these actions are performed, none of these objects are revered because of what they are in themselves. In themselves they are just locations, activities, things. But they point to or symbolize something beyond themselves— something mysterious, something that cannot be seen, something special. And in this respect they are all sacraments, symbols of something else that is mysterious and hidden, sacred and holy.

In the social sciences that study religion there are two general ways of looking at sacraments in this broader sense. Anthropologists tend to favor a sociological interpretation and historians of religion tend to favor a psychological interpretation, but these are not mutually exclusive or opposed to each other. In fact they can be considered complementary ways of looking at a rather complex human reality that is both social and psychological. Sacramental rituals in particular are usually social ceremonies, and all sacraments are designed to affect the thoughts and feelings of those who believe in them.

Theological interpretations of the meaning and reality of sacraments can be regarded in much the same way. Some would regard the explanations given by social scientists as opposed or contradictory to the explanations given by religious people themselves. After all, they argue, don't those scientific explanations tend to reduce the divine to the human level? And how can nonbelievers really understand what can only be known by faith? But the scientific and theological explanations of sacraments can also be considered complementary rather than contradictory. For sacraments can also be understood as complex realities that are both human and divine. And someone who admits that there is something very human about sacraments, but who also believes that they point to something transcendent, can take the position that the social and psychological aspects of sacraments fall within the scientific study of religion, but their transcendent aspects fall within the province of theology. Of course this neat theoretical distinction is not always observed in practice, but this does not deny that the distinction can be made. And that it has also been observed in practice is a matter of record.

2. Sacramental Rituals

Arnold van Gennep, early in the twentieth century, was one of the first anthropologists to interpret sacramental "rites of passage" as ceremonies that publicly symbolize a change in a person's social status. An adolescent who participates in a puberty ritual passes, in the eyes of the tribe, from childhood into adulthood. A candidate who is consecrated king or queen becomes, through the ordination ceremony, recognized and accepted as monarch by the subjects of the realm. Two people who participate in a wedding ceremony become, in their own minds and in the minds of their society, a married couple with all the privileges and responsibilities that their culture bestows on them.

In various cultures there are also rites of passage surrounding birth (passing into society) and death (passing out of it), as well as rituals for receiving or relinquishing property, for transferring into a different tribe or clan, for joining a special group or caste, for regaining health, and so on. In traditional cultures these transition rituals are religious ceremonies; in modern secular cultures vestiges of them remain in civil ceremonies and customs that range in formality from baby showers to presidential inaugurations, and that range in solemnity from fraternity initiations to funeral services. But they are all social rituals that publicly dramatize some change in social status.

Anthropologists and sociologists since van Gennep have also recognized that sometimes rituals do not dramatize a change in status but instead solemnize some permanent reality or value. These "rites of celebration" (like wedding anniversaries or Independence Day parades) often commemorate changes that have occurred in the past (the marriage or the revolution), but their primary focus is on the social reality that is always present but sometimes forgotten. Rather than being transition rituals, they are intensification rituals—ceremonies that call to mind beliefs and intensify values that are held by those who participate in them. In religious cultures, prayers and sacrificial offerings often commemorate the community's perpetual dependence on the deity; in secular cultures, singing the national anthem can be a reminder of a nation's values, and chanting with the cheerleaders can intensify the fans' belief that their team is the best.

Since the mid-twentieth century, Catholic theologians and educators have leaned heavily on this type of sociological analysis in explaining the meaning and function of sacraments in their church. They have suggested that sacramental ceremonies can be understood as symbolic expressions of sacred realities that are recognized and accepted by those who have faith. For example, they would say that baptism signifies a cleansing from sin and a reception into the Christian community. Likewise, the eucharist symbolizes the presence of Christ and the unity of the church in his body. And the marriage ceremony is a sign of a real change in the relationship of two persons to each other, to God, and to society. The realities symbolized are social realities because they are recognized and accepted by the believing community, but at the same time they are transcendent realities because their author and cause is God. Finally, the theological interpretation is viewed as complementary to the sociological one: it completes and goes beyond what can be learned about sacraments from sociology.

There is no doubt that the seven Catholic sacraments—and sacraments in other religions—can be understood in this way. It gives a good explanation of how common beliefs and values function in a social group, but it is not so clear about how they function within the mind of the individual believer. It helps us to understand how religious beliefs get expressed in sacramental rituals, but it is not so helpful for understanding how participating in such rituals generates and confirms beliefs. As an interpretation of social rituals it can be applied to those sacraments that are rituals—but what about sacred objects, places, and persons? And while it can offer to explain the sacraments as social experiences, it does little to help us understand them as religious experiences. To explore these other aspects of sacraments, therefore, it is necessary to turn from the sociology of religion to the psychology of religion.

3. Sacred Space, Sacred Time, Sacred Meaning

Later in the twentieth century, religion scholar Mircea Eliade analyzed how sacramental rites and objects function in a variety of religions and cultures from the most ancient to the most contemporary. For him, the key to understanding how sacraments work can be found in the descriptions that religious people give of their own religious experiences and in the explanations that they give for the sacraments they believe in. Very often these descriptions and explanations are given in mythic language, that is, in words that tell a story about the origin of the ritual or that picture how a sacred object or place is connected to a divine power. By comparing hundreds of these accounts from religions all over the world, Eliade discovered what seem to be permanent features of sacramental experiences in any religion past or present.

The most important of these features is that sacraments in all religions function as "doors to the sacred," that is, as invitations to religious or spiritual experiences. He calls such experiences "hierophanies," coined from the Greek words *hieros*, meaning sacred or holy, and *phaino*, meaning to manifest or reveal. A hierophany, then, is a manifestation of the sacred, an experienced revelation of the holy. Having such an experience is like entering into another dimension of space and time, and discovering a whole new world of meaning. The space is sacred space, the time is sacred time, the meaning is sacred meaning. Whether or not it is actually an experience of another dimension of reality—a transcendent dimension—is an open question. But the experience as a human experience is objectively real, testified to by Australian aborigines and European mystics alike.

Eliade offers a general psychological description of such religious and spiritual experiences, although he prefers to call his descriptions phenomenological rather than psychological. He wants to describe the phenomena that people experience without suggesting that they are ultimately just psychological. They may be just that, or their explanation may be ultimately supernatural. But simply describing the experiences as they appear to those who have them does not prejudice the case either way. In any event, to those who have had such experiences Eliade's descriptions are clear, and those who read them are free to add their own theological or non-theological interpretations.

According to Eliade, then, sacraments allow a person to enter into a religious or spiritual dimension of human existence. They occasion a transformation of consciousness, an alteration of a person's experience of space and time, in which things become imbued with new meaning and value. It is possible to summarize what Eliade says about the main features of sacramental experiences by talking about sacred space, sacred time, and sacred meaning.

Sacred space is experientially different from ordinary space. Our experience of space is ordinarily very homogeneous: it makes no difference whether we are here or there. We may be in a different place, but our experience of the space we inhabit is always the same: it is just space, plain ordinary space. At times, though, we go to a certain place and the space literally feels different. We enter a towering cathedral or a national shrine or a funeral parlor or the home of our childhood, and suddenly the space we find ourselves in is charged with significance. At other times something happens right where we are, and the space around us is transformed. We fall in love, and the space we inhabit becomes vibrant and alive; or we lose our job, and the space around us becomes silent and oppressing. And sometimes when we remember past events we have an internal sense that we are there again, in that special space that surrounded that event, rather than in the ordinary space that surrounds us now.

In sacramental experiences this same sort of thing happens. Catholics go to Rome, Jews go to Jerusalem, Muslims go to Mecca, and especially at the shrines the space feels different from the space at home. A religious person reading her scriptures is reminded that God is everywhere, and suddenly she finds herself in sacred space. During a religious service, even in a secular setting like a classroom or a park, those who really enter into it feel the sacredness of the space around them—a sacredness it did not have before the liturgy began. When a person experiences a hierophany, then, he or she no longer has the experience of being in a place that is just the same as every other place. Somehow the surrounding space becomes different, imbued with significance. During the hierophany the person is transported, as it were, from ordinary, unimportant, homogeneous space into sacred space, space that is experienced as special and meaningful.

Sacred time is as different from ordinary time as sacred space is from ordinary space. Ordinarily our experience of time is rather continuous. Sometimes we are busy and the time passes quickly; sometimes we are bored and it seems to drag. But it is always the same time, it is always passing, and one moment seems just like the next. But on certain occasions our consciousness of time is altered and we enter a special time, a sacred moment. Sometimes the moment is longed for, like the moment our child is born; sometime the moment is dreaded, like the moment our parent dies. But when the moment arrives, time feels different. The time spent with a close friend is often precious and experienced as such, especially when meetings are infrequent. And the time that we have to ourselves is also sometimes sacred. On other occasions our experience of time is changed even further, for it is a time when time seems to stand still. We remember when…and suddenly then is now. We feel we are back again in that time, or that the past has been brought into the present. That moment is once again with us, and we are once again in it. And it lingers; it does not pass. And it can be repeated; over and over and over again it is the same moment. It can be a moment of triumph or a moment of tragedy, a moment of fear or a moment of discovery, but it is now as real to us as it ever was. And it is always the same time: that special time, that sacred time.

In sacramental experiences the time that is experienced is similarly sacred. It can be experienced as a precious time, and it can even be experienced as a participation in an eternal moment. In prayer or meditation it can happen that a person almost tastes the value of the time being spent. At a baptism or wedding a devout Catholic can sense the sacredness of the occasion. And five times a day a pious Muslim can feel the sacredness of sacred time approaching, for they are the times of the required prayers. Moreover, there are sacramental occasions when a person passes through a sacred ritual and enters into a time which is not now but then. The tribesman chants his history of the world's creation and he feels himself there, in the beginning. The woman dances her myth of how the gods first taught her people how to till the soil, and she experiences that time as her own. But that "then" is always "now"; it is an eternal present. It is a moment that can be made present by symbolic rituals or words. The Catholic hears the words of consecration and the sacrifice of Calvary is brought into the present. The Protestant reads the Bible and the eternal truth is timelessly present. The tribal doctor mixes herbs in the proper ritual and the healing power that they were given in the past is released into the present. When a person experiences a hierophany, then, he or she experiences time as different, special, charged with importance. And sometimes the person is transfixed in another time altogether. It is a time when something meaningful happened, and suddenly once again that time is now.

In a way, sacred space is spaceless space, and sacred time is timeless time. When the nomad in search of a new home thrusts his stake into the ground and declares, "This is the center of the world!" he is not speaking of physical space but of meaningful space. The next place he performs the same ritual will be in a physically different place, but it will again become the center of his meaningful living space. And when the wandering Catholic visits a church during her vacation, she finds herself in the same sacred space that she found in her parish church. Sacred space is independent of place. Likewise when the ancients annually relived the creation of the cosmos in their new year festivals, they were celebrating the beginning not of chronological time but of meaningful time. Their festival was a reaffirmation of meaningful existence, which is why the time it spoke of could be entered into time and time again. And when the preacher proclaims, "We are saved by the blood of the Lamb!" the claim is being made that the time of salvation is not restricted to a moment in history; rather, that time is now. Sacred time is independent of duration.

Sacred meaning is meaning that is experienced as significant or valuable. The mental world we each live in is filled with meanings—ideas, suggestions, thoughts, opinions, facts, beliefs, judgments, evaluations. We get them from our parents and we pick them up in school, we need them for our work and recreation, we are bombarded with them by the media, and we even come up with some of our own. Usually they just come and go: we think something and then go on to think something else. Occasionally, though, some meaning is experienced as more valuable than others. In an emergency our knowledge of first aid becomes important to us, for example. Or we are struggling with a problem, and when the solution is found we are drenched with delight. More often, however, the meaning that is experienced as significant is an ideal rather than an idea, or an end rather than a means. We hear a speech that touches our ideals and something stirs deep within us. We see a film that reflects our hopes and aspirations and our feelings about them are intensified. Psychologically, too, there are meanings that are important for each of us. We all need to feel accepted, and it is good to feel needed. If we are to accomplish anything we must feel capable, and if we are to love we must feel loved. Finally, there are meanings that are important for the society we live in, and occasionally we sense how really important they are. Loyalty, honesty, courage, friendship—these are all value-laden meanings. So a meaning can be sacred to us because it is wanted, or because it gives direction to our lives, or because it gives us a sense of worth, or because it holds our world together.

A meaning can be sacred simply because it is significant to us personally, because it is associated with some significant person or place or event in our life such as a parent or teacher, a home or city, a vacation or wedding. We meet an old friend, and what we once meant to each other suddenly reappears in our relationship. We visit a special place from our past, and we recall what our life meant when we were there last. We rummage through the attic, and something we find brings back cherished memories and precious feelings. But a meaning can also be sacred because it is significant to us as a member of a group; it is one of the meanings that is important to us all. A family Bible, a club insignia, a school song, a national flag—each of these can revivify a meaning that is important to many people. For the most common way of entering into the experience of sacred meaning is through symbols, and symbols can be anything: gestures or actions, natural or manufactured objects, spoken or written words, pictures or sounds, persons or places. But what the symbol does is draw us out of the world of our everyday concerns and into a world of meaning that is associated with the symbol.

In this sense symbols are, or at least can be, sacraments. Some symbols never affect us; they never draw us into their world of sacred meaning. But others do, and these are the sacramental symbols. They are the occasion for a hierophany, a manifestation of something that is holy and mysterious. They are doors to sacred meaning.

In sacramental experiences, then, the meaning that is encountered is sacred meaning. It is meaningful meaning. In a personal experience it makes *my* life meaningful. In a social experience it makes *our* life meaningful. But sacred meaning, when it is experienced, is also mysterious. We do not fully comprehend it. We enter into it, we participate in it, we live it during the hierophany. Through the experiential living of that meaning we certainly understand it somewhat, but we do not understand it completely. This is why sacraments are said to be, or to reveal, mysteries. What they are symbolic of, what they refer to, is something that is experienced and dimly understood, but not fully comprehended.

Moreover, the meaning that is experienced in the sacramental event is experienced as discovered, as encountered. It is not felt to be artificial or imposed on the symbol. The meaning seems to come not from us but from or through the sacrament. It radiates out of the sacramental object or illuminates the sacramental ritual from within. It is experienced as something that is simply given, within the sacramental event. In that sense it is gratuitous; the sacred meaning does not have to appear, it does not have to be experienced. So when it does appear it is felt to be a gift, a grace. The experienced effect of the sacrament is experienced as somehow caused by something or someone else than the person who is having the experience.

Of course, sacramental symbols do not always have a profound experiential effect on those who see them or otherwise perceive them. People must believe in the effectiveness of sacraments in order for them to be effective. They must look at their sacred signs with the conviction that they can indeed have the kind of effect that they are supposed to have. Without such a conviction the sacrament can be a sterile symbol that signifies something but that does not generate a living experience of meaning. Or the experience can be minimal, like an intellectual awareness of a sacred meaning that is not fully felt. So faith and beliefs also play a role in the effectiveness of sacraments: faith in the effectiveness of the sacraments, and beliefs that specify the effects that each sacrament is supposed to have. Without the needed faith, sacraments signify but they do not effect; without the needed beliefs, the effects of the sacraments cannot be specified. In brief, faith is the key that opens the doors to the sacred.

4. A Variety of Rituals

Since the experience of sacred meaning is also connected with beliefs, it is hard to talk about the meanings of sacraments in different religions without getting specific about their beliefs. It is possible, however, to look at general kinds of sacraments and take note of the general kinds of meanings that these sacraments symbolize. Eliade points out that even in different religions the same kinds of symbols often generate the same kinds of hierophanies. Thus, for example, the sky is usually a symbol of transcendence, stones are often symbols of permanence, and plants are frequently symbols of life. Moreover, since our concern is ultimately with the sacraments in the Catholic religion, and since these are primarily symbolic rites, it is possible to limit ourselves to a brief look at some general kinds of sacramental rituals.

Water Rituals. Rituals that involve the use of water often signify life and growth, or cleansing and purification. In myths about the creation of the world, water is sometimes pictured as the element out of which other things are formed, for water itself is formless and all living things have liquid in them. In pre-Columbian Mexico women bathed newborn children and dedicated them to the goddess of the waters who gave them life. Ancient Greeks used water to wash away guilt, and Romans used it to wash away madness. Muslims even today purify themselves before entering a mosque by washing their hands and face. And Hindus bathe in the Ganges to experience physical and spiritual regeneration.

Rituals of Initiation. Among some desert tribes, newborn children are sprinkled with water as a sign of welcome into the community. Jews since the days of Abraham have circumcised their male infants as a sign of their belonging to the people of the covenant. In tribal cultures adolescents are usually initiated into the duties and responsibilities of adulthood through ritual instructions and testings and celebrations that sometimes take days or even weeks. Young Hindus begin their journey along the four stages of life by receiving a sacred cord and beginning a long period of religious instruction. In many cultures there are select or secret societies whose members are initiated into the meaning and purpose of each society through various ordeals and rites. In all such initiation rituals, those who administer them reaffirm the meaningful values in their lives, while those who participate in them are introduced to those same values.

Ritual Meals. Sharing food is frequently a sign of acceptance and communion among those who partake of sacred meals, but it can also be a sign and a means of experiencing spiritual strengthening. In primitive hunting cultures where food is scarce, the sharing of food is quite literally a sharing of life. Among agricultural peoples, harvest festivals celebrate a common accomplishment as well as thanksgiving to the mysterious realities that make food and life possible. Feasts in honor of ancestors or gods are often a means of spiritual communion with them. The Aztecs used to eat a bread made in the image of one of their gods in order to receive divine life and experience its qualities. Wine and other intoxicants were often used in primitive and ancient cultures as a means of experientially communing with gods or feeling their power. One of the purposes of the Japanese tea ceremony is the achieving of spiritual communion between host and guest.

Ritual Sacrifices. Ceremonial offerings of food, property, or even human beings often dramatize a people's feeling of dependence, and symbolize their thankfulness for what they have received. The ancient Israelites were expected to offer the firstborn of their flocks and the first fruits of their harvest to Yahweh each year, and similar practices can usually be found in other herding and farming cultures. Since blood is a sign of life, the shedding of blood is frequently an essential part of sacrificial rites. The drinking of blood can symbolize a sharing in life-giving power, and the sharing of blood can unite participants in a common spiritual bond. At times the object sacrificed represents something hateful or evil, and so its destruction symbolizes its elimination from society. At other times it represents the person or group offering the sacrifice and its destruction symbolizes absolute obedience to a god or its demands.

Atonement Rituals. Sacrifices are sometimes a means of making atonement or reparation for violations of a moral code. Cleansing with water and other rites of purification can also be sacramental means of restoring a relationship when they symbolize the washing away of an attitude that impairs that relationship. Prayer is sometimes an atonement ritual, when the purpose of the prayer is to seek forgiveness. In primitive cultures diseases and disasters are often seen as signs of divine displeasure, and sacramental rituals are employed to bring the participants back into harmony with the divine will. Confessions of guilt, as well as public lamentations, were sometimes required as conditions of atonement in ancient Middle Eastern cultures such as Israel. Finally, societies that have rituals for solemnizing contractual agreements between persons have rituals of reconciliation and reparation for reinstating an agreement that has been violated.

Healing Rituals. Health is an important human value, and so in traditional religious cultures when health is lost there are always ritual means that attempt to restore it. Although often associated with magic, rituals of healing and regeneration always involve the participants in a search for the causes of illness and a desire for overcoming it. In other words, the general meaning of all kinds of healing rituals is that life and health are extremely important. Sometimes sacred objects such as hairs or bones, pebbles or sticks, are believed to be instruments through which healing powers can be felt to operate. Sometimes sacred persons such as shamans or priests are the principal instruments. Here the objects and persons are sacramental means of entering into an experience of the meaning of health even in the midst of illness. Usually ritual incantations accompany the healing rites, and these can be exorcisms, prayers, or recitations of myths that put both the healer and the patient in contact with the experience of healing. Herbs and other natural medicines may be used, but even in these cases ritual is an important means of ensuring that they are properly prepared and applied.

Funeral Rituals. Funeral rituals in any culture dramatize the meaning that death has for those in that culture, and allow them to enter more fully into that meaning. For those who are immediately affected by the death of another person there is usually a prescribed period of mourning, which helps them make the transition from life with that person to life without him or her. The funeral ceremonies themselves reflect the particular beliefs and attitudes toward death that are found in the society. In ancient Egypt entombment with symbols of wealth and food for the journey expressed a belief in an afterlife similar to this life. In many religions burial is a sign that human beings must return to the earth from which they came, but Zoroastrians place the bodies of their dead on ceremonial towers for birds of prey because they do not want decaying flesh to contaminate the earth. In Hindu regions the dead are cremated in order to ensure that the soul does not linger but goes on to its next incarnation.

Marriage Rituals. Marriage rites are similar to funeral rites in that they represent in ritual the meaning that family life has in a culture, and enable those who participate in them to ceremonially enter into that meaning. In most religious cultures the ritual is an elaborate one which includes a preparation or period of separation and a ceremony of transition or incorporation into a new pattern of living. During the preparation period the betrothed persons begin their separation from their previous place in society, and in some cultures they are given instructions about their future marital and social responsibilities. Particular rites of separation can include negotiations between families, a pretended abduction of the bride, breaking a thread or other symbolic object, giving away things connected with childhood or with one's parental family, cutting or shaving hair, periods of fasting or seclusion, and so on. Later, by means of the transition ritual or wedding ceremony, the couple is brought together and incorporated into the social world of married adults. These wedding rites can include prayers and promises, exchanges of gifts, symbolic joining by a string of flowers, new clothes or home or both, a ceremonial meal, sexual intercourse, and so on. Through these rituals of separation and incorporation, then, it is possible for people to rediscover and reaffirm the meaning that marriage has for them.

Ordination Rituals. Rites of ordination or consecration are transition rituals which, like those of marriage, usually include symbols of separation and incorporation. Both men and women can be admitted into sacred orders depending on the culture, but the pattern and function of the ordination rituals is usually the same regardless of sex or culture: the candidate in question is separated from the world of ordinary persons and affairs, initiated into the world of sacred service, and incorporated into a class or order of sacred persons. Fitness for such service must usually be shown by a sign. Sometimes the candidate must exhibit some special behavior, like entering into trances or wanting to be alone; sometimes the candidacy is hereditary and then the sign is simply one's ancestry. Very commonly there is a period of isolation and special instruction during which the candidate learns the rituals and other services to be performed, as well as their sacred meanings. The consecration ceremony can include symbolic rituals such as taking a new name, receiving special clothing or other signs of office, and being anointed or touched by someone who already holds the office. The ritual separation and consecration thus serve to mark the candidate as a sacred person in society and to intensify the meaning of the ordination in the candidate's own mind.

5. Parallels and Precedents

There are of course many other types of rituals in the history of religions, but these at least are types that have parallels to the seven rites that Catholics call their sacraments. By summarizing the general patterns of such rituals it is possible to see that in each of the types there is a general meaning that is symbolized: the meaning is entrance into the community, of participating in its life and values, of perpetuating or serving the community, and so on. The precise meaning will be different in each specific culture or religion, and the specific rituals will differ accordingly, but the general meaning of each type of ritual is the same in each case.

Like myths, which are representations of values and attitudes in story form, rituals are expressions of values and attitudes in the form of symbolic action. Water rituals express values of life and purity; initiation rituals dramatize values of belonging and responsibility; ritual meals represent attitudes of acceptance and sharing; ritual sacrifices symbolize attitudes such as dependence and thankfulness; atonement rituals affirm the value of forgiving and being forgiven; healing rituals embody values of hope and health; funeral rituals express attitudes toward death; marriage rituals incorporate attitudes about the sexes and the family; and ordination rituals attest to the value of centering one's life around sacred meaning, as well as the value of ensuring the continuance of sacred ritual in society. And through each of these types of rituals, societies not only publicly act out the sacred meanings that are symbolized in the rituals but also their members are given the chance to renew their acquaintance with them through a more or less intense experience of sacred meaning.

As was suggested earlier in this chapter, these parallels between the seven Catholic sacraments and the sacramental practices of other religions can be interpreted in at least two different ways. Those who wish to reduce sacraments to the human meanings that they signify may view them as nothing more than dramatic representations of social values and attitudes. On the other hand, those who wish to insist that the human meaning does not exhaust the transcendent significance of the sacraments can show how the general meaning of such rites falls far short of the specifically Christian meaning of the seven sacraments. But seeing the Catholic sacraments in the context of other religious sacraments does at least show that the Catholic sacraments are not odd as religious phenomena. Other religions have sacramental rituals even though they do not label them as such. Marriage and ordination ceremonies in Protestant churches, for example, are not called sacraments. Secondly, it shows that the general meanings that Catholics find in their sacraments are not meanings that are unimportant to other religions. Belonging, forgiveness, hope, fidelity, and so on, are meanings that are sacred to peoples of many religious traditions. And thirdly, it shows that the Catholic rituals are valid human ways of entering into those meanings, reaffirming them, and deepening one's understanding of them. Rituals are not escapes from life but intensifications of it.

But comparisons such as these also raise questions for Catholics regarding the uniqueness of their sacraments and the numbering of their sacraments as seven. To begin to approach such questions we have to move now to a more specific study of the Catholic sacraments.

For Further Reading

Leonel Mitchell, *The Meaning of Ritual* (Morehouse, 1988) is a basic introduction to religious ritual and the cultural background of early Christian practices.

Marion Hatchett, *Sanctifying Life, Time and Space* (Seabury Press, 1976) is an anthropological treatment of Christian rites and other sacraments from the earliest centuries to the present.

Dermot Lane, *The Experience of God* (Paulist Press, 1981) examines the relationship between religious experience and doing theology.

Joseph Campbell and Bill Moyers, *The Power of Myth* (Doubleday, 1988) documents the recurrence of patterns of myth, symbol, and ritual through all human cultures.

Gerard Pottebaum, *The Rites of People* (Pastoral Press, 1992) is an introduction to the function and importance of ritual in people's lives.

Tom Driver, *The Magic of Ritual* (Harper San Francisco, 1991) argues that the types of rituals needed for human culture are lacking in contemporary society. (Republished by Westview Press in 1998 as *Liberating Rites*.)

David Hogue, *Remembering the Future, Imagining the Past* (Pilgrim Press, 2003) connects the scientific study of the brain with religious practices such as worship, prayer, and meditation.

Andrew Newberg, Eugene d'Aquili, and Vince Rause, *Why God Won't Go Away* (Ballantine Books, 2001) describes brain research and conclusions about the links between spiritual experience and neurobiology.

For Further Study

Classics in Religious Studies

William James, *The Varieties of Religious Experience* (Liguori/Triumph, 1991), written in 1902, is the first and most famous study attempting to describe and classify types of religious experiences.

Arnold Van Gennep, *The Rites of Passage* (University of Chicago Press, 1960), originally written in 1908, is a classic study of religious rituals.

Rudolph Otto, *The Idea of the Holy* (Oxford University Press, 1950), first published in 1917, is the classic introduction to the notion that religious experience is an encounter with the sacred and mysterious.

Joachim Wach, *Types of Religious Experience* (University of Chicago Press, 1951) discusses religious experience in the context of the history of religions.

Mircea Eliade, *The Sacred and the Profane* (Harcourt, Brace and World, 1959) is a good introduction to Eliade's work and to the notions of sacred space and time.

Ninian Smart, *The Religious Experience* (Macmillan, 1991) is the fourth edition of a frequently reissued textbook on world religions that highlights the experiential dimension of spiritual teachings and ritual practices.

Religious Experience

Sumner Twiss and Walter Cosner, eds., *Experience of the Sacred* (Brown University Press, 1992) offers a lengthy introduction to the phenomenology of religion, followed by excerpts from important writers in the field.

André Godin, *The Psychological Dynamics of Religious Experience* (Religious Education Press, 1985) analyzes the felt and observable aspects of such experiences using a variety of conceptual tools.

Wayne Proudfoot, *Religious Experience* (University of California Press, 1985) examines a variety of explanations for religious experience from the perspective of the philosophy of religion.

Bruce Riley, *The Psychology of Religious Experience in Its Personal and Institutional Dimensions* (Peter Lang, 1988) offers a thorough analysis of religious experiences as genuine human phenomena while favoring a naturalistic explanation of them.

Thomas Finn, *From Death to Rebirth* (Paulist Press, 1997) explores the process of spiritual conversion in ancient paganism, Judaism, and Christianity.

Luke Timothy Johnson, *Religious Experience in Earliest Christianity* (Augsburg Fortress, 1998) finds evidence for a long overlooked experiential basis to New Testament texts.

John Morgan-Wynne, *Holy Spirit and Religious Experience in Christian Literature ca. AD 90-200* (Paternoster Press, 2006) looks for the experiential basis of references to the Holy Spirit in biblical and other early texts.

Eugene d'Aquili and Andrew Newberg, *The Mystical Mind* (Fortress Press, 1999) describes and interprets recent scientific research into what the brain is doing in mythological thinking, in meditative activities, and in liturgical participation.

Ralph Hood, ed., *Handbook of Religious Experience* (Religious Education Press, 1995) collects 24 essays on the topic from the perspectives of faith, philosophy, psychology, and education.

Ritual and Symbol

Wendell Beane and William Doty, eds., *Myths, Rites, Symbols: A Mircea Eliade Reader* (Harper and Row, 1975) situates Eliade's understanding of sacred space and time within the context of his other works in the history of religions.

Joseph Campbell, *Historical Atlas of World Mythology* (Harper and Row, 1989), lavishly illustrates the connections between symbolic myths and rituals in primal cultures.

Thomas Fawcett, *The Symbolic Language of Religion* (Augsburg, 1971) is a clearly written and thorough examination of religious symbols, how they originate, and how they function in Christianity and other religions.

William Doty, *Mythography: The Study of Myths and Rituals* (University of Alabama Press, 1986) is an excellent and thorough introduction to the many ways that scholars examine and explain myths and rituals.

Bernhard Lang, *Sacred Games* (Yale University Press, 1997) connects six prominent patterns of Christian worship with their Christian and pre-Christian precedents.

Jean Holm and John Bowker, eds. *Rites of Passage* (Pinter Publishers, 1994) studies transition rituals in Christianity and seven other religions. *Worship* (1995) looks at private and public practices in Christianity and seven other religions.

Walter Burkert, *Ancient Mystery Cults* (Howard University Press, 1987) is a systematic treatment of the features and dynamics of mystery religions rather than a descriptive exposition of each of them.

Susan Ashbrook Harvey, *Scenting Salvation* (University of California Press, 2006) explores the sense of smell in ancient Christianity as a revelatory experience of human and divine realities.

Ritual Studies

Ronald Grimes, *Beginnings in Ritual Studies* (University Press of America, 1982) is a collection of early essays by the pioneer of contemporary ritual studies.

Catherine Bell, *Ritual: Perspectives and Dimensions* (Oxford University Press, 1997) is a thoroughly systematic treatment of ritual as it is approached in contemporary ritual studies.

Paul Bradshaw and John Melloh, *Foundations in Ritual Studies* (Baker Books, 2007) is a good introduction to the field of ritual studies through readings selected for their relevance to Christian worship.

Eric Rothenbuhler, *Ritual Communication* (Sage Publications, 1998) summarizes recent advances in ritual studies and applies them to a wide range of stylized activities.

CHAPTER II

THE BEGINNINGS OF THE CHRISTIAN SACRAMENTS

Every sacrament points to invisible and ineffable realities by means of signs and symbols.

—THEODORE OF MOPSUESTIA

What was visible in the Lord has passed over into the sacraments.

—POPE LEO THE GREAT

Catholic catechisms say that the sacraments were instituted by Christ, and theologians acknowledge a sense in which this is true. Historically speaking, however, we have to admit that there is no direct evidence that Jesus of Nazareth left his companions with a well-defined and complete set of sacramental rituals such as those that later developed in the church. On the other hand, there is ample evidence that the earliest followers of Jesus performed sacramental rituals that they believed were "from the Lord" or otherwise approved by God. They shared a special meal and prayed together, they baptized new believers and imposed hands on them, they anointed the sick and appointed leaders of the community.

How did these sacramental practices originate? In many cases we simply do not know. The records that we have, even the earliest, come from a time when these practices were already established and regarded as part of the community's religious inheritance. But the followers of Jesus lived in a world that was familiar with sacraments, and we can understand something about the beginnings of the Christian sacraments by looking first at some of their antecedents and contemporaries.

1. Israel and the Roman Empire

Judaism is not usually thought of as a sacramental religion since the focus of its worship is not on sacred rituals that are believed to have a spiritual effect. In fact, the early religious history of Israel was a constant struggle against what it saw as the nature worship and superstition of its neighbors. Time and time again the religious leaders of Israel affirmed that there was no god but Yahweh, who was above all creation and who could not be coerced by ritual magic. The sun and moon were not gods but lights. Plants and stones had no magical powers but were parts of creation over which people had power, and pictures and statues were never divine but always just the work of human hands. Thus over a period of centuries the Israelites gradually desacralized much of the world that was still sacred to their gentile contemporaries, a world filled with things that could manifest sacred meanings.

Instead of finding God in nature, the Israelites found God in history—their own history. And instead of seeing God in statues, they saw God in events—events that happened to them and their ancestors. Their prophets ridiculed the emptiness of nature worship and announced that God was present in the migration of Abraham, in the escape of the Israelites from Egypt, in their conquest of Canaan, and even in the downfall of their own kingdom. Their law forbade any attempt to make an image of Yahweh, but it commanded the yearly commemoration of those events in which the hand of God could be seen. In other words, for Israel it was not nature but history that was sacred. It was sacred history, filled with stories that put Jews in the presence of the most sacred meanings that they knew as a people: that the world is good, that it is human sinfulness which disrupts the harmony in life, that people could and should be open to the call of the transcendent, that slavery is inhuman and freedom is to be cherished, that justice and law are important but ultimately mercy and love are more important, that it is possible to be chosen and loved despite one's mistakes and failures.

In a sense, Israel's history was its most important sacrament. It revealed things to the Israelites that they simply could not believe were their own invention or discovery—things that were too true and too real to be the product of human ingenuity. Revelations like that had to come from beyond this world, from God alone. And so Israel's second most important sacrament was its scriptures, the record of that holy revelation. It was to be enshrined and venerated, read and meditated. For it was the word of God, given to Moses, sung by the psalmists, recorded by the historians, spoken through the prophets. Reading it brought one into contact with the important events of Israel's past, and pondering it in one's heart put one into contact with the God who spoke through those events.

The religion of Israel also had other sacramental aspects: sacred rituals, objects, places, and persons. The books of the Law were filled with prescriptions about rituals of worship, purification, ordination, and so on. Very often these rituals required the use of things that were "sacred unto the Lord" such as the temple, animals and utensils for sacrifices, the ark with its tablets, or holy vessels and oils. Certainly the Holy of Holies, the innermost chamber of the temple, was a sacred place, as were Mount Sinai and other locations where Yahweh's presence was revealed. In Jewish history the judges, kings, and prophets were sacred persons, as were the temple priests through whom it was possible to be in contact with God. Finally, sacramental experiences or hierophanies were not a central part of Jewish life, but the scriptures did record how Moses saw God in the burning bush, how Samuel heard God in the temple, and how Elijah felt God's presence in the gentle wind.

Thus the first followers of Jesus, who were Jewish, grew up in a unique sacramental tradition, a tradition in which God spoke to humankind through persons and events, a tradition in which sacred meaning was revealed in actions and in the record of those actions. It was also a tradition of temple rituals like offerings and sacrifices and home rituals like purifications and symbolic meals. In fact it was the ritual element of Judaism which in Jesus' time was the most prominent and perhaps the most abused. Earlier prophets had denounced such rituals as hypocritical, and Jesus himself had rebuked those who made the rituals of the Law more important than love for others.

But the first followers of Jesus also grew up in a Greek world, for the Roman Empire especially in its eastern provinces was still largely Greek in language and culture. Many of the Roman provinces and centers of trade dated back to the Greek empire of Alexander the Great. The official religion of the empire was filled with borrowings from older Greek myths, and its philosophies were descended from the philosophical schools of ancient Athens. The Jewish disciples of Jesus were acquainted with this world, and very soon there were non-Jewish converts who knew little of any other world. A few years after the death of Jesus, Paul of Tarsus was converted to the new faith and became one of its most energetic missionaries. A Jew who had been born in a Greek-speaking Roman province, Paul carried the message of Jesus out of Palestine and into Asia Minor, Greece, and Rome itself. Within a short while the non-Jewish believers in Jesus outnumbered the original Jewish believers.

Only forty years after the start of Christianity, events began to sever Christianity from its Jewish cultural roots. The Roman armies, in their attempt to stamp out a Jewish rebellion, reduced the temple in Jerusalem to rubble in AD 70, thereby eliminating the most visible symbol of Jewish unity. From then on, Jews who believed in Jesus as the messiah had no central place to worship. Jewish resistance against Roman rule persisted, however, until the year 135, when the Romans eradicated the problem by leveling the entire city of Jerusalem to the ground and forbidding anyone of Jewish ancestry to live there. These two cataclysms destroyed the religious center of Judaism and the center of Jewish Christianity; and although the followers of Moses preserved much of their culture in places where they settled, the followers of Jesus tended to adopt the cultural practices of the Greek Christian communities into which they were welcomed. Thereafter, Christianity was almost entirely Greek in its cultural outlook, except for what it preserved in the sacred writings and religious practices that dated back to its Jewish origins. Its understanding of Jesus and his message leaned heavily on the letters that Paul had written for non-Jewish Christians, and it began to borrow from Greek philosophy as it developed its own theology.

In the area of religion, however, it was neither the traditional Greek religion nor its Roman counterpart that bore the greatest similarity to Christianity. The Greek gods had lost much of their credibility when they failed to protect their homeland against the Roman legions, and the Roman gods were a collection from all parts of the empire: the diversity of the empire was represented by its pantheon of gods from Italy and the provinces. Moreover, the official Roman religion was more political than anything else. The sacred meanings that it embodied and expressed were those which were important to the preservation of the empire: loyalty and courage, family and state, agriculture and commerce. The only deity to whom all were expected to show their respect was the emperor, the living symbol of imperial unity. So those who looked for deeper meanings in life had to find them elsewhere, and they often found them in what were called mystery cults or mystery religions.

The origins of the mystery religions are still unknown. Some of them seem to go back to the time when the Romans conquered Greece in the second century before Christ; others can be traced back even farther. In one way or another, though, they appear to have been related to times when national religions such as those of the ancient Greeks or Egyptians no longer gave their followers convincing answers to the deeper questions of life and death. Many of these cults were, in fact, concerned with the meaning of death, and grew up around the mythical figure of Orpheus, who was believed to have returned safely from the nether world. Others centered around the myth of Demeter, the goddess of grains, and her daughter who was abducted by the god of the nether world and was later restored to her mother.

Common to all of these cults was the *mysterion*, a sacred ritual in which the myth was symbolically presented and its meaning was revealed. In everyday Greek, *mysterion* meant something hidden or secret, and it had no particularly religious connotation. But the central ritual of each of these cults was in fact something that was hidden, since it was closed to those who had not been initiated into the religion, and so it could be called a *mysterion*. In addition, those who knew the meaning of the rite were sworn to keep it secret, so only the initiated witnessed the rituals or knew their sacred meaning. How well they kept their secrets is attested to by how little is known about the details of the rites, but the accounts we do have are enough to confirm that these *mysteria* or mysteries were indeed sacramental rites, for they were rituals through which an important or sacred meaning was revealed. They were well respected by many, such as the Roman author Cicero, who said of them: "Nothing is higher than these mysteries. They have sweetened our characters and softened our customs; they have made us pass from the condition of savages to true humanity. They have not only shown us the way to live joyfully, but they have taught us how to die with a better hope" (*On Laws* II, 14).

There were, then, sacraments in the Greek and Roman religious world of early Christianity. There were the formal sacraments of the official state religion: oaths and offerings, oracles and auguries, public festivals and family devotions. There were also the sacraments of the mystery religions: symbolic rituals that dramatized deeper religious meanings for those who sought them. There was a time when some historians of religion suspected that the Christian sacraments might even have been an outgrowth of the pagan mysteries, but today it seems certain that they existed side by side, satisfying similar religious needs in somewhat similar fashions. But the existence of both official and unofficial sacraments in the Roman Empire is enough to show that the notion of sacramental ritual was not foreign to the non-Jewish converts to Christianity. And even if the Christians did not borrow any rituals from the Greek mysteries, they did borrow the word *mysterion* and they made it a permanent part of the Christian vocabulary.

2. The Early Christian Community

The earliest records of the Christian community are the letters that the
apostle Paul wrote to various churches between ad 50 and 65.[1] Although
they mention various sacramental actions performed by the first Christians, they do not use a single general word such as "sacraments" for them.
Among their ritual actions were baptism, the laying on of hands, and the
sharing of the Lord's supper. There were also what could be called charismatic sacraments such as tongues (talking in an unknown language) and
prophecy (speaking on behalf of God), which were not specifically rituals
even though they probably followed a stylized pattern during community
worship. Each sacramental action simply had its own name; there was no
generic name for all of them.

Greek-speaking Christians some time later began to speak of their
sacramental rituals as "mysteries," apparently borrowing the term from
the pagan mysteries, but in Paul's letters *mysterion* always had the more
everyday meaning of something that is hidden or secret. According to Paul,
God's wisdom is a mystery, which is hidden from the worldly but revealed
to those who are spiritual (1 Corinthians 2:7–13). The message that he
preaches is likewise a mystery since it was hidden from previous generations (Colossians 1:26–27). Basically that message is God's secret plan of
salvation (Ephesians 1:9–10), but more specifically it is the mystery of
Christ that was hidden but now has been made known through the Spirit
(Ephesians 3:3–6).

When Latin translations of the Bible were made for Christians who
did not speak Greek, *mysterion* was sometimes rendered as *mysterium* and
sometimes as *sacramentum*, although why the translators used two different
Latin words is still not clear. This appearance of the word *sacramentum* in
scriptural texts sometimes led medieval theologians who knew no Greek
to believe that some of these passages contained references to the Catholic
sacraments (for example, Ephesians 5:32). But the fact remains that in the
New Testament neither *sacramentum* nor the original *mysterion* ever refers
to Christian rites.

But the early Christians certainly did have rites. At least there were
things connected with their newly found faith that they repeated in roughly
the same manner each time. They ate some meals in common, and dur-

---

[1]Although not all of the letters attributed to St. Paul in the New Testament were written by him, no distinction will be made herein between the genuinely Pauline and the
deutero-Pauline epistles, which were written after AD 65.

ing the meal they would share bread and wine in memory of Jesus, as he had told them to do (1 Corinthians 11:23–27). And it was a sacramental sharing, for through it they experienced their oneness with the Lord (1 Corinthians 10:16–17). The meaning that it expressed, and in which they participated, was their unity with each other and with Christ, whom they believed would soon return in glory. For they lived that unity every day, sharing their belongings and praying together at temple and at home (Acts 3:42–47; 4:32–35).

The apostles' preaching after their Pentecost experience also tended to follow a set pattern: "This Jesus who was condemned and crucified is the Messiah whom you were expecting. He had been raised from the dead, and you should believe that he is Lord." (See Acts 2:22–36, for example.) Their preaching was a sacramental word, for it had a profound effect on many people, and it was often followed by a ritual washing that both symbolized and solidified the change that they felt in their hearts (Acts 2:37–41; 8:34–39). The meaning that this baptism expressed was their acceptance of the message that they had heard, and their unity with the death and resurrection of Christ through whom they died to their sinful ways and were reborn into a new life (Acts 8:12–13; 16:32–34). For many of them it was indeed the start of a new life, the beginning of a new way of living. Salvation was something real to them: what they were saved from was the way they used to live, and they experienced salvation both in the conversion of their own attitudes and in the shared life of their newly found community.

Probably the most amazingly effective sacramental rite in the early church was the laying on of hands, but to understand what it meant it is necessary to go back a step. The book of Acts describes how, shortly after Christ's last appearance, some of his followers underwent a spiritual experience that totally transformed their lives. It was the Jewish feast of Shavuoth or Pentecost, but since then it has also become the Christian feast of the coming of the Holy Spirit, the "birthday of the church." From a purely historical standpoint it is hard to say exactly what that experience was, but the author of that book says that those who were in the room heard what sounded like a strong wind, and then something like tongues of fire appeared over each of their heads. Suddenly they felt themselves changed inwardly, filled as it were with a new spirit, that same spirit with which Jesus had been filled. They believed it was the spirit of God. And from their viewpoint, what else could it be? What human power could fill them with such exuberance, such hope, such courage in the face of what they saw happen to their master, such understanding of what those final days really meant? What human power could make them start uttering what they felt in languages they had never heard before? It had to be the spirit of God itself, the Holy Spirit. (See Acts 2:1–4.)

What was perhaps even more astonishing to them was that they could be instrumental in bringing that spirit to others. They began to tell others their good news about Jesus, and after the listeners would accept Jesus as Lord and be baptized in his name, they would lay their hands on them and ask the Holy Spirit to fill those persons as well. The converts would then have an experience of being filled with a new spirit, and sometimes even begin to praise God in strange languages (Acts 19:4–6). Usually this imposition of hands would take place immediately after baptism, but sometimes it might have to wait until awhile later (Acts 8:14–17). Undoubtedly it was a sacramental action, for it was a symbol of something that could not be seen, of the spirit's being "poured forth" upon the converts. And it was an effective symbol, for its effects on the initiates could be seen in their behavior, as well as felt by them personally. The meaning that it expressed was the imparting of the Holy Spirit, the spirit of love, joy, peace, patience, kindness, goodness, faithfulness, gentleness, and self-control (Galatians 5:22–23). It was the confirmation of their acceptance by God, for the Father gave them the same interior spirit that he had given to his son, Jesus.

There were other sacramental actions in the early community, even though none of them seem to have had the central importance of the ones just described. Speaking in tongues, for example, was a sacramental action to those who witnessed it, as were prophesying and interpreting the scriptures (1 Corinthians 14:22–25). There were also sacramental gestures of healing, through which people felt the presence and the power of God (Acts 3:1–10; James 5:14–15). Prayer, as always, was a sacramental activity, and a mutual confession of sins was also sometimes practiced (James 5:16). These ritual actions—ritual, because they were repeated roughly the same way each time—were genuinely sacramental because they symbolized realities that were invisible and mysterious, even if the effects of those realities could be witnessed by others. Those realities were at least psychological and social: the experience of inner conversion, of being freed from guilt about the past, of feeling a new spirit within; the fact of a new community with common practices, beliefs, values. But for the first Christians, and for most Christians today, those realities were more than merely human; they were God-given, they were signs of God's graciousness, they were free gifts, they were graces.

What is important to remember is that the scriptural passages about these sacraments in the early Christian community are usually descriptions or based on descriptions of religious experiences. Although they were familiar with sacraments in the Jewish and Greek cultures, those who wrote about the early Christian sacraments had no pre-established theology that they could use to explain what they were experiencing. Instead, they had to develop their theology as they went along, relying on what they remembered of what Jesus had said and done, relying on the religious interpretations given by the spiritual leaders of the community, and relying on their own insight into what they and others experienced.

And yet the New Testament descriptions of early Christian sacramentalism are never pure descriptions. They also include theological interpretations of the experiences; for example, that sins are forgiven in baptism or that the Holy Spirit is received in the imposition of hands. But the interpretations are interpretations of experiences, of things that were felt or seen by the early followers of Jesus. Underlying all of the theologizing in the New Testament there is a record, however sketchy, of the early community's memories of Jesus and of their lives afterward.

The reason why it is important to remember that the first writings about the sacraments were related to personal and communal experiences is that in later ages Christian thinkers would often take the theology that they found in the scriptures and either use it to interpret their own experiences or use it without any reference to experience at all. When they used it to interpret their own experiences, the New Testament theology of the sacraments was often a help toward intensifying their own sacramental experiences and deepening their appreciation of them. But when they used it without any reference to experience, it sometimes led to a purely metaphysical and even a magical understanding of the sacraments: that they have an effect whether or not any effect is felt or seen. Both of these tendencies would be found in the later centuries of Christian theology.

3. The Patristic Period

Just as Americans speak of Washington, Adams, and Jefferson as "founding fathers" of their country, so Christians speak of the great church leaders in the first centuries of Christianity as "fathers of the church." The period of the fathers runs roughly from the second through the sixth century, and includes men from both the eastern and western divisions of the Roman Empire. Almost all of them were bishops. Many of them had the best education available in their day. Through their activities and writings they gave direction to church practices and Christian theology for centuries to come. In Greek they were called *pateres*, in Latin *patres*, and so the age in which they lived has come to be called the patristic period.

Under their guidance the church's sacraments developed into a set of richly symbolic rituals, and its sacramental theology grew into Christianity's first philosophical understanding of those rituals. Like the writers of the New Testament, their work was largely without precedent; they had to develop their understanding of the sacraments as they went along, checking their growing understanding against the scriptures and against the sacramental practices of their day. And like those writers, too, the fathers often developed their interpretations of the sacraments by reflecting on their own experiences with the sacraments.

Initially, as we have already seen, they did not even have a general term that they could apply to the ritual activities of the church. And so we find the earliest writers speaking of baptism and of the Lord's supper, for example, but nowhere do we find them speaking of sacraments in general. But then, in the second century, a few Christian writers began to speak about the ceremony of Christian initiation in comparison with the rituals of the pagan mystery religions. Just as outsiders were barred from witnessing the pagan mysteries, non-Christians were not allowed to be present at the final step in the Christian initiation ritual, the eucharistic celebration. And the writers felt it convenient to explain this secrecy by relating it to a religious secrecy that most of their audience knew and accepted. Clement of Alexandria, who knew about both the pagan and the Christian rites, spoke of mysteries in this sense when he described them as representations of sacred realities in signs and symbols, metaphors and allegories, that only the initiated could understand. Before long the religious rites of the Christians were also being referred to as mysteries; and when Christianity replaced the other religions in the Roman Empire, the pagan origins of the word *mysterion* were gradually forgotten. After that there were only the Christian mysteries.

But *mysterion* also had the broader meaning of something that was hidden or secret, and it continued to have this meaning as well. This was the meaning that Paul intended when he spoke of mysteries: because they had been hidden from human view until the coming of Christ, God's wisdom and plan of salvation were mysteries; and because they could not be fully comprehended, Christ's continued presence in and union with the church were mysteries. The early Christian writers realized that their religion included other mysteries as well: the mystery of how sins were forgiven in baptism or how the Spirit was received in the imposition of hands, the mystery of Christ's death and resurrection, the mystery of the Son's relation to the Father and the Spirit in the Trinity, the mystery of continued evil in the world, and so on. Christians caught a glimpse of these mysteries both in their sacred rites and in their sacred writings. According to John Chrysostom, "A mystery is present when we realize that something exists beyond the things that we are looking at" (*Commentary on 1 Corinthians* I, 7).

It was Tertullian, writing around the year 210, who first used the Latin word *sacramentum* in a Christian sense. Looking for an equivalent of the Greek word *mysterion* for his Latin-speaking audience, he adopted *sacramentum* perhaps because it already referred to Roman religious rites—and he even accused the Greek mysteries of imitating the Christian sacraments! In a discussion of the meaning of baptism, Tertullian explained that it was similar to the *sacramentum* that was administered to Roman recruits when they entered the army. The *sacramentum* was a religious initiation; so was baptism. It marked the beginning of a new way of life; so did baptism. It was an oath of allegiance to the emperor; baptism was a promise of fidelity to Christ.

Largely because of Tertullian's influence on other writers, *sacramentum* became used as a general term for the Christian ceremony of initiation which at that time included an immersion in water, an imposition of hands, and participation in the eucharistic meal. And by extension it came to be used as a general term for Christian religious rituals and everything in them like water, oil, blessings, and the like. The Latin word *mysterium* was closer in appearance to the Greek *mysterion*, but the Latin authors used it only when they wanted to speak of mysteries in the broader sense of things that were hidden from human understanding or that could not be comprehended without faith. Thus by the third century, Greek Christian writers were using *mysterion* in two different senses, but the Latin authors now had two words to use: *sacramentum* to refer to the Christian rituals, and *mysterium* to refer to the mysteries of faith. They could now speak of *sacramenta* as signs of *mysteria*.

The reason for using the Greek and Latin words rather than their English equivalents here is that it would be a mistake to suppose that at this point in history *sacramentum* was equivalent to the later Roman Catholic meaning of "sacrament." Its meaning during the patristic period was much more general. As already mentioned, a *sacramentum* could be an ecclesiastical ritual but it could also be any part of the ritual that had a symbolic significance. For Hilary of Poitiers in the fourth century, people and events in the Jewish scriptures that prefigured the Christian mysteries could be considered *sacramenta*. And for Ambrose of Milan in the same century, the Christian *sacramenta* included the feasts of Easter and Pentecost.

But however wide their scope, the *sacramenta* did include the sacred rites of the church. And the church fathers in both the east and west developed their theological understanding of the meaning of those rites in many different ways. They relied on the Bible, on their own experience of the sacramental rituals, and on what their predecessors and contemporaries said about them.

They took the Bible seriously, and in many cases, literally. If the scriptures said that baptism forgives sins, then it must be so. If at his last supper Jesus said, "This is my body," then the eucharistic bread must indeed be his body. And if in imposing their hands the apostles conferred the Holy Spirit, then when the successors of the apostles did the same, the Spirit must be conferred. For the scriptures were the word of God, and God's word was an effective word. At God's command the world was created; God gave his word that Israel would inherit the promised land, and they did; Christ told people that they would be healed, and they were miraculously cured. John Chrysostom, preaching in the fourth century, exemplifies this confidence in the power of God's word: "Let us believe God in all things and deny him nothing, even when what is said seems contrary to our judgment and our senses. We should do this in the mysteries, not looking merely at the things before our eyes but keeping his words before our mind. For his word cannot deceive, whereas our senses are easily deceived. And so, since the word says, 'This is my body,' let us be convinced and believe, and let us look at it with the eyes of the mind" (*Homilies on Matthew 82*, 4).

But the fathers did not completely deny the value of experience; in fact it was often their own religious experiences that gave them their insights into the meaning of the rituals. In other words, they did not simply deduce their theological conclusions from the scriptures; they often found those conclusions confirmed by their own experience and that of their fellow Christians. For example, they believed on the strength of scripture that baptism is a new birth (John 3:3, 5) and that those who are baptized are washed clean, sanctified, and justified (1 Corinthians 6:11). But Cyprian of Carthage testifies that he also knew this from his own experience: "As soon as the stain of my former life was washed away through baptism's birth-giving wave, a calm pure light filled my breast. And as soon as I drank of the heavenly spirit and was given a new manhood through a second maturity, in an amazing way doubts began to vanish, secrets started to reveal themselves, what was dark grew light, apparent difficulties cleared up, seeming impossibilities disappeared" (*To Donatus* 4). In another work he speaks of baptism as "the sacrament of salvation" that removes "the blemishes of sin," and again he seems to be talking from his own baptismal experience.

As bishops of their dioceses the fathers also presided over and preached about the sacramental rites in their churches. Over the course of a few hundred years baptism had evolved from a simple bathing into a richly symbolic ceremony, and the Lord's supper had developed from a simple meal into an elaborate liturgy. And it was incumbent on the educated Christian leaders to explain the meaning of these "awe-inspiring liturgies," as Theodore of Mopsuestia called them. Especially in their instructions to new Christians, the fathers often explained every detail of the liturgy, giving the sacred meaning of every word and action in the sacred space and time of the ritual. The eucharistic liturgy, for example, represented Christ offering himself to the Father, the bread and wine symbolized his body and blood, the candles stood for the light of faith, the attending deacons symbolized ministering angels, and so on. According to John Chrysostom, when the "Holy, holy, holy" is chanted, "one is as it were transported into heaven itself, for this is actually the hymn of the seraphim; and at the moment of consecration, one should stand in the presence of God with fear and trembling" (*On the Incomprehensible*). For the fathers, then, there was a close parallel between the details of the sacramental rituals and the mysterious realities that they symbolized; and by understanding the symbolism it was possible to enter into those realities experientially.

In this way the principal theologians of the early church accepted and developed the idea that *sacramenta* were effective symbols: they actually caused what they signified. Or rather it was God who ultimately caused those effects, for only God could touch people's souls, forgive their sins, impart the Spirit to them, or make the Son present to them. And only God could make people members of the church through baptism, or give them the powers of the priesthood through ordination. To these fathers the effects of the sacramental rites were patently real, for the *sacramenta* enabled Christians to participate in the sacred and mysterious realities which were of the utmost importance but beyond complete human comprehension. They believed and deeply felt their importance, and their faith told them that these realities had to be revelations of God, not inventions of human beings.

Here, too, we find the growing conviction in the church that *sacramenta* were necessary for salvation, not just the salvation that followed death but also the salvation from sin that could be experienced in this life. It was a belief that they found affirmed in scripture (see John 3:5; 6:53–56) and that they found verified in their own lives. The fathers knew this salvation firsthand, and reflecting on the way that they and others found it made them realize that it had been revealed to them primarily in their sacramental experiences. Without the *sacramenta* and especially the sacramental liturgies that opened to them the deepest meanings and values in life, salvation in a very real and practical sense seemed impossible.

4. The Sacramental Seal

As we have seen, the fathers of the church developed their sacramental theology by taking the Bible seriously and by taking their religious experiences seriously. But there were also other sources from which they constructed their understanding of the *sacramenta*. One was the sacramental practices themselves that they found in the church. They reasoned that if the church was under the continual guidance of the Holy Spirit, there must be a divine approval of these practices. This is also why they believed that it was appropriate to meditate on every element of the rituals in order to penetrate more deeply into their meaning; for if the rituals were approved by God, then every part of them must have divine approval.

Another source of their theologizing was the body of Christian beliefs that were not stated clearly and unambiguously in the Bible but that were commonly accepted as part of their religious tradition dating back to the time of the apostles. They knew, for example, that the scriptures could give rise to more than one interpretation about the nature of Christ, but the common interpretation was that he was both divine and human. And in the area of church practices they realized that the Bible was vague about the baptism of infants, but the accepted belief was that it was not improper.

A third important source of patristic theology was Greek philosophy, which suggested new ways to think about the Christian mysteries. According to Plato and Plotinus, for example, there was a dimension of reality that lay beyond the visible world and that could be understood even though it could not be seen, and the fathers often used this way of thinking when they attempted to formulate what they believed. Also, as inheritors of the Greek intellectual tradition, these Christian theologians had a philosophical faith in the rationality of the universe. Granted that there were mysteries that were beyond complete human comprehension and that even defied human logic, the fathers still shared a confidence that the mysteries could be at least partly understood and that ultimately there was nothing irrational about the wisdom of God. So they tried to develop an understanding of their sacramental practices that was logically coherent, one that took into account the biblical revelation, the traditional beliefs and practices of the church, and their own religion experiences; and in doing this they attempted to show that these diverse sources were not in conflict with one another but ultimately harmonized with one another. In short, they were trying to develop a theologically coherent explanation of what they were doing and why they were doing it.

In their attempt to do this, however, they often found it necessary to go beyond the simple descriptions and interpretations that they found in the New Testament, and to develop more philosophical explanations of Christians' sacramental practices. Many of these speculations were found wanting by later generations and have long since been forgotten, but some of them eventually became a permanent part of Catholic sacramental theology. They were philosophical theories that pulled revelation and experience, belief and practice, together into a coherent picture for the fathers and for later ages as well.

One of these theories was that of the sacramental seal, or sacramental character. It was developed in order to deal with questions that were being asked about sacramental practices during the patristic period, and it has remained a part of Catholic sacramental teaching until the present. The questions it tried to answer were ones like: What does the Bible mean when it says Christians are "sealed with the spirit"? Why are some sacramental rites, like baptism and ordination, never repeated? Does a sacramental ritual have any real effects if none are experienced? Is the effectiveness of a ritual dependent on the holiness or beliefs of the minister?

Since the notion of the sacramental seal, the idea that some sacraments imprint a spiritual mark or character on the soul, became such a central idea in later theology, and since a discussion of it involves a number of the Catholic sacraments, it would be well to treat it now rather than in the later chapters on the individual sacraments. Also, discussing it here will give us a concrete illustration of how philosophical thinking entered into Catholic sacramental theology at a very early stage of its development.

First, then, there are the biblical data with which the fathers had to contend. In the Jewish scriptures the word "seal" had primarily a literal meaning. A seal was a stamp, usually made of engraved stone, or the impression it made in clay or wax. In the ancient Near East the seal served as a sign of authority (Genesis 41:42), or as a mark of a document's authenticity (1 Kings 21:8) or legal validity (Jeremiah 32:10). The seal could also be used to secure something that could not be opened without breaking the seal (Isaiah 29:11). The impression of the seal showed that whatever it was on belonged to or came from the owner of the seal. In the Christian testament, however, this literal meaning was often extended into a poetic metaphor to signify that something belongs to or comes from God. There are the seven seals on the scroll in the book of Revelation, and the seal of God is placed on the foreheads of those who are to be spared during the final tribulation (Revelation 5:1; 7:2–4). John's gospel affirms that God set his seal on the messiah, making him God's son (John 6:27; 10:36). In his letter to the Ephesians, Paul reminds them that they have been sealed with the Holy Spirit as a promise of final salvation (Ephesians 1:13–14; 4:30), and in another letter he says that God has put his seal on the followers of Christ by sending his spirit into their hearts as a foretaste of things yet to come (2 Corinthians 1:22). In these Pauline passages especially, being sealed with the Spirit seems to be a metaphorical way of speaking about the experience of being filled with the Spirit. The first Christians felt inwardly changed, as if they had been "touched" or "stamped" by God; and extending the metaphor, they bore that "stamp of God" on their radiant faces and in their transformed lives.

But later Christian thinkers saw more in these texts than just a metaphor. And if one takes the passages from John's writings literally, the seal appears to be a reality that marks Christians as different from others, even as God's seal on Christ made him truly different from other human beings. But what exactly was this seal? What kind of reality was it? To answer these questions the fathers searched the scriptures for other passages that might illuminate the meaning of the seal. And the ones that they found most helpful were those that talked about anointing, since in many places being anointed with the Spirit seems to be another way of talking about being sealed with the Spirit. Also helpful were those places that talked about the image of God, since a seal is a stamp that leaves its image on the thing that is sealed.

For example, the passage in the letter to the Corinthians where Paul speaks about being sealed with the Spirit, reads literally: "He has anointed us and sealed us and given us the pledge of the Spirit in our hearts" (2 Corinthians 1:21–22). John, too, speaks about receiving the Spirit in terms of anointing: in one of his letters he reminds his readers that they have been anointed with the Holy One, and that this anointing remains with them, revealing the truth to them (1 John 2:20, 27). In the book of Acts, the Holy

Spirit is described as being "poured out" upon the apostles on Pentecost (Acts 2:33). In ancient Israel the king was anointed with oil, and when he was, the spirit of the Lord came upon him (1 Samuel 10:1–10; 16:10). When Jesus was baptized in the Jordan, the Holy Spirit descended on him as a sign that he was the messiah, which means literally "the anointed one" (Luke 3:21–22; 4:18–25; Acts 4:27). And in speaking about Jesus, Peter says that God anointed him with the Holy Spirit (Acts 10:38). On the basis of these texts, then, it was possible for early Christian thinkers to consider the receiving of the Holy Spirit as a kind of spiritual anointing.

There are other biblical texts that speak about receiving the Spirit in terms of becoming like God or receiving God's image, and this comes even closer to the idea of being stamped with a seal. John's gospel hints at the idea that Christ is the image of God when it quotes Jesus as saying, "Whoever has seen me has seen the Father" (John 14:9), but Paul in his letters states outright that Christ "is the image of the invisible God" (Colossians 1:15; 2 Corinthians 4:4). Humankind has also been created in the image of God (1 Corinthians 11:7; see Genesis 1:26–27), but those who receive the Spirit are changed into a new likeness of God by becoming conformed to the image of God's Son (1 Corinthians 3:18; Romans 8:29). It is like "putting on Christ" or putting on a nature that is renewed in the image of God (Galatians 3:27; Colossians 3:10). For Paul, then, becoming filled with the Spirit means somehow becoming like God, bearing God's likeness; and it is a sign to all who see it that the followers of Christ are different from other people. God's seal on Christ made him the Son, and so those who look at Christ see the image of his Father. Similarly, Christ's seal on his disciples makes them brothers and sisters and children of God, for they all bear the stamp of their Father, that is, the Spirit.

The fathers of the church, then, attempted to penetrate the meaning of the "seal of the Spirit" by reading many biblical texts such as these in the light of one another, and searching for an understanding that would illuminate them all. Eventually they came to the understanding that receiving the Holy Spirit meant somehow receiving the image of God on one's soul, or being impressed with God's seal. And since Christ himself was the image of God, receiving the seal of the Spirit meant being stamped with the likeness of Christ as well. In other words, their way of understanding the biblical metaphor was to understand it as a metaphysical reality. The seal had to be something real because the scriptures speak of the realities of faith. But it could not be a physical reality since the Spirit made no physical mark on a person's body. It therefore had to be an invisible or metaphysical reality, a spiritual image of Christ impressed on the soul of the person who received it.

But this philosophical understanding of the meaning of the seal did not develop overnight; it evolved over the course of a few centuries. Only gradually were the relevant texts singled out and read in relation to one another. Only gradually was the church's sacramental practice of pouring the water of baptism related to the pouring forth of the Spirit on the baptized. Only gradually were the anointings of the initiation and ordination rites related not only to the passages that speak about the anointing of the Spirit but also to those that speak about the seal of the Spirit.

Secondly, besides attempting to understand the meaning of the seal through scripture, the fathers also tried to understand it by relating it to other things with which they were familiar. For some of the earliest writers, the idea of the seal was related to something more visible, something in the sacramental rites themselves. The word for a seal was *sphragis*, and in colloquial Greek it meant a branding iron or the mark that it made. Sheep were branded for identification, and sometimes soldiers were branded or tattooed to prevent them from deserting. Now, since the *sphragis* could be the instrument that made the mark, writers in the second century sometimes referred to the water of baptism as the seal that gave new life. "The seal, then, is the water," says Hermas around the year 150 (*The Shepherd*, Simulitude 9). Other writers considered the seal to be the bishop's making the sign of the cross on the forehead of the baptismal candidates, or else his anointing them with oil; but it could also be the sign of the cross itself or the mark of the oil on the forehead.

More commonly, though, the seal was thought of in connection with the seal on the forehead of the elect, mentioned in the book of Revelation. It would therefore have to be some kind of spiritual seal marking a person as a follower of Christ. Cyril of Jerusalem drew upon the theme of Christ the Good Shepherd when he addressed the candidates for baptism: "Come forward and receive the mystic seal so that the Master will recognize you. Be numbered in Christ's holy and faithful flock and he will place you at his right hand" (*Cathechesis* 1, 2). Theodore of Mopsuestia compared the seal to both the shepherd's brand and the soldier's tattoo: "This signing which has been given to you is the sign that you are now marked as one of the sheep of Christ, and as a soldier of the King of heaven" (*Catechetical Homilies* 13, 17). Other fathers used other comparisons: the seal was like the seal on a document, the image on a coin, the brand on a slave, or the circumcision that marked a man as an Israelite.

These analogies could also be extended to include the idea that, like the brand or the tattoo, the seal was permanent and unremovable. In one of his writings Cyril speaks of "the holy and indelible seal," and in another he prays, "May God give you the ineradicable seal of the Holy Spirit for eternal life" (*Procatechesis* 17). For it was common church practice that a person could be baptized or ordained only once, and the comparisons with permanent physical marks helped the fathers explain why this was so: the spiritual mark could never be lost, and so it would never have to be received twice. Of course there was also a scriptural basis for this belief: baptism in the New Testament is always a once-and-for-all initiation into the Christian community. Paul exhorts his readers to live up to the meaning of their baptism even when they have fallen away from it, but he never suggests that they should be rebaptized; and 1 John 2:27 says that the anointing of the Holy Spirit "remains with you always."

Baptism, being a deliverance from sin, was also believed to be a protection from future sin, and some of the analogies suggested to the fathers why this was so. It was like the mark that God put on Cain so that he would not be killed, or like the blood that the Israelites in Egypt sprinkled on their doorposts so that they would be spared by the avenging angel. According to the book of Revelation, those who are marked with the sign of the Lamb will be spared the final tribulation. Gregory of Nazianzus, relating the seal to the oil used in the initiation ceremony, says: "If you fortify yourself with the seal, marking your body and your soul with the oil and the Spirit, what can happen to you? It is something that gives you the greatest security, even in this life" (*Orations on Baptism* 40, 5). And according to Basil of Caesaria, "When angels recognize the seal they come to our aid and deliver us from our enemies" (*Homilies on Baptism* 13, 4). Understood in this way, the seal began to be viewed as both a permanent sign and an effective sign; it seemed to have a permanent spiritual effect.

Such were the biblical data on the seal, and such were some of the fathers' attempts to explain its meaning by comparing it with other kinds of marks. But these early thinkers did not do their theologizing in a vacuum. Many of them were bishops, and they developed their ideas in association with their pastoral concerns. As shepherds of their flocks they would favor the analogy with the sheep brand. In times of persecution they might stress the analogy with the military tattoo. To discourage parents from postponing the baptism of their children, some would emphasize the spiritual protection that the seal gave. And occasionally there would be theological controversies, bringing bishops on both sides of an issue to defend their views.

The controversies that had the greatest impact on the doctrine of the seal raged around the issues of rebaptism and reordination, and lasted for over a century. It was commonly agreed, at least in the western part of the Roman Empire, that persons who had been baptized or ordained in the church were permanently affected by those rites, so that they need never—and indeed could never—be admitted to them again. But what about persons baptized by heretics who denied orthodox beliefs? And what about priests ordained by schismatics who were not in communion with the orthodox bishops? Were they really baptized and ordained, or had they participated in empty and ineffective rituals? If the former, then it seemed there would be no real difference between the true church of Christ and false churches, making any notion of spiritual authority in the church meaningless. If the latter, then it seemed that those who were outside the one true church would have to be rebaptized or reordained should they wish to join it, and yet there seemed to be no precedent for this. It was a real theological dilemma, and there were bishops on both sides of it.

Besides being a theological dilemma, it was also a juridical one. For at the height of the controversy there were rival bishops and the priests they had ordained claiming to be the rightful clergy of the same dioceses. Appeals were made by both groups to other church leaders and to civil authorities as well, asking them to decide in their favor. Juridical decisions had to be made on the question of which bishop was the legal religious authority in the diocese, and on the question of which priests were validly ordained ministers. In this way (although this was not the only reason for it) juridical terms such as "legality" and "validity" were introduced into the theology of the sacraments.

Another development in terminology connected with these juridical aspects was the way that the sacraments got spoken of as "administered" and "received," just as one would speak about administering an oath or receiving an office. The Greek word for both the external rite and the hidden reality was *mysterion*, and so when the Greek was translated into Latin it sometimes happened that both the visible rite and the invisible seal were referred to by the same Latin word, *sacramentum*. In this way it became possible to speak about the seal itself as a *sacramentum*, and "receiving the *sacramentum*" became synonymous with "receiving the seal." But if a *sacramentum* were received it must also be given, and so it seemed natural to speak of giving or administering the *sacramentum* as well. For during the controversy about rebaptism and reordination it was necessary to distinguish between those who had and those who did not have the authority to give the seal, that is, to administer the sacrament.

What sparked the controversy was the persecution of Christians under the emperor Diocletian, beginning in the year 303. In places where it was severe, some of the clergy renounced their faith, and those who held fast to their religion generally agreed that these apostates had lost all authority to function as clerics. Some of these, however, continued to baptize, and when the persecution was over the question was asked whether the people they baptized would have to be baptized again, this time by clerics in good standing. In AD 314 a council of bishops met at Arles and decided that they would not. It also decided that those who had been ordained by defecting bishops would not have to be reordained.

But there were some who would not accept those decisions, and among them was Donatus, the bishop of Carthage. The persecution had been a bitter one in northern Africa, and feelings ran high against those who had apostatized when others persevered. To complicate matters, there was another bishop of Carthage who had been ordained by a bishop who was rumored to have defected during the persecution, which was why Donatus had been ordained by some other bishops instead. Many of the African bishops sided with Donatus, and within a short time there were rival bishops in a number of cities: one who agreed with the council of Arles, and in general with the majority opinion in the church, and one who agreed with Donatus and his small, vocal minority. By and large the situation remained volatile until well into the fifth century, when the whole of North Africa was overrun by the Vandals, who put an end to the dispute by putting an end to the disputers.

The political history of the controversy is interesting, but for understanding the development of the sacraments, the theological debate that it triggered is much more important. The followers of Donatus argued that only the one, holy, catholic church had the means of salvation since the Holy Spirit did not act outside the true church of Christ. But apostates who renounced their faith and heretics who denied its truths cut themselves off from the church and therefore from the action of the Holy Spirit. Consequently, any sacramental rites they might perform were empty and useless. Put simply, they could not give what they did not have, and so their ceremonies could not bestow any spiritual benefits. If they ordained, those whom they ordained were not really priests and so they had to be reordained. And if they baptized, those whom they baptized did not receive the seal of the Spirit, they did not have their sins forgiven, and they were not really members of the church. Spiritually speaking, their baptism was simply null and void, and so those whom they baptized would have to be rebaptized in order to be saved.

The defenders of the orthodox Catholic position were hard pressed to refute these arguments. They were logically coherent and for the most part they rested on assumptions that the orthodox theologians were willing to admit. Who could deny that there was a real difference between Christian sacraments and non-Christian rites? Who could deny that Christ had promised his Spirit only to the apostles and their successors? Who could deny that there was but one true church? And who could deny that it was only in the true church of Jesus Christ that sins could be forgiven?

And yet somehow the arguments were not sound. Somehow they did not really express what the majority of Christians believed and felt about their sacraments. In most places people were never rebaptized or reordained unless the rituals themselves had been done incorrectly. There had been heretics before, and the common consensus was that those whom they baptized became members of a heretical Christian sect; they did not remain pagans. For when heretics were received back into the church they were not rebaptized; they were just forgiven and reconciled with their bishop. And what about sinners? According to this logic, since the church is holy, only those who are holy are in the church, and so anyone who sins is outside the church. This would mean that if a priest were not holy he could not give the Holy Spirit in baptism, since he could not give what he does not have. And this would in turn mean that Christians could never be certain that they were validly baptized, since they could never be sure that the priest who had performed their baptism was not a secret sinner. It was an absurd conclusion, and yet it seemed to follow logically from Donatus' position.

Theologically as well as politically it was a stalemate. The Donatists (as they came to be called) controlled many of the North African churches, and they argued incessantly that it was the other churches, not they, who were in heresy. The orthodox bishops were spread through the rest of the Roman Empire, and they were equally certain that it was the Donatists who did not represent the catholic or universal tradition. The Donatists could convince themselves that they were right, but they could not convince the rest of the church. The orthodox had tradition on their side, but they could not come up with a theological explanation that was consistent with it; they could only show that the Donatist position led to theological absurdities. The stalemate lasted for seventy years.

5. Augustine and Afterward

Augustine, the future bishop, theologian and saint, was born right in the middle of this controversy in North Africa, but for a long time he paid little attention to it. His mother was a Christian but his father was not, and initially he chose to adopt his father's attitude toward religion. A brilliant student, he was sent to study in Carthage, where he fell in love with philosophy and became a teacher of rhetoric. In his search for his own answers to life's questions he was first attracted to Manichaeism, a Persian religion, and then to neoplatonic philosophy. His teaching career took him to Rome and then to Milan, where he came under the influence of the Catholic bishop, Ambrose, and was converted to Christianity. Shortly after returning to Africa he was ordained a priest and a few years afterward he was chosen by the aging bishop of Hippo to succeed him in order to prevent the diocese from falling under Donatist control. From his consecration in 395 until his death in 430 Augustine preached and wrote on almost every aspect of the Catholic faith, becoming the most influential theologian in the Latin church for over a thousand years.

Very early in his ecclesiastical career, he addressed the questions raised by the Donatists. The logic of their position was strong, but it was not consistent with the church's practice of not rebaptizing those who had fallen away from the faith. The task that Augustine faced was to develop an explanation of the sacraments that was equally logical and yet able to justify theologically the traditional practice. And his solution was to argue from practice to theory, rather than the other way around.

Augustine reasoned that if heretics, apostates, and other sinners were never rebaptized, their baptism must somehow be permanent regardless of any sins that might be committed afterward. Moreover, if those who were baptized by heretics and others were never rebaptized, then there had to be something about baptism that was independent of the orthodoxy of the minister. At least these were the conclusions that would follow from the traditional practice of the church.

On the other hand, it was generally agreed that although one of the effects of baptism was the forgiveness of sins, and even though baptism might strengthen the Christian against future temptations to sin, still it was no guarantee of a sinless life. If baptized Christians sinned again, their baptismal innocence would be lost, and they would have to seek reconciliation with God and the church by some means other than baptism. Some theologians in Augustine's day even held that individuals who were baptized by someone who was excommunicated did not have all their sins forgiven, even though they were indeed truly baptized and could not be rebaptized. Thus there seemed to be something about baptism that was independent of the recipient and the minister, and another that was not.

Augustine's solution to the theological problem posed by the Donatists was as simple as it was ingenious: there must be *two* effects of baptism, one that was permanent, and one that could be lost through sin. The permanent effect was the seal, which all the fathers testified was indelible. The other effect was God's grace, removing sin from the soul of the baptized. Thus if Christians sinned, what they lost was God's grace, not the seal. And if people were baptized in a heretical sect, the reason why they could not receive the grace of forgiveness was that they were still, wittingly or unwittingly, in a sinful state of separation from the church until they repented of their error. If and when they did repent, that sin too would be forgiven.

But which of these—the rite, the seal, or the grace—was the sacrament? Theological terminology was still by no means standardized, but according to common usage the rite itself could certainly be considered a *sacramentum*. And by following the practice of referring to the seal as a *sacramentum*, Augustine could say that baptism by heretics and schismatics was valid because it truly conferred the seal, the *sacramentum*, the sacrament.

Moreover, by referring to the seal as the sacrament, Augustine could argue that the Donatists had simply not distinguished clearly between the sacrament and its beneficial effects, and this is why they imagined that if the full benefits of baptism were not present (for example, forgiveness of sins or union with the church) then the sacrament was not present either. That the sacrament was present even outside the church was attested to by tradition of not rebaptizing those who returned to it, just as stray sheep were not rebranded when they were found, and deserters were not given another tattoo when they returned to the army. In his writings against the Donatists, the seal and the sacrament were so closely identified with each other that Augustine could say that "an apostate does not lose his baptism" because "baptism cannot be corrupted or defiled" (*On Baptism Against the Donatists* V, 15, 20; IV, 2, 2).

But what of the Donatist argument that an apostate or heretical minister could not give what he did not have? Augustine replied that it was not the minister but the rite that conferred the seal. The seal was a sign, an image, a character; baptism imprinted this character on the recipients, making them Christians, impressed with the likeness of Christ. The seal, therefore, bore not the image of the minister but the image of Christ, and it was conferred on the recipients because the baptism was Christ's baptism. Baptism was from Christ and in Christ, and so the sacrament was Christ's, not the minister's.

Augustine's identification of the sacrament with the seal and his distinction between the sacrament and its benefits were to have three long-lasting consequences in Catholic theology. First and foremost, it focused attention on the idea that the meaning and effect of a sacramental ritual were properties of the rite and not of the minister. It did not matter whether the minister was a saint or a sinner; the meaning of the ritual was still the same. And since it was God and not the minister who caused the sacramental effect, the worthiness or unworthiness of the minister was of little importance.

Secondly, it solidified the habit of speaking about the sacraments' being administered and received. In the case of baptism what was administered and received was the seal, the indelible character imposed on the soul of the recipient. But there were also other sacramental rituals that were by custom never repeated, and Augustine's identification of the sacrament with the seal in time was extended to cover confirmation and ordination. The obvious explanation why these sacraments could not be received more than once was because in each case a special character was received, a character that confirmed the Christian in the church or marked someone as an ordained cleric. And in all three cases—baptism, confirmation, and ordination—receiving the sacrament was another way of speaking about receiving the character. It was, of course, quite natural to speak of receiving the eucharist, and in time this manner of speaking would be extended to other sacraments (for example, administering extreme unction or receiving the sacrament of penance).

Thirdly, Augustine's solution to the Donatist problem enabled Catholic theologians in later centuries to draw a general distinction between sacraments and their fruitfulness. It made it possible to speak about receiving a sacrament even when it had no noticeable effect on the recipient. If a person were validly baptized or confirmed, there was no question about whether or not he or she had received the sacrament, even if the person behaved no differently afterward. And if a person were validly ordained, there was no question about whether or not he was a priest, even if he did not live up to his calling. The rites were therefore always effective inasmuch as they conferred the sacraments; but they were not always effective in the sense of bestowing their spiritual benefits. Whether or not those benefits or graces were actually received depended on the openness and willingness of the recipient, on the disposition of his or her soul. Later theologians would refer to this secondary effectiveness of the sacraments as their "fruitfulness." They would say that the sacraments (meaning the rites) were always effective even when they were not spiritually fruitful.

But these theological technicalities were still far in the future. Before they would become part of Catholic sacramental theology there would be many centuries of debate and development. There would be debates over theological problems that Augustine never envisioned; there would be the introduction of theological terms that Augustine never used; there would be the development of the Catholic sacramental system into seven major rituals and the restriction of the term "sacrament" to just those seven. When those problems did arise and when the sacramental system did develop, the anti-Donatist writings of Augustine became a primary source of theological inspiration. But for Augustine it was enough that he had hit upon a way to show that the Catholic position on baptism and orders was logically and theologically coherent.

Many of Augustine's other writings, however, show clearly that his understanding of sacraments was quite broad, and much broader than the restricted view that developed in later centuries. In fact, it was the broadness of Augustine's view of sacraments that allowed him to look upon both the ritual and the seal as sacraments. His general understanding of a *sacramentum* was that it is a sacred sign, "a sign of a sacred thing" (*Letters* 138, 7). According to this general definition, the baptismal ceremony was a sacrament because it is a sign of entering the church, but the baptismal seal was also a sacrament because it is a sign of belonging to Christ. But these were not the only things that Augustine called *sacramenta*. For him the Lord's Prayer and the Nicene Creed, the Easter liturgy and the sign of the cross, the baptismal font and its water, the ashes of penitence and the oil of anointing were all sacraments, for each of them is a sacred sign "which, besides the impression it makes on the senses, has an inherent ability to bring some further idea to mind" (*Against Faustus* II, 1) Thus the number of possible sacraments was infinite: everything in creation was a reflection of God, and so in a sense even the universe itself was a sacrament, a sign of God. On the other hand, Augustine also taught that the number of really important sacraments in the church was relatively small, and he divided these into sacraments of the word and sacraments of action. Sacraments of the word such as sermons, prayers, and the reading of the scriptures awakened and enlivened the faith of believers. Sacraments of action such as water and wine, blessings and rituals, involved Christians in worship and other sacred mysteries. But all of them were sacraments because they helped make divine realities present to those who understood the meaning of the signs.

With the passing of Augustine an important era of sacramental theology came to a close. The rites themselves continued to develop, but for the next few centuries thinking about them continued pretty much along lines drawn by the church fathers. And in fact the way the fathers thought and spoke about the rites inevitably influenced Christianity's sacramental practices by influencing its understanding of what was going on in those practices. The fathers spoke about sacraments primarily in objective, metaphysical terms since that was the manner of speaking which their philosophical tradition demanded. So later generations came to understand sacramental practices primarily as signs of unseen metaphysical realities such as changes in one's soul or in one's spiritual relation to God and other Christians. Since the changes were unseen, faith was needed to believe in them. And since the changes were metaphysical, they were automatic: as long as the rituals were correctly performed, the spiritual effects objectively resulted.

What occurred in the first few centuries of writings about the Christian sacraments, then, was a gradual movement away from metaphorical descriptions of experienced realities to philosophical explanations of spiritual realities. The fathers took the Bible literally, and their way of taking it literally was to understand the biblical metaphors as objective facts. And yet that is not the whole story. They believed that baptism was necessary for salvation not only because the scriptures affirmed it but also because they saw people's lives being transformed by entering into the Christian community. They taught the presence of Christ in the eucharist not only because they interpreted the biblical texts literally but also because they felt a divine presence in their liturgies. They believed in the forgiveness of sins not only because scripture spoke of it but also because they experienced it in their own lives.

What these early theologians were trying to do was to articulate the meaning of their sacraments in their own day in their own way. They thought about their sacraments using the concepts of their culture, and they wrote about them using the words at their disposal. They were putting into words the sacred meanings of the rituals and symbols that they lived with, and they were verbalizing the nonverbal experiences of sacred meaning that their sacraments opened up to them.

But the words that people write live longer than the people who write them, and the meanings that they find outlast the experiences in which they find them. Thus centuries later the writings of the fathers became, in addition to the scriptures, a primary source of ideas about the meaning of the sacraments in the Catholic Church.

For Further Reading

Eugene Fisher, ed., *The Jewish Roots of Christian Liturgy* (Paulist Press, 1990) collects articles on Jewish antecedents to Christian worship, marriage, and funeral practices.

C. K. Barrett, *Church, Ministry, and Sacraments in the New Testament* (William B. Eerdmans, 1985) is a concise and readable treatment of early ecclesiastical developments.

O. C. Edwards, *How It All Began* (Seabury Press, 1973) gives an overview of the origins of Christianity, including the sacraments.

C. F. D. Moule, *Worship in the New Testament* (John Knox Press, 1961) is a short introduction to baptism, eucharist, and other practices mentioned in the Christian scriptures.

Allen Cabaniss, *Pattern in Early Christian Worship* (Mercer University Press, 1989) summarizes and comments on early documents containing descriptions of Christian worship.

Kenneth Stevenson, *The First Rites* (Liturgical Press, 1989) summarizes contemporary scholarship about what is known about early Christian worship and rituals.

R. A. Markus, *Christianity in the Roman World* (Charles Scribner's Sons, 1974) traces the growth of Christianity from a Jewish sect to its establishment as the official religion of the empire.

Jaroslav Pelikan, *The Excellent Empire* (Harper and Row, 1987) is a set of informative lectures on the decline of paganism and the rise of the Christian Roman Empire.

Norbert Brox, *A History of the Early Church* (SCM Press, 1994) puts the early development of church life and liturgy in a wider historical context.

Paul Bradshaw, *Early Christian Worship* (Liturgical Press, 1996) summarizes what scholars say about the origins and early development of baptism, eucharist, and other liturgical practices. *Reconstructing Early Christian Worship* (SPCK, 2009) is a short and readable description of worshipful praying and singing in the first four centuries.

Larry Hurtado, *At the Origins of Christian Worship* (William B. Eerdmans, 2000) draws a detailed but readable picture of pagan and Jewish practices and beliefs surrounding early Christianity.

For Further Study

Christian Worship and Theology

Frank Gavin, *The Jewish Antecedents of the Christian Sacraments* (SPCK, 1928) is one of the first books to argue that there is a close connection between early Christian practices and first-century Judaism.

Walter Brueggemann, *Worship in Ancient Israel* (Abingdon Press, 2005) is a more recent work that connects early Jewish practices with later Christian ones.

Margaret Baker, *The Great High Priest* (T & T Clark, 2003) argues that the ancient liturgy had deeper roots in Jewish temple worship than most Christians realize.

James Dunn, *Jesus and the Spirit* (Westminster Press, 1975) interprets the religious experience of Jesus and the first Christians on the basis of New Testament evidence and modern scholarship.

Valeriy Alikin, *The Earliest History of the Christian Gathering* (Brill, 2010) reviews scholarship on Christian origins in the context of the cultural practices of ancient Mediterranean societies.

Thomas Carroll and Thomas Halton, *Liturgical Practice in the Fathers* (Michael Glazier, 1988) documents the gradual development of Lent and Easter, Advent and Christmas, and other Christian feasts.

Michael Philip Penn, *Kissing Christians* (University of Pennsylvania Press, 2005) examines the role of greeting kisses and liturgical kisses in early Christianity.

Joseph Jungmann, *The Early Liturgy to the Time of Gregory the Great* (University of Notre Dame Press, 1959) gives a detailed account of the development of Christian worship during the first six centuries.

Jean Danielou, *The Bible and the Liturgy* (University of Notre Dame Press, 1956) shows how patristic writers used biblical images and philosophical ideas to explain the meaning of the Christian liturgies.

Enrico Mazza, *Mystagogy: A Theology of Liturgy in the Patristic Age* (Pueblo, 1989) is a thorough study of the instructional homilies of some of the great church fathers.

Geoffrey Lampe, *The Seal of the Spirit* (SPCK, 1967) examines and reflects on all of the early texts pertaining to this topic.

Carolyn Osiek and David Balch, *Families in the New Testament World* (Westminster John Knox, 1997) discusses house churches, community meals, marriage, and celibacy.

Paul Bradshaw, *The Search for the Origins of Christian Worship* (Oxford University Press, 1992) questions many of the assumptions that are usually made about early church rituals.

Benjamin Williams and Harold Anstall, *Orthodox Worship* (Living Light Publishing, 1989) brings out the connection between early liturgical practices and the Orthodox liturgy as it is practiced even today.

Hugh Wybrew, *The Orthodox Liturgy* (SPCK, 1989) presents a clear summary of the historical development of the Byzantine rite.

Robert Taft, *The Byzantine Rite* (Liturgical Press, 1992) summarizes developments in the Greek or Eastern liturgy from the fourth to the fifteenth century.

Paul Palmer, *Sources of Christian Theology* (2 vols., Newman Press) is a useful collection of historical texts on the sacraments from patristic to modern times. *Sacraments and Worship* (vol. 1, 1955) covers sacraments in general and the eucharist. *Sacraments and Forgiveness* (vol. 2, 1959) covers penance and the anointing of the sick.

Christian Women in Community and Worship

Jean LaPorte, *The Role of Women in Early Christianity* (Edwin Mellen Press, 1982) is a scholarly study of women as martyrs, wives, contemplatives, ministers, and as symbols of virtue and vice, based on patristic texts.

Bonnie Bowman Thurston, *The Widows* (Fortress Press, 1989) examines the qualifications and roles of women referred to as widows in the New Testament and early Christian writings.

Patricia Cox Miller, *Women in Early Christianity* (Catholic University of America Press, 2005) collects texts referring to women in dozens of Greek literary sources and introduces them with brief explanations.

Christine Trevett, *Christian Women and the Time of the Apostolic Fathers (AD c. 80-160)*, (University of Wales Press, 2006) looks at women's lives in Corinth, Rome, and Asia Minor through the lens of men's writings about problems in the church.

Carolyn Osiek and Margaret MacDonald, *A Woman's Place* (Fortress Press, 2006) scours textual and archaeological evidence of women's roles in early Christian house churches.

Reta Halteman Finger, *Of Widows and Meals* (William B. Eerdmans, 2007) analyzes scriptural evidence to reconstruct the social world of the early Christian community.

Ross Sanders, *Outrageous Women, Outrageous God* (E. J. Dwyer, 1996) vividly describes the counter-cultural qualities of the early Jesus movement as reflected in the New Testament.

Luise Schottroff, *Lydia's Impatient Sisters* (Westminster John Knox Press, 1995) reconstructs early Christian history in terms of oppression and liberation in the Greco-Roman world.

Ross Shepard Kraemer and Mary Rose D'angelo, eds., *Women and Christian Origins* (Oxford University Press, 1999) is a collection of scholarly articles by experts on various aspects of early Judeo-Christian writings.

Church History

Wayne Meeks, *The First Urban Christians* (Yale University Press, 1983) gives a sociological description of first-century Christianity, including church organization and rituals.

Henry Chadwick, *The Early Church* (Penguin Books, 1967) covers the history of Christianity from the first to the sixth century.

Jaroslav Pelikan, *The Emergence of the Catholic Tradition, 100– 600* (University of Chicago Press, 1971) discusses the theological concerns of the patristic period in their cultural and intellectual setting.

Rodney Stark, *The Rise of Christianity* (Princeton University Press, 1996) is an intriguing sociological reconstruction of the spread of Christianity through the Roman Empire. *Cities of God* (HarperCollins, 2006) uses archaeology and other evidence to show how early Christianity spread through social networks in urban areas.

W. H. C. Friend, *The Early Church: From the Beginnings to 461* (SCM Press, 1991) is a concise history that has been revised twice since its first edition in 1965.

Walter Wagner, *After the Apostles* (Fortress Press, 1994) reconstructs the second century of Christianity from how church leaders responded to the challenges of the day.

Everett Harrison, *The Apostolic Church* (William B. Eerdmans, 1985) summarizes much that can be known about first-century Christianity from the New Testament and other sources.

Justo Gonzales, *A History of Christian Thought* (3 vols., Abingdon Press, 1987) is a lengthy but useful history that includes major developments in the theology of the sacraments.

Thomas Bokenkotter, *A Concise History of the Catholic Church* (Doubleday, 2004) is a very readable general history written from a Catholic perspective.

Martin Marty, *A Short History of Christianity* (New American Library, 1959) is a very readable history written from a Protestant perspective.

Brian Moynahan, *The Faith* (Doubleday, 2002) is a lengthy and illustrated history of Christianity that reads like a novel.

Edward Engelbrecht, ed., *The Church from Age to Age* (Concordia, 2011) is a multi-authored history that includes readings from primary sources.

CHAPTER III

THE DEVELOPMENT OF THE CATHOLIC SACRAMENTS

Properly speaking, a sacrament is something that is a sign of a sacred reality pertaining to human beings; so that what is properly called a sacrament in the present sense of the word is a sign of a sacred reality that makes people holy.

—Thomas Aquinas

The Holy Roman Church maintains and teaches that there are seven ecclesiastical sacraments. One is baptism, which has already been mentioned. Another is confirmation, which bishops confer through the imposition of hands, anointing those who have been reborn. The others are penance, the Eucharist, the sacrament of orders, matrimony, and the last anointing which is administered to the sick, according to the teaching of St. James.

—Second Council of Lyons

The numbering of the Catholic sacraments as seven dates from the twelfth century. Prior to that time the word *sacramentum* still had a rather broad meaning, and it could be used to designate any number of sacred signs and symbols. By the thirteenth century the meaning of *sacramentum* had become much more restricted, and the word was used only to refer to the ecclesiastical rites listed by the Second Council of Lyons.

The medieval period was a crucial one for the Catholic sacraments in other ways, too. Their rituals became more standardized, their religious meanings became more solidified, and the theological explanations for them became more unified. During the patristic period the forms of some

51

of these rituals had varied considerably, their meanings were sometimes debated, and their theology reflected a variety of regional traditions. In the Middle Ages, however, Christians in the eastern and western parts of the old Roman Empire drifted apart and finally stopped speaking to each other. Byzantine Christianity, the Orthodox tradition, remained rooted in the patristic heritage of liturgy, theology, and regional autonomy; European Christianity, the Catholic tradition, retained its patristic roots but saw its liturgy and theology evolve in new directions under the authority of Rome. The sacraments in the Orthodox churches therefore tended to keep their diverse ancient forms, while those in the Catholic Church developed a newer, more uniform, more western style.

The first Catholic developments were in the area of sacramental practice; they began in the sixth century and continued almost imperceptibly during the next few hundred years. The rite of confirmation became separated from that of baptism. The eucharistic liturgy became a clerical affair with little lay involvement. The practice of public repentance disappeared and was replaced by private confession. Marriage became a church ceremony and came to be regarded as a sacramental rite. Ordination to the priesthood developed into a sequence of holy orders. The anointing of the sick became the anointing of the dying. By the twelfth century these sacramental practices had not only achieved a more or less stable form, but they were also becoming regarded as the principal sacraments in the church.

These practical developments were followed in later centuries by theological developments. In the thirteenth century there arose a new style of Catholic theology based on the philosophy of Aristotle. Old theological problems were reexamined and new types of answers were introduced. In time a more or less standard approach to Catholic sacramental theology appeared, and even though there were scholarly disagreements about peripheral matters, there was general agreement on all of the main issues.

It was during the Middle Ages, then, that the sacraments of the Roman Catholic Church emerged in the forms that they would retain until the twentieth century. Their number was fixed at seven, their practice became more uniform, and their general theology was established for centuries to come.

1. Seven Liturgical Sacraments

The years from the sixth to the eleventh century were hard times for the Catholic church. The intellectual centers of Italy were in ruins; the provinces in North Africa and the Middle East fell under Muslim control; the Greek provinces were isolated both geographically and culturally. The collapse of the Roman Empire in the west, the Germanic invasions, and subsequent missionary efforts in Europe left little energy for original theological work. Church leaders did what they could do to Christianize the continent, and ever so slowly their efforts succeeded. But they were practical men, with little taste for theological speculation. The missionary monks, poorly educated as they often were, brought with them only what they knew: the book of gospels, the creed, and the sacramental means of salvation. Those who remained in the monasteries copying ancient manuscripts or producing new psalters were sometimes even illiterate: they knew the shapes of the letters but they could not read them.

It was during this long period that the Catholic sacraments underwent their greatest changes. Instead of being an elaborate initiation ritual, baptism was reduced to a simple rite of water and words. Instead of being a public, once in a lifetime affair, penance became a private, repeatable sacrament. Instead of being a repeated anointing in times of illness, extreme unction became a final anointing at the time of death. And along with these changes in their ritual forms, the sacraments underwent changes in their sacred meanings, some only slightly, others more drastically.

During this period, too, the liturgical practices of the church began to center around seven major rituals: the baptism of infants and converts, the confirmation of baptism by the bishop, the rite of penitence and forgiveness, the anointing of the dying, the ordaining of priests, the uniting of people in marriage, and the eucharistic liturgy or mass. There were of course many other ritual practices: initiation ceremonies for men and women who entered monasteries, the daily chanting of psalms by monks and nuns, various types of blessings and exorcisms, the veneration of martyrs and relics, pilgrimages to sacred shrines, and other pious devotions. But there were seven which were becoming in practice, if not yet in theory, the primary liturgical sacraments of the church.

Then in the twelfth century, after the "barbarians" had been converted and Europe began to experience some relative political peace and economic prosperity, the intellectual task of understanding religion began afresh, first in the monasteries and then in the newly founded schools. For hundreds of years monks had laboriously copied and recopied fragile manuscripts to keep their contents from being lost forever. Now at last there were people who had the leisure to read them and think about what they contained. They were trying to understand for themselves what it meant to be a Christian, to have faith in God, to be a member of the church; they were trying to find explanations of the mysteries that they had been celebrating for centuries in ritual. And so they turned with renewed interest to the Bible, to the writings of the church fathers, and to the statements of the early councils.

It was an enormous undertaking. The monks and schoolmen were looking for a coherent understanding of the Christian religion, but they found themselves confronted with a bewildering variety of texts: sermons and letters, commentaries and treatises, statements of bishops and councils. And the texts did not always agree with one another in matters of theology. So in order to make some headway through this mountain of information, early medieval scholars began making summaries of what they read and collecting quotations on various subjects such as the incarnation, the Trinity, the church, and so on. Soon there were "books of sentences" or collections of opinions on every major theological topic, including the sacraments.

Early in the twelfth century there was still little agreement about the exact nature and number of the sacraments in the church. Most theologians admitted that there were "sacraments of the Old Law" such as temple sacrifices and other Jewish rituals, as well as "sacraments of the New Law" such as those found among Christians. Hugh, a monk in the Abbey of St. Victor in Paris, thought Augustine's definition of a sacrament as a sign of the sacred was too broad, and he proposed a definition that was narrower in scope; but when it came to treating the things that he considered to be sacraments he discussed not only the familiar seven but also such things as the incarnation of Christ, the church, holy water, blessed ashes, the sign of the cross, and vows. Lists of sacraments by various authors ranged from twelve all the way up to thirty. On the more conservative side, a book of sentences compiled before 1150 treated only five ecclesiastical sacraments, and Peter Abelard around the same period enumerated six, leaving out ordination.

One of the largest collections of sentences was compiled by Peter Lombard at the University of Paris. He gathered together biblical quotations and patristic texts on every major theological issue of the day, and added his own observations and conclusions about them. Published in four parts, it was both systematic and thorough, and within a relatively short time it came to be adopted as the standard theological source book for all beginning theology students. The last part contained a large section on seven principal ecclesiastical sacraments as they were practiced in the twelfth century. Because of the book's popularity and wide usage, Lombard's enumeration of the Catholic sacraments soon became accepted by theologians and preachers alike, and by the end of the next century it was accepted by regional and ecumenical (that is, universal church) councils.

But Peter Lombard's textbook did more than crystallize theological thinking around the liturgical rites of baptism, confirmation, eucharist, penance, extreme unction, matrimony, and ordination. It also offered a definition of sacraments which for the first time enabled Catholics to distinguish between these seven and other sacred signs and rituals. He wrote, "Something is properly called a sacrament because it is a sign of God's grace, and is such an image of invisible grace that it bears its likeness and exists as its cause" (*Sentences* IV, 1, 2). The seven ecclesiastical sacraments (*sacramenta*) were for him causes as well as signs of grace, and this made them different from sacramentals (*sacramentalia*) which were signs but not causes of grace. Among the sacramentals were included such things as statues and crucifixes, holy water and oils, blessings and prayers, religious promises and vows, and other church ceremonies. From that time on, then, many things that could be considered sacraments in a broad sense were no longer given the name "sacrament," and Catholic theologians began to use the word almost exclusively in reference to the familiar seven rites.

The decision to restrict the name "sacrament" to just these seven, however, was not a sudden one. For some time there had already been tendencies in this direction, and the symbolic significance of the number seven added immensely to medieval thinkers' willingness to regard Peter Lombard's list as definitive. Seven was regarded as a "perfect" number, representing as it did the unification of the natural and the supernatural, four being symbolic of creation (for example, the four human temperaments, and the four corners of the earth) and three being symbolic of the divine (for example, the three persons of the Trinity, and the resurrection on the third day). On the other hand, seven also represented the fundamental illness of the human race (that is, the seven deadly sins). It seemed appropriate, therefore, that if God were to convey spiritual healing to a sick humanity through *sacramenta*, this would be accomplished through seven such rites.

Moreover, the early medieval theologians recognized that some of the *sacramenta* were believed to have definite spiritual effects. They also observed that some of the *sacramenta* were rituals which "bore the likeness" or acted out, as it were, the meaning of the effect that they were supposed to cause. (For example, baptism washed away sins, confirmation gave an anointing of the Holy Spirit, couples being joined in marriage held each other's hand, and so on.) And it was these *sacramenta* which presented the greatest challenge in trying to explain just what they were and how they worked. It is understandable, then, that these special *sacramenta* were singled out for special treatment. When theologians argued about sacraments it was usually these sacraments that they had in mind. And so in the course of time it was these sacraments that came to be commonly regarded as *the* sacraments.

2. Sign and Reality

The twelfth and thirteenth centuries were high points of Catholic sacramental theology. Medieval thinkers succeeded in putting together the scriptural data, the patristic contributions, and the sacramental practices of their day into a logically coherent framework that proved satisfactory for centuries. But why were the medievals no longer satisfied with Augustine's broad definition of sacrament as a sign of a sacred reality? Why did they want a "proper" definition like the one offered by Peter Lombard? And why did the search for such a definition take the route that it eventually did? To begin to answer these questions we must look at an earlier theological problem and see how it was resolved.

Around the middle of the eleventh century, Berengar of Tours attacked the idea that the bread and wine consecrated at mass became literally the body and blood of Christ. He believed in the presence of Christ in the eucharist, but he believed that it was a spiritual presence. To him it was obvious that something had to be either a sign or a reality; it could not be both. Smoke is a sign of fire, but it is not fire; a crown is not a king but only a sign that the man who wears it is one. Applying this logic to the eucharist, he argued that the consecrated bread and wine either had to be signs of the body and blood of Christ or else they had to be the real body and blood of Christ. And it was equally obvious to Berengar that the consecrated bread and wine were not the real body and blood of Christ: they looked nothing at all like human flesh and blood, and besides, the real Christ had ascended bodily into heaven. Berengar's conclusion was that the bread and wine were and remained signs; they were not the real thing. And in support of his conclusion he cited Augustine: "A sacrament is a sign of a sacred reality" (*Letters* 138, 7). If the eucharist was a sacrament, he argued, it had to be a sign of Christ's body and blood, not his real body and blood.

Berengar's attack did not go unchallenged. A number of his contemporaries argued against him, and in 1059 his ecclesiastical superiors forced him to sign a confession of faith in which he admitted the real presence of

Christ in the eucharist. But the ecclesiastical reaction against Berengar did not explain how Christ became present in the bread and wine; it simply reaffirmed the church's traditional belief that they were Christ's body and blood despite the fact that they still looked like bread and wine. It took medieval theologians about a hundred years to work out a satisfactory philosophical explanation for this belief.

Berengar had assumed, as did most other theologians of his day, that there were only two elements involved in a sacramental ritual: the ritual itself and the reality that it signified, the *sacramentum* or visible sign and the *res* or real thing to which it pointed. The visible sign in the eucharist was clear enough: it was the bread and wine, together with the words of consecration, "This is my body. This is my blood," said over them during the mass. But what was the reality that the eucharist pointed to? Slowly the medieval theologians came to the conclusion that the ultimate reality signified by the eucharist was not a physical reality but a spiritual one; the ultimate purpose of consecrating the bread and wine was not to make Christ present on the altar but to receive him in communion. And so the ultimate reality, the *res* of the eucharist, was spiritual union with Christ. But what, then, was the status of the consecrated bread and wine before they were received? Were they a sacrament or a reality? The answer that was finally worked out was that they were both. Or rather, it was agreed that the bread and wine were in reality the body and blood of Christ, and that these in turn were a sign of union with the real Christ, which was to be achieved in the receiving of communion.

To Catholics of a later age this solution seemed quite natural, and yet it took decades for Catholic theologians to arrive at it. Why? One reason was the authority of Augustine. Besides his definition of a sacrament as "a sign of a sacred reality," there was also another which was attributed to him: "a visible sign of invisible grace." Both of these definitions indicated that there were only two elements in a sacrament. But if the writings of Augustine were part of the problem, they also suggested a solution. Augustine himself in his polemics against the Donatists had spoken of the seal or character received in baptism as a sacrament. The seal was, so to speak, both a reality and a sign: a reality since it was something really received, and a sign since it marked a person as belonging to Christ. And as these writings of Augustine were rediscovered and reread, the possibility of a parallel solution to the eucharistic problem became clearer.

In the end, medieval theologians developed a threefold distinction in reference to the sacraments: the *sacramentum tantum* being the element which was "only a sign," the *sacramentum et res* being the element which was "both sign and reality," and the *res tantum* being the element which was "only a reality." In reference to the eucharist, the words of consecration and the outward appearance of bread and wine could be considered as only a sign; the body and blood of Christ really present under the appearance of bread and wine could be considered as both a reality in itself and a sign pointing to the spiritual nourishment to be received in communion; and the grace of that union with Christ could be considered as a reality which was not also a sign of something else. In reference to the other sacraments, the symbolic words, gestures, and objects in the rite could be considered as the sacramental sign, the *sacramentum tantum*; something new in the soul of the subject of the rite could be considered as the sacramental reality, the *sacramentum et res*, which was received by participating in the symbolic ritual; and the spiritual benefit of receiving the sacrament, God's freely bestowed grace, could be considered as the sacred reality, the *res tantum*, which the sign pointed to and helped to cause.

Taking the lead suggested by Augustine, this triple terminology was applied first to baptism and then to the other liturgical sacraments. The baptismal seal on the soul of the recipient was not just a sacrament and it was not just God's grace; it must therefore be, the theologians reasoned, a sacramental reality produced by the rite which made it possible for the baptized person to receive the grace connected with that sacrament. But baptism was not the only sacrament that was believed to have a permanent effect on the recipient. Confirmation and ordination could likewise be received only once, and because of this it was argued that they too must bestow an indelible character on the soul. And this character, like the seal of baptism, could be considered a sacramental reality, neither pure sign nor pure grace.

It was not so easy to discover the sacramental reality bestowed by the other three liturgical sacraments of matrimony, penance, and extreme unction, since all of them could be received more than once and so none of them were believed to confer a permanent character. And yet there had to be some sacramental reality given by them, the medieval theologians reasoned, because this element had been found in four of the sacraments, and if all seven were sacraments they should all have the same essential elements. In this respect medieval thought was basically the same as classical Greek thought: it tried to understand the essential nature of things, and one of its working assumptions was that the natures of similar things were essentially similar. If, for example, one could discover the nature of one's own soul, one would possess an understanding of the essential nature of any human soul. Similarly, by understanding of the nature of virtue or sin, of the state or the church, of animals or angels, one would arrive at an essential understanding of any instance of those things. Believing that they had hit upon an understanding of the essential nature of a sacrament, therefore, medieval Catholic theologians assumed that what was true of some of them had to be true of all of them.

Medieval thought was like Greek thought in another respect, too, in that it strove for logical coherence in its theories. And having found a theory of sacraments that enabled them to give a coherent account of the eucharist, baptism, confirmation, and ordination, the theologians of the Middle Ages sought to bring that same kind of coherence to their explanations of the remaining three sacraments. In matrimony the sacramental reality produced by the rite seemed to most theologians to be the bond of marriage between the husband and wife. Marriage produced a real change in a man and a woman: it made the man a husband and it made the woman a wife. Furthermore, the marriage bond was a sign that they should be united in love the way Christ is united to the church, and that they would receive the grace they needed to fulfill their marital obligations to each other. It was harder to determine the sacramental realities involved in the remaining two sacraments. Some claimed that the sacramental reality produced by penance was the repentance of the penitent, while others held that it was reconciliation with the church; in either case the sacrament received would in turn permit the grace of God to effect the forgiveness of sins. Finally, most theologians came to agree that the sacramental reality produced by the rite of extreme unction was the commitment of the dying person to the mercy of God, and that this could have the effect of either physical recovery or spiritual strengthening.

It can be readily seen that the sacramental realities produced by the various sacramental rites were not all of the same order: one was a real change in bread and wine; three were permanent changes in the soul of the subject of the rite; three were less permanent changes. But whatever obscurity there was in the notion of the *sacramentum et res*, it was slight in comparison to the logical clarity that it brought to the medieval attempt to understand the church's sacramental system. Once the schoolmen adopted the threefold analysis of the nature of sacraments, they had a conceptual scheme that enabled them to approach an entire range of related theological questions: the nature of the sacramental character itself, the meaning of valid and invalid sacraments, the nature of sacramental causality, and many others. The notion of the sacramental reality thus became a central concept in the whole Catholic theology of sacraments. Its importance cannot be overestimated.

Perhaps the most significant result of this development was the fact that the word *sacramentum* was commonly applied to the sacramental reality produced by the rite as well as to the rite itself. Following the example of Augustine and other church fathers, the medieval theologians came to speak regularly of "administering" and "receiving" the sacraments; but when they did so they were referring to the *sacramentum* which was also a *res*, thing, a reality which could be given and received. They were referring to the sacramental reality conferred or bestowed by the rite, not to the sacramental rite itself. Thus the entire Catholic theology of the sacraments in the Middle Ages eventually became a theology of the *sacramentum et res*, a philosophical explanation of the sacramental effect that was believed to be produced by each of the church's seven major liturgical rites.

3. The Sacramental Character

The theology of the sacramental character had not developed much between the fifth and twelfth centuries, when the medievals picked up where the fathers had left off. Augustine had settled some basic questions about the baptismal seal: that it was a stamp of Christ impressed on the soul, that it could not be lost, that it could be called a *sacramentum*. Later it was generally believed that confirmation also bestowed an indelible character on the soul, and after a period of hesitation it was decided that ordination conferred such a character as well.

Now, however, in the drive to develop a comprehensive theology of the sacraments, further questions were raised: What was the exact nature of the sacramental character? Was it something real in the soul or was it just a special relationship between the soul and God? If it was something real, what kind of reality was it? Why should it be called a sacrament (for a sacrament is by definition a sign) if it was invisible? Was there a philosophical explanation for the fact that it could not be lost? Was there any difference between the baptismal character and that given by the other sacraments?

The search for answers to these and similar questions led Catholic thinkers into some of the more esoteric areas of medieval theology. Moreover, neither the answers given nor the reasons behind them were always uniform; they varied from theologian to theologian. Still, in the course of the Middle Ages a general consensus emerged around most of the major issues, and quite often the direction of that agreement can be found in the writings of Thomas Aquinas, not only because of the comprehensiveness of his theology but also because of its influence on later theologians. By focusing mainly on Aquinas, therefore, it is possible to draw a brief but fairly accurate picture of the state of Catholic sacramental theology during this period.

The main development in the theology of the sacraments in the twelfth century had been the introduction of *sacramentum et res* as a workable solution to the problem posed almost a hundred years earlier by Berengar. Both Hugh of St. Victor and Peter Lombard had used that terminology in reference to the eucharist, and it was largely through the influence of the latter's *Sentences* that it gained acceptance among other theologians and began to be applied to other sacraments. In time it became a standard term in the Catholic theological vocabulary, so when Aquinas began his career around the middle of the thirteenth century he could write: "The sacraments add two things to the soul. One is a sacramental reality like the character or some other adornment of the soul; the other is a reality only, namely grace" (*On Book IV of the Sentences* 1, 1, 4). Catholic thinkers in the thirteenth century, then, understood the character to be a *sacramentum et res*, a sacramental reality. But this presented a special problem: How could the character be rightfully called a sacrament?

Sacramentum in earlier times had referred mainly to observable rites and sacred objects; and although Augustine had argued for its applicability to the baptismal seal, he himself often used the word to refer to rituals and the things used in them. In fact, Augustine's definition of a sacrament as a visible sign of invisible grace clearly referred to observable rites and seemed to contradict the idea of the seal's being a sacrament. How could the seal be a sign of anything if it was spiritual and therefore invisible? Some theologians speculated about its being seen by God or the angels, but the more accepted solution was to give a broad interpretation to Augustine's words. "Visible" can mean either visible to the eye or visible to the mind, that is, knowable. And since it was possible to know who had the seal by knowing who had been baptized, theologians reasoned that the seal was in that sense visible. Thus Aquinas argued that the baptismal character could be known because the reception of the sacrament could be seen. And others argued that the character was visible through its observable effects: membership in the church in the case of baptism, firmness in the faith in the case of confirmation, position in the hierarchy in the case of ordination to holy orders. For example, if one looked at a man whom one knew to be ordained, what one saw was not a layman but a priest; in effect, one perceived the individual's priestly character. Similarly, people perceived Christians as different from pagans, they perceived husbands and wives as joined to one another, and so on, in effect seeing with the mind what was invisible to the eye.

The solution to this problem led naturally to the solution to the next: Were the characters given by baptism, confirmation, and ordination the same or different? As long as the character was considered to be completely invisible there was no way to answer this question. But as soon as it was decided that the character was visible through the sacramental rite and its observable effects, it was clear that the characters for each of the sacraments had to be different.

But what of the metaphysical status of the character? How was one to understand it philosophically? Granted it was a spiritual reality, some kind of impression or change wrought in the soul, how was one to understand the metaphorical words "impression," "seal," "image," "character"? Aristotelian philosophy, which the medieval theologians had adopted, gave them at least one answer immediately. Whatever the character was, the reason why the fathers had been right in calling it indelible was because the character had to be received in the human soul, which was immaterial and therefore not subject to decay. A metaphysical alteration in the soul, then, could be permanent; it could last forever and not be lost.

Aristotle's philosophy offered a number of concepts for thinking about the soul and its abilities: faculty, habit, disposition, power, activity, passion. But Aristotle, having lived before the birth of Christ, never had to deal with questions of Christian theology. Medieval thinkers thus found themselves faced with the task of deciding which of his concepts could be used to think about the nature of the character. During the first half of the thirteenth century they tried to adapt one concept and then another to their needs, but each of their proposals ran into philosophical difficulties that seemed insurmountable. It was Aquinas who finally developed an acceptable solution by reinterpreting some of Aristotle's concepts in a way that made it possible to apply them in one way to the natural order, to human nature that was fallen but not yet redeemed, and in another way to the supernatural order, to the human soul that was enlightened by faith and elevated by grace.

Although the details of Aquinas' theory of the supernaturally elevated soul were sometimes abstruse, the ideas behind it were fairly fundamental to Christianity. Just as in creation God made human beings in his own image, so now through the sacraments Christ made them anew in his own image. Christ was essentially a mediator between God and humankind, and in that sense a priest. In the words of the Epistle to the Hebrews, "...we have a great high priest who has passed through the heavens, Jesus, the Son of God,...one who in every respect has been tested as we are, yet without sin" (Hebrews 4:14–15). So Christ was truly human, but he alone of all human beings loved God so perfectly that his whole life was a continual offering to his Father, culminating in his complete self-surrender on the cross. Christ, then, was a redeemer priest; and he brought about humanity's redemption by transforming and elevating human nature, making it possible for others to be born into a new dimension of existence, that same divine dimension in which he had lived his whole life. The means of entering into and sustaining that new life he had left with his church, and these were the sacraments.

The sacramental character, therefore, was a transformation of a person's soul, a spiritual conformation to the redemptive, self-sacrificing priesthood of Christ. Augustine had spoken of the seal of baptism as the image of Christ, but for Aquinas it was not as though a person were stamped on the arm with a tattoo; rather it was as though the whole person were cast into a new mold and emerged in a new image, that of Christ, who loved and was obedient to the Father. Still, receiving the gift of new life was one thing; using that gift and living that life was another. This was why those who had been baptized could still sin, why those who had been confirmed could still deny the faith, why those who had been ordained could still live for themselves rather than God. Each sacrament brought with it a slightly different yet more complete participation in Christ's priesthood: all were called to new life, all adults were called to a mature life of faith, some were called to continue Christ's sacramental ministry in the church.

In the categories of Aristotelian philosophy, the sacramental character was therefore a power (in more contemporary language, an ability or capability), but a supernatural power that could be given only by God. The character of baptism was a liberation from the deformity of original sin, an openness to receiving the other sacraments. The character of confirmation was a power to live a life of active faith, an ability to publicly confess Christ, a capacity to participate fully in the church's worship. The character of ordination was a disposition to service in the church, a capability of preaching the gospel, a power to administer the sacraments so that others might enter and grow in the Christian life. The powers conferred by the characters were thus also orientations toward activity, just as the power of sight is oriented toward seeing, as the power of emotion is oriented toward feeling, and as the power of intelligence is oriented toward understanding. And therefore, just as in the natural order one had to open one's eyes to see, one had to open one's heart to feel, and one had to open one's mind to understand, so also in the supernatural order having the supernatural power to participate in the priesthood of Christ did not mean that the power would be automatically and always used.

In fact, there was one important difference between a person's natural powers and the supernatural powers of a Christian. The use of natural powers was an activity of the person who had them; one used one's own power to see, to feel, to understand. But the exercise of supernatural powers was always also an activity of the one who gave them, and they were God-given powers. Thus the use of those powers was always dependent on a person's openness to receiving God's gifts, and their exercise was never a purely human activity but always a cooperation with divine activity, with God acting in one's soul. One who was baptized always had to look upon others who afterward fell into sin and say with Paul, "There but for the grace of God go I." A Christian at worship thanked and praised God, yet he or she was aware that somehow this worship was also the work of the Holy Spirit within. Receiving a spiritual power through the sacraments, therefore, oriented one toward grace, but it was not the same as cooperating with it.

In summary, during the thirteenth century the sacramental character came to be understood by Aquinas and others as something real, a supernatural power that enabled a person to cooperate with God's grace. It could not be lost or destroyed because it was a power of the human soul, which was immaterial and, according to Catholic teaching, immortal. The character or power could not be seen, and yet it could be known through the sacramental rite in which it was received; and so it could legitimately be called a sign or a *sacramentum*. Finally, since the character was known through the sacramental rite, and since there were three rites, each of which signified something different, there had to be three different sacramental characters. The premises behind these conclusions could be found in scriptural and patristic texts as they were understood in the Middle Ages. The style of reasoning used was that of classical Greek thought. And the conclusions themselves made sense in the light of the sacramental practices of the medieval church and the religious beliefs and experiences of medieval Christians. But there was more to sacramental theology than the explanation of the character, and to understand it more fully it is necessary to learn more about its background.

4. Aristotle, Aquinas, and the Sacraments

If the scriptures and the fathers gave medieval theologians something to think about, it was the Greek philosopher Aristotle who gave them a way to think about it. His writings were virtually unknown to the fathers, who preferred the idealism of Plato and the sometimes mystical metaphysics of the neoplatonic philosophers. Many of his works had been preserved in the great libraries in the eastern part of the old Roman Empire, but in the seventh and eighth centuries the Muslim conquest swept westward across Africa and pushed northward into Asia Minor, and Christian Europe lost all but the names of most of them.

Some of his writings did survive in the west, however. They were a collection of works on logic, which began to be studied first in the monastery schools and then in the cathedral schools as the medieval renaissance began. Those who adopted Aristotle's logic developed a style of thinking and reasoning that soon became a trademark of the schools. Those who taught in them were known as *scholastici* or schoolmen, and their method of philosophizing came to be called scholasticism. Berengar of Tours, for example, was an early scholastic who tried to analyze the doctrine of the eucharist using Aristotelian logic.

In the meanwhile, a number of Muslim theologians had read Aristotle and had chosen him as their philosophical mentor. Then, in the twelfth century, Christian intellectuals near Moorish Spain began to learn about the missing writings of Aristotle that had been translated into Arabic. Wanting to meet Muslim theology on its own grounds, they obtained copies of the missing works and had them translated from Arabic into Latin. These translations of translations, unclear and erroneous in parts, were then brought to Paris for study, and slowly the main body of Aristotelian writings was introduced to the schools of Europe. Early in the thirteenth century copies of these writings in the original Greek were discovered in Constantinople and translated directly into Latin. And one of the first persons in the west to study the more accurate translations was the Dominican monk Thomas Aquinas.

The effect of Aristotle on the west was incalculable. In his books on psychology and biology, physics and metaphysics, politics and ethics, Christians discovered an encyclopedic knowledge of the world that was completely different from their own. And yet this Greek philosopher, born almost four centuries before Christ, was evidently a master not only of logic but also of all the sciences then known. Some church leaders feared the influence that a pagan thinker might have on students, and his works were banned from the universities more than once. Nevertheless, through the efforts of Aquinas, his teacher Albert, and others, Aristotle's ideas were gradually accepted as complementing rather than contradicting the knowledge that Christendom called its own. Eventually, Aristotelian science and philosophy were taught in all the schools and incorporated into the medieval view of reality. And Aristotle himself came to be so esteemed that the schoolmen, instead of referring to him by name, called him simply "the Philosopher."

The Aristotelian philosophical vocabulary was replete with technical terms such as "substance" and "accident," "matter" and "form," "potency" and "act." Medieval thinkers did their best to understand their meanings and then use them to develop philosophical explanations of the Christian mysteries. Transubstantiation, for example, was basically an Aristotelian way of speaking about the change of bread and wine into the body and blood of Christ: the "substance" or reality changed, while the "accidents" or appearances did not. Aquinas and the scholastics also spoke about sacramental ritual, the *sacramentum tantum*, as being composed of matter and form since according to Aristotle everything in this world was composed of matter and form, and rituals were things in this world. What Aristotle meant was that everything in the world around us has, as it were, two basic aspects. On the one hand it is sensible or experienceable in some way: it is seeable, hearable, touchable, tasteable, or smellable. On the other hand it is also intelligible or understandable: it has a meaning, we have an idea or concept of what it is. Now, what we see of something is very often the material it is made of—wood, stone, metal, and so forth; hence, Aristotle referred to the sensible aspect of things as their matter. Likewise, very often the shape of a thing gives us an idea of what it is—we tell a woman from a man or a table from a chair by their shapes; hence, Aristotle referred to the intelligible aspect of things as their form.

Theologians in the Middle Ages not only agreed with Aristotle's analysis but they also noticed that ecclesiastical rituals had something like a matter and a form to them. On the one hand, there were sensible gestures and objects used in them, and on the other, there was the meaning that the rituals had. Moreover, the meaning of the rituals was often given in words used—the pouring of water was just the pouring of water, if it were done without the words "I baptize thee...." So the scholastics used the terms "matter" and "form" as a kind of technical shorthand to talk about the experienceable and intelligible aspects of sacramental rituals.

For Aristotle, "science" meant a knowledge of the causes of things, and the scholastics endeavored to make theology a science in the Aristotelian sense of the word. Now, "cause" was also a technical word in the Aristotelian vocabulary, and broadly speaking a cause was anything on which something else depended. Thus, for example, matter and form were causes in the Aristotelian way of looking at things, since in order to be what it was a thing had to be sensible and have a certain meaning. Purposes were also causes: they were the reasons why things were made or done. Causes in the modern sense of the word—like a spark causing a fire—were also causes for Aristotle, but they were only one kind of cause. The important point to realize about the Aristotelian method of analyzing causes, however, is it worked backward, as it were, from effect to cause.

Aquinas realized this, and he applied this method of causal analysis to the sacraments. Why was this woman a Christian? Because she was baptized. What caused sins to be forgiven? Confession and the absolution of the priest. How was it that Christ is present in the eucharist? It was caused by the words of consecration over the bread and wine. Sacraments were causes in the Aristotelian sense, therefore, because various aspects of the Christian life depended on them. Moreover, different aspects of the Christian life could be traced back to different sacraments. The reason why priests were different from married people was because they had received different sacraments. The experience of the presence of Christ and a feeling of love for others could be directly related to the reception of communion. The restful resignation (or even the remarkable recovery) of a dying woman might be traced back to the fact that she had received the last rites. So it was clear to Aquinas, using this kind of causal analysis, that different spiritual effects had different sacramental causes, or to put it the more common way, that different sacraments had different effects.

Some of these effects were sacramental realities such as the character of confirmation or the bond of marriage. These were known by faith, and their cause was the sacramental ritual itself. Thus, for example, Catholics could know by faith that Christ was present in the eucharist even when they did not experience a sense of his presence. Other effects were graces, sacramental graces: the unselfish love of a husband and wife in marriage, the feeling of spiritual cleansing in confession, a happy and productive ministry in the priesthood, the spiritual gifts of wisdom, understanding, fortitude, and piety from confirmation. They were graces because they were God's free gifts; God owed them to no one. But to those who were open to receiving them, God gave them freely.

Almost every aspect of Christian life in a Christian culture such as medieval Europe could be connected in one way or another with one or another of the sacraments. Both the sacramental realities that Aquinas believed in and saw evidenced in the society around him, and the graces that he experienced and saw manifested in others, could therefore be related to sacramental rites as their causes. But Aquinas also insisted that the sacraments were not their ultimate cause. In themselves the rites were only symbolic gestures; the ultimate cause of all sacramental effects was God alone. For the sacramental realities were supernatural powers enabling a person to receive and cooperate with grace, and the sacramental graces were God-given gifts. The sacraments were, so to speak, God's instruments, vehicles, channels of grace. In Aristotelian terminology the sacraments were instrumental causes, things through which God acted in people's lives, creating and sustaining the church, bringing people to salvation, and making them holy.

But if sacraments were merely instrumental causes of grace, why did Aquinas claim that the sacraments were necessary? Why could God not bring people to salvation without intermediary symbols and gestures? In framing his answer, Aquinas once again argued from effect to cause, only this time the effect considered was the sacramental rituals themselves. Sacraments were necessary, he reasoned, because signs were a necessary part of human life. Whenever people communicated, they used signs: sounds in the air, marks on a page, and so forth. Signs were instrumental causes of knowledge; through signs people came to know what others were trying to say to them. In other words, signs were instrumental causes but they were necessary because they were needed for communication. In the same way, he argued, sacraments were instrumental causes but they too were necessary; they were signs of sacred realities that God wanted to communicate to people for their own benefit. Without signs such as the sacraments people would not come to know or experience God's salvation. It was a conclusion that made a great deal of sense in a world where books were scarce and few could read; for most Christians the sacramental liturgies were the main form of religious instruction.

Finally, since it was God who acted in and through the sacraments, it was clear to Aquinas—as it had been clear to Augustine in the case of baptism—that the real effectiveness of sacraments did not depend on the worthiness of the minister. People knew by faith that they had received sacramental realities, and they experienced in their lives sacramental graces, regardless of the sanctity of the person who performed the ritual. Early in the thirteenth century, theologians had wrestled with this question, and the main objections to saying that the sacramental effects did not depend at all on the minister or recipient came from those who envisioned cases where the rite might be performed in jest or in ignorance. Suppose, for example, that a Christian child playfully poured water over a Jewish friend's head and said the words of baptism; would the friend be baptized? Or suppose that a priest were teaching a student how to say the mass and said the words of consecration over an unnoticed piece of bread; would it automatically become the body of Christ? From considering marginal cases such as these and reflecting on liturgies that were genuinely sacramental, the scholastics came to acknowledge that intentions did play a role in sacramental rite: both the minister and the recipient must have the intention of participating in a sacramental rite, or as they would have said it, of doing what the church does. Without that intention the rite would be an empty ritual, and so there would be no spiritual effect.

Barring such bizarre circumstances, however, the scholastics generally agreed that it was the rite, not the minister, that was the cause of sacramental effects. How otherwise could one explain that most of the fathers considered the sacraments of heretics and schismatics to be valid? How otherwise could one explain the experience of union with Christ after receiving communion from a priest later discovered to be living in sin? The scholastics' way of referring to this independence of the rite from the sanctity or orthodoxy of the minister was to say that the effects of the sacraments were caused *ex opere operato*, literally, "by the work worked," or "from the doing of the thing done."

As already said, the twelfth and thirteenth centuries marked a high point in medieval theology. These two centuries saw the rediscovery of the church's patristic heritage, the organization of theology into major areas of inquiry, and the working out of an intellectual method to deal with theological problems. In the hands of theologians like Aquinas, the scholastic method provided the Catholic Church with logical and coherent explanations for the sacraments and for all the other mysteries of the Christian faith. Catholic thinkers of that age sought to explain as much as they could of their religion, without explaining it away. It was an age of *fides quaerens intellectum*, of faith seeking understanding.

But there were also other tendencies in medieval Christianity, tendencies that were more practical than theoretical. There were those who were more concerned with the proper administration of the sacraments than with the philosophical explanations of them. There were also tendencies that were more analytic than synthetic. Aquinas and the scholastics had woven a theological synthesis, but it was not perfect; and the tendency of later thinkers was to find the flaws in the system. Lastly there were events, political and otherwise, which had nothing directly to do with theology, but which made the medieval synthesis tend to be less and less relevant to what was actually happening in Christendom. It is to those tendencies that we must now turn.

5. Legalism, Nominalism, and Magic

Peter Lombard's *Sentences* was not the only medieval compendium that had a great impact on the Catholic sacraments. Around 1140 John Gratian at the University of Bologna published a comprehensive treatise on ecclesiastical or canon law in which he gathered, organized, and edited materials on almost every aspect of the church's institutional functions. The original title of the work was *The Agreement of Disagreeing Canons*, but because many church rules or canons were found in official pronouncements it was popularly known as Gratian's *Decrees*. Like the *Sentences*, it was mostly a collection of texts from other sources, but the texts included in the *Decrees* were letters, decrees, and directives of popes, bishops, and councils. Like the *Sentences*, it cited authorities on both sides of disputed issues, to which Gratian added his own opinions. Like the *Sentences*, it included a large section, the whole third part, on the sacraments, but the *Decrees* was more concerned with questions of administration (for example, whether or not lay people may baptize, or who may legally enter into marriage) than with questions of theology.

Also like the *Sentences*, soon after its appearance the *Decrees* became a primary source book for students of canon law and the main reference book for those who needed to be informed about ecclesiastical regulations. Since it contained conflicting rules and opinions it could never be adopted as an official code of canon law, but since there was as yet no unified judicial code in the western church it continued to influence ecclesiastical decisions for a number of centuries. In regard to the sacraments, it had the effect of bringing an additional measure of uniformity to the rites and the rules surrounding them.

It was only slowly that theology and canon law developed into separate disciplines, but from the very beginning there were some important differences between the theological and canonical approaches to the sacraments. Theologians were primarily concerned with understanding the sacraments and explaining how they functioned within the spiritual life of the Christian; canonists were concerned primarily with regulating the sacraments and determining how they functioned within the institutional life of the church. In theology, for example, the main effect of baptism was the reception of God's gifts, or grace; in canon law, the importance of baptism was that it made a person a member of the church with certain rights and obligations. Also, theologians were primarily interested in the essential nature of the sacraments; they sought to understand what they basically were and how they worked when they were devoutly participated in. Canonists on the other hand were primarily interested in individual sacramental acts; they sought to specify what each particular rite must contain in order for it to do its spiritual work. Thus in theology the mass was regarded as a sacramental participation in Christ's offering of himself to the Father; in canon law the mass was treated as a sacramental ritual containing certain basic elements such as prayers, readings, gestures, and the materials for consecration.

As the theological and canonical interpretations of the sacraments were developing, they influenced one another. Initially it was the theology of the sacraments that had the greater impact; later it was the other way around. Until the twelfth century, sacraments had been regarded primarily as signs rather than as causes of spiritual realities; even in the thirteenth century, influential theologians such as Bonaventure and Duns Scotus held theories that explained the sacraments as signs of rather than as causes of grace. But Aquinas insisted that this explanation did not do justice to the writings of the fathers and the testimony of the saints, and in the long run it was his causal explanation of the sacraments that the canonists accepted. Still, for Aquinas, the sacraments were primarily signs: they were effective because they were signs, and they produced their effects the same way that signs do, as instrumental causes. But for the canonists the crucial point was that they were effective signs: they were causes of sacramental realities and grace in the soul. And for them this meant that great care had to be taken to preserve the signs by administering the sacraments correctly, to ensure that they maintained their spiritual effectiveness. Put succinctly, Aquinas' insistence on the causal nature of the sacraments led canonists to insist on proper performance of the rituals.

In time, this emphasis on proper performance led paradoxically to a kind of minimalist attitude toward the sacramental rites. Instead of suggesting that sacramental liturgies should be richly symbolic and personally involving so that people could experience their spiritual effects fully, the idea of sacraments as causal signs suggested that there were certain minimum standards that had to be met if their spiritual effectiveness were not to be lost entirely. Would a baptism be effective if dirty water were used, for instance, or if the words were not properly pronounced? How much of the mass could be eliminated without affecting the transubstantiation of the bread and wine? What essentials had to be observed if extreme unction were administered in an emergency? Questions of this sort concerned the validity of the sacraments. A valid sacrament was one that met the minimum ritual requirements; if any of these requirements were not met the ritual was considered to be invalid, that is, it was not really a sacrament and it therefore had no sacramental effects.

It was agreed that in order for a ritual to be effective it must have the proper matter and form, be performed by the proper minister, and be done with the proper intention. The terms "matter" and "form" were borrowed from theology, but to the canonists the matter was simply the materials and gestures used in the rite, and the form was the prescribed words that were said. Certain kinds of oil could be used in confirmation, for example, while others could not. Again, if the priest did not make the sign of the cross over the host during mass, it would still be consecrated. Or again, a confession in which the priest omitted some of the words of absolution could still be valid. The proper minister for most of the sacraments was a priest, but there were exceptions. A layperson could validly baptize if the proper words were said while the water was poured; even a non-Christian could baptize under exceptional circumstances, as long as it was done with the intention of performing a Catholic sacramental act. A bishop was the ordinary minister of confirmation, but he could validly delegate that power to a priest. But a bishop was the only valid minister of holy orders; even if a priest performed the ordination with permission it would be invalid. The proper intention was usually the general intent to do what the church did, but it was particularly important in the case of matrimony. The bride and groom were considered the ministers of the sacrament; the priest was merely an official witness of their union. And so if a couple went through the motions of a wedding ceremony without really intending to be united in Christian marriage, the sacrament would be void and the marriage could be annulled.

What, however, was the effect that a valid sacrament was supposed to have? It was the *sacramentum et res*, the sacramental reality caused by each of the particular sacraments: the seal of baptism, the characters of confirmation and ordination, the bond of marriage, reconciliation with the church, the commitment of the soul to God, the body and blood of Christ. Canonically considered, if the sacramental ritual was validly performed, the sacramental effect occurred *ex opere operato*; that is, by virtue of the performance of the proper ritual, the sacrament caused what it signified.

But what about grace, the second effect of the sacraments? According to theologians after Aquinas, the sacraments always offered or caused grace but it was not always received. As they interpreted Aquinas' theory, sacramental grace was caused not by the observable rite, the *sacramentum tantum*, but by the sacramental reality, the *sacramentum et res*. One could infer the existence of the sacramental reality from the valid performance of the rite; but since grace was a hidden reality, a *res tantum*, given by God, one could never be certain whether or not another person had actually received sacramental graces. One could be certain that God offered the graces through the sacramental reality since God always offers divine gifts freely, but it was always possible that the person who received the sacrament was not also open to receiving the sacramental gifts.

Thus the graces caused by a sacrament came to be called its fruits. A sacrament was considered fruitful if the one who received it also received the graces appropriate to the sacrament; if in fact no grace was received, it was considered unfruitful. And what were the graces, these fruits? Certainly they could be religious experiences such as having a sense of Christ's presence in the eucharist or feeling God's mercy in penance; but they could also be other things such as children in marriage, a priest's talent for inspirational sermons, or the strength to live a virtuous life, looked upon as gifts, graces from God.

The most prevalent explanation for why a person might receive a sacrament and yet experience none or few of its graces was that the recipient did not have the proper disposition to receive them. Pride, fear, greed, love of self, or some other such attitude might be a sort of spiritual obstacle blocking cooperation with the graces that God was offering through the sacrament. Even God respected the human will, the theologians reasoned, and so God would not force supernatural gifts on anyone who was not disposed to receiving them.

This distinction between the sacramental reality and the sacramental graces also helped theologians to explain what they saw as the reviviscence of the sacraments in certain cases. Suppose, for instance, that a married man after a period of infidelity to his wife suddenly realized the anguish he was causing her and renounced his philandering; or less drastically, suppose that a baptized and confirmed Christian experienced a deeper religious conversion many years after receiving those sacraments. According to the theory of reviviscence, God had been continually offering divine grace since the time that the sacrament had been received, but it was only when the obstacle of sin or vice was removed that grace could flow through the sacramental reality into the soul. The sacrament, or rather the effects of the sacrament, had thus been revived after a period of dormancy.

The theological distinction between the sacramental reality and sacramental grace was helpful to canon lawyers as well. The sacramental reality could be considered to be unfailingly bestowed by a valid sacramental rite, and therefore who was baptized, married, or ordained could be a matter of public record. But sacramental graces were private affairs, governed by the inner disposition of the soul. No one could be sure, for example, whether the harmony between a husband and wife was a result of their natural abilities or whether it was a supernatural help from God given through the sacrament of marriage. Therefore, the canonists could consider a sacrament valid even if it did not bear fruit, that is, even if no graces were received, even if receiving the sacrament made no noticeable difference in a person's life.

The theologians and canon lawyers of the Middle Ages also drew one other important distinction in reference to the sacraments which, like the ones already mentioned, still survives in the Catholic Church's *Code of Canon Law*. This distinction regarded the liceity or legality of sacramental rites. Briefly, a sacrament was considered licit if it was administered in accordance with all of the regulations stipulated by canon law; it was considered illicit if one or more of those regulations was violated. Thus to change or omit prescribed parts of the mass would be illicit or inappropriate, and the same would be true for any of the other sacramental rites. Likewise, for a priest to celebrate mass or administer other sacraments in a diocese without the permission of the local bishop would be canonically illegal. However, in neither of these cases would the sacraments administered be considered invalid, unless the conditions for validity had also been disregarded.

This difference between validity and liceity was important because it meant that sacraments which were illicitly or improperly administered were often canonically valid. Thus if a priest from another diocese unlawfully heard a dying person's confession or administered extreme unction, those who went through the sacramental ritual unaware of his legal impediment could still be assured that they had truly received a sacrament. Even more seriously, if a deposed or heretical bishop ordained men to the priesthood, he would do so in violation of church law but the priests would be validly ordained; and the sacraments that they in turn administered would be valid even though illicit.

Although this approach to the administration of the sacraments became explicit only in the course of the development of canon law itself, the legal and theological principles behind it went back to Augustine and his position in the Donatist controversy. And by accepting the distinction between validity and liceity, Catholics today can regard the sacraments of Orthodox churches as valid even if not canonically licit. Yet if the distinction has its brighter side in an ecumenical age, it had its darker side in the Middle Ages. At a time when canon law was still in formation and rules for the proper administration of the sacraments were not yet codified, the minimalist rules for the valid administration of the sacraments, instead of being the barest acceptable standards, tended to become the norm. This is not to say that there were no beautifully performed liturgies in the Middle Ages, or that there were no devout and conscientious priests, or that there were no Catholics who reverently participated in the sacramental rites of the day. There were many, especially in the monasteries and in the cathedrals and in the university chapels. But there were also many—the peasants in the countryside, the artisans in the cities, and even the slowly growing middle class of merchants and professionals—who little understood the subtleties of canon law. Their acquaintance with the sacraments was all too often an experience of rituals reduced to their bare essentials, and their understanding of the sacraments was all too often a mechanistic idea of sacramental causality. To them, the rite produced what it signified, nothing more and nothing less: the washing away of original sin, the gifts of the Holy Spirit, the body and blood of Christ, the forgiving of mortal and venial sins, married people, priests, and spiritual readiness for death.

And there was plenty of death. In the fourteenth century, bubonic and other plagues swept across Europe, killing an estimated twenty-five million people. In some places, two thirds to three quarters of the population died within a few years, though in other places the plague took only a tenth or a fourth. And the plague was indiscriminate: it took young and old, poor and rich, saint and sinner. But those who braved the Black Death to nurse the afflicted or bury the dead took an even greater risk of infection, and they were often the young who had strength, the poor who could not escape to a less pestilent region, and the saintly who cared more for others than for themselves. The plague also made no distinction between artist and laborer, between merchant and farmer, between educated and illiterate, and in the course of that century the medieval renaissance came to an untimely end. Culture declined, trade dwindled, schools closed.

The Black Death put an end to the theological renaissance, too. Aquinas and Bonaventure had both died in 1274, long before the plague years, but there was no one who was able to continue their work, to carry on where they had left off. There might have been, among the monks and scholars of the Dominicans and the Franciscans, but many monks died tending the sick, and the schools were often vacated for fear of contamination. In addition to commenting on the *Sentences*, beginning theology students now wrote commentaries on the *summas* of the past masters, and possibly on the lately recovered writings of Aristotle. It was a tedious introduction to the divine science, but it seemed like the logical thing to do. It had worked well in the previous century, and besides, it was the only theological method that they knew.

But Aquinas' *Summa Theologica* was deceptive. It did not represent what Aquinas did, the way he had worked out his conclusions. It only presented his conclusions already worked out, along with summary reasons for and against them. One of the hallmarks of Aquinas' theological method was that it was largely inductive: he reasoned from the way things were to explanations of why they were that way. Just as Augustine had developed his theology largely by reflecting on the beliefs and practices prevalent in his day, Aquinas often drew his ideas from reflections on his own religious experience, which was that of a saintly monk. And yet his own writings, especially the *Summa*, hardly show this. His method of presenting his ideas was often more deductive in appearance, beginning from more general consideration and working toward more specific questions and applications. In his own mind he reasoned from effect to cause, but in his writings it seemed that he often moved from cause to effect. Thus God, for example, who for Aquinas was the ultimate cause of everything in the universe, was treated at the beginning of the *Summa Theologica*, while the sacraments, around which revolved his life as a priest and a monk, were treated in almost the last section, left unfinished. Aquinas and his better contemporaries knew what they were talking about when they talked about the effects of the sacraments, for they were often talking about what they had experienced in their own lives. But they did not write about their lives and their religious experiences; they wrote using the customary categories of their day: matter and form, substance and accidents, nature and grace, and so forth. And those who later read what they wrote tended to think they were talking about entities called matter and form, substances hidden under visible accidents, metaphysical objects called essences, and supernatural influxes called graces.

Thus the later scholastics erected an elaborate intellectual system of theological terms that had little or no reference to the lives that people actually led or to the religious experiences that they actually had. The sacraments that were received were spiritual realities in the soul that were neither experienced nor known except in virtue of the sacramental rites. The sacramental characters were invisible signs impressed on the soul distinguishing Christian from non-Christian, confirmed from unconfirmed, priest from layperson. The powers that the sacraments gave were hidden spiritual powers: baptism prepared the soul to receive the other sacraments, ordination gave special priestly powers, all of them gave the power to receive sacramental graces. The causal effectiveness of the sacramental rituals was guaranteed by God, who gave the graces, and by Christ through whose merits these were distributed. But the grace caused by the sacramental rituals was an unexperienced entity, given to those whose souls were properly disposed, yet hidden and unknown except by faith.

Thus the Aristotelian causal analysis that Aquinas had used was reversed. Now the first cause was the triune God, who through the incarnation of the second member of the Trinity had established the church and instituted the seven sacraments. Since the rites were divinely ordained, they worked by the power of God, and they caused their effects automatically as long as they were correctly performed. Their proper performance was guarded by canon law, which gave the conditions for their validity and liceity, enumerated their effects, and indicated their necessity. And now the sacraments were necessary for salvation not because people needed signs, but because only the Catholic Church has the sacraments, and "outside the church there is no salvation."

For the twelfth- and thirteenth-century theologians, arguments from authority had great weight, not only because their theological training began with the *Sentences* but also because quoting the scriptures and the fathers was their way of tying their own work to the ancient Christian tradition. Yet when these theologians developed their own ideas they felt no qualms about choosing one father over another, or about interpreting a text in a favorable light, because in their writings they were talking mainly about what they themselves had worked out, not about what the fathers had said. But those who followed in the fourteenth century tended to do otherwise. They followed what they believed to be the example of Aquinas and others, and since the great scholastics had always quoted authorities and only rarely referred to their own experience in their written works, they tended to argue more from authority than from experience. Thus, by following the style of the *summas* and being unaware of the style of their authors, the later scholastics tended to write about what Aquinas and the others wrote instead of thinking the way they thought. It was as though they assumed that since the answers in theology had all been worked out, all they had to do was study and comprehend them.

Those who followed this tried and proven *via antiqua*, the old way, formed themselves into schools—not new colleges or universities but schools of thought. The Dominican school followed Aquinas, the Franciscan school followed Bonaventure or Scotus, there were those who followed less well-known scholastics, and there were those who preferred Augustine. But there were also those who rejected this bookish repetition of the past and struck out on what they called the *via moderna*, the modern way. They were skeptical of the metaphysical speculations of the scholastics and the unproductive rivalries between the schools, and they sought a way to cut through both of them. The tool they chose was logic, the logic of Aristotle, used not in the service of theology but in the service for which the ancient Greek had originally intended it, that of critical reasoning. And they interpreted Aristotle's categories not as categories of reality but as categories of thought, referring only to words and the way they were used. Foremost among these new thinkers was William of Ockham, in England.

The label that was eventually given to this new way of thinking was nominalism, since it was a philosophical method that focused on words, *nomina* in Latin. The nominalists insisted that the metaphysical realism of the scholastics was a mistake. To them it was obvious that matter and form, essence and existence, substance and accidents were not real in themselves. The real things in the world were individuals: people and animals, trees and stones, and so forth. The metaphysical terms that the scholastics used were actually just concepts, abstractions, products of the mind. The scholastics had believed, for example, that there were metaphysical principles that could be used to deduce scientific knowledge about the real world, principles such as the notion that every real thing must have a cause. But the nominalists contended that these metaphysical principles were in fact logical principles, rules of thought which helped one to learn about the real world, but which said nothing directly about the real world.

One by one the metaphysical assumptions of scholastic theology came under attack. Ockham denied that it was possible to prove that there was only one God or to know anything definite about God using reason alone, although as a Catholic he still believed that God existed and as a theologian he accepted what had been revealed about God. He also denied that it was possible to prove the existence or immortality of the human soul: the soul was at best a plausible explanation for human life and activity, and immortality could be hoped for but it could not be demonstrated. Again here, though, Ockham was willing to admit that human beings have immortal souls, for this was a truth of faith; what he denied was that it was philosophically provable.

The uncertainty of metaphysics was matched by a similar uncertainty in ethics. Philosophers might use reason to discover ethical principles or formulate moral codes, but these were not strictly provable. They were simply practical guidelines, general rules that should govern human behavior in society, and philosophical reasoning could never demonstrate that they had to be true. If indeed they were true, it was only because God had willed them to be true. In fact, Ockham claimed, the whole order of creation, including the moral order, depended on the will of God. Things were the way they were because God willed them to be that way; if God had willed otherwise the world would be different, including the laws of nature and the rules of ethical behavior. If it had been the divine will, God could have made a world in which the moon was hot and the sun was cold, in which it was noble to steal from the poor and dishonorable to relieve their poverty. For if the creator was all powerful and completely free, as Christians believed, God could have produced a universe that was different from the present one, simply by willing it.

After Ockham the philosophical and theological unity of Christendom was shattered. Nominalism showed that philosophical reasoning could lead to conclusions quite different from those of theology, and it contended that reasoning itself had to deal with words and statements rather than the real world. All that could be known from experience, it claimed, was experience; everything else was metaphysical speculation. Nominalism thus succeeded in diminishing, at least in the minds of many, the credibility of scholasticism, and it opened the way for a variety of philosophical and theological approaches in the schools of fifteenth-century Europe. Some followed Meister Eckhart of Germany, preferring the intuitive truth of mystical experience to the uncertain truth of philosophy. Some continued to follow the *via antiqua*, preferring the achievements of the past to the disagreements of the present. Some developed new philosophies, preferring originality to antiquity. Some went down into skepticism, or preferred *fides sine intellectu*, faith without understanding.

Sacramental theology in the late Middle Ages could no longer depend on philosophy for its explanations, and so it turned to canon law. The words of the canonists were still the words of the great scholastics, but now they had legal rather than theological meanings. Matter and form were the things that were necessary for validity. Validity was what was required to cause the sacramental reality. The sacramental reality gave power in a legal sense: baptism gave the power to receive the other sacraments, matrimony gave the power to have lawful intercourse and legitimate children, ordination gave the power to administer the sacraments, penance gave the power to receive communion and the other sacraments worthily. In the end, a large portion of canon law dealt with the sacraments, and a large measure of sacramental theology was dependent on canon law.

Sacramental practice suffered a worse fate: it became sacramental magic. *Ex opere operato* meant that the rituals worked automatically. The priest poured the water on the infant's head, saying the right words, and the child was saved from hell. The bishop anointed the candidate for confirmation and she received an indelible mark on her soul. Two people recited their marriage vows and they were thereby bonded together for life. The priest said the words of absolution in the confessional and sins were immediately wiped away. By the words of consecration the bread and wine were suddenly transformed into the body and blood of Christ. The soul of the person who received the last rites went directly to heaven.

The magical attitude that invaded the church's liturgical sacraments also pervaded other pious practices. Special prayers to the Blessed Virgin or the saints were certain of being heard. Gazing intently at the host or crucifix could guarantee that a son would be born. Touching relics of martyrs or saints could cause miraculous healings. Chanting the proper holy phrases would keep away temptation. Making a pilgrimage to Rome or a famous shrine would earn merit in heaven. Reciting certain prayers at the proper times would cancel all the punishment one could expect after death. Making a donation to the church could release a soul from purgatory.

None of this was ever officially sanctioned by the Catholic hierarchy. None of it even entered the manuals of sacred theology or was approved by canon law. But it was going on among the people and it was condoned by the clergy. And it was setting the stage for a revolution.

For Further Reading

G. R. Evans, *Philosophy and Theology in the Middle Ages* (Routledge, 1993) is a very approachable introduction to how and why medieval thinkers thought the way they did.

Isnard Wilhelm Frank, *A Concise History of the Medieval Church* (Continuum, 1995) gives an overview of what was going on socially, politically, spiritually, and intellectually.

B. B. Price, *Medieval Thought* (Blackwell Publishers, 1992) grounds the development of scholastic theology in Greek thought and Christian spirituality.

Carl Volz, *The Medieval Church* (Abingdon Press, 1997) situates the twelfth century renaissance within the broader sweep of medieval history.

Thomas Heffernan and E. Ann Matter, eds., *The Liturgy of the Medieval Church* (Western Michigan University Press, 2001) collects articles by scholars for teachers and students of medieval theology on basic topics.

Marshall Baldwin, *The Medieval Church* (Cornell University Press, 1953) is a concise and readable history of Christianity in the Middle Ages.

Christopher Dawson, *Medieval Essays* (Doubleday Image Books, 1959) contains a number of essays on the church and medieval thought.

For Further Study

Medieval Theology

Jaroslav Pelikan, *The Growth of Medieval Theology, 600–1300* (University of Chicago Press, 1978) traces the development of scholasticism up until the synthesis of Thomas Aquinas.

Michael Haren, *Medieval Thought* (University of Toronto Press, 1992) explains how the recovery of ancient Greek philosophy provided a foundation for the development of scholasticism.

Yves Congar, *A History of Theology* (Doubleday, 1968) contains three chapters on the development and contributions of scholasticism.

G. R. Evans, ed., *The Medieval Theologians* (Blackwell, 2001) contains well-written articles on Christian thinkers from Augustine through the scholastics to the nominalists and mystics.

Ulrich Leinsle, *Introduction to Scholastic Theology* (Catholic University of America Press, 2010) is a comprehensive history of scholasticism from the early Middle Ages to the Renaissance and beyond.

Gary Macy, *The Theologies of the Eucharist in the Early Scholastic Period* (Oxford University Press, 1984) presents a detailed account of how theology was done in the Middle Ages, focusing on different interpretations of the eucharist.

Scholastic Theologians

Peter Lombard, *The Sentences: Book 4, On the Doctrine of Signs* (Pontifical Institute of Medieval Studies, 2010) is a recent translation of the medieval work that framed all discussion of the sacraments in scholastic theology and Catholic doctrine.

Philipp W. Rosemann, *The Story of a Great Medieval Book* (Broadview Press, 2007) describes how Lombard's *Sentences* came to be written and how it became the most influential textbook in the Middle Ages.

Elizabeth Rogers, *Peter Lombard and the Sacramental System* (Richwood Publishing, 1976) shows the changes that took place in numbering and defining the sacraments in the middle of the twelfth century.

Radulphus Ardens, *The Questions on the Sacraments* (Pontifical Institute of Medieval Studies, 2010) was written after Lombard and before Aquinas, showing how medieval thinkers reflected on the sacraments.

Thomas Aquinas, *Summa Theologica* contains his theology of the sacraments in Part III, Questions 60–90, and Supplement. *Summa Contra Gentiles* presents his ideas on the sacraments in more summary fashion in Book IV, Chapters 56–78.

Thomas O'Meara, *Thomas Aquinas, Theologian* (University of Notre Dame Press, 1997) is a comprehensive treatment of the thinker, his context, and his legacy.

Matthew Levering and Michael Dauphinais, eds., *Rediscovering Aquinas and the Sacraments* (Hillebrand Books, 2009) is a collection of clear essays on liturgical worship and the seven sacraments.

Peter Garland, *The Definition of Sacrament According to Saint Thomas* (University of Ottawa Press, 1959) gives a technical but clear explanation of Aquinas' understanding of sacraments as signs of grace.

John Gallagher, *Significando Causant: A Study of Sacramental Causality* (Fribourg University Press, 1965) is a thorough treatment of how Aquinas and other scholastics explained that sacraments cause grace.

Bernard Lonergan, *Grace and Freedom in Aquinas* (Herder and Herder, 1971) develops the approach to grace and causality followed in this chapter.

Medieval Church History

J. N. Hillgarth, ed., *Christianity and Paganism, 350–750* (University of Pennsylvania Press, 1986) introduces and comments on historical texts, documenting the gradual conversion of western Europe.

Richard Fletcher, *The Barbarian Conversion* (University of California Press, 1999) is a lengthy but readable narrative about the spread of Christianity into pagan Europe from 600 to 1400.

C. Warren Hollister, *Medieval Europe* (John Wiley and Sons, 1982) provides a generous supply of maps and illustrations to help explain what was happening in the Middle Ages.

Margaret Deanesly, *A History of the Medieval Church, 590–1500* (Routledge, Chapman and Hall, 1969) is a clear and often reprinted account of almost every aspect of church life in that period.

Richard Southern, *Western Society and the Church in the Middle Ages* (William B. Eerdmans, 1970) details the social and political background to the theological developments in medieval Christianity.

Francis Oakley, *The Western Church in the Later Middle Ages* (Cornell University Press, 1979) describes ecclesiastical, liturgical, and theological developments during that period.

Joseph Lynch, *The Medieval Church* (Longman, 1992) covers everything from the conversion of Europe to the invention of the printing press, with a chapter devoted to the sacraments.

John Thomson, *The Western Church in the Middle Ages* (Arnold, 1998) gives a fairly comprehensive overview of developments in Europe from the fall of Rome to the eve of the Reformation.

F. Donald Logan, *A History of the Church in the Middle Ages* (Routledge, 2002) contains helpful maps, diagrams, pictures, and bibliographies.

Stephen Wilson, *The Magical Universe* (Hambledon and London, 2000) is a thorough treatment of magical beliefs and practices in medieval Europe.

CHAPTER IV

CATHOLIC AND PROTESTANT SACRAMENTS

All true justification either begins through the sacraments, or increases through them once it is begun, or is restored through them if it is lost.
—Council of Trent

The function of the sacraments is precisely the same as the word of God.
—John Calvin

Protestantism began as an attempt to reform the Catholic Church from within. There had been other attempts during the Middle Ages; some had succeeded temporarily, others had been rejected or repressed. In the thirteenth century Francis of Assisi attempted to rebuild the church on a foundation of evangelical poverty, and many of his Friars Minor or "little brothers" dedicated themselves to serving the poor. Dominic de Guzman founded the Order of Preachers to bring the gospel to the world, and his followers became missionaries throughout Europe and scholars in universities. Around the same period the Albigensian sect in southern France protested against the immorality and worldliness of the clergy, but their theology was heretical and so they were massacred by crusaders. Peter Waldo had been a wealthy merchant in Lyons before he sold his goods and gave them to the poor, but when he preached voluntary poverty without the permission of the bishops he was excommunicated. In the fourteenth century John Wycliffe argued against ecclesiastical abuses in England, but his arguments did little to change them. John Hus aroused the national spirit of Bohemia by attacking the authority of the Roman popes and the greed of the Roman clergy, but he was convicted of heresy and burned at the stake. In fact, most reforms from the bottom up were either short lived or else they did not get to the heart of the matter. They were for the most part lay movements that had little impact on the established hierarchy.

Reforms from the top down fared little better. Between 1123 and 1517 nine general church councils met to deal primarily with clerical and political abuses, but the reforms they decreed usually went unheeded. Kings and princes appointed bishops, bishops ordained priests, and priests administered sacraments—often for a price. Canon law forbade priests to marry, so many of the clergy sought the comfort of a wife without the benefit of matrimony; some bishops even sold their priests licenses to keep concubines. Bishops themselves were often land-owning barons, and to keep their estates within the family they sometimes appointed relatives, and even their sons, to succeed them.

Bishops taxed those in their jurisdiction, and the pope taxed the bishops. The popes often as not lived in luxury; the mass of peasants lived in poverty, fear, and superstition. When reforms were actually made, new disorders usually replaced the old ones. But the impotence of even reform-minded church leaders to remedy things is shown by the number of times that councils addressed the same problems again and again.

While conditions within the church remained largely unchallenged and unchanged, however, cultural and social conditions in Europe did change, slowly at first and then more quickly. A once feudal society with fluid boundaries began to solidify into countries with their own cultural identity. The world, once thought to be flat and bounded by the borders of civilization, was discovered to be larger and stranger than previously imagined. Literacy, once a clerical privilege, began to grow among the merchant middle class, and lay students of law and medicine, philosophy and science gradually outnumbered the clerics at the universities. Books, once copied by hand, were rare and expensive, but after 1450 books printed on presses became more available and less costly. The arts, once devoted almost exclusively to the glory of God, began to explore the world and celebrate the individual. By the sixteenth century a new nationalism and a new humanism were rapidly transforming western civilization from medieval Christendom into modern Europe. Later generations hailed it as a new birth of culture and called it the Renaissance.

It was this change in Europe that finally made a change in Christianity possible. Martin Luther challenged what was passing for Catholic theology on the grounds that it was unintelligible, and what he said seemed to make sense. He attacked scholasticism for being unscriptural, and those who read the Bible saw that it was so. He denounced the corruption of the clergy and the superstition of the faithful in a vigorous attempt to spark reform in the church. But his attack was too pointed and his attitude was too adamant for Rome to tolerate, and within a few years he was excommunicated. But he also denounced the domination of the German church by the Roman hierarchy, and so some German princes protected this spokesman for their cause from the fate that had met earlier reformers. His evangelical theology won the support of the laity, his call for church reform won the support of the lower clergy, and his insistence on freedom from papal oppression won the support of the nobility. Within a few decades this reform movement in northern Germany developed a religious, moral, and political impetus that carried it into many parts of Europe. Luther's reformation was a success because it came at a time when in the spirit of the Renaissance people were beginning to sense that there could be an alternative to the medieval mentality, that individuals could think for themselves, and that states could govern their own affairs. Rome saw this movement as a rebellion against tradition and a breaking away from the church; the reformers saw it as a renewal of the church and a breaking away from Rome.

It took the Roman church twenty-five years to address the problems that precipitated the reformation, and it took another eighteen years to discuss, debate, and begin to implement its own internal reforms. When the Council of Trent first met, fewer than three dozen bishops bothered to attend, although by its final session almost two decades later it had the support of most of the remaining parts of once Catholic Europe. The council affirmed what it saw as the traditional teachings of the church and denounced those recent developments that it saw as heretical. In addition, it legislated practical reforms that eventually eliminated most of the abuses against which the reformers had protested. It prohibited bishops from presiding over several dioceses in order to collect the income from them; it put a stop to bishops appointing their own successors; it abolished many of the bishops' taxing privileges and forbade the selling of indulgences; it announced automatic penalties for priests who were living with women, or who failed to preach or administer the sacraments; it called for the establishment of seminaries and it outlined a program of priestly formation. In the area of the other sacraments besides orders, the popes who followed the council initiated a series of reforms that gradually curtailed the most flagrant abuses and superstitious practices. But by this time the authority of Rome to dictate changes within all of western Christianity was lost. Protestants had already brought reform to much of Germany, Switzerland,

Holland, and Great Britain, and they were not about to surrender what they had achieved to a foreign pope. In these countries most of the Catholic sacramental practices were either abolished or drastically simplified. They developed other sacraments in the broad sense of that term, but these were usually different from the Roman church's sacramental practices, and they did not call them sacraments. These were new forms of worship, like the Quakers' later use of sacramental silence, or else they were adaptations of older forms, like preaching and hymn singing.

From the viewpoint of the Christian church as a whole, then, the reformation marks as great a turning point in Christianity's attitude toward the sacraments as the patristic and medieval periods had been. The church fathers had sown the seeds of a sacramental system that developed in parallel but separate ways in eastern Orthodoxy and western Catholicism. Medieval theology and canon law erected the theory and practice of Christian sacramentalism into an elaborate intellectual and ritual system in the Catholic Church. The reformation demolished what remained of the medieval synthesis and abolished most of what had become misused and misunderstood sacramental practices in large portions of Europe. Among the Protestant denominations the traditional sacramental system came to be regarded as a Roman invention riddled with superstition. In response, the Catholic Church reasserted its position on the seven liturgical sacraments and curtailed the flagrant abuse of sacramental practices, but it was never able to reestablish its sacramental system within all of western Christianity. Henceforward, Roman Catholicism would continue in the medieval tradition; Protestant Christianity would develop its own tradition.

1. Luther and the Protestant Reformation

At the end of the last chapter we saw how nominalism in Catholic theology and legalism in church practice led to a mechanistic and minimalistic attitude toward the seven sacraments; and at the beginning of this chapter we have taken a quick look at some of the wider issues surrounding the Protestant reformation. The reform movement was a complex one involving a number of persons, a sequence of events, and a variety of theological positions too numerous to be treated in detail. Nevertheless, as the movement gained momentum there were some key figures and some central issues that emerged and can help to delineate the major differences between Protestant and Catholic approaches to sacraments.

On October 31, 1517, Martin Luther announced his desire to debate a number of points of Catholic doctrine by posting his opinions (so the story goes) on the cathedral door in Wittenberg. These now famous "ninety-five theses" challenged the church's position on indulgences, which were a part of the sacramental system related to penance. In the early church, public sinners had been required to perform long and severe public penances before they would be readmitted to full fellowship in the community. As time went on this discipline became more relaxed, and less stringent penances such as the recitation of the psalms were substituted for harsher ones such as fasting in sackcloth and ashes. The justification for this new practice was the belief that church leaders should be indulgent or compassionate toward sinners, and if severe penances discouraged people from reconciliation with the community then more lenient ones should be imposed instead. The penances were, in a way, punishments for sins, and these indulgences were seen as a means of tempering divine justice with Christlike mercy. During the Middle Ages, popes extended this practice by granting special indulgences to those who participated in or financially supported the crusades. But by the sixteenth century, indulgences were frequently used to entice people to donate money to the church in exchange for dubious assurances that they would not be punished for their sins in this life or the next. It was this abusive indulgence system that Luther knew, and that he set out to challenge.

Luther was an Augustinian monk who for some time had been tormented by doubts about his own personal salvation even though he often received the sacrament of penance. Plagued by temptations and a sense of his own sinfulness despite the asceticism he practiced, he was unable to experience any real assurance that he was a just person in God's eyes. But then, while meditating on Romans 1:16–17, he found the answer to his search for reassurance: the power of God saves all those who have faith, and the just person lives by faith. For Luther, this was a revelation. It was faith, not good works, that brought salvation. It was faith in God's mercy, not the performance of rituals, that assured Christians that God regarded them as just and upright. It seemed to him that the reason why he had never experienced salvation before was that, like most Christians of his day, he expected the sacraments to do their work automatically, mechanically, *ex opere operato*. And though he might struggle to believe that the sacraments were actually doing their spiritual work, his own spirit experienced few of the effects that the sacraments were supposed to cause. It was only when the scriptures opened his eyes to the necessity of living a life filled with faith in God that he began to feel—and understand—salvation. Slowly he began to question and then to reject the seemingly sterile theories of scholastic theology. Slowly he began to suspect that the church both in its theology and in its institutions had distorted the very meaning of salvation.

Armed with this personal discovery, Luther attacked the most flagrant example of mechanical salvation in his day, the sale of indulgences, and he challenged the scholastic theologians to justify the practice not with subtle theories but with the clear words of scripture. But his attack was taken as a denial of the hierarchy's authority in spiritual matters, and within a short while he was cited for heresy. Undaunted, convinced of the basic correctness of his position, and sensing the support of other reform-minded thinkers, Luther broadened his attack and began to denounce other abuses in the church. In 1520 he was excommunicated by the pope, and in response he called upon the secular authorities in Germany to reform the conditions that the ecclesiastical authorities in Rome could not or would not reform. This time Luther's call for change was heeded, and reformation in the church became a political and social fact. Rome remonstrated, but without the support of the German nobility it was powerless to reverse the process. Other voices soon joined Luther's and other places began their own reforms, especially in Switzerland and northern Europe, far removed from Rome.

Protestants and Catholics are often pictured as divided over the question of scripture and tradition, with Protestants affirming the primacy of the Bible and Catholics maintaining the importance of traditional doctrines and practices. Initially, however, the fundamental difference between the reformers and the rest of the church was not theological but philosophical: it was not a question of what they believed but of how they decided what to believe. For centuries Christians had relied on the teaching authority of the church to tell them what to believe. The early councils had formulated the major doctrines of the Christian religion and had decided which writings were to be accepted as scripture. The works of the great fathers and medieval theologians were regarded as authoritative expressions of Christian wisdom. Popes and bishops approved the liturgical practices within their jurisdiction and legislated the ecclesiastical duties of clerics and lay people. And traditional church practices were themselves invested with a certain degree of authority since the church was understood to be guided by the Holy Spirit. In short, Catholics had come to rely on the authority of the church, on its hierarchy and theologians, on its traditions and institutions, to determine the meaning of the Christian religion.

The reformers, however, came to despair in that authority. In their day church officials often served themselves instead of the church, their motives were often more political than religious, and their attitudes were often more authoritarian than pastoral. Although church practices such as the mass and the sacraments were supposed to be divinely instituted, in fact they were often perfunctory rituals that seemed almost empty of meaning. And the scholastic theology that was supposed to provide a theoretical explanation for Christian beliefs and practices seemed far removed from both. So instead of looking outside themselves for the answers to their religious questions, men like Luther began to look within. They began to trust their own religious insights more than the official pronouncements of the hierarchy. They began to rely on their own religious experience to discover the meaning of Christian doctrines and the relevance of church practices. Thus the basic difference initially between Protestants and Catholics was not a theological difference over the primacy of scripture or tradition, but a philosophical difference over the right to decide what to believe.

Ultimately many of the reformers accepted the authority of scripture over the authority of tradition because the scriptures seemed to be more authentically religious than the current tradition. The scriptures spoke to the heart and conscience in a way that scholastic theology could not. The scriptures revealed the world of the sacred in a way that the liturgical sacraments failed to do. The scriptures, understood as the word of God, spoke with an authority that bishops and popes could claim but could not rival. In short, those who like Luther discovered an experiential meaning of salvation through reading the Bible came to determine the meaning of the Christian religion by relying on their own insights rather than on the conclusions of others. And when they had to back up their insights with authoritative statements, they appealed to the authority of the Bible over the authority of the Catholic tradition. Of course the defenders of tradition also claimed to have the Bible on their side and quoted it freely, and proponents of change were not unwilling to quote from the fathers or councils whenever they could. For the Catholics, however, the ultimate authority was God's word spoken through the church; for the Protestants it was God's word spoken through the scriptures.

In a sense, then, both Catholics and Protestants argued from authority, for that was one of the accepted modes of debate in that period. But the early reformers introduced something new to the debate that had not been an important element in Christian theologizing since the days of Aquinas: the role of personal experience in interpreting statements about God and religion. The reformers expected theology to make experiential as well as logical sense, and this is where they found scholasticism wanting.

The sacraments, for example, were supposed to have certain spiritual effects, and yet often enough sacramental practices in the church at that time had little or no experiential effect on those who participated in them. Catholic theologians cited the authoritative teachings of the past to affirm the reality of those effects, but reform theologians took the apparent ineffectiveness of the sacraments as a sign that the traditional teaching had become corrupted. Arguing along the lines of scholastic theology, the Catholics defended t'he view that the sacraments were always effective because they understood the effect of the sacraments to be metaphysical, not experiential: the primary effect of a valid sacrament was the sacramental reality conferred on the soul, not an experience of grace felt by the recipient. In other words, Catholic theologians took the absence of religious experience to mean that sacramental effects were outside the realm of experience. But reform-minded theologians took exactly the same absence to mean that the sacraments did not have the effects they were supposed to have. The sense of the sacred was so lacking in Catholic sacramental practices that many reformers felt compelled to either reject them as superstitious or to interpret them in new ways.

There were of course other aspects of scholastic sacramental theology that the reformers rejected on theological rather than experiential grounds. Luther, for example, believed that the scholastics taught that people could receive God's grace in the sacraments without meeting any moral requirements at all. He took *ex opere operato* to mean that the sacraments were supposed to cause grace regardless of the intention or spiritual disposition of the recipient. But this implied that God could be controlled by rituals, that grace could be mechanically dispensed, and that salvation could be obtained without any real conversion of the heart—implications which for Luther were intolerable. Other reformers objected to the number of sacraments and sacramental practices that were supposed to be necessary for salvation. They considered the repeated infusions of grace in sacrament after sacrament as denial of salvation by Christ. If people were saved by accepting Christ and being baptized, they reasoned, then there was no need for the other sacraments; and if they were not saved by faith and baptism, then how could they be saved by even more rituals?

Very rapidly Protestant theology, or rather a number of Protestant theologies, attempted to fill the void left by a misunderstood and misused scholastic theology of the sacraments. Generally speaking the reformers all reasoned from their own experience of sacraments to an understanding that made sense in view of that experience. But their sacramental experiences were sometimes different and so the explanations they developed were likewise different. And although the reformers usually rejected scholastic theology as intellectually bankrupt, they did not always reject all of the theological assumptions that scholasticism was built on. The result was a variety of Protestant positions on the sacraments ranging from those that were very Catholic (as in the Anglican and Episcopal churches, which retained all seven sacraments) to those that were very anti-Catholic (as among the early Anabaptists and later Baptists, who rejected the practice of baptizing infants). Broadly speaking, however, reform positions on the sacraments can be divided into those that held that sacraments had divine effects, those that held that they had human effects, and those that held that they had no special effects at all.

Martin Luther, for example, believed that sacramental actions had effects that were caused by God. He believed in the real presence of Christ in the eucharist, and he believed that God saved Christians through baptism. But he insisted that it was God, not the sacraments, that caused these effects; and he contended that faith was needed to perceive and receive these effects. A sacrament was a visible sign of an invisible reality, but its power came from God and was released through the faith of the one who received it. In fact, for Luther faith was one of the three essential parts of any sacrament: "The first is the sacrament or sign, the second is its significance, and the third is the faith required by these two.... The sacrament must be external and visible, having some material form; the significance must be internal and spiritual, within the human soul; and faith must be applied to use both" (*Treatise on the Blessed Sacrament and the Brotherhood*). The sacrament was a sign, but it was the faith of the believer in God's power and goodness that made it an effective sign and enabled the person to receive God's grace through it.

John Calvin's sacramental theology was a step removed from this. For him sacraments were not channels of grace but reminders of the grace that God was always bestowing on those who were saved. They were signs of God's favor, symbolic actions that could awaken believers to a sense of the divine graciousness that was always and everywhere the same. They were testimonies of God's good will toward humanity that could open Christians to an awareness of the grace that was always present to them, if they would but receive it. For example, "Baptism attests that we have been cleansed and washed; the Eucharistic Supper, that we have been redeemed" (*Institutes of the Christian Religion* IV, 14, 22). So the sacraments neither contained nor conferred grace, but they did reflect spiritual realities, and those who devoutly participated in them became receptive to the action of the Holy Spirit: "I consider all the energy of operation as belonging to the Spirit, and the sacraments as mere instruments, which are empty and useless without its agency, but which carry a surprising efficacy when it acts and exerts its power in the heart" (*Institutes* IV, 14, 9).

Ulrich Zwingli denied that sacraments had any particular spiritual efficacy. "Sacraments are simply signs of Christian belief; through them believers indicate that they belong to the Church of Jesus and have separated themselves from unbelievers" (*On True and False Religion*). Sacraments for him were just social signs, even if they were divinely ordained; they were rites that signified God's salvation, and that Christians used to testify to their belief in that fact. But faith was an inner experience that no outward sign could cause, and salvation was the direct work of the Holy Spirit who needed no instrumental ritual. So sacraments could be no more than external representations of spiritual realities; they did not cause those realities, and they were not needed to become aware of them.

In the absence of accurate historical information about the origin and development of the sacraments, each of the major reformers did his best to formulate a coherent explanation of Christian rituals. As already mentioned, one reason why their positions on the sacraments differed was that their religious experiences differed. Those reformers who experienced personal spiritual effects through participation in sacramental rites tended to speak of them as having effects on the individual; those who saw only the social consequences of the sacraments tended to deny that they had personal effects. But when it came to formulating a theological explanation for their sacramental practices, all of the reformers turned to the only source of information that they trusted—the Bible.

The Bible, they discovered, did not speak of sacraments the way the Catholic Church did. Instead it spoke separately of baptism and the Lord's supper, and it spoke of them as ordained by Christ and commanded to be continued by his followers (Matthew 28:19; 1 Corinthians 11:23–25). For this reason some of the more radical reformers rejected even the name "sacraments," and preferred to call these rites divine ordinances. The majority of reformers, however, kept both the name and the Roman Catholic idea that sacraments were visible signs or ceremonies instituted by Christ, and on the basis of this criterion they rejected all but baptism and the Lord's supper as without any scriptural foundation.

It was true, of course, that Christ had preached a message of repentance (Matthew 4:17), and had even instructed his disciples about forgiving sins

(John 20:22–23), but the Bible mentioned no sacramental ceremony or sign of forgiveness, and so penance was ruled out as a sacramental rite. It was true also that Christ had appointed apostles to carry his message to others (Mark 16:15) and to continue the breaking of bread in his memory (Luke 22:9), but again here there was no evidence of an ordination ceremony. On the other hand, there was scriptural evidence that the early Christians did perform rituals such as imposing hands (Acts 8:17; 9:17) and anointing with oil (James 5:14), but there was no clear indication that these were personally ordained by Christ to be continued in the church forever. Lastly marriage, although undoubtedly approved by Christ (John 2:1–10), was just as certainly not instituted by him because it had existed since the days of Adam and Eve. Using this double criterion, then, that a sacrament had to be a ceremony or sign and that it had to be instituted by Christ, most of the reformers eliminated five of the seven Catholic sacraments from consideration as divinely ordained rites.

What, then, of baptism and the Lord's supper? How were these to be understood? Here the scriptural data for all the reformers were the same, and yet different reformers developed different theologies of these sacraments. Why? Again the main difference seems to have been experiential: the different personal experiences of the early reformers in connection with these rituals, and the different social experiences that reform-minded Christians had had with the old Catholic sacraments. Of course there were other influences as well. Martin Luther, the former Augustinian monk, knew that Augustine had defended infant baptism in the fourth century, and so even though he argued that salvation came through faith and not through works, he could not abandon the belief that the gift of faith could be received by children as well as adults who were baptized. How else could he justify this practice that existed in the church before the days of papal corruption? How else could he explain how his faith, seemingly long dormant, had been awakened upon reading Paul's epistle to the Romans? The Anabaptists, in contrast, ignoring or ignorant of patristic precedents, accepted Luther's doctrine of justification by faith, but refused to baptize infants because all of the baptisms mentioned in the Bible were baptisms of adults. Moreover, the scriptural admonition, "Repent and be baptized" (Acts 2:38; see Mark 16:16), seemed to indicate that personal conversion must precede baptism, and infants were not capable of making that kind of personal commitment. John Calvin had seen enough corruption in the church to conclude that baptism did not automatically save people from their sins, and the New Testament even spoke of people being saved both without and before baptism (Luke 23:43; Acts 10:47). From this he could reason that baptism was a sign of the grace that God was always offering to the elect, independently of baptism. For Ulrich Zwingli, any sacramental ceremony seemed to be a public profession of faith by those who participated in it. He observed that the sacraments presupposed faith, and so he could not agree that the sacraments caused faith.

In regard to the Lord's supper, the situation was pretty much the same. Luther's personal experience of the presence of Christ during his celebration of the mass convinced him of the real presence, and so he took the words, "This is my body. This is my blood," in a literal and Catholic sense. He did not, however, agree with the scholastic explanation in terms of transubstantiation (a change in reality from bread and wine to Christ's body and blood), but adopted a different explanation in terms of consubstantiation (the presence of both real bread and wine, and the real body and blood of Christ). Zwingli went to the opposite extreme. He denied outright what he took to be the Catholic position that Christ was physically present in the eucharist, and he took the words of Christ in a purely figurative sense. Thus for him the sacrament of the Lord's supper was simply a symbolic commemoration of Christ's last supper, and any special presence of Christ had to be merely a mental presence. Calvin steered a middle course between these extremes. His experience with the sacrament suggested that through receiving communion Christians did indeed receive spiritual nourishment for their souls, and so he regarded Zwingli's interpretation as inadequate. But he did not go as far as Luther in affirming the substantial presence of Christ in the eucharist. For him it was the power of Christ, not the body of Christ, that was present in and received in communion.

Through their attention to experience and their devotion to the scriptures, therefore, the early Protestant reformers reduced the number of rituals called sacraments to just two: baptism and the Lord's supper. And for most Protestants today this is still the case. They acknowledge only two sacraments in the Christian religion, even though the variety of Protestant positions on the sacraments is greater than the few just summarized. And yet it seems clear that in Protestant Christianity there are more sacraments than just these two, if "sacrament" is taken in the broad sense of something that can call forth an experience of the sacred. In Pentecostal denominations, for example, heartfelt preaching and the invocation of the Holy Spirit are expected to have experienceable results. In almost any Protestant church, the Sunday sermon is more than an intellectual affair, prayer is more than a recitation of words, and hymn singing is more than a group choral exercise. And in many denominations the Bible itself has become the primary sacrament. Sacred scripture, whether read privately or preached publicly, is regarded as an open door to the sacred through which God is revealed, not in a purely intellectual way but in an experiential way. The devout Christian, whether Protestant or Catholic or Orthodox, finds in the Bible the word of God, a word that can touch the heart, disturb the conscience, or comfort the soul. For Catholics and Orthodox, however, the Bible is one albeit unique sacrament among many. For many Protestants it has become the principal sacrament.

2. Trent and the Catholic Counter-Reformation

If the reformers tried to revise the sacraments, the Council of Trent sought to restore them. Finally convoked in 1545 after repeated delays, this council of the Catholic world's bishops was able to initiate the kinds of reforms that earlier councils had envisioned. It was interrupted twice, once for four years and once for ten years, partly because of political unrest in Europe and partly because of dissension within the hierarchy. Despite these interruptions, however, the council ultimately achieved its purpose and completed its work in 1563. Its purpose was primarily practical: reform within the Catholic Church. But practical reform now also meant combating the Protestant heresies, and so the council's major decrees summarized Catholic doctrine and excommunicated those who believed otherwise. It even called for a reunification of the church—but on Rome's terms, and so its call went unheeded in Protestant countries. In Catholic countries, however, Trent's decrees were definitive, and it set its stamp on Roman Catholicism for four centuries.

Most of the council's practical reforms dealt with the clergy, abolishing ecclesiastical privileges, detailing responsibilities of bishops and priests, and prescribing strict standards of conduct for them. But over half of its doctrinal decrees dealt with the sacraments. In its carefully worded statements outlining the Catholic position and in its numerous condemnations of opposing positions, the council adopted the medieval scholastic view of sacraments and rejected any other interpretations. In regard to other points of Catholic doctrine, the council made no attempt to summarize all of Catholic theology but addressed only those beliefs that had come under attack by the reformers, such as the role of scripture in the church, the doctrine of original sin, the meaning of justification, the veneration given to saints, the belief in purgatory, and the value of indulgences. The attempt was to delineate the Catholic position in these matters, with the result that the dividing line between Catholic and Protestant Christianity was drawn with unmistakable sharpness.

For example, it declared the Latin Vulgate Bible (a translation dating back to the fourth century, and in common use since the sixth) to be the authentic Catholic version, and it forbade Catholics to use any other version in the liturgy or for doing theology. Further, it accepted all of the books in the Vulgate as divinely inspired, in opposition to those Protestants who accepted a slightly shorter Old Testament based on the Hebrew Bible. And it prohibited Catholics from interpreting the scriptures in any way that would contradict established Catholic doctrines.

The question of justification had been raised by Luther and others, and so the council formulated the Catholic position on this question and forbade Catholics to preach, teach, or believe anything to the contrary. First, it outlined the Catholic teaching on original sin, a traditional way of talking about the fall of Adam and its effects on the human race. It declared that through his sin Adam had lost his original justness or righteousness and had been punished with death, that this sin was transmitted to the whole human race and put all under the bondage of the devil, and that baptism removes this sin even though it does not remove all inclinations to evil. Second, the council outlined the Catholic understanding of justification. It defined justification as "a passing from the state in which people are born children of the first Adam, to the state of grace and acceptance as children of God through the second Adam, Jesus Christ our Savior" (*Justification* 4). Even though the descendants of Adam must still physically die, they could be spiritually reborn through baptism; and if they sinned mortally after being baptized, they could regain spiritual righteousness through the sacrament of penance.

Still, the council did not regard justification as primarily a sacramental work. Rather, it saw justification as a result of the Father's mercy, merited for humankind by the passion and death of his Son, and effected in souls by the power of the Holy Spirit. It conceived of justification—the process of becoming morally just—as beginning with God's call to sinners to change their ways, and with their free decision to cooperate fully with God's grace. Thus the council agreed that people were justified through faith, in the sense that faith was needed to begin the process of salvation. But faith could not be the whole thing. Belief in God had to be followed by a confident hope in God's promises and a transforming love for God and others. Such virtues were beyond natural human attainment, but they were received from God in baptism, which also gave the power to live on a higher than natural level in avoiding sin and doing good works. Nonetheless, gifts once given and received might not be continually used, and so it was possible for Christians to fall again from righteousness even though they did not lose their faith. God still called them to a life of cooperation with grace, and if they responded to that call again through repentance and penance, they would once more be able to live by the power of the Holy Spirit instead of having to rely only on their natural abilities. Thus the council regarded justification as primarily a work of God; in scholastic terms God was the principal cause of justification, but in the church God also worked through instrumental causes called sacraments.

How did the council reach these conclusions? Like the reformers it relied on the Bible, and there is hardly a chapter in Trent's document on justification without a number of references to scripture. Like the reformers, and like the better medieval theologians, it relied also on experience, but the experience that the bishops at the council had in mind was different from the experience to which the Protestant reformers had appealed. Instead of generalizing on their own individual experiences as Luther did, they drew upon the general experience of Catholics who tried to live morally just and upright lives in the church. For them, living in the state of spiritual justness meant living in a way that was morally upright, believing in God, doing good works, and avoiding serious sins. Ultimately it meant leading a life of sanctity, of the kind of holiness lived by the saints in the church. It was not in any way based on an experience of personal salvation, for the council regarded salvation as something that was experienced only in heaven. Generally speaking, the bishops assumed that those who were just in the eyes of others were also just in the eyes of God (of course, there could be secret sinners), and so they reflected on the way that Catholics normally came to lead upright lives, and they outlined that path in their statement on justification. Unlike the reformers, however, the bishops of the council used scholastic theology to formulate what they believed happened to Christians who with God's help walked from unrighteousness to righteousness. For them this was simply a reaffirmation that traditional Catholic theology had spoken truthfully about Christian experience. To the reformers it looked like a relapse into theological jargon that had nothing to do with experience.

Part of the difficulty between Catholics and Protestants in the sixteenth century and afterward, therefore, was that they were speaking different languages. Not that Catholics used Latin and Protestants used something else; for a long time both sides wrote their theology in Latin. The difficulty was something deeper. When Catholics used words such as "justification" and "salvation," "sin" and "grace," they simply meant different things from what Protestants often meant when they used those terms.

Like the new secular philosophies that began to replace scholasticism in the modern world (rationalism in France and Germany, empiricism in England), the new Christian theologies were fresh starts. The reformers looked at things differently, and they talked about them differently. And yet the only words they had at their disposal were the traditional words, words of traditional philosophy and theology. The result was that when Protestant theologians used the old words they were often using them to express new ideas; they were giving them new meanings. When Catholic theologians read them they assumed that the words had their traditional meanings, and so what the Protestants wrote looked like obvious nonsense. The Protestants, for their part, never fully understood the Catholic theological vocabulary, which had become distorted during the decline of scholasticism. And so it seemed to them that the Catholics were the ones who were speaking nonsense.

What the Catholic theologians and bishops assembled at Trent were able to do was to restore, at least to some extent, an experiential basis to the language of Catholic theology. The experience to which they referred, however, was the traditional Catholic experience of Christianity, not the modern Protestant experience of Christianity. But if we grant that the theology of the Catholic counter-reformation (as it came to be called) was based on this experience, we can understand the vigor with which the council's bishops defended the seven sacraments. For them the Christian tradition was not only a theological tradition documented in conciliar and papal decrees but also a living tradition of church practice that extended as far into the past as anyone could remember. It was the experience of the church that they were defending, and the experience of the church, it seemed, had always included these sacraments. There was also, of course, the traditional belief (accepted by many reformers as well) that Christ had instituted the sacraments, and the council reiterated this belief as an item of Catholic doctrine. Some of the bishops even held that Christ had personally instructed his apostles to perform the rites and that they had remained unchanged for fifteen centuries, but other bishops were aware that this could not be documented from scripture, and so the exact manner of Christ's institution was left as an open question. The important point was that the traditional religious experience of the church seemed to indicate that the sacraments had always been a necessary part of Christian life, and so the council resisted any attempt to do away with them.

Of course the bishops at Trent accepted the medieval numbering of the Christian sacraments as seven, just as they accepted the medieval understanding of these sacraments. But they made no attempt to restate the entire scholastic theology of the sacraments. They limited their pronouncements to those points that had been attacked by one or another of the reformers. Among other things, they declared that the sacraments were necessary for salvation even though not all of the sacraments were needed by each individual; that the sacraments did more than just nourish faith or publicly represent it; that some sacraments bestowed an indelible character on the soul with the result that they could be received only once; that all of the sacraments contained and conferred grace and so they were not just signs of the grace that God was always offering to people; that God's grace was always offered through the sacraments even though individuals might place obstacles in the way of receiving that grace; that the grace of a sacrament was conferred by the rite itself and not by the faith of the recipient or the worthiness of the minister; that nevertheless in performing the sacramental rites, ministers had to intend to do what the church did in order for them to be effective.

This last point showed the bishops' recognition that the working of the sacraments was not mechanical, even though they understood that the effects of the sacraments were metaphysical. It meant that the words and gestures of the sacramental rites were not magical, with an independent power to work on their own. It meant that going through the motions of the ritual was not the same as the sacramental performance of the ritual. And it meant that sacramental effects could not be produced unintentionally or inadvertently.

Moreover, during this period of the counter-reformation, the understanding that ministers of the sacraments must do what the church does had another important implication. Some of those who had initially joined the reform movement were validly ordained bishops and priests. In their churches they often continued to baptize, to celebrate the mass, and to ordain, and some even retained all seven sacraments. An important question from the viewpoint of Catholic theology was: Were those Protestant sacraments valid? Did they have real sacramental effects or had they lost their spiritual power? The council's general answer was that they remained true sacraments in the Catholic sense only if the persons performing them kept the Catholic understanding of the sacraments. In other words, if bishops ordained ministers without intending to ordain them as priests in the Catholic sense, those ordinations were not valid as far as the Catholic Church was concerned. If priests said the words of consecration with only the intention of performing a memorial of Christ's last supper, the bread and wine were not sacramentally changed into the body and blood of Christ. If two Protestant Christians married with the idea that they could someday divorce and remarry, theirs was not a sacramental marriage in the eyes of the Catholic Church.

For all practical purposes, then, from the time of the Council of Trent, the Catholic Church ceased to recognize the validity of Protestant sacraments with one exception—baptism. Most Protestant churches continued to baptize their members either as infants or as adults, and most of them baptized using the formulas given in the scriptures and had an understanding of baptism based on the New Testament. In these ways Protestant baptisms were essentially the same as Catholic baptisms even though they might differ in other respects. And so these baptisms could be considered truly sacramental in the Catholic sense even if Protestants did not accept the full Catholic theology of baptism. And for that reason Protestants who later became Catholics were not to be rebaptized. Instead, they were to be treated the same way that heretics and schismatics had been treated during the patristic period, simply being welcomed into communion with Rome and confirmed in the Catholic Church.

In addition to treating the sacraments in general, the council formulated the Catholic position on each of the seven individual sacraments. To go into further detail at this point, however, would bring up matters that can be better treated in later chapters. But its general approach to these sacraments was also significant, for it indirectly imposed a standard sacramental practice and theology on all of Catholicism. It did not decree many practical reforms itself, but it did demand that Catholic bishops make whatever reforms were called for in their own dioceses. In setting strict standards for priestly conduct it gradually eliminated the worst elements from the clergy. And by requiring seminary training for all future priests it ensured that the sacraments would be better understood. Within a short time after the council, reforms in canon law imposed a greater uniformity on the practice of the sacraments. The Roman missal became the standard liturgical book for the mass throughout Catholicism, and Roman sacramentaries were adopted for the other sacraments. These books not only contained the words to be used for the church's sacramental practices but they also included rubrics or directions on how they were to be performed. In time,

Catholics would point to the uniformity of their church's sacramental practices around the world as a visible sign of its spiritual unity. And this uniformity in practice was matched by a uniformity in theory. By accepting and in effect canonizing the scholastic interpretation of the sacraments, the council practically ruled out any alternative interpretations of them within Catholicism. For the next four centuries, the only developments in sacramental theology would be refinements in peripheral matters; the central issues were settled.

One final word about indulgences. Ironically, they were the first things challenged by the reformers and the last to be treated by the Council of Trent. And its treatment was quite brief. It declared that indulgences were a legitimate practice dating back to ancient times and approved by previous councils. And it reasserted the right and power of church authorities to grant them. But it also recognized that many abuses had grown up around indulgences, and it ordered these to be corrected. As a step in this direction the council summarily abolished the office of alms collector in the church, it forbade anyone but bishops from granting indulgences, and it prohibited bishops from making almsgiving a condition for receiving an indulgence. Henceforward, indulgences would be, as they once had been, strictly spiritual matters.

3. The Modern Centuries

The two Protestant sacraments of baptism and the Lord's supper developed in the direction of greater variety after the Renaissance. As each new reform movement added its own insights to those of the early reformers, these sacraments came to be understood and practiced in more and more diverse ways. The notion that the church could and should be reformed provided a permanent rationale for breaking away from Protestant traditions, just as it had once supplied a reason for breaking away from the Roman Catholic tradition. The idea that the words of the Bible carried greater weight than the words of church leaders made it possible to introduce new changes on the authority of the scriptures continually. But what the scriptures had to say about the sacraments was in fact ambiguous and could be interpreted in different ways, so there was always room for new interpretations. Christians within the larger denominations remained in general agreement with one another, but those who broke with these churches in the name of new reforms brought ever new beliefs and practices into Protestant Christianity, and even the denominations that were able to tolerate internal reform movements often found themselves with a variety of sacramental rituals, such as the "high" and "low" churches of the Anglican communion.

In contrast, the seven liturgical sacraments of the Catholic Church underwent very little change during the modern centuries. The official Roman missal was published in 1570 and was uniformly imposed on all dioceses in communion with Rome; only those that could prove their unique eucharistic customs were at least two hundred years old were allowed to keep their own liturgies, and these were very few. Only minor changes were made in the missal or in the Roman sacramentaries until the middle of the twentieth century, when the Second Vatican Council authorized a general reform of Catholic sacramental practices.

And yet the Protestant churches were not immune from ossification, either. In Protestant Christianity as a whole there was increasing diversity in theologies and rituals, but within individual denominations imposed uniformity was often the last stage of sacramental development. After the initial period of protest, most churches reacted to the old abuses by emphasizing the importance of sacramental discipline, insisting that sacred rites be properly performed and reverently attended. The standards of proper performance varied among the denominations, as did the penalties for failing to meet them, but the fact remains that most churches erected such standards and enforced them. Thus for many, both Protestants and Catholics, the era following the reformation was just as much an era of sacramental formalism as the one that had preceded it.

Does this mean that there was no development in the Catholic sacraments for four centuries? Not at all. But it does mean that the developments in sacramental theology and practice came in areas other than those defined by the Council of Trent. In sacramental theology the principal questions seemed to be settled, and so theologians confined their speculations to secondary issues. In sacramental practice, the words and gestures of the seven ecclesiastical sacraments could not be changed without the permission of Rome, but this did not prevent the development of new sacramental practices in the church. These were not considered sacraments in the restricted Catholic sense, but they were in fact sacraments in the broad sense of being doors to the sacred.

The situation in theology was basically where it had been in the high Middle Ages, with one difference. Medieval writers such as Aquinas had proposed their theories as individuals, and other individuals were free to disagree with them and propose alternative theories, not only about the sacraments but also about other points in the Catholic religion. The only restriction was that they could not contradict Catholic doctrines that had already been defined in the church. This is why in the later Middle Ages, thinkers such as John Duns Scotus and William of Ockham could freely disagree with earlier theologians; they only had to demonstrate that their own theories were logical and coherent, and that they did not conflict with established doctrines. But during the Middle Ages the number of such doctrines had grown. Theologians could no longer debate about the number of the sacraments the way they did in the days before Peter Lombard; the Council of Lyons in 1274 decreed they were seven. Nor could they disagree about the basic nature of sacraments; the Council of Florence in 1439 taught that they were instruments of salvation that contained and conferred grace. Nor could they question whether the sacraments worked *ex opere operato*, whether three of them conferred an indelible character on the soul, or whether all of them had been instituted by Christ; these were now closed questions. Thus by the time of the Council of Trent in the mid-1500s, the main features of scholastic sacramental theology had become officially defined doctrines, or Catholic dogmas. And the bishops at Trent accepted and added to these scholastic teachings in their own doctrinal decrees.

What remained for theologians to speculate about, therefore, were things that the councils had not defined, such as the manner in which Christ instituted the sacraments, the philosophical explanation of sacramental causality, or the metaphysical nature of the sacramental character. For example, some theologians favored the position that Christ had specifically instituted each of the seven sacraments, personally instructing the apostles as to their matter and form. Others held the view that Christ had left his followers with an understanding of the meaning of the sacraments—that baptism forgives sins, that the eucharist is his body and blood, that confirmation bestows the gifts of the Holy Spirit, and so on—but had let the church determine the specific sacramental rites. On the question of how the sacraments worked, modern Catholic scholastics debated the merits of philosophical explanations that were sometimes as subtly different as their names: perfective physical causality, dispositive physical causality, dispositive intentional causality, and others. All theologians accepted the fact that each sacrament bestowed a specific sacramental reality, but they sometimes disagreed about how each sacramental reality affected souls in their relation to Christ or to the church.

Thus the dogmatic decrees of the Council of Trent did not put an end to discussion about the sacraments, but they did shift the discussion from central issues to peripheral ones. A parallel but more visible development occurred in the area of sacramental practice. The seven liturgical rites had become more standardized in the Middle Ages, and these were now fixed by the Roman missal and sacramentaries. But this did not prevent them from being embellished with ceremony and music, nor did it prevent new sacraments from emerging. These "new sacraments" were called sacramentals or devotions or pious practices, but they were indeed sacraments in the broad sense if not in the narrow Catholic sense of the term.

For instance, prayer books during the modern period were filled with devotions—collections of prayers and reflections, that focused on some aspect of the Catholic religion. There were devotions to God the Father, to the Holy Spirit, and to God's Eternal Wisdom; there were devotions to various aspects of Christ's life, especially his suffering and death on the cross; there were devotions to the mother of Christ, to her sorrows and joys, and to special saints. These devotional practices could be performed privately, or publicly on feast days and at shrines. They were encouraged by sodalities, formal and informal organizations formed to promote the daily practices of one devotion or another. Chapels were dedicated to these objects of devotion, and pilgrimages were made to these new holy places.

Devotions to Mary and to the saints had been a part of Catholicism for centuries, but now they took on a new dimension and a new importance. The Blessed Virgin was honored as the spiritual patroness and protectress of new religious movements and organizations. The ringing of the parish church bell at noon, originally a daily reminder of the hour of Christ's passion, became associated with the Angelus, a Marian prayer. In the early Middle Ages, penitents had been allowed to recite the Our Father or Lord's Prayer one hundred and fifty times if they could not read the hundred and fifty psalms. In the course of time, the Hail Mary was substituted, grouped in tens, and counted on strings of knots or beads, and this Marian rosary of repeated prayers became a popular sacramental practice. Like other devotions, the rosary could be recited privately or in public, and it was encouraged as an excellent form of parish and family prayer. As a style of repetitious prayer, it served as a sacramental mantra, freeing the mind from worldly distractions and focusing it on spiritual realities.

Another form of mantra prayer that developed in modern Catholicism was the litany. Like the rosary its beginnings lay in the Middle Ages, when communities of monks praying the psalms sometimes inserted short prayers between the verses. Litanies were lists: lists of events in Christ's life, aspects of his passion, titles by which he could be addressed, and so forth, which were recited by a prayer leader and responded to by the congregation with a brief phrase such as "Lord, have mercy," or "Hear us," or "Pray for us." Litanies of the saints likewise enumerated moments in their lives or virtues for which they were known, and litanies of Mary often included poetic titles such as "Star of the Sea" or "Mystical Rose," which had been ascribed to her in religious literature.

Devotion to the heart of Jesus began in the sixteenth century and became widespread by the eighteenth. Pictures and statues of the image known as the Sacred Heart showed a Christ figure bearing the marks of the crucifixion on his hands and feet and revealing a heart burning with love. It was a representation of Christ as a merciful savior, crucified and resurrected, human and divine, suffering and forgiving. As a sacramental image with multiple meanings, it was able to evoke a depth and range of responses perhaps equaled only by the crucifix itself. But the crucifix in medieval and Renaissance art had come to depict mainly the human agony of Christ on the cross; the image of the Sacred Heart was able to symbolize the triumph of Easter over the tragedy of Good Friday. Those who contemplated the crucifix often found themselves filled with guilt and remorse, but those who prayed before the heart of Jesus found themselves in the presence of a merciful God, ready to forgive the repentant sinner. The sacramental effects of the two images were different.

The object of greatest devotion in modern Catholicism was probably the Blessed Sacrament, the name given to the consecrated eucharistic bread. Many of the reformers had questioned or denied the doctrine of the real presence of Christ in the eucharist, and so the Council of Trent reasserted the doctrine in no uncertain terms: the bread and wine, after consecration during the mass, were really and truly Christ's body and blood. The practice of keeping consecrated bread in a tabernacle on the church altar dated from the Middle Ages. There it could be visited and venerated, and Christ could be prayed to as intimately as if he were bodily present, for to the eyes of faith, he was. During the mass, the congregation would kneel in adoration of the host, the round wafer of unleavened bread, when it was held aloft after the consecration. This practice led to that of blessing the people with the host outside of mass, and to that of placing the host in a ceremonial holder (called a monstrance) so that it could be seen and adored on special occasions. A continuous forty-hour devotion to the Blessed Sacrament developed in connection with Holy Thursday celebrations, and in the sixteenth century this devotion was separated from its original Holy Week setting to become an independent sacramental practice of uninterrupted prayer before the eucharistic host. Both the Forty Hours'

Devotion and the briefer Benediction of the Blessed Sacrament remained in popular Catholic usage until the mid-twentieth century, and they are still practiced by tradition-minded Catholics.

One sacramental practice whose influence can still be seen in Catholic churches was the Way of the Cross, also called the Stations of the Cross. Around the walls of each church were placed fourteen scenes depicting events in Christ's passion from his sentencing by Pilate to his burial in the tomb. Catholics were encouraged to meditate and pray at each station in order to become more vividly aware of the sufferings that Christ had endured out of love for each and every person.

This flowering of novel sacramental customs was due in part to the restrictions placed by the counter-reformation on the seven established sacraments. Many of the abuses of the past had resulted from the freedom that bishops and priests had had to alter the sacramental rituals. The Tridentine reforms severely curtailed that freedom and imposed a uniform sacramental practice on Catholicism. Yet, even though the words and gestures of the past were set by rubrics, local churches were still free to add their own ceremonial elaborations. Baptisms of royalty and confirmations in cathedrals, for example, were usually more prolonged and elaborate than those of commoners in rural parishes. The basic rite was prescribed and this was the sacrament proper; the embellishments were considered superfluous and nonsacramental even when they had spiritual effects on the feelings and beliefs of the participants.

The traditional sacraments were not uniformly affected by this additional sacramentalizing of the rites, however. Penance, for instance, had been restricted to a private encounter with a priest-confessor, and little could be done to elaborate on such a ritual. Matrimony, at the other extreme, could be a grandly ceremonious affair surrounding the exchange of vows essential for the official sacrament. Perhaps the best illustration of the range of added symbolism that could accompany the basic rites was the Roman mass itself. As the most frequently repeated of the ecclesiastical sacraments, it was the most commonly embellished . A simple "low mass" could be said in about twenty minutes; but basically the same liturgy could be extended by music and ceremony into a "high mass" lasting an hour or more. The music for masses became an art form in itself, and music sometimes overshadowed the simple liturgy it was meant to embellish. Yet this church music was itself a sacrament of sorts, for through it Catholics could enter into the sacred time of worship and experience the sacred meaning of the central Christian mystery more fully.

It could almost be said that during the modern period the seven ecclesiastical sacraments became a central part of Catholic doctrine but a marginal part of Catholic religious life. True, all Catholics had to be baptized when they were born, and most were confirmed while they were children. True, Catholics were obliged by canon law to attend mass every Sunday and go to confession once a year. True, most Catholics were either married in the church or ordained to serve in it. And true, most Catholics hoped to receive the last rites before they died. But in the day-to-day living of their religion, most Catholics could and did live without too much contact with the official sacraments. Even devout Catholics relied as much on sacramental devotions as on recognized sacraments like mass and confession to intensify their faith and expand their religious awareness.

Modern Catholicism inherited the fear that the sacraments could be abused and the conviction that it should not happen again. The result was that they were not abused, but some of them came close to not being used much either. Modern popes and bishops had to insist on attendance at mass and reception of communion, and they had to remind Catholics of the importance of confirmation and extreme unction since these sacraments were not absolutely necessary for salvation. On the other hand, sacramental practices such as the rosary and other devotions developed on their own, and only later found official approval and encouragement. It was as though Catholics had come to use the seven sacraments only to be assured of good standing in the eyes of God and the church, and to be guaranteed final entrance into heaven. But they used other sacramental practices to intensify their convictions and celebrate their religious beliefs.

Modern Catholicism also inherited the medieval theology of the sacraments, but it was not understood the way the medieval theologians had understood it. Early medieval sacramental theology had been an inductive explanation for liturgical practices and religious experiences; modern sacramental theology was a deductive system that took the decrees of the councils and the canons of the law as its basic postulates. In this respect, modern sacramental theology resembled later scholasticism rather than its earlier phase. The medieval stress on the importance of faith in the reception of the sacraments was downplayed during the counter-reformation, in reaction to Luther's emphasis on faith. Trent's insistence on the *ex opere operato* effectiveness of the sacraments fostered a popular conception that they worked automatically, and that all that was needed was a passive reception of the sacramental reality. Grace itself continued to be regarded as a metaphysical reality infused into the soul. And even the modern mechanistic understanding of science tended to foster the notion that the correct theological explanation of the sacraments involved an interaction of spiritual forces.

There was also another important similarity between the modern Catholic approach to the sacraments and the approach of the late medieval period. In the manuals of theology the sacraments were mainly treated as a part of moral theology, and moral theology was mainly treated as an expanded commentary on canon law. Thus Catholic sacramental practices, at least the seven ecclesiastical sacraments, tended to be looked on as moral and legal obligations rather than as doors to the experience of the sacred.

Not until the late nineteenth century did a series of developments begin to lay the foundation for an entirely different approach to the Catholic sacraments. A renewed philosophical interest in the intellectual achievement of the Middle Ages turned scholars' attention toward the original works of thinkers such as Aquinas. A renewed liturgical interest in early sacramental worship turned their attention toward the descriptions and commentaries of the pre-medieval fathers of the church. And a renewed scriptural interest in the biblical foundations of the Christian religion turned their attention toward the pre-patristic writings of the New Testament. Within a few decades these first investigations into the historical origin and development of Christianity grew into a series of movements—neoscholasticism, the liturgical movement, and the scriptural renewal—which ultimately freed Catholic theology from the nonhistorical, deductive approach that characterized its modern period.

Of course it would be a gross oversimplification to suggest that these were the only forces at work promoting a reevaluation of the Catholic sacraments. In the twentieth century, societies became less homogeneous and more pluralistic; the natural sciences became less mechanistic and more statistical; the social sciences introduced new ways of looking at people, their individual behavior, and their cultural practices. Two world wars shattered the European illusion of cultural supremacy; improved transportation brought people out of isolation and into interaction; electronic mass communication and information processing disseminated discoveries and ideas with increasing rapidity. Interdenominational cooperation among Protestant churches fostered ecumenical contacts with Roman Catholicism and a reexamination of hardened positions on both sides; new developments in philosophy made it possible to look at previous achievements within a historical perspective; the comparative study of religions suggested that Christianity was not so unique that it had nothing in common with other religions. The list could be expanded. Ultimately the list of forces promoting change in the Catholic Church would have to include all of the cultural and social changes of the twentieth century. Just as at the beginning of the patristic, medieval, and modern periods, Christianity was moving into a new era when the old answers were no longer as satisfying as they had been in the past. But this time, it was chiefly the discovery that the past had been different that made it possible to think differently in the present.

For Further Reading

William Estep, *Renaissance and Reformation* (William B. Eerdmans, 1986) situates the Protestant reformation in its cultural and historical context.

Madeleine Gray, The Protestant Reformation (Sussex Academic Press, 2003) focuses on Catholic and Protestant beliefs and practices, including the sacraments.

Andrew Atherstone, *The Reformation* (Lion Hudson, 2011) is an engaging account of early Protestantism illustrated with colorful maps, photos, and portraits.

Kurt Aland, *Four Reformers* (Augsburg, 1979) presents brief biographies of Luther, Melancthon, Zwingli, and Calvin.

William Willimon, *Word, Water, Wine and Bread: How Worship Has Changed over the Years* (Judson Press, 1980) gives special attention to Protestant developments from the reformation to the present.

Bernard Piault, *What Is a Sacrament?* (Hawthorn Books, 1963) gives a clear presentation of the modern scholastic understanding of the sacraments and their development to the time of the Council of Trent.

For Further Study

Reformation and Counter Reformation

Peter Klassen, *Europe in the Reformation* (Prentice-Hall, 1979) puts the Protestant reformation in the context of European history.

John Bossy, *Christianity in the West 1400-1700* (Oxford University Press, 1985) emphasizes the social and spiritual dimensions of the transition from medieval Christianity to the beginning of its modern expression.

Henri Daniel-Rops, *The Catholic Reformation* (E. P. Dutton, 1962) details the Roman church's attempt to reform after the loss of much of Christian Europe to Protestantism.

Michael Mullett, *The Catholic Reformation* (Routledge, 1999) describes the impact of the Council of Trent on the hierarchy, on vocations, on ordinary people, and on the arts.

R. Po-chia Hsia, *The World of Catholic Renewal 1540-1770* (Cambridge University Press, 1998) covers the tumultuous period from the Council of Trent to the suppression of the Jesuit order.

Glenn Miller, *The Modern Church* (Abingdon Press, 1997) situates developments in Roman Catholicism within the context of worldwide Christianity.

Erwin Iserloh, Joseph Glazik, and Hubert Jedin, *Reformation and Counter Reformation* (Crossroad, 1986) is volume 5 of the ten-volume *History of the Church* by Jedin, which covers the events in this and other chapters in great detail.

Lee Palmer Wandel, *The Eucharist in the Reformation* (Cambridge University Press, 2006) traces Protestant and Catholic developments in worship from before Luther to after the Council of Trent.

James White, *Protestant Worship* (Westminster John Knox, 1989) describes and analyzes nine styles of worship, their historical origins and development. *Roman Catholic Worship: Trent to Today* (Paulist Press, 1995) details developments during the modern centuries, including the beginning of the liturgical movement.

Bernard Leeming, *Principles of Sacramental Theology* (Newman Press, 1956) is a detailed exposition of the modern Catholic understanding of the sacraments as it developed in history, written from the viewpoint of scholastic and dogmatic theology.

The Church Teaches: Documents of the Church in English Translation (Herder, 1955) is a handy source of official Catholic statements on the sacraments in medieval and modern times, especially the Council of Trent.

Protestant Reformers

Martin Marty, *Martin Luther* (Penguin Books, 2004) focuses more on the life of the reformer than on his theology.

Derek Wilson, *Out of the Storm* (St. Martin's Press, 2007) is a comprehensive yet readable look at Luther's life, times, and legacy.

John Dillenberger, ed., *Martin Luther: Selections from His Writings* (Doubleday Anchor Books, 1961) contains Luther's main ideas on the sacraments and other subjects.

Hermann Sasse, *This is My Body* (Augsburg, 1959) examines Luther's arguments for the real presence of Christ, his controversy with Zwingli, and Calvin's later contribution to the discussion.

Alister McGrath, *A Life of John Calvin* (Blackwell Publishers, 1990) focuses on the social setting of the Reformation and Calvin's impact on western culture.

William Bouwsma, *John Calvin* (Oxford University Press, 1988) tries to get inside the mind of the reformer.

Hugh Thomson Kerr, ed., *A Compend of the Institutes of the Christian Religion* (Westminster Press, 1939) contains, in Book IV, John Calvin's main ideas on the sacraments.

Ronald Wallace, *Calvin's Doctrine of the Word and Sacrament* (Oliver and Boyd, 1953) explains how the reformer saw scripture, baptism, and the Lord's supper as means of revelation.

W. P. Stevens, *The Theology of Huldrych Zwingli* (Clarendon Press, 1986) contains chapters on his understanding of the sacraments, especially baptism and eucharist.

Thomas Davis, *This Is My Body* (Baker Publishing, 2008) examines Protestant understandings of the eucharist by reviewing the teachings of Luther and Calvin related to Christian worship.

Modern Catholic Spiritual Practices

John Hardon, *The History of Eucharistic Adoration* (Ave Maria, 2000) summarizes the development of this devotional practice from the perspective of the doctrine of the real presence.

Ann Taves, *The Household of Faith* (University of Notre Dame Press, 1986) describes nineteenth century devotional practices and explores their impact on the lives of Catholics and the church.

James O'Toole, ed., *Habits of Devotion* (Cornell University Press, 2004) studies prayer, Marian devotion, confession, and the mass in the lives of American Catholics in the twentieth century.

Ann Ball, *Encyclopedia of Catholic Devotions and Practices* (Our Sunday Visitor, 2003) includes terminology, feast days, saints, symbols, and sacramentals associated with traditional religiosity.

CHAPTER V

THE SACRAMENTS TODAY

The purpose of the sacraments is to sanctify people, to build up the body of Christ, and, finally, to worship God. Because they are signs they also belong in the realm of instruction....

With the passage of time, however, certain features have crept into the rites of the sacraments and sacramentals which have made their nature and purpose less clear to the people of today. Hence some changes are needed to adapt them to present-day needs.

—SECOND VATICAN COUNCIL

For the Roman Catholic Church, the Second Vatican Council marked the end of one era and the beginning of another. Before the council the Roman mass was the uniform liturgy for Catholics around the world, and it was in Latin; after the council Catholics heard the mass in their own language, and they celebrated it somewhat differently in different countries. Before the council other sacramental rites were almost identical in every country and diocese; after the council Catholics had much greater freedom in designing sacramental rituals to fit their own cultures. Before the council, scholasticism was the dominant theology of the Catholic Church; after the council Catholics developed new ways of thinking and talking about their beliefs.

In other areas not directly related to the sacraments, the change was no less dramatic. In the period before the council the authority structure of the Roman church was assumed to be pyramidal; lay people were subject to their pastors, pastors were subject to their bishops, and all were subject to the pope. During and after the council bishops began to view their authority in terms of collegiality or consensus among church leaders, priests began to understand their role less in terms of authority and more in terms of ministry, and lay people began to assume responsibilities which had long been reserved to the clergy. Also in the period before the council, Catholics officially regarded Protestants as heretics even if unofficially they respected their freedom of conscience, and they looked upon people of other religions as obstinate or at best unenlightened. But the bishops of the council began to address other Christians as their "separated brothers and sisters," they affirmed the spiritual ties between Catholics and Jews, and they acknowledged that non-Christian religions contained valid religious insights and practices.

Yet what happened at the council and what happened as a result of it did not occur instantaneously. The council took two years of preparation and another four years (1962–65) of official and unofficial meetings. The bishops in 1963 called for changes in the sacraments, but the worldwide implementation of those changes took more than a dozen years. After the council changes in the authority structure of the church occurred at different speeds in different dioceses and parishes, in some places changes never took place, and in other places changes were implemented only to be later undone. And although there have been some fundamental changes in the attitude of Catholics toward non-Catholics, ecumenical dialogue at the institutional level has not progressed much beyond the point of acknowledging similarities and respecting differences.

What happened at the council was also a long time in coming. As suggested at the end of the last chapter, developments both inside and outside the church were already forcing a reexamination of Catholic beliefs and practices. Some of those internal developments had a direct bearing on the sacraments.

1. Twentieth-Century Developments

Until the end of the nineteenth century the Catholic understanding of theology, worship, and scripture was fundamentally nonhistorical. The hierarchy and laity were largely unaware that Catholic theology had a history, or that their doctrines had not always been expressed in scholastic terms. They did not know that the mass and sacraments had been developing for centuries before their forms were frozen in time by the Council of Trent. They knew, of course, that some books of the Bible had been written before others, but they were ignorant of the actual history of their composition. At the same time, however, Christianity regarded itself as a historical religion based on factual events, and Catholicism in particular prided itself on its centuries of continuous tradition. Thus it was somewhat logical that, in attempting to meet modern challenges to the Christian faith, Catholics would turn to the study of history to support their beliefs and practices. Yet in the long run it was precisely that investigation of history which led to deep changes in those same beliefs and practices. The discovery that things had not always been the same in the past opened the possibility for things to be different in the future.

Neoscholasticism

In the modern world Catholicism was intellectually challenged by modern philosophies and ideologies. Empiricism and idealism, pragmatism and positivism, naturalism and materialism, were philosophical movements that seemed to attack the very foundation of Catholic theology. Nationalism and liberalism, socialism and democracy, were ideas that seemed incompatible with Catholic views about how society should be ordered. Utilitarianism, romanticism, and pragmatism proposed ethical norms that ran counter to traditional Catholic morality. Medieval scholasticism seemed incapable of meeting these modern challenges and most European intellectuals dismissed it as unworthy of serious consideration. Then in the 1800s some Catholic scholars began a sustained attempt to revitalize scholasticism, purge it of antiquated ideas that had been disproven by modern science, and form it into an intellectual system as coherent and comprehensive as any other. This neoscholastic movement gained papal approval in 1879 when Leo XIII called for a restoration of Christian philosophy based on the ideas of Thomas Aquinas, and in 1914 Pius X ordered all Catholic seminaries to use the *Summa Theologica* as a major source book in theology.

Before the new Catholic philosophy could be constructed, however, the old philosophy had to be recovered. Critical editions of the works of the major medieval theologians were published, translations were made, articles about them appeared in scholarly journals, and new books compared and commented on them. At first it seemed that Pope Leo's hope for a unified Christian philosophy would be realized, but as the century progressed it became apparent that medieval philosophy was not the single body of thought it had been assumed to be. Historical studies showed that there were some profound differences among the medieval scholastics, and the new scholastics seemed incapable of reconciling them. Moreover, Catholic thinkers in attempting to deal honestly with modern philosophies began to discover that these approaches raised questions that traditional scholasticism could not answer, and so they began to fit new philosophical ideas into a general scholastic framework. By the 1950s Catholic philosophers and theologians were incorporating insights from existentialism and phenomenology, as well as ideas from sociology, psychology, and other disciplines into their work. Then, when the Second Vatican Council chose to speak in pastoral rather than scholastic terms, many Catholic writers abandoned scholasticism entirely in favor of more contemporary ways of looking at the world. So although today it is still possible to distinguish between Catholic thinkers who were educated in the scholastic tradition and other currents of Catholic thought, and although scholastic thinking has enjoyed a certain resurgence among conservative theologians, it is fair to say that scholasticism is no longer the unifying force in Catholic theology that it once was.

The Liturgical Movement

The bishops at the Vatican council were more concerned with pastoral and practical matters than with the doctrinal ones, and one of the developments within the church that had aroused this concern was the liturgical movement. Like the neoscholastic movement it began in the nineteenth century out of a dissatisfaction with the way things were, it progressed through a period of research into historical origins, and it culminated in a shift away from Tridentine Catholicism. Initially the movement affected only the monks of Europe who were trying to improve their eucharistic liturgies by studying the historical background of the mass. In the 1880s, however, desire for liturgical reform began to spread beyond the monasteries, and during the first half of the twentieth century historical research by Catholic scholars steadily increased. Archives were explored, influences on the liturgy were traced, and the evolution of the Roman liturgy began to become clearer. It became apparent that the Tridentine mass was actually a composite of prayers, readings, and gestures that had become part of the church's worship at different times and that did not always agree with one another. Research into the other sacraments showed that they too did not always have the forms given them in modern times and that they had been understood differently in different periods of the church's history.

In coming to grips with this new historical information, theologians began to look for new ways to understand the liturgical sacraments. Odo Casel in Germany, for example, did extensive research into early Christian worship and developed an explanation of the sacraments which was more patristic than scholastic. He returned to the Greek fathers' practice of referring to the sacraments as mysteries, and he interpreted them as rites in which the saving activity of the risen Christ became present to those who participated in them. For Casel, genuine participation in the sacraments meant an experiential participation in the Christian mysteries rather than a reverent attention to the rituals. He argued that through the sacraments and the yearly cycle of sacred feasts, Catholics relived the mysteries of Christ and made contact with his redeeming presence. His ideas seemed unorthodox at the time, but they began a movement toward a more experiential interpretation of the sacraments in Catholic theology.

Besides these theological developments, the period between the two world wars also saw a growing concern on the part of bishops and pastors to make the Sunday liturgy more intelligible and meaningful for Catholics. Then in the late forties and into the fifties the liturgical movement gained noticeable momentum. Liturgical journals were started, institutes and courses of study were founded, national and international conferences were held on such themes as modern culture and the liturgy, liturgy and piety, and the Bible and liturgy. In 1947 Pius XII issued the first papal encyclical devoted exclusively to the liturgy, and during the next ten years Rome authorized a number of changes in Catholic worship and granted permission for modern languages to be used in some of the sacramental rituals. From there it was a short step to the Second Vatican Council's call for a thorough reexamination of the church's liturgy and an updating of its sacramental practices.

THE BIBLICAL RENEWAL

The council could not have succeeded and possibly would not have attempted such broad reforms, however, were it not for a third important development known as the scriptural movement or the biblical renewal. Until the twentieth century the Catholic Church interpreted the Bible quite literally, and it used scriptural quotations to support its doctrines with little concern that the biblical authors did not have later Catholic doctrines in mind when they wrote. Nor was Catholicism alone in this practice; most other churches took the Bible literally and used proof texts to support their doctrines as well. But in the nineteenth century some Protestant scholars began to question this approach to the scriptures, and through the first decades of the twentieth century they developed more scientific and impartial methods of interpreting the Bible.

The new methods employed language analysis, literary criticism, and archaeology to determine when and where the books of the Bible were written, whether they were in their original form or had been subsequently edited, whether their allusions to historical facts were accurate, and so on. For a long time Rome was reluctant to admit the value of these methods or permit their use in biblical studies since the hierarchy considered itself responsible for guarding the faith and properly interpreting the scriptures. But Catholic theologians repeatedly requested that they be allowed to use these methods in studying the Bible, which were already being used successfully in studying patristic and medieval texts. Finally in 1943 Pope Pius XII issued an encyclical that recognized the importance of these methods for scriptural research and granted Catholic scholars permission to use them with prudence and discretion.

During the next ten years Catholic biblical studies increased enormously, enabling theologians to reexamine the scriptural basis of Catholic beliefs and practices. This research gave additional impetus to the liturgical movement by suggesting better usage of scripture in worship, and it provided another alternative to scholasticism by suggesting biblical rather than philosophical categories for theology. By the mid-1950s most Catholic theologians had abandoned the earlier dogmatic use of the Bible and recognized a distinction between biblical statements and doctrinal statements. They agreed that statements in the Bible had to be understood in the context in which they were written, and so it was a mistake to ascribe to biblical authors the views and doctrines that developed later in Christianity. In the area of the sacraments this meant that scripture scholars no longer had to assume that modern sacramental practices were to be found in the New Testament. It also meant that sacramental theologians could approach the scriptural data more openly in attempting to understand the meaning and purpose of the sacraments.

The Human Sciences

The social sciences of psychology and sociology, as well as other scientific inquiries into human nature and behavior, supported the developments in philosophy, liturgy, and scripture that preceded the Second Vatican Council. During the decades following the council, however, and especially in the years following the revisions of the sacraments authorized by the council, insights drawn from the human sciences increasingly influenced Catholic attempts to understand the sacraments and their role in Christian life.

The scientific study of history, especially liturgical history, supplied the bishops at the council with the essential information needed to support the thesis that since the sacraments had changed in the past, they could be revised in the present, and they could again be allowed to evolve in the future. Even more practically, the growing knowledge of how the liturgy had been practiced in the past, especially during the patristic period when many of the sacraments grew to their initial maturity, gave the liturgical commissions established after the council historical examples of how the sacraments might be revised in accordance with the ancient practices of the church. Although much of the fundamental history was known to experts before the council, theologians and liturgists have continued to mine the historical data for new insights into how sacraments can and should function in the church.

The sciences of psychology and sociology, when applied to religious experience and religious ritual, enabled Catholic thinkers both during and after the Vatican council to see that there were many fundamental similarities between the ways that sacraments operate in Catholicism and the roles that parallel rituals play in other religions. Initially, this discovery provided an incentive to ecumenical dialogue and increased mutual understanding not only among Christians but also between Christians and members of other faiths. Increasingly, however, findings in psychology and sociology are being used to penetrate the individual and social dynamics of the Catholic sacraments themselves, revealing how they function in their actual performance, disclosing why they do not always have the effects that they are supposed to have, and suggesting ways to increase their spiritual and communal effectiveness.

Along these same lines, Catholic intellectuals today are using insights gleaned from linguistics and communications theory, anthropological and cultural studies, as well as interdisciplinary inquiries into symbol and myth, in their attempts to penetrate more deeply into the meaning of their own sacraments. They are discovering that in our pluralistic world it is difficult to confine the meaning that a sacrament has for people to its deliberately intended significance, that people in different places may interpret the same rituals differently, and that even people in the same location might, because of their differences in background and personality, experience a sacrament in a variety of ways. They are also learning that symbolic story and ritual are unavoidably polyvalent, that is, they inherently contain a rich variety of meanings and values, some of which are deliberately intended and some of which are unconsciously communicated. On the one hand, these discoveries pose a discouraging challenge to any attempt to see a sacrament as having only one essential meaning. But on the other hand, they simultaneously present an encouraging opportunity to allow the sacraments to speak for themselves, as it were, permitting them to reveal the Christian mysteries in increasing richness and depth.

2. Contemporary Sacramental Theology

Catholic theology underwent more change in the four decades from 1960 to 2000 than it did in the four centuries from the Council of Trent to Vatican II. In the middle of the twentieth century, Catholic theologians found themselves faced with the task of rethinking the meaning of Christianity in the contemporary world, and during the Second Vatican Council the Catholic hierarchy implicitly acknowledged the need to do so. The first stage in this theological enterprise was to recover the past. The second stage has been to redefine the religious significance of Christian doctrines for Catholics today. It is a process which is still going on, and it is affecting all the areas of Catholic theology, not just the sacraments. Theologians today are taking another look at the nature of the church, the meaning of the Trinitarian doctrines, the role of scripture and tradition, and the norms of Christian morality.

In taking this step toward redefining the religious significance of the sacraments, Catholic theologians have been unburdening themselves of the mechanistic and legalistic attitudes that dominated the modern treatment of the sacraments. They have been questioning the notion that the sacraments operate automatically on the soul, and they have been insisting that the sacraments have to be treated in a wider context than canon law. At the same time, though, in their desire to remain faithful to the Catholic tradition, they have been asking what the traditional doctrines meant, why the sacraments were said to cause grace, why Christ was said to have instituted the sacraments, and so on. In a sense, theologians today have been trying to get behind the traditional words used to explain the sacraments and to recapture the experiences that gave rise to those explanations. They have been trying to get beneath the verbal meaning of the sacraments to their experiential meaning, and then trying to put that meaning into new words.

What, then, *are* sacraments according to contemporary Catholic theology? There is no simple answer to that question. In theology books and journals, in sermons and in religion classes, Catholics find their sacraments talked about as signs of grace, as acts of Christ, as expressions of the nature of the church, as symbolic actions, as encounters with God, as celebrations of life, as participations in Jesus' worship of the Father. The list, although not endless, is extremely diverse.

Still, amidst the diversity there is a recurrent theme and a definite trend. The theme underlying all the others is that sacraments are doors to the experience of the sacred, and the basic trend is toward more experiential accounts of the sacraments.

Sacraments As Signs of Grace

The Baltimore *Catechism* definition of the sacraments called them "outward signs instituted by Christ to give grace." Catholic theology had always spoken of the sacraments as signs, but this doctrine had not been challenged by the reformers and so the Council of Trent did not insist on it. Instead, counter-reformation theology stressed the effectiveness of the sacraments, and modern Catholicism regarded them more as causes than as signs of grace. But historical research showed that the fathers and the medievals had also spoken of sacraments as sacred signs, and contemporary writers have tended to emphasize this idea, speaking of the sacraments as signs of grace, signs of Christ, signs of God's love, signs of life, signs of faith, signs of the church, and signs of spiritual transformation.

Regarding the sacraments as signs has enabled Catholic theologians to clarify the idea behind the phrase *ex opere operato*: that as a sign of what was happening, a sacramental ritual was independent of the holiness of the minister. This clarification also helped Catholics begin to overcome the notion that sacraments mechanically or magically cause something in the soul of the recipient. Still, even in speaking of the sacraments as signs, the initial tendency was to regard them as signs of unexperienced metaphysical occurrences: that baptism was a sign that a person was washed clean of original sin, that penance was a sign that God forgave the sins confessed, that the marriage ceremony was a sign of an unbreakable spiritual bond between the husband and wife. It was a step, but only a first step, toward rethinking the meaning of the Catholic sacraments.

Sacraments As Encounters With Christ

A second and more important step was taken by Edward Schillebeeckx, a Dutch theologian who wrote extensively on the sacraments during the 1950s and 1960s. More than any other person Schillebeeckx was instrumental in showing that Catholicism could develop a theology of the sacraments that was both faithful to the insights of Thomas Aquinas and free of the minimalistic tendency of late scholasticism. Like Aquinas he attempted to recapture the religious experience within the sacramental ritual and then to speak about that experience in philosophical terms, but the basic terms he chose came not from Aristotelian philosophy but from contemporary existentialism.

Schillebeeckx suggests that the closest equivalent to what happens in a sacramental experience is an existential encounter between persons. When two persons deeply encounter each other—in contrast to simply meeting each other—they discover something of the mystery that the other person is. Those who fall in love, for example, see beyond the physical appearance of the other person to a beauty and a value in that person that others cannot see. In the encounter of love they see the same outward signs that others see, but to them the words and gestures of the other person reveal a depth of reality that is ordinarily hidden from view.

For Schillebeeckx the sacraments are outward signs that reveal a transcendent, divine reality. They open up, so to speak, the possibility of falling in love with God. Jesus himself when he lived in Palestine was that same kind of sacramental sign to many of those who knew him. When they encountered him they found themselves in the presence of a mystery, but the mystery that was revealed to them was more than a human love, more than a human understanding, more than a human power. For them Jesus was a sacrament through whom they encountered the mystery of God.

Even after he died Christ remained a sacrament to those who accepted his message and believed in him. In his resurrection appearances he revealed to his first followers that the mystery they saw in him and the mystery of the God they believed in were one and the same. After he was gone from their sight they continued to sense the presence of that mystery, and they came to recognize that Jesus was now glorified as the messiah, the Christ, united with God but still active in the world.

In their turn the community of those whom Christ had called together were a sacrament to others. They preached his message and in their words God was present, touching people's hearts and transforming their lives. Through their actions Christ himself acted, healing the sick and bestowing his spirit. They were, as Christ had been, a sign of the mystery of God, and those who responded in faith to what they said and did encountered Christ as their Lord and acknowledged the gift, the grace, of God's redemptive power.

In time this church came to see itself as making the divine mystery present in the world primarily in seven ways, corresponding to seven ways that Christ himself was a sacrament of God to others: in introducing others to new life, in sharing the power of his spirit with them, in healing their illness and forgiving their sinfulness, in ministering to their religious needs, in being faithful to his Father and his church, ultimately in the action of sacrificing himself out of love. The church could have chosen other ways to collectively sacramentalize the redeeming presence and power of Christ—and indeed all Christians are called to be sacraments in the world—but as a matter of historical fact these seven were chosen as the ecclesial sacraments, the official sacraments of the church. In these seven the Christian community recognized that the redemptive mystery of Christ was present, and that those who participated in these ritual actions could encounter the source of all salvation.

In this way Schillebeeckx traces the seven traditional sacraments to the church, which is the sacrament of Christ, and to Christ himself, who is the sacrament of God. As official signs and acts of the church they are also signs and acts of Christ. They signify the redemptive action of Christ in the world, and it is the power of God's grace that is effectively communicated through them.

Moreover, by adopting the existential encounter as a philosophical model for interpreting what happens in a sacramental experience, Schillebeeckx is able to safeguard the traditional teachings of the Catholic Church about the sacraments. When they are occasions for spiritual encounters with Christ, the sacraments communicate God's grace and change people's lives. Yet even if they are not fruitful they are still valid as signs of Christ, just as the signs that can reveal the mystery of a person in fact do not when others are not open to encountering and responding to that mystery.

All deeply interpersonal encounters change a person inwardly and call for an outward response, and in the same way some sacramental encounters have a permanent effect on those who fully participate in the church's rituals. The sacramental characters of baptism, confirmation, and orders, then, are these permanent effects of the encounter with Christ, calling Christians to live a life of faith, of witness, and of service. These three sacraments signify that Christ's call for a response is real and permanent even if people do not immediately recognize who it is that is speaking to them in and through these rituals. This is particularly true of infants who, when they are baptized, are not yet capable of fully encountering Christ or responding to his call.

Schillebeeckx's success in translating the ideas of scholastic sacramental theology into more contemporary philosophical language was one of the major reasons why the bishops of Vatican II felt secure in allowing Catholic theologians to reexamine the traditional teachings of the church and to restate them in nontraditional ways. And Schillebeeckx must also be credited with an important contribution to liturgical as well as theological reform. For according to his model the essence of any sacrament is the encounter with Christ, made available to Catholics through ecclesial rites that admittedly had changed through the centuries. If, then, the outward rites had changed without their essence being lost, they could certainly be changed again. In fact it could be argued—as it was—that the hierarchy now had the responsibility to authorize a new change in the rites in order for the sacraments to be more effective signs of the encounter with Christ.

Sacraments As Symbolic Actions of the Church

In some respects the sacramental theology of Karl Rahner resembles that of Schillebeeckx, but his overall treatment is different. Writing in Germany about the same time as Schillebeeckx but continuing to refine his ideas on the sacraments well into the 1970s, Rahner was one of the most prolific of Catholicism's contemporary theologians and undoubtedly the most systematic. He attempted to rethink the entire range of Catholic doctrines using philosophical insights introduced by existentialism and phenomenology for the framework of his theological system.

One of the goals of phenomenology has been to describe the fundamental phenomena of human existence, the fundamental facts that no human being can escape, the fundamental ways that human life is lived. And the phenomenon that Rahner chose as the model for his sacramental theory was the fact that human existence is a symbolic activity.

What this means is that in every action human beings symbolize what they are. A carpenter symbolizes what he is when he works with wood, for example, and an honest person symbolizes what she is in telling the truth. Each human action embodies, so to speak, one of the many things that each human being is. But human actions sometimes do more than this. Sometimes people do things they have not done before, or that they have not done as well before. When a girl learns to swim she does something new, and becomes a swimmer; the more a boy practices juggling the better he becomes at it. In actions like these people go beyond or transcend what they were before, and in performing them they symbolize or embody something new that they are becoming.

According to Rahner this phenomenon of self-transcendence is the basic fact of human existence that traditional Catholic theologians were referring to when they talked about grace. In their view the nature of anything was simply to be what it was, and so to go beyond that nature was always gratuitous. In a way they recognized that life was full of gifts from God; any growth or development and even life itself was a gift of grace in a broad sense. But in their writings about the Christian life and the sacraments, when they spoke about grace they tended to focus on the times when people went beyond what could ordinarily be expected of them. Thus they spoke about God's grace being present in special religious experiences and in heroic acts of virtue, and they said that grace had to be present for people to believe and worship a God they did not see. Things like that simply went beyond what they considered to be naturally human.

The traditional Catholic view of Jesus can also be understood in these terms. From his birth to his death to his resurrection, Christ continually went beyond what it means to be an ordinary human being. His whole life was full of grace, for he continually transcended human nature in his words and in his actions. Furthermore, since every action of his was a symbolic action in the sense that it embodied who he was and who he was becoming, Jesus became the perfect human incarnation of God's grace. In traditional terms Jesus was God become human, a unique incarnation of God's spirit, which is the same spirit that makes all human self-transcendence possible. For Rahner this means that the distinction between the natural and the supernatural in human existence is not absolute but relative: it is fundamentally a matter of going beyond what one has already become.

In the person and the life of Jesus, however, God-given self-transcendence reached its ultimate goal, which is complete union with God. Christ showed that salvation from the stagnation and self-centeredness of sin was possible, and since he was the first and only person to do this completely, Christians have regarded him not only as God's perfect son but also as their personal savior and the redeemer of human nature. In this sense Christ was and remains a sacrament, a sure sign of what is humanly possible with the help of God's grace. Christians see that if they live like Christ they too can stretch beyond their natural abilities and limitations. And since Christ is the one who made it possible for others to do and see this, he is in one sense the source and in another sense the sign of continual human self-transcendence.

Although they do not embody God's grace as perfectly as Jesus did, those who accept Christ as their savior and live as he did become in their turn sacraments to others. Traditional theology spoke of the church as a source of salvation because through the community people were introduced to Christ and to the life of self-transcendence that he made possible. The church was thus and continues to be a sacrament, a sign of Christ and a channel of grace in the world.

In the course of history the church came to adopt seven ritual signs of God's grace. These are symbolic activities in the sense already described because when they are performed the community collectively expresses what it is and what it is becoming more fully: a community of those who are saved by grace, confirmed to live in the Spirit, willing to forgive, and so on. At the same time these are also symbolic activities for those who fully participate in them because when they consciously make these ritual activities their own they individually express who they are and who they are becoming more fully: persons who are saved by grace, living in union with Christ and the church, willing to be forgiven and healed, and so on. Thus on the one hand these ritual sacraments are expressions of the nature of the church, and on the other hand they are signs and means of grace to those who deeply enter into them. They are signs of the self-transcendence that God makes possible, and they are means of acknowledging, experiencing, and incorporating grace in daily life.

Rahner accepts the fact that there is no historical evidence in the Bible that Jesus personally instituted all seven of these church rituals, but he does not believe that it is necessary to trace each of them back to moments in the life of Jesus in order to hold the traditional doctrine that Christ instituted the sacraments. For him it is enough to show that Christ instituted a sacramental church, and since these ritual actions symbolize the grace of complete self-transcendence that Christ made possible, Christ can be said to have instituted everything that the sacraments signify and make available to others.

Still, Rahner sees this as simply a different interpretation of the doctrine of the institution of the sacraments by Christ and not a denial of the traditional doctrine. And it is this loyalty to the Catholic tradition as well as his wide-ranging ability to interpret the traditional doctrines in more contemporary terms that has won Rahner's work both acceptance and respect in contemporary Catholicism.

SACRAMENTS AS SYMBOLS OF HUMAN MEANING

Influenced by the "secular theology" of the late sixties and early seventies, some proponents of a more experiential approach to the Catholic sacraments have given them a more humanistic interpretation as well. Few Catholics have proposed an entirely secular interpretation of the sacramental rituals, but there was a distinct tendency to do so especially among religious educators in North America and Europe. Catechetics or religious education after the Second Vatican Council found itself faced with the task of explaining Christianity to a new generation of Catholics without the aid of the old and once familiar, but now outdated, catechisms. One of the ways that religious educators chose to explain the sacraments was to relate them to basic human experiences of celebration, forgiveness, sharing, and so on.

The starting point for this more humanistic theology is often a simplification of Rahner's notion that reality is not neatly divided into two parts, one natural and the other supernatural, and that grace is therefore everywhere in human experience. The immediate inference is that since there is no clear-cut distinction between the natural and the supernatural it is legitimate to talk about the sacraments in more natural, experiential terms. Even so, Catholic writers within this trend have been careful to preserve a sense of the sacred about the sacraments. Considered as symbols of sacred meanings, the sacraments are still regarded as doors to an experiential awareness of what is meaningful and precious, and in that sense sacred, in human life.

For example, the sacraments may be discussed as symbols analogous to a national flag or anthem which intensifies our awareness of what they stand for in terms of patriotic values. The Catholic rituals of initiation—not only baptism and confirmation but also the marriage and ordination ceremonies—may be compared to secular rituals by which persons are adopted into families, initiated into clubs, or sworn into public office. The eucharistic liturgy may be viewed as a parallel to a banquet given in someone's honor, or a meal of special significance as on Thanksgiving Day. Such comparisons, however, are usually just given in preparation to a discussion of the significance of the church's rituals in contrast to the others.

In this perspective the Catholic sacraments are often viewed as symbolic representations of basic human meanings and values. The sacraments are therefore invitations to be more fully human, to live up to the ideals that the rites represent such as fidelity (marriage), service (orders), conversion (reconciliation), or maturity (confirmation). They can also be viewed as ritual affirmations of basic human needs and desires such as belonging (baptism), healing (anointing), or community (eucharist). The purpose of the sacraments is thus to open our eyes to see what is always there in our life and in our experience.

Since the sacramental rituals always involve more than one person and ultimately relate the individual to the whole Catholic community, the social significance of the sacraments is often stressed. The sacraments are thus symbolic statements of what the community believes it is and hopes to be, and in this sense they are signs of the faith of the church. The traditional seven sacraments also take place at significant moments in the individual's life in the community—birth, the assuming of responsibilities, the building up and breaking down of relationships, decisions regarding one's role in the community, illness, and death—and so they offer social support to individuals by affirming common values.

For a while, this approach to the sacraments led to greater freedom and (sometimes unauthorized) experimentation with the rituals, for it was guided by the insight that if the sacraments are to be effective signs as the tradition has taught, then they must be planned and performed with an eye toward their effect on those who will participate in them. At the same time, it led to a more intensive effort to explain the symbolic meaning that can be found in the authorized rituals, for many of the sacraments employ symbolic objects, gestures, and words (wine, anointing, scriptural language, etc.) whose ancient meanings are unknown or unclear to people today. If the sacraments are to be effective signs, it was argued, Catholics have to learn to read the sign language.

Sacraments As Transformations of Human Reality

In the English-speaking world one of the main contributors to new sacramental theology has been Bernard Cooke. In his writings on the sacraments, he has presented an explanation along lines suggested by Schillebeeckx and Rahner but more overtly experiential in content.

The key notion in Cooke's interpretation of the sacraments is that meaning is constitutive of human reality. It is an insight drawn from phenomenology and developed in contemporary psychology and sociology, and it asserts that meaning enters into our very experience of reality. The way we experience reality depends on the meaning that it has for us, or to say it the other way around, the meaning that we give to our experience is part of the reality of that experience.

Some examples may make this idea clearer. Two people might live in similar circumstances, but if one person is optimistic and the other is pessimistic their whole experience of reality is different. Or again, a woman who is joyously in love experiences herself and the world quite differently from another who is seriously depressed. Psychologists also tell us that there are basic human experiences that we all have, and the meanings we attach to them consciously or unconsciously shape our image of ourselves and our picture of reality: experiences like birth, acceptance, rejection, success, failure, love, pain, health, sickness, death. And for Cooke, the purpose of the sacraments is to transform the meaning of those fundamental human experiences.

Everybody can look back at certain experiences that have shaped reality for them, but Christians point to the life, death, and resurrection of Jesus as definitive for revealing what the experience of being human is all about. For Christians Jesus was not just a man but a man in whom God spoke the ultimate word about the meaning of human life. By being completely open to that word and letting its meaning form his experience of who he was, Jesus fully became the word of God spoken into human history. In the course of his life Jesus transformed the meaning of human existence and thereby transformed the very reality of that existence. And for those who knew him and believed in him, the experience of life changed so radically that their reality too was altered. They proclaimed him as their savior, the Christ. He was for them a sacrament.

In a similar way the community of Christ's followers by their example, by their preaching, and by their ritual activities were a Christian sacrament to the ancient world. They continued to experience the presence of Jesus among them, especially when they shared a meal in his memory, and they strove to introduce others to the experience of that same transforming presence. Through telling their good news and through baptizing and laying hands on those who accepted it, they not only initiated others into the Christian experience of life but also reaffirmed the meaning of Christ to those who were already living it. In these and other sacramental rituals the community of those who came in contact with the risen Christ found ways to acquaint others with the reality of resurrection and to renew in themselves the existential experience of that meaning.

Jesus Christ in the transformation of his own human reality reinterpreted what it means to be human, making that transformation and that reinterpretation available to others for all time. The new depth of meaning that Jesus discovered has entered into human history and has made a permanent change in the reality of human existence. He opened the way to a new, resurrected life which still lies open to any man or woman who enters it in faith. And the church that traces its existence to the first disciples' experience of Jesus has always lived with sacramental means of transforming the meaning and reality of life. The traditional doctrine that Christ instituted these sacraments thus reflects the perennial Christian confidence that what believers discover in their sacramental experience was and is made available to them through Christ. The life of Jesus provided both the historical starting point and the existential meaning of the Christian sacraments.

The sacraments are the church's doors into a new realm of human meaning, a transforming meaning made available to all by the life, death, and resurrection of Christ. Baptism means dying to other interpretations of life and rising to a life charged with redemptive meaning. Confirmation marks a continuation of the new life begun in baptism. Reconciliation means accepting forgiveness from God and offering it to others. Anointing reinterprets the meaning of sickness for those who are suffering and makes death alive with possibilities. Marriage reveals the meaning of Christ's fidelity to his church. Ordination changes the meaning of service from servitude to ministry. In the eucharistic liturgy Christians discover the meaning of resurrected living for their daily experiences, and celebrate that continually rediscovered meaning.

Christianity for Cooke is fundamentally an invitation to a new way of life that leads to happiness and fulfillment, and the Catholic sacraments both introduce and intensify the Christian experience of life for those who participate in them. They are ritual actions that are truly sacramental if they make the saving significance of the risen Christ truly present.

Sacraments As Interpreted in Different Ways

Once it becomes apparent that the sacraments can be understood from a variety of perspectives, no one of which looks at everything to be seen in the church's rituals, it is possible to envision a great variety of sacramental theologies. Each of the viewpoints just discussed looks at the sacraments from a different angle, so to speak, or, to change the metaphor, examines the sacraments through a different lens. These intellectual lenses can be different philosophies such as existentialism or phenomenology (or, for that matter, scholasticism), or they can be different branches of the human sciences such as psychology or sociology. What becomes clear, however, as theologians look at the sacraments first in one way and then in another, is that there is no one interpretation of the sacraments which is so true that it excludes all the others.

While many of the sacramental theologies developed since the Second Vatican Council build on those already discussed, some do not, and a brief mention of a few of these can serve to underscore the kind of variety that is appearing in the Catholic world.

Process thought was first developed by British intellectual Alfred North Whitehead during the first half of the twentieth century, but it was not until after Vatican II that Catholics felt free to apply his philosophical ideas to theology. The fundamental assumption of Whitehead's system is that all reality, including God, is in process. Indeed, according to Whitehead, all reality is process, or a complex interweaving of processes. Of these, only the divine process is infinite in space and time, and as such, it is present to all the finite processes that Christians regard as created realities, including human life and society. By being present to and entering into human life processes, God's life-giving creativity becomes taken into the individual and social activity of human beings, and is experienced as grace.

Very often, process thinkers would contend, human beings do not acknowledge the divine life process that energizes their development as coming from God, but those who do (and this encompasses people of all religions) recognize their dependence on God and express that recognition in prayer and worship. All Christians believe that Jesus was and continues to be the one person in whom God's life was so total that he can be called both truly human and truly divine. Catholics, in addition, believe that the grace of God can be found with a special intensity in the sacraments. When they join together in a sacramental process, God's life becomes present to them in a special way, and if they open themselves up to that grace, God's reality enters into their own reality, not as perfectly as it did in Jesus, but at least to the extent that they can be truly said to grow in grace. And, because sacramental processes are communal actions of the church, participating in them does not just benefit individuals but it builds up the body of Christ, which is the divine-human continuation of Jesus in space and time.

One drawback of process theology for traditionally minded Catholics is that by portraying God as a being in process it seems to deny God's absolute transcendence or complete otherness from creatures, whose chief characteristic is that they are beings in process. Since a being in process is not yet complete, this conception would imply that God is somehow incomplete. Process thinkers are quick to reply, however, that this conception of God squares very nicely with the portrayal of God in the Bible, who is described as being in process, making one decision now and another decision later, and who becomes increasingly involved in the lives of people. For ecumenically minded Catholics, on the other hand, one benefit of process theology is that it explains how God enters not only into the lives of Christians but also into the lives of all religious people who open themselves to God's grace.

A second perspective from which the sacraments can be viewed is that of the charismatic or pentecostal movement which began involving Catholics in the 1960s. Although the movement reached the height of its popularity about a decade later, its members are still found throughout Europe and North America, it experiences periodic resurgence in various parts of the world, and it enjoys the blessing of the Catholic hierarchy.

Although most people in the charismatic movement tend to have a simple but deep faith, some of its more intellectual members have proposed what might be termed as a charismatic theology of the sacraments.

Unlike most theologies of the sacraments, which borrow concepts from other disciplines to interpret the rituals, charismatic theology uses as its interpretive lens the experience of ecstatic group prayer (see the descriptions on pages 148–149). Since these prayer experiences are sacramental in the broad sense, they readily lend themselves to being models of the sacraments in the more restricted, liturgical sense.

Two features of the charismatic prayer experience which undergird this theology of the sacraments are conversion and charisms. Conversion is an act of total openness to God and a resulting attitude of receptivity to receiving God's gifts. Charisms are those spiritual gifts received from God through the power of the Holy Spirit, just like those received by Christians in the New Testament community (see pages 27–28). Although personal charisms such as spiritual insight or deep conviction may strengthen the faith of the individual believer, ecclesial charisms such as the gifts of prophesy or preaching are given by God for the sake of the local church community.

The seven traditional sacraments, then, are those prayer experiences of the universal church which are meant to be occasions in which converted Christians receive special charisms for their own and others' spiritual benefit. Even baptism presupposes conversion. This is clear in the case of adult baptism, and in infant baptism the requisite conversion is supplied by the faith of the parents until the child can decide personally to accept Jesus Christ as Lord and Savior. In confirmation the child or adult is strengthened in faith to resist temptation and grow in spiritual maturity. In marriage and ordination the Christian receives the needed gifts to serve the family and the ecclesial community with love and fidelity. In reconciliation and anointing of the sick, the gifts offered and received are forgiveness and healing, which benefit not only the recipient but also others in that person's community. And in the eucharist the gifts are manifold: the saving mystery of Christ's death and resurrection, reconciliation with and unity with others, and the experience of communion with the Lord.

A charismatic theology of the sacraments emphasizes what other theologies tend to neglect, namely the power of the Holy Spirit, which can be known experientially and which can transform the human spirit through an attitude of deep conversion and openness to receiving God's gifts. But the strength of this theology is also its weakness, since it cannot be fully appreciated except by those who have experienced the charismatic moments that are its primary analogues for the Catholic sacraments.

A third and quite different perspective on the sacraments comes from Catholics living under oppressive political regimes in Latin America and in impoverished living conditions in Asia and Africa. During the 1970s, a new method of theologizing evolved from the practice of pastors and peasants working together to discern how the scriptures spoke to them in their frightening situation of virtual slavery and actual poverty. Subsequently named liberation theology, this approach was taken up by seminary and university professors who applied it not only to the Bible but also to the doctrines and practices of the church.

What they found in the Old Testament was a God who freed the Israelites from slavery in Egypt, a God whose prophets denounced tyranny and exploitation, a God who saved the Jews from exile in Babylonia. And what they found in the New Testament was a Christ who proclaimed that those who live in God's kingdom love and care for one another, and a community of disciples who took that message to heart by sharing with one another and carrying the good news to others. What they found, in other words, was that salvation originally meant being saved from sinful oppression in this life rather than being saved from damnation in the next.

Seen from this perspective, baptism and eucharist were originally celebrations of God's liberation: baptism welcomed those who have turned away from the sinful ways of the world and bravely trusted in the way that Jesus taught to live; the weekly eucharistic meal reaffirmed their solidarity with one another and with the Lord who had liberated them from selfishness and distrust. Likewise, attending to the sick and prayerfully anointing them with oil freed the suffering from the debilitation and isolation of illness. And ordination to ministry celebrated the liberation that is discovered in a life of service to others.

In this theological context, the church from the beginning was meant to be a place where God's liberation to new life was discovered, enacted, and celebrated, and the sacraments were rituals which the community developed for remembering and living out their lifestyle as disciples of Jesus. When the church allied itself to the power of the Roman Empire, however, and then when it became a political power itself in the Middle Ages, Christians lost sight of the socially challenging meaning of God's kingdom, the reign of God in individual lives and social structures. As a consequence, the liberating message of the scriptures became individualized and the saving power of the sacraments was highly spiritualized. Finally, when the church identified itself with colonial nations exploiting the New World, the Christian message to the conquered peoples was transformed into an ideology of accepting suffering in this life in order to obtain salvation in the next, and the church's sacramental system became in effect part of the oppressive social system by promising spiritual rewards for good behavior.

Liberation theologians, therefore, see their task as twofold. First, they are trying to free the church itself from its alliance with the ruling classes and the oppressive ideology that has been used to keep the poor politically and economically enslaved. In this task they see themselves acting in accordance with Vatican II's teaching that the church is not just the hierarchy but the whole people of God, and (as a matter of historical fact) it was not until after the Vatican council that theologians in the developing world began to implement this teaching in the way they did theology. Second, they are trying to help God's people rediscover the liberating message of the scriptures and the liberating meaning of the sacraments. As long as the gospel and the sacraments are not seen as referring to salvation in this life and the transformation of the world into God's kingdom, these theologians would contend, the oppressed peoples of the earth will never fully realize the freedom of God's sons and daughters for which Jesus died and for which the church was founded.

Although initially liberation theology was approved by the progressive hierarchy in the countries of the developing world, most of whom had been present at the Second Vatican Council, in recent years it has become regarded with suspicion by a more conservative Vatican and by bishops appointed since the council, some of whom prefer to work with rather than against the economic and political elites in their countries, and some of whom perceive this theology as a threat to the more traditional interpretation of Catholic doctrine. So serious was this perceived threat that the Roman curia ordered the closing of Latin American seminaries that taught liberation theology, and it ordered all seminaries to return to a more traditional theological curriculum. Despite the lessening of official support for the method and conclusions of liberation theology, however, it has become more respected in universities for its insights into the Bible and church history and for its contribution to theological methodology.

A fourth perspective comes out of the European intellectual movement known as postmodernism. Just as Schillebeeckx and Rahner in the middle of the twentieth century incorporated the insights of existentialists and phenomenologists into their theologies, Louis-Marie Chauvet at the end of the twentieth century used ideas from linguistic thinkers and deconstructionists to develop an understanding of sacraments as elements in a complex symbol system or language of faith. Chauvet accepts the postmodern critique of metaphysics (also called ontology), concluding that it is an illusion based on a misunderstanding of language, and he rejects "onto-theology," which is his name for the traditional way of thinking about God, grace and other spiritual realities as though they were things like other things in the world. Deconstructionists, for example, take apart the usual ways that people (especially those who speak European languages) think and talk. Such analysis exposes the cultural assumptions and linguistic presuppositions behind much of what people say, calling into question much of what they take for granted as being real and true. Chauvet therefore develops an understanding of sacramentality based on how things appear in the realm of religious belief and practice, and thus he avoids making metaphysical (or ontological) claims about how things are in reality.

Chauvet insists that believers inhabit a world of faith that is very different from the world that non-believers live in, and the faith world that Catholics live in is different from that of Protestants in that it is filled with symbols of the divine through which God is made present to them. God's presence, however, is not like the presence of things in the everyday world; it is a presence that is also an absence. Therefore, religious symbols such as the sacraments reveal the presence of what to non-believers (and, in some ways, even to believers) seems to be absent.

Along with other postmodern thinkers, Chauvet argues that what people call reality is a human construction that is structured by words and other symbols provided by the culture in which they find themselves. In this sense, language creates reality. Moreover, ritual language (a symbol system of words, gestures, images, vestments, and so on) is not informative but performative, not descriptive but evocative. The efficacy of both secular and religious rituals, therefore, is due to the way that symbolic language creates a human world and alters relationships within it. Thus aliens become citizens, civilians become soldiers, couples become married, pagans become Christians, laymen become priests, and bread and wine become the eucharist, not by being ontologically changed but through the power of language that structures and restructures reality according to the way that it is spoken about. Metaphysical explanations of sacramental effects are not needed because language itself, especially ritual language, is understood to have symbolic efficacy.

The sacraments of course do not exist in isolation but they are part of a larger symbolic network that constitutes the church. Christian faith (and especially Catholic faith) is structured sacramentally in that what is not present is made present through symbols. For this reason, the church can be said to be the fundamental sacrament in Christianity because it mediates Christian truth and meaning, thereby creating Christian faith, Christian community, and so on. Even scripture is sacramental because it is a complex linguistic symbol of the divine, and for this reason it is called God's word. In this light, reading the scriptures is a symbolic performance that makes God present to the reader through understanding, reflection, and openness to self-transformation.

Chauvet reviews traditional and contemporary claims about the sacraments and sacramentality (for example, that Christ instituted the sacraments, and that Jesus is a sacrament of God), showing that they all can be understood without having to have recourse to an outdated and implausible metaphysics. It is only this kind of dense analysis, Chauvet believes, that can demonstrate to sophisticates with a postmodern sensibility that the sacramental faith of Catholics is intellectually defensible and humanly appropriate.

Sacraments As Liturgical Acts

Since the implementation of the revised rites of the Catholic Church in the 1970s, a new form of sacramental theology known as liturgical theology has developed. Unlike sacramental theologians who tend to use the human sciences and especially philosophy as intellectual frameworks for interpreting the meaning and implications of the sacraments, liturgical theologians reflect on the sacramental liturgies themselves to discern what they reveal about the faith of the church that has created and enacted them. Although they too use the human sciences in their endeavor, liturgical theologians emphasize the ancient rubric *Lex orandi, lex credendi*: The law of prayer is the law of faith, or more freely translated, what we pray as a church is what we believe as a community.

In the words of a contemporary observer of recent developments, "Liturgical theology studies liturgical texts as privileged expressions of the church's faith. It examines as well the inner movements of faith which ritual action calls forth. It examines the correspondence between what is portrayed in ritual and what is lived by individuals and by the community. It calls on the arts, the human sciences, and pastoral experience as well as the more traditional sources of doctrine, philosophy, and liturgical history....It is open to any source and any method which serves to link worship, faith and human life" (Fink, p. 1112). Liturgical theology is thus seen by some as the successor to sacramental theology done in the traditional way of analyzing abstract theological concepts, perhaps to the neglect of concrete liturgical performance.

If the above definition is taken as descriptive of contemporary theological methodology, it would appear that a genuine shift is taking place in the way that Catholic theologians reflect on the sacraments and draw their conclusions. Many of the books that have been published on the subject since the late 1970s would thus be classified as liturgical theology rather than sacramental theology, for even though they differ from one another in many respects, they share a number of common assumptions about theological method.

The first and most basic assumption is, as it turns out, one of the fundamental assumptions underlying this very book on the history of the sacraments, namely, that the Catholic sacraments (and their parallels in other churches) are liturgical rituals. Although this way of looking at sacraments may seem obvious to some, it represents a radical shift away from the traditional understanding of sacraments as metaphysical entities that are communicated (in the traditional terminology, "administered" and "received") to a recipient from God through the instrumentality of a properly performed (or valid) liturgical ceremony.

Ordinary Catholics and, indeed, official church documents still often speak about receiving the sacraments, which is a mode of speaking that arose in the patristic period, was reinforced by the writings of Augustine, and was given metaphysical status by medieval theologians in the scholastic concept of the *sacramentum et res*, or sacramental reality. If contemporary theologians, however, are abandoning this concept in favor of what the scholastics would have called the *sacramentum tantum*, or sacramental rite, this signals as well a shift away from many other traditional concepts connected with the *sacramentum et res* in the medieval framework, such as the indelible character bestowed by baptism, the seal of the Spirit given by confirmation, the indissoluble bond of matrimony created by the wedding ceremony, and the ineradicable priestly character conferred by ordination. The chapters in Part Two of this book will in fact illustrate how this intellectual shift is taking place.

A second working assumption of the theological method employed by liturgical theologians is that liturgical texts or written rites have a special significance, embodying as they do many of the central beliefs of the church that created them. In this regard, liturgical texts are viewed as perhaps even more important for understanding the faith of the church than papal encyclicals and Vatican pronouncements, not only because they express the most fundamental beliefs of Catholicism but also because Catholics are exposed to many of the sacraments on a regular basis. The sacraments thus form the faith of Catholics as well as being formed by that faith.

This realization of the centrality of liturgy for Catholics has led to a host of books being written about the revised rites. Whether they are commentaries written for liturgical ministers, or explanations written for catechists and religion teachers, or reflections written for priests and lay people, these works are based on the premise that since the sacraments state what Catholics deeply believe, studying the texts should lead to a deeper appreciation of their faith and a greater awareness of what their faith requires of them. In recent years, in fact, a number of books and a greater number of articles have been written about the ethical implications of the sacraments for Christian living.

A third assumption of liturgical theology which follows upon the second is that attention should be given to the experience of the rituals in addition to the texts or rites. Since this experience is both inner and outer, both personal and communal, the human sciences of psychology and sociology need to be called in to help examine and interpret it. And since the experience of worship occurs in an environment that is influenced by culture, the arts of architecture and design, painting and sculpture, music and dance should be invited to enhance the felt dynamics of the rituals.

If the experience of ritual is important, then to the extent that the existing rites impede or confuse that experience, they need to be reexamined and altered. In other words, liturgical theology does not assume that the present rites are definitive and final expressions of the church's faith, but it believes that the rites should continue to be adapted to the religious needs of the people for whom they are performed. During the 1960s and 1970s such adaptations by and large took place in "experimental" liturgies, some of which had ecclesiastical approval but many of which were tried by priests without official permission. Although such local adaptations still occur in places where priests feel a need for them, liturgical theologians in the 1980s began to replace this trial-and-error method of experimentation with a more sophisticated process of examining the effectiveness of the present rituals and then suggesting changes in them or even composing new rites for consideration by liturgists and church officials.

The Catechism's Treatment of the Sacraments

During the pontificate of Pope John Paul II (1978–2005), the church's top leadership engaged in a systematic effort to slow down the hectic pace of change that occurred in the wake of Vatican II. Rome appointed theologically conservative bishops, it curtailed the relative autonomy of episcopal conferences (national and regional associations of bishops), it emphasized traditions that before the council made Catholicism unique (for example, the canonization of saints, and distinctive habits for nuns), and it issued directives returning the church to Tridentine attitudes and practices (for example, less emphasis on ecumenism and greater insistence on papal infallibility). Part of the Vatican's effort to standardize Catholic beliefs in an increasingly diverse global society was the preparation and promulgation of a new official catechism, the first Roman catechism to be issued since the Council of Trent. (The Baltimore *Catechism*, familiar to older Catholics, was an American version of that catechism, which appeared in a number of editions for adults and children.)

The *Catechism of the Catholic Church* appeared first in French in 1992 and then in other languages (including Latin) within the next few years. The English-language edition was published simultaneously by a number of Catholic publishers in 1994. Its various sections were drafted by different committees, and each committee attempted to put together a summary of Catholic beliefs that included both pre-Vatican II and Vatican II elements. The result in almost every section, including Part II, "The Celebration of the Christian Mystery," is a patchwork of faith statements from various theological perspectives that are not always compatible.

On the whole, Part II is cast in a Vatican II mold. Sacraments are set in the context of liturgy (1066–1075), and Section One on "The Sacramental Economy" (1076–1209) is built primarily on a scriptural and patristic foundation, reflecting the style and tone of many of the documents of the Second Vatican Council. In only a few places does the *Catechism* cite Tridentine doctrine or scholastic theology, notably in numbering the official sacraments as seven (1113), in affirming that they were instituted by Christ (1114), in declaring that some sacraments bestow a character or seal (1121), in explaining that the sacraments work *ex opere operato* (1128), and in insisting that for believers the sacraments are necessary for salvation (1129).

That liturgy and sacraments are celebrations of Christian mysteries (1066), in particular the paschal mystery of death and resurrection (1067), is a perspective derived largely from Odo Casel and other contributors to the liturgical movement mentioned at the beginning of this chapter. Liturgical worship is understood to be the work of Christ acting in and through the church (1071). At the same time, liturgical prayer can be seen as a blessing from God the Father in which Christ is glorified through the power of the Holy Spirit (1076–1112). Liturgy is, therefore, Trinitarian in its theological structure, as was affirmed by Vatican II's Constitution on the Sacred Liturgy.

The seven ecclesial sacraments are at one and the same time the sacraments of Christ (1114–1116), the sacraments of the church (1117–1121), the sacraments of faith (1122–1126), the sacraments of salvation (1127–1129), and the sacraments of eternal life (1130). In these subsections, the *Catechism* looks at sacraments for a variety of perspectives (scriptural, patristic, scholastic, Tridentine), juxtaposing them without attempting to reconcile them. This is a very contemporary approach to religious faith, for one characteristic of contemporary culture is the simultaneous presence of multiple viewpoints.

The chapter on "The Sacramental Celebration of the Paschal Mystery" (1135–1209) likewise contains both traditional and more recent perspectives. Liturgy, it says, is an action of the whole Christ, that is, of the entire worshiping assembly and ultimately of the whole church. Liturgical and sacramental worship are not the function of simply the priest, but it is the priest who presides at the celebration in most cases, and celebrations in the church are regulated by the liturgical year and by canon law. Although there is only one liturgy, theologically speaking, there are in fact a number of different styles of liturgy (the Roman rite, the Byzantine rite, the Coptic rite, and others) that are recognized as legitimate by the Catholic Church. Moreover, even within a given rite there can be cultural differences that allow for liturgical diversity without endangering the validity of the sacraments.

In summary, the *Catechism* treats sacraments within the context of liturgy, and it treats liturgy along the lines suggested by the Second Vatican Council. The *Catechism* also affirms some traditional Catholic theology of the sacraments, just as the bishops at Vatican II did, and just as the 1983 *Code of Canon Law* does.

THE "REFORM OF THE REFORM"

Inspired by the traditionalist values of popes John Paul II and Benedict XVI, conservatives in Europe and America pushed back against what they felt were liberal excesses in implementing changes called for in the documents of Vatican II. Having served as a prelate in communist Poland since 1958, John Paul II saw the value of a strong traditional faith and spirituality in uniting people against atheism and other secular tendencies in contemporary society. Similarly, Benedict XVI's early optimism about the council was dampened by the excesses of the youth culture in Europe and especially the student riots of 1968, leading him to favor the strength and stability of traditional Catholicism over the apparent relativism of postmodern culture.

Both church leaders sensed that developments in the church were going beyond what the council had mandated, and so both attempted to curb what they regarded as excesses and distortions. For example, the Constitution on the Sacred Liturgy had not called for the complete elimination of Latin from liturgical celebrations, nor had it insisted that priests celebrate mass facing the people, yet within a short time progressive elements in the church were insisting on these and other changes. Catholic liberals appealed to "the spirit of the council" as the basis for continued updating in theology and liturgy, but conservatives pointed to the wording of the documents as the only solid foundation for church renewal. In a sense, liberals saw the council as a springboard to continuous progress in the church and conservatives saw the council as having authorized a limited amount of progress but no more.

Pope Benedict characterized the difference by contrasting what he called the "hermeneutic of continuity" with the "hermeneutic of rupture," the former being an interpretation of the council as being closely connected with traditional Catholic beliefs and practices, and the latter being an interpretation of the council as breaking with the past and starting something new. As Cardinal Joseph Ratzinger and Prefect of the Doctrine of the Faith, he had called for "a reform of the reform" in the 1980s, meaning that the liturgical changes not mandated by the council should be examined and to some extent brought back in line with pre-conciliar practices. Already under Pope John Paul II, the Vatican had allowed greater use of the pre-conciliar Latin mass and it had encouraged traditional devotions such as Benediction of the Blessed Sacrament.

Conservative support for traditional practices is deeply rooted in what they perceive as an erosion of doctrine and even a loss of faith. Eucharistic devotions and the Latin mass fostered a sense of the sacred and an experience of mystery that was lost in the revised rituals, putting people's faith in the real presence of Christ at risk. Conservatives also attribute people's changed religious behavior with regard to other sacraments as stemming from rituals that have become too informal and even banal, for example, guitar masses, penance services with little time for individual confession, and frequent reception of the anointing of the sick. For them, the loss of traditional practices greatly contributes to a loss of traditional beliefs, and so conservatives also prefer traditional theology expressed in scholastic terms.

3. Contemporary Sacramental Practices

Since the mid-1960s the Catholic Church has been visibly changing. As already indicated, some welcomed the changes enthusiastically while others accepted them reluctantly. The changes that are occurring are not complete, however, if indeed they ever will be. Even today's conservative church leaders realize that the *aggiornamento*, or updating, that Pope John XXIII called for cannot be accomplished by a new Trent-like uniformity if Catholicism wants to remain a vibrant force in a culturally diverse and socially evolving world. The council and the post-conciliar church have accepted pluralism in ways that the Tridentine church did not: cultural pluralism which allows sacramental practices to differ in different regions of the globe, and theological pluralism which allows a variety of sacramental theologies to exist at the same time. Even though the Vatican since 1978 has been trying to regain control of renewal by slowing down the pace of change, diversity and pluralism have become permanent features on the Catholic landscape.

Moreover, there are signs that this trend toward pluralism is on the increase. Catholic bishops and liturgists in non-western countries have expressed dissatisfaction with the revision of the rites which was done under Vatican supervision during the 1970s, and which are still (with few exceptions) the only officially approved texts. These church leaders would like greater autonomy in designing sacramental rites that express the meaning of Christianity in their own cultural symbols. Although Rome insists that the revised rites allow for adaptation, its critics reply that they allow for little more than accommodating the European rites to particular circumstances. They point out that early Christianity developed distinctive rites in the culturally different regions of the Roman Empire, and some of these rites still exist not only among the Orthodox churches but also among the so-called uniate churches in Africa, the Near East, and Asia Minor. They also remind the Vatican that when the Roman church spread through western Europe, native cultures invariably altered the ancient Roman rites and sometimes even introduced entirely new sacramental practices.

The more moderate proponents of additional liturgical reform favor what they call "acculturation," or translating the essential meaning of the

Roman rites into equivalent cultural forms around the world. This sort of adaptation would allow for different texts, gestures, and vestments than the ones presently prescribed, and it would permit culturally appropriate additions to the liturgy such as the Asian custom of honoring ancestors as well as the church's saints. The more radical proponents of reform call for "inculturation," or creating new rites such as those which might have developed in their lands had Christianity been brought to them before the European rites became the norm. This type of adaptation would include elements of acculturation but go beyond that to allow for married, female, and group leadership of the church and liturgy where these are culturally appropriate, it would substitute other practices for the laying on of hands and the using of oil where these are culturally abnormal, it would use native foods instead of bread and wine for the eucharist, and it would Christianize indigenous wedding practices and marriage customs by allowing, for example, polygamy in African societies where this is a normal and respected practice.

Besides this straining toward cultural diversity on the part of liturgists in non-western countries, Catholic theologians in all parts of the world show no sign that they consider the task of understanding the sacraments as done. As has already been seen, theologians continue to develop new ways to talk about and explain the rituals of the church even in their present form. It is conceivable that in the future it will be difficult to speak about *the* Catholic sacraments or about *the* Catholic explanation of the sacraments.

For the time being, however, Catholicism's official sacraments still resemble one another around the world, and they all resemble more or less the sacramental rituals of the modern period. The revised rites have been translated into many languages but they are still translations of an official Latin text. The rubrics allow for some variations in the rituals but they also put limits on the amount of variation that is permissible. Similarly there is still a resemblance among the theories of the major sacramental theologians who were all initially trained in the scholastic tradition even though they are now stretching beyond it. Even though the 1994 *Catechism of the Catholic Church* drew from a variety of theological sources in its presentation of the sacraments, the official dogmas of Trent and other councils still define the hard edges of Catholic theology. It is therefore still possible to discuss general trends in Catholic theology and to speak about Catholic sacramental practices in general terms.

THE OFFICIAL SACRAMENTS

Something has been gained in the recent revision of the official rites and something has been lost. The principal gain has been understanding: Catholics can now more easily understand the meaning of rituals designed with an eye toward their being signs as well as causes of grace. The sacraments are now celebrated in more contemporary language and in more modern dress. Most of the rites have been simplified, eliminating prayers and gestures that had been added to the rituals in the Roman rite over the centuries. Some of them have been drastically revised, reflecting the work of historical researchers in recovering earlier forms of the rituals.

The principal loss, as already noted, has been a sense of mystery. The Latin mass, for example, whispered in a mysterious language by a priest over hidden objects on a high altar, the music from a different age and seemingly from a different world, the incense and pageantry of the more festive celebrations—all of these contributed to an awareness that something supernatural was occurring in the liturgy. And to a greater or lesser extent the same was true for the other sacramental rituals. The confessional was a fearsome place, and at the baptismal font one had the sense of a soul's being rescued from eternal sorrow. The serious solemnity of weddings and ordinations heightened one's awareness of marriage bonds and priestly powers as invisible realities conferred by visible rites. For many the medieval ceremonies were more palpably doors to the sacred, so much so that the excommunicated Archbishop Marcel Lefebvre and his followers rejected the new rites as mistaken compromises with modernity and established a schismatic church which retained the Tridentine mass and sacraments.

At the opposite extreme are those who, like the excommunicated Rev. George Stallings, insist on cultural adaptation for distinct groups such as African Americans and native Americans within the pluralistic society of the United States. Stallings led his black congregation in Washington, D. C., to break from the Catholic Church over liturgical and ministerial restrictions which he felt hampered their ability to express their faith and form a community that met their needs. More moderate are the American liturgists who argue that since the culture of the United States has grown noticeably beyond its European roots, there ought to be a distinctively American form of liturgy and worship, perhaps more like some forms of Protestant worship. They claim that the relatively low impact of the present liturgy cannot compete with high-tech stage shows, high-impact movies, and mass-appeal TV, so trying to celebrate Christian beliefs using obsolete rituals can lead only to failure and decline. Critics of American materialism and individualism, however, respond that some aspects of contemporary culture are so incompatible with the spiritual and communal ideals of the Christian gospel that there could never be a form of worship that is both fully Catholic and fully American.

The majority of American Catholics, however, pay little attention to these liturgical pressures from the right and the left. And despite a massive effort to educate the laity launched largely from the Sunday pulpit, many of them comprehend neither the scholastic nor the contemporary explanations of the sacraments. Their understanding of the sacraments is neither metaphysical nor experiential but based on the religious training they received as children. Although they are invited to participate fully in the liturgy, many still attend as silent spectators.

Some observers of contemporary culture suggest that it is not the change in the liturgy that has reduced the sense of mystery but the secularization of the whole society. As the distinction between everyday reality and sacred reality becomes less and less obvious, people develop what might be termed a form of religious dysfunctionalism. They can no longer move easily from ordinary space and time into sacred space and time. There are no longer any rituals or symbols that can move people smoothly and together from their isolated personal experience to a communal experience in which their thoughts and feelings are joined with one another and with God.

And yet this is not the whole story, for there are in fact those who have understood the reasons for the new liturgy and who do participate in it with energy and attention. For them the sense of mystery has not been entirely lost; it has rather shifted from a sense of magic to a sense of wonder. They have a deeper awareness that they must consciously enter into the liturgy if they are to discover the mystery behind its symbolism, and when they do encounter it, it is strangely familiar and still mysterious.

Although the Latin mass, celebrated in exactly the same way in every country of the globe, was once regarded as the most visible sign of Catholic unity, today many Catholics feel an even greater sense of community both with their immediate neighbors and with people who may be far away. This is due in part to the more informal structure of the modern-language liturgy which allows for greater interaction among participants and for prayers to be offered for those in need. But it is also due to a greater social awareness that comes not only through the news media but also from the pulpit in more socially involved parishes. Once the exclusively vertical dimension of liturgy is widened to include concern for what is happening in the world, a host of new issues impinge themselves on worshiping Christians: political oppression, economic injustice, natural disasters, racial and religious hatred, war, pollution, poverty, crime, and abortion. Whereas once the primary concern of Catholics at mass was for their own salvation, the new liturgy creates space for them to be concerned about the welfare of others.

The changes in the sacramental rituals and in the experience of them have also been matched by changes in attitudes and behavior. Freed from the belief that baptism does nothing except wash away original sin, some Catholic parents have been less concerned to have their children baptized within days after birth, and some priests have begun to question the custom of baptizing children of parents who show little interest in raising their children as Catholics. Confirmation in some dioceses is administered by pastors as well as by bishops, and the age for celebrating the sacrament varies from seven to eighteen. Catholics are now less legalistic about weekly attendance at mass, and they go to confession much less frequently than in earlier decades. Both of these changes are due partly to changes in the rites (some find them less meaningful than before) and partly to changes in the Catholic understanding of sin (missing Sunday mass and committing certain other offenses used to be considered grounds for eternal damnation). At the same time those who do attend the liturgy regularly tend to receive communion more often and with less doubt about their worthiness to do so. The anointing of the sick, once considered a sure sign that death was at the door, is becoming more regarded as a sacrament of healing, and instead of being administered only to the dying it is being received more frequently by the elderly and the less seriously ill.

Changes in Catholic attitudes toward marriage and ordination are also apparent. Baptized Catholics who have little intention of being active members of the church today feel less need to be married before a priest, and some pastors have questioned the value of church weddings for such persons even if they request one. Divorce and remarriage, once unthinkable for Roman Catholics, has come under discussion by canon lawyers and theologians, and with the relaxing of restrictions for annulments it is becoming more common. The Catholic priesthood seems to have regained some of the stability lost during the turbulent sixties: priests are no longer leaving the ministry so frequently, and vocations are no longer dwindling even though the ratio of lay people to available priests is continuously increasing. In the developing world, seminaries (and convents, too) are full, though this is perhaps less due to religious fervor than it is a function of opportunity for education and social status. But important issues still remain, notably the questions of allowing priests to marry and of allowing women to be ordained—questions not even seriously raised before Vatican II. Both marriage and the priesthood are being looked at in a more human and a less divine light, and this makes it possible for Catholics to be less dogmatic in their thinking despite Rome's inflexibility in these areas.

Another factor in decreasing dogmatism, not just about these sacraments but with regard to worship in general, has been ecumenism, or interfaith cooperation. Spurred by the church's "opening to the world" in Vatican II (which Roman Catholicism, coincidentally, considers to be an ecumenical council, since it drew bishops from all over the world), this movement toward unity among Christians drew wide attention in the 1960s and promoted unprecedented interaction between Protestants and Catholics in the following decades. Scholars from many denominations worked together to produce similarly worded prayers such as the Creed and the Glory to God used in Sunday worship, and they also cooperated in a new translation of the Bible. Inspired by Catholicism's massive undertaking to reform its entire liturgy, many Protestant churches undertook similar reforms, often working together and borrowing innovations from their Catholic counterparts. Catholics began to agree with Protestants that they should put more emphasis on the word of God in their worship, so now the Catholic Sunday lectionary contains three readings from the Bible instead of the former two. Catholics learned to sing traditional Protestant hymns, and priests began to devote more attention to their sermons, as Protestant ministers do. Protestants in turn gained greater respect for the Catholic celebration of the eucharist, sometimes going so far as to increase the frequency of communion services in their own churches.

Today, ecumenical worship services are held in many communities during the annual week of prayer for Christian unity, on Thanksgiving Day, and during Lent. Catholics who would never have dared to enter a Protestant church now find themselves attending Protestant services occasionally and inviting their Protestant friends to come to mass in return. Interfaith marriages, once permitted only in the rectory and with no nuptial mass, are now allowed to be celebrated in either a Catholic church or a Protestant church and to be blessed by both the priest and the minister. And baptism by immersion, once a Protestant prerogative, is practiced in some Catholic parishes. All in all, ecumenism at the local level is still going strong, despite the fact that the Vatican is less keen on ecumenical dialogue than it was immediately after the council.

The official Catholic sacraments have changed, and they are likely to do so again, for the forces of change are still at work. Nevertheless, the Roman church organization is large and its hierarchy is very tradition-minded, so official changes tend to occur only slowly and after much deliberation. This is not the case, however, with the other sacraments in the Catholic Church.

UNOFFICIAL SACRAMENTS

In the space of about ten years, from 1965 to 1975, many of modern Catholicism's unofficial sacraments all but disappeared, at least in North America and much of western Europe. The rosary, benediction of the Blessed Sacrament, devotion to Mary and the saints, and other sacramental practices of the modern church still flourish in eastern Europe and in the developing countries of Latin America, Africa, and Asia; but in the lands most affected by new ideas, technologies, and lifestyles the change has been drastic.

And it has been a genuine change. It is not as though the older sacramental practices died leaving nothing in their place, for they have indeed been replaced, sometimes in unexpected ways. But again, because of the Catholic custom of calling only the seven by the name "sacrament," these new sacraments have not been called that. But they are in fact new (or in some cases revived) ways of entering into an experience of the sacred, and in that broad sense sacramental.

Perhaps the most obvious of the unofficial sacraments are the charismatic ones. From its beginning in 1967 the Catholic charismatic or Pentecostal movement attracted the attention of Catholics by its unashamedly evangelical approach to Christianity and its rediscovery of New Testament forms of prayer and ritual. In the seventies and eighties, the movement spread to European and Latin American Catholics, and it gained acceptance by most of the Catholic hierarchy. In recent decades its popularity has declined, but charismatic prayer groups can still be found in all regions of the United States and in many parts of the world.

Members of the charismatic renewal movement usually attend a regular prayer meeting in addition to the Catholic Sunday liturgy. The meeting sometimes follows the pattern suggested in 1 Corinthians 14:26–40, but it always includes some distinctively charismatic sacramental practices. After a period of prayer, for example, a member of the group may feel moved to announce what he or she feels God wants to be said, giving the group encouragement or admonition, and in these words of prophecy the others hear the word of God being addressed to them personally and directly. Or someone at the meeting may seek spiritual or physical healing and ask to be prayed over, and the group will gather around and rest their hands on the person's head or shoulders or arms or back. While the group is praying confidently that God's healing power will cure what needs to be cured, they often sense a spiritual strength being channeled through them, and the one being prayed for feels a comforting warmth and presence. Genuine physical healings sometimes happen, but not always.

The most dramatic of charismatic practices (at least to outsiders) is called *glossolalia*, praying or speaking in tongues. An individual or the entire group may begin to utter a sequence of strange sounds that seem to be connected like words in a sentence even though they resemble no known language, and the effect on the group is sacramental. To them it is a remanifestation of what happened at the first Pentecost when the Holy Spirit filled the hearts of those in the upper room and moved them to speak in strange languages (Acts 2:4; see 10:46). Sometimes the entire group will be moved to join in, praying and proclaiming the praises of God. At other times only one will speak and the rest will wait in silence until another member of the group interprets what was said in tongues.

Pentecostal Christians both Catholic and Protestant also participate in another sacramental ritual known as baptism in the Spirit. Some Protestant groups accept it as the only authentic baptism, but Catholics who have been baptized as infants instead regard it as a release of the power of the Holy Spirit, which was first received through the official sacrament. The rite itself is simple enough: the person who wishes to be baptized in the Spirit sits or kneels, surrounded by members of the prayer community who rest their hands on him or her while praying that he or she receive the fullness of God's Spirit. The sacramental effect is at least a more vivid sense of God's presence and power, and a not uncommon effect is the ability to pray in tongues. For Catholics the ritual also marks the person's explicit entrance into the charismatic community, and is a sign of being called to live more fully in the Spirit.

The other things that happen at the prayer meeting are more common Christian phenomena—praying, singing, and reading from the Bible—but in the charismatic group these actions are more actively sacramental than in the typical church service. The religious openness of these Christians makes them much more receptive to the sacred significance of the prayers and scripture passages, and their genuine eagerness to respond to God fills their singing with a joy that is itself contagious. In fact the whole prayer meeting as it mounts in enthusiastic openness to the Holy Spirit becomes itself a sacramental liturgy, gradually gathering all those present into its sacred space and time.

Besides the Pentecostal movement, in contemporary Catholicism there are other organized movements of spiritual renewal, and some of them work sacramentally. Among the more notable ones are the Cursillo, the Marriage Encounter, and the Focolare movements.

The *Cursillo de Cristiandad*, the "short course in Christianity," is a three-day program of talks, personal sharing, and prayer designed to help Christians discover the experience of being a Christian community. It originated in Spain in the late 1940s and spread to Latin America during the 1950s. In 1961 the first English-language Cursillo was held in the United States, and since then it has become established in most American dioceses. For the twenty to forty participants of each Cursillo, it is an intensive intellectual and emotional experience of the meaning of Christianity conducted in an atmosphere that ranges from religious seriousness to friendly playfulness. It teaches what a Christian community can be by surrounding the participants with a living example of one: the Cursillo itself. By the third evening its effect on them is electric, and they return from the Cursillo charged with an experiential insight into the meaning of their religion and their church. Very often those who have attended a Cursillo become more active members of their parish communities, and so its sacramental effects are not just short-lived.

The Marriage Encounter, like the Cursillo, originated in Spain and was brought to the United States by way of Latin America in the 1960s. It too is a weekend experience, and it too is an experiential sacrament. Its focus, however, is not on the Christian community as a whole but on the community created by two married Christians. During the Marriage Encounter weekend the participants listen to some talks, engage in friendly socializing and pray together as a group, but for the most part they attend the weekend as couples, husbands and wives spending time alone together, sharing their feelings and thoughts, encountering the mystery of each other. The program is designed to free them from the kids, the neighbors, the jobs, and the thousand other things which keep them from meeting each other on a deep personal level, and to enable them to rediscover the person that they married, to be a sacrament to each other, to fall in love again, and since Christians believe that God is love, to find God again in their married love. The encounter is therefore a sacramental experience, and for many its effect is both transforming and lasting.

The Focolare Movement (a *focolare* is a place of fire and warmth) began in Italy during the Second World War, and even though it is now established on five continents it is not widely known in America. Its chief sacramental experience is the Mariapolis (literally, City of Mary), a week-long experience in Christian community living for the whole family. The week is scheduled with formal presentations and informal meetings, sharing testimonies about living the gospel, praying and worshiping, eating and playing together. It is a maieutic experience that gives birth to the sense of transcending and grace-filled presence, identified as the presence of Jesus in the midst of those who have come together in his name. So like Mary, it gives birth to Christ, but now experientially and existentially in the consciousness of those who participate in the sacrament. The movement has also founded what might be described as Christian communes, more permanent cities of Mary, but which function as live-in sacraments for those in the movement and for those who feel drawn to the mystery that it reveals.

Being a member of a religious order such as the Dominicans or Franciscans can have sacramental dimensions to the extent that the organization and its members are constant reminders of the values and ministries to which the order is dedicated. During his pontificate, Pope John Paul II gave special attention to recent orders and movements that had resisted many of the changes recommended by the Second Vatican Council, that were authoritarian in structure, and that promoted traditional devotional practices. The oldest of these is Opus Dei (meaning the work of God), a large organization of clergy and laity under the supervision of a bishop appointed by the pope, founded in 1928 and dedicated to personal piety and apostolic work. The Legion of Christ (an order of priests) and Regnum Christi (meaning the Reign of Christ, an association for single lay men and women) emphasize traditional spirituality and dedication to the mission of the church in the world. Communion and Liberation grew out of a Catholic student movement and is today predominantly a lay association based on conservative Catholic values that fosters the spiritual development of its members.

But today's unofficial sacraments are not all the products of twentieth century movements. Churches and monasteries still serve as walk-in sacraments for Catholics, and spiritual retreats ranging from a day to a month in length offer the same sort of dynamic sacramental experience as the Cursillo or Mariapolis. In the past retreats were usually silent, meditative affairs, and many still are, but for increasing numbers of Catholics the more effective sacraments seem to be those which include personal interaction and sharing. It is as though in the past silence was a sacrament in which the word of God could be heard more clearly, but today deep interpersonal communication also functions as a sacramental experience of God speaking to people.

The medieval and modern periods had their saints, and although the traditional saints are still revered in many parts of the Catholic world, they are today being joined by other saints, both official and unofficial. Not all of them are widely known (indeed, even the traditional saints are unfamiliar to most Catholic children) but for those who do know about them they are sacramental persons, revealing some dimension of the divine mystery. Catholics of various persuasions see something of God in Padre Pio, the Italian stigmatic who was canonized in 2002; Blessed Teresa of Calcutta; Dom Hélder Câmara of Brazil; Chiara Lubich of the Focolare Movement; Sofia Cavalletti of the Catechesis of the Good Shepherd; Archbishop Oscar Romero of El Salvador; Dorothy Day of *The Catholic Worker*; Maximilian Kolbe, who died in Auschwitz and was canonized in 1982; Daniel and Philip Berrigan of the peace movement; the Trappist monk Thomas Merton; and the recent popes John XXIII and John Paul II, both of whom were canonized in April 2014. Nor is the list limited to Catholics today. There are those who would consider Martin Luther King, the Dalai Lama, Nelson Mandela, and others as persons who personify and incarnate what grace can do in a human life. The ancient saints were represented in stone and stained glass; the recent ones are presented in other media.

To this list of new sacraments one could add others. For liberal American Catholics of the 1960s, civil rights marches and antiwar protests were prophetic, sacramental actions as participatory or media events. In the 1970s religious education moved away from catechism classes and toward sacramental learning experiences. In the 1980s converts to Catholicism began to be asked to participate in a renewed program of Christian initiation modeled on the sacramental effectiveness of the ancient catechumenate. In the 1990s conservative Catholics reemphasized traditional devotions such as the rosary and exposition of the Blessed Sacrament, and a number of dioceses urged reintroduction of the parish mission, the Catholic equivalent of what Evangelicals call a revival. In the twenty-first century, climate changes and financial crises have again drawn people together in mass demonstrations that spiritually connect people with one another, with fears and hopes that they share, and with sacred values such as life and security. And today the Bible is being read sacramentally by Catholics as well as Protestants.

Such a broadened notion of sacrament is certainly justified by contemporary Catholic theology. Not only theologians but also teachers and preachers speak of Christ and the church as sacraments, they accept the idea that Christians should be sacraments to the world, and they admit that sacramental experiences are not limited to participation in ecclesiastical rituals. At the same time, however, much of Catholic sacramental theology still fits the mold first cast in the Middle Ages and recast by such neoscholastics as Karl Rahner and the early Schillebeeckx. Although Bernard Cooke and others have been stretching and reshaping that mold, it is still unmistakably European rather than multicultural. And despite the attempt of Chauvet to do otherwise, Catholic thinking on sacramentality still tends to be a theology of seven sacraments rather than a theology of a sacramental universe.

Another feature of sacramental theology today is its assumption that the religious meaning or the mystery revealed by each of the seven sacraments has remained essentially the same through the twenty centuries of Christianity. It suggests that the essence of each of the sacraments has remained the same even though the rites have changed. But as we shall see in the following chapters, this does not always seem to have been the case.

For Further Reading

Sacraments

Richard McBrien, *Inside Catholicism: Rituals and Symbols Revealed* (Harper Collins, 1995) is a picture book of traditional and contemporary images.

Leonardo Boff, *Sacraments of Life, Life of the Sacraments* (Pastoral Press, 1987) is an engagingly personal description of experiences of sacramentality, mostly outside church but within the realm of the sacred.

Monika Hellwig, *The Meaning of the Sacraments* (Pflaum/Standard, 1972) explains the significance of the sacraments through an analysis of their symbolism.

Tad Guzie, *The Book of Sacramental Basics* (Paulist Press, 1981) discusses the process of celebrating lived experience by entering into symbolic rituals.

Sandra DeGidio, *Sacraments Alive* (Twenty-Third Publications, 1991) uses a broadened concept of sacramentality to review the seven sacraments.

William Bausch, *A New Look at the Sacraments* (Twenty-Third Publications, 1983) presents a historical and pastoral approach to understanding and practicing the sacraments.

Ray Noll, *Sacraments: A New Understanding for a New Generation* (Twenty-Third Publications, 1999) is a college text that reviews contemporary approaches to sacramentality and the seven sacraments.

James White, *Sacraments as God's Self-Giving* (Abingdon Press, 1983) reinterprets the meaning of grace through the experience of self-giving, pointing out the social justice implications of the sacraments.

William Roberts, *Encounters with Christ* (Paulist Press, 1985) develops an introduction to the sacraments based on the experience of encounters with persons.

Joseph Champlin, *Special Signs of Grace* (Liturgical Press, 1986) describes the revised rites and explains their meaning with examples from people's lives.

Patricia Smith, *Teaching Sacraments* (Michael Glazier, 1987) explains the contributions of recent developments in theology and the human sciences to understanding and preparing people for the sacraments.

Mary Peter McGinty, *The Sacrament of Christian Life* (Thomas More Press, 1992) views Christian rituals as celebrations of a way of living revealed by Jesus and promoted by the church.

Bill Huebsch, *Rethinking Sacraments* (Twenty-Third Publications, 1989) helps Catholics raised before Vatican II to relate the sacraments to their daily lives.

William O'Mally, *Sacraments: Rites of Passage* (Thomas More, 1995) relates the spiritual life and religious experience to contemporary culture as well as to the traditional church ceremonies.

Gregory Klein and Robert Wolfe. *Pastoral Foundations of the Sacraments* (Paulist Press, 1998) touches on the history, theology, and pastoral challenges connected with the rites.

Michael Drumm and Tom Gunning, *A Sacramental People* (Columba Press, 1999 and 2000) is a two-volume introduction to the sacraments that includes practical suggestions and specific celebrations.

Thomas Santa, *The Essential Catholic Handbook on the Sacraments* (Liguori Publications, 2001) contains everything the ordinary person would want to know about Catholic beliefs and practices associated with the sacraments.

Scott Hahn, *Swear to God* (Doubleday, 2003) shows the spiritual benefit that can be derived from taking the traditional Catholic teachings on the sacraments quite literally.

Kathy Coffey, *Immersed in the Sacred* (Ave Maria Press, 2003) furnishes a flurry of examples of sacraments in the broad sense drawn from everyday life.

Bert Ghezzi, *Sacred Passages* (Doubleday, 2003) translates Catholic teaching about the sacraments into language that people can relate to.

Roger Grainger, *'Bridging the Gap'* (Sussex Academic Press, 2012) uses concepts from psychology and sociology to show how sacraments are rites of passage into what is sacred and meaningful.

Liturgy and Worship

Joseph Lange, *Gathered Before the Lord* (Christian Classics, 1990) presents pastoral and personal reflections on the connections between liturgy and life.

Fred Krause, *Liturgy in Parish Life* (Alba House, 1979) argues for a close connection between liturgy and life to give worship vitality.

Eugene Walsh, *Celebration* (OCP Publications, 1994) offers insightful and sometimes humorous observations on contemporary liturgy.

Eugene O'Sullivan, *In His Presence* (Michael Glazier, 1980) is a refreshingly candid look at liturgy and prayer.

Joseph Champlin, *The Proper Balance* (Ave Maria Press, 1981) offers pastoral reflections on the first decade of liturgical change.

Chris Harris, *Creating Relevant Rituals* (E. J. Dwyer, 1992) is an excellent introduction to symbol and ritual, with applications to religious education.

John Maxwell, *Worship in Action* (Twenty-Third Publications, 1981) tells the story of an inner-city parish's renewal of community life and sacramental life.

Mark Searle, *Liturgy Made Simple* (Liturgical Press, 1981) is an excellent introduction to the revised mass.

Patrick Collins, *More than Meets the Eye* (Paulist Press, 1983) proposes that when done well, liturgy, like art, opens depth dimensions to experience.

William Freberger, *Liturgy: Work of the People* (Twenty-Third Publications, 1984) stresses the importance of full congregational participation in worship.

Lawrence Mick, *To Live as We Worship* (Liturgical Press, 1984) tries to bridge the gap between liturgy and life.

Austin Fleming, *Preparing for Liturgy* (Pastoral Press, 1985) is a fundamental book of theology and spirituality for liturgical planners.

Patricia Wilson-Kastner, *Sacred Drama* (Fortress Press, 1999) presents a basic yet comprehensive understanding of the contemporary experience of worship.

Regis Duffy, *An American Emmaus* (Crossroad, 1995) wrestles with issues concerning the interaction between contemporary culture and Christian liturgy.

Eugene Weil, *Gathered to Pray* (Cowley Publications, 1986) is an introduction to liturgical prayer written from an Episcopalian perspective.

Susan White, *The Spirit of Worship* (Darton, Longman and Todd, 1999) discusses liturgical spirituality from an ecumenical perspective.

Charles Miller, *Liturgy for the People of God* (Alba House, 2001) is a trilogy that describes and explains the liturgical reforms of the Second Vatican Council.

Michael Prendergast, ed., *Full, Conscious and Active Participation* (Pastoral Press, 2003) collects 25 articles written to help liturgists and musicians encourage and facilitate increased congregational worship.

Yves Congar, *At the Heart of Christian Worship* (Liturgical Press, 2010) is a collection of articles by a theologian who was very influential during the Second Vatican Council.

Anscar Chupungco, *What, Then, Is Liturgy?* (Liturgical Press, 2010) offers reflections and a memoir by a leader of the reforms after Vatican II.

For Further Study

Sacramental Theology

Edward Schillebeeckx, *Christ, the Sacrament of the Encounter with God* (Sheed and Ward, 1963) is the major presentation of his early contribution to sacramental theology.

Karl Rahner, *Foundations of the Christian Faith* (Seabury Press, 1978) contains a concise presentation of his sacramental theology in Chapter 8.

Herbert McCabe, *The New Creation* (Continuum, 2010) originally published in 1964, develops Vatican II ideas such as the People of God and the sacramentality of the world to explain the Catholic sacraments.

Michael Lawler, *Symbol and Sacrament* (Creighton University Press, 1995) weaves traditional Catholic teachings with insights from phenomenology, biblical studies, and contemporary experience.

Bernard Cooke, *Sacraments and Sacramentality* (Twenty-Third Publications, 1983) systematically explores how the sacraments influence Christians' interpretation of their experience.

Juan Luis Segundo, *The Sacraments Today* (Orbis Books, 1974) looks at the sacramental system, its history and its function, from the viewpoint of liberation theology.

Bernard Lee, *The Becoming of the Church* (Paulist Press, 1974) includes an analysis of sacramental experience using the categories of process philosophy.

Donald Gelpi, *Committed Worship* (2 vols., Liturgical Press, 1993) shows how conversion to the Christian life ought to be celebrated in the liturgical sacraments.

Kenan Osborne, *Sacramental Theology: A General Introduction* (Paulist Press, 1988) presents an overview of contemporary approaches to understanding the sacraments.

Edward Kilmartin, *Christian Liturgy: Theology and Practice* (Sheed and Ward, 1988) presents a traditional but comprehensive systematic theology of the Catholic sacraments.

William Van Roo, *The Christian Sacraments* (Editrice Pontifica Universita Gregoriana, 1992) shows a balanced approach: doctrinal yet not dogmatic, traditional yet not integralist.

Herbert Vorgrimler, *Sacramental Theology* (Liturgical Press, 1992) continues in the grand tradition, in the spirit of Vatican II, and is even somewhat ecumenical when possible.

Susan Ross, *Extravagant Affections* (Continuum, 1998) uses feminist theory from a variety of scholars to critique Catholic sacramental practice and theology.

David Power, *Sacrament: The Language of God's Giving* (Crossroad, 1999) proposes, in a way that takes postmodern critiques into account, that sacramental celebrations are language events that are at once human and divine.

Louis-Marie Chauvet, *Symbol and Sacrament* (Liturgical Press, 1995) is a thoroughly postmodern obfuscation of the Christian mysteries, abetted by phenomenology. *The Sacraments: The Word of God at the Mercy of the Body* (Liturgical Press, 2001) is a shorter version of the same thing.

Timothy Brunk, *Liturgy and Life* (Peter Lang, 2003) elaborates on the close relationship between sacraments and ethics in Chauvet's theology.

Glenn Ambrose, *The Theology of Louis-Marie Chauvet* (Ashgate, 2012) provides a more concise if not always a more lucid exposition than that found in Chauvet's own works.

German Martinez, *Signs of Freedom* (Paulist Press, 2003) combines an eclectic variety of modern and contemporary insights to develop a syncretistic theology of ontological entities.

John Colwell, *Promise and Presence* (Paternoster Press, 2005) is an ecumenical contribution by a liberal Baptist examining the implications of sacramentality as a revelatory process.

Lambert Leijssen, *With the Silent Glimmer of God's Spirit* (Paulist Press, 2007) reformulates Catholic sacramental teachings in postmodern terms that are accessible to most readers.

Liturgical Theology

Alesander Schmemann, *Introduction to Liturgical Theology* (St. Vladimir's Seminary Press, 2003) is one of the earliest works on the subject and a classic in the field, first published in1996.

Aidan Kavanagh, *On Liturgical Theology* (Pueblo, 1984) develops the thesis that theologians ought to devote more attention to the church's liturgical rituals.

David Fagerburg, *Theologia Prima* (Liturgical Training Publications, 2004) is the second edition of *What is Liturgical Theology?*, which discusses three different approaches to the field.

Kevin Irwin, *Liturgical Theology: A Primer* (Liturgical Press, 1990) is a brief introduction to liturgical theology and its primary authors in Europe and the United States. *Context and Text* (Liturgical Press, 1994) argues that liturgical theology must be based not only on liturgical texts but also on ritual performance and social context.

Gordon Lathrop, *Holy Things* (Augsburg Fortress, 1993), *Holy People* (1999), and *Holy Ground* (2003) is a trilogy that seeks to develop a wide-ranging theology of worship, the church, and the cosmos that is both accepting and critical of traditional Christian prayer practices.

Don E. Saliers, *Worship as Theology* (Abingdon Press, 1994) explores how the activity of liturgical worship is both the first theology of the church and a symbolic statement of its ultimate purpose.

Draško Dizdar, *Sheer Grace* (Paulist Press, 2008) offers a theological interpretation for many aspects of the liturgy, including sacred space and sacred time.

Catherine Vincie, *Celebrating Divine Mystery* (Liturgical Press, 2009) is an introduction to liturgical theology that emphasizes the religious meaning of what is done during eucharistic worship.

Jill Crainshaw, *Wise and Discerning Hearts* (Liturgical Press, 2000) attempts to correct perceived shortcomings of current liturgical theology with insights from the wisdom tradition of the scriptures.

Graham Hughes, *Worship as Meaning* (Cambridge University Press, 2003) attempts to articulate how meaning is expressed and communicated in contemporary public worship.

Simon Chan, *Liturgical Theology* (InterVarsity Press, 2006) argues that evangelical churches need to look more deeply at ecclesiology and liturgy, including the catechumenate.

Dwight Vogel, ed., *Primary Sources of Liturgical Theology* (Liturgical Press, 2000) is a helpful collection of early and recent articles by respected authors.

History of Liturgy and Worship

Anton Baumstark, *On the Historical Development of the Liturgy* (Liturgical Press, 2011) was the first book to document changes in Christian worship across 20 centuries, originally published in 1922.

Adolf Adam, *Foundations of Liturgy* (Liturgical Press, 1992) is a compendium of Catholic liturgical practice, with attention to the seven sacraments and other liturgical rituals.

James White, *A Brief History of Christian Worship* (Abingdon Press, 1993) provides a valuable systematic overview of the major periods in church history.

Frank Senn, *Christian Liturgy: Catholic and Evangelical* (Fortress Press, 1997) is a thorough and detailed history of Christian worship in the west, with some references to Eastern rites. *The People's Work* (Augsburg Fortress, 2006) is a social history of the liturgy that reconstructs what worship in the past looked like from the perspective of the participants.

Geoffrey Wainwright and Karen Westerfield Tucker, *The Oxford History of Christian Worship* (Oxford University Press, 2005) contains 34 articles on many aspects of worship in history.

Keith Pecklers, *Liturgy: The Illustrated History* (Paulist Press, 2012) is a lavishly produced liturgical history with maps, photographs, and drawings depicting twenty centuries of Christian worship.

Theories of Liturgy and Worship

Odo Casel, *The Mystery of Christian Worship* (Crossroad, 1999) is a classic of the liturgical movement, originally published in 1932, that related the Christian mysteries to other religions.

Bruce Morrill, ed., *Bodies of Worship* (Liturgical Press, 1999) explores the significance of individual, ecclesial, and cultural bodies in liturgical practice and experience.

Frank Senn, *New Creation* (Augsburg Fortress, 2000) is an ecumenical examination of how liturgy expresses a worldview that interprets experience and orders relationships.

Michael Kunzler, *The Church's Liturgy* (Continuum, 2001) is a compendious treatment of Catholic worship written from a very traditional perspective.

E. Byron Anderson, *Worship and Christian Identity* (Liturgical Press, 2003) explores the relationship between different types of worship and the formation of Christian faith.

Thomas Best and Dagmar Heller, *Worship Today* (WCC Publications, 2004) contains many articles describing and explaining many forms of Christian worship around the world.

Christopher Irvine, *The Art of God* (Liturgy Training Publications, 2006) explores the formative effect of worship on worshipers, especially in the practice of baptism and eucharistic liturgy.

Kendra Hotz and Matthew Mathews, *Shaping the Christian Life* (Westminster John Knox, 2006) explores how worship cultivates a wide range of religious affections through experiences of the heart.

Judith Kubicki, *The Presence of Christ in the Gathered Assembly* (Continuum, 2006) uses phenomenology, postmodern analysis, semiotics, and other disciplines to interpret this liturgical claim.

R. Kevin Seasoltz, *God's Gift Giving* (Continuum, 2007) interprets the scriptures, liturgy, and the sacraments as vehicles of God's self-giving.

Liturgical Celebration and Spirituality

Keith Pecklers, *Worship: A Primer in Christian Ritual* (Liturgical Press, 2003) covers everything from the basics of ritual to the history of the liturgy to the challenges of multiculturalism today.

Bernard Cooke and Gary Macy, *Christian Symbol and Ritual* (Oxford University Press, 2005) is an introduction to the Catholic sacraments and liturgy written for college students.

Lucien Deiss, *The Mass* (Liturgical Press, 1992) is a step-by-step analysis of the current Roman rite for the mass.

James White, *Introduction to Christian Worship* (Abingdon Press, 1990) presents an overview of all aspects of Protestant and Catholic worship.

Shawn Madigan, *Spirituality Rooted in Liturgy* (Pastoral Press, 1988) explores Christian attitudes and behaviors that arise from the experience of worship.

Frank Senn, *A Stewardship of the Mysteries* (Paulist Press, 1998) takes an ecumenical approach that appreciates Catholic, Protestant, and Orthodox traditions.

Richard Giles, *Creating Uncommon Worship* (Liturgical Press, 2004) offers liturgically sound suggestions for enhancing the experience of eucharistic worship.

Mark Searle, *Called to Participate* (Liturgical Press, 2006) is a compact and insightful introduction to liturgical worship and the developments that led to the Vatican II liturgical reforms.

Stratford Caldecott, *The Seven Sacraments* (Crossroad, 2006) is a contemporary restatement of traditional Catholic spirituality based on a mystical appreciation of symbolic realism.

David Torevell, *Liturgy and the Beauty of the Unknown* (Ashgate, 2007) argues that the experience of the divine in worship, like the experience of beauty in art, is an encounter with mystery.

Liturgical Renewal

Robert Tuzik, ed., *How Firm a Foundation* (Liturgy Training Publications, 1990) compiles informative biographies of the leaders of the liturgical movement in Europe and America.

J. D. Crichton, *Lights in the Darkness* (Liturgical Press, 1996) reviews developments in liturgical practice and scholarship from the seventeenth to the nineteenth century.

John Fenwick and Brian Spinks. *Worship in Transition* (T&T Clark, 1995) chronicles the liturgical movement in many churches from 1900 to the end of the century.

Keith Peckleers, *The Unread Vision* (Liturgical Press, 1998) relates stories of the liturgical movement in the U.S. from 1926 to 1955. *The Genius of the Roman Rite* (Liturgical Press, 2009) examines the history of the rite and the process that was used to create the English translation of the missal.

Annibale Bugnini, *The Reform of the Liturgy, 1948–1975* (Liturgical Press, 1990) is a scholarly and detailed account of how the revised rites took shape through years of research, many drafts, exhaustive negotiations, and final compromises.

Frederick McManus, ed., *Thirty Years of Liturgical Renewal* (United States Catholic Conference, 1987) documents liturgical reform in America with statements of the Bishops' Committee on the Liturgy from 1963 to 1985.

Lawrence Madden, ed., *The Awakening Church* (Liturgical Press, 1992) presents ten authors reflecting on twenty-five years of liturgical renewal in the Catholic Church.

Alcuin Reid, *The Organic Development of the Liturgy* (Ignatius Press, 2005) looks approvingly at the liturgical movement and reforms prior to Vatican II.

Massimo Faggioli, *True Reform* (Liturgical Press, 2012) is a nuanced and well-documented account of the developments that led to the reform of liturgy and ecclesiology at the Second Vatican Council.

Worship and Cultural Adaptation

Anscar Chupungco, *Cultural Adaptation of the Liturgy* (Paulist Press, 1982) argues on historical and anthropological grounds that liturgy should be allowed to evolve in culturally diverse ways. *Liturgies of the Future* (1989) shows how the process of inculturation is grounded in the spirit and documents of Vatican II.

Philip Tovey, *Inculturation: The Eucharist in Africa* (Grove Books, 1988) illustrates the meaning of inculturation with a variety of actual examples. *Inculturation of Christian Worship* (Ashgate, 2004) builds on the previous work and addresses philosophical, theological, anthropological, and linguistic issues.

Vincent Donovan, *Christianity Rediscovered* (Orbis Books, 1982) relates one missionary's discovery of the meaning and value of allowing people to develop their own sacramental rituals.

E. Elochukwu Uzukwu, *Liturgy: Truly Christian, Truly African* (Gaba Publications, 1982) argues for the creation of African rites as valid liturgical forms parallel to the Eastern rites.

F. Kabasele Lumbala, *Celebrating Jesus Christ in Africa* (Orbis Books, 1998) describes indigenous rites, or rites with uniquely African elements, for each of the sacraments.

Anthony Amadi, *Eucharistic Inculturation and Our Daily Meaningful Celebration* (Verlag Dr. Müller, 2010) argues for inculturation to overcome the divorce of worship from daily experience in Zimbabwe.

Francis Gonsalves, *Body, Bread, Blood* (ISPCK, 2000) offers Indian perspectives on the eucharist by Catholics, mostly Jesuits.

Mark Francis, *Shape a Circle Ever Wider* (Liturgy Training Publications, 2000) is an introduction to liturgical inculturation and its application to the United States.

Brian Blount and Leonora Tubbs Tisdale, eds., *Making Room at the Table* (Westminster John Knox, 2001) collects essays about the biblical and theological foundations of multicultural worship.

Worship and Women's Issues

Teresa Berger, *Women's Ways of Worship* (Liturgical Press, 1999) highlights women's contributions to early church worship and to the twentieth-century liturgical movement. *Dissident Daughters* (Westminster John Knox Press, 2001) contains writings from women around the world about new forms of worship and the reasoning behind them.

Marjorie Procter-Smith, *Praying With Our Eyes Open* (Abingdon Press, 1995) critiques the patriarchal characteristics of most public prayer and presents principles for feminist inclusive worship.

Janet Walton, *Feminist Liturgy* (Liturgical Press, 2000) contains descriptions of new liturgical forms developed by women and addressing issues of concern to them.

Susan White, *A History of Women in Christian Worship* (Pilgrim Press, 2003) describes the roles that women have played in the prayer life of church communities, mostly in modern times.

Dorothy McDougall, *The Cosmos as the Primary Sacrament* (Peter Lang, 2003) weaves together ecofeminism and the new cosmology of Thomas Berry.

Rosemary Radford Reuther, *Women-Church* (Harper and Row, 1985) surveys the thinking of radical Catholic women and worship services that they developed.

Sacraments and the Human Sciences

Nathan Mitchell, *Liturgy and the Social Sciences* (Liturgical Press, 1999) discusses the past, present, and future of liturgical studies performed from a social science perspective. *Meeting Mystery* (Orbis Books, 2006) draws from ritual studies and postmodern thinkers to discuss liturgy and sacraments.

Joseph Martos, *The Sacraments* (Liturgical Press, 2009) looks at sacramental practices from the perspectives of psychology, sociology, ritual studies, history, and spirituality.

Gerard Fourez, *Sacraments and Passages* (Ave Maria Press, 1983) uses phenomenology and sociology to detect distortions in the authentic practice and understanding of sacramental celebrations.

Frank Senn, *Christian Worship and Its Cultural Setting* (Fortress Press, 1983) uses the human sciences to analyze and improve the performance of liturgy.

Kieran Flanagan, *Sociology and Liturgy* (St. Martin's Press, 1991) analyzes liturgical spaces and actions in terms of their social effects.

Robert Browning and Roy Reed, *The Sacraments in Religious Education and Liturgy* (Religious Education Press, 1985) uses contributions from the human sciences to examine the potential of sacramental celebrations for individual and communal development.

Regis Duffy, ed., *Alternative Futures for Worship,* Volume 1: *General Introduction* (Liturgical Press, 1987) discusses the importance of the human sciences for understanding sacraments, and uses concepts from those sciences to analyze the experience of ritual.

Joyce Ann Zimmerman, *Liturgy and Hermeneutics* (Liturgical Press, 1999) shows how contemporary theories of interpretation are being used to understand liturgical texts and shape liturgical practice.

Lieven Boeve and Lambert Leijssen, eds., *Sacramental Presence in a Postmodern Context* (Leuven University Press, 2001) contains papers and responses from an interdisciplinary conference in Belgium.

Susan White, *Foundations of Christian Worship* (Westminster John Knox, 2006) takes an empirical approach to the meaning and effectiveness of liturgical services based on observation and questioning of participants.

Liturgy and Ethics

Rafael Avila, *Worship and Politics* (Orbis Books, 1977) argues that authentic Christian liturgy has ethical and even political implications.

Mark Searle, ed., *Liturgy and Social Justice* (Liturgical Press, 1980) shows how the two used to be and should again be interconnected.

Regis Duffy, *Real Presence* (Harper & Row, 1982) emphasizes the necessity of commitment and praxis for authentic sacramental worship.

William Willimon, *The Service of God* (Abingdon Press, 1983) looks at how worship, personal morality, and social ethics are interrelated.

Michael Downey, *Clothed in Christ* (Crossroad, 1987) works out the behavioral implications of the sacraments in terms of personal morality, social ethics, and pastoral practice.

Timothy Sedgwick, *Sacramental Ethics* (Fortress Press, 1987) shows how the paschal movement of the liturgy implies a Christian morality that is normative but not legalistic.

Brian Wrenn, *What Language Shall I Borrow?* (Crossroad, 1989) confronts the vexing problem of sexism in public prayers.

Duncan Forrester, Ian McDonald, and Gian Tellini. *Encounter with God* (T&T Clark, 1996) is an introduction to liturgy that emphasizes its connection to religious experience and ethical behavior.

Megan McKenna, *Rites of Justice* (Orbis Books, 1997) combines fable and reflection to insert the social ethics of the gospels into each of the seven sacraments.

Bruce Morrill, *Anamnesis as Dangerous Memory* (Liturgical Press, 2000) argues somewhat abstractly that liturgy can promote the values of the social gospel.

James Empereur and Christopher Kiesling, *The Liturgy That Does Justice* (Wipf and Stock, 2002) emphasizes the need to relate sacramental worship to the transformation of society in the spirit of the gospel.

Harmon Smith, *Where Two or Three Are Gathered* (Wipf and Stock, 2004) argues that liturgical worship ought to engender personal morality and social ethics.

Bernd Wannenwetsch, *Political Worship* (Oxford University Press, 2004) proposes that since worship entails ethical formation, the worshiping community cannot avoid political issues.

Mark Labberton, *The Dangerous Act of Worship* (InterVarsity Press, 2007) sees justice as a biblical theme that needs to pervade Sunday worship and transform the lives of churchgoers.

Sacraments and Ecumenism

Frans Jozef van Beeck, *Grounded in Love: Sacramental Theology in an Ecumenical Perspective* (University Press of America, 1981) suggests that legalistic attitudes and magical beliefs lie at the heart of many Protestant-Catholic disagreements.

Baptism, Eucharist, and Ministry (World Council of Churches, 1982), Faith and Order Paper No. 111, sometimes called the Lima document, is a carefully worded ecumenical statement of faith of many Protestant churches.

Gennadios Limouris and Nomikos Michael Vaporis, eds., *Orthodox Perspectives on Baptism, Eucharist, and Ministry* (Holy Cross Orthodox Press, 1985) contains papers delivered at a symposium addressing the Lima document.

Michael Fahey, ed., *Catholic Perspectives on Baptism, Eucharist, and Ministry* (University Press of America, 1986) is a study commissioned by the Catholic Theological Society of America.

Max Thurian, ed., *Churches Respond to BEM* (World Council of Churches, 1986) presents replies of eleven denominations to the formulation of beliefs in the Lima document.

Alexander Schmemann, *Sacraments and Orthodoxy* (Herder and Herder, 1965) is a very readable introduction to the theology of the sacraments as they are understood in the Orthodox churches.

Anthony Coniaris, *These Are the Sacraments* (Light and Life, 1981) is a basic yet complete introduction to the Orthodox understanding of the sacraments.

Casimir Kucharek, *The Sacramental Mysteries: A Byzantine Approach* (Alleluia Press, 1976) presents the history and theology of the sacraments as they are practiced in the eastern uniate churches.

James White, *The Sacraments in Protestant Practice and Faith* (Abingdon Press, 1999) compares the theology and practice of baptism and the Lord's supper among the reformers and the churches in the various traditions.

John Macquarrie, *A Guide to the Sacraments* (Continuum, 1997) is a conversational yet far-ranging treatment of the seven sacraments by an Anglican scholar.

Ronald Byars, *The Future of Protestant Worship* (Westminster John Knox, 2002) describes and analyzes the conflict between traditional and contemporary worship in Protestant churches today.

Timothy Carson, *Transforming Worship* (Chalice Press, 2003) grapples with the meaning, purpose, shape, and direction of worship in a non-liturgical church in a postmodern culture.

Leonard Vaner Zee, *Christ, Baptism and the Lord's Supper* (InterVarsity Press, 2004) argues that Evangelicals should reappraise the value of liturgical practices drawn from the scriptures and the Christian tradition.

Walter Sundberg, *Worship as Repentance* (William B. Eerdmans, 2012) draws on the Lutheran and Catholic traditions to argue against worship that does not challenge moral and spiritual complacency.

Liturgy and Canon Law

Kevin Seasoltz, *New Liturgy, New Laws* (Liturgical Press, 1980) insists that rubrics should serve and enhance worship, not restrict it.

John McDonald, *The Sacraments in the Christian Life* (St. Paul Publications, 1983) is a commentary on the new *Code of Canon Law* as it pertains to the sacraments.

David Liptak, *The New Code and the Sacraments* (Liturgical Publications, 1983) summarizes the canons and explains them.

Nicholas Halligan, *The Sacraments and Their Celebration* (Alba House, 1986) is a handbook on the valid and licit administration of the sacraments according to the new code.

Myriam Wijlens, *Sharing the Eucharist* (University Press of America, 2000) discusses the canonical and theological state of affairs with regard to intercommunion.

Huels, John, *Liturgy and Law* (Wilson & Lafleur, 2006) describes and explains the regulation of liturgical practices by canon law in the Catholic Church.

Vatican II and After

Guiseppe Alberigo, *A Brief History of Vatican II* (Orbis Books, 2006) summarizes the five-volume History of Vatican II, which he co-authored.

Xavier Rynne, *Vatican Council II* (Farrar, Straus and Giroux, 1968) is the one-volume edition of the session-by-session accounts written by a Vatican insider.

Dennis Doyle, *The Church Emerging from Vatican II* (Twenty-Third Publications, 1992) looks at trends and developments in practice, polity, and theology.

Robert Burns, *Roman Catholicism After Vatican II* (Georgetown University Press, 2001) describes the liberal developments of the sixties and seventies, followed by the conservative reaction of the eighties and nineties.

Paul Johnson, *Pope John Paul II and the Catholic Restoration* (St. Martin's Press, 1981) explains why the pope thinks reformers went too far after Vatican II.

Pierre-Marie Gy, *The Reception of Vatican II Liturgical Reforms in the Life of the Church* (Marquette University Press, 2003) is a brief sketch of the reforms by someone who knew the major liturgists at the council and afterward.

Piero Marini, *A Challenging Reform* (Liturgical Press, 2007) describes the work of implementing the vision of Vatican II, written by a Vatican insider.

Andrew Greeley, *The Catholic Revolution* (University of California Press, 2004) takes a sociological look at the council and its aftermath.

Tony Hanna, *New Ecclesial Movements* (Alba House, 2006) describes some of the organized conservative responses to liberal trends in the church.

Timothy McCarthy, *The Catholic Tradition: Before and After Vatican II* (Loyola University Press, 1994) is a thematic history of Catholicism in the twentieth century.

John O'Malley, What Happened at Vatican II (Harvard University Press, 2008) sets the four sessions of the council in the wider context of church history.

Massimo Faggioli, *Vatican II: The Battle for Meaning* (Paulist Press, 2012) examines the legacy of the council and shows how traditionalists and progressives have interpreted it differently.

Reform of the Reform

James Hitchcock, *The Recovery of the Sacred* (Ignatius Press, 1995) was one of the first books to criticize the loss of the sense of mystery in the revised Catholic mass, originally published in 1974.

Aidan Nichols, *Looking at the Liturgy* (Ignatius Press, 1996) uses contemporary ritual studies to argue against the post-Vatican II reforms of Catholic worship.

Thomas Kocik, *The Reform of the Reform?* (Ignatius Press, 2003) considers the revisions of 1969 to be a distortion of the traditional mass, set in the form of a debate between a traditionalist and one who favors the new mass.

Kenneth Whitehead, *Mass Misunderstandings* (St. Augustine Press, 2009) argues that the Vatican II liturgical reforms did more harm than good, so they need to be reformed.

László Dobszay, *The Restoration and Organic Development of the Roman Rite* (Continuum Books, 2010) describes the new rite and vernacular mass as an egregious distortion and suggests ways to return to Latin in the liturgy and sacraments.

Klaus Gamber, *The Reform of the Roman Liturgy* (Una Voce Press, 1993) praises conservative efforts to reverse the reforms of Vatican II.

David Torevell. *Losing the Sacred* (T&T Clark, 2000) believes that misguided liturgical reforms after Vatican II have led to the decline in church membership and Christian values in society.

Jonathan Robinson, *The Mass and Modernity* (Ignatius Press, 2003) regards the undermining of the liturgy to have begun with the Enlightenment and the philosophical ideas that inspired the liturgical movement since the nineteenth century.

Geoffrey Hull, *The Banished Heart* (T&T Clark, 2010) argues that the liturgical changes following Vatican II have undermined true Catholicism and have fostered heteropraxis in worship and other aspects of religion.

Laurence Paul Hemming, *Worship as a Revelation* (Burns & Oates, 2008) contends that the liturgical reforms initiated after Vatican II are so rationalistic and individualistic that they undermine deeply spiritual active participation in the sacrifice of the mass.

Denis Crouan, *The History and Future of the Roman Liturgy* (Ignatius Press, 2005) uses a detailed account of liturgical history to argue against the mistaken reforms of Vatican II.

Didier Boneterre, *The Liturgical Movement from Dom Gueranger to Annibale Bugnini* (Angelus Press, 2002) regards the analytic study of liturgy as a misguided effort to undermine true Catholic worship.

Jimmy Akin, *Mass Revision* (Catholic Answers, 2011) explains every part of the mass and insists that the church's liturgical laws are to be followed to the letter.

Martin Mosebach, *The Heresy of Formlessness* (Ignatius Press, 2006) presents many cultural and spiritual reasons for returning to the Latin mass.

Society of St. Pius X, *The Problem of the Liturgical Reform* (Angelus Press, 2001) argues from church documents and traditional theology that the Vatican II reforms are such a rupture from the past that they are invalid.

John Baldovin, *Reforming the Liturgy* (Liturgical Press, 2008) accurately summarizes the conservative critiques of the liturgical renewal but suggests that the problems are deeper than the externals of worship.

Reference Resources

Austin Flannery, ed., *Vatican Council II, The Basic Sixteen Documents: Constitutions, Decrees, Declarations* (Inclusive language edition, Costello Publishing, 1996) contains the sixteen documents issued by the council.

The Rites of the Catholic Church (2 vols., Liturgical Press, 1990) contains the complete texts and official introductions to all of the revised sacramental rites.

Allan Bouley, ed., *Catholic Rites Today* (Liturgical, 1992) is an abridged version of *The Rites*, for use by students.

Thomas O'Brien, ed., *Documents on the Liturgy, 1963–1979* (Liturgical Press, 1982) collects 554 official documents from the council, two popes, and the curia issued during the most active period of liturgical development after Vatican II.

The Liturgy Documents: A Parish Resource (Liturgy Training Publications, 1991) quotes important church documents written between 1963 and 1985, with introductions to their applicability in parish and diocesan situations.

James White, *Documents of Christian Worship* (Westminster John Knox Press, 1992) adds charts, maps, photos, and diagrams to texts surveying the history and variety of worship services.

Catechism of the Catholic Church (Libreria Editrice Vaticana, 1994) covers liturgy and the sacraments in addition to all other aspects of the Catholic faith.

Sacramentum Mundi (6 vols., Herder and Herder, 1970) is a Catholic theological encyclopedia containing concise and informative articles on the sacraments.

Aimé Georges Martimort, *The Church at Prayer* (4 vols., Liturgical Press, 1985–87) is a compact theological encyclopedia of liturgical history and current practice, with extensive documentation for further research.

J. D. Crichton, *Christian Celebration: The Mass, The Sacraments, The Prayer of the Church* (Geoffrey Chapman, 1981) is a work of careful scholarship and judicious evaluation of historical and contemporary Catholic worship.

Herman Wegman, *Christian Worship in East and West* (Pueblo, 1985) is a unique study guide to liturgical history, exhaustively listing references to primary and secondary resources under many subject headings.

Anscar Chupungco, ed., *Handbook for Liturgical Studies* (Liturgical Press), despite its name is a five-volume collection of articles by experts in liturgical history, theory, and practice: Vol. I, *Introduction to the Liturgy* (1997); Vol. II, *Fundamental Liturgy* (1998); Vol. III, *The Eucharist* (1999); Vol. IV, *Sacraments and Sacramentals* (2000); Vol. V, Liturgical Time and Space.

Cheslyn Jones, Geoffrey Wainwright, Edward Yarnold, and Paul Bradshaw, eds. *The Study of Liturgy* (Oxford University Press, 1992) covers a broad range of topics from the very particular to the very theoretical.

Peter Fink, ed., *The New Dictionary of Sacramental Worship* (Liturgical Press, 1990) contains concise articles on almost every aspect of Catholic liturgical practice and theology, with select bibliographies.

Paul Bradshow, ed., *The New Dictionary of Liturgy and Worship* (Westminster John Knox Press, 2002) is more ecumenical in scope than the previously mentioned work, and contains illustrative photographs, drawings, and diagrams.

Philip Pfatteicher, *A Dictionary of Liturgical Terms* (Trinity Press International, 1991) gives concise definitions of most of the elements in Protestant, Catholic, Anglican, and Orthodox worship.

Dennis Smolarski, *Liturgical Literacy* (Paulist Press, 1990) is a glossary of terms related to worship, from Abba to Zucchetto.

Part Two

HISTORIES OF
THE SACRAMENTS

CHAPTER VI

BAPTISM

God the Father of our Lord Jesus Christ has freed you from sin, and has given you a new birth by water and the Holy Spirit. He has made you Christians now, and has welcomed you into his holy people. As Christ was anointed Priest, Prophet, and King, so may you live always as members of his body, sharing everlasting life.

—Rite of Baptism

C hristians have baptized from the very beginning, but they were not the first to do so. John baptized in the Jordan River and converts to Judaism were also sometimes initiated through immersion in water. But for the followers of Jesus baptism assumed a special significance: for them it was a symbol of salvation and through it they entered into the mystery that Jesus had revealed to them. They entered it socially, for by being baptized they joined the community that accepted Jesus as the source of their salvation. But they also entered it intellectually, for by reflecting on the ritual of baptism they penetrated the mystery that it represented.

During the course of the Christian centuries the ritual of baptism has varied. It has been a total immersion in water, a pouring of water, and a sprinkling with water. It has been done to people before they believed in Christ and after they came to believe in him. As the practice of baptism has varied, Christians' understanding of baptism has varied, and yet through it all there is a continuity that is greater than the differences. For the theology of baptism is always a variation on the theme of salvation played in different modes and different keys in different ages.

1. Parallels and Precedents

Water is a natural symbol, not only in the sense that it is found in nature but also in the sense that it naturally lends itself to symbolizing many things. Water cleanses, and in many religions people wash themselves as a sign that they want to be or have been made clean spiritually as well as physically. Water refreshes, and in some religions bathing in rivers enables people to experience a regeneration of energy and to feel connected to the source of that energy. Water gives life, and so initiation rituals that mark the beginning of a new way of life often involve washing or immersion in water. But water also brings death, and so in some religious myths water symbolizes the chaotic state of things before life began, and in others death is the sea from across which no one returns.

Ritual washings and bathings were common in the religions of ancient Egypt and Mesopotamia. In ancient Israel persons who had sexual intercourse or who touched a dead body were considered unclean and unfit for religious worship until they went through a ritual of purification. In Palestine around the time of Christ gentiles who wanted to become Jews were initiated by circumcision, baptism, and sacrifice: by being circumcised a male convert was marked with the sign of the covenant between God and Abraham, by being immersed in water both men and women symbolically joined the Israelites who had passed through the Red Sea, and by offering sacrifice they accepted the Law given to them at Sinai. During the same period the Jewish sect called Essenes practiced a form of regular ritual washing in order to purify and sanctify themselves.

The Christian scriptures also speak of a Jew named John who preached a message of conversion and repentance, and who baptized those who accepted his call for a complete change of heart. The Greek word *bapto* means to dip or to immerse, and it is likely that John's baptism as well as early Christian baptism meant being completely submerged under water. Jesus underwent John's baptism before he began teaching in public, but the message that he preached went further than John's, and the baptism that his followers practiced took on additional meaning after his death.

2. Baptism and Christian Initiation

As far as we know, the followers of Jesus known as the apostles or the twelve never underwent Christian baptism. If they were baptized at all it was most likely with the baptism of John. The gospels also mention the apostles baptizing during the lifetime of Jesus, and if these accounts are historically accurate, this ritual was probably a sign of moral conversion similar to John the Baptist's. It is uncertain whether Jesus himself ever performed baptisms (John 3:22–23; 4:1–3). Soon after Jesus' followers began preaching the good news of his resurrection, however, they also began baptizing those who accepted that message. The author of Acts of the Apostles even traces it back to the very first day of the twelve's preaching, the Jewish feast of Pentecost (Acts 2:37–41).

The New Testament contains accounts of baptisms in a variety of settings, but in each case those who were baptized were adults who expressed their faith in Jesus beforehand (Acts 8–10). There were also cases where entire families were baptized but it is impossible to say whether small children were included in these households (Acts 16:29–33). In any event baptism of believing adults was the norm. It was also normal for those who had been baptized to have hands laid on them, but it did not happen in every case (Acts 19:1–6; 8:9–24). The immersion in water was associated with the forgiveness of sins and the imposition of hands with the reception of the Holy Spirit, but the scriptural accounts do not always draw clear lines between these actions or their meanings.

And what did baptism mean? One thing that is clear is that baptism marked a dividing line between the old and the new, between waiting for the messiah and finding him, between living with guilt and living with forgiveness, between being in a community of law and being in a community of love. For some the change was unexpected and unexplainable, especially when they found themselves with charismatic gifts like prophesying or speaking in tongues. For others the change was expected and explainable: it was the beginning of the end, the coming of the final time when God would establish a reign of justice and love over the earth. But for all of them the change was real: being baptized brought a real change in their lives that they could not deny.

Paul of Tarsus, besides being the first great missionary of this new religious movement, was also its first major theologian. More than any other Jewish Christian he was instrumental in carrying the message of Jesus to the gentiles, and in his letters to young Christian communities he articulated the meaning of that message so well that many of his writings were eventually included in the Christian scriptures. Reflecting on the experience of his own conversion and baptism as well as on the way it affected others, he strove to express in concepts and images the meaning that being baptized held for those who accepted Christ as their Lord and savior.

The focus of Paul's understanding of Christ was his death and resurrection, for in them he came to see the mystery that he himself had experienced in dying to everything he held dear and rising to a new way of life in a new community. In some way he had participated in that same mystery, and he came to realize that others who were baptized had likewise lived through it. Those who were baptized in the name of Jesus were actually baptized into Christ, he said, and into his death and resurrection. By being submerged under water they had joined Christ in dying to sin, and in coming out of the water they arose into a transformed and redeemed life. The power of sin and death was broken, and so Christians could not only experience the power of God in their lives now but they could also expect to be raised with Christ into glory (Romans 6:1–11).

Baptism was therefore like Jewish circumcision in that it stripped off the ways of the flesh and initiated a convert into the ways of the spirit (Colossians 2:11–13; Ephesians 2:1–6). Those who were baptized received the spirit of Christ, and being animated by a single spirit they were now joined in a single body (1 Corinthians 12:12–13; Ephesians 4:4–6). Just as they had taken off clothes before entering the water, they also took off maliciousness and divisiveness, and having clothed themselves in Christ they were now united with him and with each other (Galatians 3:27–28). They were joined together into a community that had been sanctified, justified, and washed clean of sin, for like the Israelites of old they had passed through a sea from slavery to freedom (1 Corinthians 6:9–11; 10:1–4).

Paul knew all too well, however, that this freedom could be abused, and that baptism was not an instant cure for human depravity. He reminded his readers that the new freedom they enjoyed was not a license to sin but a power to do good (Romans 6:12–19). The gift that they had received in baptism was not anything they had earned, but it did have to be used if it was to bear fruit (2 Corinthians 5:16–6:2; Ephesians 4:17–5:20). God had forgiven their past and saved them from their sinful ways, but this meant that they now had the grace to forgive others and to sin no more (Colossians 3:1–4:6).

Paul's theology of baptism was Christianity's first great attempt to articulate the experience of dying to the past and beginning afresh, filled with an energy and freedom that he and others had not known before. Baptism was a door into a new life, opened by faith in Jesus as the Christ and opening into a divine realm of spirit and grace. Other New Testament writings mostly composed after Paul's letters reiterate some of the ideas found in them. In two of the gospels, for example, Jesus speaks of his death as a baptism (Mark 10:38; Luke 12:50), and in another he speaks about being born again through water and the Spirit (John 3:5). Christians continued to see baptism as bringing salvation (1 Peter 3:18–22), not just for the Jews but for the whole world (Matthew 28:18–20). Still, salvation through baptism was not automatic; it had to be accompanied by faith in Christ and good works toward others (Mark 16:15–16; James 2:14–26).

Water baptism was therefore an important part of Christian initiation from the very beginning, and it continued to be as the new religion spread into the Roman Empire. The *Teaching of the Twelve Apostles*, in the early second century, mentions baptism as does a defense of Christianity written by the martyr Justin around the year 160. These accounts, however, show that some slight changes were taking place in the practice and understanding of baptism. To the preaching of the good news was added instruction on the Christian way of life. The water used was sometimes poured over the person being baptized, and the ritual itself was understood more in terms of washing and regeneration than in terms of death and resurrection. Finally, the process of Christian initiation was concluded with prayers and a sharing of the Lord's supper.

The pattern of Christian initiation described in these early writings is found again and again in later documents of the patristic period, and with each succeeding century the rituals and the practices surrounding them became more elaborate. There were also variations on this pattern developed by churches in the various centers of Christianity throughout the empire, but it is possible to piece together the main features of the patristic practices into a typical picture of Christian initiation during this era.

First of all a simple confession of faith in Christ no longer sufficed for admission to baptism. Those who had initially heard the news about Jesus were Jews who were living according to the Mosaic Law and who were awaiting a messiah, but now those who heard it were non-Jews of every sort of philosophical and religious persuasion, with a variety of personal and cultural backgrounds, from respectable and disreputable walks of life. If they were attracted by what they saw of the Christian way of life, they first had to find a member of the community who would sponsor them during a period of moral formation and who would present them for baptism after about two or three years of preparation. If they were prostitutes or pimps, makers of idols, actors or entertainers, gladiators or soldiers, they would have to find new professions before they would be considered for membership in the church. And all of those who sought baptism would have to avoid murder and violence, adultery and promiscuity, and be able to prove it. As Tertullian put it: "We are plunged into the water not in order to stop sinning but because we have stopped sinning, since we are already washed in our heart" (*On Repentance* VI, 17).

This lengthy period of preparation was known as the catechumenate, from the Greek word meaning instruction, but the instruction was ethical rather than doctrinal. Until the year 313 Christianity was officially outlawed in the Roman Empire even though unofficially it was usually tolerated, and because of the danger of persecution catechumens were told very little about the sacred mysteries of Christianity or the meeting places of the Christian community. The sponsors were thus guardians of the catechumens' reliability, that they would not betray the community in a time of crisis; but even after 313, sponsors continued to play an active role in preparing people for sacramental initiation into the church by being guarantors of their sincerity and witnesses to their lifestyle. Ordinarily any Christian could sponsor another adult, but parents usually presented their own children and masters brought their own slaves when the time for baptism arrived.

During the first three centuries the time for Christian baptism moved from right after conversion, to any Sunday before the celebration of the eucharist, to right before Easter Sunday or other special feasts like Pentecost. Liturgically it made sense to celebrate the mystery of death to sin and rebirth in the Spirit only on these feasts, but theologically it raised questions. If baptism was necessary for salvation, as both the scriptures and the fathers' own experience attested, then what about those who died before the yearly baptismal celebration? The *Apostolic Tradition* assured Christians that those who were martyred did not have to worry: they were saved by being baptized in their own blood. Some church leaders also taught that the explicit desire for baptism would save those who died of natural causes before they could be baptized, but others took a more rigorous view of the matter. In any event, children as well as adults were being baptized by the year 200, although the age of the children varied with local and family customs.

A few weeks before the annual baptism, the catechumens who were chosen for full initiation into the church began a period of more intensive preparation. They were presented to the bishop or his representative, and their worthiness for baptism was attested to by their sponsors. The responsibilities that they were now about to take upon themselves were made clear: as catechumens they could call themselves "Christians" but with baptism they would become members of "the faithful," and for those who were not faithful to God's way of life there was no second chance at baptism. When they were accepted as candidates they began to receive doctrinal instructions for the first time, listening to the words of scripture and hearing them explained along with other teachings that were part of the church's tradition. Each Sunday they were exorcised of the evil spirits that had ruled them in the past and that might tempt them again in the future: they were prayed over, blessed, touched, anointed with oil, signed with the cross on different parts of their body, or blown on by the bishop with the breath of the Holy Spirit. And with each exorcism on each succeeding week the candidates entered more fully into the consciousness of what it meant to be a Christian and of what was about to happen to them. The initiation ritual had begun, and it was building toward a climax.

As the day of their baptism drew nearer the intensity of their initiation increased. During their final week the candidates were instructed daily, their life was reexamined, and they underwent still further exorcisms and made promises to renounce the devil and his works. They were taught the Lord's Prayer, and they were given the Apostles' Creed to memorize. They were sometimes given salt to taste as a reminder that they were to become the salt of the earth. And for two days before the final ceremonies began, they fasted from food to experience a more complete dependence on God and to die further to the things of this world.

On the evening before Easter the solemn ceremonies began in the presence of the bishop and the congregation that they were about to join. It was the vigil of the feast of the Christian Passover, of Christ's passage from death to life. In the darkness they saw the paschal candle lit, the symbol of Christ, the light of the world. They heard hymns of praise and prayers of thanksgiving for the salvation that Christ had brought. They listened to readings from the Bible: about God's spirit moving over the waters at creation, about the flood's destruction of sinners and Noah's salvation by God, about the exodus of Israel through the waters of the Red Sea, about Ezekiel's vision of dry bones being brought to life by the spirit of God. They kept their vigil all through the night, in preparation for the dawn that was about to come upon them.

In the early morning light the candidates, the bishop, and his assistants went to a cistern or baptismal pool that was located in or near the place where they prayed. The water was blessed, the candidates were anointed and exorcised a final time, and they made a final renunciation of the devil and evil ways. One by one they were stripped naked, the men assisted by deacons and the women by deaconesses who went down with them into the bath. Standing in the water they were asked, "Do you believe in God, the Father Almighty, the Creator of heaven and earth?" They answered, "I do believe," and water was poured over them. They were asked again, "Do you believe in Jesus Christ, his Son, our Lord, who was brought into the world to suffer for it?" They answered again, and they were washed a second time. They were asked a third question, "Do you believe in the Holy Spirit, the Holy Church, the resurrection of the body and life everlasting?" And after their final "I do believe," water was poured over them a final time (*The Apostolic Tradition* XXI, 12–18).

Coming out of the pool, they were anointed in the name of Christ, the Anointed One, and given a white garment to wear before returning to the assembly. Symbolically they had cast off their sinful ways, they had gone down into the waters of salvation, and they had emerged to be clothed in Christ. Individually they presented themselves to the bishop who laid his hand on their head and anointed them with oil a final time as he prayed that they be filled with the Holy Spirit. They were now fully baptized and received into the church, and all that remained to complete their initiation as Christians was to join the assembled community in celebrating the Easter liturgy of the resurrection. For the eucharist, which they had never before attended, was now also their prayer of thanksgiving for the salvation that they had received.

The initiation just described was typical of the early patristic era, even though it corresponds to no single baptismal ritual of the period. There were variations from one city to the next and from one century to the next, but in each case the sacramental stages of initiation were basically the same. Baptism was an elaborate ritual, a symbolic action that stretched over a period of days. On the one hand it was an intensely individual act marking a decisive break with the past and inaugurating a new style of religious belief and practice. On the other hand it was an impressively communal act supported by sponsors, applauded by the assembly, and solemnly recognized by its leaders. Those who went through it experientially participated in the mystery of death and resurrection that it symbolized. They were told that their sinful past was dead, that they were forgiven by a gracious God, and that they were filled with the spiritual power to live free from sinfulness in the future. They heard it, and they were surrounded by others who testified that it was true. They believed it, they felt it, and they were affected by it. This baptism was a very effective sacrament.

The fathers who wrote about baptism during this period drew many of their ideas from their own experience as well as from the Bible. They spoke of baptism as being necessary for salvation not only because the scriptures affirmed it but also because they had experienced it personally and because they had witnessed it in the lives of others. Many of the fathers were bishops who presided over the baptismal ceremonies year after year, and some of them left records of their sermons to catechumens as well as more developed theological essays. What one finds in those records is variety, reflecting a variety of personal and philosophical backgrounds, for at this period of Christian history there was none but the basic minimum of doctrinal consensus concerning baptism. They agreed that baptism brought the forgiveness of sins, that it gave God's grace, and that it imparted the Holy Spirit; but beyond this they spoke of baptism in their own unique terms.

For example, Ignatius of Antioch, who died for his faith under the emperor Trajan, understood baptism simply as the beginning of a union with Christ that became more intimate through participation in the eucharist and was perfected in the death and resurrection of martyrdom. Irenaeus of Lyons, writing about the year 190, thought of baptism in terms of the renewal of all creation in Christ: receiving the Holy Spirit was the beginning of the divinization of humankind. About the same time Clement of Alexandria observed, "We who are baptized wipe away the sins which like a fog clouded the divine Spirit and blocked God's way. Our spiritual vision is now free, unrestrained and shining. It is with this inner eye that we see the Godhead when the Holy Spirit pours into us from heaven" (*The Tutor* I, 6, 28). In the third century Origen described baptism as a fire that painfully consumed everything that is worldly and purified the soul; but he also recognized that the sacramental ritual did not always have this effect: "For if someone who is still sinning comes to the bath he does not receive the forgiveness of sins" (*Homily on Luke* 21). And Tertullian summarized the meaning of the baptismal rites in this way: "The body is washed so that the soul may be cleansed, the body is anointed so that the soul may be made holy, the body is marked with the sign of the cross so that the soul may be strengthened, the body receives the laying on of hands so that the soul may be enlightened by the Spirit, the body is fed by the flesh and blood of Christ so that the soul may be nourished by God" (*On the Resurrection of the Body* 8).

During the fourth century the patristic theology of baptism became much more Pauline. Cyril of Jerusalem drew from a number of Pauline letters when he said, "Having been baptized into Christ and having put on Christ you have been conformed to the Son of God, for God predestined us to be adopted sons and made us to share the likeness of Christ's glorious body" (*Mystagogical Catechesis* III). But Cyril was also a philosopher who understood sacramental participation in a neoplatonic fashion: just as the objects we see imperfectly participate in their ideal forms, so also in going through baptism Christians participate in the perfect redemptive act of Christ. John Chrysostom and Theodore of Mopsuestia also spoke of baptism as a participation in the death and resurrection of Christ; and John further developed the idea in an analogy to a grimy statue that is melted down in the furnace of baptism, purified by the fire of the Holy Spirit, and recast in the image of Christ. According to Theodore, "When I am baptized and my head is immersed I receive the death of the Lord and I wish to receive his burial; and I thereby profess my belief in the resurrection of our Lord, for I think when I come out of the water that I have already risen, symbolically as it were" (*Homilies* 14, 5). All through this century, however, the fathers continued to be creative in their use of metaphors in speaking about baptism and its effects. And in developing their theological understanding of baptism they continued to use the metaphysical categories of Plato and the neo-Platonists to explain how all this was really happening.

Changes in baptismal practices also happened in the fourth century. After Constantine's edict in 313 it was no longer necessary to be so secretive about Christian worship, and catechumens were allowed to attend the Sunday liturgies up to the scripture readings and the homily. The restrictions on permissible occupations for Christians also began to become more relaxed, and both baptism and the eucharist were celebrated in public buildings rather than in private homes. Protected and favored by the Roman emperors, Christianity was eventually proclaimed the official religion of the empire in 380, and it was sometimes difficult to tell whether those who wished to join the church did so out of conviction or convenience. In the face of growing numbers of conversions, the lengthy catechumenate was retained but the period of immediate preparation and teaching was shortened with the expectation that people would learn more about their religion after their baptism since they were living in a Christian society.

The fathers often took the words of scripture literally and interpreted them metaphysically, and now Christians in increasing numbers began to take the traditional teachings about baptism literally and act accordingly. But the ways they reacted to these doctrines were not always the same. For example, it was commonly taught that baptism brought the forgiveness of sins and that those who were numbered among the faithful were expected to live exemplary lives. Besides, there were no provisions in church practice for a second baptism, and during this period the penitential practices for those who lapsed into immorality were quite severe. As Tertullian put it, "Anyone who realizes the importance of baptism will be more hesitant to receive it than to postpone it" (*On Baptism* 18). For this reason converts (like the emperor Constantine) often chose to remain catechumens until the end of their lives, figuring that a deathbed baptism would be more effective because it would wash away more sins. They also hoped that if they failed to be baptized before death they still might obtain eternal salvation through a desire for baptism, as some of the fathers taught was possible. Thinking along these same lines, some Christian parents delayed the baptism of their children until after adolescence. They believed that by waiting until the passions of youth had subsided their children could be baptized when there was less chance of their giving in to temptation. By the middle of the fourth century this practice was not uncommon, and among those who rose to prominence in the church as bishops, some were not baptized until they were adults (for example, Ambrose, Augustine, Basil, John Chrysostom, and Gregory of Nazianzus).

At the other extreme were those who took the doctrine of the necessity of baptism to literally mean that children who died unbaptized were lost forever with no chance of eternal salvation. This belief, together with the high rate of infant mortality, prompted some parents to baptize their children right after birth without even waiting for the yearly liturgical baptism. In northern Africa during the third century it became a common practice to baptize infants a week after they were born. Bishops who saw the moral danger in the lax practice of prolonging the catechumenate also argued in favor of early baptism, and gradually the idea of baptizing infants became widely accepted even if it was not universally practiced.

But why baptize babies? This was the theological question that the practice raised. Origen of Alexandria noticed the theological difficulty early in the third century when he pointed out that baptism was supposed to be for the remission of sins, and yet children were being baptized even before they were old enough to commit any sins. What sin could they be guilty of that would have to be forgiven? From Cyprian of Carthage came the answer: the sin of Adam. Arguing from the words of scripture (Romans 5:12–21) and the practice of the church, Cyprian contended that baptism washed away the guilt contracted by the human race in Adam's fall, and that this was why the church encouraged parents to baptize their infants. It seemed to be a satisfactory answer, but it left a further question: How was the sin of Adam inherited by his descendants? That question remained unanswered until the time of Augustine, a hundred and fifty years later.

In his controversy with the Donatists over the rebaptism, Augustine had developed the idea that in baptism Christians received a spiritual seal that was the image of Christ (see pages 43–44). The issue had raised a greater problem in the western churches than in the eastern churches because in the west the Holy Spirit had often been understood to pass through the bishop when he laid his hand on the recipients at the end of the baptismal rite, but in the east most of the fathers believed that the Spirit came through the baptismal water. According to their way of understanding it (and according to the prayers in their rites) the bishop called down the Holy Spirit to fill the water of baptism and so the Spirit worked directly through the water: as the candidates were washed externally they were also cleansed internally. But Augustine's solution to the problem was different: the minister of baptism was irrelevant not because the Spirit worked through the water but because the baptism and the seal were Christ's, not the minister's. Augustine had, then, early in his theological career, accepted the notion that everyone received something when they were baptized. And what they received was not just the Holy Spirit but also the seal of the Spirit, a spiritual configuration to Christ. It was the seal that marked them as belonging to Christ, and made them eligible to receive God's grace.

This idea was challenged by Pelagius, a British monk to whom it seemed that Augustine had gone too far, for Augustine later in his career had come to the position that without God's grace—the grace received through baptism and the other sacraments—people could not avoid falling into sin. To Pelagius this seemed like an excuse for moral laxity, even for blaming personal sins on the fact that God had withheld grace from the unbaptized. And it also seemed clear to him that there were pagans who did in fact manage to lead morally upright lives. So Pelagius believed that people were born in a state of "original grace" which was the reason for their natural goodness, and that what was lost by Adam was not this grace but a further grace, a "grace of pardon" which was won by Christ and received by sinful adults when they were baptized. Children of course were born innocent and so they had no need of baptism.

To Augustine, however, this seemed to contradict the idea that baptism was necessary for salvation, for if people could avoid serious sin without being baptized they would never have to be pardoned, and so they could be saved by their own efforts. And Pelagius' teaching also contradicted the church's practice; but how could the church be wrong in baptizing infants if it was guided by the Holy Spirit?

In responding to Pelagius, Augustine drew heavily on Cyprian's notion that all are born with the sin of Adam on their soul, and developed it even further. This "original sin," he taught, was in the soul from birth, and this is why it was essential for all persons to have this initial deformity reshaped, as it were, into the image of Christ by receiving the baptismal seal. "Why would it be necessary to form the little child in a figure of Christ's death through baptism if it were not already poisoned by the serpent's bite?" (*On the Acquisition and Remission of Sins* I, 32, 61).

As for the way this original sin was transmitted, Augustine borrowed one of the philosophical theories of his day. To the ancients it was obvious that the child received the seed of its body from its father—but where did its soul come from? Some philosophers maintained that it was reincarnated from a previous existence, others that it was created at conception or birth, and others that it was received from the father. To Augustine it was this last theory which explained how the sin of Adam was passed on to all future generations: if in human procreation the father passed something of his body and his soul to his offspring, they would inherit his sinful condition as surely as they inherited his human anatomy. And as for the fate of infants who died without baptism, Augustine drew the logical conclusion: they would be damned, although he believed that their punishment would be mild since they had not personally committed the sin for which they were being punished. In this way, then, because of Augustine's influence on later ages, Cyprian's rationale for infant baptism became an essential ingredient in the Catholic theology of baptism.

Augustine wrote against Pelagius at the beginning of the fifth century, and by the end of the same century infant baptism had become universal. Most children were baptized at the yearly Easter celebration but in some places they were baptized soon after birth. But this change in the normal age for baptism brought changes in the traditional practice of baptism, and this in turn led to changes in the common understanding of baptism. Obviously the catechumenate disappeared since babies could not be instructed on how to live a moral life. Likewise the doctrinal instructions prior to baptism faded away although some teaching on the meaning of baptism was included in the baptismal ceremony itself. But the exorcisms and anointings were retained since it was believed that they could be effective without the child's knowledge that they were being performed.

But again here a problem arose. The New Testament and the early fathers agreed that faith, not just baptism, was needed for salvation. When adults were baptized they could be asked what they believed in, as indeed they were each time they were washed in the baptismal water. Clearly now infants could not make such a response of faith. In fact it was even customary for the baptismal sponsors to speak in the child's name when it was asked to renounce the devil and when it was asked whether it believed the doctrines of the creed. And so the solution to the problem of the need for faith in baptism was suggested by the baptismal ritual itself: it was the sponsors who supplied the needed faith, at least until the child was old enough to speak for itself. Thus the role of the sponsors, or godparents as they were sometimes called, was changed: instead of being guarantors of the candidate's faith before baptism, they were now guardians of the child's faith after baptism, and they were considered responsible for making sure that the child received religious instruction and remained a good Christian as he or she grew up. This task was made somewhat easier by the fact that the penitential disciplines imposed on those who sinned after baptism were becoming more relaxed, for indulgences could be granted if severe penances prevented people from seeking reconciliation with the church. But for all practical purposes the role of the sponsors was now the exact reverse of what it had once been.

Infant baptism also brought other changes into the ritual. At the height of the patristic period the ritual washing was usually done by pouring water over the candidate standing in a pool of water, although washing by immersion was also practiced. But with infants complete immersion seemed simpler than partial immersion plus pouring, and so complete immersion returned as the most common form of the ritual and remained so in the eastern churches (located for the most part in the warm eastern Mediterranean basin). In the western churches, however, (perhaps because of colder temperatures in northern European climates) immersion eventually came to be replaced by the pouring of water over the head of the child. In the east the triple immersion was simplified into a single immersion; in the west it was simplified into a triple pouring. In time both east and west adopted the practice of having the minister pronounce a baptismal formula based on Matthew 28:19 as he washed the infant: "I baptize you in the name of the Father and of the Son and of the Holy Spirit." Thus the entire ritual came to symbolize something that was done to an infant by a single individual, instead of something that was done for an adult by a community of believers.

Finally, an important change occasioned by infant baptism—although there were other causes as well—was the separation of the traditional initiation ritual into distinct steps. During the patristic period the entire ceremony that preceded the Easter liturgy was known simply as baptism (although each dipping or pouring was also called a baptism). It included all the exorcisms and prayers and anointings besides the washing in water and the final anointing or imposition of hands by the bishop, and it was followed immediately by the initiates' first participation in the eucharist. In the eastern churches this pattern was kept, and even today when children are initiated into an Orthodox church they are washed, anointed, and given their first communion. But in the western churches the baptismal washing was separated from the final anointing by the bishop, and eventually the first reception of communion dropped out of the initiation ritual altogether. In Roman Catholicism the bishop's anointing eventually became an official sacrament called confirmation, while the ceremonial reception of first communion became an unofficial sacrament. And so what the medieval theologians were thinking about when they developed their theology of baptism was this practice of baptizing infants, divorced from the other rites that had once been part of Christian initiation.

3. Baptism in the Middle Ages

The fathers had been fairly creative in their development of an elaborate and effective initiation ritual. They had also been creative in the ways they explained its meaning: they drew ideas from the New Testament and images from the Old Testament, they made up their own metaphors and analogies to describe the spiritual experience of baptism, and they used Greek philosophy to explain how God was able to cause those spiritual effects. Undoubtedly not everyone experienced the effects of conversion and regeneration with equal intensity, and when babies were baptized they did not feel any change at all. But the fathers often took the words of scripture at face value, and if the Bible said that baptism forgives sins, it had to be so whether people experienced it or not. For them what happened at baptism was an objective fact, and because it was an objective fact it could be subjectively experienced even though it did not have to be. And as entrance into the church became easier, and as infant baptism became commonplace, it was experienced less and less. Thus by the end of the patristic period the age of creative theologizing was over, and most of the writers after the fifth century were content to repeat what the fathers had said was objectively true.

In the late fifth century the city of Rome fell to Germanic tribes that were pushing south into the empire in search of better farmlands and other spoils of war. Some of these invaders were Christians converted by early missionaries, but many of them were not and so monks were sent out from the monasteries to convert the new settlers and bring Christianity to the lands from which they came. As in many tribal cultures the chieftain was the spokesman of the whole community: his word was law, and what he did the tribe did. Thus the Christian missionaries often found it convenient to speak directly to the chieftains about the religion of Rome, and the tribal leaders were not always averse to listening. They were impressed by what they saw of the old empire, for even in ruins it was clearly a more advanced civilization than theirs, and in their desire to be more like the Romans they were sometimes willing to adopt what they perceived to be a more civilized religion. They were baptized and so were their people, sometimes hundreds at a time. And the ritual that was used to make them Christians was the rite of infant baptism without any moral catechumenate and without any doctrinal instruction, since it was the only form of baptism that the monks knew. Those who were converted individually by the missionaries fared only slightly better.

Most of those who accepted the new religion did not experience the full effects of the initiation ritual; many of them did not even understand it. But the monks labored with true missionary zeal, for to them it meant that with each baptism another soul was washed clean of original sin, marked with the character of Christ and filled with the Holy Spirit. The scriptures said it and the fathers said it, so it had to be true. The missionaries gave years of their lives and sometimes died so that others might be saved, but the meaning of salvation had shifted. Instead of salvation from a sinful life, baptism now meant salvation from original sin and the punishment due for committing other sins. Instead of marking the beginning of a new moral life, baptism promised eternal life after death. And so in the name of salvation and eternal life the monks performed the initiation ritual, baptizing, anointing, and administering the eucharist—all in Latin, a language that few of their converts spoke or comprehended.

It took awhile for the early rite of initiation to break apart into separate sacramental rituals. In the provinces of Italy baptisms were presided over by the resident bishop once or twice a year: priests usually presided over most of the baptismal ceremony but the bishop continued to perform the ritual of anointing and confirming the newly baptized into the church. Those who lived in and around the cities brought their children to the bishop's cathedral and returned home afterward; those who lived in outlying regions carried out the initiation in their local churches and then waited for a visit from the bishop to officially confirm the baptisms that had taken place the previous Easter or Pentecost. It was the beginning of the separation of the washing from the anointing, of "baptism" from "confirmation."

Toward the end of the eighth century Charlemagne, king of the Franks, consolidated an empire that covered much of present day France and Germany, and he sent to Rome for a copy of its sacramental books in an effort to bring some uniformity to the religious practices in his realm. In Rome the initiation rites that had once been performed over a period of weeks had become compressed into a short ceremony: children received three exorcisms on the Sundays before Easter, and then on Holy Saturday the baptismal water and font were blessed, the children were dipped into it three times while a confession of faith in the Trinity was said, a priest anointed their head with oil, the bishop laid his hand on them and made the sign of the cross on their forehead with another oil, and they were given communion at the liturgy of the Easter Vigil. Charlemagne issued an edict imposing this initiation ritual on all of his subjects, but since the Roman sacramentary restricted the second anointing to the bishop, they also had to adopt the Roman custom of waiting for the bishop to have their baptisms confirmed. In the churches of Spain, however, the second anointing continued to be done by the baptizing priest, although many of them conformed to the Roman custom by the thirteenth century. After that, the only other place in the west where both anointings were done by a priest was Milan, which defended its right to preserve its own liturgical customs on the grounds that they dated back to the fourth-century bishop Ambrose and hence were just as ancient as Rome's.

In the rest of Europe the imposition of the Roman custom resulted in a greater and greater separation of baptism from confirmation. The traditional teaching had been that baptism was necessary for salvation, but now "baptism" meant just that part of the rite that could be done by a priest, and so many people felt little urgency about having their children anointed by the bishop. Parents in cathedral cities (where a bishop was the pastor) had their infants confirmed as a matter of course during the annual liturgical baptism, but travel was difficult and those in the rural areas often waited several years for the bishop's visit, if he came at all.

As long as baptism was administered once a year, the sacramental books also provided a shortened form of baptism for infants who were in danger of death, but beginning in the eleventh century some bishops and councils noted that infants were always in danger of dying unexpectedly and started encouraging parents not to wait for the annual baptism at Easter. During the next century baptism soon after birth was encouraged even more, and by the thirteenth century a number of dioceses allowed infants to be baptized at any time of the year. Finally in the fourteenth century the new custom took the force of law, and episcopal and conciliar decrees in most parts of Europe ordered that infants be baptized anywhere from a day to a week after birth since it was the only means by which they could be protected from the peril of dying with original sin on their soul. And when this happened the baptismal ceremony disappeared from the Easter Vigil entirely, although the font and the water were still blessed for use during the rest of the year. The preparatory rites and ceremonies, the last vestiges of the ancient catechumenate, were reduced to a short service at the church door, and the baptism itself was now witnessed by only the godparents and relatives instead of the entire congregation. A final liturgical consequence of considering baptism as an emergency procedure was the replacement of immersion by pouring as was done in emergency baptisms, and the replacement of the triple profession of faith by the words of Christ in Matthew 28:19, which thereafter became the standard Catholic baptismal formula.

During the patristic period the newly baptized had celebrated their first eucharist as the completion of their initiation into the Christian community, and when infant baptism became the norm this practice continued. Even when baptism was separated from the Easter liturgy, babies were still given communion, but by the end of the Middle Ages the practice died out. The main reason was the increasingly realistic interpretation given to the eucharistic bread and wine. In 831 a monk named Paschase Radbert published a theological work in which he taught that the bread and wine were changed into the actual flesh and blood of Christ at the moment of consecration, and this physicalistic interpretation of the eucharist gained such wide acceptance by the eleventh century that Berengar of Tours was condemned for denying it. Some bishops began to express doubts about the propriety of infants receiving communion if they could not swallow it, and as a compromise babies were given only the consecrated wine. Some priests, fearing that a drop of the precious blood might be spilled and desecrated, even began offering them unconsecrated wine instead, but twelfth-century theologians like William of Champeaux strenuously objected to the substitute, arguing from John 6:53–56 that receiving both the flesh and blood of Christ was necessary for eternal life. By the thirteenth century, however, it had become common for lay people attending mass to receive only the consecrated host of bread because of the danger that the wine might be spilled, and indeed the fearful reverence for the host itself was becoming so great that many people were abstaining from communion altogether. As a consequence communion was given less frequently to newly baptized infants, but the practice did not die out completely until the Council of Trent in 1562 declared that little children were not obliged to receive the eucharist.

Thus during the Middle Ages Christian initiation was reduced to a water ritual and other attendant ceremonies of exorcism and anointing, administered without episcopal confirmation and without the eucharist, to infants soon after they were born. And after the eleventh century, when Christianity was firmly established as the sole religion of Europe, adult baptisms became so infrequent that in the rare cases when Jews or Moslems sought to convert to Christianity special adaptations had to be made in the rite, such as exempting them from the rubric that directed that the baptized be held in the sponsor's arms.

This, then, was the rite which the medieval theologians had in mind when they wrote about baptism and tried to understand it theologically. Its immediate effect was no longer experiential but social, namely membership in the church, although the scriptures and the fathers testified that baptism had individual spiritual effects as well. But the fathers had often interpreted the New Testament description of baptism's effects as a metaphysical account, and they had given metaphysical explanations of how baptism produced the effects that they themselves experienced and witnessed. The medieval schoolmen continued in this tradition even though their philosophical terms were now drawn from Aristotle rather than Plato. The more astute among them, like Aquinas, did their best to relate metaphysics to experience, but for many of them the metaphysical explanation of the sacraments was unrelated to religious experience: for them sacramental theology was more a matter of logic and deduction.

A good example of how logic led to metaphysical conclusions can be seen in the medieval doctrine of limbo. Augustine and some other fathers had contended that infants who died without baptism suffered eternal damnation. Some of the early schoolmen like Anselm of Canterbury agreed that this was logically consistent with the belief that baptism was necessary for salvation, but to them it seemed inconsistent with the belief that God was all-merciful: how could a loving God torment souls for a sin they did not commit? The logical answer was that God did not, and yet it was also logical that these souls did not get into heaven. So Anselm proposed a solution that was consistent with both points: the souls of unbaptized infants did not get into heaven, but they were not tortured either; their only punishment was that they would never see God, but other than that they were in a state of natural happiness. The most logical place for these almost-sinless souls to go was therefore just outside heaven, on its border (*in limbo*, in Latin). Like the idea of original sin it was a workable solution to a sticky problem.

When the first schools and universities in medieval Europe began to be formed, the clerics and scholars who studied the sacraments treated them rather unsystematically, in short works on single topics. Then early in the twelfth century Peter Abelard began to arrange philosophical and theological problems more systematically, lining up scriptural and patristic quotations on both sides of an issue, and out of this method grew the books like Lombard's *Sentences*, in which scholastic thinkers tried to deal with theological problems in a more logical and coherent fashion. In the area of the sacraments, for example, they invariably treated questions such as: what are sacraments, how many are there, what are their effects, who are the proper ministers and recipients, and so forth. Not all of the scholastics gave the same answers to these questions, but the important thing was that they had hit upon a method for dealing with them, and in the course of the twelfth and early thirteenth centuries some answers and theories were proposed that seemed to work better than others. As these were adopted by more thinkers, they formed a general philosophical framework within which the scholastic theologians dealt with the sacraments and other matters.

For instance, it became customary to define the sacraments in terms of their "matter" and "form," the materials or gestures used in the rite, and the words used or the significance that they had. Thus in the twelfth century Peter Lombard defined baptism as "a dipping or external washing of the body together with a prescribed formula of words" (*Sentences* IV, 3), and in the thirteenth century Hugh of St. Victor defined it as "water made holy by the word of God for washing away sins" (*On the Sacraments* II, 6, 2). The latter definition also shows how the symbolic action of baptism, considered in the Middle Ages to be just the washing with water, affected theological thinking about it: baptism was something that cleansed the soul from sin.

But how did the external washing produce this internal effect? The way to answer that question came with the notion of the "sacramental reality" (*sacramentum et res*), first developed to explain the reality of Christ in the eucharist and then applied to baptism and other sacraments by William of Auxerre and William of Auvergne, both teachers at the University of

Paris (see pages 57–58). Thus by the time Thomas Aquinas arrived there as a student in the middle of the thirteenth century, the list of theological questions to be dealt with on baptism had been drawn up and the key metaphysical concepts for dealing with them had been devised. Although his work was outstanding in many respects, Aquinas' treatment of those questions and his use of those concepts was typical of his day. Like most people in the Middle Ages, Aquinas was baptized in infancy, and so the experience he drew upon in developing his theology was limited to his social experience, that of living in a Christian society, and his adult religious experience. And of course like the other thinkers of the period, he expressed his insights into experience and into the scriptures and the fathers in the terms of Aristotelian metaphysics.

Aquinas understood sacraments as symbolic actions given to the church by Christ through which God communicated to people all that they needed to become holy and attain salvation, both individually and collectively. Thus sacraments were instrumental causes of grace through which God acted for the benefit of persons or the church as a whole. Baptism, confirmation, eucharist, penance, and extreme unction were the means by which individuals entered the church, were spiritually strengthened, experienced union with the church, received forgiveness of sins committed later in life, and prepared to meet God face to face. Ordination and matrimony were the means by which God ensured that the other sacraments would continue to be administered and that there would be people in the future to receive them. In its basic outline Aquinas' sacramental theology was a simple scheme, and it corresponded closely to the way the seven ecclesiastical sacraments functioned (or were supposed to function ideally) in medieval Christian society.

Baptism was thus the first step in the Christian walk of life. It was a ritual action normally performed on infants, but Aquinas knew that this initiation into Christianity could also be given to adults from his reading of the New Testament. The essential "matter" of the sacrament was the water poured or bathed in, and its essential "form" was expressed in the words, "I baptize you in the name of the Father and of the Son and of the Holy Spirit." If either of these were lacking, part of the sacramental sign was missing and so it was not a valid ritual. Ordinarily baptisms also included exorcisms, anointing, and other symbolic actions, but these were not essential parts of the baptismal rite since they could be omitted if a person were in danger of dying without the sacrament. A priest was the usual minister of baptism, but since baptism was Christ's and not the minister's, even laymen and women could baptize in emergency situations because of the necessity of the sacrament.

Baptism was, of course, necessary for salvation because it had been commanded by Christ (Matthew 28:19–20; John 3:5) and because without it one could not receive the other sacraments. Aquinas accepted the idea that children should be baptized as soon as possible to wash away original sin, but he believed that adults should be instructed first and wait until Easter to be baptized; if they died before their baptism they would be saved through their desire for it because by accepting the message of Christ they had already experienced a baptism of the spirit or interior repentance, and such a conversion could only be caused by God. Like the fathers of the church, Aquinas regarded martyrdom as a sort of baptism, and in fact he regarded it as the "most excellent" form of baptism since a martyr truly imitated Christ in his death and resurrection.

Aquinas borrowed much of Augustine's sacramental theology (as did most scholastics) including the idea of original sin and the concept of the sacramental character, but he also noticed an ambiguity in Augustine's use of the word "sacrament." It could refer to the sacramental rite or it could refer to the sacramental character, the primary spiritual effect of the rite. Earlier scholastics had sorted out the ambiguity by speaking about the rite as *sacramentum tantum*, the character as *sacramentum et res*, and the grace received as *res tantum*. As Aquinas saw it, one experienced the graces of baptism as a result of having the character, and one received the character as a result of having undergone the rite. Or as he would have expressed it, the rite was the cause of the character and the character was the cause of the graces (although God was the ultimate cause of all the effects).

Thus baptism for Aquinas, as for Augustine, had two effects. The baptismal rite produced in the soul of the recipient a sacramental reality that was a spiritual seal or image of Christ commonly referred to as the sacramental character. It was an inward configuration to Christ that eliminated the distortion of original sin (and any other sins, when an adult was baptized). But the metaphors of "image," "character," and "configuration" had to be understood spiritually, not materially, that is, they had to be understood in terms of a change they brought to the human soul or spirit. And the human spirit was for Aquinas, as it had been for Aristotle, basically the source of power in a human being: the power to live, the power to think, the power to feel, and so on, which were powers or abilities that anyone had. What baptism gave human beings, therefore, was a new set of spiritual powers, and the baptismal character was the patterned set of powers that Christians had from God to rise above their natural abilities, and that Christ had earned for the human race by incarnating them in a human life.

What were these powers? One was the power to resist temptation and avoid sin, which Adam had lost and which Christ had regained by his sinless life. The lives of the saints, too, showed that they had it. Another was the power to offer perfect worship to the one true God by living the way God desired and by offering themselves to God in the liturgy. The Israelites had had something like this power, Aquinas reasoned, since they lived according to the Law of Moses and offered sacrifices in the temple, but Christ was the first and only person to live completely in accordance with the Father's will, and only Christ offered the perfect sacrifice when he suffered and died on the cross—an action in which he was both priest and victim. Christians likewise had this power to live in accordance with Christ's law of perfect love, and they had the power to be united with Christ's perfect sacrifice in the eucharistic liturgy.

But these were not the only powers. The most fundamental were the powers (the scholastics called them virtues) of faith, hope, and love: the power to believe in God's revelation, to hope for what God had promised, and to love God above all things. In addition there were the special powers (traditionally called gifts of the Holy Spirit) of wisdom, understanding, counsel, fortitude, knowledge, piety, and fear of the Lord. There were others as well, and Aquinas considered it evident that people had these special powers whenever they did things that human beings did not ordinarily do, whenever they did things that transcended their natural powers and abilities. And how did Aquinas know that Christians had these powers? To him the answer was obvious: Christians used them, and if they used them they must have them. And it was equally clear to Aquinas why Christians were never baptized twice: once they received the character, they had these powers, and so being baptized again would not give them anything new or different.

And what about faith? What role did faith play in this process, and in the act of being baptized? What Aquinas usually meant by "faith" was the infused virtue or power to believe with conviction what God had revealed. Since this gift of faith was received in baptism, the person baptized did not have it beforehand. This could certainly be so in the case of infants, but what about adults who asked to be baptized? Aquinas reasoned that they had natural faith or trust in God, the natural virtue on which the supernatural virtue was built, but extraordinary faith could not be expected of them until after they were baptized. But by "faith" Aquinas also sometimes meant Christian beliefs, and again here infants could not be expected to have them at the time of their baptism. On the other hand, he argued, adults who were baptized ought to have the right beliefs before they were baptized. This is why they were to be instructed first, and this is why the scriptures and the fathers spoke of baptism's being preceded by a profession of faith or recitation of the creed when adults were baptized. When children were baptized this need for the right beliefs and the other truths of Christianity was supplied by the godparents and ultimately by the church into which the child was baptized. Thus baptism was in two ways a sacrament of faith: it gave the divine gift of faith in the baptismal character, and it expressed the beliefs that the godparents and the church had about salvation coming from Christ through baptism.

Baptism was for Aquinas a spiritual regeneration and incorporation into Christ, but it was a hidden regeneration occurring in the soul of the baptized infant that manifested itself only later in life, and it was a metaphysical incorporation into Christ that occurred through the reception of spiritual powers known collectively as the baptismal character. It was therefore also a participation in Christ's death and resurrection, as Paul had said, but it was fundamentally a metaphysical participation brought about by God's action on the soul. It enabled a Christian to continue participating in Christ's redemption by leading a redeemed life with the help of grace received through the other sacraments.

Aquinas' sacramental theology was in many ways a very penetrating and embracing synthesis. In penetrating to the essence of what the Christian way of life was all about, it brought together in a single perspective the current practices of the church, the teachings of the Bible and the fathers, and the nuanced philosophy of Aristotle. But it was also an imperfect synthesis, and thus many of those who came after Aquinas preferred to construct their own.

Later in the thirteenth century, for example, John Duns Scotus developed a different synthesis in which he explained sacraments not as instrumental causes of grace but as symbolic actions done by the church which provided occasions for God to give grace directly to the recipient. The connection between the action and the grace was God's promise that when these actions were performed the grace would be given. He did not accept Aquinas' interpretation of the sacramental character as a set of supernatural powers that were activated later in life, but instead he returned to a more literal acceptance of the patristic notion that the character was something impressed by God on the soul which stamped the recipient with the sign of Christ and marked him or her as a member of the church. Its existence could not be philosophically proven from scripture, he argued, but so many of the fathers had taught it that it had to be accepted on the authority of Catholic tradition.

William of Ockham in the fourteenth century accepted Scotus' notion that sacraments were best understood as signs of the dispensation of grace, but he went even further in arguing that none of the effects of baptism, including the forgiveness of sins, could be proven philosophically. Baptism was just a name for what happened when the ritual of washing was performed, and what really happened could be known only on the authority of the church.

Aquinas had managed in the cultural renaissance of the thirteenth century to construct an intellectually viable but fragile theology of the sacraments, but as medieval culture declined, the tendency to understand baptism metaphysically went down and the tendency to regard it magically went up. Theologically this was inadmissible, but in the popular mind it was so, and even theologians were people. The baptism of infants came to be considered more and more as a mystical occurrence in the soul that had to be believed in because the scriptures and the fathers and the church taught it. Its spiritual effects were utterly supernatural, although it also continued to have social effects such as making one a member of the church and legal effects such as enabling one to receive the other sacraments. But it no longer had any experiential effects, and through most of the modern period Christians both Protestant and Catholic accepted this as a given fact.

4. Baptism in Modern Times

The Protestants did not reject baptism, but they did reject the Catholic theology of baptism as they knew it. In its place the early reformers came up with a variety of positions on baptism that corresponded to the different ways that they understood the meaning of Christianity and the nature of the church. And as pointed out earlier (see page 89), they all used the Bible to prove their positions, just as the Catholics would later at the Council of Trent.

Martin Luther had been baptized as a baby, but despite his best efforts to lead a holy life he considered himself to be still sinful in the eyes of God. The Catholic sacraments of baptism and penance did not seem to have the effects that they were supposed to have: they were supposed to remove sins but somehow they did not. It was not until his interior conversion in 1513 that Luther finally felt truly forgiven by God, and in that experience were sown the seeds of his sacramental theology.

Luther's first argument with scholastic theology had focused on indulgences and the sacrament of penance, but after his excommunication from the Roman Catholic Church he engaged himself in a complete rethinking of Christian theology, including the theology of the sacraments. For Luther the central concepts that illuminated the meaning of the Christian life were grace and faith: because of the death of Christ, God had graciously forgiven the sinfulness of the human race, and by confident faith in God people were now able to acknowledge that forgiveness, experience God's saving grace, and trust in God's mercy after death. The sacraments were thus signs of God's grace but they were not effective—at least not in any life-changing way—until a person consciously and deliberately accepted that grace in faith. In other words, faith was the key that unlocked the grace that was given in the sacraments. But by "faith" and "grace" Luther meant something quite different from what the later scholastics had meant by those terms. Faith for Luther was not an intellectual conviction or a set of beliefs but a heart-felt confidence in God. And grace was not a metaphysical influx into the soul but the transcendent reality of divine love that could even be felt as the presence and the power and the mercy of God.

Could one have God's grace without knowing it? Yes, certainly, argued Luther, and his life demonstrated it. He had received grace as a child, but it was not until he meditated on Paul's letter to the Romans that his faith was awakened and he became aware of it. Receiving baptism in infancy was therefore no different from receiving communion without knowing that it was the body and blood of Christ: one received what the sign signified even if one did not have the faith needed to recognize it.

Luther relied on a passage from Augustine to explain how baptism worked: it was not just the washing but also the water joined to the word of God that made it effective. Augustine had written, "Take away the word and the water is nothing but water. But when the word is joined to the element the result is a sacrament....Where does the water get its lofty power to bathe the body and cleanse the soul if it is not through the action of the word? And not because it is spoken, but because it is believed?" (*On the Gospel of John* 80, 3). What made baptism a sacrament of grace therefore was God's word, understood not just as the baptismal formula but also as Christ's promise that those who were baptized would be saved. God had given his word that water baptism would bring salvation, and so it had to be true. But God's word also had to be believed if baptism was to be effective in a person's life.

The scholastics had taught that baptism washed all the sins out of a person's soul, but Luther knew that this was neither true to experience nor true to scripture. People seemed to be no less sinful just because they had been baptized, and Paul's letters to the Corinthians proved that this was so even in the early church. Besides, the Bible spoke not of the removal of sins but of the forgiveness of sins. What baptism brought Christians, therefore, was not a sinless soul but God's forgiveness. Through baptism they were assured that God forgave them even though they could not avoid sinning. In their own eyes they were sinners, but baptism assured them that in God's eyes they were all right. And when they accepted God's forgiving grace in faith, they knew in their heart that they were justified in the sight of God.

The Anabaptists (from the Greek word meaning to rebaptize) took Luther's doctrine of justification and pushed it even further. Relying on the facts that the New Testament spoke only of the baptism of adults and that in each case a profession of faith was required before baptism, they considered infant baptism to be a Roman Catholic invention and not a real baptism at all. According to them the church was meant to be a church not of sinners but of the saved, into which people came not by birth but by a decision of faith. And as they read the biblical evidence, this decision came before baptism, not after it. Baptism by pouring was also unscriptural, and so they recognized only baptism by complete immersion as valid.

Luther accepted the notion that baptism should be by immersion, but he refused to go along with the idea that infant baptism was worthless. In his *Large Catechism* he wrote, "Baptism is valid even without faith, for my faith does not constitute baptism but receives it" (IV, 53). But in some of his other writings he recognized the dilemma: if faith were really necessary for salvation, then baptized children who died before they were old enough to profess their faith were lost. Ultimately Luther came to the conclusion that faith, like grace, was a gift of God received in baptism even though it remained dormant until later life.

John Calvin avoided this difficulty altogether by envisioning how baptism worked in an entirely different way. He took Paul's words on pre-destination (Romans 8:28–34) to mean that God saved those whom he had elected, and concluded that this salvation was the direct work of the Holy Spirit giving them faith and making them upright. Thus, if a child were numbered among the elect, he or she was already saved whether baptized or not, and if the child were not among the elect, baptism could do nothing to save it.

But who were the elect? Ultimately no one knew except God, for those who appeared to be just and upright might in fact be sinners in secret. Nevertheless, the Bible made it clear that no one could profess faith in Jesus as Lord except by the power of the Holy Spirit (1 Corinthians 12:3), and so a public profession of faith was taken as a good indication of being among the elect. Another good indication was leading a morally good life and having a sincere fear of God's righteous judgment, and so Calvin's theology left no room for the kind of moral laxity he had seen in the Roman church. Immorality was a sign of damnation, whether one was baptized or not.

Baptism was therefore not a cause of salvation but a sign of salvation. For adults who were baptized, and for parents who had their children baptized as well, it was a sign of their faith that God's mercy and grace were already given to them, and it was a way of bearing witness to that grace. Baptism was also a way that children were admitted into the church so that their faith might be strengthened, and it was a sign that they were different from the children of non-believers.

Thus baptism did have an effect on people, but its effect was that of a sign. It was a sign that those who received it were among the elect, even if it was not an infallible sign. It was a sign that they desired to serve God and be saved by God's grace. As a sign it was therefore a cause of faith, for it served as a constant reminder both to those who witnessed the action and to those who recalled the fact of their own baptism that they had been washed clean of all guilt in the eyes of God. In Calvin's words, baptism "is given to us by the Lord as a symbol and token of our purification....It is like a properly witnessed legal document in which he assures us that all our sins are canceled and blotted out, so that they will never appear in his sight or come into his memory or be charged against us" (*Institutes of the Christian Religion* IV, 15, 1).

Ulrich Zwingli took Calvin's theology of baptism a step further still. He agreed that baptism was not an infallible sign of redemption because he had seen too many people living unredeemed lives. But he did not agree that it had any effect on people after they were baptized. It was a sign of the faith that people brought to the sacramental ceremony, but it was not a cause of any faith afterward. For Zwingli, faith like grace was completely at God's disposal, and the Holy Spirit could act directly on people's minds and hearts; God did not need to work through any ritual instruments. Still, Zwingli saw baptism and even infant baptism as perfectly allowable because it symbolized how God washed away the guilt of sin and because it was an expression of the belief that Christians should follow Christ in his death and resurrection.

The Catholic reaction to these Protestant theories was a while in coming, but when it came it was definitive. The bishops assembled at Trent in 1545 first took up the question of the Bible since the reformers had so often invoked its authority against the authority of the hierarchy. Then before dealing with the sacraments and baptism directly, they set forth the official Catholic position on original sin and justification (see pages 98–99). Since much of the Catholic theology of baptism was already stated in these decrees, the bishops did not issue a separate statement on baptism but simply enumerated and condemned what they viewed as the heretical positions of Luther, Calvin, and others.

Among the ideas condemned as heretical were the following: that the Roman church does not teach the true doctrine of baptism, that baptism is not necessary for salvation, that baptism administered by heretics is not a true baptism, that baptized persons cannot lose God's grace through sin but only through lack of faith, that those who are baptized may obey their own conscience rather than the laws of the church, that the grace of baptism covers sins committed after baptism and need only be remembered in order for a person to receive God's forgiveness, that anyone baptized in the Catholic Church should be rebaptized, that infants should not be baptized, and that children should not be compelled to lead a Christian life.

Some of the ideas condemned in this terse series of canons certainly corresponded to statements of various reformers, but these doctrinal rules and the decrees that preceded them missed the heart of the Protestant attack on the sacraments, which was that the medieval ritual had ceased to be effective for most people. Infant baptism made little difference in the way they lived, and it had little to do with anything that the reformers were willing to call genuine salvation from sin. It had become in practice, if not in theory, sacramental magic. It was supposed to wash away an invisible inherited sin, and judging from the way Christians sometimes behaved it looked as though it did not even do that. And yet baptism, the reformers all agreed, had been instituted by Christ. But why did he do it? Their various alterations and interpretations of the rite were all attempts to answer that question in a way that made sense to them and to a modern age.

To the bishops assembled at Trent this was a completely alien way of doing theology, and they had no inkling of the real reasoning behind the reformers' conclusions. What they could see, though, was that many of the reformers' teachings plainly contradicted the teachings of past councils and theologians, and so they had to be condemned as heretical. They ran against the whole medieval Catholic understanding of what it meant to be baptized and become a member of the church, of what it meant to be cleansed from original sin and given the character of Christ, of what it meant to be justified and put on the path of holiness. Thus these new ideas had to be wrong, and they had to be fought.

But the reform-minded bishops were also honest enough to admit that the reformers had a point. Even if Catholic theology could not be changed, the church itself was in need of reform. Too many Catholics including the clergy did live as though baptism made little difference to them, and so the council set out to change what it could. Most of the council's practical reforms were unrelated to the sacrament of baptism, however. For the most part the bishops ordered reforms for the clergy, relying on better leadership to make for a better church. They held to the medieval idea that Christian instruction should take place after and not before baptism, and they counted on the clergy to give that instruction to the faithful. And to ensure that Catholics in the future would receive at least a basic introduction to the doctrines of Catholicism, the council issued its own catechism in which it outlined the beliefs that all Catholics were obliged to hold.

This method of Christian instruction worked at least as well as those of the Protestants in Europe and later in colonized North America, but when the Roman church sent missionaries to other continents its effectiveness was at least open to question. Like the monks who left their monasteries to Christianize northern Europe after the fall of the Roman Empire, modern Catholic missionaries risked their lives to bring the faith to the newly discovered pagans. But by "bringing the faith" they meant first of all bringing baptism, for in an age when baptism was believed to bring salvation *ex opere operato* the primary objective was to save as many souls as possible from the fires of hell. Thousands of natives were baptized after little or no instruction in Central and South America, the main territories held by Catholic Spain and Portugal, as were thousands more in Asia and later Africa. Francis Xavier, a Jesuit missionary in India, reported that he had baptized ten thousand in December of 1543 alone, and his efforts were emulated by others. It was a far cry from the catechumenate of the early church, but no one remembered the catechumenate. The main thing was that people were hearing the message of Christ and were being saved through baptism.

5. Baptism in Contemporary Catholicism

The modern church had adopted the medieval form of baptism as normative, and it had accepted the medieval theology of baptism as definitive. There were no major developments in Catholic baptismal theology after the time of the counter-reformation and only one minor one. The fathers and the scholastics had spoken of "baptism of desire," by which they meant the desire to be baptized, but after the discovery that the world was larger than Christian Europe some Catholic theologians began to interpret this in a broader sense. It seemed unfair that millions of people should be condemned to eternal punishment just because they had never heard the message of Christ. Especially when it was learned that non-Christians were not always savage idol-worshipers and that some of their religions prescribed moral standards that matched those of Christianity, it seemed impossible to attribute such a terrible retribution to a merciful God.

So slowly "baptism of desire" came to mean a desire to lead a good and upright life, a desire to live like a Christian, so to speak, which was thwarted not by personal fault but by the church's failure to bring the sacrament to lands about which it had never heard. Some theologians postulated that these people would not be denied entrance into heaven because if they had been offered the chance to be baptized they would have accepted it. Some even suggested that God would give them a chance after they died to accept the message of Christ. But it was the first chink in the theological armor that surrounded the medieval practice of baptism.

In the increasing pluralism of the twentieth century, Catholics learned more about other Christians, too, and they were sometimes surprised to learn that babies in Baptist churches were not baptized. Then as the ecumenical movement gained momentum Catholic theologians began to study their Protestant counterparts not with an eye to refuting them but with an ear to hearing what they were saying. They discovered that there were other theologies of baptism that could be defended quite well on scriptural and philosophical grounds, even if they did not always agree with the conclusions.

Discussions among scholars about the theology of baptism in the 1950s and 1960s led theologians on both sides to reexamine the scriptural and historical data more closely. Catholics had to concede that the New Testament speaks explicitly only about the baptism of adults, for example, but Protestants who favored adult baptism had to admit that solid evidence for infant baptism went back at least to the second century of Christianity.

But the scriptural renewal in Catholic theology did more than provide fuel for the debate over infant baptism. Catholic theologians suddenly realized that the baptismal practices of the earliest Christian communities were very different from those of the modern Catholic Church, that there were close connections between early Christian baptism and the Jewish baptismal practices of the time, and that Christ's command to baptize all nations may not have been actually spoken by Jesus even though the gospel writers believed it was. They also discovered that the New Testament theology of baptism was different from the scholastic theology of baptism, and that Paul's understanding of baptism was far richer and more complex than the usual Catholic understanding of it.

Historical studies turned up equally surprising results. Catholic scholars discovered that during the patristic period Christian baptism was a richly symbolic personal and communal experience, and that there was no baptismal formula spoken by the minister of baptism. They learned that adult Christians waited years before being admitted to baptism, and that the catechumenate had been a period of strict moral preparation. They had to admit that in those days there was no standard practice in baptizing children, and that infant baptism became the rule only after Augustine's theory of original sin was taken to be a dogmatic fact. They came to realize that in the early Middle Ages Catholic infants had been baptized, confirmed, and given the eucharist in an initiation ritual which was celebrated only once or twice a year, and that baptism alone immediately after birth was a comparatively recent development. They saw as they had not seen before that ideas like limbo and purgatory (see page 344) were not metaphysical realities but theological explanations, and that even Aquinas' theology of baptism sometimes elevated medieval practice to the level of eternal truth.

By the mid-1960s most of the research had been done, but the only ones who knew about it were scholars. Some of them became advisers to the bishops at the Second Vatican Council, and they tried to persuade them to deemphasize the scholastic theory of baptism and to speak of baptism in scriptural terms instead. The bishops for the most part took this advice and used primarily Pauline language, writing that through baptism "men and women are inserted into the paschal mystery of Christ; they die with him, are buried with him, and rise with him" (Liturgy 6), they put on a new humanity and become a new creation, reborn by water and the Spirit, children of God, dead to sin and alive in Christ. But the bishops also wrote that in the sacrament it is Christ who baptizes, which is an Augustinian idea, and that Catholics by their baptismal character are consecrated into a holy priesthood to worship God in the liturgy, which is an idea that Aquinas developed. They reaffirmed the Tridentine teaching that baptisms outside the Roman church are valid, but they went beyond the Council of Trent in asserting that "Baptism therefore establishes a sacramental bond of unity among all who through it are reborn" (*Ecumenism* 22). Advised by patristic scholars and historians of the liturgy about baptismal practices in the early church, the bishops ordered the rite of infant baptism to be revised and a new rite of adult baptism to be composed. They decided that baptismal and penitential themes should be more prominent in the Lenten liturgies and that the liturgy of the Easter Vigil should once again be used for actual baptisms. They also revived the idea that a catechumenate of moral and doctrinal instruction should precede the baptism of adults, but they accepted the fact that most Catholics are baptized before they receive religious education.

Thus the council returned to a more scriptural and patristic approach to baptism, but it also did something unprecedented, for in one of its statements it took a major step toward reversing the doctrine of the necessity of baptism. In encouraging the work of missionaries in non-Christian countries the bishops restated the traditional teaching: since God wants all people to be saved and to know the truth of Christ, everyone "ought to be converted to Christ, who is made known through the preaching of the church, and they ought by baptism to become incorporated into him and into the church which is his body" (*Missionary Activity* 7). But in writing about non-Christians themselves the bishops said something very different: "Those who, through no fault of their own, do not know the Gospel of Christ or his church, but who nevertheless seek God with a sincere heart and, moved by grace, try in their actions to do his will as they know it through the dictates of their conscience—these too may attain eternal salvation. Nor does divine Providence deny the assistance necessary for salvation to those who, without any fault of theirs, have not yet arrived at an explicit knowledge of God, and who, not without grace, strive to lead a good life" (*Church* 16). By expanding on the modern conception of "baptism of desire," therefore, the world's Catholic bishops in the 1960s seemed to have accepted the notion that baptism is necessary for joining the church but it is not necessary for salvation.

Some years later, however, the Vatican under Pope John Paul II issued statements more reminiscent of the theology that was dominant before the era of ecumenism. In an official declaration issued in 2000 and titled *Dominus Iesus* (from its opening words, "The Lord Jesus"), the Congregation for the Doctrine of the Faith spoke out against relativism and indifferent-ism—the notions that religion is relative, and that it does not matter which religion one practices—and insisted on the objective truth that the followers of other religions "are in a gravely deficient situation in comparison with those who, in the Church, have the fullness of the means of salvation" (22). Although the document did not deny the possibility of salvation to non-Christians, its tone suggested that Catholic faith and baptism were more important than morality and sanctity in God's eyes. The declaration was to some extent a conservative response to liberal tendencies that had arisen after Vatican II.

The revised Rite of Baptism for Children, for example, incorporated many of the ideas that had been percolating through Catholic theology and had risen to the surface at the council. The introduction to the text as well as the prayers and symbolism of the rite puts less emphasis on washing away original sin and much more on incorporation into the body of Christ, being born to new life, and living by the light of faith. Catholic baptisms in the past usually took place a few days after birth in a private ceremony with just the godparents and perhaps the immediate family present, but to highlight the ecclesial nature of the sacrament they are often now performed within the context of a mass attended by many members of the church community. The new rite also gives a much greater role and responsibility to the parents themselves. Even before the actual baptism the parents need to arrange for it by participating in a catechetical program of theological instruction, spiritual reflection, and parental preparation. During the cer-emony itself they speak on their own behalf in formally requesting their child's reception into the church, in renouncing sin and professing their faith, and in holding the child as the water of baptism is poured on its head. Although the baptism should normally take place within a few weeks after the child's birth, if the parents cannot be present during that time the baptism may be delayed. And if neither parent is willing to ensure that the child will be brought up in the Catholic faith, a Vatican instruction issued in 1980 even insisted that the baptism should be postponed indefinitely.

However, an even greater innovation in the sacrament was to come in the Rite of Christian Initiation of Adults (RCIA), first issued from the Vatican in 1972 and translated into English in 1974, but not made manda-tory for all parishes in the United States until 1988. The refinement and implementation of the RCIA in the United States and Canada was largely the work of the North American Forum on the Catechumenate, a resource network of liturgists, catechists, and other pastoral ministers organized by

Rev. James Dunning in 1982. Until it ceased operation in 2013, the Forum sent ministry teams throughout the continent to present three-day and five-day workshops training local teams in how to prepare for and fully implement this parish and diocesan program.

Inspired by the lengthy catechumenate of the patristic period, the RCIA is not so much a rite (as its name suggests) but a four-stage process of gradual immersion into the church community, punctuated by liturgical ceremonies within and at the completion of each of the stages. The precatechumenate invites interested persons to inquire and dialogue about what it would mean for them to join the Catholic Church. If they decide to go forward, a liturgical ritual initiates them into a catechumenate of about a year, during which they receive sponsors and begin to participate in the life of the parish. They also meet regularly with the parish ministry team as they mature in their understanding of Christianity. On the first Sunday of Lent, a ceremony usually presided over by the diocesan bishop enters them into what is called a period of purification and enlightenment for deeper prayer and spiritual recollection, and on subsequent Sundays the candidates for baptism are ritually questioned and prayed for by their support community in the parish. The process reaches its high point during the Easter Vigil service, when the candidates are presented to the parish, asked to recite their baptismal promises, baptized and confirmed, and clothed in white robes to signify their new life in Christ, after which they receive the eucharist for the first time during the Easter liturgy. Then follows a period of mystagogy, during which the new Christians learn more about the faith that they have embraced and the church that they have joined. They continue to meet regularly, though perhaps not so often as before, becoming more deeply involved in the life of the community, often through being invited to participate in some service to or on behalf of the church.

Although the RCIA, being an initiation rite of the universal church, was designed primarily for use in places where the majority of people are not Christians, it has also been adapted for use in countries like the United States where most people who would become Roman Catholics have been baptized in another church. Such persons are not rebaptized, but they do go through the same initiation process and are confirmed in the Catholic Church at the Easter Vigil, along with any persons who have just been baptized at the service. The process has also been adapted for use with children, whether baptized or not, who are old enough to benefit from participation in the catechesis and liturgical rites.

Since the purpose of the RCIA is not primarily doctrinal instruction but a process of conversion or, in theological terms, spiritual death and rebirth, the rite recommends that whenever possible, candidates should be baptized by full immersion into water because it better symbolizes dying to the old self and rising to new life. As a matter of fact, many parishes now use portable baptismal pools that are at least deep enough for partial immersion during the Easter Vigil service, and some newer Catholic churches have been built with full baptismal pools in place of the traditional baptismal font. It would appear, then, that from ritual to architecture the new Rite of Christian Initiation of Adults has made its mark on Catholic parish life.

The treatment of baptism in the 1994 *Catechism of the Catholic Church* (numbers 1210–1284) reflects the attitudes of the Second Vatican Council and developments that the council promoted. At the same time, it retains vestiges of the scholastic theology of baptism, especially those elements that have been used to define Catholic doctrine.

First of all, the *Catechism* groups baptism with confirmation and eucharist, calling them "sacraments of initiation" (1212), a terminology that was adopted after Vatican II and that reflects the patristic practice of initiating adult converts through immersion in water, anointing with oil, and participation in eucharistic worship.

The treatment of baptism itself is very scriptural, beginning with what the fathers of the church called prefigurations of baptism in the Old Testament—the Spirit moving over the waters of creation, the deluge that washed away a sinful world, and the crossing of the Jordan River by the Israelites to reach the promised land (1217–1222). The stories of Jesus' baptism by John the Baptist and the command of the risen Christ to baptize and make disciples of all nations precede and follow the account of his sacrificial death, which in Mark 10:38 is referred to as a baptism (1223–1225). Baptism is attested to in Acts of the Apostles and in the Pauline epistles, showing that baptism dates back to the earliest days of the church and was understood to be the beginning of a new life (1226–1228).

In its discussion of the sacramental celebration, the *Catechism* clearly accepts adult baptism as the norm, with infant baptism viewed as derivative (1229–1255). The *Catechism* affirms that anyone can perform a baptism, although the ordinary minister is a member of the clergy (1256).

The *Catechism* implicitly accepts the scholastic theology of baptism when it switches from talking about the "celebration" of baptism to "receiving" the sacrament (1258). In the first instance, what is being referred to is the liturgical ritual or, in scholastic terms, the *sacramentum tantum*; in the second instance, the referent is the *sacramentum et res*, the sacramental reality that according to scholastic theory is received into the soul. Traditional theology is also the basis of the *Catechism's* discussion of the necessity of baptism, understood as a spiritual reality or change in the soul caused by the ritual *ex opere operato* (1257–1261).

Augustine's theology of baptism, which argued that there must be two effects of baptism, one that is permanent and one that is not, lies behind the subsection titled "The Grace of Baptism" (1262–1274). The permanent effect is understood to be an indelible spiritual mark, which Augustine called a character and which other church fathers interpreted as the seal of the Spirit referred to in the New Testament (1272–1274). Patristic and medieval ideas also lie behind the *Catechism's* assertions that baptism forgives original sin and, in the case of someone who is not an infant, personal sins as well (1263–1264). One who is baptized therefore receives the grace of justification and is a child of God and a member of the church (1265–1270). The *Catechism* apparently understands that these effects occur rather automatically, through the performance of the ritual, as was the case in the scholastic understanding of baptism. There is no explicit reference in this section to the experience of moral conversion or to any other experiential elements that are important in many contemporary theologies of baptism.

Thus in Catholicism today there is a certain tension between traditional and more contemporary theologies of baptism. Although it is clear from the *Catechism* and from Catholic canon law that the institutional church is not abandoning its scholastic heritage, many theology books and articles now speak of baptism as incorporating a person into the life of Christ that is continued in the church, and talk about original sin is greatly deemphasized. Religious educators especially have been trying to overcome the magical conception of baptism that still lingers in the minds of Catholics who were taught with the older catechism, and theologians, too, have come to speak of baptism as more a sign than a cause of grace. But if baptism is thought of as a sign rather than as a cause of grace, and if the ritual sign is now so rich in symbolism, the question needs to be asked: What does the sign mean?

The answer seems to be that the ritual of water baptism means many things, and perhaps in an age of cultural and theological pluralism this is acceptable. The rite had some very definite meanings for the writers of the New Testament, and Catholics do not want to abandon these. As baptism developed in the patristic and medieval periods it took on additional meanings, some of which are still meaningful to people. Most Catholics who have their children baptized at least see the rite as a sign of initiation into the church through which they express their faith in Christ and announce their intention to raise their children as Christians, however they understand that. For Catholics who are baptized as adults, the rite can take on additional meanings by being a sign of their personal commitment to Christ and to the way of life that he reveals to them. And for the church leaders who approve and perform the rites, the ritual of baptism expresses much of what they understand about the meaning of Christ and membership in the Christian community.

In the meantime, Catholic theologians continue to suggest meanings that participating in a baptismal ritual should reveal to those who witness it, as well as meanings that the rite can reveal in retrospect to those who were baptized in infancy. In doing this they often return to the main themes of traditional Catholic theology but give them a more contemporary interpretation. The New Testament speaks of baptism in terms of death and resurrection, and Bernard Cooke for example sees in baptism a rejection of self-centered attitudes and an acceptance of values that transform the meaning of human life toward love and service to others. Baptism in the patristic era involved a personal commitment witnessed and approved by the Christian community, and so Cooke suggests that the basic sacramental action of baptism is a profession of faith rather than a pouring of water. In the Middle Ages sacraments were understood as causes as well as signs, and he develops the idea that baptism is a sign and a cause of a person's entrance into the Christian experience of life. This is especially true when infants are baptized, he notes, for their whole experience of life and the world is shaped by the community that accepts and nourishes them. Thus the meaning of baptism in contemporary Catholic theology is still salvation, but the meaning of salvation is becoming more experiential and less metaphysical.

Fundamentally, then, baptism remains a door to the sacred for most Catholics because it is still a ritual through which they enter a religious society that stands for a sacred meaning of life and that opens the way to experiences of the sacred in childhood, adolescence, and adulthood. For parents and others who attend baptismal ceremonies the ritual can in addition disclose dimensions of their religious beliefs that are sometimes obscured, and can deepen their commitment to what they discover through their participation in it. And for those who reflect on the action of baptism and, like Paul of Tarsus, ask what it means, it can be a symbolic representation of the central mystery of Christianity.

For Further Reading

Lorna Brockett, *The Theology of Baptism* (Fides Publishers, 1971) offers a brief and readable history of baptismal theology.

Clare Watkins, *Living Baptism* (Darton, Longman & Todd, 2006) argues for conscious Christian discipleship and for reshaping the church accordingly.

Lawrence Mick, *Living Baptism Today* (Liturgical Press, 2004) offers reflections on the meaning of baptism for individuals or groups.

Paul Turner, *Ages of Initiation* (Liturgical Press, 2000) briefly summarizes changes in baptism and confirmation practices from the first century to the twentieth century.

Linda Gibler, *From the Beginning to Baptism* (Liturgical Press, 2010) explores the natural sacramentality of water, oil and fire, and their roles in Jewish and Christian rituals.

Philippe Larere, *Baptism in Water and Baptism in the Spirit* (Liturgical Press, 1993) reflects on a wide range of topics connected with baptism and the Holy Spirit.

Marianne Micks, *Deep Waters* (Crowley Publications, 1996) is a brief and clear explanation of the sacrament as it is practiced and understood in the Episcopal Church.

For Further Study

Baptism in Scripture and the Early Church

Olusina Fape, *Paul's Concept of Baptism and Its Present Implications for Believers* (Edwin Mellen Press, 1999) argues that the ritual originally signified immersion in a new lifestyle.

Oscar Cullmann, *Baptism in the New Testament* (SCM Press, 1950) gives a technical but clear treatment of various topics by a Protestant scripture scholar.

Lars Hartman, *"Into the Name of Jesus": Baptism in the Early Church* (T&T Clark, 1997) reviews the practice and meaning of baptism from before Jesus to the middle of the second century.

Joachim Jeremias, *Infant Baptism in the First Four Centuries* (Westminster Press, 1962) examines the evidence that children were baptized in early Christianity.

Ben Witherington, *Troubled Waters* (Baylor University Press, 2007) examines New Testament texts and applies them to the argument between believer's baptism and infant baptism.

Everett Ferguson, *Baptism in the Early Church* (William B. Eerdmans, 2009) is an exhaustive treatment of the ritual and its theology during the first five centuries.

Baptism in History

Aidan Kavanagh, *The Shape of Baptism* (Pueblo, 1978) summarizes the history of Christian initiation and discusses the reforms of Vatican II, emphasizing the norm of adult baptism.

Burkhard Neunheuser, *Baptism and Confirmation* (Herder and Herder, 1964) is a thorough study of Christian initiation from apostolic through modern times.

Peter Cramer, *Baptism and Change in the Early Middle Ages* (Cambridge University Press, 1993) details developments in the practice and interpretation of baptism from the patristic writers to the early scholastics.

Michael Dujarier, *A History of the Catechumenate* (Sadlier, 1979) recounts the development and decline of adult baptism during the first six centuries of Christianity.

E. C. Whitaker, ed., *Documents of the Baptismal Liturgy* (Liturgical Press, 2003) contains rites, sermons, and other works on baptism up to the ninth century.

J. D. C. Fischer, *Christian Initiation: Baptism in the Medieval West* (SPCK, 1965) documents the dissolution of Christian initiation into separate rites of baptism and confirmation.

Maxwell Johnson, *The Rites of Christian Initiation* (Liturgical Press, 1999) amplifies developments in liturgy and theology from early Christianity to today.

Edward Yarnold, *The Awe-Inspiring Rites of Initiation* (Liturgical Press, 1994) connects today's RCIA with church practices in the patristic period.

Brian Spinks, *Early and Medieval Rituals and Theologies of Baptism* (Ashgate, 2006) discusses a variety of practices and interpretations from the first to the sixteenth century. *Reformation and Modern Rituals and Theologies of Baptism* (Ashgate, 2006) does the same for the sixteenth to twentieth centuries in Protestant churches.

Raymond Burnish, *The Meaning of Baptism* (SPCK, 1985) examines early and later practices and theologies in an ecumenical spirit.

David Wright, *Infant Baptism in Historical Perspective* (Wipf and Stock, 2007) collects the author's writing on the subject in early Christianity, the reformation, and modern times.

Sacraments of Initiation

Thomas Marsh, *Gift of Community* (Michael Glazier, 1984) presents a scriptural and theological explanation of Christian initiation.

Kenan Osborne, *The Christian Sacraments of Initiation* (Paulist Press, 1987) gives scriptural, historical, and doctrinal sources for baptism, confirmation, and eucharist.

Liam Walsh, *The Sacraments of Initiation* (Geoffrey Chapman, 1988) offers a traditional Catholic understanding of baptism, confirmation, and eucharist.

David Hamilton, *Through the Waters* (T&T Clark, 1989) asks what washing, deliverance, birth, belonging, and celebration refer to in the process of conversion and Christian living.

Gabe Huck, *Infant Baptism in the Parish* (Liturgy Training Publications, 1980) explains the meaning and implementation of the Rite of Baptism for Children.

Mark Searle, *Christening: The Making of Christians* (Liturgical Press, 1980) explains the meaning, purpose, and dynamics of the revised rites of infant baptism and adolescent confirmation.

Henri Bourgeois, *On Becoming Christian* (Twenty-Third Publications, 1982) pleads that baptism and confirmation not be taken as automatically effective.

A. Theodore Eastman, *The Baptizing Community* (Seabury Press, 1982) examines the role of the congregation in the process of Christian initiation for children and adults.

Kurt Stasiak, *Return to Grace* (Liturgical Press, 1996) develops a theology for infant baptism around the concept of adoption.

Mark Searle, ed., *Alternative Futures for Worship, Volume 2: Baptism and Confirmation* (Liturgical Press, 1987) proposes that baptism be celebrated in stages, in the manner of the RCIA process, even for children.

Maxwell Johnson, ed., *Living Water, Sealing Spirit* (Liturgical Press, 1995) is a wide-ranging collection of articles on Christian initiation. *The Rites of Christian Initiation* (Liturgical Press, 1999) discusses the evolution of baptism and its interpretations from New Testament times to the present.

Paul Turner, *The Hallelujah Highway* (Liturgy Training Publications, 2000) is an illustrated history of baptism and the restoration of the catechumenate modeled on ancient church initiation practices

Michael Witczak, *The Sacrament of Baptism* (Liturgical Press, 2011) elaborates a theology of baptism from an examination of the text, prayers, and readings of the rite.

Rite of Christian Initiation of Adults

Michael Dujarier, *The Rites of Christian Initiation* (Sadlier, 1979) discusses each of the ceremonies in the RCIA in terms of historical origin and religious meaning.

Mary Pierre Ellenbracht, *The Easter Passage* (Winston Press, 1983) draws on the scriptures to explain the experience of participating in the RCIA.

Sandra DiGuido, *RCIA: The Rites Revisited* (Winston Press, 1984) gives an honest appraisal of what happens and fails to happen in RCIA programs.

Robert Duggan, ed., *Conversion and the Catechumenate* (Paulist Press, 1984) contains articles that work out the personal and social implications of the theology behind the RCIA.

Regis Duffy, *On Becoming a Catholic* (Harper & Row, 1984) walks the reader through the complexity of doctrinal and praxis issues surrounding the RCIA.

J. Michael McMahon, *The Rite of Christian Initiation of Adults* (Federation of Diocesan Liturgical Commissions, 1986) offers historical background, documentation, and pastoral reflection on the various parts of the RCIA.

James Wilde, ed., *Commentaries on the Rite of Christian Initiation of Adults* (Liturgical Training Publications, 1988) contains explanations of each of the individual rites in the RCIA.

Lawrence Mick, *RCIA: Renewing the Church As an Initiating Assembly* (Liturgical Press, 1989) is a compact introduction to the history, purpose, and process of the RCIA.

Thomas Morris, *The RCIA: Transforming the Church* (Paulist Press, 1989) is a more detailed introduction to the RCIA and its implementation in the parish.

Barbara Hixon, *RCIA Ministry* (Resource Publications, 1989) relates working in the RCIA to aspects of the ministry of Jesus in reflections on the rituals for each of the five stages.

Julia Upton, *A Church for the Next Generation* (Liturgical Press, 1990) explores the implications of taking the RCIA process as a model for sacraments in the future.

Mary Birmingham, *Year-Round Catechumenate* (Liturgy Training Publications, 2007) gives reasons for an ongoing RCIA process in the parish, and shows how to do it.

Ecumenical Considerations

Alexander Schmemann, *Of Water and the Spirit* (St. Vladimir's Seminary Press, 1974) develops an Orthodox theology of baptism by reflecting on the eastern rites.

Daniel Stevick, *By Water and the Word* (Church Publishing, 1997) looks at the biblical texts used in Catholic and Protestant baptismal liturgies.

Thomas Best, ed., *Baptism Today* (World Council of Churches, 2008) collects articles on the baptismal practices and theologies of many churches.

James Brownson, *The Promise of Baptism* (William B. Eerdmans, 2007) deals with issues surrounding baptism in Calvinist or reformed churches.

John Riggs, *Baptism in the Reformed Tradition* (Westminster John Knox Press, 2010) contrasts the historical and continuing tensions between infant baptism and believer's baptism.

Kenneth Stevenson, *The Mystery of Baptism in the Anglican Tradition* (Morehouse, 1998) looks at elements in the theology of baptism through the lives of early English divines.

Gayle Carlton Felton, *The Gift of Water* (Abingdon Press, 1992) looks at the practice and theology of baptism among American Methodists from colonial to modern times.

Susan Wood, *One Baptism* (Liturgical Press, 2009) looks for the meaning of baptism in various church traditions to find commonalities that can bring Christians together.

CHAPTER VII

CONFIRMATION

All-powerful God, Father of our Lord Jesus Christ, by water and the Holy Spirit you freed your sons and daughters from sin and gave them new life. Send your Holy Spirit upon them to be their Helper and Guide. Give them the spirit of wisdom and understanding, the spirit of right judgment and courage, the spirit of knowledge and reverence. Fill them with the spirit of wonder and awe in your presence.

—RITE OF CONFIRMATION

Confirmation as a separate sacramental ritual in western Christianity did not exist before the third century, and it did not become a regular practice in Europe until after the fifth century. The ritual did have precedents, however: the New Testament mentions that the apostles sometimes laid their hands on converts, and during patristic initiation ceremonies bishops usually anointed or imposed their hands on the heads of the candidates. This action was often associated with the Holy Spirit, who had descended on the apostles at Pentecost and who inwardly anointed those who were washed in the waters of baptism. Nevertheless it was not until the Middle Ages that the ritual action became definitely separated from baptismal initiation, that it was included among the seven official sacraments of the church, and that it received a separate theological justification. The reformers by and large rejected confirmation as a sacrament, while modern Catholicism retained both the medieval form of the rite and the scholastic explanation of it. Its position in contemporary Catholicism is unclear. The Roman church has retained the practice of baptizing its members in infancy and confirming them afterward, but the significance of the separated ritual is unsettled. The rite that is now called confirmation has meant different things in different periods of history, and theologians today are hard put to say which is the meaning of the sacrament.

1. Parallels and Precedents

Life is full of beginnings. Often they go unnoticed, but sometimes they are important enough to individuals or societies that they become ritualized and dramatized. In primitive societies birth, adolescence, marriage, death, and other events are marked by rituals that symbolize what the event means to both the individual involved and the society at large. Initiation into select groups such as leaders, priests, warriors, and artisans is accomplished by transition rituals that mark a new beginning and in a sense make it happen: it is only by passing through the ritual that a person becomes something different or assumes a new role in the society. Other rituals commemorate these new beginnings or celebrate their importance in regular, often annual, festivities. Still others are celebrations of important events like springtime or the harvest that have no known origins but that begin again every year. And as indicated in chapter 1, these initiation and intensification rituals have parallels in contemporary secular as well as religious societies.

It is difficult to say where in this pattern of cultural rituals that confirmation fits. In Christianity today confirmation (or its equivalent in non-Roman churches) is performed sometimes at the beginning of a person's entrance into the Christian community and sometimes after membership in the community has been established. The subjects of the ritual may be infants, children, adolescents or adults. They may or may not have made a personal commitment to Christ and the church, and they may or may not make one as a result of being confirmed. In some respects and for some people (notably infants and adult converts) it is an initiation ritual signifying and effecting full membership in the church. In other respects and for other people (usually children and adolescents) it is an intensification ritual signifying certain aspects of membership in the church but effecting little or no change in their personal lives or social roles. Traditionally, it is a ceremony to which a Christian is admitted but once, and in that sense it is an initiation or transition ritual. But it is hard to specify what the Christian passes from and passes to during the ceremony, and in that sense it seems more like an intensification ritual reaffirming the meaning of baptism.

The words and gestures of the sacramental ritual, even in its recently revised form, show this same confusion. The bishop speaks to the candidates of receiving the Holy Spirit, but Christians believe they have already received the Spirit through baptism. He extends his hands over them asking that they receive spiritual gifts that they may have already demonstrated publicly. He anoints them and tells them to receive the seal of the Spirit, which in patristic times was thought to be received in baptism. The candidates for their part make few verbal responses during the ceremony beyond assenting to their baptismal promises, which are administered to them as if for the first time.

So in a way there are no parallels to the separated Catholic confirmation ritual, for parallels in other religions would be initiation, transition, or intensification rituals, and the present rite is in some respects something of each. As for precedents, one may look to rituals that invoked the spirit and strength of gods on human recipients, or that symbolically transferred powers or rights through physical contact, or that dramatized special status in the community through anointing with oil. But the most important precedents for confirmation are to be found not in other religions but in early Christianity.

2. Receiving the Holy Spirit

The earliest Christian community experienced what it believed to be the spirit of God and understood itself to be guided and empowered by that spirit. The Jewish Christians saw themselves as living at the beginning of the messianic age when God's spirit would be poured out on all Israelites, when their sons and daughters would prophesy, when the young would see visions and the old would dream dreams. But the Christian experience of spiritual energy burst through the boundaries of its ethnic origins and within a short time the community acknowledged that God's spirit could be poured out on gentiles as well (Acts 10:44–48) and admitted them to full membership in the new church (Acts 15:5–29).

Almost everything that seemed to be beyond human ability and ingenuity in those early years was attributed to the power of God and the working of the Holy Spirit: the disciples' courage to preach the news of Christ's resurrection, people's willingness to accept it, miraculous cures and conversions, decisions and courses of events that led to the spread of the gospel, even the community's survival of Jewish and Roman persecution (Acts 2, 6, 8, 11, and so on). Within the community itself, the fellowship that they felt, the transformation of their lives, their release from guilt about the past, and their exuberant hope for the future were looked upon as due to the Spirit working in and through the church (Romans 8).

The ritual event that signified a person's acceptance of Christ and openness to his spirit (for the spirit of Christ and the spirit of God came to be regarded as identical) was baptism. Through baptism and entrance into the community, people ceased to be ruled by the spirits of evil and received the spirit of Christ their new Lord. They could of course succumb to temptation, but only if they refused to listen to the spirit of God in their hearts (Galatians 5; 1 Corinthians 6). For by baptism they had been born again by water and the Spirit, and they had only to live by the power of the Spirit in order to be saved (John 3; 2 Corinthians 3).

Baptism was, then, a sign that those who had accepted the message of Christ had also received the spirit of God. But there were other signs as well. Living in a spirit of love for one another, serving the community and ministering to its needs, avoiding sin and scandal, obeying religious and civil and family authority—these were all signs that Christians lived not by the power of any demonic or even human spirit but by the power of Christ and the spirit of God (Romans 12; 1 Corinthians 2; 1 John 4). In addition, charismatic utterances in prophesy or in strange languages, spiritual ecstasies and visions, religious insights and inspired teachings were looked upon as signs of the presence of God's spirit in individuals (1 Corinthians 12–14). Sometimes these charismatic manifestations of the Holy Spirit came when leaders in the community laid their hands on converts after their baptism, but sometimes they appeared without the laying on of hands (Acts 8:14–18; 9:31). In any event, the imposition of hands does not seem to have been always connected with baptism, even if it was a common practice associated with anointing by the Spirit (Acts 2:41; 9:17–19; 19:1–7). The imposition of hands was also used as a ritual for delegating responsibility and authority in the community, and although no charismatic behavior followed, those who were so delegated were understood to be empowered by the Holy Spirit (Acts 6:6; 1 Timothy 4:14).

As noted earlier, the charismatic activities and changed lives of individuals were spoken of in the New Testament as the "seal of the Spirit," the visible sign of their spiritual transformation (see pages 28 and 36). This experiential way of understanding the presence and manifestations of the spirit of God continued in some Christian communities well into the second century. Irenaeus of Lyons, for example, wrote about the importance of charismatic gifts such as prophecy, casting out devils, visions of the future, and healing the sick. For him these were signs that the Holy Spirit was truly at work in the church. Two hundred years later, however, these visible signs of the Spirit had so completely disappeared that Augustine of Hippo wrote, "Who in the present day expects that those on whom hands are laid for the bestowal of the Spirit will suddenly begin speaking in tongues?"(*On John I* 6, 10). In the absence of charismatic signs, most of the fathers looked elsewhere for what might be legitimately called the seal of the Spirit, and they found it in their own religious experiences or in their churches' baptismal liturgies.

During the first century and a half of Christianity, baptism evolved from a simple water ritual to a more complex ceremony of prayers, washings, and other symbolic actions culminating in the celebration of the eucharist. Just how and why Christian initiation developed in this direction is hard to say, but a plausible suggestion is that early church leaders borrowed the basic pattern from the Jewish initiation procedure for gentiles or pagans, which also included a period of instruction similar to the catechumenate and ended in a sacrificial meal analogous to the eucharistic meal. But whatever its historical precedents were, Christian initiation took a direction of its own. By the year 200 most of the Christian communities scattered throughout the Roman Empire had an initiation ritual that included both water baptism signifying spiritual regeneration and an additional rite signifying the reception of the Holy Spirit.

Usually this additional rite was placed after the washing or immersion, but third-century Syrian documents mention only an imposition of hands and an anointing before the water rite and nothing afterward. Evidently the church at Antioch and other places followed an initiation procedure in which the bishop touched and anointed the candidates on the head, then deacons anointed the men and deaconesses anointed the women over their whole body, and then both the men and the women were baptized with water. Some writings from the fourth century do mention a postbaptismal anointing but others do not. John Chrysostom, who was born in Antioch and later became bishop of Constantinople, also describes an initiation ceremony that included only a prebaptismal anointing. Theodore, the bishop of Mopsuestia in Syria around the same time, says that candidates were signed with a cross after coming out of the water but mentions nothing about oil. Moreover, both John and Theodore believed that the Holy Spirit came down upon the candidates during the baptism with water, as did most of the eastern church fathers. Apparently then, a number of Syrian churches until well into the fourth century had no ritual other than water baptism for the giving of the Holy Spirit to new Christians, although the anointings were sometimes seen as signifying what was about to happen.

In other eastern churches such as Jerusalem, Constantinople, and

Alexandria and in the western churches of Rome and Carthage the situation was somewhat different. Beginning in the third century, writers from those regions described initiation ceremonies that included various actions performed by the presiding bishop after the candidates came out of the baptismal pool. In some localities the bishop placed one or both hands on their head, extended one or both hands over the group of them, or made the sign of the cross on their forehead. In other places he poured oil over their head or made the sign of the cross on their forehead with oil. In still others he performed a combination of these ritual gestures. In Rome around the year of 215, for example, the bishop extended a hand over the candidates and prayed that they be filled with the Holy Spirit, then he poured oil and laid his hand on their head, made the sign of the cross on their forehead, and gave them a ritual kiss known as the kiss of peace.

The explanations of these symbolic gestures were sometimes as varied as the gestures themselves. Generally speaking, however, the actions of the bishop as the head of the local community were seen as a sign of the candidates' acceptance into the church. The extension or imposition of hands was done in symbolic imitation of the apostles' actions described in the New Testament. The pouring of oil was a symbolic representation of the anointing of the Holy Spirit that the candidates were receiving through the baptismal ceremony. The oil used was perfumed: in the east it was usually scented with myrrh and called myron, in the west it was usually scented with balsam and called chrism; and the meaning of the perfume was that Christians should be the pleasant fragrance of Christ in the world, or that they should experience the sweetness of the Lord. The sign of the cross was the sign of Christ, whom they now accepted and believed in; it was also interpreted as the sign by which they would be recognized as belonging to Christ at the time of his second coming.

Christian writers during the patristic period also gave these symbols their own individual interpretations. Cyprian of Carthage in the third century wrote, "Those who are newly baptized are presented to the head of the church; they receive the Holy Spirit through our prayer and the imposition of our hand, and they are perfected by means of the Lord's sign" (Letters 73, 9). Cyril of Jerusalem a century later described a ceremony in which the baptized were anointed on the forehead, ears, nose, and breast as a symbol of their sanctification by the Spirit in baptism, and a sign of their union with Christ "who was anointed with the spiritual oil of gladness, that is, with the Holy Spirit" (Mystagogical Catechesis III, 2). But in their sermons and religious instructions the fathers sometimes described each of the elements in the lengthy initiation ceremony and gave them spiritual interpretations that were not always meant to be taken literally. Augustine, for example, explained that catechumens were ground like wheat through the Lenten fast and exorcisms, mixed with water in baptism and formed into the body of Christ, and baked by the fire of the Holy Spirit in the anointing with chrism.

It was primarily in the western churches that theological writers began to take the symbolic actions more literally and tried to specify which spiritual effects occurred at each step in the initiation ceremony. Around the turn of the third century, Tertullian believed that those who were baptized were washed spiritually clean by an angel, and that they did not receive the Holy Spirit until the bishop laid his hand on them. Bishop Cornelius of Rome later in the same century indicated that the Holy Spirit came with the consignation or signing by the bishop on the forehead of the baptized. The council of Arles, which in 314 decided that heretics should not be rebaptized, also decided that they should receive a second imposition of hands so that they might again have the Holy Spirit, which they had lost. Hilary of Poitiers later in the fourth century spoke of baptism and the reception of the Spirit as separate actions, and said that the Holy Spirit descended on the newly initiated only after the washing of baptism. Ambrose of Milan, however, saw two operations of the Holy Spirit in the initiation ceremony: in baptism Christians received regeneration and forgiveness of sins through water and the Spirit, and in the imposition of the bishop's hand they received the seven gifts of the Spirit enumerated in Isaiah 11:2–3. Augustine knew of both an anointing and an imposition of hands, but for him it was the chrism that gave the seal of the Spirit, the imposition of hands being a sign of acceptance by the bishop and unity with the church, which could be repeated for the reconciliation of heretics and schismatics.

During the first four centuries of Christianity, then, there was no common consensus about the point at which people received the Holy Spirit during their initiation as Christians. All the fathers agreed that by the conclusion of the ceremony Christians had received the Spirit, but for some this happened during the baptismal washing, for others it happened afterward. Some did not specify when it happened but only spoke of the anointing or imposition of hands as a sign that it did happen.

At the height of the patristic period, Christian initiation was an elaborate ceremony of prayers and blessings, exorcisms and anointings, washings and other gestures, presided over by a bishop. The presence of the bishop was important since he represented both the local community and the larger church that the catechumens were joining. Sometimes, however, the bishop could not be present and so adjustments had to be made in the initiation rite. In most eastern churches priests were given the authority to act in the bishop's name and carry out the entire baptism. The oil that the priests used for anointing was myron, which had been consecrated by the bishop and which symbolized his presence at the baptism and his approval of the candidates. This procedure was sometimes carried out in the west, but not often.

In the middle of the third century, Cyprian of Carthage wrote that catechumens who were in danger of death might be baptized and anointed by a priest, but if they recovered they should be brought to the bishop for the imposition of his hand. A century later in Africa, however, when the chrism was consecrated by the bishop, he laid his hand on it, and so when it was applied by a priest the hand-laying of the bishop was believed to be transmitted by means of the chrism. Around the year 300 a council of Spanish bishops at Elvira decreed that those baptized in rural districts by a deacon must go afterward to the bishop to be perfected (that is, to have their baptism completed) by the laying on of hands. But in other parts of Spain and in many parts of France and Italy, if the baptism was performed by a priest, this episcopal perfecting of baptism was not necessary. In Rome, which had two postbaptismal anointings in its initiation ceremony, priests performed the first but only the bishop was allowed to perform the second. Pope Innocent I in 416 instructed that priests could anoint the baptized with consecrated chrism but that they were not to perform the rite of consignation with the chrism since only bishops as successors of the apostles could give the Holy Spirit. But at the council of Orange in 441 French bishops gave permission for priests to anoint the people they baptized, provided that the chrism they used was consecrated by a bishop. Thus in the west there was no uniform procedure for remedying the absence of a bishop at baptisms.

Three developments made it increasingly difficult for bishops to preside over all the baptisms that were performed in their territories. Late in the fourth century Christianity was made the official religion of the Roman Empire, and the sheer numbers of those who wanted to join the church made a bishop's presence at all these baptisms impossible since there was only one bishop in each city or diocese. Then in the fifth century Augustine's idea that baptism was necessary for the remission of original sin led to a tremendous increase in infant baptisms, and since baptism was still administered only once or twice a year, most of these had to be performed

at other churches than the episcopal cathedral. Lastly, when the missionaries were sent into northern Europe to convert the barbarians, very few
bishops went with them, and so from the sixth century onward most of
these missionary baptisms took place far from the presence of any bishop.

In the latter half of the patristic period, other changes took place in the
part of Christian initiation that was to become later known as confirmation.
In the west, the imposition of the bishop's hand was gradually replaced
by anointing or consignation as the rite by which baptism was completed,
especially in the regions where bishops were regularly unable to be present.
In the east a postbaptismal anointing likewise replaced the imposition of
hands, and in places like Syria, which earlier had no postbaptismal rite at
all, the anointing before baptism became an anointing after baptism. This
postbaptismal anointing came to be regarded as the completion or sealing
of the baptism as it was in the west, even though it was not regarded as
the point at which the Holy Spirit was given to the baptized. In Orthodox
baptisms today, which are based on the practices of the fourth and fifth
centuries, infants are "chrismated" after they are baptized and before they
are given communion. This chrismation is an anointing with the sign of
the cross on the child's forehead, eyes, nostrils, lips, ears, breast, hands,
and feet, and with each consignation the priest administering the rite says,
"The seal of the gift of the Holy Spirit." Eventually the eastern churches,
under the influence of western theology, came to regard baptism, chrismation, and the eucharist as separate sacraments of initiation even though
they were still administered in a unified ceremony.

3. From Consignation to Confirmation

In the west, the separated rite for the completion of Christian initiation
was designated by a variety of terms: signing, consignation, anointing,
perfection, consummation, and blessing. Usually the symbolic action was
a consignation, that is, an anointing with chrism in the sign of the cross.
The name "confirmation" was first used by the French councils of Riez
and Orange in 439 and 441, which gave priests permission to anoint the
children they baptized with consecrated chrism, and instructed bishops
to visit the rural areas of their dioceses regularly in order to confirm these
baptisms by the imposition of hands. It was hard to convince the peasants
in the remote countryside to bring their children to the bishop as soon as
he came within a reasonable distance, however, and so many people grew
up without having their baptisms confirmed.

To remedy the situation, somewhere around the year 460 Bishop Faustus of Riez delivered a Pentecost sermon in which he stressed the importance of this episcopal confirmation by saying that it made those who received it more fully Christians. Faustus preached that in baptism the Holy Spirit gave new life and all that was needed for innocence, but in confirmation the Spirit gave additional strength needed for the battle with sin and the devil in adulthood. In the years that followed Faustus' sermon, however, this French version of baptismal confirmation failed to catch on as a separate rite. The Germanic invasions and the breakdown of political organization made it impossible for bishops to make their regular visits, and during the next three centuries the separate episcopal rite was virtually unknown in France. Outside of the cities in which bishops resided, priests performed the whole initiation ceremony.

The situation was not much different in Spain and most of Italy. Around the year 600 Isidore of Seville wrote separately about baptism and the imposition of hands, but for the most part Christian initiation was carried out by local priests who baptized, anointed, and gave communion to children each year during the Easter Vigil. Not many years later, Pope Gregory objected to the practice of priests in Sardinia who were signing infants on the forehead with chrism, but because of local support for the custom he allowed it to continue. It was mainly in Rome that the rite of consignation was reserved to the bishop; and when Rome sent missionaries to England in the seventh century they brought this tradition with them, with the result that thousands were baptized but few were consignated.

Eventually the Roman practice found its way into France as well. When Charlemagne established his "Holy Roman Empire" in the west, one of the things he wanted for it was a uniform liturgy like that of the Byzantine Empire in the east. Pope Hadrian sent him a Roman sacramentary and in 784 Charlemagne decreed that its rites should be followed throughout his domain. To a large extent he succeeded, but since the Roman practice of episcopal consignation went against the tradition of the French churches it was resisted for a long time.

During the early 800s the French clergy began to view the growing power of the emperor and nobles as a threat to their own prerogatives such as the selection of bishops and the right to collect taxes from church lands. They tried repeatedly to enact legislation that safeguarded their rights, but since the nobility had to approve any reforms before they could become law, their attempts were futile. The only changes allowed were those that they could prove were the official practice of the church in the ancient

Roman Empire. Then around 850, after repeated attempts at reform, a group of clerics decided to remedy the situation by discovering the needed proof. They produced an ingenious piece of forgery, a collection of letters and decrees from popes and councils, some of which were known to be genuine and so gave the whole work an aura of authenticity. The rest of the items were either written by the forgers or borrowed from little known church records and attributed to Roman popes and councils of the patristic period, and these were the ones that provided the documentation that the French bishops needed. Finally, to give this collection of decretals added credibility, it was said to have been compiled by Isidore, the famous bishop of Seville, in the early 600s. Most of the false decretals had to do with the rights of bishops and their immunity from interference by civil authorities, but some of them were purely ecclesiastical regulations and contained sections on the proper administration of the sacraments.

Among these sacramental regulations were passages taken from the Pentecost sermon of Faustus and passed off as letters from Pope Urban (who lived in the third century) and Pope Melchiades (who apparently never existed). The one attributed to Urban insisted that "...all the faithful must receive the Holy Spirit after baptism through the imposition of the hand of the bishop so that they may become fully Christians." The one attributed to Melchiades suggested that episcopal confirmation had an even greater dignity than baptism because its minister held a higher office than the minister of baptism, and went on to say, "At the baptismal font the Holy Spirit bestows absolutely all that is needed to restore innocence, but in confirmation he provides an increase of grace. In baptism we are born to new life; after baptism we are confirmed for combat. In baptism we are washed; after baptism we are strengthened." Thus, it continued, those who died without confirmation were saved, but those who survived needed the assistance of confirmation to face the conflicts and battles of the world. In addition, the collection quoted Clement of Rome as insisting on the necessity of confirmation as well as baptism, and attributed the fourth-century pope Eusebius with saying that the sacrament of the imposition of hands was to be performed by no one but the successors of the apostles.

The bold enterprise of the forgers was even more successful than they had planned. Not only did it give the French clergy the legal precedents they needed to support their reforms in the empire but also the collection was soon accepted as genuine all over Europe. Its decretals attained the force of law, and the sacramental theology it contained acquired the weight of venerable tradition. Raban Maur, the abbot of Fulda in Germany, was among the first to further amplify the new theology of confirmation, writing that it gave Christians strength to witness to the faith and to speak openly about Christ. Thus by the end of the ninth century the foundation for the scholastic theology of confirmation had been laid.

Nonetheless, it was still hard to convince people to bring their children to be confirmed. Traditional theology taught that baptism was necessary for salvation, but now that confirmation by the bishop was no longer a part of baptism it was difficult to see why it was needed. Bishops were supposed to visit each parish in their diocese at least every three years, but parents often neglected to bring their children to him even when they heard he was in the area. Life was a daily struggle for existence in the medieval countryside and so home and farm duties seemed much more important than seeing the bishop, especially when confirmation might consist in nothing more than holding a child up to receive the bishop's anointing as he passed by on horseback. The bishops themselves did not always make these visitations because roads were often poor or nonexistent, and they were sometimes involved in politics that kept them home or in wars that kept them abroad. Moreover occasionally years passed between the death of one bishop and the appointment of another. The result was that some people were not confirmed until adolescence, and many were not confirmed at all. As long as baptisms were performed only once a year it was still possible for those living close to the bishop's cathedral to have their children baptized and anointed in a single ceremony, but when the fear of death without baptism led to having them baptized soon after birth, even this practice broke down. Thus in the Middle Ages the interval between birth and baptism was reduced to a few days, but the interval between baptism and confirmation was prolonged to several years.

Between the ninth and the thirteenth centuries the Roman custom of episcopal confirmation was extended through all the countries of Europe (except in Milan and some Spanish dioceses), and the French explanation of confirmation became the accepted Catholic view. The French bishops had adapted the Roman sacramentary to their own needs, and during the tenth century liturgical books produced in northern monasteries were imported by Rome and began to be used there. The changes in most of the rites were slight, but the anointing by the bishop was now referred to as "confirmation" and it was definitely separate from baptism. Other slight changes were made in the confirmation rite by the bishop of Mende, William Durand, when he supervised the production of a new edition of the Roman liturgical books for use by bishops in the thirteenth century. The older rite had called for an individual imposition of the bishop's hand on each of the candidates followed by an individual consignation with oil, and to simplify the ceremony Durand changed the individual imposition of the hand to a collective imposition or extension of the hand over all the candidates. The older rite had also instructed the bishop to give each of those confirmed the kiss of peace, which in the case of infants was often substituted with a caress on the cheek. More in keeping with the theology of the false decretals, Durand replaced this with a slap to signify that in confirmation Christians received strength for the battle against temptation and the enemies of the faith.

Many of the false decretals found their way into the influential collections of John Gratian and Peter Lombard in the twelfth century, and they were accepted at face value by students of canon law and theology thereafter. In the short section on confirmation in the *Sentences*, Lombard relied heavily on the decretals to show that confirmation was a sacrament, that its effect was the gift of the Holy Spirit given for strength, and that it could be administered only by a bishop. His listing of the sacraments was accepted as standard, and in 1274 the Second Council of Lyons named confirmation among the seven sacraments of the Roman Catholic Church.

The medieval theologians thus had no difficulty in accepting confirmation as one of the ecclesiastical sacraments, but they did have some difficulty in explaining it. For one thing, the decretals implied that confirmation was necessary, and yet the schoolmen knew from experience that many people were never confirmed. Why, then, was it necessary? It could not be necessary for salvation, because if it were, those who died without it would be damned—and what, then, was the purpose of baptism? Some scholastics reasoned that confirmation was morally necessary since Christians were obliged to defend themselves against temptation. Others concluded that it was a conditional necessity, in case one needed extra spiritual strength to fight off an especially attractive temptation to sin. Aquinas viewed it as necessary for achieving spiritual perfection since holiness could not be attained without the help of the Holy Spirit.

A second difficulty that the scholastics faced was the rite itself. If confirmation was a sacrament it had to have a definite "matter" and "form" in the Aristotelian sense of those terms. But what was the "matter" of the sacrament? Was it the laying on of both hands, the gesture described in the New Testament but now absent from the rite? Was it the imposition of a single hand as found in some liturgical books, or the extension of the bishop's hand over the candidates as found in the Roman sacramentary?

Was it the anointing with chrism, or perhaps the chrism itself? And what was the "form" of the sacrament? Was it the prayer of the bishop asking the Holy Spirit to descend upon the candidates, or the formula that he pronounced as he anointed them? In either case, which prayer or formula was the correct one, since there were different ones used in different parts of Europe? In the end, most of the scholastics agreed that the essential "matter" of confirmation was the anointing with chrism since this was found in all of the medieval rites, and that its proper "form" was the formula that the bishop pronounced as he did this. By the thirteenth century at least, the majority of sacramentaries in use gave the words of the formula as "I sign you with the sign of the cross, and I confirm you with the chrism of salvation, in the Name of the Father and of the Son and of the Holy Spirit," or words that were very similar. This formula was also found in the Roman sacramentary, and it became accepted as standard.

Another difficulty had to do with the sacrament's institution. It could not be easily shown from scripture to have been instituted by Christ as baptism could. Some contended that it had been instituted by the apostles, and that even if the apostles themselves had not used the prescribed matter and form, they had instructed their successors to do so. Others like Bonaventure believed that the rite in current use had been instituted by the church under the guidance of the Holy Spirit some time after the death of the apostles. Alexander of Hales even suggested that it had been inspired by the Holy Spirit at the council of Meaux in the ninth century. Those who like Aquinas believed that all the sacraments had to have been instituted by Christ pointed to various places in the New Testament where he might have done so, such as his breathing on the apostles with the Holy Spirit (John 20:22) or even the resting of his hand on the children who were brought to him (Mark 10:13). Aquinas himself proposed that Christ had instituted the sacrament not by performing it but by promising it (John 16:17).

Confirmation like baptism was administered only once to an individual, and so all the scholastics came to agree that confirmation must also bestow a sacramental character since they knew of no other reason why a sacrament could not be repeated. But what, then, was the sacramental character given by confirmation, and how was it different from the one given by baptism? In some of his writings Bonaventure suggested that the two characters were identical except in regard to their effects, but in others he implied that they were different because they pertained to different states of faith. Most, like Aquinas, agreed that they had to be different because the sacramental rituals that conferred them were different. Albert the Great and

Alexander of Hales viewed the character of confirmation as a configuration to Christ the King, the Christian's leader in spiritual battle. For Aquinas a sacramental character was a spiritual power oriented to perform certain actions: through the character of baptism Christians received the power to achieve salvation; through that of confirmation they received the power to attain spiritual perfection and to combat the enemies of the faith.

Aquinas' teaching about the effect of confirmation (the grace or *res*) stemmed from his theory about the nature of the character (the sacramental reality or *sacramentum et res*). The character was a power to perform actions that were beyond natural human ability, and in order to take into account the papal statements of the false decretals Aquinas reasoned that there must be a power of spiritual growth given in confirmation that is different from the power of spiritual birth given in baptism. Just as baptism did not automatically make a person good, however, neither did confirmation automatically make a person a saint. In either case a person had to cooperate continually with God's grace, and so in Aquinas' view the graces that were proper to spiritual maturity were different from those that were characteristic of spiritual infancy. And like the other schoolmen who depended on the decretals, he singled out strength in spiritual combat and boldness in professing the faith as graces that were proper to confirmation.

Some scholastics suggested that in baptism people received the Holy Spirit while in confirmation they received the seven gifts of the Spirit mentioned in Isaiah 11 and cited by Ambrose: wisdom, understanding, counsel, fortitude, knowledge, piety, and fear of the Lord. But others pointed out that it was hard to separate the Spirit from its gifts, and that these virtues were needed for salvation. Still others proposed that the gifts were received through baptism but that they were somehow strengthened through confirmation.

The scholastic theology of confirmation indirectly affected the age at which confirmation was administered, even though the main reasons why confirmation was delayed were practical rather than theoretical. The decretals and the schoolmen emphasized the importance of confirmation for publicly professing and defending the faith, and some church leaders began to wonder whether such spiritual strength was really needed in infancy. Still, the traditional practice had been confirmation as soon as possible after baptism, and for a long time infancy was seen as the desirable age. Through the thirteenth century a number of episcopal decrees urged confirmation by the age of one or two, and some even imposed penalties (such as penances or even fines) for parents who neglected their duty. In the effort to enforce confirmation some English bishops ruled that those who had not been confirmed would not be allowed to make their first communion, and at least one Italian bishop threatened pastors with excommunication if they did not regularly remind their parishioners about having their children confirmed.

Gradually, however, the appropriate age for confirmation moved upward. Since the graces of confirmation did not seem to be needed until a child could distinguish between right and wrong, various bishops and councils in the thirteenth and fourteenth centuries began to suggest "the age of discretion" as the proper time for confirmation. Churchmen did not agree, however, about when the age of discretion was reached. The council of Cologne in 1280 declared that children under the age of seven were too young to be confirmed, and various other episcopal and conciliar decrees put the age at twelve or even fourteen. Thus by the end of the Middle Ages a sacramental rite that had once been restricted almost entirely to infants was generally regarded as inappropriate for them, even though the confirmation of infants still persisted in a few scattered dioceses.

The medieval practice and theology of confirmation were canonized by the Council of Florence in 1439. In its decree for the Armenian Christians who were seeking union with Rome, the council outlined the basic doctrines of the Catholic Church, and among them was a section on the sacraments. It declared that there were seven sacraments, and that by confirmation Christians grew in grace and were strengthened in faith. It defined the matter and form of the sacrament as the scholastics had done, and it declared that the ordinary minister of the sacrament was the bishop because in the New Testament only the apostles had given the Holy Spirit through the imposition of hands. Nevertheless, it allowed that priests might be delegated to perform the rite (as they did in the eastern churches) provided that they used chrism blessed by the bishop.

4. Confirmation in Modern Times

What the Council of Florence summarized remained the Catholic understanding of confirmation throughout the modern period. The text of the rite was basically the same as the one that William Durand had published in the thirteenth century, and it survived with only one minor alteration until the twentieth century.

The practice of confirmation, however, as that of the other sacraments in the late Middle Ages, left much to be desired. Despite ecclesiastical decrees to the contrary, it was often neglected. And when the ritual was actually performed, it was usually done in the perfunctory way that had become characteristic of sacramental minimalism. Legally Catholics were obliged to be confirmed, although few could specify exactly why. Theologically it did not seem to make any difference in a person's ability to get to heaven, and morally it did not seem to make any difference in a person's life. Moreover, bishops sometimes used confirmation in the various parishes around their diocese as an opportunity to put on a show of episcopal dignity and to take up a collection.

By and large the Protestant reformers looked at what went on at confirmation and decided that it was neither Christian nor scriptural. To some it looked like another Roman ruse designed to glorify bishops and fill their pockets. To others it seemed to deny that the Holy Spirit was given in baptism or that baptism and faith were sufficient for salvation. In short, they found the Roman ritual to be a mockery of sacramentality, and they found the scholastic justification of it to be inept. In particular they pointed to the facts that its institution by Christ could not be proven from the Bible, and that the anointing with chrism did not resemble the apostles' laying on of hands either in outward appearance or inward effect.

Martin Luther was one of the most outspoken critics of the Renaissance practice of episcopal confirmation, and he dismissed as a medieval superstition the idea that it gave the Holy Spirit. Nevertheless he did see some merit in retaining something like a confirmation ceremony in a reformed church. In 1522, soon after his excommunication, he said, "I would allow confirmation as long as it was understood that God knows nothing of it, that he has said nothing about it, and that what the bishops claim for it is untrue" (*Sermon on Married Life*). For him, confirmation was an ecclesiastical ceremony on a sacramental par with rituals for the blessing of water or the consecration of churches. He was aware that the apostles had sometimes imposed hands on early converts, but he believed that they did it to bestow spiritual charisms which were no longer needed to spread the message of Christianity. If a similar ritual were to be retained in the church, it would have to have a different purpose, perhaps a more pastoral purpose. He suggested what that purpose might be in 1533: "I see nothing wrong if every pastor would examine the faith of the children to see whether it is good and sincere, lay hands on them and confirm them." Out of this suggestion grew the Lutheran practice of preparing and confirming children before they were admitted to the sacrament of the Lord's table.

Luther's proposal, however, was not novel. In some dioceses it had been customary to prepare children for confirmation by having them memorize the Our Father, the Hail Mary, the Apostles' Creed, and the Ten Commandments. John Calvin even saw this instruction and confirmation in Christianity as a clue to what confirmation had meant in the early church. Calvin believed that in patristic times there had been a sort of catechumenate for those who had been baptized as infants, and that in confirmation they were examined by the bishop, made a public profession of faith, and were approved by the laying on of hands. He also found a biblical precedent for this idea in the fact that in the New Testament the laying on of hands is always preceded by a profession of faith, and he contended that even though the imposition of hands could no longer confer spiritual charisms as it had in apostolic times, it could still be retained as a form of solemn blessing. Many churches in the Calvinist tradition still retain this type of confirmation practice.

Many other reformed churches eliminated confirmation entirely, however, since it seemed to have no meaning or purpose of its own. An exception to this rule was the Church of England, which originally broke from Rome for political rather than theological reasons and which retained all seven sacraments as well as other medieval Catholic practices. In 1549 the English practice of confirming infants was abolished, but the rule that children should be confirmed prior to their first communion was retained. Children were also to be instructed and examined in the catechism before being confirmed by the bishop. In 1552 the *Book of Common Prayer* changed the rite of confirmation from a consignation to an imposition of hands, but added a prayer that reflected the medieval theology of confirmation: the bishop was to pray that the candidates would not be ashamed to confess the faith of Christ, that they would fight under his banner against sin, and that they would continue as Christ's faithful soldiers until the end of their lives. In practice, however, Anglican Catholicism fared no better than Roman Catholicism, and confirmation was often regarded as a nice but unnecessary ritual.

The Roman Catholic reaction to the general Protestant rejection of confirmation was brief but to the point. The Council of Trent issued no doctrinal statement on confirmation, but attached to its decree on the sacraments in 1547 were canons condemning those who said that confirmation was a useless ceremony, that at one time it was just a form of catechesis and public profession of faith, that attributing spiritual power to the chrism was an offense against the Holy Spirit, or that any priest could administer the sacrament. The Catechism of the Council of Trent, issued in 1566 and the basis of all modern Catholic catechisms stated that confirmation could be given to any baptized Catholic but that it was not necessary to receive the sacrament until the age of seven even though it should not be postponed beyond the age of twelve. The catechism simply reflected Catholic practice, for in the sixteenth century a number of local councils in Italy and France had already forbidden confirmation under the age of seven. The council of Cologne in 1536 even said why: it was because a child younger than that would remember and understand little or nothing of what was done during the ceremony. Thus after Trent confirmation was administered not before seven and not later than twelve, except in some Spanish and Latin American dioceses, which kept the custom of confirming infants in connection with baptism.

The Roman rite of confirmation was modified only slightly when in the eighteenth century Pope Benedict XIV reintroduced the individual imposition of the bishop's hand into the rite. In order to reestablish a symbolic continuity with the practice described in the New Testament, the revised rite instructed the bishop to lay his hand flat on the candidate's head while signing the forehead with a thumb moistened with oil. The theology of confirmation remained unchanged until the twentieth century, however, as did Catholics' knowledge of the history of the rite. In 1907 Pius X condemned those modernists who claimed that there was no proof that the rite of confirmation was used by the apostles, as well as those who asserted that a formal distinction between baptism and confirmation did not exist in ancient Christianity.

The only other change in Catholic confirmation was in its relation to the eucharist. Through the seventeenth and eighteenth centuries confirmation was still given before communion because the age of first communion had come to be pushed back even further than that of confirmation. But during the nineteenth century a practice of giving communion before confirmation began in France and spread to Belgium, Austria, and Hungary, partly as a result of the liturgical movement that viewed the reception of communion as an integral part of the mass rather than as an occasional sign of devotion. The practice was later approved by Pope Pius X in 1910, and thereafter communion before confirmation became a regular custom in the Roman church.

5. Confirmation in the Contemporary Church

In the words of some Catholic writers, confirmation is "a sacrament in search of a theology." Twentieth-century historical research discovered the dubious foundations of the scholastic theology of confirmation, and contemporary theology has found it hard to justify a second conferring of the Holy Spirit after baptism.

The search for a better justification for confirmation began early. Around the turn of the twentieth century, some Catholic theologians tried to distinguish between the sacramental effects of baptism and confirmation by proposing that baptism gave a dynamic presence of the Holy Spirit while confirmation gave the indwelling of the Holy Spirit. Two decades later there was a brief return to Ambrose's idea that baptism gave the indwelling of the Holy Spirit but confirmation gave the seven gifts of the Spirit. During the 1940s and 1950s confirmation was sometimes viewed as the sacrament of "Catholic action," the sacrament that made young Catholics active Christians and soldiers of Christ, ready to bring the spiritual and social message of Christianity into the world. But all of these interpretations of the rite were still primarily based on the medieval practice of separated confirmation and on the modern custom of delaying confirmation until early adolescence. It was not until historical investigations spurred on by the liturgical movement showed that confirmation had once been a part of a unified ceremony of Christian initiation that most of the attempts to explain confirmation as a sacrament of Christian adolescence were abandoned.

With the liturgical movement came a return to the notion of confirmation as a completing or perfecting of baptism, and even some suggestions that the time for confirmation should be immediately after baptism as in the Orthodox churches. Confirmation was explained as the sacramental sign by which a Catholic, like the adult convert in the early church, became accepted not only by the Christian communities of family and parish but also by the diocese and the universal church represented by the bishop. The spiritual character conferred by confirmation was interpreted as a mark of the interior transformation that occurs when a person freely decides to be a member of the church and fully accepts what it means to be a Christian. Although historians could not find that the name "confirmation" was used earlier than the fifth century, liturgists and theologians pointed to the fact that an initiation ritual of hand-laying or anointing could be traced back to early patristic times and perhaps even to the apostolic church.

Most Catholic theologians were not liturgical purists, however, and during the 1960s many theologies of confirmation contained a blend of patristic, medieval, and contemporary ideas. Edward Schillebeeckx suggested that confirmation was an incorporation into the complete mystery of the church in that it was a deeper encounter with the mystery of Christ and the Holy Spirit. Karl Rahner wrote of confirmation as an assertive counterpart to passive baptism, an ecclesial symbol that those who are empowered by the Holy Spirit can transcend their own limitations and can be instruments of grace in the world. Marian Bohen viewed confirmation as a sacrament of God's love by which Christians became fully accepted as God's children in the Spirit, were sealed as brothers and sisters of Christ, and were constituted as witnesses to the Father's love for all people. Charles Davis suggested that confirmation did not change what the Holy Spirit did for Christians, but rather it changed their relation to God and the church by making them witnesses of Christ, heralds of the gospel, and prophets in the world.

The situation today is not much different. Confirmation is more and more referred to as a sign rather than as a cause of grace because it is hard to specify what exactly confirmation causes. It is spoken of as a sign of the Holy Spirit, of what the Spirit means for Catholics, and of their call to live by the power of God's spirit rather than according to the spirit of the times. The confirmation ceremony is interpreted as a celebration of Christian maturity, both in an individual and psychological sense and in a social and moral sense: it is a communal recognition that those who are confirmed have personally accepted the faith that was once accepted for them, and it is an ecclesiastical call for them to take up the responsibility of being adult disciples of Christ in the world. Perhaps the most radical approach to confirmation comes from the Catholic charismatic movement, some of whose members have suggested that confirmation should be something akin to "baptism in the Spirit," a releasing of the spiritual energies received in baptism and an experience of the presence and power of the Holy Spirit similar to what the disciples experienced on the first Pentecost.

Unfortunately, however, the Catholic rite of confirmation shows an ambiguous relation to many of these ideas. The Second Vatican Council directed that confirmation should be revised to indicate its close connection with baptism, and the result was a rite that could be used either immediately after the baptism of adults or at a later time for those who were baptized as infants. In the postbaptismal form of the rite, confirmation is clearly a completion of the initiation ceremony, but in the separated form of the rite its meaning is less clear. The bishop is instructed to remind the candidates that they are called to be witnesses to Christ and more perfect members of the church, which is reminiscent of the medieval theology of confirmation; but then the candidates renew their baptismal promises and the bishop prays that they be filled with the Holy Spirit, almost as though they had just been baptized. The few references to confirmation in the documents of Vatican II reflect this same ambiguity. Apart from the council's call for a closer connection between baptism and confirmation, the three texts in which confirmation is mentioned all refer to it in terms of strengthening by the Holy Spirit. Thus confirmation today is officially viewed both as a part of Christian initiation and as a separate sacrament with effects of its own.

Paul VI's preface to the revised rite that was issued in 1971 acknowledged that the ritual had undergone many changes, and added some new changes besides those already mentioned. Primarily the rite has been simplified and made adaptable to different circumstances. Bishops are encouraged to give pastors in mission lands and priests who baptize adults permission to administer the sacrament. The minister may now also extend his hands over all the candidates or impose his hands on each of them, depending on the number to be confirmed. The signing with chrism has been retained, but the words said during the consignation have been changed to a formula similar to the one used in the eastern churches during patristic times and still used in Orthodox and uniate (eastern rite Catholic) churches today: "Be sealed with the Gift of the Holy Spirit." The pope's preface also summarized the doctrinal theology of the sacrament: "Through the sacrament of confirmation, those who have been born anew in baptism receive the inexpressible Gift, the Holy Spirit himself, by which 'they are endowed... with special strength.' Moreover, having received the character of this sacrament, they are 'bound more intimately to the Church' and 'they are more strictly obliged to spread and defend the faith both by word and by deed as true witnesses of Christ.'" (The quotations in the pope's statement are from the documents of Vatican II.)

Neither the council's directive nor the pope's preface, however, have stemmed the theological debate about the meaning of confirmation and the best age for its reception. Catholic bishops have been authorized to select a time for confirmation that is best suited to their own cultures, and at present the usual age for confirmation ranges from as early as seven to as late as eighteen in different parts of the world. The American bishops' conference in 1972 agreed that children should be confirmed in early adolescence, around the age of ten to twelve, and for a while it was the most prevalent practice in the United States. Experimentation with the best age for confirmation continued, however, until the Vatican pressed the United States Conference of Catholic Bishops to decide on a definite age for reception of the sacrament. Since by the mid-1980s diocesan practices were ranging from before first communion to the senior year in high school, the American bishops could not reach a consensus about a narrower age range, and Rome eventually accepted their decision to designate seven to eighteen years of age as appropriate for confirmation.

Thus there is at present no uniform age for confirmation around the Catholic world, and no uniform theology of the sacrament, for disagreements about the proper age for confirmation usually go hand in hand with disagreements about the meaning of the rite. Those who are liturgically minded support an early age for confirmation in order to show its original liturgical connection with baptism. They argue that if confirmation is indeed the completion of baptism it should be administered at the time of baptism and not years later. They also point out that the separated rite involves a theological paradox since it seems to divide the reception of a single Spirit into two stages. On the other hand, those who are educationally minded often support a later age, when those who have been baptized in infancy can make a more mature decision to be confirmed in the church. Catechists also point out that delayed confirmation offers a special opportunity for the religious education not only of the children who participate in the sacrament but also of the parishes in which the sacrament is celebrated. The visit of the bishop is a chance for them to see their connection with the larger Catholic community, and attending the ceremony is a chance for them to renew their understanding of their relationship to the Holy Spirit.

The implementation of the Rite of Christian Initiation of Adults (RCIA) during the 1980s brought new voices and new ideas into the debate about the proper age for confirmation. The RCIA emphasizes the liturgical unity of the three rites of initiation (baptism, confirmation, and first eucharist), which catechumens in the patristic period passed through during a long ceremony on the night before Easter, and which are restored to their original sequence in this revised program of adult initiation. Moreover, since the RCIA pattern of initiation is now considered normative in the Catholic Church, the argument is made that the sequence of rites for all Catholics, not just adults, ought to be baptism and confirmation before the first reception of communion at the eucharist. Liturgical theologians Gerard Austin and Aidan Kavanagh argued strongly on the basis of the patristic precedent and the present RCIA practice that confirmation ought to be reunited to the baptismal rite, even if this means confirming infants immediately after their baptism.

Another answer to the question of how to restore the original sequence of the three initiation sacraments has been proposed at the pastoral level.

Some parishes and dioceses in the United States and elsewhere have begun programs that prepare children for confirmation and first communion together. During a mass that celebrates the completion of their initiation into the church, the children receive the seal of anointing from their pastor (or in some cases, the diocesan bishop), and afterward as confirmed Christians they are admitted to the eucharist. As in the RCIA, the emphasis in these programs is on preparation for the liturgical rituals and their immediate meaning for the participants. The fuller explanation of what they have experienced is given subsequently, in what the RCIA calls mystagogical catechesis, which in this case extends through childhood and adolescence into adulthood.

A quite different answer is given by theologians who reflect on the meaning of Christian initiation in today's society and conclude that full participation in the life of the church implies a willingness to be of service to the community or to act on behalf of the church in some way. Since adults who enter the church through the RCIA are led to understand that this is part of the commitment that they are making, the same should be expected of those who are baptized as infants. Seen in this light, confirmation would be reserved for persons who, some time in their early or later adulthood, decide to do more than attend church on Sundays in the living out of their Christian commitment. By presenting themselves for confirmation, they would be embracing the full meaning of their baptism into the death and resurrection of Christ, they would be acknowledging that the Spirit in its fullness is given for the sake of others, and they would be confirmed by their bishop or pastor as adult Christians committed to service in the diocese or parish. As can be seen, this approach revises the question of the proper age into a question of the proper time for confirmation.

A fourth answer, which also shifts the issue from the right age to the right time, has come from ecumenical sources. The Lutheran and Episcopal churches have both retained confirmation as a rite for catechized adolescents since the reformation period but, like the Roman Catholic Church, they have had difficulty in making it meaningful for children. In their most recent liturgical reform, therefore, they have established confirmation as a rite in which young people affirm the faith in which they were raised, but they also provide for additional rites of affirmation (similar to the first, but not called confirmation) to be celebrated at appropriate times later in life. For Episcopalians this means that members of the church may request to reaffirm their baptismal commitment before the visiting bishop when he comes for the regular confirmation of adolescents, and they may do this at any time in their lives when they feel that it would be particularly meaningful for them. For Lutherans the additional rites of affirmation are used when baptized persons from other denominations are joining the Lutheran church, and when persons who have left the Lutheran church desire to be restored to membership.

Belgian theologian Peter Fransen has suggested that a pluralistic approach to confirmation has some historical and pastoral merit. Historically both the format of the rite and the age of those who participated in it have varied, and there is no doctrinal reason why simultaneous variations in confirmation could not now replace the former sequential variations. Pastorally the church is in a variety of social and cultural situations; contemporary Catholicism is not the uniform European religion that it once was, and if it is to speak to people of diverse backgrounds and needs it has to adapt its rituals accordingly. In this way confirmation could continue to be, as some of its historical precedents were, a ritual door to the sacred meaning and experience of the Holy Spirit, the spirit of God which cannot be confined to a single set ritual and which, in the words of John's gospel, "blows where it wills."

The current diversity in practice and theory surrounding confirmation, however, are not evident in the *Catechism of the Catholic Church*. Citing Vatican II, it declares that "by the sacrament of Confirmation, [the baptized] are more perfectly bound to the Church and are enriched by a special strength of the Holy Spirit. Hence they are, as true witnesses of Christ, more strictly obliged to spread and defend the faith by word and deed" (1285, quoting from the Constitution on the Sacred Liturgy 11).

Although the *Catechism* ignores diversity in western practice, the section on confirmation is nonetheless quite sensitive to differences between the liturgical practices of Roman Catholicism and those of other churches that call themselves Catholic, the eastern rite or uniate churches. The sacramental practices of these churches are quite similar to those of the Orthodox churches, but since they are in union with the bishop of Rome, they are actually part of the worldwide Catholic Church. A catechism that purports to be for the whole church therefore needs to take their practices into account. The *Catechism* does this in paragraphs 1290–1292, 1297–1300, and 1312–1313, or in about a third of the numbered paragraphs devoted to this sacrament.

Part of the *Catechism*'s clarity on confirmation comes from the fact that, apart from some introductory paragraphs providing scriptural references for the work of the Holy Spirit and the meaning of anointing (1286–1289), its theology is largely derived from medieval scholasticism. The sacrament is something that can be "received," and the *Code of Canon Law* is cited to emphasize that "the faithful are obliged to receive this sacrament at the appropriate time" (1306, quoting canon 890). The "appropriate time" is left undefined, perhaps because in the Roman rite most people are baptized as infants and confirmed later, whereas in the eastern rites they are baptized and confirmed as infants.

The *Catechism* teaches that confirmation confers an indelible character or mark or seal of the Holy Spirit on the soul of the recipient (1295–1296, 1304–1305), but it does not explain how this seal is different from the one conferred by baptism.

The effects of the sacrament, according to the *Catechism*, are numerous. It marks a Christian as totally belonging to Christ, and it is a "promise of divine protection in the great eschatological trial" (1296); it makes Christians more deeply children of God, it unites them more firmly with Christ, it increases the gifts of the Holy Spirit, and it unites Catholics more firmly with their church; it gives a special strength to spread and defend the faith, to be witnesses to Christ, and never to be ashamed of the way he was put to death (1303). In the scholastic theology of confirmation, receiving these effects *ex opere operato* is tantamount to receiving certain spiritual powers or abilities, which should not be confused with actually using them. The fact that many confirmed Christians do not exhibit these behaviors (for example, many teenagers drop out of church after being confirmed) therefore cannot be used to disprove these claims.

The official theology of confirmation therefore remains somewhat disconnected from experience. At the same time, however, those who work with children, adolescents, and adults who are preparing for the sacramental ceremony often do their best to connect the theology of the sacrament with the experience of those whom they are teaching. For there is a prevailing sense in religious education and catechetics today that if the church's teachings about the sacraments are true, they need to make sense in terms of how people live their lives.

For Further Reading

Charles Davis, *Sacraments of Initiation* (Sheed and Ward, 1964) contains a clear account of the development of baptism and confirmation into separate sacraments.

Anne Field, *New Life* (Servant Publications, 1978) gives a flavor of what early Christians were told by the people who taught and baptized them.

Christopher Kiesling, *Confirmation and Full Life in the Spirit* (St. Anthony Messenger Press, 1973) takes a balanced look at the sacrament after Vatican II.

LaVerne Haas, *Personal Pentecost* (Abbey Press, 1973) views the sacrament as a rite of passage into Christian adulthood.

Michael Scanlan and Anne Therese Shields, *And Their Eyes Were Opened* (Word of Life, 1976) offers a charismatic approach to the sacraments, including confirmation.

Urban Holmes, *Confirmation: The Celebration of Maturity in Christ* (Seabury Press, 1975) assumes that confirmation is for teenagers coming to own their faith.

Peter Monkres and R. Kenneth Ostermiller, *The Rite of Confirmation* (United Church Press, 1995) asks many of the same questions about confirmation in the United Church of Christ that Catholics ask.

For Further Study

History and Theology

Eugene Finnegan, *Confirmation at an Impasse* (Linus Publications, 2011) offers a highly detailed history of the rite and its theology from the patristic era to the Middle Ages.

Marian Bohen, *The Mystery of Confirmation* (Herder and Herder, 1963) shows the historical and theological difficulties in developing a single consistent explanation of the sacrament.

Austin Milner, *The Theology of Confirmation* (Fides Publishers, 1971) gives a good history of the rite and the ways it has been understood.

J. D. C. Fisher, *Confirmation Then and Now* (SPCK, 1978) reviews early anointing and hand-laying practices in order to discuss recent Anglican practices.

Theodore Jungkutz, *Confirmation and the Charismata* (University Press of America, 1983) argues that since the sacrament has been understood in various ways in the past, it can have a variety of meanings in the present.

Kilian McDonnell and George Montague, *Christian Initiation and Baptism in the Holy Spirit* (Liturgical Press, 1991) collects evidence of charismatic gifts from writings in the first eight centuries.

James Dunn, *Baptism in the Holy Spirit* (SCM Press, 1970) connects New Testament evidence to contemporary Pentecostal and charismatic practices.

John Roberto, *Confirmation in the American Catholic Church* (National Conference of Diocesan Directors of Religious Education, 1978) is a commissioned study of the history, theology, and practice of the sacrament in the United States.

Kendig Brubaker Cully, ed., *Confirmation Reexamined* (Morehouse-Barlow, 1982) has articles describing and reflecting on the new confirmation practice in the Episcopal Church.

The Question of When to Confirm

Gerald Austin, *Anointing with the Spirit* (Pueblo, 1985) presents a commentary on the new rite of confirmation and offers ecumenical comparisons.

Paul Turner, *The Meaning and Practice of Confirmation* (Peter Lang, 1987) compares Protestant and Catholic positions taken in the sixteenth century with various positions taken today.

Aidan Kavanagh, *Confirmation: Origins and Reform* (Pueblo, 1988) argues that the rite of confirmation was originally only a dismissal rite performed at baptism by the bishop.

Kathy Brown and Frank Sokol, eds., *Issues in the Christian Initiation of Children* (Liturgy Training Publications, 1989) discusses issues such as the sequence of sacraments and how they are taught.

James Wilde, ed., *When Should We Confirm?* (Liturgy Training Publications, 1989) presents historical and liturgical arguments for confirmation before first communion.

Arthur Kubick, ed., *Confirming the Faith of Adolescents* (Paulist Press, 1991) contains articles in favor of retaining confirmation as a sacrament of mature Christian initiation.

Robert Browning and Roy Reed, *Models of Confirmation and Baptismal Affirmation* (Religious Education Press, 1995) reviews and compares the postbaptismal rites of seven different denominations.

CHAPTER VIII

EUCHARIST

At the time he was betrayed and entered willingly into his Passion, he took bread and, giving thanks, broke it, and gave it to his disciples, saying: Take this, all of you, and eat of it: for this is my body which will be given up for you.

In a similar way, when supper was ended, he took the chalice and, once more giving thanks, he gave it to his disciples, saying: Take this, all of you, and drink from it: for this is the chalice of my blood, the blood of the new and eternal covenant, which will be poured out for you and for many for the forgiveness of sins. Do this in memory of me.

—Eucharistic Prayer II

Christians remain divided about the meaning of Christ's words, "This is my body....This is my blood." Catholics and Orthodox take the words to mean that the eucharistic bread and wine are really his body and blood; most Protestants take them to mean that they are symbolically his body and blood. Catholic biblical scholars marshal impressive arguments proving that Christ meant his words to be taken literally; Protestant scholars examine the same texts and prove just the opposite.

It seems impossible to prove on the basis of the biblical evidence alone how Jesus meant those famous words to be taken. What can be proven, however, is that within a century or so of his death many Christians did in fact take them literally and that they looked upon those who did not as heretics. This understanding persisted in Christianity through the Middle Ages, and it was only at the beginning of the modern era that large numbers rejected the superstitions that had come to surround the eucharist and the traditional doctrine that seemed to support them. This time the forces of orthodoxy were unable to suppress what they regarded as heresy, and from then until now Protestants have generally understood the eucharist differently from the way that Catholics do.

But the word eucharist refers to more than the body and blood of Christ. It comes from the Greek word meaning to give thanks, and in the early church it designated not only the bread and wine but also the ritual of worship that surrounded their use. The history of the eucharist is therefore not just the history of sacramental objects but the history of a sacramental action.

1. Parallels and Precedents

The similarities between various aspects of the eucharist and beliefs and rituals in other religions are numerous. People of many religions claim to experience the presence of gods or spiritual beings, they offer sacrifices to deities and supernatural powers, they commemorate the memory of persons and events in the past, they share ritual meals that have sacramental significance.

REAL PRESENCE

The experience of a transcendent reality, of someone or something beyond the natural world, is not unique to Christianity. It is found in every religion both ancient and modern even though the quality and intensity of the experience may vary and the interpretations given to it are different. Many people can recall times when they felt themselves in the presence of something that seemed more than human, more than natural. It may have been a comforting or a menacing presence, it may have felt like the presence of a personal being or an impersonal force. They may have wondered what it was, or they may have (in their own mind) known what it was. They may have questioned whether it was just in their imagination or whether it came from a source beyond them. But it was a genuine experience.

In most religions such experiences tend to become localizable in time and space. During certain times of the year such as religious festivals the presence of gods or spirits is felt more strongly; during certain times of the day such as moments of prayer the experience of a transcendent presence becomes more pronounced. Sacred mountains and groves, temples and shrines are regarded as places inhabited by supernatural beings and their presence can be felt there. Pictures, statues, and other sacred objects can be so identified with what they represent that the transcendent reality is experienced as there, in the thing itself. Such times, places, and objects are all sacraments in the broad sense, for they open a door to the experience of a transcendent presence that is otherwise absent.

Often sacred times, places, and objects are permanent sacraments to those who understand and believe in their revelatory power. In many primitive religions the sky, the sun, and the moon are perennial symbols of the divine: they have no known beginnings, and their revelatory power can be felt whenever they are beheld. In modern Christianity the cross is a perennial symbol of Christ, and the Bible is the word of God whenever it is read.

But sometimes sacred times, places, and objects have to be consecrated, that is, they have to be "made sacred" before the transcendent can appear through them. Thus festivals commence with an opening ceremony and rituals begin with an initiatory prayer or blessing. Thus monuments are dedicated and churches are consecrated: before they were the handiwork of builders, now they are places where the sacred may be experienced. Thus objects related to prayer and worship are blessed, after which they should no longer be used for profane purposes: sacrificial animals and altars, ritual vestments and ornaments, prayer books and prayer beads. Through the blessing or consecration they are transformed from secular realities into sacred realities, or things through which the sacred can appear to those with faith.

SACRIFICES

In primitive religions (and in some contemporary religions with ancient origins) sacrifices ritually dramatize the meaning of human life in relation to transcendent realities. The relationship is understood as one of dependence, and sacrifices express the sacred insight that life is fragile and insecure and contingent on forces beyond human control. In making sacrifices, therefore, people of various religions acknowledge their dependence on transcendent realities, which are often represented as gods or conceived as supernatural beings. Sacrifices can sometimes express the desire to control the transcendent order of things, to influence the gods as it were; but more often they express the desire to maintain or restore a proper relationship to the acknowledged order, to conform to the will of the gods. Sacrifices like all religious rituals can be formalistic and mechanical, merely expressing the religious beliefs that are held by a society, but for those who enter deeply into the ritual meaning sacrifices can also be sacramental, experientially affecting the attitudes and behavior of the participants.

There have been and still are many kinds of religious sacrifices, but among the more common in the ancient world were gift offerings, shared offerings, and sin offerings. In a gift offering people acknowledged their dependence on a transcendent reality for the things they possessed and enjoyed. The offering was sacrificed completely, that is, it was given entirely to the god by being burned or buried or surrendered in some other way. Such a sacrifice could be an act of gratitude for what the god had given or a gesture of prayer that it might give in return for what it was receiving. In a shared offering people acknowledged their need for union with a transcendent reality in order to live or to live rightly. It was an offering of food, part of which was usually set aside for the god while the rest was eaten by those who participated in the sacrifice. The purpose of such a sacrifice could be to affirm a communal bond between the god and those who shared the sacred meal, or it could be to assimilate the symbolic qualities of the food that was eaten. By eating animals that symbolized strength, courage, wisdom, or swiftness, for example, the participants hoped to acquire those same qualities and came to believe they possessed them. In a sin offering people acknowledged their past disregard of the transcendent reality and their disobedience of the transcendent order. The sacrifice was offered for deliberate disobedience or inadvertent transgression of the moral law, and the sins or guilt of the participants might be symbolically transferred to an animal whose ritual death thus represented the obliteration of their past sins or the eradication of their guilt. Such a sacrifice could be looked upon as paying a debt or soothing the anger of the god, as well as expressing a desire to live rightly in the future.

All three types of sacrifice were practiced in the religion of ancient Israel. The Law of Moses commanded the Israelite farmers to sacrifice the first part of each year's crop as a gift to their God, Yahweh, in gratitude for the harvest and for the land he had given them (Deuteronomy 26). For their shared offerings the Israelites were instructed to burn the fat and vital organs (the parts that had a pleasing fragrance and that symbolized life) before the rest was eaten by the offerer and other guests (Leviticus 3). When offering sacrifice for the forgiveness of sins, the priest was to transfer the people's guilt to the animal by laying his hands on it before it was killed, and on the Day of Atonement each year Israelites were to offer a sacrifice that would remit the guilt for their transgressions of the Law (Leviticus 3, 16). People in the ancient Near East also made sacrifices to the gods to solemnize agreements or covenants made between two parties, and the covenant between Yahweh and his people is represented in the Jewish scriptures as being solemnized by a burnt offering and the pouring of sacrificial blood (Exodus 24).

MEALS

As has just been seen, some sacrifice rituals could also involve eating sacred food, and as a matter of fact most meal rituals in the ancient world were connected with food that had been sacrificed or consecrated in some other way. As a sacramental event the sacred meal was the most personally engaging: it affected all the senses (seeing, hearing, touching, smelling, and tasting) and it also involved memory and imagination, internal sensations of hunger and satisfaction, and social interaction among the participants. Usually the sacramental function of the meal was to affirm and intensify a bond of unity among the participants or between them and others who were not physically present. In Africa, for example, ceremonial meals strengthened the blood kinship among the members of a clan. In eastern Asia families affirmed their continuing relation to ancestors and other departed relatives by sharing certain meals with the spirits of the dead. In some tribal religions sacred meals renewed the unity between the tribe and the god who created it, or between the participants and a transcendent mystery that the meal represented. Each year the Aztecs in Mexico mixed dough with blood and shaped it into the image of one of their gods before sharing it in ritual communion.

In ancient Israel the most important ritual meal was the one that celebrated the Passover, the passing over of Yahweh who slew the firstborn of the Egyptians and the crossing over of the Hebrews from slavery to freedom through the Red Sea. Yahweh had ordered them to sacrifice a lamb and sprinkle its blood on their doorposts to protect them against death, and to eat their last meal in Egypt with unleavened bread since they would not have time to wait for it to rise (Exodus 12). The meal commemorating this event was celebrated every spring, and in Jesus' time it began with a prayer of praise and thanksgiving to God, and a first course of bitter relishes that symbolized the bitterness of the Hebrews' enslavement. Then after the story of the first Passover was read, the meal of roasted lamb was eaten with wine and unleavened bread, over which further prayers of blessing and thanks were offered. The meal ended with a psalm of praise and a final thanksgiving prayer over the last cup of wine.

This Passover supper was fundamentally a sacramental meal, a reenactment of sacred events by means of which those events became real and present to the people who shared it. Through eating the bitter herbs, Jews tasted the bitterness of their ancestors' enslavement in Egypt. Through reclining on couches as only free people were allowed, they sensed the freedom that their God had given them. Through the retelling of the story and the sharing of the meal, they remembered the events of the Exodus and in a way relived those events. For the Passover supper, to devout Jews at least, not only commemorated the past but also made it present. It enabled them to reenter those past events and to experience vividly the meaning of their salvation. And it made the God of Israel present to them in a fuller and richer way than their ordinary awareness of God's presence. This ritual meal was, then, a complex symbol into which Jews could enter and encounter the God of their ancestors. It was a door to the sacred through which they could pass from everyday profane existence into the sacred space and time of the Exodus.

But meals of sacrifice and the Passover supper were not the only ritual meals known to Jews when Jesus was alive. Religious groups within Judaism were accustomed to sharing a meal of fellowship on the day before the sabbath and other religious feasts. Like the Passover supper this fellowship meal began with prayers of thanksgiving and some appetizers or relishes. Those who were present then washed their hands, and after a more formal blessing in which the leader offered thanks to God, broke the bread and distributed it, the meal was served. After the supper there was another washing and then the leader offered a prayer of thanksgiving over a cup of wine that was then passed around to all those present. Finally before returning to their homes, the group sang a psalm together. The groups who attended these suppers also met regularly for religious devotion or works of charity in addition to attending the usual synagogue or temple services. Jesus and his disciples formed one of a number of such groups in ancient Palestine.

2. From the Last Supper to the Liturgy

The evening before he died (the day before the feast of Passover, according to the synoptic gospels) Jesus shared his last fellowship meal with his disciples. During this last supper, however, Jesus departed from the usual ritual in a few ways that Christians would long remember. At some point he took the basin of water kept for ritual hand-washing and washed his disciples' feet as a sign that they should serve one another. When he broke the bread and gave it to his friends, he indicated that it was his body that he was giving to them. And when he said the blessing over the cup of wine, he said it was the cup of a new covenant that they were sharing that night. Such were the simple beginnings of the eucharistic liturgy.

Beginnings

According to the gospel narratives Jesus appeared to his disciples a number of times after his death, and even after these appearances ceased, the disciples continued to sense his presence among them whenever they came together for their weekly meal of fellowship. Now, however, whenever they shared the bread and passed the cup they did it not just as devout Jews but also in memory of him. Like the Passover supper, though, this commemoration was more than a simple memorial. Through the eating of special foods and the retelling of the events that surrounded and followed that last supper, this "Lord's supper" (as it came to be known) was a sacramental meal which evoked not only the memory of those sacred events but also the experience of the risen messiah. The Jewish followers of Jesus continued to attend the temple and synagogue services, but as the breach between them and their religious leaders grew wider, their own small community of believers in Jesus became a new center of their religious life (Acts 2:42–47).

The earliest written record of the last supper of Jesus and the Lord's supper of the early Christians is found in a letter that the apostle Paul sent to the community in Corinth around the year 57. During the quarter of a century after Jesus' death Christians continued to meet for a weekly meal of fellowship, but evidently some of those who did not grow up in the Jewish religion began to take liberties with the supper. They were getting drunk with the wine and not sharing the food they had brought, and Paul tried to correct some of these abuses by reminding his readers of the origin and purpose of their weekly get-together (1 Corinthians 10–11). The cup that they shared was a communion with the blood of Christ and the bread that they broke was a communion with the body of Christ, and so at their meal they were to be united in a single body, not divided into selfish little groups (10:16–18). When they ate and drank together, they were supposed to do it for the glory of God, and so if they were doing it just to have a good time their meals were not really the Lord's supper (10:31; 11:17–22). The Lord's supper was a memorial of the last supper, and so it was not only a celebration of Christ's resurrection but also a commemoration of his death (11:23–26). Those who came to the meal should therefore reflect on what they were doing, so that in their sharing of the bread and the cup they would recognize the body in which they were united. Because they failed to see that they were all members of Christ's body, some of their community were suffering (11:27–32).

Paul's account is interesting both because of its brevity and because of its ambiguity. The only things he mentions about the last supper are Jesus' words over the bread and the wine and the instruction that they were to be taken in memory of him. Some biblical scholars believe that this brevity is due to the fact that when the early Christians retold the story of the last supper they tended to omit the parts of the supper that Jews would be familiar with and to include only the changes that Jesus had made in it. Other scholars note that Paul nowhere claims that the words of Jesus need to be pronounced when Christians gather to share food in his memory. Moreover, there is ambiguity in Paul's use of the word "body": sometimes it refers to the bread, sometimes it refers to the community, and the result is that there is no clear agreement among scholars whether Paul believed that Christ was present in the bread in the same way that he clearly believed that Christ was present in the community (1 Corinthians 12). The meal, the bread, and the cup were undoubtedly sacramental in the sense that by sharing them in memory and imitation of Christ the early Christians experienced a presence of their own risen Lord which was different from their ordinary awareness of him, but that presence seems to have been a pervasive presence, in the group's praying and eating, rather than a localized presence in the food.

This same brevity and ambiguity is found in three of the gospel narratives of the last supper (Matthew 26:26–29; Mark 14:22–25; Luke 22:14–20). Luke's account of Jesus' words over the bread and wine is very close to Paul's, and Matthew's account is very much like Mark's, leading scholars to suspect that there were two different versions of Jesus' words circulating in different communities. All three accounts, however, are similarly brief and omit the other details of that last meal except for words spoken between Jesus and his disciples. There is also some ambiguity to be found in these accounts. Luke like Paul relates Jesus' words over the wine as "This cup is the new covenant in my blood…" and does not clearly identify the wine with the blood of Christ. Matthew and Mark, on the other hand, do seem to make this kind of identification for both the bread and the wine when they relate Jesus' words as "This is my body….This is my blood," but as Protestant scholars are quick to point out, Jesus never actually said those words. The gospels were written in Greek but Jesus spoke Aramaic, and in that language he would have said, "This my body....This my blood," leaving out the copula "is." Thus when the synoptic gospels were written (between AD 65 and 85) Greek-speaking Christians may have already begun to identify the bread and wine with the body and blood of Christ, but it is impossible to prove that Jesus and his Jewish followers ever did so. In fact it is historically more probable that they did not, for the drinking of blood was both culturally repulsive and religiously forbidden to Jews (Leviticus 3:17; Acts 15:29). Moreover, Jews were familiar with the practice of eating symbolic foods at ritual meals such as the Passover supper, and it seems more likely that Jesus was simply extending this practice by giving the bread and wine a new meaning.

What we find in the fourth gospel is very different from what we find in Paul and the other three gospels. Although the author devotes five chapters to the last supper (John 13–17), he does not mention the bread and wine or Jesus' words over them. Instead, the author's understanding of the bread and wine seems to be found in John 6, and if this is correct, then at the time that this gospel was written (around AD 90–100) many Christians did identify the bread and wine with the body and blood of Christ. Some Protestant scholars dispute this, preferring to take Jesus' saying "I am the bread of life" in the same way that everyone takes his saying "I am the light of the world." That is, they contend that Jesus' words should be taken symbolically or figuratively rather than literally. Most Catholic scholars, on the other hand, point out that the gospel was written at a time when some Christians influenced by gnostic philosophy were refusing to take basic Christian beliefs literally. Gnosticism taught (among other things) that matter was evil, and its Christian adherents claimed that since God would never allow contamination with human flesh Jesus was not really human but God appearing as human. The fourth gospel was written partly in reaction to this view and this is why John places such great emphasis on the literal humanity and divinity of Christ. Of course the gnostic Christians also claimed that the Lord's supper could not literally be a sharing in Christ's body and blood, and seen in this light the "bread of life" discourse in John 6:22–66 seems to be a direct attack against this view. Even granting that this discourse is most likely a composition of the author and not a direct transcription of a speech by Jesus, it probably still reflects what John and other Christians at the time believed about the bread and wine taken in the Lord's supper: "My flesh is real food and my blood is real drink. He who eats my flesh and drinks my blood lives in me and I in him" (6:55–56).

By the end of the first century, therefore, Christians were beginning to relate the presence of Christ in the Lord's supper directly to the bread and wine used in the ritual meal. But this was not the only development in the early church's understanding of the Lord's supper. The first generations of Christians, especially those with Jewish backgrounds, relied extensively on ideas and images from their own tradition to explain what the bread and wine and the meal meant. Some of these interpretations are alluded to in the New Testament itself. For example, the bread was related to the manna that God gave the Israelites in the desert (Exodus 16; John 6:30–33) and the drink to the water that miraculously flowed from the rock (Exodus 17:1–7; 1 Corinthians 10:3–4). Jews who had been awaiting a messiah sometimes pictured the final times as a great banquet that God would share with the chosen people, and the communal meal shared in the presence of Christ seemed to some to be the fulfillment of that expectation (Isaiah 25, 55; Luke 22:15–20).

The most long lasting interpretations of the Lord's supper, however, were those that related it to the notion of sacrifice. Very early those who believed in Jesus as the messiah came to understand his crucifixion as a sacrificial death, an offering of himself to God, and because the Lord's supper commemorated his death as well as his triumph over death they began to view it as a sacrificial meal. The Lord's supper was the Christian continuation of Jesus' last supper and the synoptic gospel accounts of that supper refer to the blood of Christ that would be "poured out" for others. Matthew speaks of its being shed "for the forgiveness of sins" as in a sin offering, and both the gospels and Paul refer to a "new covenant" sealed in blood, which is an allusion to the idea of covenant sacrifice. The sharing of food at the Lord's supper made it possible to think of it in connection with the Jewish shared offering, and the close relationship between the last supper and the feast of Passover suggested similarities between the slaying of Jesus and the sacrifice of the paschal lamb. The Epistle to the Hebrews developed the idea of Christ's sacrificial death at great length, and it introduced the concept that Christ was both the priest who offered the sacrifice and the victim that was offered to God (4:12–10:18). The author of this work also portrayed Christ's priesthood as everlasting, suggesting that his sacrifice continued forever. And in time, as the fellowship meal was abandoned and Christian worship consisted mainly of prayers and the sharing of bread and wine, the conception of this sacramental action as a kind of sacrifice, continuing or participating in the sacrifice of Christ, became predominant in Christian theology.

EARLY DEVELOPMENTS

The disappearance of the fellowship meal from Christian communal worship was gradual. One reason for its discontinuance may have been the kinds of excesses found in Corinth, but it may also have been that the growth in the size of the groups simply made it impractical. From the beginning, the followers of Jesus met in homes—probably the larger homes of the community's more well-to-do members—but after a while even these would have been too small for everyone to have a full dinner. What remained in place of the real meal was a symbolic meal sometimes referred to as "eucharist" by early second-century writers, so named because the prayers that surrounded the sharing of the bread and wine were mostly prayers of praise and thanks to God just as they had been in the Jewish fellowship meal. The Greek verb *eucharistein* means to give thanks. Around the year 150 the real meal, when there was one, was usually held after the thanksgiving or eucharist service, and by 200 such fellowship meals were held only infrequently and on special occasions.

Another form of worship that derived from the Jewish Christian community was the sabbath morning prayer service. When it was adopted by non-Jewish Christians it retained its original format and consisted of an opening greeting by the leader ("The Lord be with you"…"And with your spirit" are Hebrew forms of address), readings from the scriptures, a sermon, prayers of petition, and a formal dismissal. By the second century, however, it had been transferred from Saturday (the Jewish sabbath) to Sunday (the day of the resurrection). Sometimes it was followed immediately by the thanksgiving service, but it could also be held separately, with the eucharist being shared in the evening. For reasons that are not explained in any early documents, the preferred time for Christians to gather for worship gradually shifted from evening to morning.

The thanksgiving service developed into a slightly longer ritual during the second century and consisted of an opening greeting by the leader, the bringing of bread and wine and other offerings by the congregation, prayers of praise and thanks to God over the gifts, the breaking of the bread and the sharing of the bread and wine, and a dismissal. Usually a reference to Christ's words at the last supper were inserted into the prayers of praise and thanks, but since the whole action was done in memory of Christ this was not always included. Thus at least some early forms of eucharistic worship did not contain what were to become known as the words of institution: "This is my body….This is my blood….Do this in memory of me."

About the year 112 Pliny the Younger, proconsul of Bythinia in Asia Minor, interrogated some people accused of being Christians and sent a letter to the emperor Trajan asking what to do about them. In his letter he reported that they met before dawn on a fixed day each week, sang a hymn to Christ their god, and bound themselves by an oath to do no wrong; then later that same day they met again for a religious meal. Around the same period, Ignatius, the second bishop of Antioch, wrote letters to other churches in which he mentioned that Sunday (the first day of the week) had been chosen to take the place of the sabbath (the seventh day of the week) and that only the bishop should preside over the eucharistic worship. The *Didache* or *Teaching of the Twelve Apostles*, a Syrian work written before 150, contains a eucharistic prayer without the words of institution and refers to the weekly meal as a sacrifice. It is from documents such as these that we get some idea of what early Christian worship was like.

In the middle of the second century a Palestinian philosopher and convert to Christianity named Justin wrote a defense of Christian practices in which he briefly described two kinds of eucharistic services found in Rome, one that came after the yearly initiation and one that was held weekly. In the former there was an offering of bread and a cup of wine and water, prayers of praise and thanksgiving by the leader to which the people responded "Amen," and a partaking of the bread and wine by all present. The latter was held on "the day of the Sun" and was joined to a prayer service. It contained readings from the writings of the prophets and apostles, an explanation or exhortation by the leader, the same prayers of praise and thanksgiving, and the sharing of the eucharistic meal. Portions of the bread were then sent to those who were absent, and a collection was taken up for the poor. As Justin describes them, the pattern of these services was set but there were no set forms for the prayers. The eucharistic or thanksgiving prayer did, however, contain a commemoration of the redemption and the words of institution.

The most complete description of early eucharistic worship in the western empire was set out in *The Apostolic Tradition*, a liturgical work usually attributed to a Roman Christian named Hippolytus who wrote in the early third century. The book outlines the order of service for the consecration of a bishop and for the initiation of catechumens, each of which was followed by a eucharistic service. The pattern of these was basically the same as that given by Justin, and although Hippolytus included examples of prayers that might be used, he emphasized that the presiding bishop should not memorize these examples but should pray according to his own abilities. The third part of *The Apostolic Tradition* also contains directions for a separate fellowship meal that was not considered to be a form of eucharistic worship. Tertullian, a North African who lived in Rome about this time, mentioned in some of his writings that Christians met for the eucharist before dawn on other days as well as Sundays, and that those who wished could take the eucharistic bread home to eat before their own meals. A half century later Cyprian of Carthage in some of his letters indicated that Christians in his area met for the eucharist daily in small groups, sometimes in connection with the evening meal.

During the first three centuries, then, the form of Christian worship evolved from a fellowship meal to a ritual meal, with prayers in the general style of the earlier Jewish thanksgiving prayers but with no set words except the words of institution. It evolved differently in different parts of the empire and in the different cities within those regions, but the basic pattern was the same in all places: an offering of gifts of bread and wine, a thanksgiving prayer over these gifts, a breaking of the bread, and a reception of the bread and wine by all present. The eucharistic service was presided over by the leader of the community, and according to the texts that have survived the prayers offered were always directed to the Father in thanksgiving for God's gifts and especially for the redemption brought by Christ. But the eucharistic worship itself was always that of the community, gathered together under the leadership of their spiritual shepherd who prayed with them rather than for them. It was a sacramental experience of communal worship offered in the presence of Christ, who became present as the community prayed and worshiped together. And what made the bread and wine sacred was the entire ritual action that repeated and commemorated what Christ had done at his last supper.

During this period as well, the interpretation of this sacramental action as a sacrifice and sacrificial meal grew more popular, partly because sacrifice was a familiar form of worship in the ancient world, and partly in response to the Roman charge that Christians were atheists because they did not offer sacrifices to any gods. As early as the turn of the second century Ignatius called the meeting place of Christians a place of sacrifice, and Justin in defending the practices of Christians referred to the eucharist as the sacrifice of the church. Around the year 200 Irenaeus spoke of Christians as being a priestly people who offered a new covenant sacrifice to God, and Tertullian described the whole service in terms of offering and sacrifice around an altar. Later in the third century Cyprian explained that both the leader and the people offered the sacrifice but that Christ was the real priest in whose sacrifice they all participated. Other documents of the same period echoed the idea that when Christians offered the eucharistic bread and wine they united themselves with the self-offering of Christ and his Father and became participants in his redemptive sacrifice.

But if Christ was the priest he was also the sacrificial victim. During their eucharistic worship Christians experienced the presence of Christ, and in their prayers of thanksgiving they understood themselves as praying with him and in offering the bread and wine to God. But Jesus had also referred to the bread and wine as his body and blood, and during the second century this identification grew stronger. John's gospel had already been written to refute the notion that Jesus was not a real human being, and some of the early fathers continued to fight against gnostic ideas by stressing the humanity of Christ and the reality of his body and blood in the eucharist. According to Ignatius, "The eucharist is the flesh and blood of our savior, the flesh that suffered for our sins and that the Father raised from the dead" (*Letter to the Smyrnaeans* 6). Justin said Christians believed that "the food that has been made eucharist through the prayer formed out of the words of Christ, and that nourishes and becomes our flesh and blood, is the flesh and blood of the same Jesus who was made incarnate" (*Apology* I, 66). Irenaeus in arguing against the gnostics wrote, "When the bread from the earth receives the invocation of God, it is no longer common bread but eucharist, having both an earthly and a heavenly reality"; the bread and wine are "the body of the Lord and the cup of his blood" (*Against Heresies* IV, 18). And Cyprian argued that those who repented for having denied their faith in time of persecution should be readmitted to the eucharist, "For how can they be expected to shed their blood for Christ unless they are allowed to share in his blood?" (*Letters* 67).

For the early fathers eucharistic worship was both an expression and a source of Christian unity. Those who joined together in common prayer were united in their worship of God and their acceptance of Jesus as their Lord. Their ritual action symbolized their unity with Christ in his passion and resurrection, and their coming together under the leadership of the bishop expressed their unity with each other and with the whole church. Their sharing of a single loaf reinforced their belief that they were indeed one body, and their identification of the bread with the body of Christ helped them to understand why they were united in a single spirit. Their sharing of the cup signified their willingness to drink the cup of suffering and martyrdom, and their identification of the wine with the blood of Christ made them more conscious of their participation in the sacrifice of

Christ. In their eucharistic worship they experienced unity with each other in the living presence of Christ: they experienced it because they believed it, and they believed it because they experienced it. Their ritual action both expressed and strengthened what they felt and believed.

LATER DEVELOPMENTS

Between the fourth and sixth centuries Christian eucharistic worship evolved from a comparatively brief and simple ritual meal into a richly elaborate ceremonial liturgy. In 313 Constantine lifted the legal ban on Christian worship and Christians became free to assemble in public. Both he and later emperors viewed Christianity as a means of bringing religious unification to an increasingly disunited empire, and in 380 Theodosius proclaimed Christianity as the official religion of the Roman state. Eucharistic worship thus became a state function as well as a religious ritual.

But the influences on Christian worship were not simply external. Early in the fourth century a North African churchman named Arius popularized the idea that Christ was not fully divine even though he came from God. According to Arius, Jesus was a superior being, the human incarnation of God's word, so he was more than an ordinary human being and in some sense divine, but he was not equal to God the Father. Most of Christianity, however, had for a long time considered Jesus as divine, and if he was not to be regarded as a second god he had to be somehow identified with the one God. To prevent the mounting theological debate from splitting his empire, Constantine summoned Christian bishops to a council at Nicaea to decide the matter. In 325 the council declared the orthodox teaching to be that Christ was "one in being" (in Greek, *homoousios*, and in Latin, *consubstantialis*) with the Father, equal to but not completely identical with God the Father. A later council declared the same to be true of the Holy Spirit, and Arius' teaching was condemned as heretical. That settled the doctrinal question as far as most bishops were concerned, but Arian ideas continued to spread in some areas and to counteract them many of the church fathers now stressed the divinity of Christ in their sermons and theological writings. The eucharistic worship of the period also reflected this change in emphasis: instead of sharing in Christ's prayer of thanksgiving to the Father, Christians began to pray directly to Christ as a member of the divine Trinity.

This change in Christian worship also led to a change in the way to which it was referred. Just as the usual name for Christian worship changed from "Lord's supper" to "eucharist" when the communal meal was dropped, now the words "offering" and "liturgy" became more common names for the ritual action. The word "eucharist" henceforth designated not the act of thanksgiving but the sacred elements of bread and wine that were offered to God. "Liturgy" comes from a Greek word that originally referred to any work done for the people, a service done for the common welfare. And as Christian worship developed more and more into a religious service done by the bishop and his assistants for the congregation, it too came to be referred to as a *leitourgia*, a liturgy.

During the period when Christianity had been a clandestine religious movement, eucharistic worship had developed a variety of styles that reflected the personal tastes of the bishops who presided over them as well as the cultural differences in the various parts of the empire. Now, when Christianity emerged into the public forum, each local church continued to preserve its own variations even though the population centers of the empire set the predominant style for the regions that surrounded them. In the east, Jerusalem, Constantinople, Antioch, and Alexandria had the greatest liturgical influence; in the west, there were two principal styles, the Roman and the Gallic. The Roman liturgy provided the pattern for Italy and North Africa; the Gallic liturgy was found in the provinces north and west of Italy, known as Gallia or Gaul in the days of the empire. Still, despite these variations the liturgies always kept the standard parts of the earlier eucharistic service: a bringing of gifts of bread and wine, a prayer over the gifts that included a recalling of the last supper, and a distribution of the bread and wine to the congregation.

Whatever changes were made in the liturgies, then, they were always additions to these standard actions or variations in the prayers that accompanied them. Very early in the development of the patristic liturgies the prayer service of readings and a sermon became a standard preparation for the weekly eucharistic service. Adult catechumens were allowed to attend this part of the liturgy, but they were dismissed after the sermon because only the faithful were allowed to witness the mystery of the eucharist and receive communion. The individual changes and variations within the liturgies themselves were many; most of them were short lived but some of them eventually found a place in the standardized liturgies of the later Catholic and Orthodox churches. Most of them too were additional prayers and ceremonies that lengthened Christian worship from less than an hour to two and sometimes to even four hours. Some of these were the results of political developments, others were the result of theological developments, still others resulted from episcopal or cultural preferences.

Politically, Christians were now free to worship in public and the growing numbers of converts made it necessary to build public places of worship. Constantine set an example by financing a large meeting hall for the congregation of Rome built in the style of the basilica, a rectangular building with a raised floor at one end that was used for ceremonies of state. Even though the basilica style was more suited to watching a ritual than participating in it, it soon became the dominant form of church architecture throughout Christendom. Moreover, as congregations grew larger their church interiors showed the signs of increasing wealth: walls were richly painted or covered with mosaics, ceilings were gilded, large marble altars took the place of tables, gold and jeweled crosses replaced wooden ones, bronze chandeliers provided light, gold and silver plates and chalices became standard. For just as the basilica had originally been designed for official state ceremonies, the new liturgy that was placed in it was becoming an official public ritual.

Fairly early in his reign Constantine gave bishops the authority to act as judges in civil suits since they were usually well educated and respected by their people. After the Roman custom they were given signs of their rank—a special cape, headgear, footwear, and a ring—and were expected to wear them at public functions. It was the first time that the clergy began to dress differently from the rest of the people, and even after the fall of Rome they kept their distinctive clothing as a sign of their status. Judges were also entitled to special ceremonial honors—to sit on a throne, to be accompanied by torches and incense in procession, to be greeted with a genuflection as a sign of respect—and since worship was a public function, these elements too were added to the liturgy.

One reason why the liturgy could become so elaborate was that Sunday, which had formerly been an ordinary working day, was made a day of rest by Constantine in 321 and Christians were suddenly free to make their worship services as long as they pleased. In addition, as Christianity became more popular, new festival days were added to the calendar and celebrated with liturgies. In the west a day in honor of Christ's birth replaced the Roman birthday of the invincible Sun on December 25, and in the east a day honoring the appearance of Christ on earth replaced the old Egyptian epiphany of the sun god Osiris on January 6. Christians had always celebrated Easter and Pentecost as special feast days, and in time new days were added to commemorate the ascension and other events in the life of Christ, to honor the apostles and the early martyrs, and to commemorate the building of churches and the ordination of bishops. Most of these were originally local feasts and many of them remained such, but some of them came to be adopted by churches throughout the empire. By the end of the fourth century many basilicas offered liturgies on almost every day of the week, although these were less well attended than the Sunday liturgies.

Many of the additions and changes in the liturgy were simply extensions of previous practices. Prayers were multiplied to include references to the Old Testament, the life of Christ, and the history of the church. Petitions for God's blessing and protection covered the emperor and the government, the local congregation and the universal church, special benefactors and persons in special need. The bringing of bread and wine turned into a procession of gifts in which people also brought oil and wax for liturgical use as well as food and clothing for the clergy and the support of the poor. Toward the end of the fourth century it became customary to recite the Lord's Prayer before the distribution of communion: "Give us this day our daily bread...."

Some of the changes, however, were the result of theological developments, and among these the reaction against Arianism had the greatest impact. As already mentioned, prayers once addressed to God the Father began to be addressed to Christ or to the Trinity, and in doxologies or hymns of praise Christ was put on a level with the Father and the Holy Spirit. Many eastern churches had prefaced their liturgies with a short penitential ritual, but this now developed into a litany of prayers each ending with "Lord, have mercy" or "Christ, have mercy." In the fifth century this custom was introduced into western liturgies but the prayers were often omitted, leaving only the short phrases asking Christ for divine mercy. Finally, the identification of the bread and wine with Christ and the identification of Christ with God began to cause a decline in the reception of communion as fewer people felt worthy or willing to risk direct contact with the creator and judge of the universe.

Generally speaking, the liturgy was celebrated in the common language of the people, and at the beginning of the patristic period the common language of the Roman Empire was Greek. But late in the fourth century universal knowledge of Greek declined, and so the liturgy was translated into a number of languages in the east and into Latin in the west. With this change in language came further changes in the names for the western liturgy. Theologically it was often designated as the "offering" or "oblation," referring to the offering of prayers and the sacred bread and wine to God. One description of the liturgy was *missarum solemnia* or "ceremonies of dismissals," referring to the dismissal of the catechumens after the sermon and the dismissal of the rest of the congregation after communion. Eventually this name was shortened to *missa* or "mass," and it became the most commonly used name in the west even though after the fifth century almost everyone was baptized in infancy and the dismissal of the catechumens was dropped from the liturgy.

Another change in the liturgy was that the prayers and the directions for performing it began to be written down. The length and complexity of episcopal liturgies in the fourth and fifth centuries changed the character of the liturgy from a spontaneous expression of worship to a stately ritual of recited prayers and organized activities. Some of the church fathers were liturgists as well as theologians, and liturgies like those composed by John Chrysostom and Basil the Great were magnificent arrangements of prayer, song, and ceremony dedicated to the worship of God. The ornate style of eastern worship can still be seen in Orthodox churches today, since many of their liturgies derive from the patristic period, but in the west the liturgy continued to evolve through the Middle Ages. Today the Roman liturgy has been greatly simplified, but in the sixth century the differences in style between the Roman mass and the eastern liturgy were not so great, and we can get a glimpse of the liturgy of the period from the Gregorian sacramentary, which describes a papal mass around the year 600.

On Sunday morning the pope rode on horseback from his residence to the basilica, accompanied by a solemn procession of the clergy who were to assist him. He dismounted and vested at the church door, and when he entered the church a psalm was sung as the procession moved toward the sanctuary. He was greeted by a kiss of peace and then he prostrated himself briefly before the altar. When he arose a choir of monks sang first the penitential "Lord, have mercy" and then a hymn of glory to God, after which the pope chanted an opening prayer. A subdeacon read the epistle and the choir responded with a chanted prayer, then a deacon read the gospel accompanied by incense and two torches. Following the sermon (if there was one) a cloth was spread on the altar while another psalm was sung, and the pope received offerings from the nobles while his assistants received those of the common people. The pope then washed his hands and went to the altar where the communion loaves and chalice were waiting. He and the other clergy gathered around the altar for the solemn eucharistic prayer, at the conclusion of which the archdeacon lifted the chalice while a doxology was chanted. After the recitation of the Lord's Prayer the pope gave the kiss of peace to his assistants who in turn passed it to the remaining clergy and the people. Then he broke off the first piece of bread and communion was distributed by rank, first to the clergy and then to the nobles and the other lay people. Communion was received standing, the bread being placed in the hand and the wine being sipped through a small tube, and again all the while a psalm was sung. At the end there was a short prayer of thanksgiving and a dismissal of the congregation, followed by the final procession out of the church.

Even from this brief description it can be seen that the liturgy was a predominantly clerical affair, centered on the bishop and his attendant priests and deacons, and accompanied by monks who led the singing. Lay people still had a role to play in the liturgy, responding to the prayers and joining in the singing at various points, bringing their donations to the altar, and receiving communion if they wished; but for many of them the liturgy was something to attend and to watch rather than something to participate in intimately. The sheer size of the basilica and the crowd it held made it impossible for most people to see or hear much of what was going on, and the ceremonial pomp with its torches and incense and processions gave the impression that they were there to witness a divine spectacle rather than to share in a commemorative meal. The patristic solemn liturgy was still an act of religious worship, but its character had shifted from what it had been when small groups of Christians gathered around a table for a thanksgiving service.

This shift in the character of Christian worship was accompanied by a corresponding shift in its interpretation. Beginning in the fourth century there was a growing tendency to give allegorical meanings to various parts of the ceremony, and some of the eastern bishops were especially fond of explaining the liturgy to their people in this way. Theodore of Mopsuestia, for example, in one of his catechetical sermons explained that the bringing out of the bread and wine represented Christ being led to his passion, that their being offered to God symbolized Christ being offered on the cross to his Father, that their resting on the altar was like the resting of Christ's body in the tomb, that the invocation of the Holy Spirit over them corresponded to the transformation of his dead body into an immortal and incorruptible body, and that their being given in communion to the faithful paralleled the way he had come to his disciples after the resurrection. The liturgy could thus be seen as a sacramental representation of Christ's passion and resurrection; but it could also be seen as a representation of an eternal heavenly liturgy offered by the Son to the Father. According to John Chrysostom, during the eucharistic prayer this invisible reality became mystically present and even the angels came to worship: "The entire sanctuary and the space around the altar are filled with the heavenly powers who come to honor Him who is present on the altar" (*On the Priesthood* VI, 4).

Few of the fathers were philosophers but many of them shared the Greek philosophical outlook of Plato and Plotinus, which viewed reality as having two dimensions of depth. The first dimension was the physical universe of tangible objects and visible actions, but behind this laid a metaphysical realm of invisible realities that could be felt and perceived by the human spirit. To the Greeks this seemed to be a plausible explanation for the fact that people looked at concrete individual objects or actions but called them by abstract and general names like "tree" or "motion." It was as though the human eye saw one thing and the human mind saw another. And so the fathers who lived in this philosophical milieu were quite comfortable with the notion that what they spiritually perceived and experienced in the liturgy were perceptions and experiences of metaphysical realities.

For the liturgies, despite their differences from the fellowship meals of the earliest Christians, were still sacramental. They still had a power to awaken in their participants a sense of the sacred and an experience of a divine presence. Indeed the splendor of the ceremony, the magnificence of the surroundings, the glitter of the altar and the vestments, the solemnity of the prayers, the resonance of the music, the aroma of the incense, and the presence of so many people gathered in a common faith for a common purpose—all these contributed to a total sacramental effect that men like the fathers, who stood at the very center of the liturgy and experienced it all, could not deny. The liturgy could make the sacred time of Christ's passion and resurrection present now; it could make the sacred space of heaven palpably real; it could make the sacred meaning of submission to God in total self-sacrifice a living experience. It was out of their participation in liturgical worship, then, that the fathers developed their theologies of the liturgy, and they exhorted both the catechumens and the faithful in their churches to enter as deeply as possible into the experience of the liturgy so that they too might become aware of the spiritual realities that it represented and revealed.

From the middle of the fourth century the spiritual realities that received the greatest attention in the writings of the fathers were divine presence and holy sacrifice. The sense of presence was still related to Christ, experienced now not as glorified messiah but as almighty God, and now increasingly focused on the sacred elements of bread and wine. And the sense of sacrifice changed from its being one that was offered in the felt presence of Jesus to the Father to its being one in which Christ's death on the cross was made present by the power of the Holy Spirit. The liturgy was thus the celebration of these sacred *mysteria*, experienced as present in and through the *sacramenta* of bread and wine, prayer and offering (see page 31).

But at what moment in the liturgy did Christ become experientially present? The earlier fathers had not been very specific, suggesting that his presence was felt all during the short eucharistic service. When this service came to be regularly preceded by the prayer service, the presence of Christ began to be related to the eucharistic or thanksgiving prayer that commenced with the offering of bread and wine to God and ended with their distribution as communion. In time, however, the beginning of Christ's mystical presence came to be specified even further. Among other things the eucharistic prayer contained a remembrance of the last supper which included the words of institution, and this was followed by a prayer asking the Holy Spirit to come down upon and sanctify the sacred elements. In the west the beginning of Christ's presence was felt in the prayer of remembrance and ultimately in the speaking of the words of institution. In the east, however, these words eventually were understood as a mere memorial of the last supper, and the beginning of Christ's presence came to be felt during the invocation of the Holy Spirit.

As the liturgical experience of the presence of Christ differed from west to east, so did the theological interpretation of that experience. The western fathers understood the words "This is my body....This is my blood" as the words of God, and they attributed to them the creative power of God's word. The tendency to do this went back at least to the time of Justin in the middle of the second century, but by the end of the fourth century it had become an accepted doctrine. The idea found its clearest expression in Ambrose of Milan: "This bread was in fact bread before the sacramental words were spoken, but at the moment of consecration it becomes the flesh of Christ. We can establish this truth by examining the words of consecration themselves. Before the consecration the words are those of the priest. He offers praise to God, he prays for the congregation, for the rulers, and for all other people. But when he is about to produce the venerable sacrament the priest stops using his own words and starts using the words of Christ. It is therefore the words of Christ that produce this sacrament, words such as those through which he created all things. So if the words of the Lord Jesus are powerful enough to make nonexistent things come into being, how much more effective must they be in changing what already exists into something else! Therefore, before the consecration the bread is not the body of Christ but after the consecration it now is the body of Christ" (*On the Sacraments* 13–20, paraphrased). Thus, for Ambrose the words of institution were also words of consecration, which when spoken made the bread and wine sacred. This same idea was echoed by Augustine of Hippo: "Once the bread that you see on the altar is sanctified by the word of God, it is the body of Christ. And once the chalice is sanctified by the word of God, what the chalice contains is the blood of Christ" (*Sermons* 227).

Some eastern fathers like John Chrysostom and Gregory of Nyssa shared this interpretation but others like Cyril of Jerusalem did not, and in the long run it was the latter view that prevailed in the east. According to Cyril, "We pray that God in his mercy will send his Holy Spirit down upon the gifts lying before him so that the Spirit might make the bread the body of Christ and the wine the blood of Christ, because if the Holy Spirit touches anything it is certainly sanctified and changed" (*Catechesis* 23, 7). Thus both views were found during the patristic period, but in the eighth century the eastern theologian John of Damascus examined the liturgical texts then in use and concluded that the words of Jesus became effective only when the Holy Spirit was called down upon the bread and wine. Because of the influence of John's authoritative study of the Greek fathers, the words of institution came to be regarded as a narrative, and in the Orthodox churches the transformation of the bread and wine came to be located in the invocation of the Holy Spirit.

In both the east and west, however, as soon as the bread and wine were made sacred they were understood to be the body and blood of Christ not in a metaphorical sense but in a metaphysical sense. After this consecration Christ was understood to be really present in the sacred elements, and his presence was experienced as a mystical reality. Most of the fathers also continued to see the sharing of the bread and wine in communion as a cause of unity with Christ and the church. Thus Cyril in the east urged the newly baptized: "Let us share in the body and blood of Christ with complete conviction. The body is given to you in the likeness of bread and the blood is given in the likeness of wine, so that by sharing in the body and blood of Christ you may become one body and one blood with Christ" (*Mystagogical Catechesis* III, 8). And Augustine in the west expressed this same idea even more vividly: "If you are the body of Christ and his members, it is your mystery that has been placed on the altar of the Lord; you receive your own mystery" (*Sermons* 272). The liturgical experience of the fathers included both an experience of union with Christ and an awareness of unity with those who participated in eucharistic worship.

But the patristic reaction against Arianism and the identification of Christ with God also led the fathers to speak about the actual presence of God in the eucharist. Thus Augustine wrote that the eucharist was not only to be received but also worshiped: "Because he lived in the flesh and it is this flesh that he has given us to eat for our salvation, no one should eat this flesh if he has not first adored it" (*On the Psalms* 98, 9). And in the east the eucharistic prayer over the elements came to be regarded as such an awe-inspiring ritual that it had to be performed in profound silence. John Chrysostom referred to the altar as a "table of holy fear" and spoke of the mysteries that became present on it as "frightful," demanding "reverence and trembling." The effect of this emphasis on the divine presence, however, was more negative than positive, and lay people began to have doubts about receiving communion at the liturgy. Chrysostom himself complained, "We stand before the altar in vain; no one comes to partake" (*Homily on Ephesians* 3, 4). And Ambrose in the west found it necessary to exhort his people to receive communion frequently and not to fall into the habit that the Greeks had of receiving only once a year.

The patristic emphasis on the sacrificial nature of the liturgy also contributed to the trend away from communion, since a sacrifice could be offered to God without everyone partaking of the sacred food. The bishop offered the sacrifice on behalf of the people, and in this sense it was always an offering of the entire congregation whether or not they ate the bread and drank the wine. And the sacrificial victim was the second person of the blessed Trinity, so there could be no doubt that it was a worthy and acceptable sacrifice whether or not the Son of God was received in communion.

So the interpretation of Christian worship as a type of sacrifice remained, but in the fourth and fifth centuries it came to be regarded less as a shared offering of thanksgiving and more as an atonement offering for sin. The idea that in the liturgy Christ was both priest and victim was not lost, but gradually the role of Christ as priest became more associated with the actions of the bishop and the role of Christ as victim became more associated with the bread and wine that were offered and then "destroyed" by being consumed. In this way the part that Christ was conceived to play in Christian worship gradually shifted from an active one to a passive one: instead of offering the sacrifice of praise and thanksgiving in and with the community that was his body, now he was thought of as being offered by the church to God the Father. Earlier generations of Christians had shared their eucharistic meal in the felt presence of the resurrected Christ, who represented the ultimate achievement of God's salvation from death to life.

Now those who attended the liturgy experienced the presence of Christ as the God-man who was sacrificed to ultimately achieve their salvation. The liturgy was turning into a door to the sacred space and time of the crucifixion, and accordingly the fathers spoke of it as a symbolic representation of the passion. Those who fully participated in the liturgy mystically participated in that sacred event, and by spiritually uniting themselves with Christ on the altar they also experienced its benefits: union with God and redemption from sin.

For the fathers of the church, then, the eucharistic liturgy both represented the mysteries of redemption and made them present to those who consciously entered into the experience of liturgical worship. The liturgy was filled with sacramental symbols which revealed the mysteries that they signified, making it possible to be in contact with the divine realities of Christ's redemptive death and resurrected presence in bread and wine. It was a participation in Christ's sacrifice of himself to the Father through which Christians became one with Christ and one with each other in offering themselves to God. As Augustine put it, the visible sacrifice was a sacrament of an invisible sacrifice, their interior surrender to God.

The general population, however, did not always share this interior appreciation of the liturgy. The wholesale conversion of the Roman Empire in the fourth century, the baptism of Christians from infancy in the fifth century, and the mass baptisms of the Germanic peoples beginning in the sixth century meant that many attended the liturgy because of custom rather than conviction. For them the liturgy was a public religious function rather than a personal religious action, an act of formal worship rather than an act of deliberate worship, the preaching of the bishops notwithstanding. But the words of the fathers remained even though the character of the liturgy changed, and the theology of the liturgy that grew out of their experience of interior worship remained even though people's experience of external worship was different from theirs.

3. The Mass and Eucharist in the Middle Ages

The style of the eastern liturgy did not change much after the sixth century; the culture of the Byzantine Roman Empire remained relatively stable throughout the Middle Ages even though its size was considerably reduced by the expansion of the religion of Islam in the seventh and eighth centuries. The churches in the east continued to use the liturgies of the great fathers, and to a large extent they continue to do so today. In the west, however, the situation was different. In Europe eucharistic worship continued to evolve until the sixteenth century, when Rome imposed liturgical uniformity on the Catholic church and the reformers developed non-traditional forms of worship within the Protestant churches.

CHANGES IN PRACTICE

The greatest single change in the western liturgy was the development of the private mass. Eucharistic worship during the first Christian centuries had primarily been a communitarian experience. For each congregation there was only one Sunday service, led by the bishop; later, in each basilica, there was only one altar and the bishop presided at every liturgy. Even in the fifth century when additional services were provided for those who could not attend the bishop's liturgy, each one was a service of public worship performed by a designated priest with assisting clergy. But in the patristic period bishops also began to celebrate the liturgy on weekdays in commemoration of martyrs and saints and events in the life of Christ, and in time there was such a commemoration for almost every day of the year. In time, too, especially as the idea of the liturgy as a sacrifice became dominant, the eucharist was sometimes offered for special reasons such as good weather or a good harvest, or the ending of an epidemic or war. When individuals asked to have their personal intentions remembered during the eucharistic prayer, they normally provided the gifts for the offertory procession, and in exchange masses were offered on days of weddings or funerals, on their anniversaries, for a safe journey, for recovery from sickness, or for similar reasons. These commemorative and petitionary liturgies came to be known as "votive" masses (from the Latin word meaning promised or devoted), and by the sixth century they outnumbered the regular Sunday liturgies. But votive masses were not yet private masses since they were usually attended by at least part of the local congregation.

The private mass, the eucharist offered by a single priest with no attending congregation, began in the monasteries and in the mission territories to which the monks were sent. Originally the monasteries had been lay institutions and visiting priests led the liturgy for them, but in the sixth century monks began to be sent as missionaries into northern Europe, and if they were to bring the mass and the sacraments they had to be ordained. Soon many monasteries were filled with great numbers of priests who could not all gather around the chapel altar to celebrate the liturgy together, and those who wanted to offer the eucharistic sacrifice daily began to do so privately. The monks naturally carried this practice with them to their mission fields where they often worked alone, and in time the "low" mass, a liturgy led by a single priest with perhaps one or two lay assistants, became the norm in most of Europe. On Sundays and feast days it was a form of public worship but on other days it was a private mass, offered out of devotion or for special intentions even when no congregation was present.

The second great factor in the development of the western liturgy was not a change at all but just the opposite. When the eastern churches sent missionaries north into the Slavic territories, the Bible and the liturgy were translated into the languages of the new converts, but this did not happen in the west. Wherever the eucharistic sacrifice was offered it was said in Latin, and since few but the clergy understood that language, the mass for most people became a religious performance to watch and listen to rather than a liturgy to participate in. Even the spoken language of Italy was being changed under the influence of Germanic migrations from the north, and priests instead of leading the people in the liturgy were now obliged to say the mass for the people. Not understanding the language, the people understood nothing about the mass except what they were told, and what they were told was that the mass was a sacrifice in which the flesh and blood of God's Son became present on the altar, was offered for their sins, and was eaten and drunk.

The uniformity of language in the mass, however, did not mean there was uniformity of style in the western liturgy. What liturgical books there were contained mainly prayers and rubrics for elaborate episcopal liturgies, and even in the parish churches of Rome priests had to improvise as best they could using the episcopal models. Outside of Rome bishops were free to compose their own liturgies, and before the beginning of the Middle Ages Spain, England, and France had liturgical styles that were very different from that of Rome. The Roman liturgy had been simplified somewhat in the reforms of Pope Gregory, but the Spanish, Celtic, and Gallic liturgies were often filled with long sequences of prayers that commemorated their own saints, implored help for their own needs, and expressed their own beliefs about the eucharistic sacrifice. Only the general format of the mass and isolated parts like the institution narrative and the Lord's Prayer were fixed; the rest was left to local custom and individual inventiveness.

Nonetheless, in the seventh century this picture began to change. When Rome sent missionaries to England, they brought Gregory's sacramentary with them, and by the end of the century the Roman-style mass had largely supplanted the older Celtic liturgy. As early as 754, Pippin, king of the Franks and Charlemagne's father, had tried to make the liturgy of Rome obligatory in his kingdom, but it was only under Charlemagne himself that the royal insistence on a more uniform liturgy in the Frankish empire began to be taken seriously. Charlemagne had Alcuin of York, a monk and the chief scholar at his court, adapt the Gregorian sacramentary to the needs of priests saying low masses, and in 784 he decreed that it should be used by all the bishops and priests in his realm. It was the beginning of the end of the traditional Gallic liturgy. Eventually the influence of Rome was felt in Spain as well, and after the eleventh century the only church that still had a distinctively different liturgical style was Milan, which continued to use the rite inherited from its early bishop, Ambrose, despite papal edicts to the contrary.

But the influence was not all one-sided. Besides the changes that Rome brought to the older European liturgies, there were many changes that were made in the Roman liturgy as it began to be used throughout Europe. Alcuin himself made some of the first by including Gallic-style prayers and ceremonies in his edition of the Gregorian sacramentary, and the French and German bishops who were obliged to use it made further alterations of their own. The Gallic liturgy, for example, was very anti-Arian in flavor since some of the southern tribes in Gaul had been converted in the fourth and fifth centuries by disciples of Arius. The orthodox bishops of the period had responded by emphasizing the presence of the divine Christ in their liturgies, and the Gallic way of doing this was now transferred to the Roman mass. A ritual confession of sinfulness was inserted into the introductory prayers, and protestations of unworthiness were added in other places. Priests made numerous signs of the cross over the bread and wine and genuflected before them in adoration after they were consecrated. In the Roman mass the eucharistic rite surrounding the words of consecration had a regulated format and so was known as the "canon," and now the prayers of the canon were whispered to protect and honor the mystery that was made present on the altar. Lay people were discouraged from taking communion lest it bring damnation rather than salvation upon their sinful souls, and even those who ventured to the altar dared not touch the body of Christ or the chalice of his blood with their hands. Instead they were fed the sacred elements by the priest, and they received them kneeling rather than standing. In some places a recitation of the creed of Nicaea was inserted between the reading of the gospel and the beginning of the canon to affirm the divinity of Christ and his unity with the Father in the Trinity.

Other customs introduced into the Roman mass also reflected the Gallic understanding of the liturgy. Prayers formerly said by the priest as one with the people were now said by the priest intervening for the people, and when he prayed he often did so with hands folded in supplication rather than with arms outstretched in thanksgiving. Since the mass was primarily understood to be a sacrifice, the sermon was seen as superfluous and was often omitted. And when a sermon was in fact preached it usually bore no relation to the scripture readings for the day because the people did not understand the Latin in which they were read. Since lay people were communicating less frequently, a loaf of bread was not needed for the mass, and a small round wafer made of flour and water was substituted in the belief that Christ's last supper had been a Passover meal with unleavened bread. This wafer was commonly referred to as the "host," from the Latin word for a sacrificial victim.

Still further changes reflected the fact that the mass was now regularly offered by a single priest rather than by a bishop with his attendant clergy, and without any lay participation in the ceremony. The one priest now recited all the prayers and scripture readings and performed all the actions that had formerly been done by other ministers. When there was no trained server to assist him, he even said the prayer responses that originally had been the people's, and that in the Gregorian liturgy had been chanted by a choir of monks. Since this mass was modeled on the private mass, there was no procession of gifts to the altar, but when it was a votive mass the priest himself collected the offering from those who had asked him to say it. There were, however, special feast days on which greater solemnity was called for, and so the elaborate episcopal mass of the Gregorian sacramentary was simplified into a more manageable "high" mass celebrated by a priest assisted by two clerics and other servers.

The Roman mass thus underwent a considerable change in style under the influence of the Frankish bishops, and eventually this new liturgy of northern Europe became the new liturgy of Rome. In the tenth century the cultural life of that city had declined to the point that it could not even produce its own books, so liturgical books were imported from northern monasteries and with them came many of the changes just described. Now the popes too celebrated the mass in the Frankish style, and hereafter whenever popes or councils, canonists or theologians referred to "the mass" they were referring to this type of mass. It was a liturgy of sacrifice and supplication rather than communion and thanksgiving, offered by a single priest rather than a bishop and presbyters, done for the people rather than with the people, said in Latin rather than in a living language, and performed mostly in silence rather than out loud.

This change in the liturgy was reflected and perpetuated in the church architecture of the Middle Ages. As early as the sixth century, altars in smaller churches and chapels were placed against the rear wall, and in larger churches and cathedrals reliquaries containing relics of saints were placed on or behind the traditional free-standing altar so that the priest had to say the canon prayers with his back to the people. Now the priest and people were in no way gathered around the altar for a sacrifice which they all offered; now the priest alone offered the sacrifice while the congregation watched. Moreover, they watched from an ever-increasing distance. Choir stalls for monks and clergy occupied the first places in front of the altar; behind these a row of columns or a decorative screen separated the sanctuary from the rest of the church; later a communion rail was added for people to kneel at while receiving the eucharist. In memory of the crucified Christ a crucifix was placed on or above the altar, and in memory of the saints the backdrop of the altar was filled with statues. Since the scriptures were no longer read to the people the priest just read them at the altar, moving the book from the "epistle side" to the "gospel side" in unconscious imitation of the days when separate lectors read on different sides of the sanctuary.

But the laity were not entirely forgotten; their role in worship was simply changed from active participation to passive inspiration and adoration. When the twelfth-century architectural invention of the pointed arch made it possible to build more spacious cathedrals, the distance between the main altar and the congregation increased even further, but side altars were added for offering private and votive masses that smaller groups could attend. The windows and walls of the Gothic cathedrals were filled with stained glass and statuary that could inspire even the illiterate, and the vaulted ceilings rose to a height that drew both eye and imagination upward toward heaven. Pulpits erected more toward the center of the nave accentuated the divorce between the sermon and the mass, but they also enabled more people to hear whatever preaching was done.

Nevertheless, by the thirteenth century the liturgy that had once been a communal prayer was now a clerical ritual separated from the congregation by barriers of language and architecture, and the theology of the Middle Ages reflected this change. For the liturgy instead of revealing the Christian mysteries had itself become a mystery in need of explanation, and the greatest mystery of all was how the bread and wine became the body and blood of Christ.

CHANGES IN THEOLOGY

The eastern fathers of the church had sometimes explained the liturgy in terms of allegory, giving a symbolic meaning to each of the liturgical actions, and for preachers in the Middle Ages this was a convenient way of giving people something edifying to think about as they watched the mass in silence. Early in the ninth century Amalar of Metz took this practice so seriously that he proposed that the real meaning of the mass was the life of Christ, symbolically represented by the various prayers and actions. According to him the opening psalm symbolized the prophets announcing the coming of Christ, the hymn of glory represented the song of the angels at his birth, the separate consecration of the bread and wine stood for Christ's death, while the dropping of a piece of host into it signified his return to life, and so on. It was one of the first medieval attempts to penetrate the mystery of the mass, and although his theory was rejected by theologians, allegorical interpretations of this sort continued to abound in popular preaching.

The only theologically acceptable view was that the mass represented just one event in the life of Christ, his redemptive death, and that it not only represented it but also mysteriously reenacted it. The words of the mass said as much, for they clearly indicated that Christ became present on the altar in the form of bread and wine, and that he was offered to God as he had offered himself on the cross. In 831 Paschase Radbert, abbot of the monastery of Corbie, took this notion of sacrifice a step further and concluded that the real flesh and blood of Christ must be physically present on the altar during the mass: by the power of God the words of consecration changed the bread and wine into the same flesh and blood that Christ had assumed when he became human. Not everyone agreed with Radbert's physicalistic interpretation of the sacrifice, but at the time it gave a convincing explanation of why priests saying the mass experienced the presence of Christ after saying the words of consecration and of how the sacrifice of the mass and the sacrifice of the cross could be one and the same.

Two centuries later Berengar of Tours challenged this interpretation of Christ's presence and offered another which to him seemed more logical. To Berengar it seemed natural to assume that things were what they appeared to be, and since the bread and wine did not change their appearance after the words of consecration were spoken, he reasoned that they must still be bread and wine. Christ's presence in the eucharist therefore had to be a spiritual, not a physical presence, and Berengar used Augustine's definition of a sacrament as "a sign of a sacred reality" to support his position. If the eucharistic bread and wine were a sacrament, he argued, they had to be a sign of Christ's body and blood, not identical with it. Besides, if the pieces of bread were really Christ's body, then logically speaking the body of Christ was in pieces, and if the wine were really his blood then his blood was not in his body.

Berengar did not deny that Christ was really present in the eucharist, nor did he deny that through the words of consecration the bread and wine were changed into the body and blood of Christ. But he did deny that Christ was physically present in the eucharist, and he did deny that the real body and blood of Christ could logically be called a sacrament. For him they were not a sacrament at all but a reality, a spiritual reality perceived by the eyes of faith and received spiritually in communion. For many of his contemporaries, however, denying the physical presence of Christ in the eucharist was equivalent to denying his real presence, and denying that the body and blood of Christ could be called a sacrament ran counter to the accepted practice of the church. A council of bishops in 1059 cited him for heresy and Berengar was forced to sign an oath admitting that "the bread and wine which are placed on the altar after the consecration are not only the sacrament but also the true body and blood of our Lord Jesus Christ, and that they are palpably handled and broken by the hands of the priest and torn by the teeth of the faithful, not simply as a sacrament but as a true fact." To them Berengar's "spiritual" interpretation of the eucharist was just as unacceptable as Amalar's "symbolic" interpretation of the mass. To them a reality was one thing, a symbol was another, and so to call the eucharist or the mass symbolic was to deny their reality. And their reality was precisely what could not be denied.

The controversy over Berengar's ideas had two main results. Theologically it led to the development of the concept of a sacramental reality, the *sacramentum et res*, by means of which the eucharistic bread and wine could be referred to as both a sacrament and a reality (see pages 57–58). Practically it led to an increased sense of realism about the eucharistic elements. Since the days of Pope Gregory, some consecrated bread had usually been reserved in a cupboard near the altar for use as viaticum (food for the journey to the next world) which could be carried to persons who were dying. It had also been customary for bishops to bow toward the reserved eucharist before beginning the liturgy, but now priests began to genuflect in reverence whenever they passed in front of it. To give it more prominence the sacrament was placed in a tabernacle or repository on the altar, and a lamp was kept lit in the sanctuary to remind those who entered the church that God was present there.

Some of Berengar's opponents had argued that Christ was not divided when the host was broken but that the whole Christ was present in every piece of bread and in every drop of wine, and this soon became the prevailing view. On the one hand it corresponded well with their sense of presence in each of the eucharistic elements, but on the other it led to some new changes in practice. Priests were required to genuflect every time they touched the host and to keep the fingers that touched it joined (lest a particle drop unnoticed) until they were rinsed after communion. Moreover, since Christ was equally present in the bread and the wine, priests stopped passing the chalice to communicants (lest a drop spill on the floor or clothing), reasoning that even those who received only the host received the whole Christ.

The growing sense of Christ's miraculous presence in the eucharist, however, led more and more people to abstain from communion altogether, and since they could not participate in the mass by hearing and responding to the prayers, their worship came to focus on the adoration of the host. Priests were asked to raise the host over their head after the consecration, and in some places people were known to cry out to the priest to hold it higher so they could see it better. Later the chalice was also elevated during the mass, and a bell was rung so that people who had been praying privately would know when to look up to adore the sacrament. Gradually the consecration and the elevation rather than the prayer of thanksgiving and the reception of communion came to be regarded as the high points of the liturgy, at least for the laity.

This physicalistic view of Christ's divine presence in the host also engendered some novel beliefs and superstitions about the eucharist. Some people believed that gazing upon the elevated host would keep away sickness or death, others that it would cure their illness or change their luck. Stories were circulated about hosts that miraculously bled after being broken by doubting priests or stabbed by sacrilegious unbelievers. There were even priests who feared for their faith because the bread and wine they consecrated still tasted like bread and wine, not like meat and blood. This interpretation raised some interesting theological questions as well. For example, if consecrated wine turned into vinegar, did Christ remain in it? And if a mouse got into the tabernacle and ate some of the reserved hosts, did it receive communion?

Many of these superstitions remained popular throughout the Middle

Ages, and many people continued to have a rather physicalistic belief in Christ's eucharistic presence. But during the reawakening of intellectual life in the twelfth and thirteenth centuries, theologians came to regard this extremely physical view as unnecessary and ultimately untenable. Aristotelian philosophy which was then being reintroduced to the west gave Christian thinkers a much more sophisticated analysis of reality, and together with a renewed study of the church fathers it enabled them to understand the presence of Christ as a metaphysical rather than a physical reality.

SCHOLASTICISM

When the scholastic theologians treated the eucharist in their writings, they often dealt with the mass only in passing. Their primary interest was in the sacrament, and for them the sacrament was not the liturgical action but the eucharistic bread and wine. The great theological issue of the day was not how Christians should worship, for the format of the mass was now pretty well set. Nor was there any real question about the nature of the mass; everyone accepted it as a representation and continuation of Christ's sacrifice on Calvary. Rather the important questions came to be two: At what point in the mass did the sacrifice take place? And how were the bread and wine changed into the body and blood of Christ?

To the first question the scholastics gave no unanimous answer. All agreed basically with Peter Lombard that what took place in the mass was "the memorial and representation of the true sacrifice and holy immolation" which Christ had made on the cross (*Sentences* IV, 12, 7). But when in the mass did the immolation or destruction of the victim occur? Some theologians proposed that it took place in the separate consecration of the bread and wine, reasoning that this represented in an "unbloody manner" Christ's death from loss of blood on the cross. Others saw the breaking of the host or its being eaten in communion as being more representative of the destruction of the victim that was needed for a sacrifice. Aquinas chose the former view, but for a different reason. All those who attended the mass were said to participate in the sacrifice but not everyone received communion, and so he regarded the sacrifice as being completed in the consecration of the elements. Ultimately there was no way to resolve the issue, and although the question was often treated, the scholastics' answer was never univocal.

As to the second question, how the bread and wine were changed into the body and blood of Christ, the scholastics did reach unanimity at least for a time. Shortly after they did, moreover, this answer came to be regarded as the only orthodox one and all other answers were branded as heretical, so even those who considered them to be more plausible refrained from proposing them. Thus the answer that has come to be identified with scholasticism is only the one called "transubstantiation," meaning a change in substance or reality. During the thirteenth century the nature of this change was rather precisely worked out in terms of Aristotelian philosophy.

The fathers of the church had also spoken of a change in the bread and wine, and they referred to the change in a variety of terms: transmutation, transfiguration, transelementation, transformation. But their chief concern was not with explaining how the change was effected but with affirming that it did in fact occur. For this reason they were usually content to say that the change in the elements took place by the power of God. If they tried to explain anything it was the presence of Christ in the eucharistic liturgy and in the bread and wine after the consecration, and those who did it were satisfied with an answer in terms of Platonic philosophy. But the scholastics were not Platonists, and ever since the days of Radbert and Berengar the question of the nature of Christ's presence had become connected with the question of the nature of the change that brought it about.

The schoolmen through the early 1200s proposed three different explanations of how the bread and wine became the body and blood of Christ. One view was that the substance of Christ was added to that of the material elements when the words of consecration were spoken. This view came to be known as "consubstantiation," meaning that both realities were present in the sacrament, and its adherents argued from the fact that the scriptures and the fathers spoke of the eucharist as bread and wine as well as the body and blood of Christ. Others, however, appealed to the philosophical notion that two substances could not occupy the same space, and they proposed that during the consecration the bread and wine were annihilated by the power of God and that the body and blood of Christ took their place. According to this "substitution" theory, one reality was replaced by another, but critics pointed out that a replacement is not the same thing as a change, and therefore the theory did not actually fit the belief that bread and wine are changed into the body and blood of Christ. Both views did, however, account for the experienced presence of a divine reality associated with the sacrament, and although neither was widely held, they were not considered heretical before 1250. When they were criticized it was on grounds that they were philosophically implausible or theologically inadequate.

The term "transubstantiation" was first used by Hildebert of Tours early in the thirteenth century and within decades it was in common usage at the University of Paris. The Fourth Lateran Council even used Hildebert's terminology in saying that the bread and wine were "transubstantiated" into the body and blood of Christ, but at the time no one took it as an ecclesiastical endorsement of the philosophical view that went under that name. In fact, some of the theologians who used this term held that what happened at the consecration was a miraculous substitution; in other words they held a substitution theory while calling it transubstantiation. Central to the scholastic theory of transubstantiation was the notion that the reality or substance of the elements truly changed, while their appearances remained those of bread and wine.

According to the Aristotelian philosophy that the scholastics adopted, a substance was anything that could exist on its own; it was a reality in its own right. Thus living things were considered to be substances, but their size, shape, color, and so forth were not, because properties like these (the scholastics called them "accidents") could not exist on their own but only in something that had those properties. The scholastics sometimes had difficulty in applying this analysis to nonliving things (for example, was earth a substance or was each particle of dirt a substance?), but for the most part it was a serviceable scientific approach to reality. Among other things it enabled scholastic thinkers to distinguish between two different types of change in the real world. Sometimes only the properties or appearance of things changed, as when a person lost weight or an animal changed its position or a leaf turned color (these were "accidental changes"). But sometimes things themselves changed from one thing into something else, as when a person died and became a corpse, or when wood burned and turned to ash, or when flour and water were baked into bread. In these cases the change was a "substantial change," a real change in substance, as they viewed it.

Now, substantial changes in ordinary experience always involved a change in the way a substance looked or behaved, that is, it also included a change in the thing's apparent properties. But the schoolmen (who were usually priests as well as scholars) also experienced another type of change: at the beginning of the mass they experienced the presence of bread and wine on the altar, but when the words of consecration were spoken they experienced a different presence, a sacred presence, the presence of Christ. For them, during the mass the reality of the bread and wine changed into the reality of Christ's body and blood, or to say it another way, the visible properties through which they perceived the reality of ordinary bread and wine became properties through which they perceived the divine reality of Christ. The consecrated bread and wine were thus sacraments in the broad and most fundamental sense: they were a door to the sacred experience of divine presence.

The scholastics analyzed this change in the reality that they experienced in terms with which they were familiar, that is, in terms of Aristotelian philosophy. It was certainly not a change in accidents, for the properties of the bread and wine remained even after the change. It therefore had to be some kind of change in reality, a substantial change. But since other substantial changes always involved some change in sensible properties, this change was unique, and so they called it by a unique name: transubstantiation.

As a philosophical theory that explained the change of the bread and wine into the body and blood of Christ, transubstantiation proved to be the most satisfactory of the three originally proposed. It agreed with what people experienced as the real presence of Christ in the eucharist; it agreed with what Christ said in the scriptures, that this was indeed his body and blood; and it agreed with the general Aristotelian analysis of reality with which the scholastics worked. Moreover it had an advantage over the older physicalistic interpretation of the change because it did not have to explain how Christ could physically fit into the eucharistic elements or how he could physically be both in heaven and on the altar. For the change that was known as transubstantiation was not conceived as a physical change but as a metaphysical change, that is, a change in reality that could be perceived by the mind even if it could not be perceived by the senses.

Around the middle of the thirteenth century, however, some scholastics began to look on transubstantiation as more than just a satisfactory theory. They were so convinced of its correctness that they began to regard the other explanations as patently erroneous, theologically false, and therefore heretical. One of these theologians was Thomas Aquinas.

Aquinas accepted the theory of transubstantiation and developed it with a philosophical sophistication that was to make it plausible to Catholic theologians even centuries later. But Aquinas' theology of the eucharist included more than an explanation for the change in the bread and wine. As a priest the mass was the daily focus of Aquinas' religious life, and as a theologian he placed the eucharist at the center of his sacramental system. Certainly this was also true of other scholastics, but since Aquinas' work was to have a more lasting influence on Catholic theology, it would be well to summarize some of the other things he said about the eucharist.

To begin with, Aquinas noted that the eucharist was different from the other sacraments in that it was not a sacred action but a sacred object: the consecrated bread and wine. With the other scholastics he shared the view that the mass itself was not a sacrament but a sacred action in which a sacrament was produced for the spiritual benefit of the church, and so in his sacramental theology he said very little about the mass and concentrated on the consecration and reception of the eucharistic elements. Thus for Aquinas and others the "matter" of the sacrament was the bread and wine, and the "form" was Christ's words spoken over them by the priest, which signified what happened to them at the moment of consecration.

Aquinas also adopted the conceptual scheme developed by earlier schoolmen that analyzed the sacraments in terms of *sacramentum tantum*, *sacramentum et res*, and *res tantum*. According to this analysis the physical appearance of the bread and wine was "only a sacrament," a sacred sign of a spiritual reality. The consecrated elements themselves were "both sacrament and reality" since they both signified the body and blood of Christ and were in fact the reality that they signified. But Aquinas differed from some of his contemporaries by identifying that which was "only a reality" not with Christ as present in the elements but with Christ as received in communion, for when the host and wine were consumed the sacrament disappeared and only the experienced reality of Christ's presence remained.

For Aquinas, then, God's purpose in giving the eucharist to the church was not to make bread and wine an object of worship (although he agreed that it was proper to venerate the sacrament) but to give Christians a means of spiritual nourishment. The reality of the sacrament was therefore a grace, the grace of union with Christ experienced in the reception of communion. Just as ordinary food was a gift from God, so also was the gift of the eucharist through which Christians were sacramentally united with Christ's body and blood and experientially united with Christ himself. Further, through this union with Christ they were united with the church, his body on earth, for union with Christ was a union in love not only with God but also with other persons. Thus Aquinas could say in one place, "The reality of this sacrament is the unity of the mystical body," and in another, "The reality of this sacrament is love, and not just the power to love but the activity of love, which is kindled in [the reception of] the sacrament" (*Summa Theologica* III, 73, 3; 79, 4).

Certainly, Aquinas admitted, Christians could experience spiritual union with Christ apart from the eucharist, but they could also receive the eucharist without experiencing Christ's love in their heart. Much depended on their inner disposition or openness to God's grace. Unrepentant sinners who took communion received Christ only sacramentally but not spiritually, and so they did not grow in love. But those who cooperated with the grace of the sacrament did grow in love, and in the measure that they did they also became less sinful. The eucharist was therefore a sacrament of redemption, for it had the effect of forgiving sin in the present and reducing the inclination to sin in the future. Moreover, the eucharist was a sacrifice as well as a sacrament, and as a sacrifice it could be offered to God for the spiritual benefit of others both living and dead. Still, for Aquinas, the spiritual effectiveness of such an offering was proportionate to the disposition of those for whom it was offered. Thus the eucharist was not automatically effective either for those who received communion or for those who had masses said for them. The actual effectiveness of the sacrament always depended on their cooperation with God's grace.

If there was anything automatic about the eucharist in Aquinas' view it was only in regard to the consecration of the elements. The priest's power to consecrate was given in his ordination, and so his ability to change bread and wine into the body and blood of Christ came from his priesthood and not from his personal holiness. The sacrament consecrated by a sinful priest was therefore just as valid as that consecrated by a saintly one, even though the spiritual benefit received by each communicant depended on his or her openness to God's grace. Although it was against church law to do so, even a heretic or a defrocked priest could validly consecrate the eucharist because the priestly character bestowed on his soul in ordination was permanent, and those who received the sacrament from such a priest truly received Christ's body and blood although they also acted contrary to church law in doing so. Thus the consecration of the elements was effected *ex opere operato*, in virtue of the action performed by a validly ordained priest, and Aquinas even held that if they were needed for communion a priest could consecrate all the bread in a market or all the wine in a barrel.

For Aquinas, then, the experienced presence of Christ in the eucharist was a result of his real presence in the sacrament under the appearance of bread and wine. That real presence was not a physical presence but a metaphysical presence, and so it could be perceived not by the eye but only by the mind. Moreover it was not a natural presence but a supernatural presence, and so it could be perceived not by unaided intelligence but only by the mind illuminated by faith. By faith in God's word and God's power over reality, Christians acknowledged that what appeared to be bread and wine were in reality Christ's body and blood. But where his body and blood were present so also was Christ, and by their openness to God's grace

Christians could experience that presence, a personal presence of Christ in the eucharist. It was a presence that could be sensed in the sacrament on the altar, but in communion it could reach the intimacy of union in love.

Later Developments

Aquinas' understanding of the eucharist, like his understanding of the other sacraments, grew out of his sacramental experiences as they were guided and formed by his faith in the doctrines of the church, his knowledge of the writings of the fathers, and his meditations on the scriptures. Such was the way theology was done at the height of the medieval renaissance in the first half of the thirteenth century. As we have already seen in earlier chapters, however, this way of doing theology did not continue and scholasticism went into an intellectual decline. Those who followed in the footsteps of the great schoolmen like Albert, Aquinas, and Bonaventure tended to neglect the relevance of religious experience and relied increasingly on texts and logic to prove their positions and deduce their conclusions. In the long run this tendency led to legalism and nominalism but its beginnings were evident even by the end of the thirteenth century.

John Duns Scotus, for example, agreed with the doctrine that the mass was a sacrifice, but for him this meant it was a repetition of Christ's sacrifice on Calvary rather than a representation of it. The earlier idea that the mass was identical with Christ's sacrifice had derived in part from the liturgical experience of self-surrender to God, which theologians interpreted as a personal participation in Christ's sacrifice of himself to the Father. But for Scotus and later writers the mass was first and foremost the official worship of the church, offered to God by priests acting on the church's behalf, and so experiential participation in the sacrifice although desirable was not deemed necessary. Even those who saw the mass as a representation of Christ's one sacrifice tended by the fifteenth century to view it as an allegorical representation or memorial of that historical event. In either case, moreover, the mass was considered to be effective on its own, producing grace and forgiving sins each time it was offered regardless of people's interior dispositions. Christians were advised to cultivate the appropriate feelings of devotion and self-surrender during the mass, but those feelings were viewed as an addition to rather than as a participation in what was going on at the altar.

The later schoolmen's grasp of Aristotelian metaphysics was also less nuanced than Aquinas', and many of them saw no philosophical reasons to prefer transubstantiation over consubstantiation as a theory explaining the eucharistic change. Consubstantiation agreed just as well with their experience of the presence of Christ in the sacrament, it did not contradict the scriptures, and it was easier to understand. Beginning with Scotus, however, theologians began to take the Fourth Lateran Council's use of the word "transubstantiated" as an ecclesiastical endorsement of transubstantiation. In the fourteenth century William of Ockham even favored consubstantiation as a philosophical explanation for the real presence, but he accepted transubstantiation as the correct theological position because he believed that it had already been defined as a dogma. Ultimately this belief became so common that those who rejected transubstantiation were looked upon as heretics, and acting on this assumption the Council of Constance in 1415 condemned John Wycliffe for teaching that the substance of the bread and wine remained in the sacrament of the altar.

Apart from these changes in the understanding of the mass as a sacrifice and the acceptance of transubstantiation on doctrinal rather than philosophical grounds, there were few developments in the theology of the eucharist during the fourteenth and fifteenth centuries. Most of the treatises written about the mass and the sacrament were devoted to questions about rubrics and to discussions about validity and liceity. The mass thus came to be regarded as an ecclesiastical ritual with certain minimum requirements that had to be met in order to produce the sacrament, and eucharistic theology became largely a matter of canon law.

During this same period popular piety continued to shift more and more toward the adoration of the host. Among other things the Fourth Lateran Council had decided that it was not necessary to receive communion regularly before the age of discretion and in so doing it implicitly approved the growing practice of not giving the eucharist to infants right after baptism. In point of fact, communion among the laity had so died out in some places that the council also felt it necessary to decree that all Christians were obligated to receive the eucharist at least once a year. On the other hand, the worship of the Blessed Sacrament (the name given to the consecrated elements) continued to grow. In the thirteenth century the feast of *Corpus Christi* (Body of Christ) was established first in France and then throughout the whole church, and later the veneration of the host expanded into solemn processions in which it was carried aloft, as well as into public adoration of the sacrament exposed on the altar. Stories about bleeding hosts and apparitions of Christ in the eucharist were widespread, and superstitious beliefs about the host's ability to effect cures and ward off evil were commonplace. In the fourteenth century people were known to rush from church to church to see a host being elevated at mass, believing that a glimpse of the sacrament would protect them from sudden death or make their business prosper on that day.

But if lay people were not very involved in eucharistic sacrifices, just the opposite was true among the clergy. Now that the mass was believed to produce spiritual benefits whether or not it was devoutly attended, private masses abounded and in larger churches with many side altars they were offered side by side in polite silence. Most of these were votive masses, offered for special intentions in return for a suitable donation, and priests sometimes said as many as eight a day. Although certain parts such as the canon had to be included in the mass for validity, there were few definite rules that had to be followed and so a number of masses could be performed one after another quite rapidly. Moreover, to satisfy the demand for votive masses, by the fifteenth century thousands of "altar priests" were being ordained to do nothing but say masses for souls in purgatory, in request for favors, and in thanksgiving for favors received. Sometimes as many as a hundred were assigned to say mass in a single church.

Thus by the end of the Middle Ages the mass had been transformed from an act of public worship to a form of clerical prayer. Instead of being offered once a week as in patristic times, it was offered many times each day. Instead of being concelebrated by the bishop and his assistant priests it was said simultaneously in the same church by many priests. Instead of being a service of scriptural readings followed by a communion service, it was a symbolic sacrifice in which the readings were not heard and communion was not distributed. Although Sunday masses still continued to be attended by the faithful, the vast majority of masses were ones that were paid for by the people and said by the priests on weekdays. By and large the mass had become a "good work" performed by priests for the spiritual benefit of the church. This was the mass that the reformers knew, and this was the mass that many of them rejected.

4. The Lord's Supper and the Modern Mass

The early Protestant reformers found themselves faced with a dilemma. On the one hand they saw that the private low mass was nothing at all like the biblical descriptions of the last supper. On the other hand they read Jesus' words over the bread and wine and his command, "Do this in commemoration of me." What was it that Christ wanted them to do, if it was not the saying of masses? To compound the difficulty, they knew practically nothing about the eucharistic worship in the first few centuries; most of the manuscripts describing them had been lost or forgotten in libraries for ages. So even though their excommunication from Catholicism meant they were free to reform the mass without Roman interference, it was not easy to envision how the mass should be reformed or what should take its place.

As a matter of fact, early Protestant worship often resembled the late medieval mass in a number of ways. Luther mainly shortened and translated the Latin mass into German, and insisted that communion be given to the laity. Calvin and others divided the mass into two services, a service of scripture readings followed by a sermon and a service in which communion was distributed. Catholic sermons in the Middle Ages had frequently focused on Christ's passion in conjunction with the sacrifice of the mass, and although the reformers by and large rejected the sacrificial nature of the mass, they accepted the idea that Christ's death was the supremely important act in the salvation of mankind, and in their sermons they often exhorted their listeners to focus on the passion to appreciate what God had done for them. Finally, since Christians in the Middle Ages had become accustomed to receiving communion very rarely, most Protestants saw no reason to receive communion daily or even weekly. In most of their churches communion services were therefore held anywhere from once a month to once a year, and the usual form of Sunday worship became a noneucharistic prayer service.

By and large, then, Protestants did not reject the eucharist (which they believed had been instituted by Christ) but they did reject the Roman mass and they replaced it with other forms of worship. They also rejected the superstitious beliefs and practices connected with the consecrated host and in so doing they eliminated the practice of reserving the sacrament in their churches and looked for new ways of interpreting the words of institution. Even the name "mass," whose origins had been lost in antiquity, was discarded in favor of new names like "the Lord's supper" and "the Lord's table" that seemed more scriptural and more appropriate for services in which people were invited to receive the sacrament. The only exception to this movement away from the mass as a frequent form of liturgical worship was the Church of England. Initially, Anglicans did not consider themselves Protestants but Catholics in all respects except for allegiance to the Roman pope, and so they kept the mass. Eventually, however, the Protestant influence was felt in England too, and Anglicans adopted other forms of worship as well.

PROTESTANT REVISIONS

Apart from the Anglicans, the reformer who had the most Catholic attitude toward the mass and eucharist was Martin Luther. His reforms were among the first in European Christianity, and at the beginning Luther was more intent on correcting abuses than in changing the very form of Christian worship. Like indulgences, masses were sometimes "sold" to people who believed that their spiritual benefits could be applied to whatever the priest intended. Among other things, people gave money for masses to be said for the release of souls from purgatory, and they sometimes even bequeathed funds for masses to be said for themselves after their death. Nor were the priests who accepted these donations entirely mercenary, for they themselves believed in the automatic effectiveness of the mass and many of them had been ordained for no other purpose than to perform this good work for the benefit of the church. To Luther, however, the practice meant that people could buy their way into heaven, and he found it scandalous: "I regard the preaching and selling of the mass as a sacrifice or good work as the greatest of all abominations" (*Confession Concerning Christ's Supper*).

For Luther the underlying cause of this practice was the scholastic notion of the mass as a sacrifice that could be offered by a priest on others' behalf, and as he knew of no other Catholic interpretation of the eucharistic sacrifice, he rejected it outright. All that could be offered to God in the mass were prayers, he argued, since Christ had offered himself once and for all on Calvary. Moreover, the consecrated bread and wine were supposed to be offered not to God but to the people, since Christ said, "Take and eat"; and because there was no sacrifice to offer to God, no priest was needed to do it. Luther did at times admit that the mass could be considered a sort of sacrifice in which Christians offered themselves to God, but he regarded this as an entirely novel idea based on his reading of New Testament passages that spoke of Christians as members of a holy priesthood (for example, 1 Peter 2:5; Hebrews 13:15–16). Even according to this interpretation, however, an ecclesiastical priesthood was not necessary since all believers were priests and so they offered the sacrifice together.

What, then, was the mass if it was not primarily a sacrifice as the Catholic Church taught? To answer this question Luther examined the New Testament accounts of the last supper in the light of his own developing theology of salvation by grace and faith. Salvation was a free gift of God but it had to be acknowledged for it to make a real difference in people's lives, and Luther saw in communion the perfect sign of that salvation and the perfect opportunity to respond to it in faith. He interpreted the words of institution as Christ's last will and testament, and the sacrament of his body and blood as the seal that confirmed and authenticated it. At the last supper Christ had said, "This is my body....This is my blood, the blood of the testament, which shall be shed for the forgiveness of sins," and so for Luther the sacrament was a sign that Christians' sins were forgiven through Christ's death on the cross. "These words and the actual eating and drinking are the main thing in the sacrament, and whoever believes these words has what they say and mean, namely, the forgiveness of sins" (*Small Catechism*). Through receiving communion, then, Christians received an assurance of their salvation, for by faith they understood the significance of the sacrament and experienced God's forgiveness despite their sinfulness.

In communion Christians also experienced the presence of Christ, and Luther was convinced that the sacrament was "the true body and blood of the Lord Christ in and under the bread and wine which we Christians are commanded by Christ's word to eat and drink" (*Large Catechism* V, 8). It was a reality that could be perceived by faith, but Luther argued that the real presence of Christ in the elements did not ultimately depend on faith. Rather, it depended on God's word spoken over the elements making them a sacrament. "The bread and wine at the supper are the true body and blood of Christ, and are received not only by good Christians but also by the wicked" (*Articles of Schmalkald* 6).

How, then, did Luther explain the change in the elements? For most people Luther believed that a philosophical explanation was unnecessary and confusing, and that it was enough to know that the change took place by the power of God's word. But for those who insisted on having an explanation, he believed that consubstantiation made a great deal more sense than transubstantiation. As he understood it, transubstantiation implied that at the words of consecration the reality of the bread and wine vanished and were replaced by the body and blood of Christ, which seemed to contradict the evidence of his senses. Yet in faith he perceived the reality of Christ in the elements, and so he concluded that in the sacrament both bread and wine and Christ's body and blood were substantially present. In support of this explanation Luther also quoted the words of scripture that spoke of communion as both bread and the body of Christ (for example, 1 Corinthians 10:16; 11:26–28).

Not all of the early reformers agreed with Luther, however, for their sacramental experiences were different and their philosophical backgrounds were less scholastic than his. John Calvin, for instance, had not been a priest before the reformation, and as a layman he rejected both the mass and the veneration of the host as empty rituals. He also had no sympathy for scholasticism, and he regarded any attempt to identify the elements with the actual flesh and blood of Christ as an abasement of Christ's glorified body, which was in heaven. But he did not deny that Christ was somehow present in the receiving of communion, and he admitted that Christians could both experience that real presence and derive spiritual benefit from it.

Calvin interpreted Christ's words at the last supper in a figurative rather than a literal sense. The bread and wine were a figure or a sign of Christ's body and blood, which were really but only spiritually received in the act of taking communion. In this sense Christ was truly meat and drink for the soul (John 6:55), for through the sacrament Christians were spiritually nourished and strengthened. "When bread is given to us as a symbol of the body of Christ we should immediately think of it in terms of this comparison: as bread nourishes, sustains and preserves the body, so the body of Christ is the only food which animates and supports the life of the soul" (*Institutes of the Christian Religion* IV, 17, 1).

But how, then, was Christ present in the sacrament? Calvin refused to say that the substance of Christ's body and blood were present in the elements, for this seemed to imply that Christ could be physically located in some place other than heaven. On the other hand, Calvin was equally insistent that Christ's presence was more than just a presence in thought or imagination, for it seemed to be too real a presence to be called purely mental or subjective. For him it was a genuine experience of transforming strength and redeeming power that seemed to come from outside himself and that Calvin could attribute only to Christ. But Calvin had no well-developed philosophical system that he could use to explain this experience, and in the end he could only say that the spiritual nourishment of Christ's body and blood were made truly present through the action of the Holy Spirit when the bread and wine were received. "If it is asked whether the bread is the body of Christ and the wine is his blood, we should reply that the bread and wine are visible signs that represent the body and blood to us, but that they are called 'body' and 'blood' because they are means by which our Lord Jesus Christ gives his body and blood to us" (*Short Treatise on the Lord's Supper* 2). For Calvin, then, the body and blood were spiritual realities which were received at the same time that communion was taken.

Luther experienced a personal presence of Christ in the sacrament; Calvin experienced the presence of Christ's strengthening and redemptive power in the sacrament. But there were also those reformers who did not experience a sacred presence in the eucharist, or who at most interpreted it as a purely mental or psychological presence, and among these was Ulrich Zwingli. For him the Lord's supper was primarily a memorial service that reminded Christians of Christ's last supper, his passion, and his death. Its purpose was to allow Christians to express their faith in their redemption by Christ and to remind them of their duty to live according to his precepts. In this memorial they used bread and wine as Christ had ordained, but Zwingli interpreted Christ's words at the last supper as meaning that the bread and wine signified his body and blood which were going to be offered on the cross, not that he was going to somehow change them into his body and blood. Thus the eucharist was in reality only plain bread and wine, but Christians were to view it as a reminder of what Christ physically endured on their behalf. "I believe that in the holy eucharist...the true body of Christ is present to the mind by faith. Those who give thanks to God for the gift he has given us in his Son recognize that he took upon himself true flesh, and that his flesh truly suffered and that he washed away our sins by his blood. Thus everything that Christ did for them becomes present, as it were, by being contemplated in faith" (*On True and False Religion* II).

Among the early Protestant reformers, therefore, there was no unified conception of what the eucharist was or how Christians should regard it in their communion services, for they each began from their own sacramental experiences and interpreted them in the light of their own understanding of Christian life and worship. Moreover, this initial diversity increased even further in the many denominations that eventually grew out of the formation as doctrinal differences (not only about the sacraments) continued to divide one group from another. In time such diversity could even sometimes be found within individual churches. In the years that followed the separation of the English church from the church of Rome, for instance, Anglican worship varied between newer, more Protestant forms and older, more medieval forms, and the Anglican theology of the eucharist varied between Calvinist and even Zwinglian interpretations and the traditional Catholic interpretation. Eventually the Church of England settled for a variety of liturgical forms and Anglican theology permitted a variety of doctrinal interpretations about the eucharist. But the result of this diversity both within single churches and within reformed Christianity as a whole was that today there is no single attitude toward the eucharist that can be characterized as the Protestant attitude.

CATHOLIC SOLIDIFICATION

The reformation had just the opposite effect on the Roman church. The variety of Protestant opinions about the eucharist forced the bishops at the Council of Trent to rethink the meaning of the sacrament and come up with a unified Catholic position. In doing this the council produced three documents on the eucharist: one on the Blessed Sacrament (1551), one on the reception of communion (1562), and one on the mass as a sacrifice (1562). The teachings in these documents were mainly those of scholastic theology, and the result was that the scholastic approach to the eucharist came to be regarded as definitive and final. Moreover, this triple division of the eucharist into sacrament, communion, and mass was embodied in the council's catechism and was perpetuated in later Catholic theology, with the result that Catholics continued to think of them separately just as they had in the late Middle Ages.

Thus in their decree on the sacrament of the eucharist, what the bishops meant by "the sacrament" was the consecrated bread and wine. This was the sacrament that Christ had instituted at the last supper and that he had given the church to remember him, to proclaim his redemptive death, and to give spiritual nourishment to souls. Eleven years later the bishops also declared that the mass had been instituted by Christ, but the mass was regarded as a sacrifice and not as a sacrament. Communion likewise was looked upon not as a sacramental action in itself but as "receiving the sacrament."

In this first decree, then, the bishops declared that "Our Lord Jesus Christ, true God and man, is truly, really and substantially contained under the appearances of bread and wine" (Eucharist 1). This presence was not necessarily a physical presence but it was a real presence, localizable in the sacrament, and not just a spiritual presence in the minds of believers. The correct understanding of the real change in the sacramental elements was the one the scholastics had called transubstantiation: "By the consecration of the bread and wine the whole substance of the bread is changed into the substance of the body of Christ our Lord, and the whole substance of the wine is changed into the substance of his blood" (Eucharist 4). This sacrament was therefore unique since it contained not only the power to make people holy but also the very author of holiness, who is God. Because of the divine nature of the sacrament it was to be treated with great reverence and publicly adored. Catholics were urged to have a strong faith in this sacred mystery, to worship it with great devotion, and to receive it frequently, but they were also admonished to be careful lest they receive it with unconfessed sins on their conscience.

The bishops believed that this understanding of the eucharist had always been the doctrine of the church, and they stated their belief in no uncertain terms. "About this venerable and divine sacrament this sacred Council teaches the correct and authentic doctrine which the universal Church has always held, which it received from Christ our Lord and his Apostles, and which it learned from the Holy Spirit..., and which it will preserve until the end of time." Accordingly, the council forbade Catholics "henceforth to believe, teach or preach anything about the most holy Eucharist which differs from what is explained and defined in this present decree" (Eucharist, intro.). It also explicitly condemned as heretical a number of the other explanations of the eucharist that had been developed by the reformers.

The council's second eucharistic decree dealt with communion, and in it the bishops defended two Catholic practices that were being challenged by the reformers. Catholics did not have to receive both the bread and the wine in order to receive Christ in communion, they contended, because the whole Christ is found in every particle and every drop and therefore in either element separately, and because Christ himself had promised eternal life to those who ate the bread (John 6:52, 59). Moreover, children did not have to receive communion before they reached the age of reason because they had been reborn through baptism and did not need the spiritual benefit of the sacrament until they were old enough to sin deliberately. The bishops admitted that in earlier times the church's customs may have been different, but they believed that God had given the successors of the apostles the authority to regulate the practices of the church, and they excommunicated those who claimed that the current practices were erroneous.

In their third decree the bishops presented the accepted understanding of the mass as a sacrifice and defended some of the liturgical practices of the day. They explained that at the last supper Christ had offered a sacrifice of his body and blood to God the Father, and had commanded that it be continued so that through it his sacrifice on the cross could be present in the church forever. In the mass, therefore, Christ offered himself in an unbloody manner just as he had offered himself on Calvary in a bloody manner. Since it was Christ's own offering of himself, it was a clean oblation that could not be defiled by any unworthiness of the minister, and it was always just as satisfying to God as Christ's death on the cross had been. The sacrifice of the mass did not detract from the importance of Christ's sacrifice on the cross but was the means by which its spiritual benefits were made available to the church, and so it could be offered to atone for the sins of the living and the dead. Moreover, its efficacy as a sacrifice did not depend on the people's participation in the mass and so they did not have to receive communion or hear it offered in their own language. Still, lay people would derive additional spiritual benefit from receiving the sacrament and from having the mass explained to them, and the bishops encouraged priests to instruct the faithful about the meaning of the sacrifice especially on Sundays and feast days. Finally, as they had done at the end of the two previous decrees, the bishops listed a number of contrary interpretations that had been developed by the reformers and condemned them as heretical.

In its doctrinal pronouncements on the eucharist, therefore, the Council of Trent did little more than consolidate the eucharistic theology of the scholastics, defend some of the genuinely sacramental practices of the church, and give that medieval theology and practice official ecclesiastical approval. Nonetheless, in their own day these rather brief documents of the council were an unprecedented intellectual accomplishment, hammered out through days and weeks of drafts, suggestions, debates, and revisions. Never before had the scholastic theology of the eucharist been compressed into such a terse synthesis. Never before had church leaders used that theology as a general criterion against which to judge the sacramental practices of the church. And never before had Christianity in the west made such a thorough attempt to unify its theology of the eucharist and to regulate its liturgical worship. For a large portion of Europe this accomplishment came too late, for the reformers were already busy perfecting their own theologies and making their own changes in Christian worship. But for those parts of Europe that remained Catholic, it was both the capstone of eight centuries of liturgical development and the foundation stone of four centuries of liturgical stability.

To be accurate, however, the council's actual accomplishments were more doctrinal than practical. Most of the bishops could agree on the theology of the eucharist and on the practices that should be retained, but many of them could not agree on which practices should be eliminated. Each diocese had its own cherished customs that might seem odd or inappropriate to outsiders, and the bishops were unwilling to lay them open to the judgment of their fellow bishops. But they were at least willing to have reform, they declared that it should take place, and they indicated the direction it should take: keep the essentials and eliminate the abuses.

They had done their work in defining what the essentials were, but they left it up to the pope and the Roman curia of advisers and administrators to decide how the abuses were to be eliminated. In doing that, however, they implicitly gave to the pope an authority over the Catholic liturgy that the bishop of Rome had never had before and ended fifteen centuries of relative episcopal independence in the area of Christian worship.

A commission appointed by the council uncovered a variety of abuses and exaggerated practices, some of which were quite prevalent and have already been mentioned: priests extorting stipends to offer masses for people, or guaranteeing that a fixed number of masses would liberate a soul from purgatory; priests saying masses many times each day, one after another, eliminating prayers and without even taking communion themselves; many masses being offered in the same church at the same time, sometimes while a congregational mass was going on at the main altar. But the commission's report also included things that were less frequent but nonetheless quite noticeable: priests elevating the chalice by placing it on their heads, dead bodies being laid on the altar during mass, people coming into the church with their dogs and falcons for the hunt, processions of the Blessed Sacrament from different churches crossing each other and breaking into brawls. The list went on, and rather than name each abuse and condemn it, Rome chose a simpler way to eliminate unwanted practices from its liturgy: it prescribed exactly what was to be done, and it prohibited Catholics from doing otherwise without its explicit permission.

In 1570 a normative edition of the Roman missal was issued under the authority of Pius V and was made mandatory for all of Catholicism. The only exceptions allowed were those dioceses and religious orders which could prove that their own liturgies had been in continuous use for more than two centuries, as in Milan. The new mass book and the directives which accompanied it gave detailed instructions for almost every aspect of the liturgy from the prayers that were to be said each day to the tone in which they were to be recited, and from the number of masses that a priest could offer on a given day to the number of signs of the cross that he should make over the bread and wine. To ensure liturgical uniformity Sixtus V in 1588 established the Congregation of Rites within the church's administrative system to interpret the rubrics and make decisions about their application. Henceforward no changes in the mass would be made without the highest ecclesiastical approval, and in fact no substantive changes were made for almost four hundred years. The Catholic mass in

1960 was almost identical, word for word and gesture for gesture, with the Roman mass of 1570.

It took awhile, however, for Rome's directives to be carried out. In the beginning many bishops resisted the new restrictions on their episcopal prerogatives, and records show that as late as 1790 more than half the dioceses in France were still performing Gallic-style liturgies at least occasionally. But the Roman authorities had a technological advantage that was unavailable during earlier attempts at liturgical reform. The invention of the printing press now made it possible to produce a uniform missal for the whole church and to make it cheaply enough that even the poorest country parish could have a copy. So the days of local variations in the liturgy were numbered, and in the long run the increasing power of the pope and increasing pressure from the Roman curia led to greater and greater conformity throughout the Catholic world.

The liturgy that Rome approved was basically the same as it had been in the Middle Ages, only now with official texts for low masses offered by a single priest and high masses offered by a priest with clerical assistants. It was a style of worship that still excluded the laity, but this seemed proper because Rome had known no other style for about nine hundred years. On the one hand this inability of the people to share in the church's official worship led to a flowering of new forms of unofficial worship such as those mentioned in chapter IV. On the other hand it led to a renewed emphasis on church music and architecture as additional sacraments with power to arouse in people a sense of the sacred. The music that had begun as plain chant in medieval times developed into polyphony during the Renaissance and into elaborate choral and orchestral works during the Baroque period, and when people went to "hear the mass" in the seventeenth and eighteenth centuries it was often the choir and not the priest to which they were referring. Church interiors also grew more elaborate, with decorative painting and sculpture designed to capture the eye and stimulate the religious imagination even while mass was going on. Altars too became more ornate, and tabernacles that had once been rather small containers for consecrated hosts now became magnificent receptacles for the Blessed Sacrament and the focal point of eucharistic piety.

But eucharistic piety for lay people was almost entirely divorced from the liturgy. Translations of the Latin missal were forbidden by Rome (partly in reaction to Protestant claims that people needed to worship in their own language) and so books written for use during mass could contain only popular presentations of the meaning of the sacrament and suggestions about how to receive its spiritual benefits. Other books contained numerous devotional prayers that could be said during the mass, and the silent saying of the rosary was suggested for those who would not or could not read. Even in those progressive places where hymn singing was allowed during low masses, the hymns usually had nothing to do with what was going on at the altar, and the only time that the congregation was expected to stop their singing or interrupt their praying was when the host and chalice were elevated. For lay people, then, the modern mass was mainly a time for private and devotional prayer except for the moment when the sacrament was adored. But the eucharist could also be worshiped outside of mass, in the tabernacle, or during exposition of the Blessed Sacrament.

For the laity, there was also very little connection between communion and the liturgy. Holy communion was often distributed before and after the mass so as not to interrupt the sacrifice, and a solemn high mass was by custom a liturgy at which no one except the priest was expected to communicate. Lay reception of communion dwindled even further in the seventeenth century when a French pietistic movement called Jansenism emphasized human sinfulness before God and suggested that people should never receive the Blessed Sacrament without first going to confession. Canon law still obliged Catholics to fulfill their "Easter duty" to receive communion once a year, but preachers encouraged people to practice "spiritual communion" when they were not prepared to receive Christ in the sacrament, and so the rule that was once laid down as a minimum became a norm instead.

LATER DEVELOPMENTS

The developments in eucharistic theology up to the twentieth century were minimal. Doctrinally as well as liturgically it looked as though Trent had had the last word, and so the only task left to theology was to clarify the truth of what the council had defined.

For example, the council had affirmed that Christ was present in the Blessed Sacrament. But how was this presence different from his presence in the world? The council had declared that "the whole Christ, body and blood, soul and divinity" was present in either the bread or the wine. But why, then, were both bread and wine needed for the sacrament? The council had implied that transubstantiation was the only acceptable explanation for the change that took place at the consecration. But why was this so, and why were other explanations unacceptable?

Some of the Tridentine doctrines about the mass were also seen to be in need of clarification. For example, how was the mass both the same as and different from Christ's death on the cross? Was the spiritual value of each mass finite or infinite? How did the grace of receiving communion differ from the grace of attending mass? How were the spiritual benefits of the mass applied to the souls of the living and to souls in purgatory? How did the mass give glory to God, and why did Christ command that it be repeated until the end of time?

Whatever answers Catholic theologians gave to these questions, however, they could be no more than corollaries to what Trent had already stated. And as a matter of fact the answers that most theologians gave did not differ much from one another, and they did not differ much from the answers of the medieval scholastics. Catholic theology, it seemed, had reached its high point in the Middle Ages, and although it might possibly be refined it could not be basically improved on.

Modern eucharistic theology was therefore mainly dogmatic and metaphysical. It was dogmatic in the sense that it defended the dogmas of Trent against the heresies of the Protestants, and was built solidly on that doctrinal foundation. And it was metaphysical in the sense that it explained things which could not be seen but which were nonetheless believed to be real. Yet it would be unfair to say that modern Catholics' faith in the eucharist and the mass was blind, or that their beliefs rested only on defined dogmas and metaphysical speculations. The dogmas themselves seemed to say merely what the church had always believed, and they seemed to be verified in the words of scripture and the writings of the fathers. The dogmas were thus authenticated by the revealed word of God and the continuous testimony of tradition. And the speculations seemed to be simply explanations of what Catholics could verify for themselves in their own religious experience when they worshiped Christ in the Blessed Sacrament or devoutly attended the sacrifice of the mass. Praying in front of the host, they could indeed experience Christ's presence, a divine presence that was unshakably and unmistakably real. And attending the mass they could in fact experience themselves as present at Christ's sacrifice on the cross and feel its redemptive graces flooding their hearts.

In modern Catholicism, therefore, the eucharist was a sacrament not only in the restricted Catholic sense but also in the broader religious sense of that term. It was a sacred object, made holy by the words of consecration, which had the power to reveal an experientially real presence to those who contemplated it with the eyes of faith. And the mass too, although theologically explained as a sacrifice, was sacramental in the broad sense, for it opened the door to an experience of sacred time and sacred meaning, the transcendent time and meaning of Christ's sacrifice on Calvary.

Yet both of these sacraments—as well as the reception of communion, which involved an intense internalization of the experience of divine presence—were uniquely modern in that they gave rise to individualistic rather than communitarian experiences of the sacred. People might adore the Blessed Sacrament together, but they each experienced the presence of Christ separately. People might attend the mass together, but the spiritual benefit they derived from it depended only on their own individual dispositions.

In the nineteenth century, however, this individualistic approach to the eucharist began to be questioned by Catholic scholars who were discovering that the liturgy before the Middle Ages had been an act of public rather than private worship, and who began to suggest that those who attended should participate in it in other ways besides devout watching. It was the beginning of the transformation of the Latin mass, a transformation that would take a hundred years to complete. And in a less obvious way it was the beginning of the end of the scholastic theology of the eucharist.

5. Liturgy and Eucharist in the Twentieth Century

Although the Catholic Church officially still recognizes the doctrines of the Council of Trent as its own, much of Catholicism is quietly laying them aside. Most of its theologians no longer speak about the mass as a sacrifice, few of its preachers and catechists urge special devotion to the Blessed Sacrament, and virtually no congregations regularly attend the Latin mass that the Tridentine dogmas defended and explained. The term "transubstantiation," once found in every Catholic catechism, is virtually unknown to younger Catholics, and even the word "mass," though still in popular use, is disappearing from the professional vocabulary of Catholic theologians and liturgists.

The immediate cause of this shift was the change in Catholic worship that resulted from the Second Vatican Council, but the beginnings of the shift were already being felt decades before in the liturgical movement (see pages 116–117). Initially this movement toward liturgical renewal was neither an organized movement nor an attempt at genuine renewal. Rather it began as an attempt at "restoration," an effort to restore to the Roman mass some of the things it seemed to have before the Council of Trent. And in the beginning it affected only the monks in a few European monasteries.

CHANGES IN THE LITURGY

Europe in the nineteenth century experienced a renewed interest in Gothic art and architecture and a reawakened curiosity in the Middle Ages. In academic circles libraries began to be searched for old manuscripts and new historical investigations began to be made into the period. As part of this general intellectual interest in the past, some Benedictine monks in France and Germany tried to find where the prayers of the Tridentine mass had come from, hoping to improve their understanding of the liturgy through an investigation of its historical origins. What they found, though, was that the mass in the early Middle Ages was different in many ways from the mass in the modern church, and that in Pope Gregory's day, for example, lay people had actually been expected to participate in the liturgy.

At first the monks tried to improve their own liturgies by restoring Gregorian chant to their celebrations of the mass, but in time others too became interested in this ancient form of church music as a third alternative to nonliturgical hymns and operatic masses. But if people were to sing parts of the mass they had to have the text, and if they were to do it well they had to understand what they were singing. In the 1880s missals for use by lay people were first allowed to be published, and some even contained translations of some of the prayers. It was not until 1897, however, that the official ban on translating the Roman missal was lifted, enabling ordinary Catholics for the first time in over a thousand years to follow everything that the priest was doing at the altar.

During the early years of the liturgical movement it was mainly the Benedictines who encouraged people to use missals rather than devotional prayer books and to pray along with the priest rather than say the rosary during the mass. But after a while the movement began to gain support from some of the hierarchy, and in 1903 Pius X gave papal approval to greater lay participation in the mass through the use of chant and more frequent reception of communion. Pius himself had a great personal devotion to Christ in the Blessed Sacrament and he worked hard to dispel the Jansenist notion that most people were not worthy enough to receive communion regularly. The Council of Trent had decided that children need not be given communion before the age of reason, and it had gradually become customary to wait until they were twelve or even sixteen before being admitted to the sacrament. But the pope saw no reason why young children should be denied the eucharist, and in 1910 he established the age for the first reception of communion at seven years. In the years that followed, "first communion" became an important ceremonial occasion for Catholic children, sometimes even rivaling confirmation, which continued to be celebrated during adolescence. Girls were dressed as "brides of Christ" with white veils and dresses, boys too were dressed more formally, and both were given presents and parties to mark the occasion. First communion thus became a modern unofficial sacrament, an almost universally practiced childhood ritual closely associated with the mass and the official sacrament of the eucharist.

In the period between the two world wars, research into the historical origins of the liturgy continued, and the movement for improving the liturgy grew primarily in Germany and Austria, Belgium and France. Yet even in those countries not all the hierarchy were in favor of altering the Tridentine tradition, and some openly criticized attempts to increase lay participation as violations of the rubrics and dangerous innovations. The Congregation of Rites was also extremely conservative in many of its rulings during this period, but gradually the results of decades of liturgical scholarship came to be recognized even in Rome. In 1947 Pius XII issued a papal encyclical in which he attempted to steer a middle course between the proponents of change and those who reacted against it, warning priests against tampering with the official liturgy but approving other attempts to make it more relevant to the laity.

Shortly before, two lengthy and detailed historical studies of the mass had been published by Josef Jungmann and Gregory Dix, and articles on the liturgy by other scholars were beginning to show the fruits of wartime research. Basically what the historians had discovered was much of what has already been discussed in this chapter: that the mass was not always in Latin, and that the language of the liturgy had been changed when people no longer spoke Greek; that it did not always have the form firmly fixed after the Council of Trent, and that regional variety had been the rule in earlier days; that the Roman-style mass had itself undergone centuries of evolution, and that many of the prayers and rituals in it had originated in other places; that in the beginning bishops had used spontaneous rather than written prayers, and that lay people in the early church had had an active role in eucharistic worship. For the advocates of liturgical improvement these discoveries were crucial because they proved beyond any doubt that the church's worship had varied considerably in the centuries before the counter-reformation and because they provided historical precedents which suggested directions that new reforms of the liturgy could take.

During the 1950s certain reforms in the liturgy in fact began to occur, but they were extremely modest. For example, some dioceses were
given permission to celebrate evening masses on Sundays and holy days,
the liturgies of Holy Week were revised to be a little more like the Lenten
practices of the patristic period, and the long hours of compulsory fasting
before communion were shortened to three and then to one hour. Then
in January 1959, John XXIII announced his intention to convoke an ecumenical council, and the world's Catholic bishops responded to the pope's
call to update the church by approving the Constitution on the Sacred
Liturgy the first conciliar document of Vatican II. It was the end of an era,
for the constitution called for changes in the liturgy more thorough than
any in over four centuries. It was even more than the liturgists had ever
dreamed possible in the period before the council, and yet it was the logical culmination of their years of research and efforts to increase popular
participation in the liturgy.

In the years following the Second Vatican Council, change replaced
sameness as a liturgical norm in the Catholic Church. In fact a series of
changes in the mass were implemented in such quick succession in the
sixties and seventies that older Catholics sometimes began to yearn for the
"good old days" when they knew what to expect when they went to church
on Sundays. First only parts of the Latin mass were translated into modern
languages, then the whole mass was translated, and finally the liturgy itself
was simplified and made more flexible. As a result, the Roman mass today
(for it is still basically a single ritual with allowable variations, all of which
have been approved by Rome) is a more biblical and eucharistic form of
worship that emphasizes scripture readings and communion rather than
the consecration. It can be celebrated by a single priest or concelebrated
by two or more priests, and it allows for the readings and other liturgical
actions to be performed by lay people as well. Almost all of the priest's
prayers are said in a tone of voice that is audible to the congregation, and
the people are expected to respond to the prayers at certain points and to
join in the recitation of other prayers such as the creed and the Our Father.

Seen from the perspective of the people in the pews, then, the change in
the Catholic mass could hardly have been more complete. Instead of being
a service that they were expected to watch from a distance, it has become a
form of worship in which they are expected to participate. Instead of being
a silent ritual, it has become one with very few moments of silence. Instead
of being a "sacrifice of the mass" at which few people communicated, it has
become a "eucharistic liturgy" at which almost everyone communicates.

And instead of being a legalistic obligation that must be fulfilled on Sunday morning, it has become a religious requirement that may be satisfied on Saturday evening as well as on Sunday.

These recent revisions have also altered the priest's role in and experience of the mass. He used to offer the mass rather privately, up at the altar with his back to the congregation, but the altar has now been moved away from the rear wall so that he faces the people and acts as a leader in public worship. His role as a preacher used to be secondary to his function as a minister of the Blessed Sacrament, but now he is supposed to give regular homilies explaining the scripture readings. His preparation for mass used to be rather cursory, since low masses did not vary much from day to day, but now he must select from a variety of alternative prayers and readings, and on weekends he often has to help design and coordinate a liturgy that is expected to have some ceremonial variety from week to week.

In many parishes, lay people have become increasingly involved in the preparation and celebration of the weekly eucharist. Liturgy teams plan for what will happen at the service, selecting among optional prayers and readings, composing prayers that reflect parishioners' personal needs and social awareness, choosing appropriate music, designing floral and symbolic arrangements for the interior of the church, and coordinating the efforts of a variety of people who work both behind the scenes and in public view. More affluent parishes even employ full- or part-time liturgy directors and music directors to oversee this planning and coordinating effort. The result is a liturgy that involves a great number of active participants: greeters who welcome parishioners as they arrive; ushers who show them to their seats, take up the collection, and help direct the people going to communion; an organist or other musicians, and a choir or a less formal singing ensemble, who provide music and lead the singing of the parishioners; lectors who introduce the liturgy, read the scriptures, and make announcements; people chosen to carry the symbolic gifts of bread and wine to the altar; acolytes and perhaps a deacon who assist the priest; eucharistic ministers who help in the distribution of communion, especially when the cup is shared in addition to the consecrated hosts; and perhaps even a hospitality committee that serves coffee and doughnuts to those who like to socialize before going home. In many ways, then, Catholics' experience of eucharistic worship is quite different from what it was before the council, and this is true for laity and clergy alike.

Initially it was thought that both the rate of change and the variety to which it gave rise would increase in the future. The Second Vatican

Council approved the notions of liturgical change and variety in principle, and since the council itself sanctioned only certain changes and limited variety, some critics pointed out difficulties in the revisions. The new rubrics allowed the mass to be adapted to special needs and occasions: for weddings and funerals, for teenagers and children, for formal church celebrations and for informal home gatherings. But even this adaptability did not seem to be enough in a Catholic world that included a bewildering diversity of national and regional, racial and cultural, economic and social groups. Could a single style of liturgy be the best form of worship day after day and week after week for so many who are so different? This is the question that liturgists and theologians began to ask, and some have even answered it in the negative. Bishops, too, especially those in nonwestern countries, were aware that in the period before Trent their predecessors enjoyed greater freedom in liturgical affairs, and in the 1970s some dared to suggest a return to regional autonomy in matters of worship. During the 1980s and 1990s, however, expansive growth in variety was curtailed both through the appointment of more conservative bishops and through Vatican directives that disallowed certain earlier experimentation.

One of these directives was issued in 2001 regarding the proper implementation of the Constitution on the Sacred Liturgy. Known by its Latin name, *Liturgiam Authenticam* (meaning authentic liturgy), it revised the norms for translating liturgical texts from Latin into modern languages that had been in place since 1969. In general, it said that the earlier practice of translating the words of the mass into modern phrases that captured the sense of the original was no longer acceptable, and that scripture passages used in the mass should be guided by what is said in the Latin translation of the Bible. In particular, it insisted that translators follow the word order of the master Latin text, that they seek to preserve the dignity, beauty, and doctrinal precision of the Latin, and that they avoid inclusive language when talking about human beings as well as gender-neutral language when talking about God. It allowed that a very literal translation may at times sound odd, but it suggested that any departure from ordinary language could be used as an opportunity for catechesis.

Around the same time, the International Commission on English in the Liturgy (ICEL) that had created the first English translation of the mass was disbanded and replaced by one that was more attuned to the new directives from Rome. This commission produced a revised translation that was gradually approved by English-speaking episcopal conferences around the world and that was adopted in the United States in 2011. Among other things, the large *Roman Missal* replaced the thinner liturgical books that had been in use after the council, and laity were instructed to reply "And with your spirit" instead of "And also with you" when the priest said "The Lord be with you." Although the publication of the new missal aroused strong feelings in favor and against the more traditional language, both sides in the liturgy debate were somewhat surprised by the fact that the revised mass texts had neither the positive effects that conservatives had hoped for nor the deleterious effects that liberals had anticipated.

Undaunted, conservative Catholics continue to press for what Benedict XVI called a "new liturgical movement" that would bring mass translations more in line with the missals that had been in use before Vatican II, and they applauded the pope's lifting of restrictions on the use of the 1962 Latin mass. They believe that active participation in the liturgy, which the bishops at the council had called for, includes reverent silence and inward appreciation of the eucharistic mystery, as well as greater use of Gregorian chant to foster deeply worshipful attitudes. Above all, they deplore what they perceive as a secularist mentality and a fascination with worldly fashions that detract from the authentic worship embodied in the traditional mass that was the same for all Latin rite Catholics around the world.

Notwithstanding, great autonomy continues to be exercised in places where a shortage of priests raises the need for deacons or lay people to lead Catholics in public prayer. Without the authority to preside at the eucharist, these pastoral ministers must create new forms of worship such as communion services using already consecrated hosts, or scripture services suggestive of what might be found in Protestant congregations. Critics of this situation point out the irony of losing the eucharist as the central form of Catholic worship at a time when the liturgy has been revised to make it more accessible to people, and they sometimes fault the Vatican for not relaxing the rule of celibacy so that more priests might be ordained. On the other hand, there are those who even prefer this type of situation, saying that it gives added significance to the eucharist when it is able to be celebrated, and that in the meantime it provides for greater freedom and variety in worship.

The initial impetus for change and variety had not come from pastoral sensitivity or practical necessity, however, but from the liturgical movement and from the historical facts it had uncovered about the eucharistic liturgy in earlier eras. Before Vatican II those facts suggested that other forms of the mass were possible and that development could occur again as it had in the past. They also suggested that other explanations of the eucharist were possible besides the scholastic one, and the shift toward nonscholastic philosophies and biblical theology in the twentieth century showed how that possibility might be realized. In the ten years prior to the council, this shift in Catholic thinking about the eucharist was slight, but it was definite enough to justify the changes in eucharistic practice that have already taken place. In the years since the council, the shift has become more noticeable and it is suggesting changes that are yet to come.

CHANGES IN EUCHARISTIC THEOLOGY

The main direction in recent years has been toward a reunification of thinking about the Blessed Sacrament, communion, and the mass. Today Catholic theologians prefer to speak of the mass as the eucharistic liturgy, and there is a tendency to regard it as a single sacramental action so that eucharistic theology today is as much a theology of the liturgy as it is of the consecrated elements. In the 1950s, however, the theology of the eucharist was still primarily a theology of the Blessed Sacrament, and the first step toward a new eucharistic theology was a reexamination of what happened during the consecration.

The Catholic explanation of the consecration since the Middle Ages had been given in terms of transubstantiation: the appearances of the bread and wine remained while their substance or reality changed into the body and blood of Christ. In 1955, however, F. J. Leenhardt proposed that the consecration could also be explained by another theory that came to be known as "transfinalization." The basic idea behind it was that the "final reality" of any created thing is determined by its maker and not by what it is made of. A carpenter who made a cabinet, for example, made something whose final reality was a cabinet even though he made it out of wood. He had actually produced something new, since before only the wood existed but now there was a new reality, brought into being through the intention of its creator. In an analogous way one could understand the eucharist, Leenhardt suggested, since it started out as bread and wine but its final reality was different. It was something new brought into being through the intention of its creator, for Jesus Christ, who instituted the sacrament, had intended that the bread and wine should become his body and blood. Of course there was an important difference between the two cases since the artifact was made by a human action while the sacrament was produced by the power of God, but the whole point of the analogy was that God could in fact change the final reality of the bread and wine since he was the ultimate author of all creation.

Leenhardt was a Protestant theologian who presented his theory in an ecumenical spirit, hoping that it might be an explanation that both Protestants and Catholics could agree on. For many Protestants, however, the theory explained too much since it suggested a real change in the elements about which they could not agree. And for most Catholic theologians the theory explained too little since it admitted that the elements were changed without fully explaining how the change took place. But Leenhardt's theory did show that it might be possible to explain the consecration in other ways besides transubstantiation, and in the following years theologians continued to explore that possibility.

A theory that gained wider acceptance in Catholic theological circles was called "transignification." It was developed in a number of ways by various authors using philosophical categories from existentialism and phenomenology such as those discussed in chapter V. The basic philosophical idea behind it was that significance or meaning is a constitutive element of reality as it is known to human beings, and this is especially true of human realities like attitudes and relationships. Such human realities are embodied and expressed in symbolic actions such as gestures and words, and they are known through the meaning that those actions have for people. The words "I love you," for example, embody and express one human reality, while a slap on the face embodies and expresses quite another. But sometimes symbolic actions can mean more than one thing, and in these cases they can embody and express very different realities. Obeying an order, for example, can be a symbolic action signifying either willing agreement or unwilling compliance: the meaning of the action and the human reality involved are different in the two cases. Finally, the meaning of a symbolic action can change, and the human reality that is signified changes with it. Young men wore long hair in the 1960s as a sign of rebellion against society, for example, but when they did so in the 1970s it was more usually a sign of their social conformity. By the 1990s the length of a man's hair symbolized a lifestyle choice rather than a social statement.

Symbolic actions, therefore, can embody and express—and in that sense reveal—things that cannot be directly seen but are nonetheless real, and theologians like Schillebeeckx, Rahner, and Cooke have used this philosophical insight in developing their understanding of the Catholic sacraments. Looked at in this way the sacraments are symbolic actions, ritual actions of words and gestures, which embody and reveal not only human realities but also divine realities. They are signs through which God's grace and presence are communicated and through which people come in contact with the transcendent realities that the sacraments signify. Yet these same theologians recognize (as earlier Catholic thinkers did not) that many of the symbolic actions called sacraments were not invented by Jesus: baptisms, sacred meals, marriage, and ordination rites, for example, already existed in ancient Judaism. What Jesus did then in "instituting" the sacraments (either directly or through the church) was to change the significance of these actions, giving them new meanings and enabling them to reveal the same divine mysteries that he himself incarnated and revealed during his lifetime. In this sense, then, most of the sacraments were instituted not by direct invention but by transignification: Christ changed the significance that existing rituals had for those who believed in him and in doing so changed the realities that they embodied and revealed.

With respect to the eucharist, the proponents of transignification suggest that at the last supper Christ changed the meaning of a common Jewish ritual to a memorial of his death and resurrection, and that he changed the meaning of the bread and wine from what they signified for Jews to a sacrament of his body and blood. But since meaning is an intrinsic aspect of reality as it is known to human beings, by changing the meaning of the ritual and the elements he thereby transformed their reality, making them objectively and for all time signs through which he would be present in the church and through which Christians could personally encounter him. In parallel fashion the reality of the bread and wine is changed during the mass not in any physical way but in a way that is nonetheless real, for as soon as they signify the body and blood of Christ they become sacramental, embodying and revealing Christ's presence in a way that is experienceably real. In other words, when the meaning of the elements changes, their reality changes for those who have faith in Christ and accept the new meaning that he gave them, whereas for those without faith and who are unaware of their divinely given meaning, they appear to remain bread and wine.

Despite its apparent orthodoxy, the Catholic hierarchy has had some difficulty in accepting transignification as an explanation for the eucharist. To many of them, including Pope Paul VI in his encyclical on *The Mystery of Faith*, transubstantiation seems to be part and parcel of the Catholic belief in the real presence, and so to change the explanation of it seems tantamount to changing the doctrine itself. In addition, words like "meaning" and "significance" seem to be very subjective, suggesting that the only change in the eucharist is in the mind rather than in the sacramental elements themselves, and this is an explanation that was explicitly rejected by the Council of Trent. After historians demonstrated that transubstantiation had never been proclaimed a doctrine of the faith by any pope or council, however, many theologians came to accept transignification as a possible theory even if they did not endorse it.

Another reason for theological tolerance had to do with changes in the theology of the mass itself, changes that were proposed by the same theologians whose earlier ideas had been accepted by many of the bishops at the council. Researchers in the liturgical movement discovered not only earlier forms but also earlier theologies of the eucharist in the patristic era, and when theologians began to incorporate them in their own writings, church leaders had to admit that these too were part of the Catholic heritage. At the same time scholars in the biblical movement rediscovered the connection between the last supper and the scriptural ideas of covenant, meal, and Passover, and since these connections were found in the Bible the hierarchy had no objection to them. Slowly it became clear that for twelve hundred years Christians had been able to talk about the eucharist without speaking of it in terms of transubstantiation, and that the scholastic understanding of the mass was somewhat narrow when seen in the light of the entire Catholic tradition.

Since the Second Vatican Council, then, Catholic theology has been explicitly attempting to recover the patristic and scriptural understanding of the eucharist and to translate it into terms that make sense to people today. At the same time, it has been gradually abandoning the Tridentine insistence on transubstantiation and on the mass as a sacrifice in favor of other interpretations that are equally Catholic but less scholastic. And in doing this it has been shifting its attention from the Blessed Sacrament as an object of worship to the entire liturgy as an act of worship.

The general direction of these changes could already be seen in Vatican II's Constitution on the Sacred Liturgy in 1963. The council spoke of the eucharist in scriptural rather than scholastic terms and it placed the liturgy in the context of the mystery of Christ's death and resurrection as the fathers had often done. It reiterated the Catholic belief in the real presence of Christ in the Blessed Sacrament, but not before it had emphasized the presence of Christ in the church and in the entire eucharistic liturgy. According to the council document the mass is, then, an action of Christ and an action of the church. It is an action of Christ because he initiated it and continues to be present in it through his presence in the worshiping community. As the word of God he is present in the reading of scripture at each mass and he addresses himself to all those who listen with faith in him. He is also present sacramentally in the bread and wine that are of-

fered to God in praise and thanksgiving and that are distributed as a sign
of spiritual communion with him. But the mass is also an action of the
church, for it is in and through the community's worship that Christ's action
takes place. Christians join themselves to Christ's redemptive sacrifice by
offering themselves in praise and thanksgiving to God the Father just as
Jesus had done at the last supper. And by fully participating in the liturgy
they most fully express what the church is and hopes to be: united with
Christ and responsive to his word.

Of all the themes that the council developed in connection with the
eucharist, the one which appears the most in its other documents is unity:
the unity of each Christian with Christ and the unity of all Christians with
one another. "Really sharing in the body of the Lord in the breaking of the
Eucharistic bread, we are taken up into communion with him and with
one other" (*Church* 7). As Paul said, Christians are the body of Christ, and
so by sharing in the eucharist they both affirm and become what they are.
In Christ Catholics are united not only with one another but also with all
other Christians, and it is "the wonderful sacrament of the Eucharist by
which the unity of the Church is both signified and brought about" (*Ecumenism* 2). The mass is "a supper of brotherly and sisterly communion
and a foretaste of the heavenly banquet" (*Church in the Modern World* 38),
and so it should be "the center and culmination of the entire life of the
Christian community" (*Bishops* 30). According to the documents of the
council, therefore, the eucharistic liturgy was to be understood as a sign
of Christian unity, and it was largely with this theme in mind that the mass
was revised to invite greater congregational participation.

In the years following the council, theologians continued to emphasize the biblical and patristic meanings of the eucharist without rejecting the scholastic interpretations still familiar to many Catholics. They
continued to explore the ideas that the eucharist is a meal and as such a
sign of sharing with others, that it is a memorial of the last supper and
as such a sign of participation in Christ's death and resurrection, that it
is an act of thanksgiving and as such a communal action of the entire
congregation. They continued to elaborate on the prayers and rituals that
have become a part of the mass through the centuries: on the penitential
rite, on the readings and responses, on the hymn of glory and the profession of faith, on the prayers of petition and the offering of gifts. The first
effect of these theological reflections was the church-wide revision of the
mass in the late 1960s and the early 1970s, but they continued to affect
the celebration of the liturgy in individual dioceses and parishes around

the world. For the eucharist had been shown to have not one but many meanings, any one or combination of which can be highlighted during a particular mass.

Liturgical theology, starting in the 1980s, carried these developments ever further, as theologians reflected on the experience of the renewed liturgy in the light of both historical scholarship and the teachings of the Second Vatican Council. The council had broadened the notion of Christ's presence to include not only his sacramental presence in the bread and wine but also his presence as the word of God in the scripture readings of the mass, and indeed his presence as the risen Lord in the assembly of believers. Since these are ideas that were prominent in the early centuries of Christianity, liturgical theologians prefer not to engage in the type of metaphysical theologizing that emerged in the Middle Ages; instead they talk about the liturgy in scriptural and liturgical terms. In other words, they talk about what is happening in the liturgy and do not use philosophy to explain how it is happening. By looking at the entire liturgy instead of focusing on the consecration of the bread and wine, they develop what might be called a theology of eucharistic worship rather than a theology of eucharistic change.

From the perspective of liturgical theology, then, the eucharist is a prayerful action of an assembled Christian community, gathered as the body of Christ in remembrance of his death and resurrection in which they continue to participate, and united with one another as they worship God the Father in the power of the Holy Spirit. The whole assembly is thus the principal actor in the liturgy, making eucharistic worship happen, rather than the priest who presides at the liturgical action. The worshiping community makes it possible for Christ to be present in the proclaiming of God's word in the scriptures, in the thanksgiving that it offers to the Father, in the remembrance of Jesus' last supper, and in the giving and receiving of the eucharistic bread and wine. The community's worship is a memorial of the life, death, and resurrection of Christ, which they continue to experience in their lives; it is sacrificial because they are united with Jesus in his offering of his will to God and his life to others; and it is a sign of God's kingdom to come as a foretaste of the caring and love that join people into God's family.

The section on the eucharist in the 1994 *Catechism of the Catholic Church* reflects many of the developments that took place during the preceding decades. Its approach is predominantly scriptural and patristic, liturgical and spiritual, with a minimal amount of reference to scholastic theology. Traditional Catholic doctrines on the eucharist are firmly embedded in this section, but they do not dominate the treatment. Given the centrality of Catholic worship, it is not surprising that the *Catechism* devotes more attention to it than to any other sacrament, almost a hundred numbered paragraphs (1322–1419). Moreover, its emphasis is on the eucharist as an act of worship rather than on eucharist as an object of devotion. In this respect its treatment continues the approach taken by the bishops at the Second Vatican Council.

After noting that the eucharist is the third of the sacraments of initiation (1322), the *Catechism* drops all reference to the eucharist's role in Christian initiation and focuses instead on its role in weekly and even daily Catholic worship. Using an often-cited phrase of the Constitution on the Sacred Liturgy, the *Catechism* characterizes the eucharist as "the source and summit of the Christian life" (1324; the quotation is from *Liturgy* 11). Acknowledging the "inexhaustible richness of this sacrament," it reviews the many terms used to refer to it: eucharist, Lord's supper, sacrifice, liturgy, communion, and mass (1328–1332).

As the *Catechism* does for the other sacraments, it reviews references to the eucharist in the scriptures, first looking at precedents primarily in the Old Testament (1334–1336) and then recounting the institution of the eucharist in the New Testament (1337–1344). The *Catechism* devotes only three paragraphs to the history of the mass (1345–1347), but it gives a somewhat lengthy explanation of the liturgical dynamics of eucharistic worship, that is, the movement of the celebration from the initial gathering of the assembly to the reception of communion (1348–1355).

Within this liturgical context, the Trinitarian structure of eucharistic worship is noted (1356–1358), followed by explanations of how the mass offers praise and thanksgiving to God the Father (1359–1361), how it is a memorial of and participation in Christ's sacrificial death (1362–1372), and of how Christ is made present by the power of the Holy Spirit (1373–1381). It is here that the *Catechism* treats traditional Catholic teachings such as the mass as a sacrifice and the real presence of Christ both in the liturgy and in the consecrated bread and wine. Its treatment reflects recent developments in liturgical and systematic theology, and transubstantiation is mentioned only once, in a quotation from the Council of Trent (1376).

The *Catechism* concludes with a lengthy subsection on holy communion (1382–1401) and a less lengthy subsection on the eucharist as an eschatological sign (1402–1405). Most of the treatment of communion focuses on eucharistic spirituality, that is, interior self-preparation for communion, spiritual encounter with and union with Christ through the reception of communion, and the spiritual benefits of this encounter. Although the *Catechism* in this subsection utilizes some very traditional terminology, its treatment is devotional rather than scholastic when it talks about the fruits of communion being union with Christ, forgiveness of sins, removal of the inclination to sin, constitution of the church, unity with other Christians, and commitment to the poor. These themes lead naturally to the concluding paragraphs on the eschatological nature of the eucharist in which the spiritual experience of communion is regarded as a taste of what heaven will be like.

At its present stage of development, therefore, the eucharistic liturgy is a multivalent religious ritual, that is, it is a complex sacramental sign that can express and reveal a variety of Christian values and meanings. For traditionalists it can still be primarily an act of private devotion focused on the real presence of Christ in the host. For those in tune with the changes implemented after Vatican II it is fundamentally an act of public worship, a common prayer of thanksgiving, and a celebration of Christian unity. For the majority of Catholics, however, the meaning they find in any particular liturgy and the value they derive from it varies from mass to mass. Sometimes the scripture readings or the homily may reveal a new dimension of the Christian mystery, sometimes a prayer they listen to or say aloud may intensify their awareness of their relation to God and to others, sometimes the actions of those at the altar or those around them may silently illuminate the purpose for which they have gathered together. Sometimes the occasion for the liturgy, the place in which it is celebrated, or the persons who take part in it may say as much or more to individual participants as the prescribed prayers, the prepared readings, or the ritual actions. And for those who are inwardly ready for the liturgy when it begins and who are receptive to whatever may disclose itself to them as it progresses, the mass can reveal a rhythmic sequence of transcendent meanings in sacred space and time.

It is as though the eucharist today is not a single door to the sacred but a multiple door to sacred truth and mysterious reality. In its long and varied history it has opened to Christians the reality of divine presence and the inner truth of Christ's death and resurrection. Its bread and wine have symbolized the sacred significance of being united as in one body and of being poured out in sacrifice like blood. Its multitude of prayers have defined the meaning of Christian life and articulated the range of Christian experience from abject sinfulness to joyful holiness. Its interchangeable readings from the Bible have laid open the full sweep of the Judeo-Christian understanding of God and humanity, of good and evil, of life and death.

At various points in its history, eucharistic worship has emphasized now one and now another facet of the Christian mystery, sometimes clearly and sometimes obscurely. Today, however, an awareness of that history has opened the possibility of a multifaceted awareness of that same mystery, the mystery that Christ incarnated in his life and that Catholics find in the Bible and the other sacraments. In its root, perhaps, it is a single mystery but in its manifestations it is complex, revealing a sacred dimension to almost every aspect of human existence. And the eucharist as a constantly repeated and variable liturgy is the only Catholic sacrament of the seven that can unlock the door to the rich complexity of that simple mystery.

For Further Reading

Eucharistic Liturgy

Adolf Adam, *The Eucharistic Celebration* (Liturgical Press, 1994) explains the meaning and purpose of each of the parts of the mass.

William Marrevee, *The Popular Guide to the Mass* (Pastoral Press, 1992) is actually a fairly sophisticated even if brief explanation of eucharistic worship.

Ralph Keifer, *Blessed and Broken* (Michael Glazier, 1982) develops a contemporary theology of the eucharist based on the experience of public worship.

Gail Ramshaw, *Words Around the Table* (Liturgy Training Publications, 1991) offers poetic yet scholarly reflections on various aspects of Sunday eucharist.

Frank Anderson, *Making the Eucharist Matter* (Ave Maria Press, 1998) is intended to help Catholics find more meaning in the mass.

Kevin Irwin, *Responses to 101 Questions on the Mass* (Paulist Press, 1999) addresses basic liturgical and theological matters for people with little background in Catholic worship.

Lawrence Mick, *Forming the Assembly to Celebrate the Mass* (Liturgy Training Publications, 2002) presents the spiritual dynamics of liturgical worship in each part of the mass.

Jeremy Driscoll, *What Happens at Mass* (Liturgy Training Publications, 2005) gives a fairly detailed description of each part of the mass, presenting its liturgical purpose and meaning.

John Laurence, *The Sacrament of the Eucharist* (Liturgical Press, 2012) provides theological background and commentary on the eucharistic liturgy.

Joseph Lionel, *New Missal, Same Mass* (Academia Press, 2011) offers an apologetic for the third edition of *The Roman Missal* and its English translation.

Eucharistic History

Jean Lebon, *How to Understand the Liturgy* (Crossroad, 1988) offers a basic yet somewhat sophisticated introduction to the history, theology, and practical celebration of the eucharist.

Robert Cabié, *History of the Mass* (Pastoral Press, 1992) includes intriguing excerpts from writings contemporary with the developments being described.

Alfred McBride, *A Short History of the Mass* (St. Anthony Messenger Press, 2006) is a multifaceted treatment with sidebars, stories, and discussion questions.

Mary Durkin, *The Eucharist* (Thomas More Press, 1990) reviews the contemporary understanding of sacraments and presents a history of the eucharist in nontechnical language.

Tad Guzie, *Jesus and the Eucharist* (Paulist Press, 1974) takes a look at Catholic beliefs in the light of history and comparative religions.

Eucharistic Doctrine

Fidelis Stoeckl, *John Paul II and the Mystery of the Eucharist* (Paulines, 2006) presents a synthesis of the pope's teachings, based on his writings and addresses.

Francis Arinze, *Celebrating the Holy Eucharist* (Ignatius Press, 2006) presents church teachings and policies with clarity and reasonableness.

Christoph Schönborn, *The Source of Life* (Crossroad Publishing, 2007) is a very readable exposition of Catholic teaching on the mass and the Blessed Sacrament.

Robert Barron, *Eucharist* (Orbis Books, 2008) contains reflections on the eucharist as sacred meal, as sacrifice, and as sacramental reality.

Ralph McMichael, *Eucharist: A Guide for the Perplexed* (T&T Clark, 2010) offers general reflections on the sacrament by a writer in the Anglican tradition.

Donald Wuerl and Mike Aquilina, *The Mass* (Doubleday, 2011) is an exposition of Catholic worship for people who need an introduction to the basics.

Eucharistic Spirituality

Paul Bernier, *Eucharist: Celebrating Its Rhythms in Our Lives* (Ave Maria Press, 1993) moves through each of the parts of the mass, explaining how participants should prayerfully enter into it.

Theodore Dobson, *Say But the Word* (Paulist Press, 1984) presents a spirituality of the eucharist based on Jungian psychology, suggesting how the mass can facilitate a process of inner transformation.

Kenneth Stevenson, *Accept This Offering* (Liturgical Press, 1989) explains how the dynamics of the eucharist can be understood as an act of sacrificial worship.

Thomas Keating, *The Mystery of Christ* (Continuum, 1994) explains the ability of the mass to foster spiritual experience through the cycle of the liturgical year.

Tony Kelly, *The Bread of God* (Liguori Publications, 2001) proposes that eucharistic imagination is needed to appreciate the implications of the sacrament.

David Pearson, *No Wonder They Call It the Real Presence* (Servant Publications, 2002) presents testimonies of people who have encountered Christ in the Blessed Sacrament.

Dennis Billy, *Eucharist* (Twenty-Third Publications, 2004) explores various facets of eucharistic practice and spirituality.

Miriam Therese Winter, *Eucharist with a small "e"* (Orbis Books, 2005) means living with the spirit of Jesus, according to his values, sharing his compassion and concerns.

Vinny Flynn, *7 Secrets of the Eucharist* (MercySong, 2006) combines traditional teaching and personal experience in discussing doctrine and spirituality.

Kenan Osborne, *Community, Eucharist, and Spirituality* (Liguori Publications, 2007) argues that genuine eucharist occurs only in a community whose members love one another.

Joan Ridley, *In the Presence* (Liguori Publications, 2010) explains devotion to the Blessed Sacrament and describes the practice of eucharistic adoration.

Bruce Morrill, *Encountering Christ in the Eucharist* (Paulist Press, 2012) is an ecumenically sensitive explanation of the liturgy from a Catholic perspective.

For Further Study

Scripture and Theology

G. D. Kilpatrick, *The Eucharist in Bible and Liturgy* (Cambridge University Press, 1983) sheds light on Jesus' last supper and early Christian communal meals.

Xavier Léon-Dufour, *Sharing the Eucharistic Bread* (Paulist Press, 1987) is a thorough exegetical examination of all the texts in the New Testament related to the eucharist.

Jerome Kodell, *The Eucharist in the New Testament* (Michael Glazier, 1988) summarizes contemporary scripture scholarship about the texts relating to the last supper of Jesus, and other meals.

Markus Barth, *Rediscovering the Lord's Supper* (John Knox Press, 1988) uses insightful scholarship to reach some surprising liturgical conclusions.

Eugene LaVerdiere, *Dining in the Kingdom of God* (Liturgy Training Publications, 1994) explores the biblical meaning of the eucharist as presented in the Gospel According to Luke. *The Breaking of Bread* (Liturgy Training Publications, 1998) does the same with regard to Acts of the Apostles, also written by Luke.

Dennis Smith, *From Symposium to Eucharist* (Fortress Press, 2003) situates the Lord's supper of the early church in the context of Greek, Roman, and Jewish banquets.

Martin Stringer, *Rethinking the Origins of the Eucharist* (SCM Press, 2011) argues that the weekly eucharistic meal did not become a universal practice until the second century.

History and Theology—Overviews

Edward Foley, *From Age to Age* (Liturgical Press, 2008) is a thorough introduction to the history of eucharistic liturgy and theology, covering architecture, music, books, and visuals.

Josef Jungmann, *The Mass* (Liturgical Press, 1976) is a historical, theological, liturgical, and pastoral treatment of the eucharistic liturgy that summarizes and updates his more detailed work, *The Mass of the Roman Rite*.

Gregory Dix, *The Shape of the Liturgy* (Dacre Press, Adam and Charles Black, 1945) is a very thorough examination of the history and meaning of the eucharist, covering Anglican as well as Roman developments.

Theodore Klauser, *A Short History of the Western Liturgy* (Oxford University Press, 1969) is an excellent one-volume treatment of almost all aspects of church worship.

Lucien Deiss, *Early Sources of the Liturgy* (Alba House, 1967) contains translations of texts dating from the second to the fifth century.

Aidan Nichols, *The Holy Eucharist* (Veritas Publications, 1991) is a small book with a large number of texts, giving clear explanations of historical debates about theological issues.

Owen Cummings, *Eucharistic Doctors* (Paulist Press, 2005) summarizes the eucharistic theologies of Christian writers in the patristic, medieval, reformation, and modern ages.

Paul Bradshaw and Maxwell Johnson, *The Eucharistic Liturgies* (Liturgical Press, 2012) looks at the evolution and interpretation of eucharistic forms of worship from the beginning to the present.

History and Theology—Early Centuries

Enrico Mazza, *The Origins of the Eucharistic Prayer* (Liturgical Press, 1995) discusses early Christian liturgical texts but does not provide them in translation to any great length.

Paul Bradshaw, *Eucharistic Origins* (Oxford University Press, 2004) summarizes the scholarly reconstruction of early Christian meal rituals and their interpretation from the first to the fourth century.

Dennis Billy, *The Beauty of the Eucharist* (New City Press, 2010) explains the theology and spirituality revealed in 23 writings from the patristic period.

Robert Daly, *The Origins of the Christian Doctrine of Sacrifice* (Fortress Press, 1978) shows how the ancient notion of religious sacrifice became applied to Christian worship.

Kenneth Stevenson, *Eucharist and Offering* (Pueblo Books, 1986) shows how the language of sacrifice was used quite early to describe the eucharist, but that the understanding of sacrifice shifted over the course of centuries.

Michael McGuckian, *The Holy Sacrifice of the Mass* (Liturgical Training Publications, 2005) points out that sacrifices in the ancient world were ceremonies of offering food, after which the food was shared by those in attendance.

John Koenig, *The Feast of the World's Redemption* (Trinity Press International, 2000) argues that in their fellowship meals, Christians during the first decades felt the presence of their risen Lord as they celebrated the spread of God's kingdom.

Andrew Gerakas, *The Origin and Development of the Holy Eucharist* (Alba House, 2006) argues in favor of intercommunion between the Catholic and Orthodox churches, based on their early history.

History and Theology—Middle Ages

Henri de Lubac, *Corpus Mysticum* (University of Notre Dame Press, 2006), originally published in 1944, shows that the term "mystical body" referred to both the eucharist and the church during different periods in the Middle Ages.

Neil Xavier O'Donohue, *The Eucharist in Pre-Norman Ireland* (University of Notre Dame Press, 2011) looks at medieval missals and penitentials to reconstruct Irish liturgical worship before the eleventh century.

Gary Macy, *The Theologies of the Eucharist in the Early Scholastic Period* (Clarendon Press, 1984) documents a wide spectrum of interpretations and appreciations in the Middle Ages. *The Banquet's Wisdom* (Paulist Press, 1992) offers a highly readable account of how the eucharistic liturgy has been understood by Christians through the centuries.

William Crockett, *Eucharist: Symbol of Transformation* (Pueblo, 1989) is a scholarly and ecumenical presentation of the history and theology of the change brought about in and through the eucharist.

Marilyn McCord Adams, *Some Late Medieval Theories of the Eucharist* (Oxford University Press, 2010) explains the intricacies of sacramental causality and transubstantiation in greater detail than most people can stand.

History and Theology—Modern Period

Charles Journet, *The Mass* (St. Augustine Press, 2008) presents the traditional theology of the mass as an unbloody sacrifice and explains the reasoning behind transubstantiation, originally written in 1958.

Stephen Clark, *Catholics and the Eucharist* (Servant Publications, 2000) presents a traditional understanding of the mass, with explanations of basic concepts and terminology, using church teachings and scripture references.

James O'Connor, *The Hidden Manna* (Ignatius Press, 2005) traces the evolution of Catholic thinking toward the Tridentine doctrines and their affirmation by recent popes.

James Collins, *The Mass as a Sacrifice* (Alba House, 2007) summarizes the Tridentine doctrine with reference to earlier writings and later papal teachings.

Roch Kereszty, *Wedding Feast of the Lamb* (Hillenbrand Books, 2004) is a very readable presentation of a modern theology of the eucharist supported by scripture texts and writings from the Catholic tradition.

Marcel Lefebvre, *The Mass of All Time* (Angelus Press, 2007) presents the author's ideas about the eucharistic sacrifice and the departure of Vatican II from traditional teachings.

Michael Gaudoin-Parker, *The Real Presence Through the Ages* (Alba House, 1993) collects and comments on citations from Christian writers who have experienced Christ in the eucharist.

Benedict Groeschel and James Monti, *In the Presence of Our Lord* (Our Sunday Visitor, 1997) connects the history of eucharistic theology with the Catholic tradition of devotion to Christ in the sacrament.

Nathan Mitchell, *Cult and Controversy* (Pueblo, 1982) is a detailed study of the emergence and decline of devotion to the Blessed Sacrament.

Joseph Dougherty, *From Altar-Throne to Table* (Scarecrow Press, 2010) summarizes the history of infrequent communion and details Pope Pius X's gradual success in encouraging weekly and even daily communion.

Charles Caspers, Gerard Lukken, and Gerard Rouwhorst, eds., *Bread of Heaven* (Kok Pharos, 1995) meticulously describes and documents practices and beliefs about holy communion through the ages.

Michael O'Carroll, *Corpus Christi: An Encyclopedia of the Eucharist* (Michael Glazier, 1988) contains entries providing a wealth of historical and theological information related to the sacrament.

History and Theology—Contemporary Period

Joseph Powers, *Eucharistic Theology* (Seabury Press, 1967) summarizes the biblical background, liturgical and doctrinal history, and recent theology up to Vatican II.

Edward Schillebeeckx, *The Eucharist* (Sheed and Ward, 1968) examines the Council of Trent's decrees on the eucharist and gives an interpretation of the doctrine of real presence in terms of transignification.

David Power, *The Sacrifice We Offer* (Crossroad, 1987) argues that the scholastic theology of the eucharist, dogmatically affirmed by the Council of Trent, can and should be reinterpreted today. *The Eucharistic Mystery* (1992) critiques traditional eucharistic theologies and suggests that participants in liturgical worship play an important role in constituting its meaning.

Kevin Irwin, *Models of the Eucharist* (Paulist Press, 2005) develops a many-sided theology based both on the liturgy itself and on Catholic teachings about the eucharist.

Ghislain Lafont, *Eucharist: The Meal and the Word* (Paulist Press, 2008) offers a meditative analysis of the symbolism of the mass following ideas contributed by French postmodern thinkers.

Liturgy and Theology

Johannes Emminghaus, *The Eucharist: Essence, Form, Celebration* (Liturgical Press, 1997) is a historical and liturgical introduction to the meaning, structure, and celebration of the mass.

Kevin Seasoltz, *Living Bread, Saving Cup* (Liturgical Press, 1982) is a helpful collection of articles published in *Worship* from 1965 to 1980.

Ralph Keifer, *The Mass in Time of Doubt* (Pastoral Press, 1983) offers a commentary on the revised rite, bringing in many contemporary issues.

Nathan Mitchell, *Eucharist As Sacrament of Initiation* (Liturgy Training Publications, 1995) grounds the practice of eucharistic meals in Jesus' practice of eating with sinners and his proclamation of the kingdom of God.

Bernard Lee, ed., *Alternative Futures for Worship, Volume 3: The Eucharist* (Liturgical Press, 1987) explores what eucharistic worship might be like if celebrated in an intentional Christian community unlike the average parish.

M. Basil Pennington, *The Eucharist* (Liguori Publications, 2000) offers mystagogical reflection on liturgical symbolism, paying attention to both western and eastern rites.

Nathan Mitchell, *Real Presence* (Liturgy Training Publications, 2001) addresses contemporary liturgical and theological issues in a collection of essays on the eucharist.

Thomas Fisch, ed., *Primary Readings on the Eucharist* (Liturgical Press, 2004) is a collection of essays foundational to contemporary liturgical studies.

Keith Pecklers, *Dynamic Equivalence* (Liturgical Press, 2003) presents historical arguments in favor of liturgical language that is closer to vernacular speech than to Latin syntax.

Christopher Carstens and Douglas Martis, *Mystical Body, Mystical Voice* (Liturgical Training Publications, 2011) offers an apologetic for the new *Roman Missal* in language that is as clear as that of the missal itself.

Ethical Dimensions

Monika Hellwig, *The Eucharist and the Hunger of the World* (Sheed and Ward, 1992) examines traditional ideas such as sacrifice, blessing, and sacrament to explain the social dimensions of the mass, originally published in 1976.

Tissa Balasuriya, *The Eucharist and Human Liberation* (Orbis Books, 1977) examines the liturgy from a Third World perspective and finds in it a spiritual force for social reform.

Rafael Avila, *Worship and Politics* (Orbis Books, 1977) argues that the Lord's supper of the early Christians had social and political implications that were lost as the liturgy became theologized and spiritualized.

Jean Stromberg, ed., *Sharing One Bread, Sharing One Mission* (World Council of Churches, 1983) presents articles that draw attention to the meaning of eucharist for Christian ministry to others.

Joseph Grassi, *Broken Bread and Broken Bodies* (Orbis Books, 1985) argues that authentically celebrating the eucharist entails ministry to the hungry and oppressed.

Anne Primavesi and Jennifer Henderson, *Our God Has No Favorites* (Resource Publications, 1989) develops a feminist liberation theology of the eucharist based on Jesus' table fellowship with the marginalized.

Francis Moloney, *A Body Broken for a Broken People* (Collins Dove, 1990) argues that, since Jesus broke bread with sinful people, canonical requirements for receiving communion are unscriptural distortions.

William Cavanagh, *Torture and Eucharist* (Blackwell Publishers, 1998) points out connections between historical developments in eucharistic worship and the rise of the Catholic Church as an authoritarian institution.

Patrick McCormick, *A Banqueter's Guide to the All-Night Soup Kitchen of the Kingdom of God* (Liturgical Press, 2004) draws connections between being thankful for God's blessings and serving the poor and marginalized, as Jesus did.

Dennis Billy and James Keating, *The Way of Mystery* (Paulist Press, 2006) promotes the eucharist as a means of entering into the paschal mystery and moral living.

Andrea Bieler and Luise Schottroff, *The Eucharist* (Fortress Press, 2007) is a lengthy theological reflection on eucharistic worship in the context of a low Christology and a heightened awareness of political and economic realities.

Margaret Scott, *The Eucharist and Social Justice* (Paulist Press, 2009) argues from scripture, the rite, and personal experience that the liturgy is meant to transform awareness and relationships.

Ecumenical Dimensions

Irenée-Henri Dalmais, *Eastern Liturgies* (Hawthorn Books, 1960) offers a survey of the history and variety of liturgical and sacramental practices in the eastern churches.

Max Thurian, *The Mystery of the Eucharist* (William B. Eerdmans, 1984) tries to develop an ecumenical theology of the eucharist based on what is central to Orthodox, Catholic, and Protestant faith.

John Reuman, *The Supper of the Lord* (Fortress Press, 1985) describes the way many Protestants arrived at an ecumenical convergence in their understanding of the eucharist.

Ernest Falardeau, *One Bread and Cup* (Michael Glazier, 1987) points out similarities and differences in churches' spiritualities and theologies of the eucharist.

Alexander Schmemann, *The Eucharist* (St. Vladimir's Seminary Press, 1988) presents an Orthodox understanding of the eucharist through an extended commentary on the traditional liturgy.

Dennis Smith and Hal Taussig, *Many Tables* (Trinity Press International, 1990) uses variety in first century worship to argue for diversity and creativity in eucharistic practice today.

Horton Davies, *Bread of Life and Cup of Joy* (William B. Eerdmans, 1993) compares eucharistic prayers of different church traditions.

Philippe Larere, *The Lord's Supper* (Liturgical Press, 1993) summarizes the history and theology of the eucharist so that Catholics, Orthodox, and Protestants can discuss it together.

Thomas Davis, *The Clearest Promises of God* (AMS Press, 1995) shows how Calvin's thoughts about the Lord's supper developed over more than thirty years of writing.

Jeffrey Vander Wilt, *A Church Without Borders* (Liturgical Press, 1998) correlates inclusivistic and exclusivistic eucharistic policies with differing understandings of church.

Michael Welker, *What Happens in Holy Communion?* (William B. Eerdmans, 2000) is a scholarly comparison of different liturgical and theological traditions, reaching toward ecumenical convergence.

Jean-Marie-Roger Tillard, *Flesh of the Church, Flesh of Christ* (Liturgical Press, 2001) argues that the spiritual communion among Christians is the ground of their sharing eucharistic communion.

Kenneth Stevenson, *Do This: The Shape, Style and Meaning of the Eucharist* (Canterbury Press, 2002) looks at the eucharist from pastoral, doctrinal, and liturgical perspectives.

Roch Kereszty, *Rediscovering the Eucharist* (Paulist Press, 2003) presents papers and responses written by Catholic, Protestant, and Orthodox scholars at a conference focusing on the eucharist as a sacrifice.

Jeffrey Vander Wilt, *Communion with Non-Catholic Christians* (Liturgical Press, 2003) lays out the pros and cons of more open eucharistic sharing among different bodies of Christians.

Walter Kasper, *Sacrament of Unity* (Crossroad Publishing, 2004) presents reflections on ecumenical fellowship and communion by a member of the Catholic hierarchy.

Gordon Smith, *A Holy Meal* (Baker Publishing, 2005) is an ecumenical reflection on the Lord's supper and eucharist as a central Christian ritual.

James Puglisi, ed., *Liturgical Renewal as a Way to Christian Unity* (Liturgical Press, 2005) collects essays written by Protestants and Catholics who feel excluded from the process of liturgical cooperation due to conservative Vatican policies.

Owen Cummings, *Canterbury Cousins* (Paulist Press, 2007) summarizes the eucharistic theologies of a dozen contemporary Anglican theologians.

Ben Witherington, *Making a Meal of It* (Baylor University Press, 2007) suggests ways to bring a greater sense of community to the practice of the Lord's supper.

George Hunsinger, *The Eucharist and Ecumenism* (Cambridge University Press, 2008) attempts to reconcile doctrinal difference over the real presence of Christ, eucharist as a sacrifice, the eucharistic minister, and implications for social morality.

CHAPTER IX

RECONCILIATION

God, the Father of mercies, through the death and resurrection of his Son has reconciled the world to himself and sent the Holy Spirit among us for the forgiveness of sins. Through the ministry of the Church may God give you pardon and peace, and I absolve you from your sins in the name of the Father, and of the Son, and of the Holy Spirit.

—RITE OF PENANCE

There have been many sacraments of forgiveness and reconciliation in the history of Catholicism. Private confession evolved during the Middle Ages and became dominant in the modern church; other rituals preceded and were contemporary with it; still others are emerging today.

Baptism was the first sacramental ritual to be clearly associated with the forgiveness of sins. In early Christianity those who were baptized believed and felt themselves to be freed from their sinful past and reconciled with God. Bishops in the first centuries imposed their hands on heretics and schismatics who renounced their deviant beliefs and sought reunion with the orthodox community. It was a sign through which they accepted the forgiveness of God and through which they were forgiven by the church. The eucharistic liturgy was a repeated sign that Christians were united with Christ despite their sinfulness and that they were to be united with one another in faith and forgiveness. When the mass came to be understood and experienced as a sacrifice, the bread and wine were often seen as a sin offering, and in the Middle Ages theologians such as Thomas Aquinas spoke of devout participation in the sacrifice as a purification from personal sinfulness. Also in the Middle Ages the anointing of the sick came to be

317

explained and experienced as an occasion for spiritual rather than physical healing, and indulgences which began as commutations of ecclesiastical penalties ended up as cancellations of divine punishment. And throughout Christian history, prayer and the reading of scripture, fasting and physical self-discipline, almsgiving and other works of charity have been sacramental actions through which people could discover, experience, and practice the conquest of sin.

Amidst all these sacraments, however, there has usually been one in every age that stood out from the others. Whatever form it took, it combined an admission of guilt, interior and exterior acts of repentance, and an assurance of divine forgiveness given to the penitent. In the modern church it was administered privately by a priest and received by all Catholics perhaps once a year. In the patristic period it was publicly presided over by a bishop and undergone by only the most notorious sinners, and only once in a lifetime. Until medieval times the assurance of God's forgiveness could be given by a layperson; afterward it became an exclusive prerogative of the clergy. In recent times the works of repentance were usually brief prayers; in ancient times they were usually lengthy acts of mortification. But despite these differences the common elements of confession, repentance, and forgiveness were always found in one form or another, and they are still found in the Catholic ritual of reconciliation long known as penance.

The word itself comes from the Latin *paenitentia*, meaning repentance or penitence, an interior turning away from sinful attitudes and actions. Originally it meant the same as the Greek *metanoia*, which also means conversion or change of heart, but it later came to be applied to outward acts of repentance and to the whole ecclesiastical discipline of public penitence. In the Middle Ages the recognized *sacramentum paenitentiae* (sacrament of repentance) became private confession, absolution from guilt, and assigned works of penitence. When church Latin was translated into English these works were usually referred to as penances, and the ecclesiastical rite itself was called the sacrament of penance, penance being a shortened form of the word penitence.

As the ritual evolved it reflected changing conceptions of sin and forgiveness, and in turn it generated new explanations of how sins were forgiven in the church. All sin was ultimately, of course, an offense against God that required divine forgiveness, but what this meant abstractly and how it was interpreted concretely varied significantly through the centuries.

1. Parallels and Precedents

Today we think of crime and punishment as essentially secular, but in primitive and ancient cultures both were primarily religious. In primitive societies much of what we now would call law was social custom reinforced by religious myth. In ancient civilization laws were often understood as given by the gods, and so violations of them were sins as well as crimes. The role of punishment was therefore also religious. It helped preserve the divinely established order by discouraging violations, it reintegrated offenders into the order of society, and if necessary it safeguarded the sacred order by exiling or executing those who disrupted it.

Corresponding to the external social order was the internal moral order, the right order of things as perceived by the individual conscience. Deviations from the order brought feelings of guilt and anxiety to those who violated it, and even if they did not, the punishments of religious societies were designed both to make the offenders aware of their guilt and to give them the means of rectifying their conscience. Mild forms of punishment included temporary exclusions from religious worship, rituals of purification, and sacrifices such as sin offerings. More severe forms included public prayer and fasting, self-disfigurement and other signs of remorse, social ostracism, physical torture, and even death.

It is important to remember, however, that these ritual means of preserving the social and moral order were always in some sense sacramental, even if today we do not perceive them as such. Most laws were understood to be divine laws, handed down by the gods or their representatives on earth, and so the ritual penalties for violating them served as reminders of the sacred order to both offenders and onlookers. Participation in a rectification ritual was supposed to heighten people's awareness of their sins, intensify their respect for the moral code, and reinforce their conviction to live up to it in the future. Even the ritual of execution did this, at least for those who witnessed it. This is not to deny that ritual penalties could not become legalistic and unsacramental; they often did. But for those who viewed moral behavior as a sacred responsibility, they could and did serve as sacraments of reconciliation with the demands of society and the will of the gods.

Ancient Israel was a religious society in the sense described, even if many aspects of Jewish daily life had become secularized by the beginning of the Christian era. Its most ancient laws were religious laws, handed down from Yahweh through Moses and other prophets. Transgressions of those laws were therefore also sins, violations of the covenant between Yahweh and the chosen people, disruptions in the relationship between a divine person and human persons. And the penalties for those transgressions were not merely punishments meted out by society but sacraments of moral rectification and reconciliation. Sacrifices and sin offerings, prayers and lamentations, fastings and fines, property restitutions and corporal punishments were all intended to restore the covenant relationship between a holy God and a people who had fallen from the holiness that their God demanded of them. The Torah, the Law of Moses, was therefore a written sacrament through which the personal will of Yahweh was revealed to the people, and Jewish law was essentially an elaborate sacramental system even though it could (as the later prophets said it did) degenerate into legalism and empty ritual.

Around the time that Jesus lived, many of the penitential practices prescribed by the Torah were still in force. Individual infractions of the law, whether intentional or unintentional, had to be rectified through individual acts of repentance that were described in the scriptures or prescribed by the rabbis who tried to clarify the law where the Torah was vague. In addition, on the Day of Atonement each year the high priest had to confess his sins and the sins of the people to God before offering the sacrifice that would symbolize their sincerity and willingness to rectify their lives (Leviticus 16:21; Nehemiah 1:6–7). Confession was also prescribed by the Torah for certain individual sins (Leviticus 5:1–6; Numbers 5:6–7), and some early rabbinical books suggested that the confession of sins to a rabbi was a sign of sincere repentance. Since sacrifices could be offered only in the temple at Jerusalem, Jews living outside the city sought reconciliation with God through other means, and the rabbis recommended prayer, fasting, sleeping on the ground, wearing sackcloth and ashes, and almsgiving as penitential practices. The Torah ordered idolators to be expelled from the community (Deuteronomy 13:16) and the rabbis expanded on this practice by excluding notorious sinners from the synagogue and readmitting them when they repented and mended their ways.

2. Repentance and Reconciliation in Early Christianity

The earliest Christian penitential practices did not differ greatly from their Jewish predecessors. Around AD 57 Paul wrote that he was shocked to hear that the community in Corinth had not expelled one of its members for marrying his stepmother, a practice that was expressly forbidden by the

Torah (Leviticus 18:8). They were to be a holy community, free of wickedness, and Paul counseled them to cast out from their midst those who worshiped idols, who got drunk, who charged interest on loans, and who fell into other immoral practices (1 Corinthians 5:1–13). Evidently they took his advice, for a short while later he wrote again telling them to reinstate someone whom they had ostracized. He had been punished enough, said Paul, and now they should show their ability to love and forgive a brother Christian (2 Corinthians 2:5–11). In Paul's mind the purpose of such treatment was familial correction, to let sinners know they were in the wrong, and so it was not to be done indiscriminately but only after fair warning had been given (2 Thessalonians 2:6–15; Titus 3:10).

This practice of restricting someone from normal intercourse with the community and later lifting the restriction was known in rabbinical writings as "binding and loosing." The rabbis did it on the authority of Jewish law, but the early Christians saw themselves as doing it on the authority of Christ. Matthew's gospel depicts Jesus as telling his disciples to ostracize those who will not listen to milder corrections, and it portrays him as giving to Peter the "keys of the kingdom" with heavenly power to bind and loose people on earth (Matthew 16:19; 18:15–18). Neither the gospels nor the other New Testament writings indicate that there was any specific ritual connected with this discipline, although Paul does say that it should be done "by the power of the Lord Jesus" when the community is gathered together (1 Corinthians 5:4–5).

Evidently the only ritual of forgiveness known to the earliest Christian community was baptism, and today biblical scholars view almost all the texts that speak of a call to repentance as a call to baptism and moral rectitude after baptism. Even the words of Jesus to the disciples about the forgiving and retaining of sins (John 20:22–23) are seen as referring to baptism or the discipline of binding and loosing rather than to a special sacrament of penance in the later Catholic sense. This is not to say, however, that the practices of familial correction were not sacramental in the broad sense. They were, or they at least could be, for those to whom they opened a door to reconciliation with the community, with their own conscience, and ultimately with God.

It is in this broad sense, too, that Jesus was a sacrament of divine forgiveness to many of those who met him. He began his ministry with a call to repentance (Mark 1:15), and to those who showed sorrow for their sinfulness he announced that they were forgiven by the power of God (Luke 5:18–26; 7:36–50). He visited with sinners, explaining that he had been sent to the "lost sheep" of Israel (Matthew 7:24), and he spoke in parables about his heavenly Father's constant love even for those who strayed (Luke 15). When asked how many times one person should forgive another he said, in effect, "every time," and he taught that people should love even their enemies (Matthew 18:22; 5:43–48). The New Testament writers saw Jesus' mission as reconciling humankind to God: the name given to him meant in Hebrew "Yahweh saves," and his blood was poured out "for the forgiveness of sins" (Matthew 1:21; 26:28). Salvation from sin came through baptism and fellowship in the community, but ultimately it came from God through Christ (John 1:1–18; Ephesians 1–2; Hebrews 2).

In this same broad sacramental sense the early Christian community was a sacrament of reconciliation to those who heard its message of salvation and to those who tried to live up to it. Its leaders announced good news of divine pardon to all who would listen, and they exhorted those who believed it to live forgiven and redeemed lives. None of the epistle writers had any doubts about the sinfulness of Christians even after baptism, but they all believed that the community contained the means for overcoming sin. Paul had to continuously reprove his converts for their moral lapses, and he vividly described the inner war that the followers of Christ had to fight between their spiritual and their unspiritual self (Romans 6–8; Ephesians 4–6). John announced flatly, "If we say that we have no sin, we deceive ourselves, and the truth is not in us," but he went on to say that those who acknowledged their sins would be forgiven by God (1 John 1:8–10). James made this more concrete, advising his readers to "confess your sins to one another, and pray for one another" (James 5:16). And even if this practice was not a sacrament in the restricted medieval sense of the word, it at least was sacramental in the sense of being a way to experience divine forgiveness and healing.

The whole tenor of the New Testament was one of mercy for repentant sinners; there does not seem to be any sin that God would not forgive. And yet there are a few texts that seem to say the contrary. Matthew 12:32 speaks about a "sin against the Holy Spirit" which will not be forgiven, 1 John 5:16 talks of a "deadly sin" for which Christians are not to pray, and Hebrews 6:6 argues that those who have "mocked Christ" cannot be spiritually renewed a second time. What was this "unforgivable sin"? Christian theologians have speculated about it for close to twenty centuries, but the simplest answer seems to be the most plausible: it was unrepented sin, the sin of turning away from God (or God's messiah) without asking for forgiveness. Because no pardon was asked, no pardon could be given. In concrete terms it was the sin of quitting the community of those who had been saved through baptism and the Spirit, and returning to Judaism or paganism. Since the early Christians expected the second coming of Christ at any moment, there was no question of a second repentance and reconversion.

But the second coming did not come, and in the second century church leaders had to face the problem of converts who had left the community and later sought to be readmitted. Some took a hard line and would not allow readmission, basing their position on generations of tradition. Others, however, were more compassionate and envisioned the possibility of a second conversion after baptism. Early in the second century a Christian named Hermas (about whom we know little except that he lived in Rome) wrote a work called *The Shepherd* on Christian morality and repentance. In it Hermas recounted a revelation given to him by an angel who told him that God had mercifully provided that sinners who turned from their evil ways should be received back into the community, "but not repeatedly, for there is only one repentance for the servants of God" (*The Shepherd*, Mandate 4, 1). Whether Hermas intended to introduce a new practice or justify an already existing practice is hard to say, but it is clear that at the time there were those who disapproved of it. In any event, by the middle of the century other churches, too, were readmitting people who had fallen into immorality or renounced their religion and wanted to return. None of the writers of the period described a formal ritual of readmission, but since the practice was regarded as a sort of second baptism, those who underwent it had to offer proof of their sincerity and moral conversion just like catechumens. After this conversion, as after their baptism, they were to live uprightly, "but if some sin and repent repeatedly it will do them no good, for such people are not likely to live" (Mandate 4, 3). Clement of Alexandria agreed with Hermas that fallen Christians could be forgiven after their baptism—but only once, for to fall and repent repeatedly would make a mockery of God's mercy.

The only formal ritual of repentance during this period was an acknowledgment of sin that was sometimes made at the beginning of Christian worship. *The Teaching of the Twelve Apostles* directed, "Confess your sins in the assembly and do not come to your prayers with a guilty conscience" (4, 14). This was not a detailing of sins but a general admission of sinfulness through which Christians acknowledged that they still needed to be forgiven even though they had been redeemed by Christ. Other writings recommended fasting and giving aid to the poor as works through which Christians might demonstrate and develop detachment from sinful habits.

Ignatius of Antioch and other second-century bishops continued to speak of fraternal correction and praying for others as means of combating sin, and Polycarp of Smyrna wrote that pastors should be compassionate and merciful to the sheep in Christ's flock who went astray. The New Testament practice of excommunicating and reinstating sinners was also continued, but here again there seems to have been no prescribed way of doing this; when and how it was done was left up to the individual bishop and local custom. And again, these were probably all sacramental practices, at least in the broad sense of that term.

By the third century, however, a general pattern for the public rec-onciliation of known sinners began to appear in many churches. Those who wanted to rejoin the community went to the bishop and confessed their error, but before they could be readmitted to the ranks of the faithful they had to reform their lives. Like catechumens they were excluded from eucharistic worship but admitted to the prayer service of scripture read-ing and pastoral instruction. And like catechumens they had to wait until the bishop and the community were convinced that their conversion was complete. But unlike catechumens they had to perform works of repen-tance, fasting and praying and giving alms to the poor to show that their repentance was sincere. In some places they were prayed over weekly so that the spirit of evil might be exorcised from their lives. In others they were given guardians like baptismal sponsors who counseled them and testified to the community that they had reformed. The period of their penitence could be a few weeks or a few years depending on the penitential customs of their community, and when it was all over the bishop imposed his hands on them as he had done after their baptism. In some places this signified that they were receiving back the Spirit which they had lost by turning away from God, in others it was taken as a sign of forgiveness by their spiritual father and pastor, but it always meant that they were now reunited with the community and welcomed back into eucharistic com-munion with their Lord.

This public penitence was sacramental, for it was a sign both to those who witnessed it and to those who endured it that God was merciful to the contrite and that the church was a place where people could find salvation from their sinful ways. And it was an effective sacrament, for by the conversion of the heart that it demanded, the communal support that it provided, and the public approval that it gave to repentance, it brought about a real release from sin—if not from all sin, at least from scandal-ous behavior. Origen of Alexandria described it as a "remission of sins through repentance during which the sinner bathes his bed in tears and his tears become his bread by day and night, and during which he is not ashamed to show his sin to the priest of the Lord and ask for the remedy" (*On Leviticus* 2). Like the process of baptism it was an extended discipline through which people discovered the meaning of Christian morality and came to experience the forgiveness of God, but unlike baptism it was a rare occurrence in the early church. The rigors of one baptism were enough for most people, and those who sought—or needed to seek—this "second and more laborious baptism" were few.

The time that it was most often sought was right after a period of persecution. Religious persecutions in the Roman Empire were (with a few notable exceptions) local and brief, but when they did occur they were usually severe enough to cause a number of Christians to renounce their faith under pressure. After it was over, some of the apostates would seek readmission to the church, but others shrank from the demands of public repentance. Tertullian, in a work written at the end of a persecution in North Africa, acknowledged that penitents might feel humiliated by having to openly confess their guilt and seek the church's forgiveness, but to those who objected to the practice he asked, "Is it better to be damned in secret than to be absolved in public?" (*On Penitence* 16, 8).

The first empire-wide persecution of Christians took place in 249–50 under the emperor Decius, and it aroused a storm of controversy over ecclesiastical reconciliation afterward. Some Christians had openly offered sacrifices to the Roman gods; others had paid for certificates saying they had done so; and some of those who renounced their faith had second thoughts about it, and obtained letters from more stalwart Christians who were about to be martyred. In these "letters of peace" the martyrs promised to intercede in heaven for their weaker comrades and asked the church to show compassion on them. Some bishops valued the prayers of the martyrs so highly that they immediately reconciled letter holders without making them undergo public penitence. Others were astonished by this leniency and demanded the full penitential discipline for all who had lapsed. Still others, led by a churchman named Novatian in Rome, argued that apostasy was the "unforgivable sin" mentioned in the scriptures, and that the bishops had no power to forgive those who had denied Christ.

A similar debate had arisen over adultery and other sins earlier in the century. A Christian sect led by a layman named Montanus believed that the second coming was imminent and that only the pure would be saved. He claimed to have received this revelation while under the ecstatic inspiration of the Holy Spirit, and his followers preached the necessity of strict moral conduct including sexual abstinence in the period before the final tribulation. In the latter part of his life Tertullian joined this sect and was persuaded that to keep themselves pure Christians should not even associate with pagans in business, politics, or the army. He was indignant at what he regarded as the lax attitude of church leaders toward sin, and through his influence as a writer he challenged the bishops' right to forgive the "deadly sins" of adultery, murder, and idolatry. Such sins might be forgiven by God, he argued, but the church should not, lest it encourage others to sin.

At the one extreme, then, were the rigorists who claimed that excommunication for sins like apostasy and adultery should be permanent; at the other extreme were the bishops who generously readmitted people who seemed to be sorry for what they had done. What was to be the church's policy toward penitents? Local bishops were relatively independent and could set their own policies, but for the sake of regional unity some bishops met in council to discuss the issue. In 251 North African bishops decided in favor of both forgiveness and severity: those who held certificates of sacrifice were to be readmitted to communion after a lengthy period of penitence; those who had actually offered sacrifice during the persecution were to be admitted to the penitential discipline but reconciled only at the end of their life; those who had obtained "letters of peace" from martyrs were not to be excused from public repentance but their penance might be mitigated in some cases. But as for those who did not do penance and asked for reconciliation only when they were dying, they were to be left to the mercy of God. In Rome a similar council condemned the extremes of Novatian but adopted a similarly strict policy toward apostates, and in the years that followed, other bishops and other churches imposed similar burdens on adulterers and fornicators, murderers and thieves in response to the rigorism of the Montanists.

In some places penitents were required to stay away from public amusements; in others they were forbidden to hold public office or were barred from the clergy; in still others they had to abstain from marital intercourse during the whole penitential period. The lengths of assigned penances increased in many places from a few weeks or months to three, five, and even ten years; and occasionally for heinous offenses like bestiality or abortion penances of twenty or thirty years were imposed. During the Diocletian persecution in the early 300s the Spanish Council of Elvira declared that those who had offered sacrifice to the gods could not receive communion, "not even at the end, for their action is the greatest of all crimes," and it imposed the same penalty for seventeen other serious sins. Moreover, ecclesiastical forgiveness could still be received only once, and those who committed another notorious offense after they had been reconciled with the church were excluded forever from the eucharistic table. Fortunately for most Christians, however, they never had to endure the discipline of penitence since they never did anything that would warrant it.

And what was the relationship between ecclesiastical forgiveness and divine forgiveness during this period? The theological understanding seems to have remained what it was in New Testament times, namely that the leaders of the church had the power to "bind" and "loosen" ecclesiastical sanctions and that those who were reconciled with the church were also forgiven by God. But most bishops did not see their forgiveness as "causing" divine forgiveness; rather, it was the other way around. Divine forgiveness always came to those who turned from sin and mended their ways, and the church simply declared that they were forgiven by God when it was sure that they had truly reformed. Reconciliation with the church, then, was a sign that reconciliation with God had already taken place. Like Tertullian a half century earlier, Cyprian of Carthage urged apostates to seek reconciliation "while their confession can still be accepted, and while the satisfaction and forgiveness granted through the priests can be received by God" (*On the Lapsed* 28). Cyprian believed that ecclesiastical forgiveness was needed for divine forgiveness even though God alone could forgive sins, but his reason was that the removal of sin occurred not in the rite of reconciliation but in the process of repentance that preceded it. Until the conversion of sinners was complete (and the bishop's imposition of hands was a sign that it was), they could not be forgiven by the church because they were not yet forgiven by God.

In 313 the last great persecution was over, and a decade later Constantine called the world's bishops to a meeting at Nicaea to bring greater unity to church doctrines and practices. The bishops approved the now traditional notion of a single repentance after baptism, and against the teachings of the rigorists they affirmed the legitimacy of reconciling apostates and adulterers after public repentance. More significantly, however, they took an unprecedented step regarding those who were dying before they could complete their penance or who relapsed after once receiving reconciliation: "If anyone is departing from this life and asks to receive the eucharist, the bishop should make an investigation and grant the permission, no matter who asks it" (Canon 13). It was a small but important move toward modifying the church's rigid rule about only one reconciliation for Christians.

In the decades that followed, however, the general direction of ecclesiastical penitence was toward greater strictness and legalism. In the Christianized Roman Empire the penitential system came to be regulated by an increasing number of conciliar decisions and episcopal directives which in time acquired the force of church rules or canons, and so the procedure was sometimes called canonical penance. During the fourth century, bishops were given the right to act as judges in civil suits and their decisions had legal force, and as this happened their decisions in matters of church discipline were increasingly regarded as spiritual laws: as judges they acted in the name of the emperor, as bishops they acted in the name of God. As a result, sin—which had earlier been thought of as a break in the relationship of love and trust between members of the community, and as a violation of the covenant relationship between the community and God—was increasingly conceived of in legal terms, as a breaking of a divine law or the violation of an ecclesiastical law. In a similar way, repentance—which had originally been understood as a reconversion, a change of heart that was needed to reestablish the relationship—was regarded more and more as a penalty imposed for violating the law. Long and severe penances were often seen in the same light as criminal sentences: they were needed to satisfy the demands of the law, to expiate or pay for the offense committed, or to fulfill the requirements of divine justice.

This slow but definite change in the official attitude toward sin and repentance brought with it a correspondingly definite change in theology. Whereas earlier fathers like Cyprian saw the process of repentance as the means by which sin was eliminated in the penitent and forgiven by God, later fathers of the church tended to speak of penitence as a prelude to forgiveness, which occurred in the final act of reconciliation. In the middle of the fourth century, Athanasius wrote, "Just as individuals are enlightened by the Holy Spirit when they are baptized by a priest, so those who confess their sins with a repentant heart obtain their remission from the priest" (*On the Gospel of Luke* 19). Later in the same century Ambrose pointed to the same parallel between baptism and public penitence: "Why do you baptize if sins cannot be forgiven through human beings? Certainly in baptism there is forgiveness of all sins. What difference does it make then whether priests claim this right which has been given to them by arguing from baptism or from the penitential discipline?" (*On Penitence* I, 8). And for Ambrose the parallel was perfect, not only because there was only one baptism and one public penitence but also because in both cases ministers forgave sins not by their own power but in the name of God and by the power of the Holy Spirit.

Perhaps more than any other church father, Augustine, like Cyprian before him, acknowledged that sins were cleansed from one's life and soul not in a single act but through heartfelt contribution and repeated acts of penitence. And yet for Augustine, too, forgiveness for serious sins required the discipline of public repentance that was imposed by the bishop. Private repentance was not enough: "Those who govern the church appoint times of penitence with good reason, so that satisfaction may also be made to the church in which the sins are remitted. For outside the church there is no remission of sins" (*Enchiridion* 65). He believed so strongly in the efficacy and necessity of both baptism and ecclesiastical reconciliation that when the Vandals were threatening to overrun Africa he implored the priests in his diocese not to desert their posts, lest people die without being released from their sins. For Augustine, like the other bishops of the period, took the words of Christ in John's gospel to mean literally that only they, as successors of the apostles, had the power to forgive and retain certain sins. And they understood Christ's promise of the power of the keys to "bind" and "loose" in Matthew's gospel in a parallel sense, as referring not to an authority to impose or lift sanctions in the church but to a supernatural power to hold people to or release them from their sins. As John Chrysostom expressed it, "Priests have a power to bind and loose, to forgive and retain sins, which is not even given to the angels. It is a power given to them by God through the promise of Christ" (*On the Priesthood* III, 5, paraphrased).

This understanding of the priestly power to administer divine forgiveness found its most articulate spokesman in Leo I, pope and bishop of Rome from 440 to 461. Writing to one of his fellow bishops he explained, "God's bountiful mercy has come to help stumbling sinners regain hope of eternal life not only through the grace of baptism but through the medicine of penitence as well....These remedies which come from the goodness of God have been so arranged that his pardon cannot be obtained without the intercession of priests. For Jesus Christ, the mediator between God and humankind, has given those who are placed over the Church the power to grant the discipline of penitence to those who confess, and to admit those who have been purified by wholesome reparation through the gate of reconciliation to the reception of the sacraments" (*Letters* 18, 3). Leo readily granted that those who were dying should be reconciled even if they had not completed their penance, but he also believed that

unreconciled penitents died without forgiveness and were liable to
God's judgment.

Yet despite this tendency toward legalism, the purpose of penitence,
whether privately undertaken for lighter sins or publicly endured for
weightier ones, was still sacramental. It was an arduous road to the remission of sin, a release from the bondage of self-interest, a cleansing from the
servitude of self-indulgence. Penitence, as it was experienced and conceived
in patristic times, was a path of discipline that led through the eradication
of morally destructive and socially disruptive behavior to a life of love for
God and service to others. Like the sacrament of baptism it was a lengthy
corridor that led from the confines of guilt and remorse to the freedom of
acceptance and forgiveness. At least it was meant to be that. In practice,
however, it did not always look that way to ordinary Christians. To them
penitence, especially canonical penitence, often looked more like something
to be avoided at all costs.

The fathers before the Council of Nicaea had distinguished between
the ordinary sinfulness that would be counteracted by personal acts of
penitence and extraordinary sinfulness that required public penitence,
but there had been no uniform agreement about which sins called for this
drastic procedure. Roughly this same state of affairs remained in the period
of canonical penance, for although all agreed that apostasy, adultery, and
murder demanded ecclesiastical forgiveness, there was no general consensus
in the empire about which other sins were serious enough to demand it.
Canonical letters and decrees from individual bishops and regional councils
contained regulations assigning penances for dozens of capital sins, but
not all agreed about which sins were capital offenses. Some distinguished
between deliberate and involuntary acts; others distinguished between sins
against the Ten Commandments and other sins; most just followed local
custom in deciding which sins called for public repentance and which did
not. And in assigning the kind and amount of penance to be performed,
most bishops followed the canonical norms they were aware of, adapting
them as particular cases demanded.

The actual discipline could thus vary from one locality to the next, but
the general procedure that was followed was basically the same throughout
the fourth and fifth centuries. First, anyone who had committed a canonically grievous offense went to the bishop and asked what had to be done
in order to be forgiven. The bishop decided whether the sin was serious
enough to warrant public repentance, and if it was he assigned the penitential works that were to be performed. In some places people sought the

advice of a monk or some other spiritual guide first, and in larger cities priests were sometimes appointed to perform this function for the bishop. Secondly, these self-acknowledged sinners were enrolled in the "order of penitents," sometimes in a brief liturgical ceremony, which set them apart from the rest of the community and excluded them from the eucharist. For a period of weeks or years they performed penances and were watched, counseled, and prayed over by the other members of the congregation, and sometimes they received special exorcisms at regular intervals, just as the catechumens did. Finally, the penitents were received back into full communion with the church in a public ceremony that might require them to renounce their sinfulness, ask God's mercy, and be exorcised a final time. In the ritual of reconciliation the bishop readmitted the penitents to the ranks of the faithful usually by imposing his hands on them, but in some places by anointing them with oil, for both acts signified the forgiveness of sin and the reception of the Holy Spirit.

A contemporary account of this penitential procedure has been left by the historian Hermias Sozomen. Writing in the middle of the fifth century, he portrays the penitents at a Roman liturgy standing together "with downcast eyes and mournful faces." Then, "wailing and lamenting they throw themselves prostrate on the floor. Looking at them with tears in his eyes, the bishop hurries towards them and likewise falls to the floor. The church echoes with loud cries and the whole congregation is filled with tears. After this the bishop gets up and raises those who are prostrate, and after praying for the penitents in a befitting manner he dismisses them. Then each one individually performs the difficult works for as long as the bishop has assigned, either fasting, or not bathing, or abstaining from meat, or doing other things that have been prescribed. When they have paid their penalty like a debt, on the day appointed they are acquitted of their sin and take their places in the congregation" (*Ecclesiastical History* VII, 16).

The lot of the penitents was not a happy one, nor was it meant to be. Not only were they expected to demonstrate their remorse "with downcast eyes and mournful faces," but they were also marked out as sinners by what they sometimes had to wear: sackcloth made of goat hair, to symbolize their separation from the sheep of Christ's flock; chains, to signify their bondage to sin; rags, to dramatize their poverty of virtue. Some had to cut their hair short like slaves, to show that they were slaves to Satan; others had to sprinkle themselves with ashes, to show they were spiritually dead like Adam, and cast out from the paradise of the church. Penances usually included increased amounts of prayer and the recitation of psalms, but they

also included eating and sleeping less, to lessen the penitents' attachment
to the things of this world; contributing alms to the poor, to purge them
of the desire for wealth; refraining from marital relations, to purify them of
the passions of the flesh; renouncing involvement in business or politics,
to remove them from obvious temptations to sin again. And of course as
public sinners they were not allowed to share in the "communion of saints,"
that is, the eucharist.

Originally this exclusion from the eucharist simply meant that the
penitents were dismissed, along with the catechumens, after the readings
and sermon of the Sunday liturgy. But as the penitential periods became
longer, they were sometimes divided into several stages. In North Africa
and other places in the west there were two stages in the penitential discipline: those who had not yet proven their willingness to reform their lives
were treated like catechumens and dismissed after the sermon; those who
had been officially admitted to ecclesiastical penitence could remain for
the entire liturgy, but they were segregated from the rest of the congregation, and they could neither offer the gifts nor receive communion. In Asia
Minor and other places in the east there were four grades in the order of
penitents: "weepers" had to remain outside the church and implore the
prayers of the faithful; "hearers" could stay at the back of the church, but
only for the liturgy of the word; "kneelers" could come further into the
church and receive the bishop's blessing before being dismissed with the
catechumens; "standers" could remain for the entire liturgy but could not
receive communion until they were restored to the status of communicant.

It was a richly symbolic and impressively rigorous system, but it did not
last. Its origins lay in the church of the martyrs, when becoming a Christian
meant risking life and property, and when being excommunicated seemed
to be a fate worse than death. But now Christianity was the official religion
of the Roman Empire. Many of those who entered the church did not feel
any great call to holiness, and the idealistic morality of the early church
was being replaced by a more practical one. If few people undertook public
repentance in the early days, now even fewer did. Despite the canons on
the books and the insistence of bishops that even serious sins committed
in secret required ecclesiastical forgiveness, not many came forward, and
in most places only the most notorious offenders were publicly excommunicated.

The majority of Christians, of course, felt no need for public penitence,
for although they were not great saints they were not great sinners either.
They sought the remission of their sins in the customary ways of prayer

and almsgiving, by fasting at the times appointed, and by attending the eucharistic sacrifice. Some of those who, because of the nature or publicity of their sin, felt obliged to become penitents, found it more convenient to be halfhearted about it and hope for final forgiveness on their deathbed. Some people simply waited until old age before enrolling in the order of penitents. Some even avoided the problem altogether and, like the emperor Constantine, put off being baptized until the end of their life.

One reason for avoiding public penitence was obviously its harshness. Another reason was the social stigma that had come to be attached to it: instead of giving sinners the community's support in their attempt to re-form, the penitential discipline now often brought them the community's contempt. A third reason was the fact that ecclesiastical reconciliation could be received only once, so those who feared they would fall again naturally postponed asking for it as long as they could. Some pastorally minded bishops even encouraged this practice. John Chrysostom, the bishop of Constantinople at the turn of the fifth century, tried a different approach and instead offered repeated forgiveness to those who needed it. His devotion to his people won him their love, but his disregard for this and other established customs so scandalized other churchmen that they brought charges against him and had him deposed.

A fourth reason had to do with the canonical effects of public penitence especially in the western churches. Even after receiving reconciliation, penitents were sometimes bound by various canons to observe certain restrictions for the remainder of their lives. From the middle of the fourth century, reconciled penitents could often not marry, not have sexual rela-tions with their spouse if they were already married, not engage in business or military service, or not hold public or ecclesiastical office; and by the end of the fifth century they were often barred by the canons from all of these things. The original intent of these canons was, of course, to prevent sinners from relapsing, but in time they seemed to cause more problems than they solved. As bishop Caesarius of Arles rhetorically asked in the sixth century, "If I am an officer in the army and have a wife, how can I possibly do penance?" (*Sermons* 258). In response, he counseled a penitential life rather than ecclesiastical penance, until shortly before death. Other bishops prohibited young people from being admitted to public penitence, and two French councils decreed that married people could be admitted only with the consent of their spouse.

At the close of the patristic era, then, canonical penance had little or no effect on the lives of ordinary Christians, but the rigors of the penitential system did have some unexpected side effects. Since at least the fourth century, bishops and priests were forbidden to become penitents because the social stigma attached to public penitence might bring disgrace to the priesthood. Instead, clerics who committed serious sins were required to undergo a different discipline called "degradation" under which they were forced to retire from public life and perform penitential works, perhaps in a monastery, for the duration of their punishment. According to the church's regulations, therefore, clerics could not become penitents and penitents could not become clerics, and the result was that during this period few priests—and certainly no bishops—ever received public penance.

Again unexpectedly, the rule forbidding sexual relations after admission to the order of penitents was one of the factors that led to the rise of clerical celibacy in the west. Since around the fourth century the men who went out into the desert and countryside to live as hermits and monks had led a life of voluntary penitence in the pursuit of holiness, and in doing so they gave up the same things that penitents were required to renounce: marriage, wealth, public careers, and so forth. In time, as ecclesiastical penance came to be practiced as a ritual for the dying, penitence during one's lifetime came to be reassociated with the desire for holiness, and in the fifth century young men who were about to enter the clergy or the monastic life began to undergo voluntarily a penitential discipline similar to public penitence for the sake of spiritual perfection. One of the canonical consequences of this discipline was that those who went through it were forbidden to marry, and eventually what began as a self-imposed practice became a law of the Latin church.

A liturgical consequence developed from the fact that during this same period the number of adult candidates for baptism was declining and so there were fewer and fewer catechumens to take part in the tradition of public prayer and fasting from Ash Wednesday to Easter Sunday. To make up for their numbers, clerics and monks who were not eligible to enter the order of penitents became devotional penitents as part of their pursuit of spiritual perfection. By the fifth century in Rome, even lay people who had committed no sins requiring public repentance were becoming ceremonial penitents during the weeks before Easter. Gradually, this devotional practice spread from Rome to other dioceses until, by the tenth century, Christians everywhere were expected to become penitents during Lent.

A third and equally lasting consequence of the decline of the canonical penance system was the rise of a new, unofficial sacrament of penitence that eventually replaced the old one. As early as the third century, devout

Christians were sometimes encouraged to reveal the condition of their soul to a spiritual "guide" or "physician" who would give them direction in works of prayer and repentance. They did this to lead more holy lives, and the person to whom they went was not necessarily a priest. Later, those who left the world for a life of penitence were similarly advised to have an experienced monk as a "spiritual father" to whom they regularly confessed their sins and shortcomings in order to receive guidance in their effort to achieve sanctity. After this revelation of conscience the older monk might fast and pray with his charge, and at the end assure him or her of God's mercy and forgiveness. Most of the monks were, of course, lay people, and this practice of theirs was not a sacrament in the strict Catholic sense, but it was a sacramental activity in the broad sense. To those who used it—and by the sixth century people outside the monasteries also sometimes had monk confessors—it was a sign of God's fatherly concern and a door to the experience of spiritual regeneration and divine forgiveness.

3. Confession and Penance in the Middle Ages

In the early years of the fifth century a young Christian living in the Roman colony of Britain was captured by a band of sea raiders and carried off to slavery in Ireland. A few years later he managed to escape, and after a brief visit home he made his way to Auxerre in France where he joined a recently founded monastery. Around the age of forty he was consecrated a bishop and charged with the mission of bringing Christianity to the land of his captivity. His Celtic name was Sucat, but he is better remembered under his Roman name, Patrick. By the time he died in 461 the country had a thriving new religion. Its priests were mostly monks, some brought from the continent, others converted and ordained in Ireland. It had a style of liturgy that was distinctively Celtic even though it was performed in Latin. It also had a penitential discipline that was unlike any other in Christianity.

Canonical penitence was gradually disappearing from Christian life in Europe even though some of its rigid regulations were often relaxed in an effort to encourage more people to seek ecclesiastical forgiveness. In Italy, for example, the penitential period was reduced to the forty days of Lent, with penitents being signed with ashes on Ash Wednesday and reconciled on Holy Thursday, but these new leniencies did little to change the habit of asking for reconciliation only near death, when the penance imposed would be even lighter. Hardly anyone did lengthy penances anymore, except in the monasteries. There the ideal of the penitential life and the practice of private confession continued, and the monks who became missionaries to Ireland brought both their ideals and their practices with them.

There were no cities on the island and so Christian life centered around the monasteries. From them, the monks traveled out to the countryside bringing baptism and the mass and preaching the forgiveness of sins. But the wild clansfolk did not adjust easily to the moral norms of the new religion, and in their daily affairs they continued to behave much as they had before being converted. To make matters worse, the monasteries were few and far between, and the itinerant preachers could not always be on hand to bring them the church's assurance of forgiveness on their deathbed. To remedy the situation the monks prescribed the same means that they themselves used to overcome their sins and make satisfaction for them during their lifetime: private, repeated confession and continuous works of penitence. On one trip they would hear the confessions of those who had seriously violated God's or the church's commandments, and assign them their penance. On the next trip, or whenever the penance was completed, they would pray with the penitents, asking for God's merciful pardon. Since there was no official excommunication or reconciliation with the church, however, and since the monks were not bishops, the sign of forgiveness was a blessing rather than an imposition of hands. To bring some measure of fairness and uniformity to this widely scattered practice, the monks composed books containing lists of sins and the appropriate penances for each of them. For less serious sins they recommended that the people confess their sins to each other and perform lesser works of mortification, just as the monks were accustomed to doing.

By the early sixth century the British Isles had begun to recover from the tribal invasions that had led to the fall of the Roman Empire in the west, and so when Rome sent missionary monks northward many of their British and Irish counterparts left their monasteries as well to help with the conversion of the continent. Within a few decades they traveled prodigious distances, founding monasteries, building churches, and establishing schools in France, Spain, Germany, Switzerland, and even northern Italy. And wherever they went they brought with them the penitential system that their predecessors had introduced so successfully into Ireland.

The method met with equal success among the peasants of Europe, for it promised a salvation that baptism could no longer assure: salvation from divine punishment for sins committed in adulthood. And unlike the older form of canonical penance it could even offer forgiveness for less than capital sins, for there was no sin that could not be confessed and expiated, hopefully before the hour of death. There were those among the European clergy, however, to whom the new discipline looked like an unscrupulous cheapening of divine forgiveness, not to mention that it directly violated the tradition of only one repentance after baptism. A regional council in Toledo, for example, declared in 589: "We have learned that in some of the churches in Spain the faithful are doing penance not in accordance with the canonical rule but in another detestable way, that is, they ask a priest to grant them pardon as many times as it pleases them to sin. We wish to put an end to this abominable presumption, and accordingly this sacred council declares that penances should be given in the manner prescribed by the ancient canons." But the novel practice continued despite ecclesiastical disapproval, and by 650 a similar council in Chalon, France, approved confession to priests as "a medicine for the soul" and "helpful to people."

Nor was it really true that the new discipline was simply an easy way to make reparation for sins and avoid the fires of hell. As the zealous monks envisioned it, repentance was an elementary requirement of the gospel that they preached, and so the penitence that they prescribed was intended to have a lasting effect on those who underwent it. Many of the penances meted out were in fact quite severe, and in their own harsh way they served as a deterrent to sin and crime in a world where civil law was almost nonexistent.

As the practice grew, so did the number of penitential books that were used in various parts of Europe. The penalties that they assigned were not the same everywhere but generally speaking they tried to make the punishment fit the crime, at least in intensity if not always in kind. Typical penances included: for thievery, restoration of the stolen goods plus compensation; for adultery and other sexual sins, payment of damages to the injured party plus total abstinence from intercourse; for fighting and bloodshed, scourging and a prohibition to carry weapons; for murder and other crimes that might arouse vengeance, compulsory pilgrimage (a euphemism for exile). Other penances included traditional penitential practices such as fasting, abstaining from tasty foods, days or nights spent in prayer or the recitation of psalms, and giving alms to the poor. Commonly sinners were also excluded from taking communion until their penance was accomplished, as in the canonical system.

Besides being intense, penances could also be quite lengthy, but the duration of the penance was often dependent on the guilt involved, measured by the number of times the sin was committed, the amount of premeditation it involved, and whether or not it was actually accomplished.

For instance, repeated drunkenness drew a greater penalty than one night's revelry, and a successful theft was punished more severely than plotting to steal. Penances could vary from a few days for a simple lie, to a few years for harming another's reputation, to life for lying under oath. Generally crimes committed against clerics brought harsher penances than those committed against lay people, but crimes committed by clerics themselves were also treated more severely. According to one penitential book, the murder of a cleric required ten years of penance, three of which were to be spent on bread and water, but the murder of a layperson required only seven years, again with three on bread and water. According to another book, if a priest invited a woman to commit adultery but was refused, he had to do penance for a year and a half on bread and water plus an additional year without wine and meat, but if a layman did the same thing he had to do penance for only forty days. For the clergy were God's representatives, and accordingly both sins against them and sins by them were more offensive to God and incurred more guilt.

The penitential books often emphasized that penances were truly effective only when they brought genuine contrition and a change of heart, but interior repentance was harder to judge than external compliance, and the system tended to perpetuate the legalistic attitude on morality that had arisen earlier in the church. The tables of assignable penances constituted a code of law, and the confessors themselves were cast in the role of judges who weighed the severity of the sin, pronounced the sentence, and later assured the penitents that their debt had been paid. God was conceived as a king who issued commands for the welfare of his subjects, sin was a violation of God's law that demanded punishment, and penances were means of satisfying the demands of divine justice. It was a harsh system of justice and its conception of morality was crude, but it worked well in carrying civilization through the Dark Ages.

At times the penances for individual sins were so lengthy that some penitents could not make satisfaction for all their sins in a single lifetime, and so the system also developed an ingenious method of commutations whereby shorter and more intense penances could be substituted for longer and milder ones. For instance, a year of mild fasting could be commuted to three days of complete abstinence and continuous recitation of the psalms in the Bible; and for those who could not read, three hundred genuflections and three hundred lashes could be substituted for reciting the hundred and fifty psalms. Celtic tribal law had also allowed a fine to be substituted for almost any other penalty, and when this custom was taken into the Irish penitential system it meant that almost any penance could be replaced by the payment of alms. In pre-Christian Ireland it had also been possible for an individual to accept the punishment for another's crime, and some penitential books similarly allowed a person to perform a penance for someone physically unable to do it. In time, however, the idea of substitutions led to some extraordinary abuses of the system, and one tenth-century English record, for example, showed how a wealthy landowner could accomplish a seven-year fast by hiring a small army to do it for him in three days. The idea of substitutions was also part of the rationale behind the selling of indulgences, which led to similar abuses in later centuries.

Such misuses of private penitence made some bishops want to return to the older system of canonical penitence over which they had more direct control. Penitential books were being copied and composed faster than the bishops could keep track of them, and in the hands of ill-educated priests they were being used as though they gave magical prescriptions for divine forgiveness. When Charlemagne received a copy of the Gregorian sacramentary from Pope Hadrian, it contained no provision for repeated private confession since the practice was unknown in Rome, and in 813, separate councils at Tours, Rheims, and Chalon called for the restoration of the ancient penitential discipline in the French church. But the new practice had already become an established tradition, and the bishops who were intent on reform had to accept a compromise: public penitence for public sins, and private penitence for private sins. It was difficult to put this neat distinction into practice, however. In small towns most people knew what everyone else did sooner or later, and so it was hard to say which sins were public and which ones were private. As a result private penitence continued to be the more common practice, and it was not until the eleventh century that the hierarchy at last succeeded in having the penitential books withdrawn from circulation.

Other bishops took a different approach to the abuses of private penitence and, instead of attempting to abolish it, they tried to regulate it by church laws. From the eighth century various bishops and councils began to recommend confession for grave sins before the reception of communion, and some diocesan canons even made confession obligatory for everyone one to three times a year regardless of the seriousness of their sins. Eventually this kind of legislation became so common that the Fourth Lateran Council of bishops from the whole Latin church decreed that all Catholics who committed serious sins had to confess them to their pastors within a year. Thus by 1215 the practice of repeated private confession to priests, which had begun as an unofficial sacrament and which had been denounced as contrary to tradition, had become an official sacrament of repentance in western Christianity. Solemn public penitence and reconciliation remained under the jurisdiction of the bishops for crimes that incurred official excommunication, but even this practice died out by the end of the Middle Ages. In modern times certain sins were "reserved to the bishop" for the granting of absolution, the last vestige of what had once been an entirely episcopal prerogative.

At the beginning of the Middle Ages "reconciliation with the altar," like reconciliation with the church in the canonical penance system, had been granted only after the completion of the assigned penance. During the ninth century, however, the liturgical reformers in Charlemagne's empire, in an attempt to bring confession under greater clerical control, insisted that penitents receive absolution from a priest rather than assurances of God's forgiveness from a monk or nun or pious layperson. But since people who were used to the monastic practice often did not return to be formally absolved from the obligation to do penance, French priests were told to bestow absolution right after hearing the penitent's confession. In this same period, priests in other parts of Europe began admitting penitents to communion after only part of the lengthy penance was done, once they were sure of the penitents' sincerity. Moreover, if penitents were dying, priests would usually reconcile them and pray for God's forgiveness right after hearing their confession, as was the custom with canonical penance. But during the tenth century, for fear that any penitent might die without the priestly assurance of God's forgiveness, some churchmen began to recommend reconciliation right after confession in all cases, and by the end of the century the once emergency procedure had become a standard practice. Penances were still assigned, but now they had to be performed after the rite of reconciliation.

This practice, however, raised a theological question: What if penitents died before completing their penance? Would they be admitted to heaven even though they had not paid the full penalty for their sins? All the priests could do was to pray that God would absolve them from paying the debt in full, as they did for dying penitents. In addition, since priests were the ones who assigned the penances, many of them began to follow the French practice of granting absolution from unperformed penances, after praying for the penitent's forgiveness by God. In time the prayer for forgiveness dropped out of the ritual of reconciliation altogether and the words of absolution were applied not to the penance but to the sins themselves. Thus in the course of some two hundred years, from around 1000 to 1200, the words that the priest said after hearing the penitent's confession changed completely in the Latin church from a prayer for divine forgiveness (such as "May God have mercy on you and forgive you your sins") to a statement of priestly absolution (such as "I absolve you from your sins in the name of the Father and of the Son and of the Holy Spirit").

By the time that the schoolmen in the twelfth century began trying to explain the church's sacramental practices, these changes in ecclesiastical penitence were all but complete. Now penitents were absolved from their sins immediately after confession. Now penitents could seek absolution as often as they sinned. And now the penances were performed after absolution rather than before. Furthermore, after the penitential books were withdrawn from use in the eleventh century, the imposed penances had gotten lighter and shorter, and so the power of remitting sins, once attributed to lengthy and severe periods of penance, came to be regarded as something that had to be found in the ritual of confession itself.

Admitting one's faults to another human being is never easy in any age, and in the age of early scholasticism it seemed to the majority of theologians that the "power of remitting sins," the effective cause of being loosed from the sins of one's past, was to be found in the shame and sorrow felt in the act of confessing. Peter Abelard, who lived when the ritual of reconciliation still included both a prayer for forgiveness and a statement of absolution, taught that perfect contrition motivated by the love of God effectively removed sins from one's soul and that the priest's absolution referred only to the satisfaction that had to be made for them. When God saw this interior penitence, God forgave the sins, said Abelard; it was not the priest who forgave them. This belief in the value of contrition led some theologians to suggest that confession merited more forgiveness if it was made to several persons before being made to a priest, while others suggested that if no priest was available confession could be made to a layperson to obtain God's forgiveness. Among those who held this latter view was Peter Lombard.

In Lombard's listing of the Catholic sacraments, the primary "sacrament of penitence" was private confession; by this time episcopal reconciliation was rare and was needed only in case of excommunication. In doing this he simply reflected the practices of his own day, but since his book of *Sentences* was so widely used by subsequent students of theology, he set the pattern for the treatment of sacramental forgiveness in the rest of the Middle Ages. He was among the first to try to fit confession into the conceptual scheme of *sacramentum tantum*, *sacramentum et res*, and *res tantum*, since he regarded contrition as the effective element in confession he excluded absolution from his definition of the sacrament altogether. For him the outward acts performed by the penitent were the sacramental sign; they were a sign of penitence, which was both an experienced reality and a sign that sins were forgiven; and God's forgiveness was the reality that resulted from confession and contrition. The role of the priest was simply to assure penitents that their sins were forgiven, to assign appropriate penances, and perhaps to remit some of the punishment by the granting of absolution. If the priest was a bishop, he could also readmit penitents into the church, but in Lombard's opinion this, like the other actions of the priest, occurred only after the sacramental confession. Most of the other twelfth-century scholastics agreed with Lombard, as they did with Abelard, that in confession sin was removed by contrition and forgiven by God.

Some of the other scholastics did not agree, however. Hugh and Richard of the School of St. Victor argued that if the priest forgave the punishment due for sins he effectively forgave the sins themselves. Their opinion reflected the fact that the words of absolution were now more frequently being applied to the sins confessed, and as their interpretation of the ritual became more accepted this practice increased even further. When it was objected that only God could forgive sins, Hugh replied that this power had been given by Christ to the apostles and to their successors in the priesthood. Thus when priests forgave sins they did not do so by their own power but by the power of God that had been entrusted to them. That Christ had intended his priests to forgive sins was clear from the words of John 20:23, and that he had given them the power of loosing people from their sins was equally evident from Matthew 18:18. It was the "power of the keys" mentioned in Matthew 16:19, now understood not as the power to exclude or admit people to the Christian community but as the power to exclude or admit them to heaven. Of course once this interpretation of the priest's absolution was accepted—and the words of the ritual seemed to warrant it—confession to a layperson could no longer be viewed as having any value for the remission of sins, for only priests had the authority to pronounce the words of absolution.

Both of these explanations of confession—the one contending that contrition caused the remission of sins and the other that absolution was the effective cause—were taught in the schools of Europe at the beginning of the thirteenth century. Numerous attempts were made to reconcile the two positions, and in the course of the debate some distinctions emerged that were to be important in later theology.

The first was a distinction between "mortal" and "venial" sins. The distinction had long been made in Christian theology between serious and less serious sins, and in the early church it was primarily a distinction between sins that required public penitence and those that did not. Some sins were so serious that they were considered to be "death to the soul" inasmuch as those who died unrepentant and unreconciled with the church after having committed them were excluded from salvation. Other sins were considered less serious and were therefore pardonable (the original meaning of "venial") without public penitence. During the period of the penitential books there was no public reconciliation except in unusual circumstances, but the monks who preached private confession also warned that some sins were so deadly that those who died in them would never see God. Although during the Middle Ages it was never worked out in detail just which sins were mortal and which ones were not, most theologians agreed that some sins, if committed with knowledge and premeditation, involved such a complete rejection of God that they would be punished forever in hell, while others were less serious offenses and therefore might be forgiven after death.

The second distinction was between "imperfect" and "perfect" contrition. The scholastics recognized that feelings of sorrow for having sinned could be motivated either by a fear of divine punishment or by a realization that sin had no place in the heart of one who loved God. The former they named imperfect contrition since it did not necessarily change people's behavior; even hardened criminals could regret that they were going to be punished eventually for their sins. The latter was named perfect contrition, and it designated a depth of repentance which so changed people's outlook on life that they resolved never to sin again. Imperfect contrition, then, was insufficient to lead people to renounce their sins and lead lives of holiness, though it might motivate them to sin less often or to avoid mortal sins. Perfect contrition, on the other hand, was strong enough to cause a conversion away from sin and toward God. It was a deliberate break with the sins of one's past, even if due to weakness and temptation one did fall into sin again in the future.

The third distinction had to do with the punishment of sins. During the patristic era works of penitence were originally meant to bring about conversion from a life of sin, but they gradually took on legalistic overtones of being penalties for sins, and during the early Middle Ages these overtones became the dominant theme of the penances prescribed by the penitential books. As long as the penances had to be completed before reconciliation, penitents could be assured that they had paid the penalty for their sins and priests could, in emergencies, pray that God would absolve them from any penance they had left undone. Once absolution became a forgiveness of sins that was administered before the performance of the penance, however, it became necessary to rethink the relationship between forgiveness and punishment. After all, how could the sins be truly forgiven if a punishment still had to be paid for them? The scholastic answer was a distinction between "temporal" and "eternal" punishment. The distinction had a precedent in the fact that penance done over a period of time had earlier been seen as a substitute for everlasting punishment after death, but it was now used to explain why penance had to be done after sins had been forgiven in confession: absolution forgave the eternal punishment that was due for sin but not the temporal punishment. By the power of the keys priests could assure sinners that God's mercy released them from the punishment of hell, but God's justice remained to be satisfied by penances performed over a period of time.

But what if the penance was left undone, or was insufficient? Earlier, in the period when penances were seen as a means of purifying the soul and purging it of sin, theologians had speculated that a final purgation after death would have to complete the purification of the soul before it could enter heaven, since according to Matthew 5:8 only the pure of heart could see God. This "purgatory" was now viewed as the place where the temporal punishment due to sin would be expiated, and especially as penances imposed after confession grew shorter and easier they were believed to remit only part of that punishment. The rest of the agonizing purification, if not accomplished by actual penitence in this life, would have to be undergone in the next.

By the time Thomas Aquinas went to school at the University of Paris, most of the conceptual tools needed to analyze and explain how confession worked had already been developed, but the key theological question had not yet been answered: What precisely was the sacrament of repentance? Was it the acts of the penitent or the action of the priest? Aquinas' answer was a simple one as it was obvious in the light of current practice: he said it was both. On the one hand he admitted the value of contrition and penitential works; on the other, he acknowledged that the words of absolution were an essential part of the sacramental ritual as he knew it. As a result of his treatment of the sacrament, all of the elements in the ecclesiastical procedure of forgiveness came to be subsumed under the name *paenitentia*, in English, "penance." What Aquinas had to show was how the various elements were interrelated.

According to Aquinas penance was a sacrament because it signified something sacred, the renunciation and forgiveness of sins, which could not happen without God's help. The "matter" of the sacrament consisted in the actions of the penitent and the priest: the penitent confessed and felt sorrow for these sins, the priest listened and pronounced the absolution, the penitent performed the assigned penance. The "form" of the sacrament was found in the words "I absolve you from your sins..." for they signified the hidden reality of divine forgiveness that was effected by the rite. As a sacrament of the church, penance was necessary for salvation, but not absolutely necessary; Aquinas agreed with his predecessors that sins could also be remitted by perfect contrition even without the priest's absolution. But the sacrament had been instituted by Christ to be a help especially for those in mortal sin, who otherwise might be unable to renounce their sinfulness and be reconciled with God.

Aquinas' integrated approach to penance made him insist that contrition was needed for the sacrament to be truly effective. In other words, contrition was a necessary part of the "matter" of the sacrament; without it the ritual would be merely a formality effecting no real remission of sins. Moreover, the sorrow for sin had to be perfect contrition; imperfect contrition might motivate a person to go to confession, but only the love of God would lead to true repentance and the remission of sin, and so Aquinas believed that the specific grace of the sacrament was the gift of perfect contrition. This grace was the ability to be sorry for having offended a just and merciful God, which God granted to those who devoutly sought forgiveness through the means supplied by the church.

Yet Aquinas knew from experience that confessing a sin and receiving absolution did not necessarily eliminate it from a person's life. In his understanding of human behavior, vice like virtue was a habit, and unless the sinful habit was broken the sinful act would be committed again. Aquinas and his contemporaries called this lingering proneness to sin "the remnants of sin," and he saw the purpose of the assigned penance as helping to eradicate such inclinations from the soul. By performing works of penitence the remaining sinfulness in a person was gradually eliminated and would not have to be purged after death. Again here, however, it was not enough to go through the motions of performing the penance; it was only effective in removing the remnants of sin if it was done with a penitential attitude of love and sorrow for having offended God.

As Aquinas envisioned it, the penance was a sacramental step in the Christian journey toward a just and holy life. To understand his view of the effectiveness of the sacrament, one must see it from the perspective of those who in fact succeeded in becoming morally good people. In the eyes of a medieval theologian, how did this happen? It happened by individuals being baptized into the church and living lives in cooperation with God's grace. If they sinned mortally and turned from God, they lost that supernatural help and were left dependent on their own natural abilities. But such abilities were not enough to turn sinners back to God, and so if in fact they felt contrition and desired to mend their ways it must be that God was offering them the grace of repentance. If they cooperated with this grace they admitted their guilt and confessed their sins, at least to God but ideally in the sacrament, for the priest had the power to absolve them from those sins and assign them penances that would help them remain truly contrite and eventually eliminate the tendency to commit such sins again. From this perspective, then, the sacrament of penance was an effective cause of the remission of sins. It was the occasion for encounters with God's forgiving and redeeming grace, and in the measure that people continued to cooperate with that grace, they eventually replaced the sinful habits of vice with the good habits of virtue.

Aquinas of course also believed that penance was effective because Christ had promised the power of forgiving sins to his church, and that priests exercised this power in their performance of the sacrament. His analysis of the penitential process, however, shows that he had an experiential grasp of what the sacrament entailed, and that in coming to his conclusions he worked inductively from experience as well as deductively from the scriptures and the practices of the church. In this respect he had more in common with the earlier scholastics, who saw contrition as the effective element in confession, than with the later scholastics, who tended to deduce its effectiveness from the words of absolution.

John Duns Scotus, for example, was born while Aquinas was still alive, but his approach to the sacrament was much more deductive and legalistic than Aquinas' had been. Basically he agreed with Hugh and Richard of St. Victor that the effectiveness of the sacrament was based on the power of the keys given by Christ to the apostles and their successors, and transmitted by bishops to priests in their ordination. But Scotus also went beyond those early schoolmen and contended that the sacrament consisted entirely of the exercise of that power: "Penance is absolution, that is, a definitive judgment absolving the guilty" (*Oxford Commentary* IV, 14, 4). In Scotus's view neither confession nor contrition were parts of the sacrament; rather he regarded these merely as preconditions for receiving absolution. Likewise, he regarded the assigned penance as something that was done after the reception of the sacrament itself.

Aquinas and other scholastics had taught that imperfect contrition was sufficient to bring people to confession but that perfect contrition, which was caused by God's grace, was needed for sins to be truly remitted. Scotus borrowed this same schema but denied that there was any discernible difference between the two types of contrition. One was simply sorrow without God's grace, the other was sorrow that contained God's grace; but grace was a metaphysical entity that could not be experienced, and so people could never tell whether their contrition was perfect or imperfect. At the most, Scotus admitted that there might be degrees in the intensity of contrition, and outside the sacrament God could will to bestow grace on a soul that was sufficiently contrite, thus canceling out its sins. But since no one could be sure whether their sorrow was intense enough to merit forgiveness, Christ had instituted the sacrament as a sure way to receive the grace that turned imperfect contrition into perfect contrition. All that was needed was some degree of sorrow for sins, and God would abide by the scriptural promise to forgive sins by infusing the needed grace when the words of absolution were pronounced.

In this way the idea that the sacrament worked *ex opere operato*, which had originally meant that its effectiveness was independent of the holiness of the priest, came to mean that its effectiveness was almost automatic. For Scotus, however, this was simply an indication of how merciful God was: God had agreed to forgive sins by absolution rather than by requiring everyone to have perfect contrition for each and every sin. It was a surer way to salvation, and because the church recognized this it had made regular confession a legal obligation for all Christians.

Scotus also conceived of sin in legal rather than experiential terms, and he spoke of it as a violation of divine commandments rather than as a turning away from God in one's heart. A person who committed a sinful act therefore incurred a liability to punishment that remained even after receiving absolution, and for Scotus this is what was meant by "the remnants of sin." Because Christ had earned forgiveness for the sins of humankind by dying on the cross, a merciful God granted this forgiveness in the sacrament, but God's justice also demanded that every fault be punished. This punishment could be voluntarily endured in this life, but if it were not it would be involuntarily suffered after death. The purpose of the penance assigned in confession was therefore to shorten one's time in purgatory, but since no one could be sure how much temporal punishment was due for each sin, no one could be certain that the penance performed was enough to cancel it.

Churchmen in the later Middle Ages often accepted Aquinas' definition of the sacrament because it covered more parts of the ritual, but their understanding of its purpose and operation was closer to that of Scotus. For most theologians the purpose of penance was to forgive the sins of those who did not have perfect contrition for their sins and to remit part of the temporal punishment that was due for them, and it worked primarily through the act of absolution. In time, absolution came to be regarded as the only essential part of the sacrament, and the only thing that was needed for its valid administration. Confession, contrition, and the assigned penance were thus nonessential, although they were needed for the sacrament to be "fruitful," that is, to make any real difference in a person's behavior.

In this way, then, penance came to be identified more and more with the priest's absolution, and it even became common to speak of receiving absolution as "receiving the sacrament." In theory it effected the forgiveness of sins, but in practice it ceased to have any noticeable effect on people's lives. No great repentance was needed to receive it, it could be repeated if need be, and the obligation to perform the assigned penance could be fulfilled even by doing it quite mechanically. In addition, the penances were by this time quite mild (usually the recitation of some prayers) and gave no guarantee that they remitted more than part of the temporal punishment that was due for sins that had been confessed. Most Christians had to look forward to spending at least part of eternity in purgatory, and since there was no longer any sacramental means of escaping God's punishment, they turned increasingly toward a legal means: indulgences.

The general idea behind indulgences went back to the patristic period when bishops could, if the case warranted it, lighten the severity of public penitence that had to be done before reconciliation in the church. In the era of canonical penitence this leniency was extended primarily to those who asked for reconciliation when they were dying, since they obviously did not have time to perform a lengthy penance. And in the period when the penitential books were used, the idea of tempering divine justice with divine mercy was the main theological motive behind the practice of substituting shorter penances for longer ones. Up through the beginning of the Middle

Ages, however, this *indulgentia* or compassion was seen as extending only to actual penances that had to be performed before the end of a person's life, and it was offered to people only individually.

The theological justification for this practice was the power of the keys, in virtue of which bishops (and later, priests) imposed and released people from ecclesiastical sanctions and other penances. In the eleventh century, however, the practice took a step forward when bishops in France began to grant reprieves from certain amounts of undone penance to anyone who contributed to the support of designated churches and monasteries. Initially these reductions in penance amounted to only a few days, but sometimes bishops allowed a donation to substitute for several months or years of penance, and in 1095 Pope Urban II offered a "plenary" or full indulgence first to all those who went off to fight in a crusade and later to all those who financially supported it. Theoretically this kind of indulgence was supposed to be a substitute for all the penance that a person had to perform for confessed sins, but since penances were often seen as penalties for sins, the plenary indulgence was soon perceived as full payment of the penalties. Furthermore, as penances on earth began to be equated with temporal punishment in purgatory, indulgences began to be viewed as substitutions for penalties that would be incurred in the hereafter.

As the granting and obtaining of indulgences became more popular, some theologians like Peter Abelard in the twelfth century denounced them as excuses for greed on the part of bishops and laziness on the part of penitents, but the bishops countered by asserting the power of the keys and the practice continued. Since they were unable to deny the bishops' contention, the schoolmen gradually accepted the legitimacy of the practice, but it did present a theological problem in that there seemed to be little proportion between the small sums of money contributed and the debt of punishment that was remitted by them. The problem was solved early in the thirteenth century when Hugh of St. Cher suggested that the donations were not substitutions for penances at all but simply prerequisites for gaining the indulgences. The indulgences themselves came from the church's "treasury of spiritual merits" accumulated by the meritorious suffering of Christ, who had never sinned, and of the saints, who had done more penance than they needed in order to pay for their sins. Because they had the power of the keys, then, bishops could unlock this spiritual treasury of the church and apply the infinite merits of Christ and the superfluous merits of the saints to whomever they deemed worthy to receive them. Ordinarily these were persons who contributed to the church's financial needs, but they could also be persons who did other pious deeds such as making a pilgrimage or performing some other spiritual devotion.

At the beginning the indulgences could be applied only to the punishment due for sins confessed by the individual who received them, but during the thirteenth century some people began acquiring more indulgences than they could use for themselves and applying them to souls in purgatory. Theologians debated whether or not this could actually be done, but while the debate continued the practice grew, and eventually the theologians who favored the idea argued that the merits in the church's treasury could even cover the punishment of unconfessed sins in the case of departed souls. Once this happened the popularity of indulgences increased even further: people could use them to shorten the temporal punishment of their relatives in purgatory, and bishops could use them to build and repair churches and monasteries, schools and hospitals. But the money that the bishops collected did not always get used for the purposes they announced, and after a while the sale of indulgences became an indispensable source of church income.

Only the popes, however, could grant plenary indulgences, and in the fourteenth and fifteenth centuries sales of papal indulgences became more frequent. In 1447 Calixtus III suggested that these too might be applied to souls in purgatory, and in 1476 Sixtus IV issued an indulgence expressly for their benefit. Even though the spiritual value of such indulgences was still debated by theologians, the clerics who were given the job of collecting the revenues often had no scruples about passing them off as infallible aids for the departed. Contemporary critics satirized these collectors as street vendors hawking, "When in the box a coin does ring, a soul from out the fire will spring," but the practice continued despite its obvious abuses.

In 1515 Pope Leo X announced yet another indulgence (there had been others) for the rebuilding of St. Peter's basilica in Rome. Collectors in Germany poured over the countryside under the direction of the archbishop of Mainz, and they had been profitably proclaiming the new pardon of souls for over a year when a monk in the course of hearing confessions learned that the real purpose of the indulgence was to enable the archbishop to pay the pope for appointing him to the diocese after he already held two others. Outraged by the duplicity and the scandalous way in which the indulgence was being preached, he denounced the whole practice of indulgences and the theology behind them, and announced that he was willing to debate publicly no less than ninety-five points on the topic. The monk's name, of course, was Martin Luther.

4. The Modern Sacrament of Penance

When Leo X excommunicated Luther from the Catholic Church in 1520, the bill of excommunication also condemned forty-one of his ideas, including six on indulgences and twelve on penance. Luther had denied the existence of any treasury of merits out of which the church could pay penalties due for sins, and he had caricatured indulgences as little more than "pious frauds" that duped the gullible. Neither Luther nor the other reformers ever saw any merit in indulgences, but all were not so straightforward in their rejection of penance. Most of the reformers consigned the sacrament to the category of useless Roman inventions, and eventually confession all but disappeared from Protestant Christianity. At the beginning of the reformation, however, at least some saw the confession of sins as valuable, whether or not they considered it a sacrament.

Luther himself was somewhat ambivalent about the sacramentality of confession. Certainly at the beginning of his break from Rome he still believed it was a sacrament in the Catholic sense, but by the end of his life he no longer considered it a sacrament instituted by Christ similar to baptism and communion. If confession was a sacrament at all it was only a sacrament in the broad sense, a sacrament instituted by the church, through which Christians could experience the forgiveness of God. But no matter which kind of sacrament it was, Luther never stopped urging his followers to confess their sins and to resist all attempts by other reformers to do away with the practice: "Yes, I would rather bear the pope's tyranny of fasting, ceremony, vestments, serving trays, capes, and whatever else I could stand without doing violence to my faith, than have confession taken from Christians" (Letter to Osiander).

But Luther did not admit any automatic *ex opere operato* value to absolution even in his early period. Most Catholic theologians at the time accepted the Scotist theory of penance but some continued to claim that only an intense experience of contrition brought true forgiveness of sins, and for Luther this was the correct explanation of confession. As he saw it, those who felt sorrow for their sins and feared God's punishment went to the sacrament repentant and asking for mercy. They confessed their sins in shame and humiliation, and when they heard the words of absolution they realized God's readiness to spare the repentant sinner and felt released from the burden of their sins. In his own words, "Christ placed absolution in the mouth of his church and has commended it to release us from our sins. Therefore when our heart feels the burden of our sins and aches for consolation, we who are Christians find an undeniable refuge when we hear the word of God and learn that God, through the ministry of a human being, releases us and absolves us from our sins" (*Large Catechism*, "Short Exhortation to Confession").

Luther's analysis of confession also differed in some other important ways from the usual Catholic theories of the period. For one thing he insisted that Christians approach the sacrament with active faith and confidence in God's mercy; without that kind of faith, going through the ritual would be a mere formality and the sacrament would be ineffective. On the other hand, Luther claimed that sinners did not merit God's forgiveness by the degree of contrition that they felt; Christ's redemptive death on the cross had earned God's forgiveness once and for all. Sincere confession simply enabled Christians to realize that forgiveness covered their own personal sins, and it allowed them to rejoice that their sins would not be charged against them. The effect of the sacrament therefore was the "grace of forgiveness," interpreted not as a metaphysical cleansing of the soul but as an experience of peace and joy that came from faith in God's mercy. And since Christ had already atoned for all sins by shedding his own blood, Christians did not have to fear further punishment in a purgatory that was nowhere mentioned in the Bible. In fact, argued Luther, doing penance for sins after confession insinuated that something was lacking in the satisfaction that Christ had made for sins on Calvary.

So Luther was not against confession, but he did attack what he called "the false penance of the papists" who "lead the people to confide in their own works" and "do not mention Christ or faith" (*Articles of Schmalkalden*). As he experienced and taught it, penance did not remit sins in the sense that it eliminated them from one's life and washed them from one's soul, for he recognized that even after confession he himself remained bound by his sinful habits and was prone to sin again. Being a Christian meant therefore being *simul justus et peccator*, simultaneously just and a sinner, justified by the grace of God but still sinful despite one's best attempts to be good. Thus confession did not actually forgive sins but it was a sacramental way of realizing that sins were forgiven and of being freed from the burdensome fear of punishment. It was not a "good work" that Christians did to have their sins forgiven but a door to the joyful experience of forgiveness.

Like his Catholic contemporaries, Luther saw the words of absolution as the sacramental sign of God's forgiveness, but unlike them he did not believe that only a priest could give absolution. In his view what made the words effective was not the power of the person who said them but the faith of the person who heard them, and so Christians could confess their sins to one another and receive assurance of divine forgiveness from any layperson. However, since Luther did not believe that Christ himself had instituted private confession he could not insist that his followers practice it, and despite his protests they began to discard confession even during his lifetime. Eventually the only confession of sins that remained in the Lutheran churches was a general admission of sinfulness that was made at the beginning of Sunday worship.

John Calvin, too, saw no scriptural basis for private confession since "the ceremonies of the sacraments can be appointed only by God" and the Bible did not describe any ceremony other than baptism for the forgiveness of sins (*Institutes of the Christian Religion* IV, 19, 16). In addition, he found it strangely contradictory that the Catholic hierarchy claimed to have the power of the keys to the kingdom of heaven and yet they demanded penance or punishment in purgatory for sins that were presumably forgiven. He believed that confession as an early church practice had arisen in response to the apostle James's suggestion that Christians should confess their sins to one another, and he was familiar enough with the writings of some of the fathers to recognize that there had been some form of penitential discipline in early Christianity. But he also realized that whatever the discipline had been, it was nothing like private confession in the sixteenth century, and from his studies he concluded that the power of binding and loosing referred not to sins but to ecclesiastical sanctions that were imposed on public sinners.

Still, Calvin agreed that it was a good thing to feel repentance for sins provided that this did not lead to despair and forgetfulness of the forgiveness that God had promised to the elect. If anything, then, the practice of confession should be a means of bringing relief from the guilt that Christians might feel because of their sinfulness, and it should be a way of receiving reassurance that their sins were blotted out by the blood of Christ. Calvin's attitude toward confession was in this respect much like Luther's, and like Luther he did not see why priests should be needed to continue this Christian practice. "Scripture does not specify anyone to whom we should unburden ourselves and so it leaves us free to choose from among the faithful someone who seems worthy to hear our confession. Nevertheless, because pastors must above all be suited for this, it is better for us to address ourselves to them" (*Institutes* III, 4, 12).

Calvin therefore denied the sacramentality of confession in the strict Catholic sense, but he admitted its sacramental value in the broad sense of being a way to intensify one's awareness of God's mercy and experience God's forgiveness. Christians could, of course, receive reassurance of pardon for their sins when general absolution was given in the name of Christ at their public worship, but Calvin maintained that "individual absolution is no less effective and beneficial when those who need assurance in their conscience make use of it" (*Institutes* III, 4, 14). What he particularly objected to was the Roman insistence on obligatory confession and the medieval practice of enumerating sins in detail, both of which he believed had turned a worthwhile Christian custom into an ecclesiastical form of mental torture. So Calvin made private confession a purely voluntary practice, and with nothing but his own personal approval to recommend it, confession eventually disappeared from Calvinist churches as thoroughly as it did from Lutheran ones.

In England the original reformers retained the practice of private confession but made it nonobligatory, and Archbishop Cranmer in the 1552 revision of the *Book of Common Prayer* recommended it to the sick and dying for the relief of their conscience. Its status as a sacrament was unclear, however, and although English priests still received the power of absolution at their ordination many Anglican theologians adopted the position that penance was a "lesser" sacrament than baptism or the eucharist, a sacrament of the church but not a sacrament instituted by Christ. Private confession continued to be widely practiced in the seventeenth century, but after that its popularity declined, and by the beginning of the nineteenth century it was no longer an important part of the Anglican tradition. It remained a ritual for the sick and dying, but was not usually practiced in times of health.

If the Protestant reformers doubted the strict sacramentality of confession, however, the Catholic bishops of the counter-reformation certainly did not, and the Council of Trent in 1551 reaffirmed the medieval understanding of penance as the only orthodox one. And because of what they viewed as blatant distortions of the sacrament by Luther and Calvin, the bishops set forth the Catholic doctrine of penance in a rather lengthy document containing nine chapters of exposition and fifteen canons condemning heresies.

The bishops were convinced of the correctness of their position partly because private confession had been a Catholic practice from time immemorial, and partly because when they read the word *paenitentia* in the New Testament and patristic writings they often assumed that it referred to penance rather than penitence. The bishops did not know much about the penitential practices of the early church and they were unaware of the changes that had occurred in them through the beginning of the Middle Ages. Since the time of Aquinas, *paenitentia* had designated the sacrament, and since the time of Scotus the essence of the sacrament had been identified with absolution, and so it seemed that Christ's command to forgive sins in John 20 was a divine endorsement of the medieval ritual, that the apostle's recommendation in James 5 referred to private confession, and that the fathers' calls to penitence were exhortations to receive the sacrament. As far as the bishops knew, therefore, penance in the form of private confession had been an official sacrament of the church since the time of its foundation, and any attempts to undermine it had to be vigorously opposed.

In their theology of the sacrament the Catholic bishops situated penance, as Aquinas had done, in the context of justification, that is, they saw it as part of the process by which a Christian became a just and hopefully a holy person. As they explained it, penance had been instituted by God for the benefit of those who fell into sin after being baptized. Baptism forgave original sin, but divine wisdom saw that help was needed for overcoming further sins, and the sacrament provided the means by which these were both forgiven and eliminated. The forgiveness was effected through the words of absolution, but contrition, confession, and assigned works of penance were also needed for the remnants of sin to be fully eliminated. By receiving the sacrament regularly, then, Christians could expect to grow in grace in this life and be accepted by God in the next.

Since the Middle Ages Catholic theologians had insisted on the importance of contrition for the remission of sins, and the Catholic bishops at Trent also insisted on it for confession. Those who approached the sacrament were expected to examine their conscience, "pondering the seriousness of their sins, their number and foulness, the loss of eternal happiness and the eternal damnation that they incurred" (*Penance*, Canon 5). Confession was not to be a perfunctory affair but an occasion for real soul searching and a step toward a more holy life. On the other hand, confession did not require such deep remorse that penitents had to feel terror stricken, and the council condemned those Protestants who claimed that the Catholic practice was impossible because it did. The bishops admitted the traditional distinction between different kinds of contrition, and they allowed that perfect contrition motivated by the love of God rather than the fear of punishment could bring forgiveness of sins even without confession to a priest. But in their view such perfect contrition also had to include the desire to receive the sacrament that God had ordained for forgiveness through the church. And so in the end, all contrition ultimately led to confession.

In regard to confession itself, the council declared, "The universal Church has always understood that the Lord instituted the integral confession of sins, and that divine law makes it necessary for all those who lapse after their baptism" (*Penance*, Chapter 5). By "integral confession" was meant the enumeration of all mortal sins "specifically and particularly," along with "those circumstances which alter the character of the sin." Venial sins on the other hand did not have to be confessed since they could be atoned for in other ways, but the council recommended confessing them as a "proper and advantageous" act of religious devotion.

The reason why all unconfessed mortal sins had to be enumerated had to do with the way penance had come to be treated in canon law. Theologically, penance was understood to remit the eternal punishment only for confessed sins, and so any mortal sins that were not mentioned by the penitent could not be forgiven by the priest. Canonically, absolution was understood to be "the equivalent of a judicial act in which the priest acted like a judge in pronouncing sentence" (*Penance*, Chapter 6). In order to judge correctly, therefore, priests had to hear all the evidence, otherwise "the judges do not adequately know the sins and they cannot properly assess their gravity, nor can they impose on the penitents the penance they ought to impose" (Chapter 5). The words of absolution were not merely an announcement of forgiveness by God but a pronouncement of forgiveness by the priest acting in God's name. Their use was an exercise of the power of the keys that Christ had promised to the church, and such sacred power had to be used judiciously.

In this same legalistic light, penances performed after confession were looked on mainly as a means of making satisfaction for sins: "We should not have our sins forgiven without any satisfaction, for otherwise we would be tempted to regard sins lightly and offend the Holy Spirit by falling into more serious sins" (*Penance*, Chapter 8). For this reason priests were warned not to "wink at sins and deal too indulgently with penitents" by imposing "very light works for very serious sins." Clearly the bishops recognized that assigned penances were a deterrent to crime and even a remedy for wicked habits, but primarily they were a "sure way of averting the threatening punishments of God" that waited in purgatory for those who did not pay for their sins before they died. At the same time, however, the bishops were careful to insist that "the satisfaction which we make for sins is something which is done only through Christ Jesus." Contrary to the claims of the reformers, doing penance after confession did not imply that something was lacking in the satisfaction made by Christ's death, but it was the divinely established way of making sure that the merits he had earned were applied to those who deserved them.

In the end, then, the Council of Trent's approach to penance was both theological and canonical, and it was hard to keep the two apart. Theologically the forgiveness of sins was needed for salvation, but since the beginning of the Middle Ages the sacramental administration of that forgiveness had become bound up with the church's judicial system, and by the end of the Middle Ages the theology of penance had become inseparable from its treatment in canon law. What the reformers had tried to do in effect was to isolate the sacramentality of confession from the legalities connected with its administration, but the Catholic bishops could not make that distinction and so they viewed an attack on one as an attack on the other. In the long run the reformers failed in their attempt, for without the support of divine or church law the practice of purely sacramental confession fell into disuse. On the Catholic side, the reform-minded bishops almost failed as well, but for a different reason. They attempted to cure the ills of the church's penitential system by legislation, and eventually the way they treated it became the way it was treated in modern Catholicism.

Henceforth the confession of mortal sins would be primarily regarded as a matter of divine law, supported by the ecclesiastical law to confess them within a year after they were committed. Those who committed only venial sins were legally exempted from both laws, although they were encouraged to make use of the sacrament to receive absolution and make the necessary satisfaction for them. If penitents were not sure whether their sins were mortal or venial, prudent application of the law dictated that they follow the safer course by going to confession and letting the priest be the judge. Priests themselves were to be better trained in both divine and church law so that they could execute their responsibility as administrators of absolution with knowledge and fairness. To safeguard against the injudicious use of the sacrament, canon law ordained that priests could hear confessions only within the jurisdiction of bishops who gave them permission to do so, and it clarified the distinction between sins that priests could validly absolve, those that were reserved to the decision of the bishop, and those that could be forgiven only by the pope.

After the council most of the changes in the administration of ecclesiastical forgiveness were legislated for the spiritual protection of penitents. In 1567 Pius V ordered the cancellation of every indulgence for which money had to be offered so that Catholics could not be deceived into thinking that they could buy their way into heaven. The revision of the Roman sacramentary in 1614 made it mandatory for priests to listen to confessions from behind a screen, partly to ensure the anonymity of those who came to confess serious sins and partly to protect women who confessed sexual sins from being solicited. Weak or unscrupulous confessors who did so anyway were automatically suspended from saying mass and hearing confessions, and priests who revealed sins that were confessed to them were placed under an excommunication that could be lifted only by appealing to Rome.

Some of the bishops at the council had expressed the hope that private confession could become a vehicle for giving spiritual counseling to the faithful, but outside of monasteries and convents this hardly ever happened. The legalities that surrounded the sacrament tended to ensure that it would remain a tribunal of clerical judgment, and as cities in Europe grew larger it became impossible for priests in large parishes to know most of their parishioners well enough to give them individual guidance. By and large confession remained what it had become in the Middle Ages: the usual preparation for communion, which was received once a year. It was not until the twentieth century, when Pius X urged Catholics to receive communion more often, that lay people began to go to confession more often as well, acting on the assumption that they had to confess their sins each time they wanted to receive the eucharist. Theologically this was a mistaken assumption, but many of the clergy were not aware that it was, and those who were saw no harm in the mistake as long as it brought people to the sacrament of penance.

Yet it would be incorrect to suppose that confession and absolution were not sacramental in the broad sense in modern Catholicism. True, confession for many became just another requirement of church law, and making satisfaction for sins often seemed no different from paying the penalty for breaking other laws. True, those who had to reveal their secret sins to another human being sometimes felt more shame and humiliation than divine forgiveness. And true, there was a great tendency to treat the words of absolution like sacramental magic, a mystical incantation that could free a soul from untold suffering in the life hereafter when pronounced by a man who had been given the power to say them. But it is also true that for many Catholics the sacrament of penance was genuinely sacramental, a sacred door through which they could enter a realm of justice and mercy unlike any that they knew on earth. For them it was a sacrament of honesty and truth, for it demanded a soul-searching in which nothing needed to be hidden since nothing could indeed be hidden from God. It was a sacrament of freedom, for it called for a conversion from habits of sin and it brought a liberation from guilt over past wrongs that could not be undone. And it was a sacrament of reconciliation, for it announced forgiveness by God and it invited forgiveness of oneself and others. For those who sought spiritual perfection in the clerical or religious life, it could be a process through which they reached beyond themselves and touched the goal of their personal growth. And for those thousands who flocked to saintly confessors of the period like John Vianney in France it could be a ritual through which they experienced the meaning of God's mercy in a dramatic and personal way.

But the experience of penance, whether it was mechanical or sacramental, had little effect on the theology of penance. The dogmatic understanding of the sacrament had been set by the council and there was little that could be done to alter or add to it. After Trent, there were only two theological controversies over penance and they both took place in the seventeenth century. One stemmed from the pietist movement promoted by Cornelius Jansen, a professor of theology at Louvain in Belgium, who wanted a return to more rigorous penitential practices like refusing sinners communion until after they had performed their penance. The Jansenists denied that imperfect contrition was enough to merit forgiveness by either God or the church, and for this and other insinuations that the church's sacramental practices were not valid they were eventually condemned by Rome. The other controversy stemmed from the fact that the bishops at Trent had avoided settling a fine theological point that was still being debated by scholastics at the time, namely, whether imperfect contrition for mortal sins was enough for having them forgiven by absolution, or whether imperfect contrition had to be elevated by grace to perfect contrition for mortal sins to be forgiven. One school of theologians appealed to Trent's teaching that imperfect contrition was sufficient for approaching the sacrament; the other school argued that what was sufficient for approaching the sacrament was not sufficient for the effective reception of the sacrament. Those who favored the sufficiency of imperfect contrition accused their opponents of Jansenism; those who believed that only perfect contrition could remit mortal sins called their opponents laxists. At one point the dispute between the two theological camps got so heated that Pope Alexander VII issued a decree prohibiting both schools from publicly condemning each other until the matter was settled by Rome. But it never was, and so the argument continued, a little more quietly this time, until the twentieth century.

5. Sacramental Reconciliation in the Church Today

What finally brought the argument to an end was the fact that after the Second Vatican Council theologians abandoned the scholastic approach to penance, which effectively eliminated both sides of the debate. Even before the council, however, there were signs that the Tridentine theology of sin and confession had somehow lost contact with reality in the contemporary world. Catholic intellectuals realized that neither individuals nor societies were as simple as scholastic theories presumed them to be, and so the neat division of sins into mortal and venial sins, as well as the categorizing of sins according to the commandments they violated, did not seem to do justice to the complexity of human motives and actions. Acts like eating meat on Friday or missing mass on Sunday had come to be considered mortal sins, but now theologians began to question seriously whether such otherwise innocuous behavior could actually merit eternal damnation. And when Rome relaxed its laws about fasting before communion and not eating meat on Friday, ordinary Catholics began wondering, too. Was sin really just a matter of breaking the law, so that if the law were changed what used to be sinful would suddenly be unsinful?

As long as sin had been understood in legal metaphors it was not hard to equate goodness with obeying the law, sin with breaking the law, and purgatory with punishment for sin. But psychologists and other social scientists in the twentieth century began to explore human motivations more deeply, existentialists and phenomenologists began to explain ethics in terms of internal decisions rather than external actions, and even theologians began to suggest that Christian morality had to be based on more than canon law and the Ten Commandments. In the 1950s, for example, Bernard Häring spoke of the "law of Christ" as an ethical ideal that went far beyond the bounds of legalistic morality, and Joseph Fuchs and others proposed that mortal sin was more a matter of making a "fundamental option" for evil than a matter of violating a moral code.

This move away from traditional moral concepts got an added impetus from biblical theology when more careful scripture scholarship discovered that the basic moral category of the Bible was not law but covenant. For centuries Christians had read the Old Testament in the light of their own western legalistic mentality, but a more scientific study of Middle Eastern culture and Hebrew forms of thought revealed that the basis of law in ancient Israel was the covenant between Yahweh and the chosen people. A covenant was basically a pact, an agreement that established a personal relationship between two parties. The covenant might be spelled out in terms of dos and don'ts, but living up to those commandments was primarily a matter of living up to a personal agreement rather than obeying a law. Likewise, breaking those commandments was primarily a matter of breaking a personal relationship rather than disobeying a law. The discovery gave Catholic theologians a whole new way of thinking about morality.

Around the same time, personalist philosophy was proposing that interpersonal relationships had to be understood on a deeper level than social interaction, and personalist psychology was suggesting that there was more to moral development than adjusting to society's norms. In the 1960s an Anglican theologian, Joseph Fletcher, aroused the attention of Catholics and Protestants alike by proposing a new Christian morality under the name "situation ethics." Its sole criterion for judging the morality of an action was whether or not it was motivated by love, and it considered the concrete situation in which the action was performed as more important than abstract moral codes. Catholic theologians rejected Fletcher's theory as too simple to do justice to complex ethical problems, but most of them also respected his effort to deal with morality in terms of intentions and relationships rather than actions and laws.

The late sixties and early seventies were also years of social unrest and social protest, and the conscience of Catholics and other Americans was pricked by the sudden realization that black people had been denied their civil rights for centuries, that millions lived in poverty in a land of affluence, and that civilians were being slaughtered in a war in southeast Asia. How could it happen in a country of "good Christians"? What did traditional Catholic morality, so long focused on the laws of the church and the Ten Commandments, have to say about these larger issues? And what relevance did the practice of private confession with its enumeration of personal sins have in the face of social sin, a sinfulness which no one could personally confess but for which all were collectively responsible? How could penance wipe away the guilt of social injustice? It seemed that it could not.

It is perhaps significant that the Second Vatican Council, apart from its directive to revise the confessional ritual along with the other sacramental rites, said nothing about the sacrament of penance that had not been said in traditional Catholic theology, and what it did say about it was very little. The bishops had been educated in the tradition of private confession and individual absolution, and at least up to the time of the council this type of forgiveness ritual still seemed viable and in no danger of being abandoned by contemporary Catholics. But the bishops also learned what church historians had been discovering about penance for the previous twenty years: that during the patristic period ecclesiastical reconciliation had been a public ritual, that it had not been a very frequent practice, and that a Christian could be admitted to it only once during a lifetime; that during the Middle Ages a new private ritual had been introduced from Ireland, that it had only later won acceptance by Rome, and that originally confessors did   not forgive sins but only prayed that God would forgive them; that in modern times the Protestant reformers reacted against scandalous abuses in the penitential system, that the Council of Trent corrected most of them but retained a rather legalistic attitude toward sin and forgiveness, and that the council had been mistaken in assuming that repeated private confession dated back to the days of the apostles. In light of these discoveries, the bishops of Vatican II had to admit that the practice of penance had changed in the past and so it could change again in the present. But they said nothing specific about the direction that the change should take.

The ecumenical movement, which had been fostering friendlier relations between the Catholic and the Orthodox churches, suggested some new directions and possibilities. Since the time of their final break with Rome in the Middle Ages, the eastern churches had retained a belief in seven sacraments and Rome even recognized the validity of those sacraments. Yet the way they were practiced and the way they were understood was sometimes very different from their Catholic counterparts. Like the churches in the west, the eastern churches had eventually dropped the ancient principle of restricting sacramental reconciliation to only once in a lifetime, but their equivalent of the sacrament of penance bore little resemblance to the modern Catholic practice. Most Orthodox churches, for example, regarded the general confession of sinfulness at the beginning of the eucharistic liturgy as a sacramental rite, and most Orthodox Christians sought reconciliation with God primarily through this communal ritual. Those who went to confession privately did so only infrequently, and usually as a preparation for receiving communion, perhaps once a year. When they did, they did not confess all their sins or even all their serious sins, but only the ones that weighed most heavily on their conscience and for which they wanted assurance of God's forgiveness. When they received that assurance from the priest, he did not absolve them from their sins but simply prayed for God's mercy and forgiveness, and he did not assign any penitential works unless the penitents wanted to do them. Overall, then, the eastern churches had no conception of confession as a judicial act, and they did not think of penances as making satisfaction for temporal punishment. For them, if the sins were forgiven by God, they were simply forgiven, and the purpose of penitential works was not to pay a debt but to grow in holiness.

If Rome recognized these practices as sacramental, then Rome could revise its own ritual of penance, making it less individual and more communal, less legalistic and more liturgical, less concerned with the enumeration of sins and more concerned with conversion of the heart. A liturgical commission set to work on the revision keeping in mind the Tridentine rite, examples from the eastern churches and older western forms of penance, and suggestions from biblical theology and contemporary philosophy about the meaning of sin and forgiveness. The result was not one but three forms of the rite—one individual and private, one communal and public, and one combined form—which were published in 1973 and officially substituted for the rite of 1614 three years later. The new forms of the rite stressed the idea of reconciliation rather than absolution, they encouraged the use of scripture in addition to the prescribed prayers, and they allowed for flexibility in each of the forms.

The private form was an adaptation of the Tridentine rite, but it could now be performed with priest and penitent facing each other rather than separated by a screen, in an atmosphere of pastoral counseling rather than ecclesiastical judgment. The words of absolution spoken by the priest were prefaced by a prayer asking for God's mercy and pardon, and priests were encouraged to assign more meaningful penances than the rote recitation of a few short prayers. The semi-private form of the sacrament began with a penitential prayer service with appropriate hymns and readings from the Bible, after which the congregation was invited to make their individual confessions privately. The public form was a communal penance service for those situations when there were too many people or not enough time for individual confessions. After an opening ceremony of prayers, scripture readings, and a call to reconciliation, the congregation would be invited to silently confess their sins to God, and then the priest would ask for God's pardon and absolution on all those present. People who had their sins absolved in this way, however, were still supposed to see a priest privately afterward, for personal counseling and spiritual direction.

But these changes in the sacramental ritual came all but too late for most Catholics. Frequent confession had been a common practice through the beginning of the 1960s, when lines of penitents could still be seen in most parish churches every Saturday evening, at least in the United States. But with the coming of the council, the new air of freedom in Catholicism, and the theological debates about the nature of sin and forgiveness that were publicized in the Catholic press, the confession lines dwindled and by the end of the decade many priests were finding other things to do on Saturday afternoons. As already mentioned, there was a growing uncertainty among Catholics about what was sinful and what was not, and a growing dissatisfaction with the church's traditional emphasis on individual sins to the neglect of social sins like racism and the exploitation of the poor, militarism, and the arms race. But the single moral issue that probably led more Catholic lay people to question the nature and necessity of confession was not a global one but a personal one: birth control.

Traditional Catholic theology had viewed the begetting of children as the primary purpose of marriage, and any way of preventing the birth of children besides abstaining from intercourse had been considered sinful. Then in 1960 medical technology introduced the contraceptive pill, and although Catholic theologians were undecided about the morality of using it, the church's hierarchy decided it was an "artificial" and not a "natural" method of birth control and hence sinful. Women who began using the pill for reasons they considered legitimate felt obliged to discuss it in confession, but many confessors believed there was nothing to discuss: if women wanted to be forgiven they would have to renounce their sin. Many married Catholics, however, did not see anything sinful about it, and some who were concerned about the global population explosion even viewed it as virtuous rather than sinful. In time, Catholics simply stopped mentioning birth control in the confessional, and the image of the priest as the final arbiter in moral matters began to be discarded.

Other disagreements between contemporary theologians and the tradition-minded hierarchy, especially in the area of sexual morality, added to the Catholic confusion about what was sinful and what was not. Lay people could no longer go to the priest and say, "Bless me, father, for I have sinned…" because they were not always sure about the morality of what they were doing. And the responses they got from different confessors were not always the same: it seemed that now the priests were not sure either. Theologians emphasized the importance of personal responsibility in moral decisions, and even the council had sanctioned the rather modern idea of freedom of conscience. More often than ever before, Catholics felt they had to decide things for themselves according to their own conscience rather than according to clear and certain moral precepts. On top of it all, the hierarchy's general ambivalence about war, civil rights, and poverty left many Catholics looking to others for moral leadership and they no longer turned to their clergy for moral guidance as they had in the past. They took their marriage problems to counselors rather than pastors; they took their personal problems to therapists rather than priests; and in increasing numbers, to make their peace with God they did it directly, without the aid of the church's official sacrament.

In ten short years, then, the traditional penitential system simply broke down, especially among the educated classes of America and Europe, but to a greater or lesser extent in other parts of the world as well. For a variety of reasons the Tridentine form of confession stopped being an effective sacrament for many Catholics, and the newer forms, although they aroused some interest and hope when they were first introduced, were unable to take its place. The situation led some theologians to speculate that perhaps the future of penance will be not unlike its ancient past, when Christians sought sacramental reconciliation with God and the church very infrequently, if ever.

For a while, after the promulgation of the revised rite of penance with its three different forms, some bishops, especially in developing countries, put more emphasis on communal penance rather than private penance. In some countries of South America, for instance, where priests are scarce and few people go to private confession, the public form of the rite became a regular and well-attended practice. Church officials in Rome, however, fearing that the communal penance service might displace individual confession and absolution as the principal form of the sacrament, issued injunctions against its being used except in cases of severe emergency. The revised *Code of Canon Law*, issued in 1983, added a requirement that penitents who receive general absolution must confess their serious sins to a priest as soon as possible afterward. These restrictions effectively put an end to the third form of penance as a pastoral option, but they did little to encourage people to return to private confession in any great numbers.

Faced on the one hand with few individual penitents and on the other hand with the inability to offer communal penance, some resourceful bishops and priests have encouraged the creation of penance services in which general absolution is not offered, especially during the penitential seasons of Lent and Advent. In the United States these have not met with great success, but in some small communities in Latin America they are becoming more popular. Also becoming more widespread is the practice of seeking spiritual direction from lay people who are formally trained for that ministry or, in countries where such training is not available, from people who are known for their pastoral wisdom. Since the process of spiritual direction usually entails revealing one's sins and shortcomings, and receiving assurance of God's forgiveness as well as advice from the director, it is not unlike the practice of the medieval monks who acted as spiritual fathers for novices and people near the monastery, in the days before most monks were ordained as priests. Thus one path that reconciliation is taking may retrace a path that it took many centuries ago, with one important difference: today many spiritual directors are women.

A question that was raised in the 1970s concerned the future of first penance for children. Advances in child psychology reinforced observations by religious educators that children who were being taught to go to confession before they made their first communion around the age of seven or eight were for the most part incapable of having a sense of personal responsibility for sinful acts. Although beliefs inherited from Jansenism (see page 291) had made confession before communion a normal practice, canon law at that time did not prescribe any sequence for these sacraments, so bishops in the United States and elsewhere accepted the advice that the first celebration of reconciliation be postponed at least until the age of ten. More than half the parishes in the United States adopted this new practice, and religious educators reported that not only was their catechesis with the older children more successful, but they were also able to address the Jansenistic attitudes of the children's parents.

Complaints to the Vatican from unconvinced parents, however, brought a reply that the practice to be followed was that decreed by Pope Pius X in 1910. But since the pope's decree had only stated that children from the age of seven could be admitted to the two sacraments (and had said nothing about their sequence), the matter remained unclear for several years while letters passed between the United States Conference of Catholic Bishops and the Vatican. Although Rome's preference was decidedly in favor of confession before first communion, it was unable to prove its case from canon law or papal decrees. When the new *Code of Canon Law* was issued by Pope John Paul II, it seemed to assume that children would normally go to confession before making their first communion, but a careful reading of the relevant canons revealed that the law does not require it. The situation is therefore much the same as it was before, and in the absence of clear legislation one way or the other, the future of this issue remains ambiguous.

A more positive development pointing to the future of the sacrament has been the creation of a program for estranged Catholics who feel a desire to rejoin the institutional church. Called *Re-Membering Church* by its originators in the North American Forum for the Catechumenate, it is modeled on the catechetical and liturgical process used in the new Rite of Christian Initiation of Adults, although its historical roots go back to the order of penitents in the patristic period (just as the RCIA does). Use of the program has grown significantly in the United States and Canada since its introduction in the early 1980s, and although proposals have been made that it be officially adopted by the church, it remains still a parish or diocesan endeavor. Persons participating in the program are invited to begin the sacrament of reconciliation on Ash Wednesday with the understanding that they will not receive absolution right away, following the ancient practice of the order of penitents. Lent for them is a time of prayerful sharing in a small group with others who have been alienated from the church, under the guidance of a team of ministers, most of whom are lay people. After four weeks of personal catechesis and inner healing, the penitents are absolved and receive the eucharist at the Mass of the Lord's Supper on Holy Thursday. They then receive additional catechesis after Easter until the feast of Pentecost, when they are called to make a commitment of service in the parish. By and large, Re-Membering Church is one of the more hopeful directions that the sacrament is taking.

There have been few additional developments in this sacrament during the 1990s, and its treatment in the *Catechism of the Catholic Church* reflects Rome's understanding of the sacrament during the pontificate of John Paul II. The tradition-conscious pope emphasized private confession over the other two forms of the sacrament, and this is reflected in the *Catechism* produced under his direction. This section (1422–1498) is therefore very traditional in its doctrinal aspects and its use of terminology from scholastic theology, but it is also very untraditional in that it focuses on the pastoral and spiritual aspects of going to confession rather than on the juridical aspects.

Acknowledging that the sacrament is known by many names (penance, reconciliation, confession, sacrament of conversion, sacrament of forgiveness), the *Catechism* explains its necessity and purpose, noting the New Testament's many calls for moral conversion, even of the already baptized, and pointing out that conversion of the heart is not simply a human effort but a work of God's grace (1422–1433). Moreover, moral conversion and development take place through many activities of the Christian life (fasting, prayer, reading the scriptures, and so forth) and not through the liturgical sacrament alone (1434–1439).

Sin is defined in relational terms as a rupture of communion with God and a breakdown in community, which is why conversion requires both

God's forgiveness and reconciliation with the church (1440). The *Catechism* insists that only God forgives sins, but the sacrament is an essential means of seeking and obtaining that forgiveness (1441–1445). At one point the *Catechism* says flatly, "Reconciliation with the Church is inseparable from reconciliation with God" (1445), which seems to imply that reconciliation with God is impossible without going to confession, except that the *Catechism* has already acknowledged that moral conversion and growth take place in many ways (1434–1439). This betrays a hidden assumption, common in many traditional discussions of the sacrament and explicit in canon law, that the type of sin being referred to here is a complete severance of a person's relationship with God and the church, or what was tradition- ally known as mortal sin. This is made clear in the *Catechism's* discussion of the confession of sins (1455–1458).

The process of going to confession is described in traditional terms such as perfect and imperfect contrition, examination of conscience, mortal and venial sins, making satisfaction for sins, and so forth (1450–1460), and the ministry of the ecclesial sacrament is restricted to priests (1461–1467). Likewise the effects of the sacrament are described in objective terms, *ex opere operato*, with little attention given to the subjective process that rec- onciliation may actually entail.

A full subsection (1471–1479) is devoted to indulgences despite the fact that few Catholics in Europe and North America still think in these terms, and there is little evidence that such concepts inform the thinking of most Catholics in other parts of the world. A final subsection (1480–1484) is devoted to the ways that the sacrament can be celebrated other than private confession as hitherto described: in the Byzantine (eastern rite) liturgy, in a communal penance service that invites people to individual confession, and in a service of general confession and absolution. The subsection closes, however, with a renewed emphasis on individual confession.

Regardless of official attempts to return to the practices of the past, however, penance in the future will have to be liturgically and perhaps also theologically diverse. In technologically advanced cultures where the level of education is high, the sacrament will need to be a more sophisticated sign of reconciliation and forgiveness, perhaps one that in a liturgical set- ting enables people to recognize and overcome their estrangement from one another, and in doing that recognize and overcome their estrangement from God. In less advanced cultures the traditional legal metaphors for sin and forgiveness may yet be appropriate, for being forgiven by a human authority can still be a sacramental sign of being forgiven by a divine author of law and morality. And in non-western cultures, whether technologically advanced or not, Catholics may have to find their own cultural metaphors for forgiveness and reconciliation, and develop liturgical symbols that speak to them of God's mercy and pardon as clearly as the western sacrament once spoke to Catholic Europe.

So the sacrament of repentance and conversion in the church seems to be in a state of transition. It is still officially called penance, but it bears little outward resemblance to private penance in the Middle Ages and public penance in the ancient world. Inwardly, too, both of those were sacraments of penitence, of sorrowful satisfaction for sins, and today such feelings seem foreign both culturally and theologically. Moreover, the present forms of the rite do not yet seem capable of being effective sacraments for many, although undoubtedly they are effective for some. Theologically they speak of mercy and pardon, conversion and repentance. Liturgically they symbolize in words and gestures the Christian ideals of forgiving and being forgiven, of unity and reconciliation. But the symbols too often, in the experience of many Catholics, are representative rather than effective: they signify something sacred but they do not effect what they signify, and in this sense they are not adequately sacramental.

And yet the prospects for the future are not bleak but hopeful. For some time, priests and bishops have been expanding on the freedom given them in the new rites, altering them to make them more effective in their own local situations. For some time, liturgists have been expressing their dissatisfaction with the present revisions and have been suggesting new ones for the church as a whole. And for some time, theologians have been speaking of penance not in terms of absolution from sin but in terms of reconversion and reconciliation. They remind their readers that Jesus was a living sacrament of spiritual healing for those who knew him, and that the early Christian community had been a vital sign of forgiveness in the face of persecution, of fraternal love in a world of armed suspicion, and of personal concern for the welfare of others. If the history of the sacrament is a reliable precedent, it should be only a matter of time before sacramental practice again matches sacramental theory.

For Further Reading

Tad Guzie and John McIlhon, *The Forgiveness of Sin* (Thomas More Press, 1979) examines the meaning of sacrament and forgiveness in the light of the new rite for confession.

Léonce Hamelin, *Reconciliation in the Church* (Liturgical Press, 1980) discusses reasons for the sacrament and explains the three forms of the new rite.

James Dallen, *Removing the Barriers* (Liturgy Training Publications, 1991) tries to reclaim some of the sacrament's past functions and explore some future possibilities.

Quentin Donahue and Linda Shapiro, *Bless Me, Father, For I Have Sinned* (Donald I. Fine, 1984) proves that history can be humorous and that theology can be undertaken by ordinary people.

Sandra DeGidio, *Reconciliation: Sacrament with a Future* (St. Anthony Messenger Press, 1985) is a compact introduction to the sacrament and its theology today.

Patrick Brennan, *Penance and Reconciliation* (Thomas More Press, 1986) looks at the past history, present practice, and future possibilities of the sacrament.

Kevin Doran, *More Joy in Heaven!* (Liturgical Press, 1988) is a sensible and occasionally humorous introduction to the meaning and practice of confession.

Domiciano Fernandez, *The Father's Forgiveness* (Liturgical Press, 1991) argues that general absolution without individual confession should be more widely practiced in the Catholic Church.

George Maloney, *Your Sins Are Forgiven You* (Alba House, 1994) offers a scriptural and spiritual reintroduction to the sacrament for those who no longer find it meaningful.

Julia Upton, *A Time for Embracing* (Liturgical Press, 1999) faces the complex issues connected with sacramental reconciliation without offering simple answers.

Jim Forest, *Confession: Doorway to Forgiveness* (Orbis Books, 2002) contains a kaleidoscope of history, scripture, stories, and spiritual direction.

Scott Hahn, *Lord, Have Mercy* (Doubleday, 2003) weaves stories of personal experiences and a literal reading of the scriptures into a conservative theology and spirituality of confession.

Christopher Walsh, *The Untapped Power of the Sacrament of Penance* (St. Anthony Messenger Press, 2005) is a pastoral discussion of the sacrament, its contemporary difficulties, and its potential for moral conversion and spiritual growth.

Loughlan Sofield, Carroll Juliano, and Gregory Aymond, *Facing Forgiveness* (Ave Maria Press, 2007) is an introduction to the process of forgiveness and reconciliation, primarily through stories.

Robert Morneau, *Reconciliation* (Orbis Books, 2007) presents a basic understanding of sin and the sacrament for individual spirituality.

Antoinette Bosco, *Radical Forgiveness* (Orbis Books, 2009) reflects on the need to forgive in the face of unforgiveable evil.

For Further Study

History and Theology

Ronald Witherup, *Conversion in the New Testament* (Liturgical Press, 1994) summarizes the process of interior transformation as described in the gospels and epistles.

Kenan Osborne, *Reconciliation and Justification* (Paulist Press, 1990) thoroughly examines the history of the sacrament in light of the theological issue of justification.

James Dallen, *The Reconciling Community* (Pueblo, 1986) offers a detailed and documented history of the sacrament, and a complete commentary on the revised rite.

Ladislas Orsy, *The Evolving Church and the Sacrament of Penance* (Dimension Books, 1978) looks at the larger issue of change in the church, using penance as an example.

Monika Hellwig, *Sign of Reconciliation and Conversion* (Michael Glazier, 1982) discusses the major aspects of the sacrament historically and theologically.

Bernhard Poschmann, *Penance and the Anointing of the Sick* (Herder and Herder, 1964) presents a scholarly and detailed account of the history of penance before Vatican II, with chapters on indulgences and the anointing of the sick.

Annemarie Kidder, *Making Confession, Hearing Confession* (Liturgical Press, 2010) looks at the history from an ecumenical perspective, emphasizing the process of repentance rather than the performance of the ritual.

Hugh Connolly, *The Irish Penitentials* (Four Courts Press, 1995) explains the Celtic understanding of moral conversion in terms related to the heart rather than in legalistic terms.

Ludwig Bieler, ed., *The Irish Penitentials* (Institute for Advanced Studies, 1963) contains the Latin text and English translation of over a dozen manuscripts listing sins and the penances they incur.

Sarah Hamilton, *The Practice of Penance 900-1050* (Boydell & Brewer, 2001) argues that public repentance and private confession existed side by side well into the Middle Ages.

Eric Luijten, *Sacramental Forgiveness as the Gift of God* (Peeters, 2003) is a scholarly monograph written to refute the mechanistic notions of sacramental forgiveness that are sometimes blamed on Aquinas.

Liturgical and Pastoral Dimensions

The Rite of Penance: Commentaries (Liturgical Conference, 1975, 1976, 1978) comprises three volumes with a variety of articles on understanding, implementing, and evaluating the new rite.

Clement Tierney, *The Sacrament of Penance and Reconciliation* (Costello, 1983) offers a scholarly investigation of the theology underlying the revised rite of penance.

Richard Gula, *To Walk Together Again* (Paulist Press, 1984) clearly articulates the contemporary Catholic understanding of the sacrament and its theology.

Bernard Cooke, *Reconciled Sinners: Healing Human Brokenness* (Twenty-Third Publications, 1986) discusses many dimensions of sin and the need for personal, liturgical, and social reconciliation.

Peter Fink, ed., *Alternative Futures for Worship, Volume 4: Reconciliation* (Liturgical Press, 1987) contains articles on the history, psychology, and theology of reconciliation, as well as suggestions for new liturgical rites.

Arthur Barker Chappell, *Regular Confession* (Peter Lang, 1992) explains how this practice can aid continuous conversion and spiritual growth.

David Coffey, *The Sacrament of Reconciliation* (Liturgical Press, 2001) is an exercise in liturgical theology inasmuch as it is primarily a reflection on the current rite of penance.

David Steere, *Rediscovering Confession* (Routledge, 2009) approaches the topic as a therapeutic experience, both personal and interpersonal.

Social Dimensions

Ronald Kraybill, *Repairing the Breach* (Herald Press, 1981) says that Christians can and should be instruments of reconciliation in conflicts between individuals and between groups.

Robert Schreiter, *Reconciliation: Mission and Ministry in a Changing Social Order* (Orbis Books, 1992) shows how Christians can develop social ministries of reconciliation. *The Ministry of Reconciliation* (1998) uses the stories of Jesus' resurrection to provide insight into the process of social reconciliation today.

Gregory Baum and Harold Wells, eds., *The Reconciliation of Peoples* (Orbis Books, 1997) looks at the church's role (or lack of it) in mediating social conflict and violence.

John De Gruchy, *Reconciliation: Restoring Justice* (Fortress Press, 2002) explores the theology and politics of social reconciliation based on the experience of South Africa after apartheid.

Brian Cox, *Faith-Based Reconciliation* (Xlibris, 2007) uses gospel values to address prejudice and hatred based on ethnic or religious identity.

Emmanuel Katongole and Chris Rice, *Reconciling All Things* (InterVarsity Press, 2008) presents a vision for implementing ways to reconcile people divided by race, class, violence, or prejudice.

Ecumenical Dimensions

Max Thurian, *Confession* (SCM Press, 1958) examines the meaning and practice of confession from the perspective of the reformed churches.

Clarke Hyde, *To Declare God's Forgiveness* (Morehouse Barlow, 1984) offers a pastoral theology of the sacrament as it is practiced in the Anglican church.

Martin Smith, *Reconciliation* (Cowley Publications, 1985) discusses the hows and whys of confession in the Episcopal church.

Theodore Jennings, *The Liturgy of Liberation* (Abingdon Press, 1988) discusses the confession of sins in public worship, in pastoral counseling, and in Protestant ritual.

Martin Dudley and Geoffrey Rowell, *Confession and Absolution* (Liturgical Press, 1990) contains historical and pastoral articles written in an ecumenical spirit, with special emphasis given to the Church of England.

John Chryssavgis, *Repentence and Confession in the Orthodox Church* (Holy Cross Orthodox Press, 1990) introduces and documents the Orthodox understanding of the sacrament.

R. Scott Appleby, *The Ambivalence of the Sacred* (Roman & Littlefield, 2000) studies the role of religion in inciting and reducing violence, especially in today's world of fundamentalism and extremism.

The Meaning of Sin

Ted Peters, *Sin: Radical Evil in Soul and Society* (William B. Eerdmans, 1994) is a systematic treatment of sin, combining traditional and contemporary insights into individual and social evil.

Eugene Maly, *Sin: Biblical Perspectives* (Pflaum/Standard, 1973) uses modern scripture scholarship to reevaluate the Christian concept of sin and forgiveness.

James Gaffney, *Sin Reconsidered* (Paulist Press, 1983) contrasts the traditional idea of sins as wrongful actions with a broader notion of sin as a lack of proper relationship.

Patrick McCormick, *Sin as Addiction* (Paulist Press, 1989) proposes addiction as a disease model of both individual and social sinfulness.

Sean Fagan, *What Happened to Sin?* (Columba Press, 2008) is a rather clear book on a sometimes murky subject, originally published as *Has Sin Changed?* in 1978.

Gary Anderson, *Sin: A History* (Yale University Press, 2009) is actually a history of the language used to talk about sin and therefore about redemption by Christ.

Tatha Wiley, *Original Sin* (Paulist Press, 2002) investigates the origin and development of the concept, and reviews contemporary interpretations of its meaning.

Alan Jacobs, *Original Sin: A Cultural History* (HarperCollins, 2008) offers a literary approach to the pervasive propensity of human beings to do evil.

Kay Carmichael, *Sin and Forgiveness* (Ashgate, 2003) attempts to understand wrongdoing and responses to it in a post-Christian society.

The Order of Penitents

James Lopresti, *Penance: A Reform Proposal for the Rite* (Pastoral Press, 1987) outlines how a new form for the rite of penance could be developed for inviting the alienated to return to membership in the church.

Lawrence Mick, *Penance: The Once and Future Sacrament* (Liturgical Press, 1987) reviews the history of the sacrament and suggests ways that it can be restructured to meet new needs.

Joseph Favazza, *The Order of Penitents: Historical Roots and Pastoral Future* (Liturgical Press, 1987) presents a detailed investigation into the ancient practice and a brief proposal for a contemporary version of it.

CHAPTER X

ANOINTING

Lord God, loving Father, you bring healing to the sick through your Son Jesus Christ. Hear us as we pray to you in faith, and send us the Holy Spirit, our Helper and Friend, upon this oil, which nature has provided to serve the needs of your children. May your blessing come upon all who are anointed with this oil, that they may be freed from pain and illness and made well again in body, mind and soul.

—Rite of Anointing of the Sick

The first known ecclesiastical rite for anointing sick Christians dates from the ninth century. Before that time blessed oil had long been regarded as a sacramental substance through which God could effect physical cures, but until then there was no official ritual for applying it. Its purpose was to heal the body and strengthen the spirit of the afflicted, and it could be used by lay people as well as clerics. In the early Middle Ages administration of the oil was reserved to priests, and the rite in which it was used eventually became a sacrament for the dying. It was under this form that it came to be numbered among the seven Catholic sacraments. Modern church doctrine agreed in principle that it was a sacrament for the sick, but in practice it was given only to people who were not likely to recover from their sickness. In contemporary Catholicism the modern rite based on the late medieval one has been replaced with a rite that reflects the more ancient understanding of anointing with oil. Thus the original purpose of the ninth-century ritual has been restored, and it is now considered to be a sacrament of spiritual and physical healing.

1. Parallels and Precedents

In most religions of the world disease and death are viewed as mysterious violations of the way things ought to be. They are mysteries because they are not fully understood, and this is so in both primitive and technological cultures. Most people even today do not understand the technical pathology of disease and death, and even those who do can ask questions about them that science and medicine cannot answer: What is the meaning of it? Does it have any purpose? Why this? Why now? Why me? When they are experienced from within, sickness and dying raise more questions than we have answers for. And when they are witnessed from without, the situation is not much different, especially when they come to those who are close to us.

In our own way we look for answers to those questions, and when we find them (if we do) they make our suffering a little more bearable. We find a meaning for what before seemed meaningless, we make some sense out of what seemed so senseless, and the meaning that we find is precious because it gives us something that we did not have before: a strength to face what is strange and threatening, a way of coping with pain or loss, a means of making the intolerable tolerable. In its own way it is a meaning that is sacred for us, for it is a meaning that helps us to understand and live with what we recognize as a mystery. The meaning may be unique and personal, like the reason I have cancer or the meaning of my mother's death, but it may also be a shared social meaning, like the purpose of suffering in the world or the reason we all have to die.

In primitive and ancient societies people asked the same questions that we ask today about sickness and misfortune, suffering and death. The answers they found meaningful were often expressed in religious rituals and myths—rituals through which they enacted their response to the mystery they could not fully comprehend, and myths in which they embodied in story form the little that they did comprehend. Generally speaking the religious response to sickness and death has been to assert that they should not be, they are not normal, they are violations of the sacred order in which health and life are preserved. And myths in many religions contrast the way things should be with the way things are, sometimes by narrating how the present disordered state of affairs came about. The biblical story of the Fall in the book of Genesis is but one example of this idea that can also be found in myths of the Middle East, Africa, and Asia.

The Genesis myth also illustrates two features of the ancient attitude toward life and health, sickness and death. The first is that it was holistic, for it was part of a holistic view of reality. Life was not physical or spiritual but both, for people were not bodies or souls but living beings. Likewise health and sickness were not just physical: it was the whole person that was sick. And the world in which people lived was both a physical and a moral universe: things happened or behaved in certain ways because they were supposed to, they were obeying a sacred order. Conversely, when that well-integrated order was upset the effects were both physical (destruction) and moral (evil).

The second feature was tied to the first, and it was understood that if one part of this interconnected web of reality was disturbed the effects were not isolated but were felt by other parts as well. Again the biblical myth illustrates this when it portrays suffering and death coming into the world as the result of an act of disobedience. In primitive and ancient cultures a sickness or injury was often seen as resulting from something that a person did wrong, like violating a taboo or not behaving properly. For in this holistic view there was but one order in the universe, and it was both material and spiritual.

But if disruptions of the sacred order were both physical and moral, then it was necessary to restore that order by means that were both physical and moral. In treating sickness and injury, natural medicines and even surgery could be used, but they were used in conjunction with prayers and incantations to discover the moral cause of the evil and set it right. And the religious rituals which surrounded the preparation and use of these remedies both ensured that the treatments were properly applied and reminded the patients of the importance of reintegration with the sacred order to bring about recovery.

Primitive and ancient responses to illness were therefore sacramental as well as medicinal. They were symbolic affirmations of the value of life and health, expressions of dependence on realities that were beyond human control, embodiments of beliefs in demonic forces that could cause disease and divine agents that could cure it. In primitive societies they were a sort of sacramental and medicinal magic that could be easily misunderstood and misused because the area of mystery was so great and the amount that was known was so small. Medically speaking they were probably ineffective more often than not, but it was the only medicine that people had, and it did work sometimes. But sacramentally speaking they were always effective, for they always explained the meaning of what was happening, even when it happened that the patient died.

In a similar way, funeral rituals have always been and still are sacramental. Whether they are simple and stark or elaborate and gaudy, they dramatize the meaning of life and death as it is comprehended within a given culture or subculture. Psychologically they help people to come to terms with the fact of death and to release their feelings of bereavement. Sociologically they provide an acceptable way for people to mourn for those they loved and to make the transition to life without them. But sacramentally they also express beliefs and hopes that make death bearable, and allow the people who participate in the ceremonies to rediscover and reaffirm those sacred meanings. In some societies preparation rituals before death perform that same sacramental function for people who are dying and for those who are watching them die.

As is clear from Genesis and its other scriptures, ancient Israel had a holistic attitude toward life and health, disease and death. A long life, many children, and prosperity were seen as signs of moral goodness and God's favor; an early or painful death, barrenness, and misfortune were evils that either afflicted the wicked or showed up the hidden sins of the just. The author of the book of Job questioned this simple view by portraying the plight of a good person who suffered for no apparent reason, but he had no solution to the problem other than the assertion that God's ways were not to be questioned. Death itself was seen as the unavoidable result of human sinfulness, and what happened after death was unknown or at best uncertain. Sickness could be treated with herbal medicines and wounds could be washed with wine or oil, but the most reliable treatment was prayer and repentance since all healing was in the hands of God (Psalms 32, 38, 88, 91).

After the fall of the Israelite kingdom and the destruction of the temple in 587 BC, some prophetic writers began to envision a time in the future when God would reestablish the kingdom, this time not in Jerusalem but in the whole world. The horrors of death, slavery, and exile that the Israelites had endured seemed to deny the justice of God, for they far outweighed whatever sins the Israelites could have committed to bring on such punishment. Some believed that Yahweh himself would come as king, others expected a savior to be sent, but they all looked forward to the day when the just would be vindicated and only the wicked would be destroyed. In the messianic age God would demonstrate divine power over evil and the forces of sin by eliminating hunger and disease and the other plagues of the innocent. Some religious thinkers even speculated that in the final days the just would be raised from their graves to share in the glory of God. It was partly as a result of expectations like these that some Jews hailed Jesus of Nazareth as the Christ, and proclaimed that the kingdom of God was at hand.

2. Healing and Anointing in the Early Church

The New Testament is filled with accounts of Jesus' miracles: of how he cured the lame and the blind, cleansed lepers, cast out demons, and even raised the dead. In later ages Christians used these accounts to prove that Jesus was God, but for those who first believed in him they were signs that he was the messiah sent from God and that the messianic age had begun (Matthew 4:23–25; 12:28; Luke 7:18–23). To those he cured and to those who saw what he did, his works were a miraculous sign of God's power over sickness and evil, and he himself was a living sacrament of God's compassion on those who suffered. He healed by word and by touch, and he brought to others a healing presence through which they became inwardly renewed as well as outwardly cured (Luke 19:1–10; John 9:1–39).

The disciples of Jesus shared in his ministry of healing, and the gospels recount that he sent them out into the countryside to cure the sick and preach the good news of God's kingdom (Luke 9:1–6; 10:1–10). One text even mentions that they "anointed many sick people with oil and cured them" (Mark 6:13), indicating that they used oil as a sacramental substance in their healing ministry. Scripture scholars point out, however, that this may reflect the practice of the community in which the gospel was written forty years later rather than the practice of the disciples during Jesus' own lifetime.

There are indications in the other New Testament books that physical healing continued to be a sign through which people came to believe in Jesus as the messiah. Peter and Paul are both credited with effecting cures while preaching the good news of Christ (Acts 3:1–10; 14:8–18). Among the believers themselves, charismatic healing seems to have been a sign that the reign of God had begun in the church, and Paul mentions healing and miracles as spiritual gifts that God gave individuals for the benefit of the community (1 Corinthians 12:9–10). Apparently in Jerusalem Christians used prayer and oil in their healing ministry, for the apostle James recommended the practice to other communities in one of his letters: "Are any among you sick? They should call for the elders of the church and have them pray over them, anointing them with oil in the name of the Lord. The prayer of faith will save the sick, and the Lord will raise them up; and anyone who has committed any sins will be forgiven" (James 5:14–15). Evidently, too, James and other Jewish Christians continued to see a connection between sin and suffering, just as the Israelites had.

The indications of a healing ministry during the next few centuries are scant, but they are definite enough to say that it continued in some form in a number of places. After the time of the apostles Christian healing was usually associated with oil, and the main evidence that we have for it comes from liturgical texts for the blessing of oil. *The Apostolic Tradition*, attributed to Hippolytus of Rome in the early third century, contains a prayer over oil that was brought to be blessed during the eucharistic liturgy. The presiding bishop prayed that "it may give strength to all who taste it and strength to all who use it" (V, 2), and after the liturgy it was taken home by the faithful to be used as an internal or external medicine. Olive oil in the ancient world was commonly used for medicinal purposes, but Christians regarded their blessed oil as an especially effective remedy. In a letter from around the same period, Tertullian mentions that he knew of a Christian who even cured a pagan with oil.

There are no other surviving texts from the third century, but some liturgical documents of the fourth century imply that the oil that was blessed for anointing catechumens might also have been used in other exorcisms for curing spiritual and physical sickness. Around the middle of the century Serapion, the bishop of Thmuis in Egypt, composed a prayer for the blessing of oil, bread, and water, that they might through the power of God become "a means of removing every sickness and disease, of warding off every demon, of routing every unclean spirit, of keeping away every evil spirit, of banishing every fever, chill and fatigue,…a medicine of life and salvation bringing health and soundness of soul and body and spirit, leading to perfect well being" (*Prayer Book* 29). Another liturgical book called *The Apostolic Constitutions*, composed in Syria around 380, contains a similar prayer over offerings of oil and water, that God would give them the power to produce health and drive away demons.

Only two early writers are known to have commented on the passage from the Epistle of James that refers to the anointing of the sick, Origen in the third century and John Chrysostom in the fourth century. Both of them, however, apparently took it as a reference not to physical sickness but to spiritual sickness because they both spoke of it in conjunction with ecclesiastical reconciliation. In their day penitents were often anointed when they were given exorcisms, and since the passage ends with a statement about forgiveness of sins, they interpreted it as referring to the process of public penitence. That they did not see it as a reference to a priestly anointing of the sick is indirect evidence that at least in Alexandria and Antioch there was no established ecclesiastical rite connected with physical illness.

The earliest clear patristic reference to oil being used by priests to anoint the sick comes from the fifth century. In 416 Pope Innocent I wrote to a nearby bishop, Decent of Gubbio, who wanted to know whether the passage in James was about the physically sick, and if so, how the anointing should be practiced. Apparently the church in Rome had such a custom, for Innocent's reply was straightforward and detailed: "There is no doubt that the passage speaks about the faithful who are sick and who can be anointed with the oil of chrism that is prepared by the bishop. Not only priests but all Christians may use this oil for anointing, when either they or members of their household have need of it" (*Letters* 25, 8). He cautioned, however, that the oil should not be given to those who were doing public penance since it was "a kind of sacrament" and penitents were not allowed to receive the other sacraments.

By the fifth century Alexandria and Antioch had definitely adopted the practice of anointing the sick. Around 428 Cyril of Alexandria berated Christians who resorted to pagan magicians and sorcerers when they were sick and advised them to call in the elders of the church instead. In the middle of the century Victor of Antioch also cited the Epistle of James in support of praying over and anointing the sick, but in his opinion the prayers were the effective element in the practice; the oil was just a symbol of the healing that God would bring about in response to prayer. Eventually, however, in the Christian east most churches developed an ecclesiastical ritual of psalms and hymns, blessing of the oil, and anointings to be performed by up to seven priests for those who sought release from physical and spiritual illness.

By the sixth century the practice had also become customary in some parts of France, and Caesarius of Arles preached a number of sermons exhorting those in his diocese to make use of it. Like Innocent he believed that lay people should use the consecrated oil themselves. And like Cyril he found himself fighting against the religious practices that had existed in his region before the coming of Christianity, for he tells how the people went to magic fountains and trees, used amulets and mystical marks, and asked fortunetellers and sorcerers for help when they were sick. "How much better and more helpful it would be if they ran to the church and received the body and blood of Christ, and reverently anointed themselves and their family with holy oil! According to the words of the Apostle James they would receive not only health of body but also pardon of sins" (*Sermons* 279).

During the patristic period, therefore, oil was indeed a sacrament of physical and spiritual health, at least in some parts of the Roman Empire and perhaps in others. It was a sacrament in the broad sense, for it symbolized the healing power of the Holy Spirit, whose activity was often described as a spiritual anointing. It was also considered to be an effective sign by those who believed that in virtue of its consecration it contained the spiritual power that it signified, and in this sense Innocent referred to it as a *sacramentum* similar to the *sacramenta* of the eucharistic bread and wine. But it was also believed to be effective because it sometimes did what it was supposed to do, and stories written by contemporaries about holy people during that period tell of miraculous cures brought about by anointing with oil. Some of them seem a bit exaggerated but others seem quite credible in light of modern faith healing and charismatic practices.

Rufinus in his *Ecclesiastical History* relates that while visiting hermits in the desert near Alexandria around 375, he saw five of them heal the withered body of a man by anointing him all over with oil in the name of Christ. In his stories of the desert fathers, Palladius says that the monk Macarius cured a paralyzed woman who was brought to him by anointing her and praying over her continuously for twenty days. He also tells of a holy monk named Benjamin who had received the gift of healing people on whom he laid hands or to whom he gave oil that he had blessed. Sulpicius Severus wrote a biography of Martin, the fourth-century bishop of Tours, shortly after the saint's death, and recounted a number of miraculous cures that Martin brought about by prayer and the use of blessed oil.

According to other sources, the monk Pachomius healed a girl possessed by a demon by blessing oil which others then used to anoint her whole body, and John of Lycopolis in the deserts of Egypt cured blindness and fever by anointing people with oil that he blessed himself. According to the stories, then, Pachomius and John blessed their own oil even though neither of them were bishops. Germain of Auxerre was, however, and in the fifth century he distributed consecrated oil to people who were suffering from an epidemic, apparently with positive results. In her ministry of healing, Geneviève of Paris used oil blessed by her bishop to bring health to the sick in her care. In the sixth century Eugene, the abbot of Condat in Burgundy, had a gift of healing by his touch, but to spare sick people the journey to his monastery he sometimes sent holy oil out to them through which they were cured. The abbess Monegunde of Tours had a similar gift, and before she died in 570 the nuns of her community asked her to bless oil which they used afterward to cure the people who continued to come to them for relief from their ills.

3. From Anointing the Sick to Anointing the Dying

During the seventh and eighth centuries, stories continued to be told about monks and other saints, mostly in France, who used oil in effecting miraculous cures. Laumer, the first abbot of Corbion, was said to have cured the paralyzed and insane by signing them with oil in the form of a cross. And Austreberta, the abbess of Pavilly, was reported to have saved the life of a nun who had been caught in the collapse of a building by anointing her. Whatever the historical truth behind these stories is, they at least show that through the beginning of the Middle Ages Christians viewed and used oil as a sacrament of healing. Sometimes the anointing was done by a priest, but not always; and it was often done with oil that had been blessed by a bishop, but not always. Most likely the anointing was always accompanied by prayer, but there is no record that there was any specific form for this prayer, even when the oil was used by a cleric.

A British monk and church historian named Bede wrote the first known commentary on the full Epistle of James, and in his section on chapter five he described the practice of anointing in early eighth-century England. It was identical with the French practice except that only consecrated oil could be used, and since he knew of no other practice he assumed it was also the same as the practice that James had in mind when he wrote his epistle.

Other documents of the period show that people asked for oil to cure almost every physical, mental, and spiritual disorder: paralysis, lameness, blindness, speech and hearing impediments, fever, headaches, pains in various parts of the body, abscesses, sores, bites, poisoning, derangement, mania, possession, enchantments, and spells. But people did not request anointing if they felt they were dying. If they were, they asked for reconciliation and the eucharist.

As it happened, however, when people received reconciliation from the church on their deathbed they were also anointed. Public penitence during the patristic period had often included anointings of exorcism to drive out the spirits of evil, and when ecclesiastical reconciliation became a deathbed ritual, the once lengthy penitential practice was usually contracted into a single ceremony that began with the penitent's confession, was followed with an anointing of exorcism, and concluded with a prayer of forgiveness. Unlike the nonclerical use of oil for healing, this anointing was an exclusively priestly function, and the fact that the passage on anointing in James 5 spoke of calling in the elders or presbyters and the forgiveness of sins led some churchmen in the later eighth century to suggest in their sermons that this was the practice to which the scriptural text was referring. (In the Middle Ages the words "presbyter" and "priest" were practically synonymous, and New Testament texts referring to presbyters—that is, elders—were often taken as referring to priests.) As a consequence, lay people began to shy away from asking priests to anoint them because anyone who recovered after receiving the penitential anointing was bound by the ancient canons prohibiting business pursuits, marital relations, and so on (see page 333). This, combined with the fact that in the Middle Ages serious illnesses were often fatal, led to priestly anointings being done more and more only when people were dying. The custom of private anointing for healing by lay people, however, continued until the beginning of the ninth century.

This was a period of organizational reform in Charlemagne's "Holy Roman Empire," and under its impetus bishops began to meet in councils and issue regulations for more uniform church practices. In 813, for example, the second council of Chalon in France declared that the anointing of the sick by the priests with oil blessed by the bishop was to be taken more seriously, and around the same time priests in Germany were told that they should carry the holy oil with them whenever they traveled in case they might need to use it. Then when the emperor ordered all his bishops to adopt the Gregorian sacramentary, his court scholar, Alcuin of York, added a supplement of prayers and rituals that were lacking in the original sacramentary that Charlemagne had gotten from Rome. It included, among other things, a newly composed rite for the priestly anointing of the sick, and Alcuin put it in the section of the supplement that also contained prayers for the dying and the rite for final reconciliation.

In the years that followed, the revised sacramentary began to be used throughout the Frankish empire, and most bishops in northern Europe simply assumed that the supplement was part of the liturgical book that had been composed under Pope Gregory. Moreover, in their effort to adopt what seemed to be the official sacramental practices of Rome, many bishops emphasized the importance of priestly anointing and prohibited the practice of lay anointing. The actual prayers for the anointing of the sick at this time still asked for healing and recovery, and the rubrics that accompanied them called for the rite to be repeated for seven days if need be. The anointing itself was to be done by signing a cross with oil on various parts of the body, with special attention to the part that was most in pain. But in fact the rite was usually performed only for the seriously sick and in conjunction with other rituals for the dying.

The order in which these rituals were performed was taken from the letter of Innocent I, which the bishops knew about from their collections of papal decretals. Innocent had said that the oil should not be given to unreconciled penitents and so, for example, the council of Mainz in 847 decreed that those who were in danger of death should make their last confession before being anointed and then receive their last communion, viaticum. The anointing itself was interpreted as a "consolation of the church" offered to those who did not have time to do penance for their sins. A similar rule was enacted by the council of Pavia in 850, which also suggested in accordance with James 5:15 that through the anointing sins were forgiven and, sometimes as a result, health was restored. By the end of the ninth century, then, the "last rites" of the Frankish church were reconciliation, anointing, and viaticum.

Up till this time the church in Rome actually had no ritual of any sort for administering oil to the sick, although it did have a ceremony for blessing oil on Holy Thursday which was then used by clerics and lay people as the need arose. But now Rome's liturgical books were in sorry shape due to a lack of skilled copyists, and so in the tenth century the Gregorian sacramentary was brought back to Rome along with the changes that had been made in it by Alcuin. Moreover, the new sacramentary seemed better suited to the needs of the times than the old one that had been composed in the late patristic period, and so the revised sacramentary was adopted and the original one fell into disuse. In this way, then, the last rites of the Frankish church became the last rites of the Roman church as well.

In the meanwhile, the ritual for anointing was undergoing even further changes in the land where it had been first introduced. Especially in the monasteries, where sick monks were often attended by their fellow priests, anointing developed into a communal ritual that was performed not in the monk's cell but in the monastery chapel. When this practice spread beyond the monastery walls, the anointing became a long ceremony that required the attendance of three or more priests who recited various prayers and penitential psalms, sprinkled the sick with holy water, signed them with ashes and anointed them with oil, commended their souls to God, and gave them communion. In fact, however, the more elaborate the ritual became the less often it was used. For one thing, it had to be performed in church, and sometimes people were too sick to be carried there. For another, it was customary for priests to receive a stipend for their services, and many people could not afford to pay for one priest, much less several.

By being associated with reconciliation and death, anointing had taken on a rather penitential character, but through the eleventh century the prayers that accompanied it still asked for physical recovery as well as the forgiveness of sins. In the twelfth century, however, this began to change. Since the anointing was rarely given to people who were expected to recover from their illness, the prayers for physical healing were gradually dropped from the rite and were replaced with ones that spoke only of the remission of sins and the hope of salvation. Sometimes these prayers were borrowed from exorcism formulas in old liturgical books; sometimes they were composed by those who inserted them into the rites themselves. But they were always attempts to make the words of the ritual correspond more closely to what it appeared to be: an anointing in preparation for death.

Of course as this happened the actions of the ritual also changed somewhat. The oil that had once been applied to the parts of the body in need of healing now began to be applied to just the senses, hands, and feet, along with a prayer that God would forgive the sins committed through the various organs of the body. And in the twelfth century the sequence in which the last rites were administered was changed as well: the anointing was put at the end, after reconciliation and communion. Now it was no longer viaticum but anointing that was seen as the ultimate preparation for entrance into the next world. It was the last anointing that people received in their lifetime and the last anointing of the church. And so in the Middle Ages it came to be called simply that: last anointing, *extrema unctio*, extreme unction.

When the early schoolmen began to classify and study the *sacramenta* of the church, extreme unction was sometimes included among them. For one thing, it was already an established liturgical ritual, and for another, it was believed to have its own proper spiritual effect, namely, preparation of the soul for the next life. In addition, Innocent I had referred to the oil as "a kind of *sacramentum*" in his letter to the bishop of Gubbio. It was for these reasons that Peter Lombard included it in his book of *Sentences* and since, as we have seen, his list of sacraments became accepted as standard, extreme unction came to be counted as one of the seven sacraments of Catholicism.

The rite that Lombard had in mind when he classified it as a sacrament was the solemn anointing that was done in a church by several priests. All the early scholastics agreed that the "matter" of this sacrament was oil that was blessed by a bishop, but there was still some disagreement about its "form" since there was no set form for the words that were said during the anointing; the prayer formulas varied in different parts of Europe. There was also therefore some disagreement about the effects of the sacrament because in the twelfth century some formulas still referred to physical healing in addition to the forgiveness of sins. Moreover, though most people died after being anointed some did not, and so it seemed that at least in some cases the sacrament could effect a physical cure. Some theologians suggested that the prayers were for healing of the body, which might happen, but that the anointing was for the healing of the soul, which always happened. According to Hugh of St. Victor, sickness afflicted the body as a result of sin, and so when sins were forgiven through the sacrament it sometimes happened that the body was cured. Hugh believed, however, that this would not occur unless God saw that recovery would be spiritually beneficial for the person who was ill.

The twelfth-century schoolmen also disagreed about who should receive the anointing and when it should be done. Should it be given to children, to the insane, to people who were unconscious? Should it be given at the onslaught of the disease or after it had run its course? Did it have to be requested, or could it be given to someone who was too weak to resist? About one question, however, there was hardly any disagreement, and it concerned the origin of the sacrament. They almost unanimously agreed that it had been instituted by the apostles.

In the thirteenth century three things happened to extreme unction that made the work of theologians much easier. First, in many places the rite itself was simplified to make it more available and easier to administer, and only one priest was needed to do the anointing. Second, the anointing came to be given only at the end of a sickness, when death seemed imminent. Third, the prayers asking for physical healing were not included in the simplified rite, and the standard formula used during the anointing came to be some variation of the prayer, "Through this holy anointing and his tender mercy, may the Lord forgive whatever sins you have committed by sight, by hearing…," and so forth as the oil was signed on the various parts of the body. It was in this form that the sacrament eventually made its way into the Roman sacramentary to replace the older, more complex form. And it was this form of the sacrament that the scholastics of the high Middle Ages had in mind when they developed their explanation of extreme unction.

In one respect the medieval theologians necessarily had to do their thinking about this sacrament in an experiential vacuum: none of them had ever experienced any effects of the sacrament since none of them had ever received it. But in another respect they did have an experiential basis for their theologizing, namely, what they saw and heard when they witnessed the rite being performed. What they had to do was find a way of explaining it that fit in with their experience and understanding of the other sacraments.

But right away this presented a problem. Here was a ritual that seemed to be for the forgiveness of sins, but there was also another ritual for the forgiveness of sins—penance. Not only that, but most people who were dying confessed their sins and received absolution shortly before being anointed. What, then, was the difference between these sacraments? Some theologians like Alexander of Hales believed that since baptism washed away original sin and penance remitted mortal sins, extreme unction should forgive venial sins, especially those that had not been confessed. But others like Albert the Great saw a better solution in the scholastic distinction between sin and the remnants of sin, which had been introduced to explain why the inclination to commit sins remained even after they were forgiven by absolution. Alexander was a monk in the religious order of Franciscans; Albert was a member of the Order of Preachers, the Dominicans. And since there was no obvious way to solve the problem, Franciscan theologians tended to adopt Alexander's solution and Dominicans tended to follow Albert.

Thomas Aquinas' theology of extreme unction differed very little from that of his fellow Dominicans, if for no other reason than that most of what he said about it is contained in his *Commentary on the Sentences of Peter Lombard*, written when he was twenty-five and still a student at the University of Paris. (He died in the midst of writing the treatise on the sacraments in the *Summa Theologica*, which was later finished by other Dominicans using ideas drawn from Aquinas' earlier work.) Like his teacher, Albert, Aquinas taught that the primary effect of the sacrament was the elimination of the remnants of sin, those sinful habits which lingered in a person's soul after sins were committed and which prevented it from entering the heavenly state that was reserved for the perfect. Secondarily, extreme unction could also effect physical healing if the disease was the result of sinful habits, and it could even be effective in the remission of unconfessed sins if the sick person cooperated with the grace of the sacrament. Albert also believed that Christ himself had instituted all the sacraments, but since there was no mention of his doing so in the gospels, Aquinas reasoned that he must have left it to James and the other apostles to make it known to the church.

In Aquinas' vision of the church's sacramental system, extreme unction was the last in a series of liturgical rites through which Christians were offered the grace to overcome sin and prepare themselves for their ultimate destination: the glory of heaven and the vision of God. It had been instituted by Christ as a means of spiritual healing, just as baptism was a means of spiritual cleansing and penance was a means of spiritual renewal. Like the other sacraments, its purpose was to cure the sickness of sin in the soul; the oil, which was a healing medicine, signified this, and the prayer which was said during the anointing asked for it. Furthermore, the sacrament was always effective in offering God's grace because the words of the scripture promised, "The prayer of faith will save the sick." Yet still, the persons who received that grace had to cooperate with it by inwardly repudiating their sinful tendencies, the remnants of sin, and turning to God in an attitude of repentant love. For this reason Aquinas believed that the sacrament should not be given to children and others who would not understand what the anointing and the words signified, since they would not be able to cooperate with the grace that was offered through it. He did not even consider the question of whether it should be given to someone who was unconscious.

For Bonaventure and the other Franciscan theologians, the purpose of extreme unction was the same as the Dominicans saw it—a preparation for final glory and entrance into heaven—but they explained the way the sacrament achieved this purpose differently. According to Bonaventure the sacramental rite worked by helping the dying receive forgiveness for venial sins that were often left unmentioned in confession, even in the last confession which preceded the last anointing. The grace that was offered in the sacrament enabled the recipients to perform supernatural acts of love and devotion that canceled out those sins, thus removing the last obstacles to complete abandonment to God. Thus Bonaventure held, as Aquinas did, that the sacrament should never be given to those who were healthy, but he also went further and added that it should not be given to people who might recover from their illness lest the purpose of the sacrament be thwarted. It should only be given when death was imminent, to those who were on their way to the next life.

Bonaventure and Aquinas both died in the same year, 1274, and the theologians who came after them tended to repeat their teachings about the sacraments without going through the same inductive reasoning or giving the same sort of experiential interpretation. In the fourteenth and fifteenth centuries, theologians accepted the idea that extreme unction was a final preparation for eternal glory and that, however it worked, the special grace it conferred eliminated all obstacles to entering heaven. But the later scholastics did not see why, if the sacrament was effective *ex opere operato*, receiving it should call for any great interior response in the recipients. In fact, such a requirement for receiving the grace of the sacrament seemed unfair since those who were anointed were usually at the point of death and in no condition to make such a response. Many therefore contended that the sacrament could be validly received even by those who were unconscious, as long as their soul was disposed to receiving God's grace. As a Franciscan, John Duns Scotus held that the spiritual effect of extreme unction was the remission of venial sins, but as a believer in the automatic efficacy of the sacraments, he argued that the anointing was the most effective when those who received it were so far gone that they were no longer capable of sinning.

In 1438 the Catholic bishops of Europe assembled in Florence for the purpose of reuniting the Roman and Greek churches, which had been officially separated since 1054. They did not actually succeed since the split was never healed except on paper, but at the time reunion with other schismatic churches seemed possible as well. In 1439 the council prepared a general statement of Catholic doctrine for delegates of the Armenian church, and it included a section on the sacraments. It listed extreme unction as the fifth of the sacraments and pointed out that it was given only to the sick who were in danger of dying. They were anointed on the senses and the hands and feet, using a formula such as the one that began to be used two centuries earlier. The minister of the sacrament was a priest, and its effect was the healing of the soul and sometimes the body, if this were spiritually beneficial. In support of its teaching on the sacrament the council cited James 5:14–15.

4. The Modern Sacrament of Extreme Unction

Because of its inclusion among the seven ecclesiastical sacraments, theologians in the later Middle Ages unanimously agreed that extreme unction had been instituted by Christ and not the apostles, since it could not be a sacrament at all without divine institution. But despite its status as an official sacrament the last anointing was in fact never received by most Catholics. In some places the rite was still fairly elaborate and costly, which prevented people from requesting it. There were also theologians who had argued that the sacrament was invalid unless it was administered just before death, and by waiting till the last moment before calling for a priest many people died before one arrived. So in most cases extreme unction was received only by those who could afford to have priests attend them during their final illness.

It was partly because the sacrament was not used much by ordinary Christians that the Protestant reformers felt few qualms about rejecting it, but their main reason for doing so was its absence from the Bible. Whereas the Catholics argued that since extreme unction was a sacrament it must have been instituted by Christ even though there was no record of it, the Protestants turned this around and argued that since there was no record of its being instituted by Christ, extreme unction could not be a sacrament.

Martin Luther and John Calvin both denied that the reference to anointing in the Epistle of James could be used to support extreme unction. Luther even called the scholastics' use of the text to prove the existence of the sacrament utter nonsense. As he saw it, James was speaking about anointing for healing, but the scholastics only spoke about anointing for dying. Still, he believed that as a ritual of the church it might have some spiritual value for those who asked for it when they were sick or dying. Even though it was not a sacrament of Christ, anointing could still be considered a sacrament of the church, like the use of holy water. Those who received it in faith could experience peace of soul and forgiveness of their sins, said Luther, but it had to be remembered that the consolation they felt came not from any power in the rite but as a result of their confidence in God and their faith in divine mercy.

Calvin was not nearly as tolerant of the Catholic practice of extreme unction. In his *Institutes of the Christian Religion* he dismissed it as "hypocritical play acting" by which priests tried to make themselves look like apostles (IV, 18). In support of his position he pointed to the stark differences between James 5 and what was done by Catholic priests: James spoke of anointing the sick, but the priests anointed those who were half-dead; James said nothing about blessed oil, but the priests would use nothing but episcopally consecrated oil; James did not indicate that the oil forgave sins, but the priests attributed the wondrous power of remission to the anointing itself. What, then, was the anointing to which the scripture text referred? According to Calvin it was a miraculous gift of healing that had been given to the church at the beginning to draw attention to the power of God in the preaching of the gospel. It was a gift that did not need the use of oil, for the disciples often worked miracles without it. But when the gospel was accepted and the church was well established in the world, Christians no longer received the gift of healing so that they would rely more firmly on the word of God and the inner power of the Holy Spirit.

The English church's solution to the problem was unique: doctrinally it admitted the existence of unction as a sacrament, but practically it eliminated it from the rituals of the church. In 1563 the *Thirty-nine Articles of Religion* ranked it among "the five commonly called sacraments" that were not of divine institution, and until 1552 the *Book of Common Prayer* contained a rite for administering sacramental unction to the sick. In that year, however, the rite was omitted from the new edition of the prayer book, and it was not replaced until 1928 when a brief prayer for anointing was reintroduced. The discrepancy between doctrine and practice was finally eliminated when a fuller rite for the sacrament of unction was composed for the most recent edition of the *Book of Common Prayer*, but it emphasized physical rather than spiritual healing.

Needless to say, none of these interpretations was acceptable to the Council of Trent. Even though they recognized that Catholics sometimes used extreme unction as an excuse for not having to lead morally good lives, the bishops of the council did not believe that this misconception of the purpose of the sacrament undermined its true function in the church. And even though they deplored the excesses that sometimes came with the custom of stipends, they did not believe that the greed of some priests outweighed the spiritual benefits that the anointing brought to souls. So even though they agreed that the popular understanding and abusive practices of the sacrament might be in need of reform, the bishops did not believe that anything could or should be changed in the basic doctrine or ritual of the sacrament. What was needed was a clear and definitive exposition, such as they had given for the other sacraments.

In the same session of the council that issued the long document on penance, the Catholic bishops approved a much shorter one on extreme unction, noting that the two sacraments were closely related. Extreme unction, they said, was the completion of penance and indeed of the whole Christian life, which should be one of continual penitence and turning toward God. Like penance it was a sign of God's mercy, for it enabled Christians to be forgiven for their sins and assured of salvation. They allowed that the institution of the sacrament by Christ was only hinted at in his sending out of the apostles to heal and anoint (Mark 6:13), but Jesus had certainly ordained that priests should anoint the sick for the forgiveness of sins since the practice was clearly commanded by no less an apostle than the brother of the Lord (James 5:14–15). The grace of the sacrament removed both sin and the remnants of sin from the soul, and because of this it brought courage and confidence to the dying and occasionally even bodily health to the sick. In accordance with the apostle's teaching the anointing was to be given only to the sick, "especially to those who are so dangerously ill that they seem to be at the point of leaving this life" (*Extreme Unction* 3). Finally, in order to highlight what they perceived as the most dangerous heresies of the reformers, the bishops unequivocally condemned all those who contradicted the true Catholic doctrine by teaching any of the following: that extreme unction was not a sacrament instituted by Christ; that it was merely a rite invented later in the church; that it did not confer grace, forgive sins, or comfort the sick; that in times past it had only been for physical healing; that the present practice of the Roman church was not what the apostle James had in mind; that the "presbyters" mentioned in his epistle were not ordained priests but lay elders of the church; that anyone besides priests could be proper ministers of the sacrament.

During the centuries that followed the Council of Trent there was no change at all in the Catholic doctrine of extreme unction, and hardly any change in its practice. In the official sacramentary of 1614 a standard, simplified rite was adopted, putting an end to the local variations and elaborate rituals that had been allowed in the Middle Ages. The medieval question about whether children should receive the sacrament was settled by practice rather than by decree in the seventeenth century, when it became customary to anoint only those who had reached the age of discretion. Before they attained the use of reason, it was believed, children were not capable of committing serious sins and so there would be little purpose in anointing them. In practice this meant that children were able to receive the sacrament when they were considered old enough to make their first confession, which was anywhere from seven to sixteen years of age depending on where they lived.

There was also some question among canon lawyers about whether people who were apparently dead could be given the sacrament. Some argued that the patient had to show some signs of life if the anointing was to have any spiritual effect on the soul. Others countered that the soul could linger in the body for some time even after vital functions such as respiration and heartbeat had ceased. In the long run the safer course was chosen, and since there was no sure way of determining the exact moment of death, priests were advised to conditionally anoint those who were apparently but not certainly dead, in case the soul had not yet departed.

The only theological question about extreme unction that remained open was a minor one concerning the effects of the sacrament. The bishops at Trent saw no compelling reason to accept either the Dominican or the Franciscan explanation to the exclusion of the other, and so they declared that the sacrament had the power both to forgive sins and to remove the remnants of sin. But the two schools of thought were not content with this diplomatic solution to the problem, and so they continued their theological debate by arguing over which of the two was the primary and which was the secondary effect of the anointing. Finally Pope Benedict XIV perceived that the question was truly moot and the argument was getting nowhere, so in 1747 he made a plenary indulgence available to all those who were anointed. Thereafter, there would be no doubt that those who received the sacrament with the proper disposition were fully absolved both from their sins and from any punishment that was due for them.

But what of extreme unction's sacramentality in the broad sense? It had been defined as a sacrament in the scholastic sense of having metaphysical effects, but did it have any experiential effects as well? Undoubtedly it did, although it may not have had the same effects on all those who underwent or witnessed a final anointing. At least to those who received it while conscious, extreme unction could indeed be a sign of God's mercy and forgiveness as envisaged by the Council of Trent. And to those who saw the rite being performed it could be a similar sign, bringing some consolation to the bereaved that those whom they lost through death were assured of eternal life. In this sense it was a transition ritual, a rite of passage, which enabled the dying to enter the final phase of their life with inner strength and peace, and which enabled friends and relatives to make the emotionally difficult transition from living with their loved ones to living without them.

And for the Catholic Church as a whole, the sacrament of extreme unction was also an intensification ritual, a rite of celebration, for despite the somber shadow that lay over the Christian meaning of death since the Middle Ages, the church through its official sacrament for the dying continued to affirm that death was not the final meaning of life. Institutionally Catholicism affirmed that the victory of death over human beings was only apparent, and that its sting was gone forever for anyone who turned from the death of sin to a life of grace. Theologically it affirmed that the transcendent order of reality was indeed gracious, for God took care of those who lived upright lives and God would show mercy on those who repented and sought salvation even if only in their final moments.

The anointing of the sick, then, which had begun in the patristic era as a door to the sacred meaning of sickness, became in the modern church a door to the sacred meaning of death. And yet the meanings that were discovered in both cases were not totally dissimilar. Through the sacramental use of oil in the early church, Christians acknowledged that their physical well-being ultimately depended on a gracious and loving God, and they sometimes experienced the existential meaning of their belief in the health that was miraculously restored to them. Through the liturgical anointing of the modern church Catholics similarly acknowledged that their spiritual well-being ultimately depended on a merciful and saving God, and they sometimes experienced the existential meaning of their belief in the security and strength they felt when death was upon them.

5. Return to Anointing of the Sick

Sacraments sometimes say more than their creators intend, and so it was with the liturgical sacrament of extreme unction. It was intended to express the Christian meaning of death, and to ensure that the transition from this life to the next would be touched with hope rather than despair, and yet for many Catholics it was not perceived that way. Since the sacrament was not supposed to be received until the end, calling for a priest to perform the last rites was often a sign that hope was lost, that there was no chance of regaining health. Even when around the turn of the twentieth century the canonical rule about the imminent danger of death was relaxed somewhat, Catholics still dreaded to ask for a priest to anoint themselves or their loved ones, since it was a sign that they had given up all hope of recovery.

The same discrepancy was found in Catholicism's unofficial sacraments for the dead, funeral services and funeral masses. The liturgical texts asserted the hope of final glory and reminded Christians that Christ had said, "I am the resurrection and the life. Those who believe in me, even though they die, will live, and all who live and believe in me will never die" (John 11:25–26). But the liturgies were celebrated in black vestments, the prayers for the deceased often pleaded for God's mercy as though it might not be granted, other texts announced the destruction of sinners as well as the salvation of the faithful, and the chants that accompanied them were mournful rather than confident in tone. And yet at the time it seemed so right, for no one knew that it had ever been different.

But later in the century this picture of the meaning of death and the sacraments of death began to change, first among Catholic academics and then among the hierarchy as well. Biblical scholars observed that the New Testament meaning of death was less doleful than the medieval interpretation of it, and that the "kingdom of God" spoken of by the gospels was not a place of celestial reward but a reign of the Spirit that began on earth. Liturgical scholars pointed out the discrepancy between the affirmative meaning of the scriptural texts and the negative meaning of the ecclesiastical rites for the dying and the dead. Catholic philosophers noted the theoretical shortcomings of the traditional conception of death and the afterlife, especially as it pertained to punishment and purgatory. And historians described the differences between the sacramental practices of the early church and those of later Christianity.

It was not until the 1950s, however, that this research began to have a noticeable impact on the Catholic understanding of extreme unction. Until then most theologians believed that all that was needed was a deeper understanding of the existing rituals, or perhaps a slight adjustment in the wording of the rites to bring them more in line with contemporary scholarship. But in that decade articles began to appear in Catholic theological journals questioning the restriction of the sacrament to the dying and suggesting that it should be given for any serious sickness. As the results of the historical research accumulated, theologians became more aware of the meaning of anointing in the early church, and they realized that the Tridentine ritual bore little resemblance to the sacramental use of oil in the patristic period. Some criticized the idea that the purpose of the sacrament was to prepare the soul for the next life; others argued that the sacrament should and could have physical as well as spiritual effects if it were administered for other than terminal illnesses. Gradually the momentum grew that extreme unction should not be regarded as a sacrament for the dying but as a sacrament for the seriously sick, and that perhaps even the medieval name "extreme unction" was misleading. Theologians such as Charles Davis also proposed that the last sacrament for Catholics should not be anointing but communion, as it had been before the twelfth century.

Those in the liturgical movement who wanted a reexamination of the sacrament got additional support from studying the liturgical texts of the Orthodox churches. Anointing in the east had never developed the way it had in the west, and so there its purpose had remained closer to what it had been in the patristic period. Over the centuries many of the eastern churches had come to reserve the administration of the oil to priests, but its meaning was primarily physical rather than spiritual healing. Usually the anointing was performed in church rather than on the deathbed, and those who received it did not have to be mortally sick. In fact in some churches the oil was even given to prevent illness, not only to cure it.

When the world's Catholic bishops assembled for the Second Vatican Council, therefore, it was clear to the ones who knew about these developments that something had to be done about the traditional practice of extreme unction. Little was said about the sacrament in the various council documents, but the council included extreme unction in its general revision of sacramental rites, and it directed that the new rite should correspond more to the ancient than the modern practice of the church: " 'Extreme Unction,' which may also and more fittingly be called 'Anointing of the Sick,' is not a sacrament intended only for those who are at the point of death. Hence, it is certain that as soon as any of the faithful begins to be in danger of death from sickness or old age, this is already a suitable time for them to receive this sacrament" (*Liturgy* 73). The council also directed that the prayers accompanying the anointing should be changed accordingly, and it ordered that the earlier sequence of the last rites should be restored so that, if in fact they were dying, Catholics would be anointed before and not after they received viaticum.

The direction that the new rite took actually went beyond the modest alterations suggested by the council, although it was certainly in keeping with the council's instructions. After being prepared by a liturgical commission it replaced the old rite in 1974, and like most of the other revised rites it contains various forms for use on different occasions. Those for whom this indeed might be their last anointing are to celebrate the sacrament in conjunction with confession, if they desire it, and communion. Those who wish to be anointed during less serious illnesses may do so either alone at home or in a hospital, or together with others in a communal celebration in church. If their illness perdures, comes back, or gets worse, they can be anointed again as often as they might benefit from it. And in all these forms the emphasis is on healing and strengthening rather than on the forgiving of sins. The oil is not placed on the five senses but on the forehead and hands, and the prayer to be said during the anointing now reads, "Through this holy anointing may the Lord in his love and mercy help you with the grace of the Holy Spirit. May the Lord who frees you from sin save you and raise you up." Also, the priest may use blessed oil, or he may bless the oil himself just before the anointing.

But the truly major revision of the sacrament has not been in the rite but in the pastoral context in which it is placed. The canon law for extreme unction had simply reminded pastors of their duty to anoint Catholics who were in danger of death. But now the instructions for the new rite direct that anointing should not be an isolated ritual but should take place within a total pastoral ministry to the sick. Priests should visit not just the dying but all those in their care who are suffering, and they should not just anoint them but counsel them, pray with them, read the scriptures together, bring them communion regularly, and listen to their confession when they desire it. They should also extend their ministry, including that of anointing, to the chronically ill, the aged and infirm, and those who are about to undergo surgery, even if there is no imminent danger of death.

Moreover, the pastoral context has been widened to include not only priests but also the broader Christian community. Lay people are reminded that they too have a ministry to the sick, to give them support and encouragement and physical care. For this reason relatives and friends, nurses and doctors, are invited to take part in the sacramental ministry of the priest by praying with him when he comes for his visit. When the sacrament is celebrated communally in a church or hospital or nursing home, all those present are asked to participate in the ceremony as a sign of their concern for those who need their help. If the situation permits, communal anointing can even be performed within a eucharistic liturgy attended both by the ill and by those who care about them.

In this context the purpose of the sacrament is to bring spiritual strength to those who are physically ill, not only by reminding them that they are loved and forgiven by God but also by reassuring them of God's concern for their physical well-being. The meaning of the sacrament is that God is offering the anointed person the grace to overcome anxiety and despair, to find comfort in an uncomfortable situation, to be healed and whole even if their body is diseased or broken. The effect of the sacrament should therefore be a personal encounter with God as a transcendent source of strength and power, and a trusting cooperation with the grace of inner and outer healing. It is a sacrament that calls for awareness and so it may be offered to children and even to the mentally ill who can understand and acknowledge God's desire for their recovery. It is a sacrament that calls for faith, which can find meaning in suffering and hope even in death. It is a sacrament that calls for a response, and so it can be a means of personal growth and even physical recovery.

And yet the anointing of the sick in its present forms is not entirely free from the ambivalence that is found in some of the other revised sacramental rites, for while it is now primarily a sacrament of the sick it is still also a sacrament of the dying. The rite allows for a number of variations depending on circumstances, and most of its prayers speak of spiritual and physical healing, but in the form of the rite for those who are near death the prayers speak mainly of spiritual healing and divine forgiveness. The action of anointing is the same in all cases, but the specific meaning of the anointing seems to be different depending on the circumstances. It is as though there were now two sacraments of anointing in Catholicism, one that corresponds in form and meaning to the patristic and early medieval anointing of the sick, and one that corresponds in form and meaning to the late medieval and modern anointing of the dying.

This ambivalence is also present in the way that the anointing of the sick is treated in the 1994 *Catechism of the Catholic Church*, for in most of the section that treats this sacrament (1499–1532) it is regarded as a sacrament for the sick, but at the end it is also regarded as being for those who are dying. In this respect the *Catechism* summarizes well the sacrament's practice and theology that are expressed in the new rite.

As is the case with its treatment of sacramental reconciliation, the *Catechism's* treatment of anointing is pastoral in tone and scholastic in its theology. After an initial review of the place of illness in human life and God's concern for people's suffering (1499–1509), the *Catechism* asserts that James 5:14–15 refers to this sacrament, it acknowledges that in times past it was called extreme unction and was given almost exclusively at the point of death, and that the rite has been recently revised (1510–1513). That the *Catechism's* operative theology in this section is scholastic theology can be discerned from the way the section talks about the sacrament's being "conferred" (1512) and "received" (1514–1516). In these instances, what is being referred to can only be the *sacramentum et res*. When the sacrament is spoken of as being "celebrated" (1517–1519), however, the reference is to the *sacramentum tantum*.

The *Catechism* affirms the Catholic tradition of restricting the administration of the sacrament to ordained priests (1516), but it also affirms Vatican II's approval of the sacrament for anyone who is seriously ill (1515) and it acknowledges recent pastoral developments such as encouraging the sacramental celebration in a variety of life settings and liturgical contexts (1517). The *Catechism* enumerates the effects of the sacrament as strengthening by the Holy Spirit, the forgiveness of sins, union with the passion of Christ, spiritual unity with the church, and preparation for the final journey (1520–1523). Finally, viaticum or last communion is mentioned as appropriate and beneficial for those who are dying (1524–1525).

If sacraments are understood in the broad sense, the current ambivalence can be tolerated, for in the broad sense the meaning and effects of sacraments are experiential rather than doctrinal. That is, the meaning of a given ritual as it is actually performed is not confined to the traditional meaning of the symbols used or the objective meaning of the words that are said. It is rather the existential meaning that occurs in the consciousness of those who actively participate in the sacramental ritual, either by undergoing it themselves or by responding to its performance for others. Likewise, the effects of a given ritual are the effects that it actually has on these participants, both those for whom it is performed and those who share in its performance.

In this broad sense, then, there is a fundamental similarity to all the present forms of anointing, whether it is done for the sick or for the dying, and whether it is done for one person singly or for many at the same time. It is an assertion that neither disease nor death are ultimate, nor need they be overpowering; they are not to be feared but faced; they are not to be escaped but lived through. It is an affirmation for Christians that they are not alone in their suffering, that there are others who care about them in their time of need, and that these others are sacraments of a transcendent love and source of strength that is always with them. It is an opportunity for self-integration, for reconciliation with their own physical and spiritual limits, with their own infirmity, with their own death. It is an expression of the Christian meaning of life even in the midst of pain and even in the shadow of death. It is a statement of the Christian belief in resurrection, whether it occurs in this life or the one that is to come. How that affirmation is made, how that opportunity is taken, and how that statement is interpreted may vary from one person to the next, and yet the symbolic ritual of anointing remains a sacramental door that opens the way to any and all of them.

In this broad sense, too, Catholicism has other, unofficial doors to the experience of healing, comfort in suffering, and consolation in death which, unlike anointing, have equivalents in other branches of Christianity and in other religions as well. For centuries prayer and the reading of scripture have been Christian sacraments of inner healing and ways of discovering meaning within suffering and bereavement. More recently, pentecostal Christians, including charismatic Catholics, have developed informal sacramental rituals of inner and outer healing that are sometimes strikingly effective, such as the "healing of memories" through which persons are freed of long-standing hatred or guilt or fear or anxiety, and such as the healing of physical disorders through charismatic prayer and the laying on of hands. Closer to the realm of common Catholic experience, however, are the liturgical rituals that are performed after a person has died: the funeral mass and burial rites. In their recently revised form they affirm an understanding of death that is more biblical than medieval, and they express more clearly than the older rites that the Christian meaning of death is not judgment but forgiveness, not fear but hope. In this sense they are sacramentally parallel to anointing, especially to the form of the rite for the last anointing. For although they are not officially recognized as such, they too are Catholic sacraments that give meaning to the mystery of death.

For Further Study

History and Healing

John Pilch, *Healing in the New Testament* (Fortress Press, 2000) looks at gospel accounts in light of cultural perceptions of sickness and wellness. *Visions of Healing in the Acts of the Apostles* (Liturgical Press, 2004) correlates biblical descriptions of extraordinary events with scientific studies of similar events.

Amanda Porterfield, *Healing in the History of Christianity* (Oxford University Press, 2005) traces practices of spiritual and physical healing from Jesus to the present.

Andrew Daunton-Fear, *Healing in the Early Church* (Wipf and Stock, 2009) summarizes texts from the first five centuries about physical cures and exorcisms in Christianity.

Francis MacNutt, *The Nearly Perfect Crime* (Chosen Books, 2005) describes how the ministry of healing was lost and even suppressed in the church.

Sacramental Anointing

James Empereur, *Prophetic Anointing* (Michael Glazier, 1982) insightfully discusses the history, theology, and pastoral dimensions of the sacrament.

Charles Gusmer, *And You Visited Me* (Pueblo, 1984) documents the history of the sacrament of anointing the sick, explains the revised rites for the sick and dying, and discusses ministering to them.

Martin Dudley and Geoffrey Rowell, *The Oil of Gladness* (Liturgical Press, 1993) surveys the use of oils in the Christian tradition, not just for anointing the sick but for other rituals as well.

John Ziegler, *Let Them Anoint the Sick* (Liturgical Press, 1987) recounts the history of the sacrament and argues that deacons and others ought to be allowed to perform the anointing.

Peter Fink, ed., *Alternative Futures for Worship, Volume 7: Anointing of the Sick* (Liturgical Press, 1987) contains articles on the experience, ritualizing, and history of healing, as well as suggestions for new liturgical rites.

Genevieve Glen, ed., *Recovering the Riches of Anointing* (Liturgical Press, 2001) looks at a variety of issues from historical, theological, and pastoral perspectives.

Lizette Larson-Miller, *The Sacrament of Anointing of the Sick* (Liturgical Press, 2005) offers an overview and commentary on the rite in the context of pastoral care.

John Kasza, *Understanding Sacramental Healing* (Liturgy Training Publications, 2007) looks at the history, practice, and theology of the sacrament from an institutional perspective.

Bruce Morrill, *Divine Worship and Human Healing* (Liturgical Press, 2009) develops a liturgical theology of sacramental ministry to the sick and the bereaved, based on the Catholic rites.

Paul Meyendorff, *The Anointing of the Sick* (St. Vladimir's Seminary Press, 2009) examines the rite of anointing in the Orthodox tradition in light of history, theology, and pastoral practice.

Pastoral Care

Gerald Niklas and Charlotte Stefanics, *Ministry to the Sick* (Alba House, 1982) discusses the value of presence, prayer, and sacraments in the pastoral care of the hospitalized.

Tom Coyle, ed., *Christian Ministry to the Sick* (Geoffrey Chapman, 1986) contains articles on the new rite and many of its pastoral dimensions.

Leo Thomas and Jan Alkire, *Healing as a Parish Ministry* (Ave Maria Press, 1992) discusses spirituality, health, religious healing, ministry, community, prayer teams, worship, and other basics.

Barbara Schlemon, Dennis Lynn, and Matthew Lynn, *To Heal as Jesus Healed* (Ave Maria Press, 1978) discusses how the rite of anointing can be integrated into the ministry of healing.

Carolyn Headley, *The Laying on of Hands and Anointing in the Ministry for Wholeness and Healing* (Grove Books, 2002) touches on the practice and its theological foundation.

Stephen Muse, ed., *Raising Lazarus* (Holy Cross Orthodox Press, 2004) is a collection of diverse articles on psychological, spiritual, and emotional healing in the Orthodox tradition.

Bruce Epperly, *Healing Worship* (Pilgrim Press, 2006) is a practical guide to the ministry of healing in individual and group settings.

Holistic Health and Healing

James Lapsley, *Salvation and Health* (Westminster Press, 1972) discusses how these concepts got separated and can be reintegrated with one another.

Morton Kelsy, *Healing and Christianity* (Augsburg Fortress, 1995) is a classic study of Jesus' healing ministry, the history of Christian healing, and spiritual healing today.

Joseph Champlin, *Healing in the Catholic Church* (Our Sunday Visitor, 1985) reviews the entire spectrum of healing in Catholicism from miraculous cures at Lourdes to charismatic healing to anointing of the sick.

Francis MacNutt, *Healing* (Ave Maria Press, 1974) relates Jesus' ministry of healing to spiritual and physical healing in charismatic and sacramental settings. *The Power to Heal* (1977) expands on the author's earlier book, providing additional theological and practical reflection on healing.

John Sanford, *Healing and Wholeness* (Paulist Press, 1977) relates the ancient understanding of spiritual well-being to the modern concept of psychological health through the psychoanalytic theory of Carl Jung. *Healing Body and Soul* (Westminster John Knox, 1992) discusses parallels between the meaning of illness in the gospels and in psychotherapy.

Dennis and Matthew Linn, *Healing Life's Hurts* (Paulist Press, 1978) describes possibilities of emotional and physical healing through the process of the healing of memories.

John Wilkinson, *Health and Healing* (Handsel Press, 1980) investigates the New Testament accounts of healing in light of the holistic concept of health found in the scriptures.

Benedict Heron, *Channels of Healing Prayer* (Ave Maria Press, 1992) gives practical advice about praying for healing, as well as a chapter on sacraments and healing.

Emily Gardiner Neal, *Celebration of Healing* (Cowley Publications, 1992) presents selections from the author's seven books based on her involvement in the healing ministry.

Bruce Epperly, *God's Touch* (Westminster John Knox Press, 2001) is an introduction to holistic health and healing from a Christian perspective.

Verna Benner Carson and Harold Koenig, *Spiritual Caregiving* (Templeton Foundation Press, 2004) argues that spiritual care should be integrated into physical caregiving and explains how it can be done at the practical level.

Lawrence Sullivan, ed., *Healing and Restoring* (Macmillan, 1989) contains articles about health and medicine by scholars from different religious traditions.

Fraser Watts, ed., *Spiritual Healing* (Cambridge University Press, 2011) is a balanced but eclectic review of spiritual practices and their effect on psychological and physical healing.

Christian Funerals

Geoffrey Rowell, *The Liturgy of Christian Burial* (SPCK, 1977) looks at Christian funeral rites from the earliest days to the present.

Chris Aridas, *Catholic Funerals: The Church's Ministry of Hope* (Crossroad, 1998) explains the Catholic funeral rite (The Order of Christian Funerals) and relates it to the grieving process.

Richard Rutherford, *The Death of a Christian* (Pueblo, 1980) describes the historical development of Christian wake and burial practices, and explains the recently revised Catholic funeral rites.

Michael Marchal, *Parish Funerals* (Liturgy Training Publications, 1987) walks the reader through the revised Order of Christian Funerals.

Anthony Sherman, ed., *Rites of Death and Dying* (Liturgical Press, 1988) offers three commentaries on the rites and their meaning in the church today.

CHAPTER XI

MARRIAGE

Father, you have made the union of man and woman so holy a mystery
that it symbolizes the marriage of Christ and his Church....
Father, keep them always true to your commandments. Keep them
faithful in marriage and let them be living examples of Christian life.
Give them the strength which comes from the gospel so that they may
be witnesses of Christ to others. Bless them with children and help them
to be good parents. May they live to see their children's children. And,
after a happy old age, grant them the fullness of life with the saints in
the kingdom of heaven.

—RITE OF MARRIAGE

Relatively early in the history of Christianity, marriage was regarded as a sacrament in the broad sense, but it was only in the twelfth century that it came to be regarded as a sacrament in the same sense as baptism and the other official sacraments. In fact, before the eleventh century there was no such thing as a Christian wedding ceremony in the Latin church, and throughout the Middle Ages there was no single church ritual for solemnizing marriages between Christians. It was only after the Council of Trent, because of the need to eliminate abuses in the practice of clandestine or secret marriages, that a standard Catholic wedding rite came into existence.

Parallel to the absence of any church ceremony for uniting Christians in marriage was the absence of any uniform ecclesiastical regulations regarding marriage during the early centuries of Christianity. As long as the Roman Empire lasted—and it lasted longer in the east than in the west—church leaders relied primarily on the civil government to regulate marriage and divorce between Christians and non-Christians alike. It was only when the imperial government was no longer able to enforce its own statutes that Christian bishops began to take legal control over marriage and make it an official church function. In the west, church leaders eventually adopted the position that marriages between Christians could not be dissolved by anything but death; in the east they followed the civil practice of allowing the dissolution of marriages in certain cases. To safeguard the permanence of marriage, Roman Catholicism gradually developed an elaborate system of church laws and ecclesiastical courts, which was challenged by the Protestant reformers as being unscriptural and unnecessary. Today some Catholic theologians and canon lawyers are themselves asking whether it might be better to let the legal regulation of marriage revert back to civic control, without denying that church weddings are important communal celebrations or that Christian marriages are sacramental.

1. Parallels and Precedents

The origins of marriage are as obscure as the origins of the human race itself. Certainly they both started sometime and somewhere since they are both here today. But whether humankind began with an original pair or with a widely scattered population is not known and perhaps never will be known with certainty. And whether marriage began with promiscuity or fidelity, monogamy or polygamy, matriarchy or patriarchy, is a historical question that likewise may never be answered.

In prehistoric and ancient cultures, however, marriage in some form or other was already well established as part of the network of relationships that bound people together in kinship and friendship, by occupation and social position. As an accepted custom it had a variety of forms in different parts of the world at different times, and marriage practices through the ages seem to have been just as diverse as the cultures in which they were found. But whether marriages were permanent or temporary, headed by men or women, joining clans or individuals, marriage was always a socially institutionalized way of defining relationships between the sexes, of establishing rights and responsibilities for parents and offspring, of providing for cohesiveness and continuity in society. Such things were important in every culture whether it was nomadic or sedentary in its lifestyle, hunting or farming for its existence, tribal or urbanized in its organization. And since social relationships were so important, the marriage customs that surrounded and supported them were revered and sacred, and in that broad sense, religious.

In early Rome, for example, marriage was a religious affair, but the religion was that of the family; there was as yet no official state religion uniting the various clans that lived in central Italy. The father of each family acted as priest and preserver of his household religion, which included reverence for the gods of the home and respect for the spirits of departed ancestors. Besides leading his family in worship, one of the Roman father's chief duties was to provide children (primarily sons) to continue the family religion. In primitive times girls had been captured from neighboring clans to continue the family line, but eventually this practice gave way to a less violent one of arranged marriages: fathers obtained wives for their sons in exchange for a "bride price" that compensated the girl's family for the loss of a skilled and fertile member. After she was escorted by her father to her new home, the bride was now only ritually abducted by the husband, who carried her over the threshold of his home and fed her a piece of sacred cake, which inducted her into her new religion and established her communion with her husband's family gods.

At the beginning the Roman family was absolutely patriarchal: the father was not only the head of the household but he also possessed all of his family's legal rights; his wife and children had none. He could beat and punish them as he saw fit; he could sell his children into slavery and even put them to death; his wife's personal property became his, and he could divorce her if she did not live up to his expectations, especially if she failed to provide him with male heirs. And although such extreme exercises of paternal power may have been rare because of social pressure, they were legally permissible and they were in fact practiced.

What changed the social status of women and children as well as the institution of marriage was war. When the Romans began to extend their republic throughout Italy and build their empire in the Mediterranean, men were often away for long periods of time, and sometimes they did not return home. Women learned to manage their family's affairs and children began to make decisions that used to be made for them. The older family values were replaced by more nationalistic ones, and the individual religion of hearth and home gave way to a state religion of glory and gods. Many of the traditional wedding customs were kept, like handing over the bride and eating the cake, but they no longer had the religious meaning that they had in the past. The wedding was still primarily a family affair, but now a betrothal ring took the place of the bride price, and the marriage was based on the mutual consent of the partners themselves and not on the consent of their parents. At the wedding ceremony the bride was usually dressed in white with a red veil and perhaps a garland of flowers in the fashion of the Greeks, and when she and her husband gave their consent to each other it was customary for them to join their right hands, but there was no legal formula they had to use and there was no special religious significance attached to this action. If they invited a Roman priest to their wedding it was only to offer a sacrifice to the gods or to divine their prospects for a happy future, and if they got married without a family celebration Roman law presumed they were husband and wife if they lived together for a year. But marriage by consent also implied divorce by consent, and by the second century BC divorces were not uncommon at least among the upper classes. And like marriage, divorce was a private affair that could be initiated and carried out by either partner; it did not require the approval of any civil authority or the judgment of any court.

But women in the Roman world were never entirely equal to men before the law, nor were they socially equal to men in the Middle East, which was also largely patriarchal. In ancient Israel marriage was a family matter that was arranged by fathers for their children usually when they were adolescents. The Jewish scriptures say little about marriage customs and nothing at all about wedding ceremonies since marriages were private agreements and weddings were not public religious functions. Most Israelite men had only one wife, but those who could afford the bride price and maintenance of more than one sometimes had more. Women had few legal rights, and when they were married off they in effect were transferred from the property of their father to that of their husband. Adultery was forbidden by the Torah, for example, not because it was sexually immoral but because it violated the property rights of the woman's father or husband, and even the Ten Commandments placed coveting a neighbor's wife on the same footing as coveting his goods (Exodus 20:17).

At the height of the Israelite kingdom in the tenth century BC, much of the early Hebrew folklore was collected into books, including the Genesis story of the first man and woman. At the time, however, this story was not taken as a divine endorsement of monogamy since Solomon and other kings had many wives and concubines. But after the conquest of the kingdom by Assyria and Babylonia, the later Israelite prophets pondered the lesson to be learned from that tragedy, and they began to propose that Yahweh had punished his people for not living up to their calling as a chosen people. They were supposed to be a holy people with high moral standards, being just and merciful to all, and not chasing after the false gods of wealth and power. And as part of the new morality that they preached, some of the prophets began to propose that the moral ideal in marriage was faithful love between a husband and one wife. Ezekiel 16 described the relationship between Yahweh and Israel as the marriage of a man who had given his wife everything, only to be deserted by her, and Hosea 1–3 portrayed Israel as a faithless prostitute married to Yahweh, who was still faithful to her and longed to take her back. The Song of Songs extolled the ecstasy of love between a bride and her beloved, and Tobit 6–8 presented the perfect marriage as one bound by the love of one man for one woman. The wisdom literature of Sirach 25–26 described the dangers and rewards of domestic life, and the book of Proverbs 5–7 and 31 praised the virtues of the perfect wife and advised husbands against adultery.

The prophet Malachi (2:16) denounced the men who divorced their Jewish wives to marry daughters of the conquerors, but apart from this divorce was an accepted, even if regretted, way to end an unhappy marriage. If a wife had sexual relations with another man her husband could divorce her, and if he caught her in the act he could have her stoned to death (Deuteronomy 22:22–24). Jewish law was fair-minded inasmuch as it also called for the death of a male accomplice in adultery, but in the case of divorce only the husband had a legal right to demand it. A woman who wanted to be freed from her husband had to ask him to grant her a divorce, and if he refused she was obliged to stay with him. Divorce in the ancient world always included the possibility of remarriage, but in Jewish law there was an exception to this: a woman who was divorced a second time could not remarry her first husband (Deuteronomy 24:1–4).

The Torah allowed a man to give his wife a writ of dismissal if she was guilty of "impropriety," and at the beginning of the Christian era there were two schools of thought about how serious the misconduct had to be for her husband to justifiably divorce her. The followers of Rabbi Shammai authorized divorce only for blatantly shameful behavior, such as adultery; the followers of Rabbi Hillel permitted divorce for almost anything she did that displeased her husband.

2. Early Christian Marriage

Jesus said very little about marriage and divorce, but what he did say put him squarely in opposition to both rabbinical schools. In Luke's gospel Jesus' denunciation of divorce and remarriage is apodictic: "Anyone who divorces his wife and marries another commits adultery, and whoever marries a woman divorced from her husband commits adultery" (16:18).

Mark's gospel contains the same short statement by Jesus, but attaches it to an argument between Jesus and Jewish religious leaders on the question of divorce (10:1–12). Against their insistence that the Torah permitted divorce, Jesus replied that Moses had allowed it only because the Israelites in his day were so hardhearted. Using the book of Genesis as the basis of his own teaching, Jesus went on: "But from the beginning of creation, God made them male and female. For this reason a man shall leave his father and mother, and the two shall become one flesh. So they are no longer two, but one flesh. Therefore, what God has joined together, let no one separate." In the opinion of most scripture scholars today, what Jesus taught about the permanence of marriage was a radical departure from the traditional Jewish acceptance of divorce.

But then how do the scholars explain the fact that Matthew's gospel contains both the short statement by Jesus (5:31–32) and his argument with the Jewish leaders (19:3–9), but that in both of these places Jesus seems to allow divorce and remarriage (at least for the husbands) in certain cases? In Matthew's version of the argument the religious leaders question Jesus about the possible grounds for divorce, apparently trying to get him to side with either Shammai or Hillel. Jesus' first answer is that God never intended the separation of men and women, but then he goes on to say that remarriage after divorce is tantamount to adultery except in the case of immorality.

The texts in Matthew raise a number of questions. Are the passages written by Luke and Mark closer to the words of Jesus, or the passages written by Matthew? What is the reason for the difference between the texts? And what is the immorality referred to?

Many if not all scholars, both Catholic and Protestant, agree that the original teaching of Jesus is found in Luke and Mark. That is to say, Jesus taught that divorce was wrong, that God did not intend it to happen, and that he himself saw it as falling far short of moral perfection. Jesus' standards of morality were high, his call to perfection was revolutionary, and he often presented his teachings in radical, absolute statements. In his "sermon on the mount," for example, Jesus proclaimed that anger is a capital offense, that lust is equivalent to adultery, that swearing oaths is wrong, and that loving one's enemies is right. No less forthrightly he commanded his followers to do good only in secret, to renounce wealth, to avoid judging people, and to cut off any part of their body that sins (Matthew 5–7). In this manner, then, Jesus also preached an ideal of lasting fidelity in marriage, and he proposed it as a norm for all those who heeded his call to moral perfection.

The gospel of Matthew was written in its present form around the year 85, and when it was composed its final author (who was not the apostle Matthew) modified the earlier, stark saying of Jesus by adding the words "except for immorality" to Christ's apodictic condemnation of divorce in Matthew 19. Many scholars theorize that the author was a Jewish Christian writing for other Jewish converts, and that he simply wrote down the teachings of Jesus as it was understood at that time in his Jewish Christian community, which allowed divorce in certain cases and believed that this was in conformity with Christ's teaching.

But what were those cases? The Greek word *porneia* can be translated as "immorality" or "indecency," but it can also be translated as "adultery" or "fornication," and some scholars believe that the Jewish Christians continued in the tradition of Rabbi Shammai and allowed husbands to divorce their wives for serious sexual misconduct. Other scholars suggest that the early community continued the Jewish practice of not allowing a pagan convert to Judaism to keep his wife if she had been related to him before they were married. The Torah regarded marriages between certain close relatives as indecent (Leviticus 18:6–18), and according to this interpretation the author of Matthew is indicating that he did not believe that Jesus prohibited divorce in this situation, which might arise if a pagan wished to join a community of Christians who still followed the Law of Moses. No matter which interpretation is accepted, however, it seems that at least some Christians allowed divorce for certain reasons at the time that the gospels were written.

Paul, too, stressed the ideal of marital fidelity, but he also allowed divorce in certain situations. On the one hand he acknowledged that according to Christ, "the wife should not separate from her husband (but if she does separate, let her remain unmarried or else be reconciled to her husband), and that the husband should not divorce his wife" (1 Corinthians 7:10–11; see also Romans 7:2–3). On the other hand he viewed marriages to non-Christians as fraught with spiritual dangers, and he ventured the opinion that if a Christian brother or sister were married to an unbeliever who wanted a divorce, he or she might grant it and be free to marry again (1 Corinthians 7:12–16; 2 Corinthians 6:14–18). Ideally the Christian spouses should be a source of salvation for their marriage partners; but Paul reluctantly admitted that this might not always be possible.

Much of what Paul had to say about marriage is found in 1 Corinthians 7, but it has to be read in the light of his belief that "the present form of this world is passing away" (7:31) and that the second coming of Christ would happen soon. Thus Paul advised the Christians in Corinth not to make any great changes in their lives and to devote their full attention to the things of the Lord. Those who were married should stay married; and if they abstained from intercourse it should be only for a time, to devote themselves to prayer, and only by mutual consent. Those who were single should stay single; it was no sin to get married, but it was better to remain celibate. The same advice applied to widows: it was better for them to remain free, but if they could not get along without a man they should marry again.

Some time later Paul (or a disciple of his) wrote to the community at Ephesus, and this time he devoted a section of his letter to the way husbands and wives should behave toward one another (Ephesians 5:21–33). He accepted the patriarchal marriage system of his own day, including the notion that the relationship of wife to husband was not the same as the relationship of husband to wife. But he saw no reason why those relationships could not be lived "in the Lord," the way Christ gave himself in love to the church and the way the church submitted in love to Christ. Wives should regard their husbands as their head, and be obedient to them in all things; husbands should regard their wives as their own body, caring for them and looking after them. So in the marriage relationship between husband and wife Paul saw an image of the spiritual relationship between Christ and the church. It was, he said, "a great mystery," for it was a reflection of an even greater mystery.

This understanding of Christian marriage was echoed in 1 Peter 3:1–7, and apart from this there is not much more in the New Testament explicitly about marriage. One of the so-called pastoral epistles written in Paul's name again mentioned widows, but this time the author advised that the younger ones should remarry (1 Timothy 5:14). Writing toward the end of the first century, the author no longer urged celibacy for those who were engaged in the Lord's work; instead he insisted that the leaders in the church should be men of character, who were faithful to their wives and able to manage their own households (1 Timothy 3:1–13).

Little is known about Christian wedding and marriage customs in the decades that immediately followed the writing of the New Testament. Most Christians were adult converts from Judaism and other religions, and presumably many of them were married according to their own customs before they were baptized. Some of them were not, however, and around the year 110 Ignatius of Antioch wrote in a letter that "those who are married should be united with the consent of their bishop, to be sure that they are marrying according to the Lord and not to satisfy their lust" (*To Polycarp* 5). But there is no indication that this was a widespread practice; probably most young people needed only the consent of their parents, and Roman law allowed those who were old enough to give their own consent. Still, the idealism of the first generations of Christians was high, and evidently Jesus' statement against divorce continued to be taken as a moral norm. Writing in Rome later in the second century, Hermas counseled that if a woman had extramarital affairs her husband could leave her, but that he should then live alone and not remarry.

Around the beginning of the next century, Tertullian wrote, "How shall we ever be able to describe the happiness of a marriage which the church supports, which is confirmed in the eucharistic offering, and which is sealed by the blessing? Such a marriage is proclaimed by the angels and ratified by the Father in heaven" (*To His Wife* 2, 9). Tertullian may have been speaking of a Christian wedding ceremony here, but it is more likely that he was referring to the blessing in the weekly eucharistic liturgy and the support which all Christian marriages could expect to receive from the community. None of the liturgical books of the period mention a wedding ceremony of any sort, and all other indications suggest that at this time Christian marriage was still regarded as a personal and family affair, something that was contracted privately but lived openly "in the Lord." Despite his praise for Christian marriage, however, Tertullian was also the first non-Jewish Christian to suggest that there were limits to Christ's prohibition against divorce: "A marriage is permanent unless it is justifiably dissolved, and so to marry again while a marriage is undissolved is to commit adultery" (*Against Marcion* IV, 34). In other words, anyone who put aside his wife without having a just reason for divorcing her was an adulterer if he married again, according to his interpretation of the gospels.

Around the same period Clement of Alexandria and other church leaders felt compelled to defend the institution of marriage against attacks by Christian and non-Christian gnostic sects which taught that sexual relations were evil and so marriage was to be avoided. According to Clement, "Marriage in accordance with the word of God is holy because it is a union that is subject to God, contracted with a sincere heart and full fidelity by those who have been washed and purified by the water of baptism and who have the same hope" (*Miscellanies* IV, 20). Nevertheless, he advised married people to spend their days in prayer and spiritual reading, and to lie with each other only after supper. And in his view, their sexual relations would be without sin only if they were performed with control and restraint. In a similar vein, Origen extolled marriage as a divine gift created by God through which people could achieve salvation, but he also believed that married people temporarily lost the Holy Spirit during intercourse, for "the matter does not require the presence of the Holy Spirit, nor would it be fitting" (*Homilies on the Book of Numbers* 6). Some of the early fathers, then, despite their defense of marriage, had some difficulty in reconciling the social institution with the sexual behavior that it necessarily involved.

On the issue of divorce, Origen noted that some church leaders in his day acted "outside holy scripture" by allowing divorced women to remarry while their husbands were still living, but he conceded, "They did not act wholly unreasonably because apparently they tolerated something outside of what has been prescribed and handed down to us in order to prevent something worse from happening," like living with another man without marrying him (*Commentary on Matthew* XIV, 23). The reason this is noteworthy is that it was becoming common to interpret Matthew 5:32 and 19:9 as condoning divorce in the case of adultery and allowing the man to remarry—but not the woman. Since Roman law permitted any divorced person to remarry, the only thing that would have prevented Christians from doing so was a clear scriptural injunction against it. The gospels were clear in forbidding an adulterous wife from remarrying, but they seemed to be ambiguous about her husband, and so men who remarried in such cases were not considered to be acting "outside holy scripture."

During the first three centuries of Christianity, then, the fathers of the church did not say much about marriage, but when they did they talked about it as an important aspect of Christian life, not as an ecclesiastical institution. When Christians married they did so according to the civil laws of the time, in a traditional family ceremony, and often without any special church blessing on their union. The early Christian writers implicitly accepted the government's right to regulate marriage and divorce, and when they spoke about marriage they usually limited themselves to pastoral matters, affirming the goodness of marriage, urging Christians to marry within their own community, and warning them not to get drunk and unruly at wedding feasts. The bishops did not approve of divorce but they did not absolutely prohibit it, and they even allowed remarriage in some places that we know of and perhaps others.

Even after the edict of toleration by the emperor Constantine in 313, the great patristic writers said little about marriage compared to the amounts they wrote about other liturgical and doctrinal matters. For one thing, there was no liturgical ceremony for marriage as there was for baptism and eucharist, and so nothing had to be said to explain or defend it. For another, the Christian teaching on marriage was not complicated, and apart from the periodic bouts with gnostic sects, there were no great doctrinal controversies over marriage to call forth a flood of literature on the subject. All of the bishops agreed that sexual licentiousness and easy divorce were wrong, and they sometimes spoke out against what they perceived as the pagan immorality of the Roman world. They all agreed that marriage was a divine institution sanctioned by Christ, and they sometimes cited the biblical account of creation and Jesus' miracle at the wedding at Cana (John 2:1–11) to prove their point. But by and large they continued to regard marriage as a mundane matter in which Christians were expected to follow the norms of the gospels and epistles no less than in their other daily affairs.

This meant that the legal regulation of marriage and divorce was left to the government, and even though Constantine gave bishops the authority to act as civil magistrates, there is little indication that they were given any marriage cases to decide. Marriage under Roman law was still by the mutual consent of the parties involved (which in rural areas often meant the consent of the parents), and divorces came into court only when they were contested or involved property litigation. But the Roman government itself was concerned about marriage for its own reasons, and since the time of the emperor Augustus it had passed laws to discourage the childless marriages that were becoming more frequent among the aristocracy, and to encourage larger families by means of financial and other incentives. Now the emperor Constantine tried to eliminate the injustice of many one-sided divorces by making it illegal for men or women to reject their spouses for trivial reasons. In 331 he passed a law that allowed a woman to be left only if she were an adulteress, a procuress, or a dealer in medicines and poisons, and that allowed a man to be left only if he were a murderer, a dealer in medicines and poisons, or a violator of tombs. Those who abandoned their spouses for other reasons could lose their property and their right to remarry, but the law said nothing and imposed no sanctions against the traditional practice of divorce by agreement.

The Christian bishops, on the other hand, recognized only adultery as grounds for divorce. The regional council of Elvira in Spain in the early 300s prohibited a woman from remarrying if she left an unfaithful spouse but said nothing prohibiting a man from doing so. A similar council at Arles in France in 314 declared that young men who caught their wives in adultery should be counseled not to remarry, though it was not forbidden. Later in the century an unknown Christian author in Italy wrote that it was clear from the scriptures that a woman who was divorced for adultery could not marry again, but that nothing prevented the husband from doing so. Thus in the west, many churchmen recognized infidelity as grounds for divorce, and some even allowed injured husbands to remarry.

The same situation—and the same double standard—existed for Christians in the eastern part of the Roman Empire. Writing around 375, Basil of Caesaria summarized the current church regulations on marriage and divorce that he knew, and offered some of his own suggestions to a fellow bishop. According to Basil, "The Lord's statement that married persons may not leave their spouses except on account of immorality should, according to logic, apply equally to both men and women. However, the custom is different, and women are treated with greater severity" (*Letters* 188). For example, the wife of an unfaithful husband was obliged to remain with him, but the husband of an unfaithful wife could leave her. It was true that a man who committed adultery had to enroll in the order of penitents, but she could not leave him and remarry even if he physically abused her. If she did so she was considered an adulteress and had to do penance for her sin, but the man she left could remarry without any further ecclesiastical penalty. Even a man who abandoned his wife just to marry another woman could be readmitted to the ranks of the faithful after doing penance for seven years. Furthermore, a woman who was unjustly deserted by her husband would be regarded as an adulteress if she remarried, but a man who was unjustly deserted by his wife could be forgiven if he remarried. Noted Basil, "It is not easy to find a reason for this difference in treatment, but such is the prevailing custom" (*Letters* 199).

Even if divorce and remarriage in the case of adultery was not universally taught during the patristic era, many bishops accepted it particularly in the eastern part of the Roman Empire, although they sometimes imposed a period of penance on the persons involved. Those who took advantage of their civil right to divorce by consent and then remarry, for example, were often treated as adulterers in the penitential system, but their second marriage was generally recognized as legal and binding. This is not to say that divorces were frequent among Christians, but it does show that they were possible and that there was no universally recognized prohibition against divorce at this time. In any case, churchmen during this period had no legal say in the matter of marriages, divorces, and remarriages, and so they had to deal with these happenings as pastoral rather than legal matters.

Many of the church fathers were against second marriages of any sort even by widows and widowers, not only because of Paul's advice against it but also because the gnostic movements sometimes tried to prove their moral superiority by rigorously forbidding them. Promiscuity, prostitution, and lewd public entertainments in the cities even led Roman philosophers of the period to insist that the only legitimate purpose of sex was to found a family, and so Christian writers were sometimes hard put to defend why people should remarry if they already had children. Gradually, sexual abstinence became increasingly associated with moral perfection, but most bishops tended to follow Paul's lead by only discouraging and not denouncing second marriages. The sole exception to this trend was divorce and remarriage by converts to Christianity. Paul had sanctioned separation by mutual consent if pagan husbands or wives strongly opposed their spouse's new religion, and bishops still allowed Christians who were divorced under these circumstances to marry again.

Even after Christianity was made the official religion of the Roman Empire in 380, there was no great change in the civil marriage laws, though some Christian writers continued to denounce the ease with which people could obtain divorces even under a Christian emperor. It was not until 449 that Theodosius II passed a law prohibiting consensual divorce, but at the same time he expanded the list of legitimate grounds for leaving one's spouse to include robbery, kidnapping, treason, and other serious crimes, and for the first time it became legal for a woman to divorce her husband for adultery. This change in the law reflected a growing tendency among the bishops in the east to interpret the *porneia* of Matthew 19:9 as any kind of gross immorality, as well as their concern that innocent wives should not suffer because of the sins of their husbands.

The outlawing of divorce by mutual consent did not last, however, and later Christian emperors made it possible again. Then in the sixth century Justinian brought about a sweeping reform in the laws of the eastern part of the Roman Empire, including the laws on marriage and divorce. According to the Code of Justinian the basis of marriage was mutual affection between the sexes, but like any other human contracts marriages should be able to be made and unmade according to law. The code provided for nearly equal grounds for divorce by either husbands or wives, and for the first time in Roman law the children of dissolved marriages were specifically provided for. The traditional grounds for one-sided divorce were reaffirmed, and to them was added impotence, absence due to enslavement, and "the renunciation of marriage" by entering a monastery. Couples could also divorce by mutual consent if one of them wanted to pursue the spiritual perfection of the monastic life. In short, permanent marriage was still regarded as the ideal, but the law provided practical norms for those who could not or would not live up to it.

This late Roman attitude was generally accepted by the churches of Greece, Asia Minor, Syria, Palestine, and Egypt, which had already become more involved in the marriage practices of those regions. On the whole marriage was still primarily a family and secular affair with the bride's father playing the chief role in the wedding ceremony. Though there were local variations, the usual custom was that on the wedding day the father handed over his daughter to the groom in her own family's house, after which the bridal party walked in procession to her new husband's house for concluding ceremonies and a wedding feast. The principal part of the ceremony was the handing over of the bride, during which her right hand was placed in the groom's, and the draping of a garland of flowers over the couple to symbolize their happy union. There were no official words that had to be spoken, and there was no ecclesiastical blessing that had to be given to make the marriage legal and binding.

Late in the fourth century, however, it became customary in some places in the east for a priest or bishop to give his blessing to the newly wedded couple either during the wedding feast or even on the day beforehand. This blessing was usually considered something of an honor, showing the clergy's approval of the marriage, and it was not given if the bride or groom had been married before. Then in the fifth century, especially in Greece and Asia Minor, the clergy began to take a more active role in the main ceremony itself, in some places joining the couple's hands together, in other places putting the garland over them, and in others doing both. Gradually the wedding ceremony developed into a liturgical action in which the priest joined the couple in marriage and blessed their union, but still this ceremony was not mandatory and through the seventh century Christians could still get married in a purely secular ceremony.

By the eighth century, liturgical weddings had become quite common in the east, and they were usually performed in a church rather than in a home as before. New civil legislation was passed recognizing this new form of wedding ceremony as legally valid, and in later centuries other laws required that a priest officiate at all weddings. Marriage in the Greek church (for by this time the rest of the eastern part of the Roman Empire had been conquered by the Muslims) thus became an ecclesiastical ceremony, and in the view of eastern theologians the priest's blessing was essential for the joining of two people in a Christian, sacramental marriage.

This same view persists in the Orthodox churches today, for which marriage is a sacrament of Christian transformation, a transition ritual from one state in life to another which both effects that transition and symbolizes its spiritual goal. Just as baptism both initiates a person into the kingdom of God and symbolizes the sinless way that life in the kingdom should be lived, so marriage unites and consecrates two persons in fidelity to each other and symbolizes the love and respect that married people should always have for each other. That relationship, as Paul said, is like the relationship between Christ and the church, and so just as by baptism Christians enter into and participate in the mystery of the redemption, so also by marriage Christians enter into and participate in the mystery of union with Christ. It is a true earthly union of one man with one woman, which both symbolizes and takes place within the spiritual union of one Lord with the one church.

It sometimes happens, however, that Christians do not live up to their spiritual calling, that they do not live up to what was symbolized and initiated in their baptism and marriage, and it sometimes happens drastically and publicly as in the case of apostasy or divorce. When it does happen the church does not approve of it but it does recognize it as a fact. Christians should not renounce their faith, and they should not be divorced, but when these things happen they must be recognized as realities, and ways must be found to deal with the persons involved justly and mercifully. In the case of lapsed Christians, the way is always left open to reconciliation with the church, and in the case of divorced Christians the way is left open to reconciliation with each other or, if that is not possible, to remarriage.

For the most part, Orthodox churches do not grant divorces but they do allow for the possibility that Christians might receive a civil divorce and later want to remarry. Rather than exclude the innocent and repentant from communion in the church, then, they allow divorced Christians to remarry in the church as a concession to human needs and imperfections even though this second marriage cannot symbolize, as the first one did, the union between the one head and the one body of the church. Thus this second marriage is recognized as a real marriage but it is not necessarily regarded as a sacramental marriage, for it is not a full sign of the unique and eternal commitment that the first one promised to be. It is an approach to marriage that focuses on the liturgical aspects of the sacrament rather than on its juridical aspects, for such is the early church tradition out of which it grew.

There was, however, another church tradition regarding marriage. It developed not in the east but in the western half of the Roman Empire, and it developed along quite different lines.

Initially in the west, as in the east, marriage between Christians involved no distinct wedding ceremony. A Christian marriage was simply one that was contracted between two Christians by their mutual consent and lived "in the Lord." In the fourth century, however, once Christians could practice their religion openly, bishops and priests were sometimes invited to wedding feasts and to bestow their blessing on the newly wedded couple after the family marriage ceremonies were concluded. Sometimes this blessing was given instead during a eucharistic liturgy a day or more after the wedding itself. As in the east, the priest's blessing was usually given as a favor to the family or as a sign of his approval on the marriage; it was not a standard or universal practice. In some places the bishop or priest occasionally participated in the wedding ceremony itself by draping a veil over the newly united couple, a custom that was parallel to the practice of garlanding in the east. Bishop Ambrose of Milan even insisted that "marriage should be sanctified by the priestly veil and blessing" (*Letters* 19), but there is no other evidence that the veiling was ordinarily done by a cleric during this period.

Shortly before the end of the fourth century, however, Pope Siricius ordered that all clerics under his jurisdiction must henceforth have their marriages solemnized by a priest, and Innocent I at the beginning of the next century issued another decree to the same effect. Around the year 400, then, the only Latin Christians who had to receive an ecclesiastical blessing on their marriage were priests and deacons.

Ambrose was also the first Christian churchman to write that no marriage should be dissolved for any reason, and to insist that not even men had the right to remarry as long as their wives were alive. "You dismiss your wife as though you had a right to do this because the human law does not forbid it. But the law of God does forbid it. You should be standing in fear of God, but instead you obey human rulers. Listen to the word of God, whom those who make the laws are supposed to obey: 'What God has joined together, let no one separate'" (*Commentary on Luke* VIII, 5). Ambrose would not even allow divorce and remarriage in the case of adultery. And his firm stand on the permanence of marriage was taken up by one of his converts to Christianity, Augustine, later the bishop of Hippo in North Africa and one of the greatest influences on the early schoolmen in the Middle Ages.

Augustine's attitude toward marriage was an ambivalent one. On the one hand he viewed it as a beneficial social institution, necessary for the preservation of society and the continuation of the human race, and sanctioned by God since the creation of the first man and woman. On the other hand he saw sexual desire as a dangerous and destructive human energy that could tear society apart if it were not kept within bounds. As a young man he had had two mistresses and a child by one of them, but he had also been attracted by the moral asceticism of the Manichaean religion, to which he had belonged for a time. He was the first and only patristic author to write extensively about sex and marriage, and in the end he affirmed that marriage was good even though sex was not.

It was an attitude that was common among the intellectuals of his day. The Stoic philosophers taught that strong impulses should be controlled in order to have peace of soul and harmony in society, and that the only justification for intercourse was to produce offspring. The Manichaeans and other gnostics were often sexual puritans, condemning sensuality as evil and even forbidding marriage among the devout members of their sects. Christian ascetics like the hermits and monks of the desert sought to quench the desires of the flesh in order to free their minds for prayers and meditation. A number of the fathers of the church, including Gregory of Nyssa and John Chrysostom, taught that intercourse and childbearing were the result of Adam and Eve's fall from grace, and that if they had not sinned God would have populated the earth in some other way. Virginity for both men and women was extolled as the way of perfection for those who sought first the kingdom of God and wished to devote themselves to the things of the Lord. In Augustine's mind sexual desire was evil, a result of original sin, so those who gave in to it cooperated with evil and committed a further sin, even in marriage: "A man who is too ardent a lover of his wife is an adulterer, if the pleasure he finds in her is sought for its own sake" (*Against Julian* II, 7).

According to Augustine, therefore, only those who remained unmarried could successfully avoid the sin that almost always accompanied the use of sex. Those who were married usually committed at least a slight sin when they engaged in sexual intercourse, but they could be excused if they did it for the right reason. "Those who use the shameful sex appetite in a legitimate way make good use of evil, but those who use it in other ways make evil use of evil" (*On Marriage and Concupiscence* II, 21). And for Augustine, as for the Stoics, the only fully legitimate reason for having sexual relations was to produce children.

Children were thus the first of the good things in marriage that counterbalanced the necessary use of sex. Another was the faithfulness that it fostered between a man and a woman, so that they did not seek sex for pleasure with other partners. These two benefits could even be found in pagan marriages, said Augustine, but Christians also received a third benefit that was mentioned by Paul in one of his epistles: it was a sacred sign, a *sacramentum*, of the union between Christ and the church. Augustine read the New Testament in Latin, not Greek, and in Ephesians 5:32 Paul's word *mysterion* had been translated into Latin as *sacramentum* (see page 26). Augustine took it to mean that marriage was a visible sign of the invisible union between Christ and his spouse, the church. But he also saw a deeper meaning in the word by understanding it in the sense that a soldier's pledge of loyalty was called a *sacramentum*: it was a sign of perpetual fidelity. In this sense it was something similar to the sacramental character that Christians received in baptism. As baptism formed the soul in the image of Christ's death and resurrection, so marriage formed the soul in the image of Christ's eternal union with the church; and just as Christians could not be rebaptized and receive another image of Christ, so spouses could not remarry and receive another image of that eternal union. The *sacramentum* of marriage was therefore not only a sacred sign of a divine reality but it was also a sacred bond between husband and wife. And like the sacramentum of baptism, it was something permanent, or nearly so: "The marriage bond is dissolved only by the death of one of the partners" (*On the Benefit of Marriage* 24).

It was this invisible *sacramentum*, argued Augustine, that reminded Christians that they should be faithful even to a partner who was not. Marriage between Christians therefore should not be disrupted even in the case of adultery; instead, like the prophet Hosea in the Old Testament, Christians should try to win back an erring spouse. If it happened that the visible sign of this union was broken by their being separated, they still had no right to remarry, for the invisible sign of their union, the bond that was formed in the image of Christ's union with the church, remained. And if they did take another partner while their first spouse was still living, the *sacramentum* of their first marriage marked them as adulterers.

Augustine presented a strong theological case for the prohibition of divorce and remarriage, and the council of Carthage which he attended in 407 reflected his position by forbidding divorced men as well as divorced women to remarry. It would be some centuries, however, before the Latin church would turn to Augustine's writings to justify an absolute prohibition against remarriage by either spouse while the other remained alive.

Jerome, a scripture scholar and contemporary of Augustine, spoke out strongly against remarriage after divorce, but he spoke out much more strongly in the case of women than men. He took Christ's words in the Bible as an absolute prohibition for women: "A husband may commit adultery and sodomy, he may be stained with every conceivable crime, and his wife may even have left him because of his vices. Yet he is still her husband, and she may not remarry anyone else as long as he lives" (*Letters* 55). But for men who had divorced unfaithful wives he had a different warning: "If you have been made miserable by your first marriage, why do you expose yourself to the peril of a new one?" (*Commentary on Matthew* 19). He even insisted on scriptural grounds that a man should not continue to live with an adulterous wife, although he was equally insistent that nothing but adultery was a valid reason for separation.

In the opinion of Pope Innocent I, those who divorced by mutual consent as the civil law allowed were both adulterers if they remarried, regardless if they were men or women. He was equally clear in affirming that a woman who had been legally dismissed for adultery could not remarry as long as her husband was alive, but he apparently held that a husband in that case could remarry. Around the year 415 he wrote to a Roman magistrate about a woman who had been carried off by barbarian invaders some time before and had returned later, only to find her husband remarried. Claiming to be his rightful wife, she appealed to her bishop and Innocent agreed with her: "The arrangement with the second woman cannot be legitimate since the first wife is still alive and she was never dismissed by means of a divorce" (*Letters* 36). Presumably if her husband had divorced her (since women in captivity were usually violated) Innocent would have considered the second marriage legitimate.

Later in the century bishops began to get even more involved in marriage cases as the Germanic invasions led to a breakdown of Roman civil authority. The council of Vannes in France in 461 decided that husbands who left their wives and remarried without providing proof of adultery should be barred from communion. And a similar council at Agde in 506 imposed the same penalty on men who failed to justify their divorce before an ecclesiastical court before they remarried. At the close of the patristic period in the west, then, Christian bishops were becoming legally involved with marriage, and there was still no universally recognized prohibition against divorce and remarriage for both sexes. And apart from Augustine, no one spoke of marriage as a sacrament.

3. From Secular to Ecclesiastical Marriage

With the coming of the Dark Ages in Europe after the fall of the Roman Empire, churchmen were called upon more and more to decide marriage cases. Centuries before, Constantine had given them authority to act as judges in certain civil matters, and now that authority grew as the regular judicial system collapsed. Bishops also began to issue canonical regulations about persons who should not marry because they were too closely related. Initially the churchmen simply adopted the prevailing Roman customs, although they sometimes added prohibitions that were found in the Old Testament. Later they incorporated the customs of the invading Germanic peoples into the church's laws. These customs varied somewhat from tribe to tribe, but generally speaking persons who were more closely related than the seventh degree of kinship (for example, second cousins) were not allowed to marry legally.

Moreover, just as the bishops had earlier accepted Roman wedding customs, so they now also accepted the marriage practices of the Germanic peoples who settled within the old Roman provinces. Again these varied from tribe to tribe, although they, too, followed a general cultural pattern. Marriages were basically property arrangements by which a man purchased a woman from her father or some other family guardian to be his wife. The arrangement involved a mutual exchange of gifts, spoken and sometimes written agreements between the groom and the bride's guardian. In many places brides were betrothed ahead of time in return for a token of earnestness such as a small sum of money or a ring from the prospective husband, which would be forfeited if the marriage did not take place as agreed. On the wedding day the guardian handed over the woman and her dowry of personal possessions to her new husband, and received the bride price as compensation for the loss her family incurred by allowing her to leave it. After the wedding feast that was celebrated by the relatives and other witnesses to the marriage, the bride and groom entered a specially prepared wedding chamber for their first act of intercourse, which formally sealed the arrangement.

Throughout this early period, then, marriage was still a family matter similar to what it had been in the Roman Empire, and the clergy were not involved in wedding ceremonies except as guests. Bishops in their sermons and letters tried to impress their people with the Christian ideal of marriage found in the New Testament, and they sometimes urged them to have their marriages blessed by the clergy, but again this blessing was not essential to the marriage itself. In some places it was given during the wedding feast, in others it was a blessing of the wedding chamber, and in others it was a blessing during a mass after the wedding. Some bishops in southern Europe also suggested that the Roman custom of veiling the bridal couple should be done by a priest, but it was not a very common practice.

Just as churchmen were not officially involved in weddings, so also they were not officially involved in divorces when they occurred. However, some divorces ran counter to accepted Christian practices, and when they occurred those who were responsible for them had to confess their sin and do penance for it. The penitential books from the early Middle Ages (see page 337) show that divorce was more accepted in some places than others, but almost all allowed husbands to dismiss unfaithful wives and marry again. An Irish penitential book written in the seventh century instructed that if one spouse allowed the other to enter the service of God in a monastery or convent, he or she was free to remarry. The penitential of Theodore, archbishop of Canterbury in the same century, gave the following prescriptions: a husband could divorce an adulterous wife and marry again; the wife in that case could remarry after doing penance for five years; a man who was deserted by his wife could remarry after two years, provided he had his bishop's consent; a woman whose husband was imprisoned for a serious crime could remarry, but again only with the bishop's consent; a man whose wife was abducted by an enemy could remarry, and if the wife later returned she could also remarry; freed slaves who could not purchase their spouse's freedom were allowed to marry free persons. Other penitential books on the continent contained similar provisions.

The penitential books contained only unofficial guidelines to be followed in the administration of private penance, but conciliar and other church documents contained more official regulations. Again here these were not uniform, and ecclesiastical practices during this period ranged from extreme strictness to extreme laxness, but at least they show that there was no universal prohibition against divorce. In Spain the third and fourth councils of Toledo in 589 and 633 invoked the "Pauline privilege" in allowing Christian converts from Judaism to remarry. Irish councils in the seventh century allowed husbands of unfaithful wives to remarry, and although the council of Hereford in England in 673 advised against remarriage it did not forbid it. In eighth-century France the council of Compiègne allowed men whose wives committed adultery to remarry, and it allowed women whose husbands contracted leprosy to remarry with their husband's consent. In 752 the council of Verberie enacted legislation that allowed both men and women to remarry if their spouse committed adultery with a relative, and it prohibited those who committed the sin from marrying each other or anyone else. It also permitted a man to divorce and remarry if his wife plotted to kill him, or if he had to leave his homeland permanently and his wife refused to go with him. Pope Gregory II in 725 advised Boniface, the missionary bishop to Germany, that if a wife were too sick to perform her wifely duty it was best that her husband practice continence, but if this was impossible he might have another wife provided that he took care of the first one. Boniface himself recognized desertion as grounds for divorce, as well as adultery and entrance into a convent or monastery. Other popes of the period, however, protested against what they considered to be unlawful divorces, and the Italian council of Friuli in 791 strictly forbade divorced men to remarry even if their wife had been unfaithful.

One reason why churchmen became involved in marriage and divorce cases, especially after the popes started sending missionaries into northern Europe, was the difference between Roman and Germanic marriage customs. According to Roman tradition marriage was by consent, and after the consent was given by either the spouses or their guardians the marriage was considered legal and binding. In the Frankish and Germanic tradition, however, the giving of consent came at the betrothal, and the marriage was not considered to be completed or consummated until the first act of intercourse had taken place. Moreover, it was customary for parents to consent to the marriage of their children months and even years before they would begin to live together as husband and wife. This was particularly prevalent among the nobility, who often arranged such marriages as a means of securing allies or settling territorial disputes between them. But it sometimes happened that one of the betrothed spouses would undermine the parental arrangement by marrying someone else before the arranged marriage could be consummated. Bishops who were asked to settle these and similar cases could follow either the Roman or the Germanic tradition in coming to their decision. Under Roman law the arranged marriage was the binding one and the subsequent marriage was adultery, but according to Germanic custom the arrangement between the parents was only a non-binding betrothal and the second marriage was the real one. Even before any marriage was arranged, young people might consent to each other in marriage and then claim that they were not free to marry the partners their parents picked out for them, whereupon the parents might appeal to the episcopal court for a decision. In still other cases people sought to rid themselves of unwanted spouses by claiming that they had secretly contracted a previous marriage, which would make their present marriage unlawful. The legal question that had to be decided in each case was: Which marriage was the real marriage? And underlying the practical matters was the more theoretical question: Are marriages ratified by consent or by intercourse? For a long time there was no uniform answer to that theoretical question, and both episcopal and royal courts decided the practical matters according to which tradition they were accustomed to follow.

As Charlemagne initiated legal reforms in his European empire, both church and civil governments made an effort to impose stricter standards for marriage. Late in the eighth century the regional council in Verneuil decreed that both nobles and commoners should have public weddings, and a similar council in Bavaria instructed priests to make sure that people who wanted to marry were legally free to do so. In 802 Charlemagne himself passed a law requiring all proposed marriages to be examined for legal restrictions (such as previous marriages or close family relationships) before the wedding could take place. When the false decretals of Isidore were "discovered" in the middle of the ninth century, they contained documents purportedly from the patristic period aimed against the practice of clandestine marriage. A decree attributed to Pope Evaristus in the second century read, "A legitimate marriage cannot take place unless the woman's legal guardians are asked for their consent,….and only if the priest gives her the customary blessing in connection with the prayers and offering of the mass." Another decree represented the third-century pope Calixtus as saying that a marriage was legal only if it was blessed by a priest and the bride price was paid. The proponents of reform in the Frankish empire used these spurious documents to support their efforts to outlaw secret or clandestine marriages, and they were partially successful. Laws were passed making marriages legal only if guardians gave their consent and were present at the wedding.

In the meanwhile, however, Rome continued to follow its own tradition. In 866 Pope Nicholas I sent a letter to missionaries in the Balkans who had asked about the Greek church's contention that Christian marriages were not valid unless they were performed and blessed by a priest. In his reply Nicholas described the wedding customs that had become prevalent in Rome: the wedding ceremony took place in the absence of any church authorities and consisted primarily in the exchange of consent between the partners; afterward there was a special mass at which the bride and groom were covered with a veil and given a nuptial blessing. In Nicholas's opinion, however, a marriage was legal and binding even without any public or liturgical ceremony: "If anyone's marriage is in question, all that is needed is that they gave their consent, as the law demands. If this consent is lacking in a marriage then all the other celebrations count for nothing, even if intercourse has occurred" (*Letters* 97). According to Rome, then, it was the couple's consent, not their betrothal by their parents or their blessing by a priest, that legally established the marriage.

Charlemagne had wanted Roman practices to become normative in his empire, and in the years that followed, a Roman-style nuptial liturgy sometimes began to be included in the festivities that followed a wedding, though it was never very prevalent. Moreover, the pope's insistence that only consent constituted a marriage was initially ignored or largely unknown in the rest of Europe. Hincmar, the bishop of Rheims during this period, decided a number of marriage and divorce cases among the Frankish nobility, and he generally followed the opinion of the false decretals that legal marriages had to be publicly contracted. He also followed the Germanic tradition in ruling that marriages had to be consummated by sexual intercourse, and he allowed that people who had been given in marriage but who had not yet lived together could be legally divorced.

For a while, divorce regulations in northern Europe became more stringent under the impetus of ecclesiastical reform. As early as 829 a council of bishops at Paris decreed that divorced persons of both sexes could not remarry even if the divorce had been granted for adultery. By the end of the century a number of other councils in France and Germany passed similar prohibitions, and the penitential books were revised accordingly. But at the same time in Italy, popes and local councils continued to allow divorce and remarriage in certain circumstances, especially adultery and entering the religious life. Then in the next two centuries the trend in northern Europe reversed itself, and councils at Bourges, Worms, and Tours again allowed remarriages in cases of adultery and desertion.

During this same period, moreover, ecclesiastical courts were slowly gaining exclusive jurisdiction over marriage and divorce cases. As Charlemagne's short-lived empire dissolved into a disunited array of local principalities, more and more marriage cases were appealed to church tribunals. Eventually the secular courts came to be bypassed altogether, and by the year 1000 all marriages in Europe effectively came under the jurisdictional power of the church.

There was as yet no obligatory church ceremony connected with marriage, but in the eleventh century this began to change. In order to ensure that marriages took place legally and in front of witnesses, bishops invoked the texts of popes Evaristus and Calixtus in the false decretals to demand that all weddings be solemnly blessed by a priest. It gradually became customary to hold weddings near a church, so that the newly married couple could go inside immediately afterward to obtain the priest's blessing. Eventually this developed into a wedding ceremony that was performed at the church door and was followed by a nuptial mass inside the church during which the marriage was blessed. At the beginning of this development the clergy were present at the ceremony only as official witnesses and to give the required blessing, but as the years progressed priests began to assume some of the functions once relegated to the guardians and the spouses themselves, and many of the once secular customs in the wedding ceremony became part of an ecclesiastical wedding ritual.

By the twelfth century in various parts of Europe there was an established church wedding ceremony that was conducted entirely by the clergy, and although there were numerous local variations it generally conformed to the following pattern. At the entrance to the church the priest asked the bride and groom if they consented to the marriage. The father of the bride then handed his daughter to the groom and gave him her dowry, although in many places the priest performed this function instead. The priest then blessed the ring that was given to the bride, after which he gave his blessing to the marriage. During the nuptial mass in the church itself the bride was veiled and blessed, after which the priest gave the husband the ritual kiss of peace, who passed it to his wife. In some places the priest also pronounced an additional blessing over the wedding chamber after the day's festivities had concluded.

Along with the church's liturgical and legal involvement in marriage came a growing body of ecclesiastical laws about pre-marriage kinship, the wedding ceremony itself, and the social consequences of marriage and divorce. The medieval system of government and inheritance emphasized property rights and blood relationships arising from marriage, making it important for ecclesiastical judges to know who was legally free to marry, who was married to whom, and who could have their marriage legally dissolved. In the eleventh century the discovery and circulation of the Code of Justinian led to increasing acceptance of the idea that marriage came about by the consent of the partners, and this idea was reflected in the new rituals for church weddings in which the priest asked the bride and groom, not their parents, for their consent to the marriage. But the growth of the consent theory also led to an increase in the number of clandestine marriages, which brought legal difficulties about the legitimacy of children and their right to inherit their father's property, as well as pastoral difficulties when women and children were deserted by men who claimed they had never intended to establish a marriage.

In response to these difficulties some church lawyers defended a different theory about when a marriage legally took place, based on the old Germanic notion that intercourse was needed to ratify a marriage. As it was taken up and developed by the law faculty at the University of Bologna, this theory proposed that a real marriage did not exist unless and until the couple had sexual relations. But the opposing theory, that consent alone made a marriage, also had its staunch defenders, mainly at the University of Paris.

Around 1140 John Gratian in Bologna published his collection of canonical regulations commonly known as the *Decrees* in which he tried to bring some order into the sometimes conflicting decrees and decisions of popes and councils dating back to the patristic era. He was aware of the two schools of thought about what constituted a marriage, and he tried to harmonize them by suggesting that the consent of the spouses or their parents (in the case of betrothal) contracted a marriage and that sexual intercourse completed or consummated it. His opinion was that a marriage could be legally dissolved before it was consummated but not afterward, and in this respect he sided with the Bologna school. But he also agreed with the Paris school's contention that a binding marriage could be made in secret, without any public ceremony or priestly blessing. In his opinion such a marriage would be illicit or irregular because it flouted the laws of the church, but it would nonetheless be a real marriage, initiated by consent and consummated by intercourse.

Gratian's work clarified but did not settle the issue. In Italy, for example, church courts continued to dissolve marriages if it could be proven that no sexual relations had taken place, but in France the courts refused to dissolve any marriage once the partners' consent had been given. It was not until later in the twelfth century, when a noted canon lawyer of the period became Pope Alexander III, that a definitive solution was worked out and legislated for the whole Latin church. Because it offered a clearer criterion of an intended marriage between two individuals, Alexander sided with the ancient Roman practice that was defended by the Paris school, and he decreed that the consent given by the two partners themselves was all that was needed for the existence of a real marriage. This consent was viewed as an act of conferring on each other the legal right to marital relations even if they did not occur, and so from the moment of consent there was a true marriage contract between the two partners. In and of itself it was an unbreakable contract, but since the church had jurisdiction over it by the power of the keys, it could also be nullified or annulled by a competent ecclesiastical authority if sexual relations between the spouses had not yet taken place.

The decision of Alexander III became the legal practice of the Catholic Church. It was reinforced by further papal decrees in the thirteenth century and has remained in effect in canon law since then. With the exception of the "Pauline privilege" by which non-Christian marriages could be dissolved if one of the spouses converted to Catholicism, henceforward the church would grant no divorces whatever. Henceforward the marriage bond would be considered indissoluble not only as a Christian ideal but also as a rule of law. Henceforward if Catholics wanted to be freed from their spouses they would have to prove that their marriage contract should be nullified, declared to be nonexistent, either for lack of intercourse or for some other canonically acceptable reason.

But the pope's decision and the support it received in subsequent centuries did not rest only on the practical needs of ecclesiastical courts. Rather, the indissolubility of Christian marriage in the mind of Alexander and later churchmen rested also on a firm theological ground, the sacramentality of Christian marriage. For it was precisely around this time—the late twelfth century and the early thirteenth century—that marriage came to be viewed as one of the church's seven official sacraments.

What John Gratian did for canon law in his *Decrees*, Peter Lombard did for theology in his *Sentences*. Lombard's collection of theological texts did not solve many of the theological problems of the Middle Ages but it did go a long way toward defining what they were and how they should be treated. Marriage was treated in the section on the sacraments, for by this time in mid-twelfth-century France there was an established Christian ritual for marriage that was not unlike the other rituals that Lombard classified as sacramental.

When the book of *Sentences* was first published, however, many theologians still had difficulty in accepting the idea that marriage was a sacrament in the strict sense which was then being developed, and Lombard himself believed that it was different from the other six sacraments in that it was a sign of something sacred but not a cause of grace. One reason for the difficulty was that marriages involved financial arrangements, and if marriage was counted as a sacrament like the others it looked as though grace could be bought and sold. Another reason they hesitated to call marriage a sacrament was that it obviously existed before the coming of Christ, and so it could hardly be said to be a purely Christian institution like the other seven. But the third reason was the most crucial, and it was that marriage involved sexual intercourse.

Throughout the early Middle Ages most churchmen held virginity in higher esteem than marriage. On the one hand Christians could not deny that God had told Adam and Eve to increase and multiply, and so marriage itself had to be good. But on the other hand marriage, as Paul said, distracted one from the things of the Lord, and he seemed to suggest that people should marry only if they could not quench the fire of sexual desire. So marriage in the Middle Ages was often viewed negatively as a remedy against the desires of the flesh rather than positively as a way to become holy, and those desires themselves were viewed as sinful or at best danger-ous. Some bishops who blessed newly married couples recommended that they abstain from intercourse for three days out of respect for the blessing; others told them not to come to church for a month after the wedding, or at least not to come to communion with their bodies and souls still un-clean from intercourse. Most writers held that sexual activity which was motivated by anything but the desire for children was sinful, but most of them also believed that even here children could not be conceived without the stain of carnal pleasure.

So the western theological tradition through the eleventh century taught that marriage was good even though sexual activity was usually sin-ful. Three things in that century, however, forced them to reexamine that view. The first was the rise of a religious sect in southern France which, like the Manichaeans in the patristic period, taught that matter was evil and so marriage was sinful because it brought new material beings into the world. The Albigensians (so named because many lived around the town of Albi) did not accept the Christian concept of God, they denied the value of church rituals, and their leaders attacked the Catholic clergy as corrupt, so they were first denounced and later burned as heretics. In combating the Albigensian view of marriage Christian writers began to propose more strongly than before that intercourse for the sake of having children was positively good. The second thing that happened during this century was the development of a Christian wedding ritual which, by the presence of the clergy and the blessing they gave, implied that the church officially sanctioned sexual relations in marriage. And the third thing was the rediscovery of the writings of Augustine on marriage in which he de-veloped the idea that marriage was a *sacramentum*. To the early schoolmen it seemed to suggest that marriage was a sacrament in the same way that baptism and the eucharist were sacraments.

Augustine had taught that marriage was a *sacramentum* in two ways. It was a sign of the union between Christ and his church, and it was also a sacred pledge between husband and wife, a bond of fidelity between them that could not be dissolved except by death. It was something like a character on the souls of the spouses that permanently united them, and it was this permanence of their union that symbolized the eternal union of Christ and the church. It seemed to the schoolmen, therefore, that the Christian marriage ritual should be open to the same kind of analysis that they gave to the other sacraments, namely that in marriage there was a *sacramentum*, a sacred sign, a *sacramentum et res*, a sacramental reality, and a *res*, a real grace that was conferred in the rite. It took most of the twelfth century for the scholastics to satisfactorily fit marriage into this scheme, but by the time they did it the Catholic concept of sacramental marriage had become the theological basis for the canonical prohibition against divorce.

But what was the *sacramentum*, the sacramental sign in marriage? At the beginning it seemed to many of the schoolmen that it should be the priest's blessing since in the wedding ritual it corresponded to the part that was played by the priest in the other sacramental rites. Later, others suggested that it should be the physical act of intercourse between the spouses since this physical union could be taken as a sign of the spiritual union between the incarnate Christ and his spouse, the church. Still others felt it should be the spiritual unity of the married couple since this union of wills was closer to the actual way that Christ and the church were united with each other. However, each of these suggestions met with difficulties and had to be abandoned. It was objected that the priest's blessing could not be the sacramental sign because some people were truly married even though they never received the blessing, for example, people who married in secret. The schoolmen who still believed that sexual relations even in marriage were venially sinful objected to intercourse's being considered the sign because this would paradoxically raise a sinful act to the dignity of a sacrament. And it was objected that the union of wills in the married life could not be the sacramental sign because sometimes this spiritual unity was minimal at the beginning of a marriage and altogether lacking later on.

Eventually, because of the growing acceptance of the consent theory of the canon lawyers, the *sacramentum* in a sacramental marriage came to be viewed as the consent that the spouses gave to each other at the beginning of their married life. This mutual consent was something that had to be present in all canonically valid marriages, even those that were unlawfully contracted in secret. Both the canonists in Paris and Pope Alexander in Rome insisted that a real marriage existed from the moment that the consent was given, and theologians such as Hugh of St. Victor argued that a real marriage would have to be possible even without consummation in intercourse since according to tradition Joseph and the Virgin Mary had been truly married even though they had never had sexual relations. In addition, locating the *sacramentum* in the mutual consent kept it within the wedding ritual for most Christian marriages, and it made it possible to look upon the union of wills in a happy married life as a "fruit" of the sacrament even if it was not the sacrament itself.

But the greatest theological consequence of seeing the act of consent as the *sacramentum* in marriage was that it made it possible to regard the marriage contract or bond as the *sacramentum et res*. According to canon law the bond of marriage was a legal reality that came into existence when the two spouses consented to bind themselves to each other in a marital union. Now, in theology, the bond of marriage could also be understood as a metaphysical reality that existed in the souls of the spouses from the moment that they spoke the words of the sacramental sign. Following the lead of Augustine, the scholastics argued that this metaphysical bond was unbreakable since it was a sign of the equally unbreakable union between Christ and the church. It was not, as in the early church, that marriage as a sacred reality should not be dissolved; now it was argued that the marriage bond as a sacramental reality could not be dissolved. According to the church fathers the dissolution of marriage was possible but not permissible; according to the schoolmen it was not permissible because it was not possible. Thus the absolute Catholic prohibition against divorce arose in the twelfth century both as a canonical regulation supported by sacramental theory, and as a theological doctrine buttressed by ecclesiastical law. The two came hand in hand.

Even through the beginning of the thirteenth century, however, many theologians found it hard to admit that marriage as a sacrament conferred grace like the other sacraments. The traditional view of marriage was that it was more of a hindrance than a help toward holiness, a remedy for the sin of fornication rather than a means of receiving grace. Many theologians accepted Augustine's idea that original sin was transmitted from one generation to the next through the act of intercourse, and so even sexual relations for the sake of having children were often seen as a mixed blessing. Alexander of Hales was the first medieval theologian to reason that since marriage was a sacrament and since all the sacraments bestowed grace, then marriage must do so as well. But William of Auxerre believed that if any grace came from marriage it must be only a grace to avoid sin, not a grace to grow in holiness. William of Auvergne and Bonaventure both agreed that the effect of the sacrament must be some sort of grace, but both of them also held that the grace came through the priest's blessing.

Nevertheless, under the influence of reasoning like Alexander's and the desire to fit all the sacraments into a single conceptual scheme, theologians from Thomas Aquinas onward admitted that the sacrament gave a positive assistance toward holiness in the married state of life. That grace was first of all a grace of fidelity, an ability to be faithful to one's marriage vow, to resist temptations to adultery and desertion despite the hardships of married life. It was also even more positively a grace of spiritual unity between the husband and the wife, enabling him to love and care for her as Christ did the church, and enabling her to honor and obey him as the church did her Lord. It was true, of course, that even non-Christians could be faithful to one another and achieve marital harmony, but for Aquinas Christians were called to an ideal of constant fidelity and perfect love that could not be attained without the supernatural power of God's grace.

Aquinas also realized as did the other scholastics that marriage existed long before the coming of Christ, but for him this was no different from the fact that washing existed before the institution of baptism or that anointing existed before the sacraments that used oil. It was thus, like the other sacraments, something natural that had been raised in the church to the level of a sacramental sign through which grace might be received. But this also meant for Aquinas that the *sacramentum* in marriage was not just the act of mutual consent in the wedding ritual but the marriage itself, which came into existence through the giving of consent, was sealed by the act of intercourse, and continued for the remainder of one's life. As a sacramental sign it was therefore permanent, as was the sacramental reality of the marriage bond that was created by consent and made permanent through consummation. As a natural institution marriage was ordered to the good of nature, the perpetuation of the human race, and was regulated by natural laws that resulted in the birth of children. As a social institution it was ordered to the good of society, the perpetuation of the family and the state, and was regulated by civil laws that governed the political, social, and economic responsibilities of married persons. And as a sacrament it was ordered to the good of the church, the perpetuation of the community of those who loved, worshiped, and obeyed the one true God, and was regulated by the divine laws that governed the reception of grace and growth in spiritual perfection. The "matter" of the sacrament was therefore the human reality of marriage as a natural and social institution since this was the natural element, like water or oil, out of which it was made. And the "form" of the sacrament consisted of the words of mutual consent spoken by the spouses, since these were what signified the enduring fidelity that would exist between them, just as it existed between Christ and the church.

Most of the other things that Aquinas had to say about marriage—and this was true of the other schoolmen as well—had to do with the ecclesiastical regulation of marriage, with the laws governing who may and may not lawfully marry, with regulations regarding betrothal and inheritance, and so on. For marriage in the Middle Ages was viewed not so much as a personal relationship but as a social reality, an agreement between persons with attendant rights and responsibilities. Thus Aquinas and the other thirteenth-century scholastics occasionally spoke of marriage as a contract, and in the centuries that followed the legal terminology of canon law was further incorporated into the sacramental theology of marriage.

John Duns Scotus, for instance, conceived of marriage as a contract that gave people a right to have sexual relations for the purpose of raising a family, and from this he drew the inference that intercourse in marriage was legitimate not only for begetting children but also for protecting the marriage bond. A woman was bound in justice to give her husband what was his by right, he reasoned, and so she had to grant his requests lest he be tempted to bring discord into the marriage by satisfying his desires with someone else. Other theologians in the fourteenth and fifteenth centuries also came to accept this argument, and by the sixteenth century it was commonly taught that not every act of intercourse had to be performed with the intention of having children. Married people could ask for sex without blame, provided they did it not out of lust but only to relieve their natural needs.

Scotus was also the first theologian to teach that the minister of the sacrament was not the priest but the couple that was getting married. According to canon law people who wed without a priest were validly married even though they went about it illegally, and according to theology people who were validly married received the sacrament. It followed, therefore, that the bride and groom had to be the ones who administered the sacrament to each other when they gave their consent to the marriage. In the fourteenth and fifteenth centuries this view became more widely accepted, but even in the sixteenth century some theologians still maintained that the priest was the minister of the sacrament, for in many places the priest not only handed over the bride to the groom during the wedding ceremony but he also said, "I join you in the name of the Father and of the Son and of the Holy Spirit."

One thing that did not change, however, was the official prohibition against divorce. In the decree that was drawn up for the Armenian Christians during the Council of Florence in 1439, marriage was listed among the seven sacraments of the Roman church and explained as a sign of the union between Christ and the church. It adopted Augustine's summary of the benefits of marriage as the procreation and education of children, fidelity between the spouses, and the indissolubility of the sacramental bond. It granted that individuals might receive a legal separation if one of them was unfaithful, but denied that either one of them could marry again "since the bond of marriage lawfully contracted is perpetual."

Nonetheless, Christians in certain cases did separate and remarry. The hierarchy no longer allowed divorces but ecclesiastical courts were now empowered to grant annulments to those who could prove that their present marriage was invalid by canonical standards. If a married man could provide evidence, for example, that he had previously consented to marry someone else, the court could decide that the first marriage was valid even though unlawful and that the present marriage was therefore null and void. Marriage within certain degrees of kinship was also regarded as grounds for annulment even after years of marriage. But the closeness of prohibited relationships varied in different parts of Europe, and so a marriage that might be upheld in one country might be annulled in another. And if the blood relationship or secret marriage was difficult to prove, ecclesiastical courts were sometimes open to being persuaded by financial considerations, generously but discreetly offered.

4. Marriage in the Modern Church

The granting of annulments in dubious cases, for the wealthy and the nobility in particular, was one of the scandals in the Renaissance that led the early reformers to protest against the hierarchy's regulation of marriage. It was not that they denied the sacredness of marriage or disagreed with the practice of church weddings, but they did revolt against the complex canonical legislation that determined who could and could not marry, and they did doubt the justice of the legal system that allowed dispensations from the law and annulments of established marriages. They could find no justification in the scriptures for most of the ecclesiastical laws about marriage, and when humanist scholars discovered that the early church did not have civil jurisdiction in marriage cases, some of the reformers even charged that Rome had turned it into a sacrament just in order to get legal control over it. Most of them called for a more biblical attitude toward marriage, which usually meant a return to allowing divorce in certain cases.

According to Martin Luther, given that marriage existed since the beginning of the world, "there is no reason why it should be called a sacrament of the new law and the sole property of the church" (*Babylonian Captivity of the Church* 5). Marriage existed even among non-Christian peoples, and there was no record of any such sacrament's being instituted in the New Testament. The Latin text of Ephesians 5:32–33 could not be used to prove the existence of the sacrament, he argued, because *sacramentum* in that text was only a translation of the Greek word *mysterion*, and in that passage Paul was speaking metaphorically about the mysterious union of Christ and the church, not literally about the marriage bond between men and women. So there was no reason to believe that people received any special grace from God just because they were married.

Marriage certainly was instituted by God, said Luther, but not as a sacrament in the Roman Catholic sense of that term. Rather it was a natural and social institution that accordingly fell under natural and civil law, not church law. "No one can deny that marriage is an external and secular matter, like food and clothing, houses and land, subject to civil supervision" (*On Matrimonial Matters*). Thus the church should "leave each city and state to its own customs and practices in this regard" (*Short Catechism*, Preface). The role of the clergy should be to advise and counsel Christians about marriage, not to pass laws about it and judge marriage cases. Civil governments, on the other hand, had a right to make marriage laws because all authority ultimately came from God, and so in the secular world they acted in God's name. They could not be expected to pass laws that were in strict conformity with the ideals of the gospel, but at the same time they were morally obliged to keep within the bounds set by the laws of nature in enacting legislation for the good of society.

Luther said that he personally detested divorce, but that as a Christian he had to admit that Christ allowed divorce in the case of adultery, and that as a pastor he was inclined to permit it in other serious cases that seemed to have a scriptural justification. Paul, for instance, had allowed the Christian spouses of unbelievers to remarry, and Luther believed this principle could also be followed if a person acted like an unbeliever and deserted his or her family. Why, he argued, should the innocent suffer for a spouse's wickedness? In his own eyes he saw more harm done to innocent individuals by ecclesiastical annulments, and he saw a greater violation of Jesus' injunction not to sever what God had joined together when the church courts nullified marriages not on moral grounds but on legal technicalities.

John Calvin, like Luther, agreed that marriage was not a sacrament. "It is not enough that marriage should be from God for it to be considered a sacrament, but it is required that there should also be an external ceremony appointed by God for the purpose of confirming a promise" such as the promise of salvation that was confirmed by baptism (*Institutes of the Christian Religion* IV, 19, 34). But in the case of marriage there was no such ceremony and no such promise mentioned in the New Testament. Calvin also believed, therefore, that marriage laws fell within the jurisdiction of civil and not ecclesiastical authorities, but unlike Luther he contended that governments were morally obliged to make marriage and divorce laws in strict conformity with Christian principles. As far as he could see, the only two scriptural grounds for divorce were adultery and acting like a pagan by deserting one's family. Moreover, in these cases only the innocent spouse should be allowed to remarry.

Despite the divorces of Henry VIII that were granted after the English church's break from Rome, Anglican canon law prohibited divorce and remarriage until the middle of the nineteenth century. Nonetheless, English theologians generally agreed with the other reformers that divorce was possible in certain cases, and so when civil courts granted them from the seventeenth century onward, those who were divorced were allowed to remarry in the church. Initially only adultery, deliberate desertion, prolonged absence, and cruelty were recognized as legitimate grounds for divorce, but in later centuries these grounds were expanded. Throughout all this time, however, marriage continued to be commonly regarded as a sacrament, though only as a sacrament of the church and one that was not instituted by Christ. The English church also continued to uphold the validity of clandestine marriages, as the Roman church had, until the British parliament passed a law in 1754 requiring weddings to be celebrated in a church, with few legal exceptions.

The response of the Roman church to the views of the reformers was slow but deliberate. The Council of Trent did not take up the question of marriage until its last session in 1563, but when it did it attempted to vindicate both the sacramentality of marriage and the church's right to regulate it. In a brief statement presenting the Catholic doctrine on marriage, the bishops of the council affirmed that God had made the bond of marriage unbreakable when he made the first man and woman, and that Christ had both reaffirmed this and made marriage a sacrament whose grace raised natural love to perfect love. Thus Christian marriage was superior to other marriages, and for this reason "our holy Fathers, the councils and the tradition of the universal Church have always taught that marriage should be counted among the sacraments of the New Law." To this doctrinal statement the bishops then added a series of canons condemning anyone who taught the following heresies: that marriage was not a sacrament instituted by Christ which gave grace; that the church does not have the power to regulate who can and cannot legally marry, and to grant dispensations from these regulations; that ecclesiastical courts cannot annul unconsummated marriages or render judgments about other marriage cases; that the church was wrong in teaching that the marriage bond cannot be dissolved for any reason including adultery, or in forbidding remarriage, or in permitting spouses to legally separate without remarrying.

But the bishops also saw that the reaffirmation of traditional doctrine was not all that was needed to make sure that the sacrament was respected and properly administered. The greatest threat to the sacredness of marriage was the continuing practice of clandestine marriages that enabled people to enter unions which they later renounced, and that allowed them to seek annulments of public marriages on sometimes doubtful grounds. And so the bishops at Trent decided to take a drastic step. In a separate decree they recognized the validity of all previous clandestine marriages but declared that henceforth no Christian marriage would be valid and sacramental unless it was contracted in the presence of a priest and two witnesses. Those who tried to contract a marriage in any other way would be guilty of a grave sin and treated as adulterers. Furthermore, all marriages now had to be publicly announced three weeks in advance and entered into the parish records afterward in order to be considered canonically legal.

The bishops' decree effectively put an end to clandestine marriages in the Catholic Church, but their institution of a legal requirement for valid marriages—the giving of consent before a priest and two witnesses—raised additional questions for theologians and canon lawyers.

The first was the reappearance of an old question, namely, who was the minister of the sacrament of marriage? In the Middle Ages the possibility that marriages could be contracted without a church ceremony and even without any witnesses led most theologians to conclude that the ministers of the sacramental bond were the couple themselves, though some theologians thought otherwise. These argued that the priest was the minister of the sacrament, and so clandestine marriages were real but not sacramental since no priest joined the marriage or blessed the union. Then in the sixteenth century a Spanish theologian named Melchior Cano developed a theory that in marriage the mutual consent of the partners was the "matter" of the sacrament, while the priest's blessing was the "form." This implied that people could validly marry (as in Protestant countries) even though they did not receive a valid sacrament (since the required form was not followed). It also implied that the priest was the minister of the sacrament since without his presence, which the Catholic Church now demanded, the marriage was non-sacramental.

According to Cano's theory, then, the marriage contract was something separate and distinct from the sacrament, and it continued to be defended by Catholic theologians in the seventeenth and eighteenth centuries who wanted to agree that civil governments had the right to make laws governing the secular aspects of marriage even though the church's hierarchy had sole jurisdiction over the sacramental aspects of marriage. These theologians were in the minority, however, for the hierarchy had had complete control over all aspects of marriage for so long that most theologians and canonists continued to assert that only the Roman church had the right to make marriage laws for Christians. Even though Protestant heretics disobeyed those laws they were not really freed from them, the majority argued, for by their baptism they belonged to the church, and the one true church was the Roman Catholic Church. This church's laws, therefore, applied to all baptized persons whether or not they acknowledged and followed them.

Those who were not under the control of the Catholic hierarchy, however, thought and acted differently. At the beginning of the Protestant era other Christian churches developed their own wedding ceremonies and considered them valid, and as a matter of fact for over two centuries afterward almost all marriages in Europe were church marriages. But late in the eighteenth century this picture began to change. In France the revolution of 1789 brought an end to the ecclesiastical control of marriage, and the Napoleonic code of 1792 made civil weddings mandatory for all French citizens. During the next century almost all the other countries in Europe began to allow people to marry before a civil magistrate rather than a priest or minister, even though most of them did not require it as the French did. And of course governments also continued to regulate the other secular aspects of marriage and divorce (legal registration, inheritance rights, and so forth) as they had done even before the French revolution.

These developments forced the Catholic hierarchy to reexamine the official teaching on marriage and determine more precisely when and how the sacrament was conferred. Technically, according to canon law, all baptized persons who were not married in accordance with Trent's decree were living in sin because their marriages were not canonically valid. But Catholic bishops in Protestant countries began complaining to Rome that this put them in the awkward position of having to regard all Christians who were not married in the Catholic Church as adulterers and their children as illegitimate. The popes by this time realized that the Protestant reformation and the civil regulation of marriage were not going to be reversed, and they allowed that the Tridentine decree should be taken as applying only to those who were baptized Catholics and thus still under the legal jurisdiction of the hierarchy.

But what of non-Catholic marriages? Were they, too, sacramental? Even though Rome had reluctantly relinquished control over many of the secular aspects of marriage to other authorities, it did not see how it could surrender its position on the sacramentality of Christian marriage. The church had long recognized that baptisms even by heretics and schismatics were sacramentally valid, and now Rome followed a similar course with regard to non-Catholic marriages. In 1852 Pope Pius IX reacted to the claim of civil governments that all marriages between their citizens were legally dissolvable by declaring that since sacramental marriage was instituted by Christ, "There can be no marriage between Catholics which is not at the same time a sacrament; and consequently any other union between Christian men and women, even a civil marriage, is nothing but shameful and mortally sinful concubinage if it is not a sacrament" (Address, *Acerbissimum vobiscum*). In other words, marriages between Christians were either both valid and sacramental or else they were not marriages at all. The same position was reaffirmed by Leo XIII in 1880: "In Christian marriage the contract cannot be separated from the sacrament, and for this reason the contract cannot be a true and lawful one without being a sacrament as well" (Encyclical, *Arcanum divinae sapientiae*).

One of the reasons why the popes could be confident that the sacrament was identical with the marriage contract was that by this time historical research had shown that through the early Middle Ages the priest's blessing did not have to be given for a marriage to be valid; all that was needed was the mutual consent of the couple. This consent, then, established the contract or bond between the two parties, and so at the same time it had to be the act which established the marriage as sacramental. The theory that the sacrament was conferred by the priest was therefore no longer tenable. Since the contract was established through the giving of consent, the sacrament had to be administered by the bride and groom to each other. And since the sacrament was administered by the bride and groom, even non-Catholic Christians would confer the sacrament on each other whenever they contracted a valid marriage.

But this conclusion raised even further questions for canon lawyers. Were marriages between Christians and non-Christians sacramental as well? If non-Christians became Catholics did they have to be married again, or did their prior marriage automatically become a sacramental one in virtue of their baptism? If non-Catholic Christians divorced and remarried, was their second marriage valid, sacramental, both, or neither? Could a legally divorced non-Catholic validly marry a single Catholic? Could a divorced non-Christian do this? Suppose a Christian of another denomination became a Catholic and was divorced because of this by the non-Catholic spouse. Could the "Pauline privilege" be applied to this case so the Catholic could remarry? Or suppose that two non-Christians were married and divorced, and later became Catholics. Were they free to remarry or was their previous non-Christian union now sacramental and indissoluble in virtue of their baptism? Questions such as these were actually raised before Catholic marriage courts. They were sent to Rome from countries wherever Catholicism was established, but especially from bishops in Protestant and mission countries. They were cases that had to be decided, and the decisions set precedents for future cases. The ecclesiastical regulation of marriage was becoming more complex than it had ever been.

At the same time, however, the Catholic theology of marriage remained relatively simple. Marriage was a sacrament instituted by Christ in which two legally competent persons became permanently united as husband and wife. The *sacramentum tantum* was the giving of consent, the external rite in which they agreed to the marriage and took each other as their spouse. The *sacramentum et res* was the marriage contract, the sacramental reality that both symbolized the permanent union between Christ and the church and permanently united the couple in the bond of marriage. The *res tantum* was the grace that the couple received to be faithful to each other as Christian spouses, and to fulfill their duties as parents. The primary purpose of marriage was the procreation and education of children; its secondary purpose was the spiritual perfection of the spouses by means of the grace of the sacrament, the mutual support they gave to each other, and the morally permissible satisfaction of their sexual needs.

5. Marriage in Contemporary Catholicism

Through the beginning of the twentieth century the medieval concept of marriage remained relatively unchallenged in the Catholic Church. Whatever challenges there were came from without, and for the most part church leaders reacted by regarding them as dangers to the sacredness of Christian marriage. The Protestant rejection of the sacramentality of marriage was one such challenge; civil governments' regulation of marriage and acceptance of divorce was another. The romantic movement in the eighteenth century exalted erotic love over marital fidelity, and popular writers in the nineteenth century applauded the idea of marrying for no other reason than love. To some extent the church adapted, admitting the rights of governments when it could no longer deny them, and allowing that sexual relations in marriage had some secondary purpose besides conceiving children. But for the most part the official Catholic attitude toward marriage continued to emphasize legal rights and social responsibilities, for that had been the European attitude toward marriage during the centuries when the official doctrines were formed.

During the twentieth century, however, western society began to undergo a change the likes of which it had not seen since the fall of the Roman Empire and the rise of medieval society. Its roots were found in the Renaissance humanism of the sixteenth century, the rise of secular nations in the seventeenth century, the industrial revolution in the eighteenth century, and the expansion of the natural and social sciences in the nineteenth century, but it was not until the twentieth century that these developments and the changes they caused began to noticeably alter the basic values and norms of western civilization.

For hundreds of years Catholics could officially ignore the social transformation that was going on around them. The majority lived mainly in the non-industrialized countries of Europe and in religious isolation elsewhere. Their intellectuals studied and taught the philosophy and theology of the Middle Ages, and they critiqued modern ideas from that perspective. Their church leaders concerned themselves with ecclesiastical affairs and remained aloof from the things of this world. But in the twentieth century this social transformation reached into the everyday lives of Catholics, and it affected the ideas and attitudes of Catholic intellectuals and church leaders alike. Now the challenge to the medieval concept of marriage came from within the church itself, and it could not be ignored.

During the first half of the twentieth century, the nature and function of marriage in the west began to change. Before then, marriage was a social duty; now, it was an individual right. Before then, it was done in compliance with parents' wishes; now, it was done for personal love. Before then, love was expected to begin after the wedding; now, it was expected to precede it. There were parallel changes in the nature and function of the family. Before, it was an extended family with three generations of relatives living in the same house, or at least close to one another; now, it was a nuclear family with parents and children having less and less contact with uncles and aunts, grandparents and cousins. Before, the family was the basic unit of society: families lived and worked together; children were educated, trades were learned, recreation was provided, and most human needs were met, all within and by the family. Now, the family was becoming but one social unit among many: people had jobs that took them away from the people they lived with, children went to schools, most occupations could no longer be learned from one's parents, recreation was brought in by printed or electronic media or sought outside the home, and most human needs except the most basic ones of nurturing and affection were met by people outside the family. In short, marriage was coming to be seen mainly as an expression of love between a man and woman, and the family was no longer needed to educate children the way things used to be.

After the Second World War Catholic thinkers who were influenced by existentialist and personalist philosophy began to reappraise the traditional teaching that marriage was primarily for the procreation and education of children. Contemporary experience suggested that this was no longer so, and social sciences like psychology and sociology suggested that sex had a much deeper significance in human life than biological reproduction. Catholic personalists primarily in Germany proposed that Christian marriage should, therefore, be redefined to better fit the contemporary experience and understanding of marriage. As Herbert Doms and others saw it, marriage and sex had meaning in themselves, and so they did not have to get their meaning or justification from the children that resulted from intercourse. The meaning of marriage was the unity of two persons in a common life of sharing and commitment, and the meaning of intercourse was the physical and spiritual self-giving that occurred in the intimate union of two persons in love. Thus the primary purpose of marriage was the personal fulfillment and mutual growth of the spouses that occurred not only through their sexual relations but also through all the interpersonal relations of their married life. Children were thus secondary to the meaning and purpose of marriage, and even though they were to be loved and nurtured for their own sake, neither children nor the absence of children affected the primary meaning of marital and sexual union.

Rome's overall response to this inversion of the traditional Catholic teaching was negative, and various Vatican offices reaffirmed the doctrine that the primary purpose of marriage was the begetting and raising of children. But Pope Pius XII saw some merit in the personalist approach to marriage, and in some of his speeches he granted that interpersonal values like commitment and fulfillment were essential even if they were secondary in Christian marriage. Taking this as an official acceptance of their efforts if not always of their views, other theologians such as Josef Fuchs and Bernard Häring continued to explore the long-neglected personal aspects of marriage in their writings. Some tried to avoid the classic dichotomy between primary and secondary ends in marriage and preferred a more integrated approach. Others tried to translate the traditional scholastic teaching into more contemporary language. All of them tried to move away from a legalistic theology of marriage and sex and toward one that was more scriptural, more personal, and more related to contemporary married life.

This change in attitude was reflected in the documents of Vatican II. The council devoted an entire chapter of its Pastoral Constitution on the Church in the Modern World to problems of marriage and the family, and although it did not reverse the traditional Catholic teaching on marriage, it did adopt a more personalistic perspective toward sex. In particular the council avoided speaking of marriage as a contract or legal bond and instead referred to it in sociological, personal, and biblical terms. It spoke of marriage as a social and divine institution, an agreement between persons, an intimate partnership, a union in love, a community, and a covenant.

Thus on the one hand the council reasserted that "by its very nature, the institution of matrimony and married love are ordered to the procreation and education of the offspring and it is in them that it finds its crowning glory" (*Church in the Modern World* 48). But on the other hand it affirmed that love between spouses is "eminently human" and "embraces the good of the whole person." This total love "is uniquely expressed and perfected by the exercise of the acts proper to marriage," for "the truly human performance of these acts fosters the self-giving they signify and enriches the spouses in joy and gratitude" (49). It was because marriage was such a noble and sacred calling that Christian spouses are "fortified and, as it were, consecrated for the duties and dignity of their state by a special sacrament." Through this sacrament "spouses are penetrated with the spirit of Christ and their whole life is suffused by faith, hope and charity" (48). The sacramental nature of marriage, the unity of love, and the welfare of children all imply that marriage is indissoluble. "Thus the man and woman, who 'are no longer two but one,' help and serve each other by their marriage partnership; they become conscious of their unity and experience it more deeply from day to day. The intimate union of marriage, as a mutual giving of two persons, and the good of the children demand total fidelity from the spouses and require an unbreakable unity between them" (48).

In other documents the council also referred to the traditional analogy from Paul's letter to the Ephesians. Thus, "in virtue of the sacrament of Matrimony by which they signify and share in the mystery of the unity and fruitful love between Christ and the church, Christian married couples help one another to attain holiness" (*Church* 11). And in its Decree on the Apostolate of the Laity the council spoke of the sacramentality of marriage in an even broader sense, saying that Christian couples should be signs to each other, their children, and the world of the mystery of Christ and the church by the testimony of their love for each other and their concern for those in need.

As with the other official sacraments, the Catholic marriage rite was revised to allow greater flexibility in different circumstances and more adaptability to personal preferences. Since 1969 couples may choose from a variety of scriptural passages to be read if the wedding is celebrated during a nuptial mass, and they may use a number of different formulas to express their consent to each other in marriage. In some places they are allowed to include poems and other non-scriptural readings that have a special meaning for them, and even to compose their own marriage vows as long as they express the basic Christian understanding of marriage. Bishops in mission countries are encouraged to incorporate native customs into the wedding ceremony as far as possible, and even to draw up new rituals that express the meaning of Christian marriage in the symbols and gestures of their own culture. And church regulations have been revised so that non-Catholics in interfaith marriages may have their own minister as well as a priest preside at their wedding in the Catholic Church, a practice that was prohibited in the past.

Immediately after the council in the mid-1960s the theology and the ecclesiastical regulation of Catholic marriage both tended to become more liberal, moving away from a uniformly legalistic understanding of marriage and toward a more person-centered theory and practice. Since the 1980s, however, church involvement with marriage has become more cautious and conservative even though Catholic thinking about marriage as expressed in scholarly and popular publications has for the most part remained more liberal. In theology there has been a shift away from the nineteenth-century identification of the sacrament with the marriage bond or contract and toward a more liturgical and scriptural identification of the sacrament with the marriage itself. According to Edward Schillebeeckx, the wedding ritual should be an occasion for personally encountering the felt reality of divine love in and through the human love that two people have for each other, and for affirming the meaning of Christian marriage as a union in covenant and cooperation. But beyond that, the marriage itself should continue to be a sacramental sign of God's redeeming activity in human life and of the fidelity and devotion between Christ and the church. Karl Rahner takes this a step further and sees Christian marriage as a unique sign of the incarnation, of the mystery that the transcendent reality of God became flesh in the person and life of Christ, just as men and women incarnate the transforming reality of divine grace in their total love for one another. Marriage is, therefore, a way in which the church, as Christ's continued presence on earth, comes into being; it is an actualization of the nature of the church in and through the everyday incarnate love that married persons have for each other. For Bernard Cooke, too, love in the family is a sacrament of divine love in the same way that Jesus was a sacrament of God to those who knew him, and in the same way that the early Christian community was a sacrament of Christ to the ancient world. On the one hand sexual love is a natural symbol of the life-giving power of divine love in that it is full of vitality and leads to the creation of new life. On the other hand the fidelity and care that two persons have for each other symbolizes the transcendent meaning that God's love has for all persons, and in the measure that that meaning shines forth from the shared life of married persons their marriage is a sacrament to others of the transforming power of grace.

The 1980 synod of bishops which discussed the family in contemporary society and the Apostolic Exhortation on the Family issued by John Paul II the following year describe marriage in similar personalistic terms. Even the 1983 *Code of Canon Law* defines marriage as "a covenant by which a man and a woman establish between themselves a partnership of the whole of life," reflecting the theology of the Vatican council. And instead of insisting that the primary purpose of marriage is children, the new code says that marriage is for both "the good of the spouses and the procreation and education of children" (can. 1055, 1). At the same time, however, the code continues to speak of marriage in legal metaphors, claiming that "a matrimonial contract cannot validly exist between baptized persons unless it is also a sacrament" (can. 1055, 2), and this raises problems. For example, if two people who were baptized in the Catholic Church are no longer practicing their faith, they are not able to be validly married: on the one hand, if they marry civilly their marriage is canonically invalid because as Catholics they are bound by the church's law to marry before a priest; but on the other hand, since they are no longer practicing their faith they cannot have a Catholic wedding. The law also states that one of the essential properties of marriage is indissolubility (can. 1056), but at the same time it continues to permit the church to dissolve valid marriages in cases where one spouse becomes a Christian (the "Pauline privilege," which had previously been extended to cover other circumstances under the rubric of the "Petrine privilege") and in marriages between baptized persons if sexual intercourse has not yet occurred (cans. 1141–1150).

The 1994 *Catechism of the Catholic Church* maintains the tension between pastoral and legalistic approaches to marriage. The opening paragraph on the sacrament of marriage (1601) sounds very pastoral, for example, but in fact it is a quotation from canon 1055. Also, the *Catechism* speaks of the relationship between the spouses as "marriage," but it uses the more archaic term "matrimony" (derived from the Latin *matrimonia*, used in the *Code of Canon Law*) when referring to the sacrament. Marriage is defined as "a partnership of the whole of life" and "a community of life and love," but it is also an institution that is endowed by God "with its own proper laws" (1603).

The *Catechism*'s use of scripture often reflects advances in biblical scholarship (see pages 117–118), but in its discussion of marriage its use of scripture tends to be isogesis, attributing later meanings to earlier texts, rather than exegesis, which attempts to discover the original meanings of texts. The biblical account of the creation of Adam and Eve seems to be taken literally and somewhat legalistically, as are New Testament references to that account, to prove that from the very beginning marriage was indissoluble, even though after the Fall the original "order of creation" was seriously disturbed and God mercifully allowed for divorce under Jewish law (1602–1611). Christ, however, raised marriage to the dignity of a sacrament, thus restoring the original order of creation and giving people the spiritual assistance needed to live marriage the way God intended from the beginning (1612–1615). The *Catechism* does not use Ephesians 5:32 to prove that marriage is a sacrament, the way Augustine and the scholastics did; instead, the text is taken as implying the sacramentality of marriage, referring as it does to the relationship between Christ and the church (1616–1617).

In its discussion of the celebration of marriage, the *Catechism* makes reference to both the Roman rite and the eastern uniate rites, insisting that the spouses "mutually confer upon each other the sacrament of Matrimony by expressing their consent before the church" (1623) even though in the eastern rite ceremony there is no exchange of vows but a symbolic crowning of the spouses by the officiating priest (1621–1624). The discussion of matrimonial consent continues through a lengthy subsection (1625–1637) in which most of the footnotes refer to the *Code of Canon Law*.

The *Catechism's* treatment of these effects of the sacrament returns to a more pastoral tone, but the underlying theology is undeniably that of medieval scholasticism. The first effect of the exchange of mutual consent (the *sacramentum tantum*) ratified by sexual consummation is the marriage bond (the *sacramentum et res*), which is indissoluble according to divine law (1638–1639). This sacramental reality is the source of a special grace (the *res tantum*), which perfects the couple's love and strengthens their indissoluble unity, making it possible for them to bear each other's burdens, forgiving and submitting to one another through the tribulations and joys of married life (1641–1642). Moreover, conjugal love (the term used in official Catholic documents for sexual lovemaking) requires indissolubility, fidelity, and openness to fertility: an indissoluble union is the only appropriate relationship for sexual intercourse, faithfulness of both spouses promotes the deeper meaning of sexual activity, and openness to fertility (that is, intercourse without contraceptives) conforms to the natural order as intended by God (1643–1654). The Christian family thus becomes a "domestic church" in which parents and children exercise the priesthood of the baptized in a special way (1655–1657) without diminishing the dignity of single persons (1658) or denying the value of celibacy and virginity for the sake of the kingdom of (1618–1620).

Despite the Catholic Church's strong defense of its traditional teachings, progressive theologians and pastorally minded canon lawyers have been raising further questions about marriage. Is it necessary or even possible to hold that the bond of marriage is a metaphysical entity, as Augustine and the medieval theologians believed, which cannot be broken except by the death of one of the spouses? If it is not, is the indissolubility of marriage a moral ideal rather than a divine law, as it seems to have been at the time of Jesus and during the first millennium of Christianity? Or could the bond of marriage be a psychological and social reality that only gradually achieves indissolubility, as some Catholic thinkers are today suggesting? And why is it not possible, some African voices are asking, for the church to recognize as valid the practice of polygamous marriage which is common in some regions on that continent? If the church had developed in Africa instead of in Europe, they argue, polygamy would have been regarded as normal and church laws today would reflect that fact. As it stands, wealthy Africans who have more than one wife and many children must divorce all their wives except one and disown many of their children if they want to become Catholics.

The African situation is but one cultural case in point that is stretching the official Catholic position on marriage. Another is the situation in the United States, where an estimated one half of marriages being contracted today will end in divorce, not because of deliberate sinfulness but because American society does not provide many young people with the interpersonal skills needed for an intimate, life-long relationship. Some theologians have proposed a return to the tradition of the fathers that has been preserved in the Orthodox churches, which regards the permanence of marriage as a norm that allows for exceptions. Others have proposed even more radically that marriage is sacramental when it embodies and expresses the kind of love that exists between Christ and the church, and that such a marriage would necessarily be permanent because the love within it would be faithful, forgiving, and self-sacrificing. But if the marriage no longer embodied and expressed that kind of love, it would in fact be no longer sacramental, and by the same token it would be liable to end in divorce.

Married Catholics, however, have not waited for such theological suggestions to win official church approval, and the divorce rate among American Catholics, for example, is now about as high as it is for other Americans. Nevertheless, according to present canon law they are not free to remarry and so if they do they are automatically excluded from the sacraments and denied reconciliation until they renounce their adultery. For many of them the matter simply ends there, and they cease being Catholics. But others who have wanted to be reinstated into full membership in the church have tried in increasing numbers to have their first marriage officially annulled.

From the time of the Council of Trent the grounds for annulment were quite well defined and they were interpreted rather strictly. Marriage contacts could be declared null and void only if one of the parties did not fully consent to the marriage (for example, if they were coerced), or if they were not able to fulfill their marital obligations (for example, if they could not perform the act of intercourse), or if they had not received a dispensation from one of the canonical impediments to a valid marriage (for example, if they were too closely related). In recent years, however, ecclesiastical courts have been interpreting the grounds for annulment more broadly to mean that if a person was psychologically unable to give a full and mature consent or was emotionally incapable of making a lifetime commitment to another person, then a valid marriage may not have existed from the very beginning. But these broader grounds are quite vague, and they are now in fact sometimes used to nullify marriages that have fallen apart for many of the same reasons that civil courts recognize in granting divorces.

At the present time, then, the only way that Catholics can remarry and remain in the church is to have their first marriage annulled, a lengthy and involved process. Despite the willingness of canon lawyers to examine every case for possible grounds, most legally divorced Catholics (some estimates range as high as ninety percent) are either unaware that they might be able to obtain an annulment, or they are unwilling to go through the equivalent of another divorce procedure, this time in an ecclesiastical court. Over and above this, canonists themselves have noted that if more Catholics petitioned to have their marriages annulled the courts would simply be unable to handle the case load. Some have questioned the way that some marriages are now annulled through what amounts to legal loopholes in canon law, and have been wondering whether the Catholic hierarchy should recognize that church annulments are often being used to legitimate civil divorces. Still others, a minority, have questioned the value and relevance of the whole ecclesiastical judicial system that researches and tries marriage cases, and have recommended that it be dismantled. They would allow marriage and divorce to revert back to civil control, as in the early church, and have the clergy concern themselves only with the pastoral and religious aspects of Christian marriage.

There does not seem to be an easy way out of the dilemma. For the past eight hundred years or so the Catholic Church has vigorously maintained that a validly contracted marriage is indissoluble not only by church law but also by divine law. It has become a part of Catholic doctrine, and to change it would call into question the infallibility of the church. During the same period of time the church's judicial system has grown into an elaborate structure of laws and courts intended to safeguard the integrity of marriage. It has become a part of the institutional church, and so to change it would call for a more radical reappraisal than the one that occurred at Vatican II. On the other hand, the historical justification for the present doctrine and judicial system has been called into question by biblical and patristic research. The theological justification for the metaphysical permanence of the marriage bond has been lost in the shift from scholastic to personalist philosophy, and it has been called into question by the view that the sacrament of marriage is not a legally binding contract but a living relationship between two people. And the practical justification for the impossibility of divorce has been called into question by the fact that the prohibition no longer deters Catholics from obtaining divorces but rather prevents them from remaining Catholics.

But if the dilemma cannot be resolved, steps can be taken to avoid it. The Catholic Church has been doing much more than in the past to prepare its members for marriage. In America, for example, Catholic high schools and colleges teach courses not only on the theology of marriage but also on the practical requirements and consequences of being married. The new *Code of Canon Law* states that the local church should provide assistance for those seeking to be married, and many dioceses have therefore established marriage preparation programs for engaged couples in which priests and other professionals talk to them about the realities and responsibilities of marriage. In addition, the Christian Family Movement, Marriage Encounter, and similar organizations offer group support for maintaining and enriching married life. Yet at the same time, these official and unofficial programs are only partially successful at best. It would seem that much remains to be done if the dilemma is to be averted.

And what of marriage as a "door to the sacred"? Is it that now? Or has it ever been that? It is, and it has been, despite the fact that much of the history of marriage in the Catholic Church has been a legal history, and despite the fact that the sacramental theology of marriage was for a long time formulated in juridicial terms. Marriage has been a sacrament in the broad sense in two different ways. One of them began in the patristic period, the other in the Middle Ages.

In the very first centuries, Paul's passage on marriage in Ephesians was not used to exemplify the union between Christ and the church, but rather Christ's sacrifice for the church and the church's obedience to Christ were used to exemplify how husbands and wives should behave toward each other. Thus marriage was considered to be sacred but not sacramental since the starting point of the analogy was the divine relationship, which was then used to illustrate the human relationship. Augustine, however, took the analogy both ways: he saw the human relationship as a sign of the divine relationship, and the divine relationship as a sign of the human relationship. Still, his emphasis was on the latter, and so he used the everlasting union between Christ and the church to argue for a permanent union between husband and wife. In the Middle Ages the Pauline analogy continued to be taken mainly in this way, but once marriage was understood to be a sacrament in the strict Catholic sense theologians also began to view it as a sacrament in the broader sense of being a sign of the incarnate spiritual union of Christ and the church. This way of looking at marriage continued in the modern church, and in recent times it has even been emphasized by Catholic theologians who want to affirm the sacramentality of marriage while avoiding the legalism of earlier sacramental theology. Today the analogy is used in books and sermons to bring Catholics to a deeper awareness of what their relationship to Christ and to each other is and ought to be.

Nonetheless, an understanding of marriage that is based on the quality of the relationship rather than on physical or legal considerations raises as many questions as it resolves. If a sacramental marriage is one in which the spouses give themselves to one another in sacrificial love, and in which their dedication to one another reflects the mutual self-giving of Christ and the church, it could be theoretically possible for two people of the same sex to engage in such a caring relationship. Could such a relationship be considered sacramental in a spiritual sense even if it is not allowed to be called a marriage under church law? And how are Catholics to regard same-sex relationships that are given the status of marriage in other churches and in civil law? Such further questions about the sacramentality of marriage have yet to be debated.

The second way in which marriage has been and remains a sacrament in the broad sense is in the sacramental wedding ceremony. It began in the Middle Ages, evolved through a variety of forms, became stabilized during the Tridentine reforms, and is now evolving again. But wedding ceremonies are always sacramental, at least in the broad sense of being celebrations of the sacred value of marriage, whatever it may be in a given culture, as well as in the sense of being rituals of initiation to a new style of life that is honored and meaningful, supported by social custom and religious tradition. In these same ways Christian wedding ceremonies have always been sacramental, for they have celebrated the sacred value of marriage in a Christian culture, and they have initiated men and women into a style of life that was to be modeled on the relationship between Christ and the church. In medieval and modern times that lifestyle was often understood to be authoritative and faithful on the part of the husband and submissive and dutiful on the part of the wife, for Christ was seen as Lord and master and the church was seen as servant and mistress. In contemporary times that lifestyle is more often understood to be one of constant self-giving on the part of both husband and wife, for Christ and the church are both seen as incarnations of transcendent love. But however the value and meaning of Christian marriage are understood, the wedding ceremony is always an important and meaningful occasion. Its words and gestures, even the bearing and expressions of its participants, symbolize to the bride and groom and the others who are present the meaning and importance of what is happening and what is about to happen to this couple. They are being transformed, and they are going to be transformed even further. And the wedding is a door through which they enter into that sacred transformation.

For Further Reading

Broad Approaches

Evelyn and James Whitehead, *Marrying Well* (Doubleday, 1981) discusses thoroughly almost every aspect of marriage from a variety of perspectives.

Challon and William Roberts, *Partners in Intimacy* (Paulist Press, 1988) touches on all the bases for discussing contemporary marriage, including its religious dimensions.

Jack Dominian, *Marriage, Faith and Love* (Crossroad, 1982) is a thorough and well-written exposition of the many dimensions of marriage in contemporary society.

Thomas Martin, *The Challenge of Christian Marriage* (Paulist Press, 1990) is a readable textbook that covers a wide range of topics.

Diane and Richard Garland, *Beyond Companionship* (Westminster Press, 1986) balances psychology, sociology, and theology to understand the challenge of Christian marriage today.

Jean-Pierre Bagot, *How to Understand Marriage* (Crossroad, 1987) presents the history and Catholic theology of marriage in a positive and uncritical manner.

Kieran Scott and Michael Warren, eds., *Perspectives on Marriage* (Oxford University Press, 1993) offers a fine selection of pieces from books and periodicals on a broad range of topics.

Kathy Heskin, *Marriage: A Spiritual Journey* (Twenty-Third Publications, 2002) looks at many facets of marriage through the lens of one couple's experience.

Peter Jeffery, *The Mystery of Christian Marriage* (Paulist Press, 2006) affirms the traditional theology of marriage as well as current church teachings on related topics.

Particular Topics

Jack Dominian, *Dynamics of Marriage* (Twenty-Third Publications, 1993) looks at marriage from a Christian perspective as an interpersonal relationship that promotes growth.

William Johnson Everett, *Blessed Be the Bond* (Fortress Press, 1985) develops a Christian understanding of marriage as communion, covenant, vocation, and sacrament.

Denise Lardner Carmody, *Caring for Marriage* (Paulist Press, 1985) is a prolonged essay on the biblical meaning of *agape* in light of contemporary feminist concerns.

John Garvey, *The Ways We Are Together* (Thomas More Press, 1983) offers insightful sketches on marriage, family, and sexuality.

Denise and John Carmody, *Becoming One Flesh* (The Upper Room, 1984) contains thoughtful and practical reflections on ways to grow personally and religiously through marriage.

Michael Lawler and William Roberts, eds., *Christian Marriage and Family* (Liturgical Press, 1996) contains articles on theological and pastoral dimensions of marriage.

Mary van Balen Holt, *Marriage: A Covenant of Seasons* (Liguori Publications, 1993) presents reflections on the experience of marriage through the natural changes in the relationship.

Christopher Reilly, *Making Your Marriage Work* (Twenty-Third Publications, 1989) describes the knowledge and skills that couples need in order to have a satisfying and lasting relationship.

Leif Kehrwald, *Marriage and the Spirituality of Intimacy* (St. Anthony Messenger Press, 1996) is an experience-based discussion of healthy close relationships by a Catholic family minister.

David Thomas, *Written on Scrolls, Inscribed in Hearts* (Abbey Press, 1989) presents thoughts about marriage based on the author's experience of life and knowledge of scripture.

Christopher West, *Good News about Sex and Marriage* (Servant Books, 2000) is a frank and non-dogmatic explanation of Catholic teachings in this area.

Richard Gaillardetz, *A Daring Promise* (Crossroad, 2002) presents a spirituality of marriage based on living the paschal mystery in intimate companionship based on divine love.

Michael Lawler, *Marriage and the Catholic Church* (Liturgical Press, 2002) looks at a number of issues over which there is some disagreement among Catholics.

For Further Study

General History

Edward Schillebeeckx, *Marriage: Human Reality and Saving Mystery* (Sheed and Ward, 1965) is a thorough examination of the scriptural and historical background for the Catholic teaching on marriage.

Theodore Mackin, *What Is Marriage?* (Paulist Press, 1982) examines the human institution and social reality of marriage through the ages, giving special attention to Christian customs and beliefs.

Philip Lyndon Reynolds, *Marriage in the Western Church* (E. J. Brill, 1994) is a detailed historical treatment of the gradual Christianization of marriage in the Roman Empire and early medieval Europe.

David and Vera Mace, *The Sacred Fire* (Abingdon Press, 1986) is a very readable history of Christian marriage from biblical to modern times.

Thomas Martin, *The Challenge of Christian Marriage* (Paulist Press, 1990) looks at how marriage has been understood and lived in the succession of Christian cultures from New Testament times to the present.

Peter Coleman, *Christian Attitudes to Marriage* (SCM Press, 2004) is a lucid history of the institution from ancient to modern times, with comparisons to Judaism.

Douglas Letson, ed., *Sex and Marriage in the Catholic Tradition* (Novalis, 2001) is a historical overview that draws together fifty church documents, articles, and excerpts.

Glenn Olsen, ed., *Christian Marriage* (Crossroad, 2001) is a collection of studies covering the history of marriage from biblical to contemporary society.

Matthew Levering, ed., *On Marriage and the Family* (Rowman & Littlefield, 2005) collects texts from the second to the twentieth century on the Catholic understanding of marriage.

Historical Periods

Frances and Joseph Gies, *Marriage and Family in the Middle Ages* (Harper and Row, 1987) documents, among other things, the church's struggle to gain control over marriage in the twelfth century.

Georges Duby, *The Knight, the Lady and the Priest* (Pantheon Books, 1983) examines the development of the modern Catholic understanding of marriage during the eleventh and twelfth centuries.

Jacqueline Murray, ed., *Love, Marriage and Family in the Middle Ages* (Broadview Press, 2001) translates original texts giving insights into medieval life.

Conor McCarthy, ed., *Love, Sex and Marriage in the Middle Ages* (Routledge, 2004) collects excerpts ranging from Augustine in the fourth century to Chaucer in the fourteenth.

Philip Reynolds and John Witte, eds., *To Have and to Hold* (Cambridge University Press, 2007) is a collection of scholarly articles on marriage in medieval Europe.

John Witte, *From Sacrament to Contract* (Westminster John Knox, 2012) exposes the understanding of marriage in five different Christian traditions through an analysis of modern church and civil laws.

Theology

David Thomas, *Christian Marriage* (Michael Glazier, 1983) presents a well-rounded theology of marriage, including a summary of the history of Christian marriage.

Theodore Mackin, *The Marital Sacrament* (Paulist Press, 1989) exhaustively investigates the development of marriage as a sacrament from biblical times to the present day.

Elizabeth and Louis Tetlow, *Partners in Service* (University Press of America, 1983) develops a biblical theology of marriage as a sacramental relationship that participates in the mission of the church to serve others.

Michael Lawler, *Marriage and Sacrament* (Liturgical Press, 1993) develops an understanding of marriage based on experience, psychology, scripture, history, and canon law.

Joseph Kerns, *The Theology of Marriage* (Sheed and Ward, 1964) is traditional in its approach but is full of illuminating historical references.

Walter Kasper, *Theology of Christian Marriage* (Crossroad, 1991) explains the Catholic doctrines of sacramentality and indissolubility while acknowledging the pastoral problems they entail in contemporary society.

William Roberts, *Commitment to Partnership* (Paulist Press, 1987) is a fine collection of serious essays on the theology and reality of marriage in the Catholic Church today.

Kenneth Stevenson, *To Join Together: The Rite of Marriage* (Pueblo, 1987) examines the development and theology of the present Catholic wedding ceremony.

Peter Elliott, *What God Has Joined* (Alba House, 1990) explains and defends the traditional Catholic teaching on the sacramentality of marriage.

Ramón García de Haro, *Marriage and Family in the Documents of the Magisterium* (Ignatius Press, 1993) documents the official Catholic teaching on marriage since the sixteenth century.

William Urbine and William Seifert, *On Life and Love* (Twenty-Third Publications, 1993) gives an overview of the Catholic teaching on marriage and family, and summarizes nineteen church documents.

Margaret Monahan Hogan, *Marriage as a Relationship* (Marquette University Press, 2002) traces the recent evolution of official Catholic teachings on marriage through an analysis of church documents.

Florence Caffrey Bourg, *Where Two or Three Are Gathered* (University of Notre Dame Press, 2004) examines the family as a domestic church from a variety of perspectives.

Richard Hogan and John LeVoir, *Covenant of Love* (Doubleday, 1985) is an exposition of Pope John Paul II's writings on marriage, the family and sexuality.

Carl Anderson and José Granados, *Called to Love* (Doubleday, 2009) presents John Paul II's theology of the body in the context of love, especially in marriage.

William May, *Marriage: The Rock on Which the Family Is Built* (Ignatius Press, 2009) celebrates the ideal which, when it is lived, provides a solid basis for human relationships.

Mark Pilon, *Magnum Mysterium* (Alba House, 2010) is a detailed presentation of the traditional Catholic teaching on marriage and related issues.

Todd Salzman, Thomas Kelly and John O'Keefe, eds., *Marriage in the Catholic Tradition* (Crossroad, 2004) collects two dozen recent articles on marriage in scripture, in the early church, in canon law and theology, and in contemporary society.

Charles Curran and Julie Hanlon Rubio, eds., *Marriage* (Paulist Press, 2009) is a collection of articles by well-known authors on the morality of marriage and related issues.

John Meyendorff, *Marriage: An Orthodox Perspective* (St. Vladimir's Seminary Press, 1975) clearly presents the tradition and thinking of the Orthodox churches about marriage and related issues.

Eugene Hillman, *Polygamy Reconsidered* (Orbis Books, 1975) argues that the traditional Christian rejection of plural marriage is culturally conditioned and shows little understanding of African society.

Divorce, Remarriage, and Annulment

Victor Pospishil, *Divorce and Remarriage: Towards a New Catholic Teaching* (Herder and Herder, 1967) is a ground-breaking study of the scriptural, historical, and theological issues surrounding Catholic remarriage.

Lawrence Wrenn, ed., *Divorce and Remarriage in the Catholic Church* (Newman Press, 1973) has articles that take a further look at the scriptural, historical, and contemporary aspects of marriage and divorce. *The Invalid Marriage* (Canon Law Society of America, 1998) provides technical explanations of the various grounds for annulment in the 1983 *Code of Canon Law*.

Theodore Mackin, *Divorce and Remarriage* (Paulist Press, 1984) thoroughly investigates how marital breakdown has been regarded down through the Christian centuries.

Raymond Collins, *Divorce in the New Testament* (Liturgical Press, 1992) thoroughly examines the divorce texts in Paul and the synoptics, with an extensive review of recent scholarship.

Kevin Kelly, *Divorce and Second Marriage* (Geoffrey Chapman, 1996) takes a personalistic approach and argues that Catholics who remarry without an annulment may participate in the life of the church.

John Catoir, *Where Do You Stand With the Church?* (Alba House, 1996) steers between canonical rigidity and pastoral permissiveness in discussing the situation of divorced Catholics.

James Young, *Divorcing, Believing, Belonging* (Paulist Press, 1984) contains stories, reflections, and suggestions for Catholics suffering from marital breakdown today.

Gerald Coleman, *Divorce and Remarriage in the Catholic Church* (Paulist Press, 1988) presents historical, pastoral, and theological perspectives in a clear and sensitive treatment of the subject.

William Roberts, ed., *Divorce and Remarriage* (Sheed and Ward, 1990) is a collection of stimulating articles on the religious, moral, and psychological dimensions of these two issues.

Joseph Zwack, *Annulment: Your Chance to Remarry Within the Catholic Church* (Harper & Row, 1983) is a handy and well-written guide to the ins and outs of the annulment process.

Ida Iris Miranda, *Undoing the "I Do"* (Resource Publications, 2002) addresses basic Catholic teachings about marriage and annulments, and offers practical advice about the annulment process.

Barry Brunsman, *New Hope for Divorced Catholics* (Harper and Row, 1985) challenges the theory of indissolubility that conceives of marriage in terms of validity and makes annulment a legal necessity.

John Hosie, *Catholics, Divorce and Remarriage* (E. J. Dwyer, 1991) is a short, clearly written book about the social, legal, psychological, and spiritual dimensions of marriage transition.

Michael Smith Foster, *Annulment: The Wedding that Was* (Paulist Press, 1999) gives answers to questions about marriage and annulment in Catholic canon law.

Edward Peters, *Annulments and the Catholic Church* (Ascension Press, 2004) does pretty much the same thing.

Pierre Hégy and Joseph Martos, eds., *Catholic Divorce* (Crossroad, 2000) contains articles that are critical of the theory of indissolubility and the policy of requiring annulments.

Richard Jenks, *Divorce, Annulments, and the Catholic Church* (Haworth Press, 2002) is a sociological examination of the process based on questionnaires given to married and divorced Catholics.

Canon Law

Bernard Siegle, *Marriage According to the New Code of Canon Law* (Alba House, 1986) is just what the title says it is.

Ladislas Orsy, *Marriage in Canon Law* (Michael Glazier, 1986) examines the canons on marriage in the new code and discusses the problems left unresolved.

John McAreavy, *The Canon Law of Marriage and the Family* (Four Courts Press, 1997) is a detailed commentary on canons 1055–1165 and other parts of the Code dealing with marriage.

Sexuality and Intimacy

Evelyn and James Whitehead, *A Sense of Sexuality* (Crossroad, 1994) places sexuality within the context of intimacy, partnership, and marriage.

Mike and Joyce Grace, *A Joyful Meeting* (International Marriage Encounter, 1980) offers earthy, humorous, and balanced advice about sexuality in marriage.

Morton and Barbara Kelsey, *Sacrament of Sexuality* (Amity House, 1986) suggests that if sexuality is sacramental, it can be a healthy part of integral spiritual development.

Andrew and Judith Lester, *It Takes Two* (Westminster John Knox, 1998) gives direction to couples who intend to achieve and maintain an intimate relationship.

Joan Meyer Anzia and Mary Durkin, *Marital Intimacy: A Catholic Perspective* (Loyola University Press, 1980) skillfully blends research, theology, and experience into a developmental description of sexual intimacy.

Thomas Tyrrell, *The Adventure of Intimacy* (Twenty-Third Publications, 1994) is partly autobiographical, partly philosophical, partly spiritual, and partly theological.

Charles Gallagher and others, *Embodied in Love* (Crossroad, 1987) develops a sacramental spirituality for married persons based on the dynamics of sexual intimacy.

William May, *Sex, Marriage, and Chastity* (Franciscan Herald Press, 1981) presents a reasoned exposition of the official Catholic doctrine on sexual behavior within and outside marriage.

Raymond Dennehy, ed., *Christian Married Love* (Ignatius Press, 1981) selects essays that explain and defend papal teaching on sex, marriage, and birth control.

Mary Durkin, *Feast of Love* (Loyola University Press, 1983) expands on Pope John Paul II's teachings on intimacy and sexuality in marriage.

Mary Rousseau and Charles Gallagher, *Sex Is Holy* (Element, 1991) is a theological and pastoral presentation of the Catholic understanding of sexuality within marriage.

John Kippley, *Sex and the Marriage Covenant* (Couple to Couple League International, 1991) argues that since marriage is the only legitimate context for sexual intercourse, artificial birth control is immoral.

Vincent Genovesi, *In Pursuit of Love: Catholic Morality and Human Sexuality* (Liturgical Press, 1996) is a through treatment that presents both sides of debated issues.

Thomas Fox, *Sexuality and Catholicism* (George Braziller, 1995) reports on issues and the controversies surrounding them, presenting official and dissenting views.

Mary Anne McPherson Oliver, *Conjugal Spirituality* (Sheed and Ward, 1994) develops a spirituality for married persons that includes their relationships to one another, to God, and to others.

Margaret Farley, *Just Love* (Continuum, 2006) uses a multidisciplinary approach to develop a framework for examining the ethical dimension of sexual relationships among Christians.

Todd Salzmann and Michael Lawler, *Sexual Ethics* (Georgetown University Press, 2012) develops a moral appreciation for sex and marriage that acknowledges the Catholic tradition but also admits its shortcomings.

Marriage and Religious Diversity

George Kilcourse, *Double Belonging* (Paulist Press, 1992) covers a wide range of topics from individual and institutional perspectives regarding marriages between persons who are active in two different Christian churches.

Michael Lawler, *Ecumenical Marriage and Remarriage* (Twenty-Third Publications, 1990) treats practical, pastoral, theological, and canonical dimensions of the issue.

Phyllis Airhart and Margaret Lamberts Bendroth, eds., *Faith Traditions and the Family* (Westminster John Knox, 1996) discusses family life and values within a wide variety of (mostly Christian) religious traditions.

Anton Vrame, ed., *Intermarriage: Orthodox Perspectives* (Holy Cross Orthodox Press, 1997) collects papers from a conference that covered many aspects of this contemporary reality.

John Bush and Patrick Cooney, eds., *Interchurch Families* (Westminster John Knox Press, 2002) is an ecumenical summary of beliefs and guidelines issued by Presbyterian and Catholic leaders.

Same-Sex Marriage

Francis DeBernardo, *Marriage Equality* (New Ways Ministry, 2011) is a defense of same gender marriage based on Catholic teachings about human dignity, respect for persons, and the primacy of conscience.

Dale O'Leary, *One Man, One Woman* (Sophia Institute Press, 2007) argues strenuously against homosexual behavior and same sex marriage using data from psychology and sociology.

Gene Robinson, *God Believes in Love* (Alfred A. Knopf, 2012) is a frank discussion of gay marriage by an Episcopal bishop.

Daniel Hauser, *Marriage and Christian Life* (University Press of America, 2005) regards male-female sexuality as the only acceptable foundation for marriage.

CHAPTER XII

ORDINATION

We ask you, all powerful Father, give these servants of yours the dignity of the presbyterate. Renew the Spirit of holiness within them. By your divine gift may they attain the second order in the hierarchy and exemplify right conduct in their lives.

May they be our fellow-workers, so that the words of the gospel may reach the farthest parts of the earth, and all nations, gathered together in Christ, may become one holy people of God.

—RITE OF ORDINATION

The earliest Christian community contained a variety of ministries, but priesthood was not one of them. The only priesthood that Jesus and his immediate followers apparently recognized was the ministry of the Jewish temple priests. Nevertheless, before the end of the first century, Christian writers likened Jesus' death on the cross to a priestly sacrifice, and by the middle of the third century those who presided over eucharistic worship were beginning to be perceived as priestly ministers. This identification of ministry and priesthood eventually grew so strong in the patristic and medieval periods that almost all those engaged in official church ministries had to be ordained as priests. At the beginning of the modern era, however, many Protestant Christians rejected the idea that eucharistic worship was a sort of sacrifice, and with it they rejected the need for a special priestly office in the church. Instead, they conceived of ministry in more pastoral terms and emphasized scripture reading and preaching in their worship. Catholics, on the other hand, insisted on the priestly character of Christian ministry, which by this time had become traditional, and all of the official ministries in the Roman church continued to be reserved to men who were ordained priests. It is only recently, in the light of biblical and other historical evidence, that the Catholic equation of ministry and priesthood has begun to be reexamined, and that other people besides priests have been encouraged to engage in ministries for which priestly ordination is not necessary.

This thumbnail sketch, however, hardly does justice to the complex history of priestly orders in Catholicism, which in many ways parallels the complex history of the other sacraments. For one thing, in the Middle Ages there were several such orders (seven, to be exact) which came to be regarded as sacramental. For another, these sacramental orders came to be defined almost exclusively in terms of a power to administer the other official sacraments. Moreover, ordination is closely connected with the concept of the sacramental character, since like baptism and confirmation it can be undergone only once. It is intimately associated with eucharist, penance, and anointing since only those in orders can offer the mass or administer absolution or anoint the sick. It is even related to marriage, not only because Catholics are required to have a priest present at their wedding but also because those priests are unable to marry. Finally, just as a broadening of the notion of sacrament is today forcing Catholics to reexamine the nature and function of the traditional sacraments, so also a broadening understanding of ministry is leading them to take another look at many of the things they used to take for granted about the priesthood.

In addition, the question of ordination raises further questions about authority in the Catholic Church, since traditionally the clergy have had authority over the laity and the clergy themselves have been ranked in a hierarchy of power and jurisdiction. It also raises questions about the nature of the church, about the function of ministry in the church, and about the relation of the Catholic Church and its hierarchy to other Christian churches and their clergy.

Not all of these connections can be explored and not all of these questions can be pursued in a single chapter. But hopefully a historical introduction to the Catholic priesthood can provide a perspective from which to view the present and envision a possible future for ordained ministries in the church.

1. Parallels and Precedents

Like sacraments in the broad sense, all religions have priests or equivalent persons who play special roles in their societies. Very often their functions are sacramental: the supervision or performance of sacramental rituals through which people enter the world of the sacred. Sometimes they themselves are sacramental, and their very presence is a sign to others of a dimension of reality that lies beyond the visible world of everyday experience. But they can also be involved in religion in ways that are not immediately sacramental, preserving and interpreting the knowledge that is sacred to their tradition, writing it down, teaching it to others. And their authority in the area of religion often extends into other areas, enabling them to act as rulers and judges in matters which are not strictly religious but which are sacred to the society in which they live. Nevertheless, in all these ways priests and their equivalents—shamans, diviners, healers, sorcerers, witches, gurus, prophets, rabbis, imams, and so on—act as mediators of the sacred, persons through which the sacred can be experienced or better understood or properly lived.

According to the customs of their own tradition, personal mediators of the sacred can be young or old, male or female. Sometimes they act independently, sometimes they function only together in groups. Sometimes their priestly position in society is permanent and their main occupation in life is to mediate the sacred, but sometimes it is temporary and they function as mediators only for a while, or perhaps they perform their priestly functions only at certain sacred times each year. In some societies they may be born into their role, in others they enter it only by being chosen.

Even in situations where priesthood is hereditary, however, there is usually some initiation through which a person must pass before publicly functioning as a sacred mediator. In cultures where heads of families or clans act as priests, they must at least be initiated into adulthood, instructed about their duties, and wait until they establish their own families. In cultures where sacred persons form a separate group, they must usually undergo a lengthy initiation. First they are singled out from the other members of society by being designated as candidates or even by being made to live apart. Next they make the transition from being profane persons to being sacred persons by passing through a period of indoctrination and testing during which they learn their new role and are judged to be fit or unfit for it. Finally they are incorporated into their new social class or religious caste in a public ceremony during which they are ritually approved by those who already belong to the group, are accepted by the other members of society, and receive tokens of their new position or power. It is a sacramental ceremony both in the sense that it symbolizes sacred values and meanings, and in the sense that it effects their entrance into a sacred social role.

Sacred persons in primitive cultures performed a variety of social functions. They preserved their tribe's accumulated wisdom in myths, proverbs,
and parables. They passed on practical knowledge by leading their society
in time-tested rituals for hunting, fishing, farming, and building. They
safeguarded the means for maintaining the sacred order needed to preserve
life through physical healing, moral judgment, and communication with
the transcendent.

In ancient civilizations, however, many common human activities lost
their religious aura and became part of an increasingly secular culture. To
the extent that these things were still important and in that sense sacred,
they were still associated with gods and spirits who might be invoked to
guard and bless them, and when things went wrong a priest might be
asked to divine the cause and prescribe a ritual remedy. But by and large
the role of sacred persons in civilizations like Egypt, Greece, and Rome
was becoming more restricted. The knowledge that they preserved was
often more philosophical and moral than practical, and the rituals that
they performed were often more related to the realm of the spirit than
to ordinary activities. Even in this more limited role, however, they still
functioned as mediators, either by representing their people to the gods
in prayer or by representing the gods to the people in blessing, teaching,
and moral judgment.

In Rome before the days of the empire, for example, the father of each
household acted as priest in offering prayer and sacrifice to his family
gods and representing their will in the decisions he made for those under
his jurisdiction. Later, as family religion declined and national religion
replaced it, various groups of priests and priestesses took care of temples
and shrines, spoke for the gods through religious utterances and oracles,
and offered prayers and sacrifices to the gods on behalf of the nation and
individuals who requested them. The religious function of the Roman
priesthood was therefore primarily *cultus*, quite literally the cultivation of
the relationship between certain gods and their worshipers, in the interest
of *pietas* or the duty to maintain the established order between the divine
and human realms of reality. Piety also demanded the protection and
vigilance of the gods when vows were made and oaths were taken, but for
these sacred occasions there was no separate cultic priesthood. Instead,
civil administrators or magistrates functioned as priests by accepting the
pledges as made to the god and solemnizing it with a brief spoken formula
or in a ritual such as the burning of incense.

In early Israel as in early Rome there was no distinct priesthood. The father of each family or the head of each clan functioned as priest in offering prayer and sacrifice to Yahweh, and national leaders such as Moses and David sometimes led the people in worship as persons with sacred authority. After the exodus from Egypt, however, various families began to assume regular priestly functions, first at shrines to Yahweh throughout the country and then at the temple built by Solomon in the tenth century BC. Chief among these, at least for a while, were the clan of Aaron and the tribe of Levi (Exodus 28–29; 32:25–29). Priesthood in Judaism was therefore largely hereditary and so ceremonies of initiation did not make men priests although they were still sometimes ritually anointed with oil and dressed in priestly garments before they actually exercised their sacred ministry (Leviticus 8–9). Priests were expected to lead exemplary lives and be respected by the people since they were engaged in the service of God, but in some ways too the whole nation was considered a "kingdom of priests" since they were a chosen people who were called to holiness (Leviticus 19, 21).

Originally, Jewish priests were responsible for a number of sacred functions: they divined the will of God by casting lots and by other means; they preserved, taught, and interpreted the Mosaic Law, the Torah; they took care of the holy places, guarded the temple treasury, accepted gifts made to God, and officiated over ritual sacrifices. During the period of the Israelite monarchy, however, prophets began to replace priests as persons who spoke for God, and after the exile in Babylonia scribes and rabbis assumed the sacred tasks of preserving and teaching the traditions of Judaism. This left the temple ministry as the main duty of the hereditary priesthood after the sixth century BC. On important holy days the high priest offered the sacrifices prescribed by the Torah on behalf of the whole people, while other priests performed the same function for individuals and on less solemn occasions.

But priests, prophets, and rabbis were not the only important persons in later Judaism. In every rural town and in every city district, Jewish communities were organized and governed by groups of elders who managed the local assembly or synagogue, saw to it that the needy were not neglected, acted as judges in disputes between individuals, and dealt with the gentile authorities on behalf of their people. These elders were not necessarily the oldest men in the community but they were men of mature age who were known for their administrative ability and moral character, and who were respected for their knowledge and observance of the Law. Generally they were chosen and appointed with the people's approval, and at least by the

Roman era they were formally inducted into their office in a ceremony that
included a laying on of hands.

2. Christian Ministries and Sacred Orders

In the sense that Jesus was a sacramental person he was also a priestly
person, that is to say, a mediator of God to those who believed in him.
He was a prophetic person who like the Jewish prophets before him and
John the Baptist in his own day spoke in the name of Yahweh, saying what
God would want people to hear and doing what God would do to help
them. By his words he announced a message of salvation that only God
could give, by his deeds he testified to the coming of a kingdom in which
God would reign in human hearts and lives. He spoke with authority in
interpreting the scriptures and was called "rabbi" even by his opponents.
He was a teacher who could fashion parables for farmers and dilemmas
for lawyers. He claimed what appeared to be a sacrilegious closeness to
God and yet in his preaching and his healing, even by his presence and
his person, he seemed to manifest the power and mercy of the one he
addressed intimately as Abba. He exercised religious leadership, forming
a community of followers around him, sharing his insights with them,
showing and telling them how to behave. Nonetheless he seemed to conceive of his life's work not in terms of power but in terms of service, and
on at least one occasion he is said to have told those who followed him
that if they wanted to be great they would have to be servants to others.
In this sense, then, Jesus saw his mission as one of ministry even though
it involved authority and leadership.

The earliest disciples of Jesus, especially the twelve who were closest
to him, continued to exercise authority and leadership among the Jews
who believed in him, but like their crucified master they also conceived
of their role as one of ministry or service. In some respects these twelve
functioned as elders in a new but somewhat unorthodox Jewish community
in Jerusalem, overseeing the welfare of those who belonged to it, acting
as teachers and preachers to people inside and outside the community,
representing the community before Jewish and Roman authorities, and
making joint decisions about Christian beliefs and practices (Acts 4–6, 8,
10, 15). In other respects they continued the ministry of Jesus and acted
as his envoys even as they did during his lifetime, announcing the coming
of the kingdom, proclaiming Jesus as the messiah, healing the sick, pronouncing God's judgment on sinners and God's forgiveness for those who

repented (Acts 2–6, 9–15). At the beginning, the disciple Peter enjoyed a certain prominence and acted as a speaker for the group; later James, a brother of Jesus who was not one of the twelve, seems to have been the chief elder in Jerusalem (Acts 1:15–26; 15:13–21). In neither case, however, did the leaders act alone; important decisions were made by the elders acting together, with the approval of the community.

These twelve formed part of a larger group of believers who were engaged in some sort of activity that continued and extended the work of Jesus. In later years the names of these activities and the groups who performed them would become titles in a more organized church, but almost all of them were originally common words which in Greek described what various people were doing. For example, the group of twelve were sometimes referred to as *apostoloi*, meaning emissaries or ambassadors, since they had been sent by Christ to carry his message throughout Palestine. The work they did was described as *diakonia*, meaning ministry or service, but so also was the work of those who helped them, or who served the community in other ways by being envoys, elders, or even distributors of food and clothing to the poor. Elders in cities outside Jerusalem were sometimes called *episkopoi*, meaning supervisors or overseers, since their ministry was to see to the welfare and good order of the whole community which was placed in their care. In many places there seem to have been *proph tes*, meaning spokespersons or proclaimers, people who during worship or as part of their missionary work spoke for the Lord and made his message known to others.

Besides the twelve, then, there were other *apostoloi* or apostles who were sent out as emissaries from the Jerusalem community to other cities, bringing the word of the resurrected Christ to the world. Paul of Tarsus was certainly one of them, as was his companion Barnabas and some others who are mentioned by name in the New Testament (Acts 14:14; Romans 16:7). As Paul saw it, apostles were more like missionaries than envoys, for they carried the Christian message throughout the then-known world, but to be fit for this ministry a person had to have seen the risen Lord so that he could bear witness to what he himself had experienced (1 Corinthians 9:1; Acts 1:22). If Paul's work is any model for what others were doing at the time (though we have few records of this), apostles were itinerant evangelists who traveled from one city to another making converts, establishing communities, placing others in charge, and then moving on but keeping in contact through letters and messengers.

In each city these missionary leaders appointed elders to oversee the affairs of the community, and at least at the beginning the words for elder and supervisor (*presbyteros* and *episkopos*) were interchangeable (Acts 14:23; 20:17, 28). Later the term *episkopos* was used to designate the presiding elder or council president, but in many ways he was one among equals, since the responsibilities of the elders were roughly the same for all (1 Peter 5:2–5). They were to watch over the community, guarding it like shepherds, preaching the gospel and teaching the doctrine that they had received, settling disputes within the community, making sure that the needy were taken care of, and in general seeing that the other ministries were properly carried out. In order to perform their administrative task well, supervisors and other elders were supposed to have the same qualities as a good head of a family: he should be able to manage his own household, be a "one-woman man," and have children who were obedient and well behaved; in addition, he should have a good reputation, be even tempered, sensible, moderate in his habits, friendly and hospitable, and not too fond of money (1 Timothy 3:1–7; Titus 1:6–9).

Other appointed ministers (*diakonoi*) who served the internal needs of the community were to have similar qualifications, being good family men, sober, and trustworthy. If they were women they should likewise be respectable, discreet, and reliable (1 Timothy 3:8–13). People in these positions, as well as elders and supervisors, were usually appointed to their ministries, sometimes with the approval of the community that they were to serve. They also seem to have received their commission by being prayed over and having hands laid on them, much as elders did in traditional Jewish communities (Acts 6:1–6; 13:1–3; 1 Timothy 4:14; 5:22). This would have been a sacramental action in the broad sense, but there is no indication that it was believed to convey any special spiritual power. As a matter of fact, the authors of the New Testament do not seem to have been very concerned about who had the right to perform sacramental actions like baptizing, hand-laying, or presiding over the Lord's supper, though presumably there were people who knew how to do them and these were in some way leaders in the community. Nor were the authors very explicit about how these persons received that right, for although there are gospel texts indicating that Jesus told the twelve and other disciples to do these things, there are no texts which show that the authority to do them was passed on to others by a necessary and well-defined rite such as the laying on of hands.

In any event, there were other ministries in the early church which may or may not have been confirmed by an imposition of hands, but at least there is no mention of it. There were widows who were supported by the community and who in return performed works of hospitality and charity, and there were other women who were designated more loosely as helpers or simply ministers (1 Timothy 5:9–13; Philippians 4:3; Romans 16:1–16). Women were also teachers and prophets, but these ministries whether performed by women or men seem to have been regarded as charisms or gifts of the Spirit rather than church-appointed ministries (Acts 18:26; 21:9; 1 Corinthians 11:15). Some thought, however, that women without these gifts were to remain silent at prayer meetings. (1 Corinthians 14:34–35; 1 Timothy 2:11–12 even extends this prohibition to all women.) The gifts themselves could be exercised at meetings or whenever the Spirit inspired them to be used. Prophets, for example, were inspired speakers who might exercise their ministry during worship or whenever the Spirit moved them. Similarly teachers might instruct individuals privately or explain various teachings in the assembly. Other spiritual charisms included almsgiving and serving the needy, administrating and preaching, wisdom and faith, healing and working miracles, speaking in tongues and interpreting what was said in tongues (Romans 12:4–8; 1 Corinthians 12:4–11). Those who exercised these gifts performed a ministry or service, for they were given not for the benefit of the ones who had them but for the good of the community (1 Corinthians 12:12–30; Ephesians 4:11–12). Undoubtedly some of these ministries were sacramental; prophesy, healing, and speaking in tongues, for example, could arouse an immediate awareness of God's sacred presence in those who witnessed them. Those who performed them, however, were not necessarily elders or organizational leaders, so in that sense they were lay ministries. Nor were these gifts and ministries mutually exclusive; pastors, for instance, were expected to be good administrators and teachers as well.

Among all these named ministries, however, there was no specifically priestly ministry, no priesthood in the later Catholic sense. One reason for this is that priesthood at this time was identified with the ritual offering of animal and other sacrifices to God, and there was no one in the community designated to do this. Another reason is that the first generation of Christians, who were almost all Jews, accepted the legitimacy of the Jewish priesthood, and showed this by continuing to worship at the temple. But in AD 70 the temple was razed to the ground by the Roman army and the Jewish cultic priesthood ceased to exist. As Jews, those who believed that Jesus was the messiah had to ask themselves what this could possibly mean. Why had the almighty God allowed this to happen? How could this terrible desecration be part of God's plan for Israel?

Some time after the destruction of the temple, a Jewish Christian liv-ing in Italy composed a response to these troubling questions, perhaps intending it to be circulated among his fellow believers who were now dispersed throughout the empire. His name was not recorded, but his work became known as the Epistle to the Hebrews when it was included among the inspired documents of the New Testament. In it he developed the idea that Jesus' crucifixion was a sacrifice that replaced the need for temple offerings; it was a sacrifice that had been made once and for all, for it offered to God the perfect victim and the one who offered it was a perfect priest. That priest was Jesus, not a high priest by ancestry but a high priest of a new and eternal covenant between God and a new chosen people, a high priest of the same order as Melchizedek, whose priest-hood had no beginning and no end. The church was, therefore, a new Israel with a new priesthood and a new high priest who by his perfect life and sacrificial death had become the perfect mediator between God and humankind (Hebrews 3:1—10:18).

Through faith in Jesus and reception of the Spirit, then, Christians could experience a complete release from sin, which was something that the old repeated sacrifices could not accomplish. Moreover, by offering praises to God in their worship and by sharing their possessions with one another, Christians continued to make sacrifices that were pleasing to God (Hebrews 13:15–16). Other early writers took up this notion that what Christians did through their worship and their daily lives was a priestly activity of a holy people (1 Peter 2:1–10). They were a nation of priests who served God and who would reign with Christ at the end of time (Revelation 1:6; 5:10; 20:6). And so by the end of the first century, Christians had developed an understanding of priesthood that was based on but went beyond their Jew-ish heritage. There were no specific Christians who were called priests, but Christ himself was regarded as the high priest of the new religion and in a spiritual sense all believers were part of a priestly people called to honor God by praise and self-sacrifice.

During the second and third centuries, however, there were further developments in Christian ministry and self-understanding which led to a greater specification of roles in the church and to the identification of one of those roles as a priestly ministry. Elders, for example, were known in Greek as *presbyteroi* or "presbyters," and as the first generation of witnesses and apostles disappeared their role as leaders in the community and preservers of the tradition began to grow in importance. In some places the presiding elder or chief presbyter was the only one called *episkopos* or "bishop" since he was a general overseer of church affairs.[2] He was also the one who usually presided at the community's eucharistic worship, and as the eucharist began to be regarded as a sacrifice, the bishop's liturgical role began to be regarded as a priestly function (see pages 251–252). Other ministers were known as *diakonoi*, but as the church grew and their work became more specialized the designation "deacon" was used more as a title and less as a general descriptive term. By the end of the third century Christianity had an emerging organizational structure headed by presbyters, bishops, and deacons.

The development was gradual, however. Around the year 95 Christians in Corinth were apparently still supervised by a group of presbyters or elders without any single person in charge, and Clement of Rome sent them a letter protesting the way they had unfairly ousted some of their presbyters from office. And Rome itself, even with a presiding elder like Clement, kept its presbyterian form of church administration until the middle of the second century.

The same was true in most other cities, although not in Antioch. By about 110 the bishop there was clearly the one in charge with deacons as his administrative assistants and a council of presbyters as his personal advisors. Ignatius saw himself as standing in for Christ both at worship and in matters of doctrine. "No one should do anything that pertains to the church without the bishop's permission. The only proper eucharist is one that is celebrated by the bishop or one of his representatives. Whenever the bishop presides the whole community should be present, just as the whole church is present wherever Jesus Christ is. Nor is it right to conduct baptisms or communal meals without the bishop. Nevertheless, whatever has his approval also has God's approval, and so you can be sure that it is proper and true" (*Letter to the Smyrnaeans* 8). In Ignatius' eyes the bishop's authority in the local community was supreme, subject only to God, and unity with him in faith and practice was equivalent to unity with Christ himself.

One reason Ignatius and other bishops began to insist on episcopal authority and church unity was that the loose organization of the early church made it very difficult to keep a check on variations in doctrine and practice that were starting to spring up. A growing body of Christian literature encompassed not only the books contained in the present New Testament but also other gospels and letters, and there was as yet no uni-

---

[2]The word *bishop* comes from the Greek *episkopos* by way of the Latin *episcopus* and later the shortened Anglo-Saxon *biscop*.

versal consensus about which of them should be considered scriptural. Itinerant apostles and prophets still carried the Christian message to distant places, and normally when they came to an established community they were honored and allowed to preside over the Lord's supper. But sometimes the message they preached did not square with what the presbyters taught, and this led to internal dissensions. Sometimes charismatic prophets like Montanus and his followers claimed to have received new revelations directly from the Holy Spirit that flatly contradicted accepted doctrines. Other gnostics (the name derives from a Greek word meaning to know) also claimed to have a source of divine knowledge besides the received tradition, but often as not their knowledge ran counter to what most Christians believed in faith.

As a result, church leaders in established communities began to emphasize the importance of teaching what they had received from those apostles who had known the Lord. Moreover, since they safeguarded the apostolic doctrine they began to view themselves as "successors of the apostles" in matters of faith. Irenaeus of Lyons, for instance, saw himself as the guardian of a tradition that he had received from Polycarp of Smyrna, who had known the apostle John. And he regarded the bishop of Rome as a similar guardian of orthodoxy, since that community had been founded in the days of Peter and Paul. "We have a duty to obey the elders in the church since they are successors of the apostles and along with their succession as overseers have certainly been granted the spiritual gift of truth by the Father" (*Against Heresies* IV, 26, 2). The central importance of the bishop was stressed even more forcibly by Cyprian of Carthage a little while later: "You must realize that the bishop is where the church is and the church is where the bishop is, and that whoever is not with the bishop is not in the church" (*Letters* 66, 8). By the end of the second century, therefore, prophets as inspired teachers were being looked on with mistrust and the role of teacher in the church was increasingly assumed by the bishops. During the following century charismatic prophecy in the church as a recognized ministry slowly disappeared altogether.

But the need to check unorthodox teachings was not the only reason that bishops gained importance. Christian communities were growing from a few families in each city to a few hundred and in some metropolitan areas to a few thousand. In order to maintain all the ministries, more organization was needed, but about the only organizational structure known in the ancient world was an authoritarian one. Families were patriarchies and governments were monarchies, and so as local churches became more organized it seemed natural to have one person at the top overseeing all of the community's affairs.

As a new administrative pattern emerged in the third century, then, the bishop was at the top. In some places like Carthage in North Africa he still worked closely with the presbyters and did not make major decisions without their consent; in other places like Antioch in Syria he asked for their advice but for the most part he acted independently. But it was the bishop himself now who was responsible for the well being of the local church. He was its pastor, the shepherd of his flock. He kept it from wandering into heresy and he protected it as best he could against attacks by nonbelievers. He was the community's chief spokesman and its chief teacher. He taught the faithful during his sermon at the liturgy and he taught the catechumens who were preparing for baptism, or at least he supervised what and how they were taught. He acted as prophet when he preached the moral ideals of the Christian life and he acted as judge when he admitted new members to that life or reconciled old ones who had fallen away from it. He played the central role in community worship, leading it in prayer, receiving and offering its gifts of bread and wine to God. And as the worship over which he presided began to be viewed as a sacrifice of sorts, the bishop came to be viewed and sometimes spoken of as a priest, at least in his liturgical function. He was also the community's chief administrator, making liturgical arrangements, supervising the training of assistants, seeing to it that care was given to the needy.

Clearly the episcopacy was becoming a full-time occupation. At the beginning apostles, elders, supervisors, and others had performed their ministry in addition to whatever else they did for a living. Paul, for example, had been a tent maker, and in one of his letters Clement warned the ministers in Rome against being financial burdens on the community. But now in both the east and west bishops no longer had time to earn their own income and it was becoming accepted that they and their families should be supported by the offerings of the faithful.

Within a short time, even being released for full-time ministry was not enough. Bishops needed full-time assistance, and deacons were chosen to give it. Quite early in the development of the diaconate those who served the internal needs of the community had come under the supervision of the presbyters; then, as a single elder assumed more responsibility for directing the church's ministries, those called deacons came under his direct supervision. They were his special assistants especially in liturgical and financial matters, reading the scriptures and administering communion

during the liturgy, leading catechumens through the baptismal ritual, receiving and distributing goods to the needy, collecting contributions and
disbursing church funds.

Two documents written early in the third century indicate that during
this period the role of deacons was shifting from serving the community
to serving the bishop, even though by assisting the bishop in his ministry
they still ministered to the needs of the church. Both these documents
were ecclesiastical handbooks of sorts, outlining the duties and functions
of church ministers in liturgical and non-liturgical matters. *The Apostolic
Tradition*, which may date from the early third century, described deacons
as the bishop's personal aides in the eucharistic and baptismal liturgy, in
supervising church properties, and in caring for the sick. *The Instructions
of the Apostles*, a later work that originated in Syria, described them as servants and extensions of the bishop in his ministry to his people. They were
the bishop's eyes and ears, since the people were not supposed to bother
him with all their personal requests but they were to speak to the deacons
instead. They did anointings and other things at baptisms that the bishop
himself could not do for everyone, and they helped keep order during
the liturgy by guiding people to their proper places, leading them in their
prayer responses, and making sure that no one whispered or laughed or
fell asleep. In the east more than in the west deaconesses did for women
what deacons did for men, leading the women's section at prayer, anointing
and dressing women at baptisms, attending to the needs of widows and
other women in the community.

Being as visible as they were at liturgical functions and in charge of
practical ministries that served the community, deacons were often the most
powerful figures in the local church next to the bishop himself. In many
places they were the chief representatives of the people to the bishop and
his main executive officers. As vehicles of the bishop's ministry they were
allowed to baptize in times of emergency and sometimes even allowed to
reconcile penitents who were in danger of dying. Later on bishops would
complain that the deacons were abusing their power and steps would be
taken to curb it, but for the time being the diaconate was in the ascendancy.

As the prestige of the deacons went up, however, that of the presbyters
went down. Originally, elders had been associates of the one presiding elder
in a joint ministry of overseeing the community, but as the supervisor's
role became more liturgical and administrative the role of the other elders
became more subordinate and advisory. In the western part of the empire
they continued to have some functions independent of the bishop and acted

as a sort of parish council in each city; in the east they tended to be more completely under the bishop's authority and acted more like his personal board of advisors. In most places the presbyters sat alongside the bishop at the weekly celebrations of the eucharist, but in the east this was an honorary and passive role; in the west they sometimes placed their hands over the bread and wine along with the bishop and distributed communion. In the west, too, they occasionally presided over prayer services, eucharistic celebrations, and communal meals, but only in the bishop's absence and only with his permission. By and large, however, theirs was not a full-time ministry and unlike bishops and deacons the presbyters continued to hold regular jobs to support themselves and their families.

But how were these ministers chosen, and how were they appointed to their various ministries? Probably the first elders and supervisors in each community were appointed by the missionary apostle who founded it, but afterward it was common for local churches to select their own leaders. By the second century bishops and presbyters were usually elected by the people in the west, but in the eastern churches sometimes only the bishops were elected and the presbyters were appointed by him. During the third century bishops and presbyters were still usually elected, but there was a growing tendency in both the east and west to make the elections more limited. In some places the bishop had to be selected from among the presbyters; in others only the presbyters voted, and they generally picked someone from among their own number; in still others bishops from neighboring churches, especially those in large metropolitan areas, had a strong voice in the selection. But the people continued to have some voice in the matter since they were usually asked to approve those who were chosen as bishops and presbyters. Deacons, however, were simply appointed to their ministry by the bishop and did not need to have the people's explicit approval.

One thing that bishops, presbyters, and deacons had in common, though, was that they were all initiated into their service through a ritual laying on of hands. Some type of hand-laying became standard perhaps quite early, but *The Apostolic Tradition* is the first written record of formal ordination ceremonies. That document shows that the rite for conferring each ministry was an imposition of hands accompanied by a prayer, but how it was done and the prayer that went with it were different in each case. A bishop was ordained by the local presbyters and neighboring bishops, one of whom prayed that God would enable the candidate to serve the church as pastor and high priest with authority to offer the eucharistic gifts, to bind and loose, and to assign ministries to others. A presbyter had hands imposed on him by other presbyters and the local bishop, who prayed that God would give him the grace to counsel and govern the church with a pure heart. A deacon, however, received only the hand of his bishop since he was to be the bishop's servant and he was not the equal of the presbyters. At this period in history, then, there was a ritual initiation to these ministries, but the ordination consisted of a sign of approval and delegation of responsibility along with a petition for divine assistance, and the presbyterate and diaconate were not yet thought of as priestly ministries.

Nevertheless, the fact that they were "ordained" made these ministers members of a distinct "order" within the church. They therefore began to be regarded as "clergy," as persons who were set aside for sacred functions like the Roman priests and magistrates or the Jewish priests and Levites. During the third century it became more common to refer to bishops as priests, and occasionally even presbyters who were allowed to substitute for the bishop were seen as performing priestly functions. Cyprian of Carthage, for example, viewed the bishop as one who was "honored by the divine priesthood" and ordained to "service of the altar and sacrifice" (*Letters* 1, 1). And by the end of the third century Christians were becoming quite accustomed to calling their liturgical minister a "priest"—in Greek *hiereys*, and in Latin *sacerdos*.

But if the clergy were sacred persons they had to lead lives that were worthy of their calling, and during the second century Christian writers continued to insist that church leaders be persons of good moral character. Then, during the third century, as Christian ministers became regarded as belonging to a different order in the church, they began to be expected to behave not only well but differently, especially in the area of sex and marriage. The apostle Paul had praised the value of celibacy for those who were fully dedicated to the service of the Lord (1 Corinthians 7:32–38), and the gospels themselves praised those who had given up wife and family for the sake of the kingdom (Matthew 19:12, 29). Now, some began to apply these texts to those who were engaged in full-time ministry. Also during this period, Paul's criterion that a church leader should be a "one-woman man" began to be taken as meaning that bishops, presbyters, and deacons should not be married more than once. Montanists and other gnostics even regarded sex as impure, and so they demanded sexual abstinence of the church's leaders, who were supposed to be holy. And even more orthodox Christians began to compare bishops and deacons with the Jewish priests and Levites who were supposed to refrain from sexual intercourse whenever they served at the altar (Leviticus 22:3–6). But by and large Christian ministers continued to marry, even those who were ritually ordained to service.

In addition to bishops and presbyters, deacons and deaconesses, there was also an increasing number of other ministers in the church who were not ordained but only appointed to their functions. These became needed as communities grew larger, and initially they were viewed not as clergy but as lay ministers. "Subdeacons" helped the deacons in their practical ministries, "exorcists" assisted at rituals of initiation and repentance, "lectors" were appointed to read the scriptures loud and clear during worship, "porters" were assigned janitorial and guard duties, "acolytes" accompanied the bishop and acted as secretaries and messengers. The development of these specialized ministries was gradual and uneven, but they existed in most major churches by the end of the third century. Many communities also had official orders of "widows" and "virgins" who were appointed to pray for the church or to take care of the sick and needy. "Teachers" were assigned to instruct catechumens, and those with exceptional ability were sometimes allowed to preach to the faithful. Clement and Origen, for example, were both laymen who taught and wrote at the catechetical school of Alexandria (although they were also eventually ordained as presbyters). But the tendency to restrict specific ministries to specific orders or offices in the church was growing. In addition, there was a tendency to link these offices sequentially, so that together they provided a lengthy period of training through which individuals moved from lower to higher orders, and which were eventually referred to as holy orders.

These tendencies were confirmed and continued in the fourth and fifth centuries, with the result that those who performed official functions in the church came to be numbered among the clergy and only the clergy were allowed to perform these functions. The only exception to this was the deaconesses. Even though they were a distinct ministerial group, even though in some places they were ordained by a laying on of hands, and even though the notion that clerics should be married only once was applied to them, churchmen from the Council of Nicaea (in 325) onward ruled that female deacons were not to be counted among the clergy. Instead, deaconesses were considered as laypersons with a special church ministry, and there are indications that these women were sometimes the wives of bishops, presbyters, and deacons. Eventually, however, as male ministers in the church began to remain celibate and as ministry began to be associated with priesthood, the female diaconate disappeared. There are few records of deaconesses in the west after the fifth century, and the same is true of the east after the sixth century.

It was mainly during the fourth century, however, that a new type of priestly ministry began to appear. That was a pivotal period in church history, for it began with the last lengthy persecution of Christians under the emperor Diocletian and it ended with Christianity's being named the official religion of the state by the emperor Theodosius. Constantine's edict of toleration in 313 put an end to the persecution, and very quickly Christianity became the favored religion of a government that was trying to maintain the unity of an increasingly divided and unwieldy empire. The conversion of adults increased rapidly and with it rose the need for more ecclesiastical ministers. Bishops in large cities were no longer able to celebrate a single eucharist for their growing communities, nor were they able to reach all the outlying districts even for baptisms.

One early solution to the problem was the appointment of deacons to prepare catechumens and administer smaller churches in the bishop's name, but deacons still had to wait for the bishop to preside over the weekly liturgy and the initiation of new Christians. Another solution that was tried for a while in the east was the ordaining of assistant bishops to act as priests and pastors in rural areas while remaining under the supervision of the metropolitan bishop who ordained them. But the notion that bishops were the supreme authority in their own communities led many of the assistants to act quite independently, and this plan was quickly shelved. A third solution worked out much better in terms of preserving the authority of established bishops and therefore, as they saw it, the unity of regional churches. Presbyters already shared a certain dignity with bishops in that they were at least nominally "elders" in the church, and there was ample precedent for their presiding over the eucharist and other functions in the bishop's absence. More importantly, though, they had little independent authority, for in many places their bishops not only ordained but even selected them. The presbyters therefore were a readily available body of ordained clergy who could substitute for the bishop while remaining under his direction. And with increasing frequency presbyters were appointed to preside at eucharistic and baptismal liturgies at which the bishop could not be present.

In this way the role of presbyters in the church was drastically altered. Whereas before they were mainly a council of advisors who worked together in a single community, now they were individuals who acted alone in separate parishes. Whereas before they had few liturgical duties, now their duties were primarily liturgical. And whereas before their authority had come partly from being accepted by their fellow presbyters and approved by the people, now it was seen as coming entirely from the bishop. Like the deacons, presbyters were becoming regarded as extensions of the bishop's ministry.

Also like the deacons, presbyters were not allowed to do everything that the bishops could do. Theirs was a delegated ministry, and they were delegated to preside over the weekly eucharist and the yearly baptism as the bishop's representative. In Rome and other places in the west, bishops kept a symbolic unity with the presbyters by sending a piece of consecrated bread from his altar to the surrounding churches to be dropped in the chalice during the eucharistic service. As another sign of symbolic unity presbyters did not complete the initiation ritual and new Christians had to wait for the bishop's visit to receive the final consignation with oil. In both the west and east, moreover, some functions were never or seldom ever delegated to presbyters. They were not allowed to consecrate chrism, ordain ministers, or make other ecclesiastical appointments. Nor were they allowed to assign public penances or to reconcile penitents unless they were on their deathbed. Often, too, bishops reserved to themselves the right to preach in public, and in some places presbyters were even forbidden to preach without the express permission of their bishop.

Part of the reason for this restriction was the bishops' earnest attempt to keep heresy, witting or unwitting, to a minimum. But part of it was also the presbyters' lack of education. They were not trained in public speaking and they often did not have much theological training; the main requirement for ordination as a presbyter was a good moral life plus a knowledge of the required rituals. And these new presbyters frequently came from the lower classes of society, which did not afford them much education. Bishops on the other hand usually came from the upper classes. Their role as community leaders made the talented and skilled more obvious choices in the beginning, and as bishops began to play a greater part in the selection and ordination of other bishops the system became self-perpetuating. It was the beginning of a clear division between "upper" and "lower" clergy.

Moreover, just as in earlier times bishops had been regarded as priests because they offered the gifts in the eucharistic sacrifice, now presbyters, too, began to be looked on as priests because of their role in the liturgy. But if both bishops and presbyters were to be thought of as priests, some distinction had to be made between them since they did not hold the same position in the church. In the fourth century presbyters were often referred to as "priests" while bishops were given the more exclusive title of "high priest." In the fifth century the word presbyter became almost synonymous with "priest" even though officially presbyters were still regarded as "priests of the second order." Thereafter the Latin terms *presbyter* and *sacerdos* were practically interchangeable since all presbyters were priests and all priests were presbyters (including bishops, who were usually ordained both as presbyters and as bishops).[3]

In the meanwhile the diaconate as a separate ministry was gradually disappearing. Although bishops in larger cities still kept permanent deacons as part of their administrative and liturgical staff, many of the deacons' earlier ministries to the people at large were slowly being taken over by the presbyters who were now appointed to serve them. To some extent the deacons brought this on themselves when they tended to abuse their authority to the vexation of the bishops who appointed them. To a greater extent, though, the decline of the diaconate was due to the circumstances of the times. Bishops needed assistants who could officiate at the liturgy, and deacons were not empowered to do this. In order to provide more priests for the people, therefore, some bishops took to ordaining deacons as presbyters, thereby making the presbyterate look like a higher rank rather than a different type of ministry. In addition, since presbyters were now seen as sharing in the priesthood of the bishop, the diaconate no longer seemed as important as the presbyterate, and deacons were sometimes even appointed to assist presbyters as well as bishops. By the fifth century the diaconate was beginning to be viewed as a step toward the priesthood and after the sixth century the permanent diaconate all but vanished.

The same thing happened to other ecclesiastical ministries, especially those connected with official church functions. Subdeacons were now perceived as being on the road to the diaconate, while porters and lectors, exorcists and acolytes, were looked upon as eventual candidates for the priesthood. Moreover, those who performed these functions came to be increasingly regarded as clerics themselves, and their ministries instead of being separate and permanent became sequential and temporary. They were no longer duties performed by lay members of the community but rather they were offices in an increasingly organized church administration. Admission to each office came through a ceremonial induction and brought with it not just duties but privileges. In time the order of clergy became

---

[3]The English word "priest" comes from the Greek presbyteros through the Latin presbyter and the shortened early form prester.

a graded series of orders, paralleling the graded ranks in the Roman civil service, with porters at the bottom and bishops at the top. In time, too, this hierarchical arrangement came to be regarded as divinely ordained so that only those who had advanced through the ranks, so to speak, could be admitted to the higher offices. The term "holy orders" thus referred to the ranks or levels in the church's hierarchy: just as the army had military ranks or orders, just as the government had administrative levels or orders, so the church had ecclesiastical offices or holy orders.

This reservation of ministry to those who were members of the clergy had a number of social as well as theological repercussions. The Roman Empire had had priests before its official sanction of Christianity, and now that bishops and presbyters were being regarded as priests they were given many of the same social privileges that the former priests had enjoyed. They were exempted from military service and they were excused from certain civic obligations; for example, they did not have to pay taxes on their property whether it belonged to the church or to them personally. These privileges, along with the honor that is usually given to mediators of the sacred in any culture, turned the Christian clergy into a distinct group who appeared to be socially and even morally superior to the mass of the faithful. At one time, supervisors, teachers, and others had been chosen for their ministries because they had an ability to perform them; now those who were ordained to these ministries were thought of as having these abilities by reason of their office. Lectors had once been chosen for their reading ability, for example, but now they were considered as empowered to read in virtue of their ordination. Similarly bishops had once been elected because they seemed to have the gifts of administering and teaching, but now those who held the episcopal office were considered to have such gifts as well as the right to use them simply because they were bishops. As clergy their function was to teach, rule, and sanctify the faithful and so they had to have the qualities needed to fulfill their duties. Those in clerical orders, therefore, were perceived as having knowledge, power, and holiness that set them apart from ordinary Christians. But this recognition that the clergy were different also brought with it demands that the clergy be different. Bishops and presbyters especially were expected to be models of Christian virtue for their people to follow. And those in any order were expected to do their work well, for that was the duty of their office and they received the grace necessary to fulfill it. So the separation of the clergy from the laity brought with it responsibilities as well as privileges.

Bishops more than any other were expected to have the spiritual gifts or graces needed to be leaders in the church, and so those who did not seem to have them were sometimes attacked as unworthy or even deposed from their office. It was also reasoning like this that lay, in part, behind the Donatist controversy which lasted from the third to the fifth century (see pages 41–42). Donatus had argued that bishops and priests who became apostates or heretics had evidently lost the Holy Spirit and its gifts, and so they could not communicate it to others through ordination or even baptism. But as possession of the Spirit and spiritual gifts came to be viewed as a function of office rather than lifestyle, the exercise and transmission of those gifts came to be viewed as independent of the worthiness of the minister.

In other ways, too, bishops were perceived as special persons because during the patristic period many of them were just that. Some of them were outstanding preachers and theologians, earning for themselves the eventual title "fathers of the church." Many of them since the days of Constantine were civil magistrates who probated wills and estates, provided for orphans, settled grievances against the clergy (who were immune from state prosecution), and arbitrated differences between clerics themselves. As members of a ruling class they had power that set them above the people. As members of a wealthy class they had property that most people did not have. And as members of a priestly class they had the honor and respect due a cultic priesthood.

For quite some time as well bishops and deacons had been different from other Christians in that they were engaged in full-time ministry and were financially supported by the community. Now this same exemption from worldly affairs was seen as applying to presbyters and other clerics. Jewish priests and Levites had been supported by the offerings that they received, and since the Jewish priesthood was becoming viewed as the forerunner of the Christian priesthood in the service of the one true God, it did not seem proper to have Christian ministers earning their own living. Some local councils even forbade the clergy in their provinces from engaging in business for profit; others simply admonished them not to spend more time making money than serving their people. These regulations were easier to legislate than to put into practice, however. Often enough they were easy for bishops to follow since bishops were sometimes independently wealthy, and even if they were not their election put the resources of a whole diocese at their disposal. But presbyters in rural areas often came from the people they served and the people they served were often poor. And besides, since more people in the Roman Empire were now born into their religion, presbyters no longer had to instruct catechumens or set up social services and so their ministry was largely limited to cultic worship, which did not take much of their time. By and large the clergy remained active in other than clerical affairs: the lower clergy still had to earn their own living by farming or practicing a trade, and the upper clergy managed their own or the church's wealth as landlords and bankers besides continuing to act as civil magistrates.

Although bishops had been wearing the insignia of their civil office during the liturgy since the middle of the fourth century, clerics were not supposed to wear any distinctive clothing at other times as late as 428. In that year Pope Celestine wrote to some bishops in southern Gaul reminding them that they should be distinguishable from other Christians by their life and teaching, not by their dress. Nevertheless, later in the fifth century clerics in many parts of the empire took to wearing a long robe as a sign of their status in society rather than the short tunic that was worn by ordinary people. It was the beginning of a distinctive style of clerical dress that was to last until modern times.

This conception that the clergy were different from the faithful not just in terms of their ministry but also in a deeper spiritual sense also found its way into Christian theology during the fourth and fifth centuries. Some of the eastern fathers reflected on the scriptures in the light of their own experience of ministry and saw themselves and other priests as revealers and dispensers of divine mysteries, as necessary intermediaries between God and humankind. In the first theological treatise devoted entirely to the Christian ministry, John Chrysostom wrote: "No one can enter the kingdom of heaven without being born again by water and the spirit, and anyone who does not eat the flesh of the Lord will not have eternal life. However, the only way we can receive these good things is through the consecrated hands of priests. It is the priests who bring us to spiritual birth through baptism....They also have the power to free us from sins committed after baptism" (*On the Priesthood* III, 5–6). Priests were therefore human instruments through which God acted, but since God could act perfectly even through imperfect instruments, their personal shortcomings did not matter. No person was worthy of the honor to be such a sacred instrument, and so the moral faults of priests did not impede the Holy Spirit from acting through their hands just as they did not stop God's word from coming through their mouths. Those who listened to their priests, therefore, heard the voice of God speaking to their hearts, and those who rejected what their priests did for them rejected both the authority and the grace of God.

According to the Greek fathers, then, priests were sacramental persons through whom God acted in all their ministerial functions. They were made such by their ordination as priests, by that same spiritual power which changed water into baptism, stones into a sacred altar, and bread into the body of Christ. The word spoken by the ordaining bishop was a divine word, said Gregory of Nyssa: "The power of that divine word bestows a special dignity on the priest, and the blessing separates him from the ranks of the people. Yesterday he was but one of the crowd, but now he has been appointed to govern and preside, heal and instruct. Outwardly he looks like he did before, but inwardly he is transformed by an invisible power and grace" (*On the Baptism of Christ*).

These same sentiments were echoed in the Latin west in the writings of Augustine, who conceived the interior transformation of the priest as analogous to what happened to every Christian at baptism. Writing against the Donatists he argued that presbyters ordained by unworthy ministers did not have to be reordained because at their ordination they received a spiritual character, an image of the priestly Christ, not from the ordaining minister but from Christ himself. Like the seal of baptism this priestly character was a *sacramentum*, a sacred sign impressed on the soul once and for all: "Each is a sacrament and each is given by a sort of consecration, one when a man is baptized and the other when he is ordained. For this reason neither one is allowed to be repeated in the church of God" (*Against Parmenian* 2, 13). Like the bond of marriage this character was a sign of who the priest was and what he was called to be: "If a priest is degraded from his office because of some offense, the sacrament of the Lord which he once received will not be lost, though it may remain to his judgment" (*On the Benefit of Marriage* 24, 32). And this was why even a bad priest was still a minister of true sacraments and the true word of God, for it was Christ who acted through his gestures and it was God's word that he proclaimed when he performed his priestly duties.

What the fathers wrote about the priesthood applied primarily to the bishops' priesthood, although by extension it applied to the priesthood of the presbyters as well. But this extension of priestly ministry to the presbyterate began to raise an important theological question, namely, what was the difference between these two priesthoods? A number of fathers taught that there was none, or if there were it was very slight since all priests were sharers in the one priesthood of Christ. The scripture scholar Jerome saw that in New Testament times *presbyteros* and *episkopos* had been interchangeable terms, and so he reasoned that the difference between priests and bishops must have arisen later in the church, not by divine ordinance but2 because of a practical need to have one presbyter in charge. John Chrysostom came to the same conclusion from his reading of Paul's epistles: "There is no great difference between presbyters and bishops. Both had held positions as teachers and presidents in the church, and what he said about bishops can also be applied to presbyters. For they are only superior in having the power to ordain, and appear to have no other advantage over presbyters" (*Homilies* 11). The difference between the two orders, therefore, was a difference in authority and jurisdiction, not a difference in priesthood. Their priestly powers were the same, for both could baptize and consecrate the eucharist and preach the word of God. But the authoritative power of the bishop was greater since he had greater responsibility in the church: he was the pastor of a larger flock and the spiritual shepherd of all the people under his jurisdiction, he was in charge of preserving the unity of the church and the integrity of the faith, and so he had to supervise the presbyters and insure that their priestly ministry continued in the church.

One thing about which all the fathers were agreed, however, was that the transmission of clerical power came through ordination, and that ordination consisted in the imposition of hands. Ordination had always been a sacred ritual for it was an initiation into a sacred ministry, but now in the patristic period it came to be understood as something more. As Gregory indicated and Augustine reaffirmed, the imposition of hands effected a metaphysical transformation in the one ordained. It was a work of the Holy Spirit, caused by the power of God's word spoken by and through the ordaining minister. When bishops ordained bishops they gave them—or rather, transmitted to them—the spiritual power to be teachers and rulers of the church, and to ordain others. And when bishops ordained presbyters they likewise transmitted to them the power to be priests of the new covenant, sharing the priesthood of Christ in the order of Melchizedek, the priesthood which supplanted and was superior to the priesthood of Aaron and Levi because it offered to God the perfect sacrifice.

But if the Christian priesthood were a newer and greater priesthood than that of the Jewish priests and Levites, then it seemed logical that Christian clerics would be called to a greater holiness than the priests of the old covenant. Holiness in the ancient world, however, was closely connected with purity, and purity among other things meant sexual abstinence. Thus with the evolution of Christian ministry into a cultic priesthood came a demand for sexual purity and ultimately for celibacy.

Originally, of course, almost all Christian ministers had married. Even though some early writers like Tertullian praised those who preferred to be "wedded to God," most Christian communities in the second and third centuries followed the advice of the New Testament's pastoral epistles and chose good family men as leaders. Even as late as 393 the council of Hippo in Africa admonished bishops to be strict with their sons, not letting them attend immoral entertainments and not allowing them to marry pagans or heretics. In the fourth century the virtual self-selection of bishops from among the upper classes led in some cases to the establishment of episcopal dynasties, especially in the east. Gregory of Nyssa succeeded his father as bishop, and two of his cousins were also bishops. And Polycrates of Ephesus at one point defended his knowledge of ancient tradition by reminding his critics that he was the eighth generation of his family to serve as bishop in that region.

Nevertheless, in the third century Montanists, Manichaeans, and other gnostics began to propose that intercourse and procreation were sinful, and the stoic philosophers suggested that sexual desire was something to be suppressed. Later, Augustine and others argued that lust was the result of an original sin that was transmitted from one generation to another through sexual intercourse. Many of these groups and individuals encouraged continence and extolled virginity as means of achieving spiritual perfection, while they disparaged marriage as anything from absolutely evil to morally tolerable. Christians themselves sometimes cited scriptural texts which supported the notion that the perfect should remain virginal although weaker persons were allowed to marry (for example, Matthew 19:10–12, and 1 Corinthians 7:8–9).

As early as the opening decades of the fourth century, local councils of bishops at Ancyra and Neocaesarea in the east and at Elvira and Arles in the west passed canons restricting the freedom of clerics in those regions either to marry or, if they were already married, to have sexual relations with their wives. A proposal in the same vein was presented at the General Council of Nicaea in 325, but the motion was defeated.

Within a half century, however, the increasing tendency to view the eucharist as a sacrifice and to regard liturgical ministers as priests led churchmen especially in the west to suggest that the Jewish laws forbidding ministers to have marital relations during their service in the temple should be applied to the Christian clergy. Ambrose of Milan even argued that since Christian priests served at the altar all their lives (unlike their Jewish predecessors, who served only periodically) they should live in a state of perpetual continence. "You have received the grace of the sacred ministry with an untouched body, an undefiled modesty and an unfamiliarity with carnal relations. You are aware that you must continue in a ministry which is unhampered and spotless, one which should not be profaned by conjugal intercourse." And after describing how the Israelites were supposed to purify themselves by washing their clothes before participating in a sacrifice, Ambrose went on: "If even the people were forbidden to take part in the offering without having washed their clothes, would you dare to make an offering for others with a defiled mind and body? Would you dare act as their minister?" (*On the Duties of Ministers* I, 50).

The ideal of sexual continence, however, was not always seen as requiring an unmarried clergy. Through the end of the fourth century in the west it was more often taken to mean that married clerics should stop living with their wives, or at least stop having sexual relations. Local councils at Rome, Turin, Toledo, and Carthage passed canons to that effect, usually denying promotion to those who obviously disregarded the regulations by having children. The canons applied not only to priests but also to deacons, since they, too, served at the altar. And the theological rationale for them was summed up by Innocent I in the year 404: "Priests and deacons should have no sexual relations with their wives since they are engaged in the demands of a daily ministry. For it is written [in the book of Leviticus]: 'You shall be holy, for I the Lord your God am holy'" (*Letter to Victricius*). Needless to say, however, the regulations were easier to follow and enforce if those who wished to enter the clergy did not marry to begin with, and so the ideal of continence gradually became an ideal of celibacy.

In the east the notion of ritual purity was never taken to mean complete abstinence, perhaps because the eucharistic liturgy was usually not celebrated more than weekly. Some churches insisted that those who were already in clerical orders should not marry but others did not, and *The Apostolic Constitutions* composed in Syria expressly forbade bishops, priests, and deacons to leave their wives on the pretext of piety. Toward the end of the fourth century, however, many eastern churches began to choose monks who were known for their holiness as bishops. The monks, even though they were not yet ordained, were already vowed to a life of celibacy, and so they remained celibate during their episcopacy. Not all eastern bishops were monks, however, and not all of them were unmarried, for the emperor Justinian in the sixth century found it necessary to pass laws making it illegal for children of bishops to inherit church property. Finally in 692 a council of eastern bishops met in Constantinople to compose general norms for the clergy in their churches. They agreed that married men could be admitted to clerical orders but that unmarried clerics had to remain unmarried. However, married priests and deacons had to abstain from sexual relations with their wives on days when they presided at the liturgy, and when they traveled in Latin rite countries. Lastly, any married priest who became a bishop had to separate from his wife by mutual consent, and she had to retire to a distant monastery. This last canon eventually guaranteed that only celibate priests and widowers would be nominated to the episcopacy, and all of these norms have remained in effect in Orthodox churches until the present day.

In the Latin west the canonical norms of continence and celibacy remained in effect through the fifth century in the churches which had them, supported on the one hand by the patristic theology of the priesthood and on the other hand by a growing belief that Christian holiness meant renouncing the things of this world. Originally those who rejected what they perceived as the worldliness of imperial Christianity were lay people, ascetics who fled to the deserts of Egypt to find God in solitude. But it was not long before they were joined by others who founded monastic communities, first for men and later for women, first throughout the east and then also in the west. Those who entered the monasteries dedicated themselves to the pursuit of holiness, giving up all material comforts and pleasures including sex. They led a life of penitence even though they had not been notorious sinners, and eventually those who joined their communities were often inducted into this way of life through a sacramental ritual similar to the one used for public penitents (see page 334). They were, in effect, a new type of prophet in the church, speaking out by their words and actions against the temptations of materialism and power, and witnessing by their lives to the gospel ideals of poverty and simplicity.

Bishops were not monks, but many bishops were impressed by the monks' spirit of heroic asceticism and they sometimes encouraged the foundation of monasteries within their territories and appointed presbyters to serve as chaplains for them. They also sometimes had unmarried clerics join together in monastery-like communities where they could be trained in their duties, instructed in theology, and introduced to the ideal of ascetic holiness. Augustine and other bishops even lived this common life with some of their clergy, encouraging them not only to sanctity but also to celibacy. For a while at least a celibate clergy seemed a real possibility.

But it was not to last. As Christian populations increased, more and more presbyters had to live further away from the bishops and their community houses, and once again many of them married. And as the Germanic invasions swept through Europe and North Africa, both civil and ecclesiastical laws became harder to enforce, including the canons commanding continence. Still, the monastic seed had been planted in the soil of the priesthood. It would grow again in the seventh century when monks were ordained priests in order to complete the conversion of Europe and again in the ninth-century reforms begun under Charlemagne, but it would not really flower until the monk who became Gregory VII brought about a widespread reform of the clergy in the eleventh century and succeeded for the first time in mandating celibacy for all the priests in the Catholic Church.

3. Holy Orders in the Middle Ages

The city of Rome fell to the Visigoths in 410, and in 476 the last emperor in the west was deposed and sent off to Constantinople, the capital of the eastern part of the Roman Empire, by his Germanic conquerors. The churches in the east continued to be protected by the imperial government, but those in the west now found themselves in a historically unique situation. There was no longer any central government in Europe and so the bishops themselves began to exercise more authority in their territories.

Nor were the bishops totally unprepared for this new role. They were already some of the best educated men in their society since they often came from upper-class families. They were already rulers of sorts, not only because of their authority in the church but also because they had had civil responsibilities in the old empire. And they were already administrators of lands and other wealth that their churches had accumulated from private and public donations. They were also a self-perpetuating government, for the popular election of bishops was a thing of the past, and now bishops were either appointed by their predecessor or chosen by nearby bishops. (The major exception to this was Rome, where bishops continued to be elected by the presbyters who were the pastors of the parish churches in the city. To this day, Catholic cardinals are titular pastors of Roman parishes, in virtue of which they are entitled to elect the pope.)

But the bishops had no armies. The Roman legions were gone. And so the bishops had come to terms with the Germanic invaders as best they could, first by negotiation and later by alliance as the tribes settled down in the former provinces. Slowly as the new inhabitants intermarried with the old and accepted their religion, a new Europe began to emerge, and bishops began to see themselves as the spiritual rulers of a Christian society. The bishops were the vicars of Christ on earth, governing God's people with the consent and support of their own local leaders, concerned for their temporal needs, and guiding them on the path to salvation.

To prove the antiquity and legitimacy of their authority, early medieval bishops often tried to trace their ancestry, as Irenaeus had done centuries before, back through the apostles to Christ himself. And since many European churches had been founded by missionaries sent out from Rome, which claimed the apostle Peter as its first bishop, that city retained much of the prestige that it had had when it was the center of the empire. Even during the days of the empire the bishop of Rome had been regarded as a touchstone of orthodoxy in the west, just as the patriarchs of Constantinople and other major churches had been regarded in the east. At that time the bishop of Rome had had no administrative authority over the bishops in the provinces, but since the middle of the fifth century the Roman bishops had had an increasingly strong voice in the selection of provincial bishops. And now as bishops began to be seen more as rulers than as shepherds of their people, the bishop of Rome began to be seen as the bishop of bishops, the source of episcopal authority in the church.

This impression was heightened after the sixth century because in many cases it was true. Gregory I and popes after him sent missionary monks, some of whom they ordained bishops, northward into Germany, France, and Britain to convert the native populations there, and since popes had appointed them, they and their successors owed their authority directly and indirectly to the bishop of Rome. Later in the eighth and ninth centuries the popes in Italy allied themselves with the Frankish rulers of central Europe, and Charlemagne himself increased the prestige of Rome by approving its liturgical customs and canon laws for use in his empire. And after the breakdown of that empire during the succeeding centuries, the only central authority left in Europe was that of the papacy. It was not always a strong authority, but it was central to European Christianity.

Thanks to donations of land by Pippin and his son Charlemagne, the bishop of Rome was also the sovereign ruler of central Italy. Bishops elsewhere had similar though not such extensive holdings surrounded by the claims of barons, dukes, and other nobles as medieval Europe became a feudal society. The feudal system was basically a pyramid, with peasants at the bottom being protected by and paying taxes to local landlords, who along with others had a similar relation to their lords, who in turn owed allegiance to their own overlords, and so on up to the sovereign ruler of the region. Medieval bishops fit into this picture by being lords of their own estates as well as by being the ecclesiastical leaders of the clergy in their dioceses, which extended beyond the boundaries of the church's property. From their lands they derived an income, to their subjects they owed whatever protection and social services they could provide, and to their sovereigns they owed loyalty and service. (Church lands were usually exempt from taxes.)

There were thus two lines of authority in feudal Europe. Political authority traced itself down from the sovereigns through their vassal lords to the peasants. Spiritual authority traced itself down from the bishops through the lower clergy to the faithful. But these two lines of authority often intermingled since the bishops, as members of the upper classes, were often as not sons and nephews, cousins and brothers, of the secular rulers. So the lord bishops played a dual role in society, and characteristically they were nominated for their office by their sovereign but ordained by their fellow bishops. Both church and state preferred celibate bishops—the church to keep its property intact and the state to keep the bishops from establishing dynasties—but since church and state were often related by blood it was sometimes mutually advantageous to let a bishop's son succeed him. Otherwise the bishop's children might be landless and reduced to peasantry.

Although they were still ordained as priests, bishops were now primarily rulers. They offered the mass in their cathedral parish, presided over baptisms, and ordained clergy when they were needed, but primarily they were administrators. Occasionally they met in council with other bishops of the region, but when they did it was usually to discuss disciplinary and not doctrinal matters. On their own lands the lord bishops supervised the collecting of revenues, the care of church buildings, and the renting of farmlands. Some of them maintained orphanages for the homeless and hostels for travelers; others organized charities for the poor. To help them in their work they had an administrative staff of clerics, at the top of which was a curia of advisors or department heads. Like other nobles they presided over their own court, discussing matters of state, issuing directives for their subjects, and judging cases that were brought to their attention. Like other nobles, too, they sometimes went to war either to protect their territories or to expand them. And like other nobles they did not have too much contact with the common people but appointed others to act in their name.

Those whom they appointed to perform ecclesiastical duties were almost always priests, since by now the diaconate had disappeared as a permanent order in all but a few places. Priests who worked in the cathedral and other city parishes were often, like their lord bishop, members of a distinct social group, separated from the laity by their dress, their special duties, and the Latin language in which they performed them. Priests who worked in country parishes, however, lived and worked with the people they served, and except for when they performed their priestly functions they were not much different from other rural peasants. They were not well educated, but they did have to know how to read the mass or recite it by heart, and how to administer the other sacraments. Their main duties were therefore not pastoral but liturgical: baptizing infants, offering the eucharistic sacrifice, hearing confessions, giving blessings, presiding at funerals. They did little preaching, except to remind the faithful of their sacramental and moral obligations. So they spent most of their time earning a living to support themselves and their families, when they had them, usually by farming or practicing a trade.

The lord bishops were expected to provide chapels and priests for the peasants who lived on church lands, but the lords of other lands were expected to do the same for their own subjects. Thus many of the smaller churches in the early Middle Ages were owned by lay people, since they were in the villages that the nobles controlled, and the income that the churches received in the form of offerings went to them as landowners. In return the nobles maintained the church buildings and paid the salaries of the priests, whom they often appointed and then sent to the neighboring bishop to train and ordain. But the priests' functions were mainly cultic and took only a small part of their time, and so those who lived on the lord's private estate were often employed as clerks and stewards while those who lived in the villages supplemented their small income in other ways. Moreover, if they performed their priestly functions well, there was a good chance that they might prevail upon their lord to let one of their sons succeed them, especially if he was already trained.

Most people in the early Middle Ages, therefore, were probably served by married clergy, and they were probably unaware of the ancient canons that forbade priests to have intercourse with their wives. In many ways medieval priests were more like the cultic ministers of ancient Israel than like the professional pastors of early Christianity, and so a married clergy seemed quite natural. In fact, bishops and local councils occasionally complained about the marriage regulations that were so impossible to enforce, and they sometimes justified their complaints by appealing to the Old Testament evidence that priests and Levites had married, as well as the New Testament evidence that Peter and other early church leaders had had wives.

The one group of clerics that usually did not marry were the monks, who lived in monastic communities rather than alone, and who vowed (as monks, not as priests) to remain celibate. Of course this did not always prevent the monks from taking wives or concubines, but periodic reforms of the monasteries like the one that took place under Charlemagne kept the ideal of celibacy in the forefront. Also, as the monasteries grew in size and number the monastic idea of holiness became the medieval model of Christian perfection, and since priests were supposed to be holy men, it became a model for the Christian priesthood as well.

It was also the monks who reestablished and maintained many of the ministries that had once been performed by lay people and ordinary clergy during the first Christian centuries. They were teachers, keeping alive the arts of reading and writing, preserving and copying, manuscripts of the Bible and liturgical books, and establishing schools that eventually provided the educational basis for medieval universities. They were prophets, preaching conversion and repentance and carrying private confession into the countryside during the early Middle Ages, and bearing witness to a spiritual lifestyle of total dedication to God. They were servants, caring for the sick and poor in their monasteries, and sometimes founding separate institutions for this work.

Eventually new religious orders were founded by charismatic figures to carry out new and even novel ministries that the regular clergy and established orders seemed to be overlooking. The Knights Templars protected pilgrims to the Holy Land after the first crusade, and as priests served as chaplains during the later ones. The Trinitarians dedicated themselves to the ransoming of Christians who were taken captive and sold as slaves during these wars. The Dominicans and Franciscans were originally founded to preach the gospel, the Dominicans to the Albigensians and the Fransiscans to the poor, but their work as teachers gradually led many of their members to become professional theologians. Women, too, were newly attracted by this resurgence in religious life, and even though they were not allowed to be clerics they still pursued the same spiritual ideals of prayer and service. The monastic influence was even felt by the regular clergy, who sometimes organized themselves into semi-monastic communities serving the major cathedrals. Some of these new orders like the Templars and the Franciscans were originally lay groups, but the now traditional identification of ministry and priesthood led most of their later members to be ordained, even if the only specifically priestly function they performed was the saying of daily mass. And many of these orders were very much unlike the older cloistered communities in that they deliberately engaged themselves in active ministries that took them out of their communal residences. Yet the general pattern of life that they followed and the spiritual ideal that they aimed at in their ministry and priesthood was a monastic one.

Most of these new developments occurred in the twelfth and thirteenth centuries, but their roots lay in the eleventh-century reforms of the traditional monasteries and the clergy in general. The monastic reform was largely a spiritual one, calling the monks to return to the lives of austerity and holiness for which the monasteries had originally been founded. But the clerical reform was also motivated by political considerations, and it was initiated by the first of the great medieval popes, Gregory VII, himself a monk. Since the early Middle Ages the power of lay nobles over church offices and lands had been growing, and the tendency of churchmen to pass their titles and holdings on to members of their own family was as great as it had ever been. But the political power of the popes had also been growing since the days of Charlemagne, and now Gregory perceived the power of the nobles and the independence of the bishops as a threat to the medieval ideal of a Christian society headed by the bishops and ultimately by the bishop of Rome. Through years of continuous persuasion and pressure (which were also continued by his successors) Gregory began to ensure that bishops would owe their allegiance to the pope rather than to their sovereign by having them elected by other bishops rather than appointed by lay lords, and he insisted that the ancient canons regarding clerical continence be strictly enforced. Under the impetus of reform, priests also began to be forbidden to engage in certain occupations that were considered unworthy of their calling—like being brewers or bartenders, tailors or perfumers, money changers or tax collectors—and they were encouraged to live as much as possible on the offerings of their parishioners.

The eleventh and twelfth centuries also saw a great increase in ecclesiastical organization, and the more organized the church became the more the lines of authority ultimately led to Rome. Canon laws were collected and classified by Gratian and others, and conflicting regulations were weeded out. Some types of legal disputes had already been able to be appealed to Rome, and now Rome assumed even greater authority in deciding what the laws of the church would be. The papal curia expanded in size and influence as it began to take on administrative duties for the whole church and not just the diocese of Rome. And the presbytery of Roman pastors developed into the college of cardinals, a collection of European church-men who not only elected the pope but also influenced worldwide church policy. Increasingly it seemed that all authority in the church was vested in the bishop of Rome, and that all power in the church flowed from the pope through the bishops to the priests.

This same period also saw the popes call the first general councils to meet in over two hundred and fifty years. The church's bishops assembled in the Lateran basilica in Rome four times in less than a hundred years, from 1123 to 1215, and each time they dealt with matters of church discipline. They decreed as universal laws of the church that lay people could not hold church property or make appointments to church offices. They prohibited church lands and offices from being hereditary. They established procedures for the election of the pope and they set standards for those who could be appointed bishops and ordained priests. They suspended clerics who flagrantly disregarded the church's laws or behaved immorally, and they tightened the accountability of priests to bishops and bishops to the pope. On the matter of clerical marriage the First Lateran Council prohibited those in holy orders from marrying at all, and it ordered all married priests to renounce their wives and do penance. The Second Lateran Council fifteen years later took a step further and declared that marriages of clerics were not only illegal but also invalid. Henceforth such marriages would be re-garded as nonexistent in the eyes of the church, unless those who asked to marry first received a special dispensation from Rome and were willingly suspended from all priestly duties. It was not until the hierarchy had taken legal control of marriage, therefore, that they had a legally enforceable way of controlling clerical marriage (see pages 430–431). And even though this new and more stringent law sometimes continued to be violated, it signaled the end of the married priesthood in the Catholic Church.

These developments in Christian ministry during the early Middle Ages were reflected in the changes of the ordination ritual between the sixth and the thirteenth centuries. In the sixth century priests were still ordained with a laying on of hands, as was the practice in the patristic period. In the later Roman Empire, however, one way to invest people into positions of authority had been to dress them in the insignia of their office, and since Christian ministers now wore special clothing during liturgical functions this practice was extended to clerics as well. In seventh-century Spain, for example, deacons were dressed in an alb and stole during their ordination, priests were again given the stole but also the chasuble which only they wore, and bishops were invested with a stole, ring, and crosier (miters were not introduced until the eleventh century). Gradually the custom spread to France and Germany and eventually into Italy. The practice was a visible expression of the idea that ministry in the church was an office bestowed by one in authority.

In feudal society another way of investing people into positions of authority was to give them symbolic tokens of their responsibilities. Rulers, for example, were given crowns and scepters, and now those in holy orders began to be given signs of their duties at their ordination. Porters thus received a key, lectors a book of the epistles, and acolytes a candle; deacons were given a book of the gospels, which they were now empowered to read at mass, and priests were given a paten and chalice with bread and wine as symbolic of their power to consecrate the eucharist. In addition, the priests' hands began to be anointed with oil during their ordination, partly in imitation of Old Testament precedents and partly in recognition of the priests' sacred power to consecrate and touch the body of Christ.

The fact that ordination was understood as a conferral of power was also reflected in the prayers that were said by the ordaining bishop. Priests were seen as receiving the power to offer the mass and, later, to forgive sins. Bishops were seen as receiving the power to rule and sanctify the church, and thus to pass laws and ordain others to the priesthood. But since the height of priestly power was now considered to be the power to consecrate and offer the eucharist, bishops were not believed to receive any additional priestly powers when they were elevated to their office. What they received, then, was not a power of orders but a power of jurisdiction, and the episcopacy was no longer regarded as a distinct priestly order or ministry.

These new ordination rituals and the theology that accompanied them made their way into Rome the same way that the medieval ritual for confirmation did. In the eighth century Charlemagne had asked for and received a copy of the Gregorian sacramentary from Rome, which was then adapted to meet the needs of priests and bishops in the Frankish empire. In the tenth century the altered sacramentary was brought back to Rome, where it succeeded in replacing the original one, and in the eleventh and twelfth centuries the new rituals were diffused through Europe in the drive toward clerical reform and compliance with the customs of Rome. To make them easier to handle, the rites that were performed only by bishops were separated from the others and put into a separate book, which continued to be revised slightly wherever it was used. The last significant revision was made by William Durand toward the end of the thirteenth century. In his revision of the ordination rite all of the various actions that had come to signify the conferral of the priesthood were arranged in a liturgically orderly way, and his book became widely adopted throughout Europe (including Rome) during the following century. After that, there were no major changes in the Catholic ordination rite until the twentieth century.

Even before Durand's revision of the rite, however, the inclusion of so many distinct actions in the ordination ceremony posed a problem for scholastic theologians. At which point in the ceremony was the priesthood conferred—at the imposition of hands, the vesting, the anointing, or the giving of the chalice and paten? Some like Bonaventure argued that the imposition of hands had to be the essential part of the rite since it went back to the days of the apostles. Others like Aquinas believed that the essential ritual was the handing over of the liturgical instruments since these more clearly signified the transmission of priestly power. In the end most tended to agree with Aquinas, but it remained a theologically open question since there was no clear way to decide the issue. In the Roman ordination ceremony all four actions were performed, and whatever the precise moment of ordination was, Catholic theologians all agreed that when they were completed a priest was fully ordained.

A second and more complicated problem had to do with the status of ordination as a sacrament. On the one hand there were many "orders" of ministry in the church—lay monks and nuns, abbots and abbesses, bishops and priests—and all those in them were initiated into their new states of life through rituals that were sacramental in the broad Augustinian sense, that is, they were sacred signs. Did this mean that each of these rituals was to be considered a sacrament in the more narrow and technical sense which was then being developed? On the other hand the order of priesthood posed an additional difficulty since it was conferred in a series of stages—seven by most counts, eight or nine by others—each of which also had its own ordination ritual. Was the sacrament of clerical orders therefore one or many? And if it was restricted to priestly orders, was the sacrament received in stages as each of the orders was conferred, or was it received only at the ordination to the priesthood itself? And if it was completely received by the time of ordination to the priesthood, what did bishops receive when they were ordained? Was episcopal consecration a sacrament or not?

Sometimes the early schoolmen did not even include ordination in their lists of the sacraments because up till that time orders and the regulations that surrounded them were treated in canon law, not theology. But the priesthood itself was a theological matter since it was intimately connected with the administration of the other sacraments, and by the twelfth century most scholastics believed that it should be treated as a sacrament in the strict sense. Peter Lombard in his collection of *Sentences* helped clear up some of the confusion by distinguishing "sacraments" from "sacramentals," sacred rites which conferred the grace that they signified from those which did not, and by including non-priestly ordinations in the class of sacramentals. Hugh of St. Victor also contributed to the solution by conceiving the priesthood in terms of seven holy orders (porter, lector, exorcist, acolyte, subdeacon, deacon, priest), designating the monastic custom of tonsure as a sacramental, and regarding the episcopacy as a special "dignity in order" rather than as a separate and higher order. Moreover, since there was only one Christian priesthood there had to be only one sacrament of the priesthood even though it was received in several stages, the last being the fullest. It was a solution that was both plausible and workable, and by the end of the twelfth century it was generally accepted.

But how, then, was the sacrament of holy orders to be understood? Lombard defined it simply as "a seal of the church by means of which spiritual power is conferred on the person ordained" (*Sentences* IV, 53). Essentially it was a priestly power, the power to consecrate the eucharist and to offer the mass, and some theologians such as Alexander of Hales even defined it exclusively in relation to the eucharistic sacrifice. If the sacrament was defined in relation to the mass it was easy to explain why bishops did not belong to a separate order since they did not have any more power over the eucharist than a simple priest had. On the other hand this narrow understanding of priesthood did not so easily explain why some priestly powers, like the forgiveness of sins, were not directly related to the eucharist, nor did it explain why some functions, like confirmation and ordination, were considered priestly functions even though they were reserved to the bishop. To overcome the first difficulty it was necessary to generalize on the priest's role in the mass and view it as a type of mediation between God and human beings. In the mass the priest brought Christ himself to people in the form of communion, but in parallel ways he brought the Holy Spirit in baptism and he brought God's forgiveness in penance. To overcome the second difficulty it was necessary to conclude that every priest had the power to confirm and ordain, although only bishops had the authority to do so. Even though the priest's power came ultimately from God, it came through the ordaining bishop, and since bishops had the authority to rule the church they could legitimately delegate some functions to priests while retaining others to themselves. Only bishops, then, had the fullness of the priesthood; ordinary priests had all the powers of the priesthood but they did not have the authority to use them without the bishop's permission. This explanation also squared with the fact that according to canon law priests were not even allowed to offer the mass or hear confessions without the permission of the bishop whose diocese they were in.

The third main problem that the scholastics settled had to do with reordination. Although Augustine had settled the question of rebaptism toward the end of the fourth century, official opinion on the question of reordination remained divided throughout the early Middle Ages. Some argued as the Donatists had that excommunicated and sinful bishops lost the Holy Spirit and hence could not give what they did not have. Others argued that since the power of the priesthood was given by God and not by the bishop, the bishop's status or holiness could not affect the ordinations he performed. Sometimes popes and other bishops readmitted heretical priests to communion with Rome without reordaining them; at other times they insisted on it. Sometimes in their power struggles rival factions of bishops would declare that their opponents' orders were null and void, and if they won they would force them to be reordained; but this did not always happen. During some periods it was commonly held that ordinations by bishops who had bought their office had to be repeated; but this was not true during other periods. Up until the twelfth century, then, there was no common or consistent opinion on the question of reordination.

During the twelfth century, however, three things happened which helped settle the matter. The first was the development of the distinction between power and authority, enabling theologians to explain that sinful and heretical bishops retained their power to ordain even though they lost their authority to do so. The second was the parallel development of the distinction between validity and liceity, enabling canonists to explain that ordinations by such bishops were still valid or true ordinations even though they were improper or contrary to church law (see page 74). The third was the rediscovery of Augustine's idea of the sacramental character and his application of it to the priesthood. And as soon as ordination was understood to confer an indelible character just as baptism did, it logically followed that once the priesthood was received it could never be lost. By the thirteenth century all the major scholastics accepted the idea that ordination conferred a sacramental character, and from then on reordination was a thing of the past.

In a sense, Aquinas' theology of the priesthood was an expansion on

the idea of the sacramental character. According to him, the priestly character that was received through ordination was, like the baptismal character, a
spiritual configuration to Christ. In this case, however, the image of Christ
that was received was that of Christ the high priest, Christ of the Epistle to
the Hebrews, and Christ seen as priest in instituting the eucharist and offering himself in sacrifice on the cross. Christ was the perfect mediator between
God and humankind not only because he had both a divine and human
nature but also because as a human being he surrendered himself perfectly
to the will of the Father. Through his act of self-sacrifice he made it possible
for others to live in complete union with God, and through his institution
of the eucharist he made it possible for others to experience communion
with God. Those who made the eucharist present in the church, therefore,
brought God to humanity and humanity to God even as Christ did.

To Aquinas it was evident that this sacred power was not given to all
but only to those who were ordained as priests, for only they were allowed
to offer the mass, and the words of their ordination spoke of the bestowal
of priestly power. Thus when they performed their priestly functions the
divine mediation occurred not by any human power but by divine power,
a power given to human beings in the form of a spiritual character. It was
a metaphysical transformation of their very soul which could never be
undone, a gift of God's grace that gave them the power to mediate God's
grace to others. It was received partly with each order on the way to the
priesthood since each of these orders was oriented toward the priesthood.
It was received completely in the ordination to the priesthood itself, for
only the priest could do what Christ did in forgiving sins and giving
himself sacramentally to others. It was activated whenever the priest by
the power of his order performed a sacramental act. But it was activated
perfectly when he performed the perfect act of worship and supreme act
of mediation, the mass.

Since it was a power given to priests by God it was a supernatural
power, and neither its reception nor its exercise depended on their natural
talents or personal holiness. It was given to them not for themselves but
for others, to be mediators of grace through their sacramental actions in
the church. As human beings they might receive the sacramental character
unworthily and they might use its power imperfectly, but as priests they
received it absolutely and its operation was infallible.

In many ways, then, the scholastic theology of the priesthood was both
a reflection of and a reflection on priestly ministry as it existed in the Middle
Ages. It reflected the way that ministry was performed, closely connected

with the eucharist and the other sacraments. It reflected the process of becoming a priest, it reflected the regulations that affected priests, and it reflected the activities that were regarded as priestly in the church. And as Bonaventure and Albert, Aquinas and others reflected on their inner and outer experience of the priestly ministry, they constructed a theology of the priesthood that was consistent both with that experience and with what they found in the scriptures and the writings of the fathers of the church. Ministry was conceived primarily in terms of sacramental ministry because at that time that is what it was, and sacramental ministry was conceived basically in terms of priestly ministry because all those who administered the sacraments were priests.

And yet priests performed almost every other ministry in the church as well. As bishops they ruled over the church in the name of Christ, teaching it through episcopal pronouncements and conciliar decrees, guarding it from heresy, providing it with the means of salvation by ordaining further priests. As professors in the universities they taught the church how to understand God and the scriptures and the sacraments. As canon lawyers they preserved order in the church, determining the relation between the moral law and ecclesiastical law and refining both to fit every situation. As bureaucrats in various church offices they kept the machinery of the Christian society functioning. As preachers they reminded Christian Europe of its obligations to God and the church, and as missionaries they brought the truth of Christianity to those who had not yet heard it. About the only ones who served the church who were not priests were lay monks and nuns, but their work was not regarded as an ecclesiastical ministry. In medieval Christianity, therefore, it was the priests who were the primary mediators between God and humans in almost every aspect of Christian life. But their priesthood was conceived almost entirely in terms of sacramental, liturgical, cultic ministry. All their other functions were thought of not in terms of priesthood but in terms of authority, office, and jurisdiction.

This way of understanding priesthood continued into the fourteenth and fifteenth centuries. According to Scotus, Ockham, and others the essential power of the priest was to change bread and wine into the body and blood of Christ. Most theologians included preaching and administration of the other sacraments in their definition of priestly functions, but some did not. They preferred to limit the priestly function to offering sacrifice and to speak of the other duties as ministerial functions, indirectly preparing the way for the Protestant rejection of priesthood but retention of ministry in the church.

But if the theology of the priesthood remained relatively unchanged in the later Middle Ages, the reality of the priesthood did not, and speaking in very broad terms we can say that it got caught in the cultural decline of the fourteenth century and in the power struggles of the fifteenth century. The intellectual renaissance that had seen the rise of the medieval universities had actually reached very few, and priests in the cities and rural areas were once again as poorly educated as they had ever been. Both they and the people they served often took the scholastic theory of *ex opere operato* to mean that the mass and sacraments worked automatically, even magically, in bringing God to earth and bringing Christians to heaven. Dozens of priests—in some places hundreds—were ordained every year just to say votive masses, and the laws restricting them from holding worldly jobs made them an economic burden on their communities. The moral reform that had seen the institution of celibacy as a clerical ideal meant that priests could not validly marry, but it could not prevent them from taking common law wives. The main difference was that now Christians knew that their priests were supposed to remain chaste, and the fact that they often did not reduced their credibility when they preached obedience to the laws of God and the church. The revival of religious life that had seen the rise of great monasteries and the founding of new orders eventually lost its momentum. Monks left their cloisters to wander the countryside in search of stipends, and the charitable and evangelical works of the religious orders were often left undone.

Still, the idea remained that priests were engaged in a holy ministry and were therefore supposed to lead exemplary lives. Local and even general councils called for clerical reforms, but even when they came they were often short lived. Occasionally, too, laity and priests such as Peter Waldo in France, John Wycliffe in England, and John Hus in Bohemia denounced the way the clergy neglected their duties and benefited from special privileges. But their protests were seen as doctrinal denials of priestly power and political threats to episcopal authority, and so they were ignored. And when they could not be ignored, they were suppressed.

Most bishops in fact were not interested in reform but as "princes of the church" were eager to increase their wealth and maintain their power. Those who could do it sometimes got themselves appointed to two and even three dioceses so they could collect the revenues from them. Often they did not even live in their own dioceses but preferred to live in southern France, where it was warmer, or in Italy, where they could engage in papal politics. The office of cardinal was especially attractive to those who could afford it, for the cardinals elected the pope from among their own number. This also made the office attractive to European kings and nobles who often had their own choices appointed cardinals in order to influence papal elections and policies. In the early fourteenth century, the college of cardinals got packed with Frenchmen and the popes from 1309 to 1376—all of them French—lived in Avignon instead of Rome. Then from 1378 to 1409 there were two popes at the same time, and from 1409 to 1415 there were three, with two of them living outside Rome, each elected by rival factions of cardinals backed by different European monarchs. The unity of the church which was once symbolized by the papacy was lost, and even when a single pope by common consent again took up residence in Rome, the papacy, cardinalate, and episcopacy continued to be political and financial appointments. Understandably, those who received those offices were more interested in ecclesiastical power and church revenues than in the spiritual welfare of the church.

4. The Modern Catholic Priesthood

Part of the reason, then, that the Protestant reformation succeeded was because the nobles of northern Europe were tired of having to pay political and financial tribute to the pope in Rome. Prior to the sixteenth century, heretics and other disturbers of the church's peace were punished by civil governments in exchange for the hierarchy's support of their secular authority over their subjects. But when the German nobility sensed that the people and even many of the clergy agreed with Martin Luther that the church should be reformed, they seized the opportunity to let Germans do the reforming and free themselves of interference from Italy. The political benefit was that they no longer had to contend with the power of the popes; the economic benefit was that they no longer had to pay Rome for favors, and by turning monasteries and episcopal estates into public lands they could now collect the revenues for themselves. And once the German reformation succeeded and other kings saw that the popes were powerless to stop it, they allowed and sometimes promoted similar reforms in their own countries.

Luther himself, of course, had no intention of breaking politically or even spiritually from Rome, at least not at the beginning. His initial call was for reform of the church "in its head and members," and it was not until 1520 when the pope excommunicated him that he finally decided that the members of the church were better off without an earthly head. He even allowed bishops in his model of the church, not as rulers of the faithful and bestowers of supernatural powers on the clergy, but as supervisors of the church's ministries much as he envisioned they had been in the first centuries of Christianity.

As for the priesthood, Luther believed that it was a valid ministry in the church—but only that and no more. He saw no reason to believe that priests were metaphysically changed into superior Christians with special powers by their ordination. Whatever happened through the sacraments, he argued, happened by divine rather than human power, and so all Christians could act as God's instruments in virtue of their baptism. He saw no scriptural evidence that something like a sacramental character was given to priests, and he took Christ's words to baptize, preach, and continue the eucharist as being directed to the church, not to a privileged group within the church. Thus any Christian could legitimately do these things, and it was only for reasons of church order that certain Christians were selected, trained, and commissioned by the community to perform these functions as ministries in the church.

Underlying Luther's conception of the ministerial priesthood was his own interpretation of the "priesthood of all believers" based on texts such as 1 Peter 2:5. The New Testament spoke most clearly of the priesthood of Christ in the Epistle to the Hebrews, and so if Christians were called to be a holy and a priestly people it meant that they all shared in Christ's priesthood, and a separate cultic priesthood was not necessary. Indeed, if one accepted that Christ's priestly sacrifice on the cross had won salvation for all, then it seemed impossible to repeat that redemptive action, and a priesthood ordained to perpetuate Christ's sacrifice in something like the mass had to be at best a mistake and at worst a sign of how far the Roman church had wandered from the truth. The only difference between the clergy and other Christians, therefore, was that they felt called by God and were commissioned by the community to perform certain functions in the church, and so if they failed to perform them they could be removed from their office and their ministry given to others.

Chief among these functions was preaching, the ministry of the word. All priesthood was mediation between God and human beings, Luther reasoned, but nothing revealed God better than the reading of the Bible, and nothing brought people closer to God better than the careful explanation of it. Secondly priests were supposed to be pastors, shepherds of their people, guiding them on the paths of righteousness, seeking them when they strayed. Only thirdly were they to be ministers of the sacraments, for sacraments were ineffective without faith and faith had to be kindled by preaching and fanned by pastoral zeal.

John Calvin likewise included liturgical and sacramental functions in his understanding of ministry, but he refused to call the church's ministers "priests" because he rejected the idea of the eucharist as a sacrifice and he insisted that only Christ himself and Christians in general had a scriptural right to the title "priest." Moreover, his reading of the New Testament led him to distinguish a variety of ministries in the church, not all of which had to be performed by the same person. Pastors were to be primarily preachers of repentance and proclaimers of the gospel of salvation. Teachers were those who because of their talents and training were better able to explain the scriptures and show how they applied to daily life. Elders and deacons were to be supervisors of the church and administrators of practical affairs, thus freeing pastors and teachers to be full-time ministers of the word.

For Calvin these were ordained ministries in the sense that they were ordained by God in the Bible and also in the sense that those who performed them were called by God to serve the church. Unlike Luther, therefore, Calvin did not see the ordained ministry as an extension of the priesthood of the faithful but as a call or vocation from above, even though candidates for the ministry were to be approved by the church before they were appointed to ministerial offices. So the ultimate judge of ministers' worthiness as well as their work was God alone, but God's Spirit acted in and though the church discerning who was to be called to which ministry.

In this way, then, Calvin provided a radical alternative to the medieval model of church organization based on bishops and priests. It was a model that not only seemed to have existed in the early church but also seemed to be needed in Switzerland where Calvin resided. For over a century Swiss bishops had been weak and ineffective appointees of the local nobility, and so if the reform of the church was to succeed in places with little or no episcopal leadership, there had to be an alternative way of organizing and appointing ministries in the church, and Calvin believed he found it in the New Testament. The churches that were founded in the Calvinist tradition, therefore, had no use for bishops and simply eliminated the episcopacy as a distinct office. Presbyterians created senates of elected elders or presbyters with administrative jurisdiction over clusters of local churches. Congregationalists went even further and insisted that the elders of each individual congregation had the ultimate authority, subject only to the authority of the Bible as the Spirit led them to interpret it.

At the other extreme, the Anglican Church kept the episcopal model of church organization almost entirely intact. When Henry VIII broke with the pope and proclaimed himself head of the church in England his motives were political rather than religious, and almost every bishop in the House of Lords agreed that he had the right to do so. Their motives were also political—to free the English church from foreign domination—and they felt no pressure to alter the traditional form of church government in which they played an integral part. Likewise their understanding of orders and the powers that they conferred remained essentially Catholic. In the years that followed Henry's death, however, the more radical ideas of the continental reformers began to influence English churchmen. Opinions were divided between those who held to the traditional Catholic view of priesthood, especially in regard to the power of consecrating the eucharist, and those who accepted the Protestant view of ministry as primarily pastoral and the eucharist as a memorial rather than a sacrifice. In the end, both views were tolerated, but the episcopal structure of the church in England remained as it was. Officially, ordination was still regarded as a sacrament, though one which was not directly instituted by Christ, and English bishops continued to ordain priests to a sacramental ministry. However, not all Anglican bishops and priests continued to accept the Catholic belief in transubstantiation and, from a Catholic viewpoint at least, this cast doubt upon the validity of their priesthood since they were not necessarily ordained with the intention of "doing what the church does" in offering the mass (see pages 99–100).

During the sixteenth century, then, most of the reformers rejected the medieval style of church ministry and the scholastic theories that supported it. They discounted the notion that authority in the church was funneled from Christ through the pope to the bishops to the priests, and they rejected the claim that this arrangement was divinely ordained. They found little evidence in the scriptures that ranks of holy orders existed in the early church, and they objected to the way that people were ordained to ministries (such as the diaconate) that they never really performed. They saw no reason to believe that ordination made the ordained better than other Christians or gave them supernatural powers or made them ministers for life, and so they dismissed the concept of the sacramental character as an invention of the medieval clergy. They observed that the law of celibacy was more often a cause of scandal than edification in the church, and since they abandoned the idea of the eucharist as a priestly sacrifice they saw no grounds for applying the Old Testament rules of ritual purity to Christian ministers. Even the English church, which kept the mass, allowed its priests to marry at the beginning of the seventeenth century.

In place of the priestly ministry of cult and ritual the reformers substituted a pastoral ministry of preaching and teaching, not only because of the superstition that often surrounded the sacraments but also because of the way they conceived of salvation. Salvation came through conversion and faith in God's word, and so Christians had a right to hear the scriptures and ministers had a duty to explain them. In a way, then, the Bible (now translated into modern language) was introduced as a verbal sacrament replacing the ritual sacraments of traditional Christianity. It was the means through which the Holy Spirit entered one's heart and enlightened one's mind. Preaching itself was expected to be sacramentally inspiring and uplifting. Explaining God's teachings was a means of deepening faith and commitment, and exhorting people to follow God's commandments was supposed to be an effective protection against sin.

In a similar way the Protestants did not do away with sacramental ordination but they changed the form and meaning of ordination to fit their new interpretation of Christian ministry. True, they rejected the scholastic theory of ordination as a sacrament in the strict Catholic sense. But reformers from the time of Luther onward recognized the need for some sort of ceremonial initiation into the ministry. As a transition ritual it marked a person's entrance into a special office or service in the church. As an intensification ritual it expressed the meaning of that office and symbolized what that service was conceived to be. Its ceremonial style and symbolic content necessarily varied from one denomination to the next, but whatever shape it took it was still a sacrament in the broad sense.

In the polemical atmosphere of the reformation, however, neither Protestants nor Catholics perceived what was going on as a reshaping of sacramental ministry and ordination. Protestants saw themselves as rejecting a medieval priesthood and returning to earlier and more biblical forms of ministry. And Catholics viewed the Protestants as rejecting a divinely established priesthood and adopting new and unorthodox forms of ministry.

It is therefore understandable that at the Council of Trent the Catholic bishops defended the traditional doctrines of priesthood and orders and condemned those who seemed to be introducing strange ideas about ecclesiastical ministry. Much of what the bishops had to say about ministry was put into their decrees on the other sacraments, defining what the priest's role was in each of them and defending the right and duty of priests to administer them. And some of the things they would have liked to have said about the hierarchy and ordination were still theologically disputed topics (such as the relation of church councils to the authority of the pope, and the nature of episcopal consecration) about which they could not reach a consensus. So the bishops kept their doctrinal decree on ordination brief and to the point in refuting the major attacks of the reformers.

First and foremost they defended the existence of the Catholic priesthood and the ministry of those on whom it was bestowed. Since the eucharist was a sacrifice instituted by Christ, they argued, there had to be a new priesthood which replaced that of the Old Testament. In its earlier decree on the mass as a sacrifice the council had affirmed that Christ made the apostles priests at his last supper, and now the bishops explained that that priesthood gave the apostles and their successors the power to consecrate, offer, and administer his body and blood. Likewise in its decree on penance the council had affirmed that after his resurrection Christ gave the apostles the power to forgive and retain sins, and now the bishops reaffirmed that that power also was granted to their successors.

Those who received the priesthood had to pass through several lower orders, some of which, like the diaconate, were mentioned in the scriptures and the rest of which were clearly attested to in the writings of the fathers. Similarly the existence of ordination as a sacramental rite could be proven from ancient documents of the church, and the fact that it bestowed grace could be shown from biblical texts such as 2 Timothy 1:6. This sacramental rite also imparted an indelible character that marked those who received it as priests forever, and made them different from lay people. Among priests themselves there were various grades, and in this hierarchy bishops were superior to simple priests. The bishops were successors of the apostles in a special way in that they had authority to rule over the church, so only they could confirm, ordain, and perform other sacred functions.

Anyone who denied the power of the bishops or claimed that ministers of the word and sacraments could be commissioned without their approval, therefore, had to be condemned. Likewise anyone who denied the existence of the priesthood, its institution by Christ, its sacramental nature, or its various powers and orders had to be regarded as a heretic. And although the council did not say anything about celibacy in its decree on the priesthood, in its decree on matrimony it did reassert that the church had a right to prohibit clerics from marrying.

Thus the Council of Trent reaffirmed the existence of a priestly ministry in the Catholic Church, and identified that ministry with the performance of cultic and sacramental functions. It also reaffirmed the existence of a ruling ministry performed by priests who were bishops and who were different from ordinary priests not because they had more priestly powers but because they had more authority in the church. The council therefore left a number of technical questions open which were to draw the attention of later theologians: Could priests be given the authority to confirm and ordain? Were the other orders besides the priesthood instituted by Christ, and were their ordination rites sacramental in the strict sense, that is, did they confer grace? Was the sacrament of the priesthood conferred by the laying on of hands or the handing over of the chalice and paten? But the major questions about the Catholic ministry were settled, or at least they appeared to be.

Still, the theological questions were only half the issue that had been raised by the reformers. They had also attacked the careless way that priests performed their duties, the abuse of episcopal authority, and the immorality of the clergy in general. Again, the bishops of the council attempted to deal with these in a number of reform decrees throughout the eighteen-year length of the council, and they left some reforms to be spelled out by their successors. But they did recognize many of the disorders that the reformers complained about and they set about to rectify them. They ordered bishops to reside in their own territories and prohibited them from holding more than one diocese. As priests they had to be pastors of their people, preachers of the word, and ministers of the sacraments, not just ecclesiastical administrators. As bishops they were to see to it that these same things were done by the priests under their jurisdiction, and they were to make sure in the future that candidates for the priesthood were fit for the ministry and well trained in their duties. Finally, they were to see to it that they themselves and the other clergy led exemplary moral lives befitting priests and ministers of Christ.

By and large the Council of Trent and the popes who came after it succeeded in bringing about a reformed and better educated clergy than that which had existed during the Middle Ages. The imposition of uniform rites for all the sacraments including the mass ensured that priests would not take liberties with their sacramental functions. The establishment of seminaries in almost every diocese ensured that priests would be better versed in theology and canon law. Priests were required to pray more, for besides having to offer the mass every day they were also required to read from the breviary, a book of psalms and lessons that grew out of the monastic practice of daily prayer. They were also required to preach at least on

Sundays and feast days, and even though preaching remained secondary to the sacraments in their ministry, priests in general did more and better preaching in the period after the council than in the period before it.

But priests also continued to dominate the other ministries in the church, and in this respect there was little change in the pattern of ministry that was established in the fourth century and reinforced in the Middle Ages. As rulers of the church, bishops were responsible for organizing and coordinating all of the teaching and charitable ministries in their dioceses, and those who were appointed to perform them were mostly priests. During the counter-reformation of the sixteenth and seventeenth centuries, there was a resurgence of religious orders founded to do teaching and missionary work, but the majority of those in them, like the Jesuits, were priests. Just as in the Middle Ages there were also orders of lay brothers and sisters, who labored in schools and hospitals at home and in mission hands, and who often worked with children and the poor. Just as in the Middle Ages they led celibate lives, lived under canonical rules, and were initiated into their orders through special rituals. They needed the approval of local bishops to do their work, and their religious superiors were ultimately accountable to the pope. But again, although they lived lives of service, their work was not officially recognized as ministry, for ministry continued to be identified with priesthood, even when priests were engaged in other than priestly activities.

For the most part, though, parish priests were encouraged to remove themselves from public life and its dangers to the soul. Starting in the seventeenth century Catholic writers (all priests) began to portray the ideal priestly lifestyle as a very monastic one, even when priests had to live alone in country parishes. They were supposed to live lives of total surrender to God and so they were to separate themselves from worldly things and avoid the temptations of sex, power, and wealth. Particularly in the eighteenth century when ecclesiastical influence in Catholic countries led to a growing anticlericalism, and in the nineteenth century when civil governments began to take over many things once done by the church (like the regulation of marriage, the organization of health care and education and other social services), the ideal priestly ministry was portrayed as one that revolved around the mass and the sacraments. In the nineteenth century, too, bishops who were still landed gentry lost most of their territory to the rising tide of nationalism, and even the pope lost his political control over central Italy. From then on, bishops and priests alike were more clearly limited to being spiritual leaders. Except for the upper echelons of the hierarchy, priests were not supposed to engage in political activity, and when they preached they were to concern themselves with the salvation of souls and not with the conditions of the world. Priests were holy ministers concerned with holy things, sacramental persons as well as administers of sacraments, and they were expected to be completely dedicated to their work.

They were also expected to be completely obedient to their superiors, and the reform of the clergy in the centuries after Trent was made possible by the general acceptance of the belief that government in the church was a divinely established hierarchy. The Tridentine reform came from the top down, from the council and popes, through the bishops and superiors of religious orders, to the diocesan priests and members of religious orders. Each church organization was a pyramid headed by a superior who was in turn part of a larger pyramid with its own ecclesiastical superior. At the top of each pyramid was a bishop or his equivalent, and at the apex of the whole ecclesiastical structure was the pope, aided by a bureaucracy of curial offices each headed by a cardinal. Church government was therefore a monarchy, just as most civil governments were through the nineteenth century, and it commanded the same fidelity and allegiance that any monarchy did.

In a way, it even commanded more allegiance than a monarchy, for in the modern church obedience to one's superior was equated with obedience to God. The pope as vicar of Christ spoke for God to the whole church, and the various departments of the curia made decisions that were binding in conscience for all Catholics. Authority (portrayed and perceived as divine authority) filtered from the top down through ordination and other ecclesiastical appointments, and at each level it was monarchial and absolute. Priests in each diocese owed obedience to their bishop, for their ministry was seen as an extension of his, and their authorization to exercise their priesthood depended completely on him. Those in religious orders even made a vow of obedience when they entered their order, and the voice of their religious superior was to be regarded as the voice of God. And at the local level, lay Catholics were expected to show the same respect to their clergy, for God spoke through the church and the church spoke through its priests.

The modern period, then, which for the Catholic Church lasted from the Council of Trent to the Second Vatican Council, was a period of great institutional stability. This stability was largely due to the ecclesiastical reforms initiated by the bishops at Trent and maintained for four centuries by the monarchial organization of the hierarchy. The stability was reflected in the stability of Catholic theology through the middle of the twentieth

century, including its theology of the priesthood. And its monarchial organization was reflected in the paternalistic style of its ministry. And as long
as the world did not change, or did not seem to be changing, all was well.

5. Ministries in the Church Today

But the world was indeed changing. From the self-imposed seclusion of
the Catholic clergy the scope of that change was not apparent at first. For
a long while into the twentieth century it looked as though the ministerial
needs of the Catholic Church could be met by its priests and nuns, and
the traditional understanding of ministry was not questioned. Those who
sought spiritual perfection were expected to join the priesthood or one
of the religious orders and to give their lives completely to God and the
church by prayer and service, celibacy and obedience. Lay people in the
church were therefore never ministers; they were the ones ministered to.

As with the other sacraments, the first hint that the modern Catholic
theology of the priesthood might have to be reexamined came from historical studies. Early research showed that the handing over of liturgical
instruments had been added to the ritual of ordination only in the early
Middle Ages, and in 1947 Pope Pius XII instructed that the imposition
of hands should therefore be considered the essential element in the rite.
But the results of later research were not so easy to reconcile. Some documents showed that during the patristic period deacons had sometimes
been ordained bishops without first being ordained priests. Did this mean
that episcopal consecration conferred priestly powers and not just a higher
office? Other records, however, showed that during the Middle Ages some
popes had authorized abbots (who were not bishops) to ordain deacons
and priests. Did this mean that priests had, or at least could be given,
episcopal powers without being consecrated? The picture was no longer
as clear as it had once been.

Further research turned up more potentially disconcerting evidence:
that before the fourth century priests had been "presbyters," with few
liturgical functions, and that only the bishops had been called "priests"
(*sacerdotes*); that the most ancient ordination rites did not speak of a conferral of priestly power but only prayed for a reception of spiritual gifts;
that the minor orders of porter, lector, and so on had originally been lay
ministries and only later became steps to the priesthood; that the monastic
ideal of spiritual perfection was added to the priesthood only gradually,
and that before the twelfth century many if not most priests and bishops

were married; that the bishop of Rome had influence rather than authority during the first centuries of Christianity, and that it was only during the Middle Ages that the papacy became a position of power. In its own way the study of the Bible was also becoming more historical, trying to reconstruct the situation in which the scriptures were written, and new biblical research made further disturbing suggestions: that there was no officially recognized priesthood in the early Christian community and that the apostles and other disciples did not think of themselves as priests; that many of the ministries in the early church were charismatic activities rather than appointed offices; that most of the texts used to prove the divine institution of a cultic priesthood and an authoritarian church structure in later centuries were not understood to mean that when they were written. It was therefore evident that the church had changed, but as long as Catholicism considered itself to be the one true church under the guidance of the Holy Spirit, it could reason that the later developments showed the direction that God wanted the church to eventually take. The fullness of God's plan for the church may not have been completely evident from the very beginning, it could be argued, but this did not mean that historical studies could affect doctrinal truths.

But by the middle of the century other more practical concerns began to raise other questions about the traditional views of the priesthood, ministry, and authority in the church. If priests were ordained to administer the sacraments, for example, then why were so many ordained clerics engaged in non-sacramental ministries as teachers and administrators whose only sacramental function was saying mass? And if priests were also supposed to be pastors, how could those who were professionally engaged in these activities fulfill their pastoral role as well? On the other hand, if some priests wanted to extend their pastoral ministry by taking jobs in factories and other places that brought them closer to their people, why were these occupations forbidden while others were approved? Was the priests' specialized training in philosophy and theology and their seclusion in seminaries and rectories making them lose contact with the realities that Catholics faced every day? Bishops, too, especially those outside Europe and North America, had questions that arose out of their unique situations. Did mission territories and foreign dioceses have to remain under such close scrutiny by Rome? Couldn't bishops by themselves or in local councils make decisions for their own regions? Was the pattern of ministry that developed in medieval Europe to be taken as the perpetual norm for the universal church? Wouldn't a married clergy be better for remote country villages, and wouldn't lifting the law of celibacy encourage more native vocations? Did all of the church's official ministers have to be priests, or couldn't something like the ancient diaconate at least be reintroduced to help priests with their work?

When the Second Vatican Council convened in 1962, however, most of these questions were still academic since the theology of the priesthood and the structure of ministry in the church were still the same as they had been for centuries. And although the tone of the council's official statements was more pastoral than doctrinal, the role of priests in the church was restated in largely traditional terms. The Dogmatic Constitution on the Church affirmed that priests were equal to bishops in priestly dignity even though they did "not have the supreme degree of the episcopal office" and had to "depend on the bishops for the exercise of their power" (28). They were therefore "cooperators," "aids," and "instruments" of the bishop in the exercise of his pastoral office. Their function as priests was first and foremost the celebration of the eucharistic liturgy, but the administration of the other sacraments was also important, and they were to lead the faithful by their preaching and example as well. The Decree on the Ministry and Life of Priests explained that through their connection with bishops priests were successors of the apostles and inheritors of the priestly ministry that Christ had bequeathed to his church. They were therefore ministers of Christ in service to others, preaching during the liturgy and also teaching groups and individuals in a variety of circumstances. For this reason they were to be men of prayer, seekers of spiritual perfection, and imitators of Christ. They must be open to the Spirit but also obedient to God's will, zealous in carrying out their assignments, and committed to the values of priestly celibacy and evangelical poverty. Finally, to strengthen their personal life and support their public ministry, they should set aside time each year for a spiritual retreat, theological study, and vacation.

But the council also added new emphasis to the role of priests as pastors and ministers outside of liturgical situations, and its decree stressed the importance of a fraternal relationship among priests and between priests and their bishop. Priests were to consider preaching, teaching, and counseling as essential and not added to their priestly functions. They were to foster a spirit of Christian community in their parishes and to entrust lay people with responsibilities that allowed them to be more active members of the church. Since they were united in a sacramental brotherhood with other priests and their bishop, they should establish both formal and informal associations for communication and support, and they should assist one another as much as possible. To help future priests prepare for their expanded ministry in the church, the Decree on Priestly Formation added that seminary training was to be revised to include more emphasis on biblical and pastoral studies, to give more attention to the social sciences, and to allow more contact between seminarians and the society around them.

Perhaps the greatest change in official attitude came in the council's approach to bishops. In the past bishops were often viewed as rulers; Vatican II pictured them primarily as pastors. In the past their subordination to Rome was often emphasized; now their responsibility and authority in their own dioceses was given more attention. In the past they were regarded as priests who had been elevated to a higher office; here, following the findings of patristic studies, the episcopal office was regarded as primary. Thus the episcopacy and not the priesthood was theologically the highest grade in holy orders, not something non-sacramental added on to the priesthood.

The third chapter of the Dogmatic Constitution on the Church talked about the hierarchical structure of the church and the role of bishops in it. Bishops were to consider themselves shepherds of Christ's flock, successors of the apostles who worked together with (rather than under) the successor of Peter in bringing about the kingdom of God on earth. Although they had helpers in their ministry, the bishop's duty was to do everything necessary to spread the message of Christ and provide for the life of the church. They had authority not only singly in their own dioceses but also collegially in their own regions, even though that authority always had to be exercised in unity with the whole church and especially with the bishop of Rome. Their duties were to preach the gospel, teach authentic Catholic doctrine, be judges in matters of faith and morals, supervise the sacramental ministry and, in general, be centers of unity and cooperation in the church. The council's separate document on The Pastoral Office of Bishops in the Church expanded on many of these same points, adding that bishops should be spiritual fathers to their people, brothers to their fellow priests, and friends to the poor. They were to adapt the universal message of Christ to the particular needs of their own people, and in doing this they were to cooperate actively with other bishops, seek the collaboration of their own priests, and invite the help of lay people and those in religious orders. The Constitution on the Sacred Liturgy described bishops as the high priests of their own churches and granted them much more autonomy than they had in the past for determining local styles of worship. In a sense, then, the pyramidal organization of the church was being flattened out somewhat, and the sharp lines of authority were being softened in the light of a new emphasis on cooperation rather than obedience.

Vatican II also did much to broaden the Catholic Church's concept of ministry, not only by defining priesthood and episcopacy in more pastoral terms but also by taking new steps to include others in the ministry of the church. The council called for a restoration of the permanent diaconate as a ministry of service that was open to older married men as well as to younger celibates, and in the years since the council deacons have been ordained to help priests in liturgical and other parish ministries. They have been especially important in mission lands where priests are scarce, enabling native Catholics to become in effect members of the clergy, doing many of the things that priests used to do, but without such long training and without having to be unmarried. The council also recognized the work of those in religious orders as ministries of prayer and service, and in its statement on the Decree on the Apostolate of the Laity reassured ordinary Catholics that they, too, shared in the mission of Christ and called them to a more active role in the church's ministries.

But the Second Vatican Council was just the beginning of a vast restructuring and rethinking of ministry in the Catholic Church. Hearing the official call to a more pastoral service, diocesan and religious priests and nuns began to move out of their traditional roles and into new ones. The movement was cautious at first, then more deliberate in the socially conscious climate of the late 1960s and early 1970s. In the United States they moved into racial ghettos and rural slums, becoming involved in social work and the civil rights movement. In Europe they identified themselves with the working-class poor who had long been disenchanted with the church. In Central and South America they began to work overtly and covertly against oppressive dictatorships. The council had also called for a renewal of established religious orders, and when the orders began to reexamine their missions and lifestyles many of them no longer found it necessary to work exclusively in schools and hospitals and other established institutions. Most of them also stopped wearing the distinctive religious habits that had traditionally marked them out from the rest of society, and even priests took to wearing non-clerical clothes. The clear and distinct lines that had once separated ministers from non-ministers in Catholicism were becoming blurred.

The sixties and seventies were also a time for questioning authority in the church, and this, too, had repercussions in the area of ministry. The results of scholarly scriptural studies led Catholics to question the hierarchy's competence to make authoritative pronouncements on the teachings of the Bible. Historical research led others to wonder about the monarchial organization of the church, about the centralizing of power in Rome, and about the infallibility of the pope. Philosophical developments led others to abandon the scholastic conception of priesthood and ministry in terms of power and authority and to conceive of them in more personalist terms of community and service. Ecumenical contacts forced Catholics to admit that in large measure the Protestant reformation had been an honest revolt against corruption and ineptitude in the Renaissance church, and that the new forms of ministry that they had developed had some merit to them. Catholics in democratic countries began to wonder whether their priests and bishops should not be less paternalistic and dictatorial. The clear identification of ministry with authority was becoming hazy.

Even the liturgical renewal following the ecumenical council fostered a breakdown of the traditional concept of ministry, especially priestly and ruling ministry. Encouraged to participate in the liturgy, Catholics no longer felt that the priest was performing a service at the altar which was uniquely his and not theirs, and when lay people were allowed to read at mass and distribute communion, this sense of the priest's uniqueness dwindled even further. The changing conception of morality that led to a revision of the sacrament of penance also led to doubts about the clergy's omniscience in moral matters and made the priest seem less indispensable for the forgiveness of sins. And the changing attitudes of Catholics toward sex and marriage made them wonder about the hierarchy's official positions on premarital sex, birth control, divorce, and even clerical celibacy, especially when priests themselves were divided on these issues. The position of the priest as dispenser of the sacraments and authority in religious matters was getting shaky.

Priests who had once found themselves at the virtual center of Catholic religious life now sometimes felt displaced and uncertain about their role in the church, despite the assurances of the conciliar documents. Some professionals who had been "part-time priests" mainly saying masses on Sundays decided to leave their liturgical work and devote themselves fully to their other occupations. Others who believed that clerical celibacy no longer agreed with their vision of themselves or their goals in life left the priesthood in order to marry. Still others found themselves at odds for one reason or another with a still authoritarian hierarchy and asked to be relieved of their clerical duties. Despite the permanence of the priestly character which they had received at their ordination, priests asked for and received permission to be laicized, that is, to live their lives as lay people. And there were those who did not wait for permission, but just left.

The exodus from the priesthood was not great in terms of percentages but it was noticeable in terms of numbers. And the cloud over the priesthood also made young men hesitate about a priestly vocation, making applications for the seminary go down. So the crisis of priests leaving was matched with an impending crisis of fewer new priests to replace old ones. A similar set of crises was faced by the religious orders. Authority, celibacy, the rapidness of change for some and the slowness of change for others, the desire to pursue other interests, an uncertainty about the role of religious in the church—all these and other factors led many of those in orders to leave and become lay Catholics. Institutions that had once been staffed predominantly by religious orders had to close or hire lay help. More and more lay people were drawn into service ministries of the church, sometimes as volunteers, sometimes as salaried workers. And not infrequently the lay people in them, particularly in professional positions, were ex-priests or ex-nuns.

What was the status of these new lay workers in the church? And what was the work in which they were engaged? Was it not a ministry of some sort? In a sense they were performing the same functions that two decades before (and for centuries before that) had been the exclusive province of the clergy and religious orders. They were working in Catholic hospitals, homes for the aged, and other charitable institutions: Weren't these ministries of service? They were teaching religion in Catholic schools and parish religious education programs, they were teaching theology in Catholic colleges and writing theological books and articles: Weren't these teaching ministries? They were working with the underprivileged, with adolescents and adults, with single, married, and divorced Catholics, and with families: Weren't these community-building ministries? They were serving as institutional administrators, on parish councils and diocesan committees: Weren't these in some way governing ministries? They were serving at and around the altar, assisting priests, reading during the liturgy, writing and performing music, and leading congregational singing: Weren't these liturgical ministries? They were speaking out on public issues that they believed should be the concern of Christians, issues like peace and justice, racial and sexual discrimination, poverty and oppression, abortion and capital punishment: Weren't these prophetic ministries? By the mid-1970s the easy identification of priesthood and ministry had to be abandoned in theory, for it had already been abandoned in practice.

But this in turn raised further questions about the identity of the priest and the meaning of ordination. Granted that today priests in many parts of the world still perform many of the functions once reserved to them, the fact is that now there is a plurality of ministers in the church doing things that priests alone used to do, and so the priesthood can no longer be defined in terms of a large set of exclusively priestly functions. Ministry in the church has become a plurality of ministries, sometimes performed by priests and sometimes not. At present the only duties reserved exclusively to priests in virtue of their ordination are some liturgical and most of the sacramental ministries. At present bishops also reserve the right to confirm (though priests are now also sometimes delegated to do this) and ordain, and by their consecration as bishops they also see themselves as having the ultimate responsibility and authority in the church.

This leaves priests as priests with an exclusively sacramental ministry, for by their ordination they alone have the power to consecrate the eucharist, to administer absolution, and to perform other sacramental functions. But with the decline of scholastic theology it no longer makes sense as it once did to speak of priests receiving the power of transubstantiation or absolution. Even the definition of priesthood in terms of exclusively priestly "powers" seems to be problematic.

Likewise the bishop's ordination once was and still is conceived in terms of powers, primarily to ordain and to govern the church. And yet as priestly ordination is seen less and less as conferring supernatural powers, the imposition of the bishop's hand can no longer be viewed as imparting those powers from the bishop to the priest. Thus the revised Roman ritual for ordination, for example, speaks of priestly office and dignity, but not priestly power. In addition, the present plurality of ministers and ministries in the church makes the ordination of priests appear somewhat anomalous, for there are now many ministers in the church, including some liturgical ministers, who are not ordained.

This leaves the bishop's power to govern the church, but even this is open to questioning. When communities were small, as in the first few centuries of Christianity, patriarchal bishops such as Ignatius of Antioch could indeed exercise paternal power over their individual churches. This was also true at the height of the patristic period when Christian communities grew large through increased conversions, and bishops used legislation and the delegation of authority to extend their power. Also as a group the bishops oversaw the development of Christian doctrines and the establishment of church practices when they acted together in councils. During the Middle

Ages, individual bishops for the most part ruled the church, either by their own power or with the backing of secular and papal power. And in the modern period, although bishops no longer ruled the lives of Christians as thoroughly as they had in medieval times, they were still the undisputed rulers (with their authority coming from the pope and ultimately from God) of the religious, moral, and intellectual lives of Catholics.

But the picture is now quite changed, and bishops no longer have even the spiritual power that they once had. As the modern individualism that inspired Protestantism has entered into Catholic religious thinking, Catholics no longer look solely to the clergy and the official sacraments for their salvation. As individualism and personalism exert greater influence on matters of conscience, Catholics no longer depend on their priests for forgiveness or on their bishops for moral decisions. And as education becomes less a clerical privilege and more a social right, Catholics no longer leave intellectual leadership to the hierarchy as they once did. The bishops, therefore, although they are still the supervisors of the church's official institutions and the guardians of its official doctrines, are no longer the rulers of the church in any comprehensive sense.

What then? Has the ordination of deacons, priests, and bishops lost all its meaning? Not necessarily. But the meaning of ordination can no longer be identified with power, either with priestly power or with regulatory power, because growing numbers of Catholics no longer live in a world permeated with clerical power. Little by little they are losing their sense that priests by their own supernatural power make Christ present during the liturgy. And they have little or no experience of bishops as persons invested with divine power. Furthermore, Catholics in increasing numbers no longer conceive of ministry in terms of power but in terms of service. And so it makes less and less sense to them to think of ordination as a conferral of power.

So the meaning of ordination is not necessarily lost, even though its sacramental association with power is diminishing. Instead, the meaning of ordination is changing, just as the meaning of the other official sacraments is changing. It is changing to one of service, a meaning which it has always had but which is now becoming primary. As a liturgical ceremony it is still sacramental in the broad sense, as well as being an official Catholic sacrament, for it is both an intensification ritual and a transition ritual. For those who participate in and witness it, it is a symbolic acting out in word and gesture of the sacred meanings of ministry and commitment, expressing the Christian beliefs that the spirit of service and the Spirit of God are one and the same, that Jesus Christ died and still lives in his church to bring salvation to others, that God as a caring and loving Father ministers to the world through the ministry of human beings. And for those who go through it, it marks a person's public entrance into a life of ministry, changing him in his own eyes and in the eyes of his community, making him an official representative of the institutional church and calling him to be a personal sacrament of Christ.

At the same time, the medieval identification of ordination with cultic priesthood is disappearing, though it still lives in the minds of more conservative Catholics, especially the conservative hierarchy. Because ordination is no longer intrinsically connected to cultic priesthood, the theological justification for clerical celibacy has vanished. The historical origins of the laws of continence and celibacy are now known. That Old Testament texts were misapplied to the Christian priesthood is no longer disputed. Christ's invitation to renounce all for the sake of the kingdom can no longer be used to impose sexual renunciation on a few. And Paul's exhortation to celibacy can no longer be used to justify a binding ecclesiastical law. In brief, the historical and scriptural underpinnings of clerical celibacy have been eroded by recent scholarship. Nevertheless, in 1967 Pope Paul VI officially reaffirmed the spiritual values of sexual continence in a special encyclical and refused to allow any revision of the church's law forbidding priests to marry. While not denying that for some people a single life can be a means of a more total dedication to God and the church, a number of Catholics, including priests, now believe that the main reasons for continuing the norm of celibacy are practical and sociological: practical, because unmarried clergy can be more easily trained, maintained, and transferred from one post to another; sociological, because some Catholics are still unwilling or unable to accept the idea of a married clergy.

Likewise, with the change in the meaning of ministry and ordination, the traditional prohibition against women in the clergy has lost much of its theological foundation. Granted that the rising insistence of women to be admitted to orders has been more a product of the women's liberation movement than the result of abstract theological reflection, the fact remains that the scriptural and historical arguments against ordaining women are not that strong and that the major arguments are cultural and psychological. It is true that Christ was a man, that all the apostles were men, and that a number of scriptural texts can be used to support the claim that women should not hold positions of authority in the church. And it is equally true that historically women have never been allowed to be priests and that the first general council of the church ruled that female deacons were not to be counted as members of the clergy. But it is also true that the sex of Jesus and the apostles is today not a very compelling theological argument, that the dominance of men in the early church can be explained as a cultural bias rather than a divine decision, and that an equal number of scriptural texts can be used to support the position that sex as such should make no difference in the choosing of the church's ministers. And it is also true that women did serve in various ministries in the early church, that some of them were ordained, and that before the Council of Nicaea they were in some places regarded as members of the clergy. To a number of Catholic writers, therefore, the exclusion of women from the ordained ministry seems to be more the result of traditional exclusion of women from positions of social authority and cultic leadership than the result of an innate incompatibility between femaleness and priestly ministry.

In fact, women have never been excluded from all ministries in the church; they have been excluded from only one: the ministry of liturgical leadership and sacramental administration. As abbesses and superiors of religious orders, they exercised a ministry of governing and authority, though never before over men. But now as women become engaged in a greater variety of ministries (including pastoral ministry) which give them some authority over men in the church, and as women are allowed to perform liturgical functions besides directly serving at the altar, the only ministries from which they are specifically excluded are those which, in the scholastic order of things, required the possession of special priestly powers. And so here, too, a growing number of Catholics find it hard to justify the traditional prohibition against ordaining women. Nevertheless, there has been no appreciable change in the official Catholic position regarding the ordination of women or married men to the priesthood since the Vatican Council. In 1976 the Congregation for the Doctrine of the Faith reiterated the Roman church's official stand against the ordination of women, and in the years since then the Vatican has become less enthusiastic about ecumenical dialogue with churches that permit women to be ordained. In 1994 Pope John Paul II declared that the church has no authority to ordain women, and later documents suggested that this should be regarded as an infallible teaching of the church.

Inconsistencies between teaching and practice, however, have tended to undermine papal credibility and authority. For example, although Rome has remained steadfast in its general policy of not allowing priests to marry, there are now in fact some married priests in the Catholic Church. This first occurred when the Vatican allowed married priests from the Anglican and Episcopal churches (some of whom left when their church ordained women) to join the Roman communion. This exception to the rule was then extended to other Protestant ministers who were willing to convert to Catholicism if they could be ordained as priests even though they already had wives and families. Thus the Church's policy seems to be that Catholics who are married cannot be ordained, but non-Catholics who are married can become Catholic priests.

But if married Catholic men cannot become priests, they can now become deacons. Today there are thousands of married deacons in the church, and in the United States there are two to three times as many deacon candidates in training as there are seminarians for the priesthood. Pope Paul VI reestablished the permanent diaconate in 1967 in accordance with the decision of the council, but it was not until formation programs were established in the 1980s that the number of deacons began to grow. Envisioned as a service ministry along lines suggested by the opening verses of chapter 6 of the Acts of the Apostles, the restored diaconate also incorporates elements found in the diaconate during the patristic era. Thus although the ministry of today's deacon is primarily pastoral (for example, caring for parishioners or working for social justice), it is also liturgical (preaching at mass and performing baptisms), it can be catechetical (teaching or leading discussions), and it can also be administrative (coordinating parish programs and even supervising a whole parish). Since many permanent deacons are married and have other occupations in addition to their ministry, they provide an example of how it is possible to combine family and business life with service in the church. In many respects they appear to be just like lay people, but since they are in fact ordained, their presence in the church is helping Catholics reevaluate the meaning of ordination in terms of service.

It is conceivable that some time in the future permanent deacons will be the first invited to become married priests. For although celibate priests are not leaving the ministry in great numbers anymore, there are not enough seminarians to replace the priests who die or retire each year. Even in countries in which vocations are increasing, the Catholic population is increasing at a faster rate so that proportionately the availability of priests around the world is steadily declining. In the United States the shortage of priests was first felt in the rural areas of the west and south, but in the early years of the twenty-first century it is also becoming noticeable in the urban areas of the north and east. And in the United States, at least, the rule of celibacy does seem to be a deciding factor in the diminished number of vocations to the priesthood, since other denominations with a married clergy are not suffering from a shortage of candidates for the ministry.

Still, there must be other factors causing the decline in vocations to the priesthood. A number of these have been suggested: the permanent commitment that the priesthood calls for in a society where most people change jobs and professions regularly; the increasing availability of other opportunities to be of service to people both in the church and in the helping professions; the decreased social status of priests in a more affluent and educated society; the failure of Catholic mothers to encourage their sons, as well as the failure of priests themselves to encourage Catholic boys, to join the priesthood; the periodic scandals caused by revelations of homosexual and heterosexual misconduct by priests; the general secularization of contemporary culture; the perception of the institutional church as being authoritarian and inflexible. It would appear that the cause is not simple but complex—a combination of many factors.

The last factor mentioned seems to be exacerbated by the conservative stance that the church has taken in a number of areas, among which the denying of the priesthood to women and married men is only one. The inability to show flexibility in areas of sexual morality, the unwillingness to permit public dissent from the church's current teachings, the imposition of an oath of fidelity on those who teach and preach for the church, the censuring of creative theologians and the questioning of liberal bishops, the closing of non-traditional seminaries in Latin America, the alliance between the official church and the wealthy ruling classes in poor countries, the increasing centralization of ecclesiastical power in the Vatican, and the corresponding decrease in autonomy for regional conferences of bishops—all these policies and actions either taken or continued in the 1980s and 1990s have led to a perception that the institutional church might not be the most congenial of employers.

Another development, more in the United States than in other parts of the world, have been highly publicized scandals involving priests who sexually abused children, primarily younger boys. Statistically, most sex abuse takes place in families and is committed by relatives and friends, and in fact the rate of sex abuse by Protestant ministers and other professionals who have access to children is about the same as the pedophilia rate for priests, but the law suits against priests gained wide public notoriety partly because of the perceived betrayal of trust by supposedly holy men, partly because of the large number of cases that came to light in a relatively short period of time, and partly because the large financial settlements paid to victims forced some dioceses into bankruptcy. News stories about boys being molested by priests began to appear in 1985, but it was not until 2002 that the issue gained widespread public attention and the American bishops adopted what amounts to a zero tolerance policy toward child abuse not only by clergy but also by other church employees.

The net effect of all these factors and perceptions, then, has been a steady relative decline in the number of young men willing to commit their lives to the service of the church in the priesthood. Yet not all Catholics regard the decrease in vocations as a problem, for they see that opportunities to serve the church are growing in other ways, and they believe in a church in which not just priests but all baptized persons are invited into ministry. They agree that the Vatican is going through a phase of conservative response to the initially liberal developments of the Second Vatican Council, but they do not see this trend as permanent. They point out, for instance, that Rome's insistence on celibacy in the traditional male priesthood is in fact rapidly declericalizing the church and that in the future more and more lay people, women and men, married and single, will be in positions of ministry and decision making. As that trend continues, the ministries once centralized in the priesthood will become more and more dispersed throughout the faithful in the church.

Quite possibly in the future church, priests (whether they are celibate or married, male or female) will continue to be those liturgical and pastoral ministers for which specialized and somewhat lengthy preparation is needed. The ministry of the word, preaching and teaching the Christian message in a way that is both knowledgeable and prophetic, both informed and inspiring, will probably require persons who are professionally if not perpetually engaged in their work. Likewise, the ministry of pastoral leadership, creating caring communities, overseeing service ministries for the congregation, serving as a spiritual mentor and personal counselor, will also require professionally trained persons at the local level. Because of the theological background required for both these ministries, they could be joined in one role, but not necessarily, since their other demands are different. Logically, too, the ministry of liturgical leadership could be joined to them for both symbolic and practical reasons, but again not necessarily. Possibly in places where full-time pastors and preachers are not available or not needed, part-time ministers could be designated to lead congregational worship just as deacons are now allowed to baptize and preside at weddings and funerals. Or when persons with talents in one area do not have skills in the others, or when the time demanded for one area does not leave time for the others, these ministries might also be separated.

Nor is there any reason why persons who are called to these various ministries should not be ordained to perform them. Their ordinations would be more varied than the ordination to the priesthood is now, for the service to which they are called would be more specific. Even today in some places catechists and lectors and distributors of communion are publicly initiated into their ministry through ceremonies that are sacramental in the broad sense, just as those who join religious communities are officially admitted to their way of life through rituals that are analogous to ordination. And the church's administrative officers, even if in the future they are not clerics in the traditional sense, could still be inducted into their office by means of sacramental ceremonies, parallel to the swearing in of public officials or the investiture of college presidents, but religious in nature and Christian in meaning.

But not all ministers would have to be ordained, either. In fact today they often are not, for ministry is no longer restricted to officially designated ministers in the church. A broadened notion of ministry implies that all Christians are called to be ministers in some sense, especially if the Christian life is understood to be a life of service to others. And such ministry in the broad sense is sacramental in the broad sense, for it is an expression of a sacred meaning which is already being lived and a sign of that sacred reality to others. It is thus a continuation of Christ's ministry, which was also sacramental in the broad sense. And in this sense, too, all ministry is a priestly ministry, a mediation between God and human beings, bringing both closer to each, incarnating the one and divinizing the other.

Notwithstanding, the authors of the Catechism of the Catholic Church have a much more traditional attitude toward priesthood and ordination. If Catholics' understanding of ministry has been changing since the Second Vatican Council in response to shifts in the practice and experience of ministry, these changes have not yet reached those who formulate its official teachings and speak publicly on its behalf. In few areas is there such a wide gap between what most educated Catholics believe and what they are told to believe, perhaps because the day-to-day experience of priesthood (both the experience of priests themselves and the experience of those to whom they minister) is visibly different from the experience of cardinals and other church officials who work for the Vatican. Also, since political power in the Catholic Church has for centuries been closely connected with priestly power, it is understandable that the church's leadership would be reluctant to rethink the meaning of ministry in any way that might call the church's hierarchical structure into question.

The *Catechism's* sections on ordination (1536–1600) therefore exhibit few signs of developments in pastoral practice and theological thinking that took place in the twentieth century. From the very beginning of the section the focus is on priestly power (1538), and this focus is maintained throughout (see especially 1551, 1564, 1584, 1592). Similarly, the concept of the sacramental character, first introduced by Augustine to explain the unrepeatability of baptism and extended in the Middle Ages to confirmation and holy orders, features prominently in this section (1558, 1563, 1570, 1580, 1597). Although echoes of Vatican II are heard in the *Catechism's* insistence that priesthood is a ministry of service (1551), it is clear that this service entails the exercise of clerical power, with bishops, priests, and deacons doing for the church what lay people, lacking such power, cannot do for themselves (1547, 1552, 1555–1558, 1563–1566, 1570, 1576, 1581–1584, 1592).

This having been noted, what the *Catechism* says about the sacrament is quite understandable. After stating that ordination bestows a sacred power that comes from Christ, the *Catechism* presents the cultic priesthood of the Jewish temple as a pre-figuring of the Catholic priesthood (1538–1543). The Epistle to the Hebrews teaches that Christ is the one high priest, but the scriptures also refer to Christians as a priestly people. Christian laity and clergy therefore participate in the one priesthood of Christ, but in different ways: lay people through baptism, priests and bishops through ordination (1544–1547). Those in holy orders act in the power and place of Christ in his role as head of the church, and they therefore lead the body of Christ in prayer and in offering sacrifice (1548–1553).

The *Catechism* presents the teaching of the Second Vatican Council that there are three degrees of holy orders: the episcopate, the presbyterate, and the diaconate. All three are conferred by ordination, and there is only one sacrament; however, ordination bestows on bishops and priests participation in Christ's priestly ministry whereas it bestows on deacons participation in his ministry of service (1554). Bishops receive the fullness of the sacrament (that is, the full sacramental reality) and so receive the power to teach, rule, and sanctify as agents of Christ and successors of the apostles (1555–1561). Priests are ordained to be co-workers of their bishop, and they receive the power to preach the gospel and offer the sacrifice in the eucharistic cult (1562–1568). Deacons are ordained to assist bishops and priests in a variety of clerical duties and charitable services (1569–1571).

All three degrees of ordination confer a sacramental character and unite the ordained in a sacramental brotherhood.

Only a bishop, as successor of the apostles, can confer this sacrament, and only baptized males can receive it. The *Catechism* insists that no one has a right to this sacrament, indirectly addressing the claims of women and married men that they should not be excluded from ordination. The rule of celibacy for bishops and priests is affirmed, although a different rule for eastern rite churches is acknowledged (1575–1580).

The *Catechism* appeals to the scholastic concept of the sacramental reality (*sacramentum et res*), calling it an indelible character that permanently marks the soul of the ordained, even though they may for good reason be discharged from performing their priestly duties. It is this spiritual configuration to Christ that gives priests the power to act in Christ's name regardless of their personal worthiness or unworthiness (1581–1584). The sacrament also makes available to the ordained a special grace (*res tantum*) proper to each of the ranks: bishops receive the grace to guide and defend the church, to proclaim the gospel, and to be a model for others; priests receive the grace to proclaim the gospel, to offer the eucharistic sacrifice, and to perform baptisms; deacons receive the grace to proclaim the gospel, to assist in the liturgy, and to perform works of charity (1585–1589). The *Catechism* does not explain how the *res tantum* differs from the *sacramentum et res*, nor the apparent overlap in the graces specific to each order.

It is clear that the *Catechism*'s vision of ordination is firmly rooted in the Middle Ages even though the world is moving rapidly from modernity into what is being called a postmodern culture. Medieval culture was strongly hierarchical, the divisions in medieval society were few and rigid, and the medieval mentality had no difficulty believing in the magical transformations of alchemy. This rise of modern culture in the sixteenth century led Catholicism to wall itself off from developments in science and politics, and the Tridentine church survived as a fortress of stability through four centuries of social change. The Second Vatican Council moved the church forward in many areas, but not with regard to the priesthood. As already mentioned, Rome has resisted changing its practice with regard to priestly celibacy and the ordination of women, even so far as to declare the matter closed. Even though official discussion of this issue has been halted, however, unofficial discussion continues in the wider church, and the issue of ordaining women as deacons remains open because it is clear that there were women deacons during the first centuries of Christianity. Thus in the twenty-first century, as the pace and scope of change increase and globalize, the Catholic Church is attempting to adapt its ministerial practices to the needs of the times (witness the explosion in the number of lay ministers, many of whom are women) and simultaneously to maintain a theology of priestly ministry that arose centuries ago in very different circumstances. How long the church can live with this tension between practice and theory is unknown. One lesson is clear, however, from the history of ordination and the other liturgical sacraments: in the dialectic between theory and practice, changes in sacramental theology more often follow changes in church practice than the other way around.

Catholicism has proven itself to be very resilient as it has moved through a succession of cultures, originating in the Jewish culture of the eastern Mediterranean, adapting to the Greco-Roman culture of the Roman Empire, transforming and being transformed by the Germanic culture of medieval Europe, and maintaining itself against the forces of modernity while becoming a potent spiritual force in the modern world. If the history of the Catholic Church and its sacraments provides a reliable precedent, therefore, the ongoing developments in ministry described earlier will eventually be reflected in its theology of ordination.

For Further Reading

Paul Edwards, *Theology of the Priesthood* (Clergy Book Service, 1974) is a concise, historical, and witty essay on the role of priests in Catholicism.

William Bausch, *Ministry: Traditions, Tensions, Transitions* (Twenty-Third Publications, 1982) looks at what is happening today in the light of history and offers practical suggestions for the future.

Daniel Donovan, *What Are They Saying About the Ministerial Priesthood?* (Paulist Press, 1992) is a summary of the theology of ministry since Vatican II.

Bernard Häring, *Priesthood Imperiled* (Liguori/Triumph, 1996) interweaves personal, scriptural, historical, theological, and moral reflections on current church policies and practices.

Donald Cozzens, *The Changing Face of the Priesthood* (Liturgical Press, 2000) articulates what is happening to the ordained ministry with data from psychology, sociology, and the experience of priests.

Donald Goergen, ed., *Being a Priest Today* (Liturgical Press, 1992) is a collection of well-written articles on a wide range of topics related to priesthood.

William Perri, *A Radical Challenge for Priesthood Today* (Twenty-Third Publications, 1996) suggests that traditional priesthood is dying, in preparation for a transformation and rebirth in the future.

Terrence Sweeney, *A Church Divided* (Prometheus Books, 1992) is based on surveys of Catholic clergy and laity about priestly celibacy and the ordination of women.

Richard Schoenherr and Lawerence *Young, Full Pews and Empty Altars* (University of Wisconsin Press, 1993) documents the growing priest shortage in the United States.

Thomas Kane, *Priests Are People, Too!* (Thomas More, 2002) contains personal vignettes and autobiographies that show the human side of ministry.

Andrew Greeley, *Priests: A Calling in Crisis* (University of Chicago Press, 2004) provides a snapshot of priests in the U.S. based on sociological data and insightful analysis.

Gerald Coleman, *Catholic Priesthood* (Liguori Publications, 2006) discusses priestly vocation and training in clear and practical terms.

Christopher Ruddy, *Tested in Every Way* (Crossroad, 2006) reports on a conference covering many aspects of priesthood in the church.

David Bohr, *The Diocesan Priest* (Liturgical Press, 2009) sets forth the traditional understanding of priesthood as dating back to the New Testament and exercising supernatural powers received in ordination.

Ronald Witherup, *Gold Tested in Fire* (Liturgical Press, 2012) uses scripture and history to re-envision the priest as shepherd, poet, sage, and teacher.

For Further Study

History—General

Bernard Cooke, *Ministry to Word and Sacraments* (Fortress Press, 1976) is a scholarly and thorough treatment of the history and theology of ministry which also provides background for understanding the development of the other sacraments in relation to the priesthood.

Kenan Osborne, *Priesthood: A History of Ordained Ministry in the Roman Catholic Church* (Paulist Press, 1988) is a thorough, detailed, and balanced exposition of the subject.

Patrick Dunn, *Priesthood: A Reexamination of the Roman Catholic Theology of the Presbyterate* (Alba House, 1990) documents the history of ordained ministry and discusses the contemporary situation in some detail.

Paul Bernier, *Ministry in the Church* (Twenty-Third Publications, 1992) uses historical analysis to shed light on the meaning and practice of ministry and priesthood today.

Leon Streider, *The Promise of Obedience* (Liturgical Press, 2001) looks at the promise made to the local bishop in the ordination rite from its first beginnings to the present.

History—Early Church

David Bartlett, *Ministry in the New Testament* (Fortress Press, 1993) connects Catholic and Protestant statements on ministry with biblical principles and values.

Marjorie Warkentin, *Ordination: A Biblical-Historical View* (William B. Eerdmans, 1982) traces the ritual of laying on of hands from its Jewish precedents to its early Christian developments.

Pheme Perkins, *Ministry in the Pauline Churches* (Paulist Press, 1982) examines the diverse roles and functions of ministers during the first decades of Christianity.

Raymond Brown, *Priest and Bishop: Some Biblical Reflections* (Paulist Press, 1970) examines the New Testament for the origins of the Catholic clergy.

Nathan Mitchell, *Mission and Ministry* (Michael Glazier, 1982) presents the history and theology of ordained ministry, with special emphasis on the first three centuries of Christianity.

John Zizioulas, *Eucharist, Bishop, Church* (Holy Cross Orthodox Press, 2001) Uses writings from the first three centuries to argue that church unity is grounded in spiritual union with Christ in the liturgy led by a single bishop.

James Mohler, *The Origin and Evolution of Priesthood* (Alba House, 1970) shows the development from the early Christian community to the fifth century.

Carl Volz, *Pastoral Life and Practice in the Early Church* (Fortress Press, 1990) looks at the office and functions of the pastor during the first five centuries, including the pastoral role of women.

John Gibaut, *The Cursus Honorum* (Peter Lang, 2000) is a comprehensive study of the development of sequential ordination in the patristic and medieval periods.

Peter Norton, *Episcopal Elections 250-600* (Oxford University Press, 2007) examines the procedures, benefits, and drawbacks of electing bishops during the patristic period.

Sharon McMillan, *Episcopal Ordination and Ecclesial Consensus* (Liturgical Press, 2005) describes how the right of local churches to elect or consent to the appointment of their own bishops was lost as the power of the papacy increased.

Theology

Thomas O'Meara, *Theology of Ministry* (Paulist Press, 1999) develops an understanding of ministry that embraces clerical and lay, professional and volunteer service in the church.

Michael Lawler, *A Theology of Ministry* (Sheed and Ward, 1990) is a solid introduction to the different meanings and types of ministry in the church today.

David Power, *Ministers of Christ and His Church* (Geoffrey Chapman, 1969) is a detailed study of the theology of pastoral ministry from early Christian times to recent times.

Edward Schillebeeckx, *Ministry: Leadership in the Community of Jesus Christ* (Crossroad, 1981) looks at current issues concerning the priesthood in the light of New Testament and historical precedents. *The Church with a Human Face* (1985) revises the argument of the previous book and challenges Catholics to rethink the meaning and practice of ministry.

Donald Goergen and Ann Garrido, eds., *The Theology of Priesthood* (Liturgical Press, 2000) contains papers from a colloquium sponsored by the Dominican order.

Susan Wood, *Sacramental Orders* (Liturgical Press, 2000) offers a commentary on the ordination rites as well as a theology of the orders of bishop, priest, and deacon.

Jean Galot, *Theology of the Priesthood* (Ignatius Press, 1984) presents a contemporary understanding of the Catholic priesthood developed along rather traditional lines.

Gisbert Greshake, *The Meaning of Christian Priesthood* (Christian Classics, 1989) argues that there is an essential difference between priest and laity in virtue of priestly ordination and consecration.

Michael Richards, *A People of Priests* (Darton, Longman and Todd, 1995) tries to pin down the difference between the priesthood of the presbyterate and the priesthood of the faithful.

Avery Dulles, The *Priestly Office* (Paulist Press, 1997) contains five lectures to priests, reflecting on the Catholic understanding of priesthood.

Thomas Acklin, *The Unchanging Heart of the Priesthood* (Emmaus Road, 2005) offers a traditional understanding of priesthood as resulting from an ontological transformation of the ordained.

Matthew Levering, ed., *On the Priesthood* (Rowman and Littlefield, 2003) is a modest selection of historical texts about the priesthood, episcopacy, and papacy. *Christ and the Catholic Priesthood* (Hillenbrand Books, 2010) argues that Christ founded the priesthood for a church that reflects the hierarchical nature of the Trinity.

Ministerial Life and Spirituality

Richard McBrien, *Ministry: A Theological, Pastoral Handbook* (Harper and Row, 1987) discusses ministry from a broad perspective and proposes a fundamental spirituality for ministry.

Priests for the New Millennium (USCCB, 2000) is a collection of essays on the ministerial priesthood by American bishops.

Robert Kinast, *Sacramental Pastoral Care* (Pueblo, 1984) explores the role of the priest in sacramental ministry through reflection on case studies.

Elaine Ramshaw, *Ritual and Pastoral Care* (Fortress Press, 1987) examines the central role that ministers play in their function as leaders of church rituals.

Mark O'Keefe, *The Ordination of a Priest* (Abbey Press, 1999) draws implications from the rite of ordination for priestly life and spirituality.

Basil Pennington and Carl Arico, *Living Our Priesthood Today* (Our Sunday Visitor, 1987) presents reflections by two priests on the charism and ministry of priesthood in the contemporary church.

John Fogarty, *The Catholic Priest: His Identity and Values* (Sheed and Ward, 1988) analyzes the beliefs and values of priests through the results of a sociological survey.

William Maestri, *A Priest to Turn To* (Alba House, 1989) proposes biblical models for priests in their pastoral roles today.

Douglas Morin, *Instrument of Peace* (Alba House, 1989) discusses spiritual growth through prayer and meditation, celibacy and friendship, sacramental and pastoral ministry.

Thomas Rausch, *Priesthood Today* (Paulist Press, 1992) reviews the changing situation of American Catholic priests in the decades following Vatican II.

Timothy Dolan, *Priests for the Third Millennium* (Our Sunday Visitor, 2000) collects conferences given to Catholic seminarians in Rome in the 1990s.

George Guiver et al., *Priests in a People's Church* (SPCK, 2001) looks from an Anglican perspective at issues pertinent to all churches that have ordained clergy.

George Aschenberger, *Quickening the Fire in Our Midst* (Loyola Press, 2002) develops an understanding of identity and spirituality tailored to the active and collaborative.

Dominic Grassi, *Still Called by Name* (Loyola Press, 2003) offers personal reflections on the challenges and rewards of being a priest.

Howard Bleichner, *View from the Altar* (Crossroad, 2004) contrasts many aspects of priestly life and ministry before and after the Second Vatican Council.

Michael Hehir, *The Lost Art of Walking on Water* (Paulist Press, 2004) deals honestly with priestly life and well-being in the wake of clergy shortages and sex scandals.

Stephen Rossetti, *The Joy of Priesthood* (Ave Maria Press, 2005) discusses why most priests find great satisfaction in their ministry. *Born of the Eucharist* (Ave Maria Press, 2009) collects reflections by priests and bishops on how their spiritual life is nourished by the sacrament. *Why Priests Are Happy* (Ave Maria Press, 2011) presents the findings of a survey of priests in the United States.

Marriage and Celibacy

Jean-Paul Audet, *Structures of the Christian Priesthood* (Macmillan, 1968) discusses the development of priestly lifestyle from marriage to celibacy.

William Bassett and Peter Huizing, eds., *Celibacy in the Church* (Herder and Herder, 1972) contains a good collection of articles on past and recent aspects of the issue.

Anne Llewellyn Barstow, *Married Priests and the Reforming Papacy* (Edwin Mellin Press, 1982) traces the history of clerical marriage through the first centuries of Christianity and the increasing devaluation of sexuality in the late Roman world.

Charles Gallagher and Thomas Vandenberg, *The Celibacy Myth* (Crossroad, 1987) is a positive presentation of celibacy as a special charism in, of, and for the church.

Joseph Fichter, *The Pastoral Provisions—Married Catholic Priests* (Sheed & Ward, 1989) discusses the acceptance of married Anglican and Episcopalian clergy into the Roman Catholic Church.

Christian Cochini, *Apostolic Origins of Priestly Celibacy* (Ignatius Press, 1990) equates celibacy with sexual continence in marriage to argue for celibacy after ordination.

Joseph Fichter, *Wives of Catholic Clergy* (Sheed and Ward, 1992) looks at the history and current practice of priests having wives, and of the treatment of women in relation to clergy.

Heinz-J. Vogels, *Celibacy—Gift or Law?* (Sheed and Ward, 1993) argues that if celibacy is a special charism, it cannot be mandated for all.

Alfons Maria Stickler, *The Case for Clerical Celibacy* (Ignatius Press, 1995) makes it case partly by ignoring married clergy in the early church.

A. W. Richard Sipe, *Celibacy* (Liguori Publications, 1996) talks in plain language about sexuality, personal development, and spirituality. *Celibacy in Crisis* (Brunner-Routeledge, 2003) examines problems associated with a celibate priesthood, including sexual relations with women, men, and minors. *Living the Celibate Life* (Liguori Publications, 2004) affirms the possibility and goodness of a celibate lifestyle.

Stanley Jaki, *Theology of Priestly Celibacy* (Christendom Press, 1997) develops a balanced and nuanced understanding of the relationship between priesthood and celibacy.

Stefan Heid, *Celibacy in the Early Church* (Ignatius Press, 2000) presents sometimes strained arguments that Catholic clergy practiced celibacy since the time of the apostles.

Joseph Allen, ed., *Vested in Grace* (Holy Cross Orthodox Press, 2001) offers articles on married clergy in Orthodox churches in the past and present.

Richard Schoenherr, *Goodbye Father* (Oxford University Press, 2002) argues that changing the rule of celibacy would lead to a more inclusive church by softening the patriarchy inherent in hierarchical structures.

Michael Crosby, *Rethinking Celibacy, Reclaiming the Church* (Wipf and Stock, 2003) argues that imposed celibacy is a means of maintaining control that has become a dysfunctional structure of clericalism and authoritarianism.

William Phipps, *Clerical Celibacy* (Continuum, 2004) is a history of the practice from pre-Christian times to the present.

Donald Cozzens, *Freeing Celibacy* (Liturgical Press, 2006) examines the many rewards of celibacy but suggests that it should be optional.

Helen Parish, *Clerical Celibacy in the West* (Ashgate, 2009) is a detailed historical study of celibacy, focusing especially on medieval Catholicism and early Protestantism.

John Cavadini, ed., *The Charism of Priestly Celibacy* (Ave Maria Press, 2012) assembles recent articles in support of celibacy and showing that it can be a healthy and happy lifestyle.

Permanent Deacons

Edward Echlin, *The Deacon in the Church* (Alba House, 1971) is a brief but thorough history of the diaconate from apostolic times to the present.

Norbert Brockman, *Ordained to Service* (Exposition Press, 1976) is another brief and clear presentation of the development and meaning of the permanent diaconate.

Patrick McCaslin and Michael Lawler, eds., *Sacrament of Service* (Paulist Press, 1986) compares the intended vision and the actual reality of the permanent diaconate.

Timothy Shugrue, *Service Ministry of the Deacon* (United States Catholic Conference, 1988) summarizes the official understanding of the nature and role of the permanent diaconate in the American church.

Lynn Sherman, *The Deacon in the Church* (Alba House, 1991) looks at the diaconate in history, describes its restoration after Vatican II, and recounts personal experiences in the ministry.

James Barnett, *The Diaconate: A Full and Equal Order* (Trinity Press International, 1995) offers a detailed history of the diaconate and a description of the restored diaconate in the Roman Catholic and Episcopal churches.

Owen Cummings, *Deacons and the Church* (Paulist Press, 2004) is a well-rounded treatment that touches on the history, theology, and practical dimensions of diaconal ministry.

Michael Kwatera, *The Liturgical Ministry of Deacons* (Liturgical Press, 2005) describes the duties of deacons in a wide range of liturgical settings.

James Keating, ed., *The Deacon Reader* (Paulist Press, 2006) is a readable collection written mostly by deacons and priests.

Kenan Osborne, *The Permanent Diaconate* (Paulist Press, 2007) examines this revived ministry in the context of Vatican II ecclesiology and post-conciliar developments.

William Ditewig, *The Emerging Diaconate* (Paulist Press, 2007) presents a detailed picture of the permanent diaconate in America and develops a theology of diaconal ordination. With Michael Tkacik, eds., *Forming Deacons* (Paulist Press, 2010) collects articles on the human, spiritual, intellectual, and pastoral dimensions of diaconal training.

The Ordination of Women—Historical Background

Haye van der Meer, *Women Priests in the Church?* (Temple University Press, 1973) examines biblical, patristic, and doctrinal texts usually invoked against the ordination of women.

Roger Gryson, *The Ministry of Women in the Early Church* (Liturgical Press, 1976) supplies a balanced view of the historical data from the first to the sixth century.

Elizabeth Tetlow, *Women and Ministry in the New Testament* (Paulist Press, 1980) develops evidence from scriptural sources that women played important roles in early Christian communities.

Ben Witherington, *Women in the Earliest Churches* (Cambridge University Press, 1988) discusses and documents women's leadership roles during the first Christian centuries.

Karen Torjesen, *When Women Were Priests* (Harper San Francisco, 1990) claims that women held leadership positions in early Christianity, but most of these were lost by the fourth century.

Ute Eisen, *Women Officeholders in Early Christianity* (Liturgical Press, 2000) investigates the diverse roles that women played in the apostolic and patristic periods, using evidence from official documents, other writings, and inscriptions.

Bernard Cooke and Gary Macy, eds., *The Ordination of Women in a Medieval Context* (Scarecrow Press, 2002) reprints two scholarly articles on the ordination of women up to and after the twelfth century.

John Wijngaards, *No Women in Holy Orders?* (Canterbury Press, 2002) examines manuscript evidence from the third century onward regarding the ordination of women as deacons. *Women Deacons in the Early Church* (Crossroad, 2006) translates 35 historical documents and provides a scholarly commentary on the issue.

Ida Ramig, *The Priestly Office of Women* (Scarecrow Press, 2004) traces the origins of sex discrimination against women's ordination to the publication of Gratian's *Decree* in the twelfth century.

Kevin Madigan and Carolyn Osiek, *Ordained Women in the Early Church* (Johns Hopkins University Press, 2005) documents and comments on references to women as deacons and presbyters through the eighth century.

Gary Macy, *The Hidden History of Women's Ordination* (Oxford University Press, 2008) uses medieval documents to show that deaconesses, abbesses, and other female ministers were ordained until the twelfth century.

The Ordination of Women—Official Teaching

Sacred Congregation for the Doctrine of the Faith, *Declaration on the Question of the Admission of Women to the Ministerial Priesthood* (USCC, 1977) provides the text and an official commentary on the position of the Catholic Church and the reasons supporting that position.

Leonard and Arlene Swidler, eds., *Women Priests: A Catholic Commentary on the Vatican Declaration* (Paulist Press, 1977) collects fifty articles by Catholic scholars who critique one or another aspect of the reasoning and conclusion of the declaration.

Carroll Stuhlmueller, ed., *Women and Priesthood* (Liturgical press, 1978) contains additional articles responding to the Vatican declaration on the admission of women to the priesthood.

David Maloney, *The Church Cannot Ordain Women to the Priesthood* (Franciscan Herald Press, 1978) is a short apologia in plain language for the Vatican's declaration on the ordination of women.

Manfred Hauke, *Women in the Priesthood?* (Ignatius Press, 1988) argues on historical, doctrinal, and ontological grounds that women are incapable of being ordained priests.

John Paul II, *Ordinatio Sacerdotalis* (USCC, 1994) is an official restatement of the Catholic Church's position on the impossibility of ordaining women set forth in 1976.

Simone St. Pierre, *The Struggle to Serve* (McFarland, 1994) contrasts Catholic restrictions on the ordination of women with scriptural, historical, and theological arguments for women's ministry.

Elisabeth Schüssler Fiorenza and Hermann Häring, eds., *The Non-Ordination of Women and the Politics of Power* (Orbis Books, 1999) presents articles critical of the Vatican's policies and procedures.

John Wijngaards, *The Ordination of Women in the Catholic Church* (Continuum, 2001) analyzes the prohibition of women's ordination and attacks it head-on.

Gerhard Ludwig Müller, *Priesthood and Diaconate* (Ignatius Press, 2002) explains why the Catholic Church does not ordain women to either of these holy orders.

Deborah Halter, *The Papal "No"* (Crossroad, 2004) is a comprehensive history and theology of both sides of the women's ordination issue in the Catholic Church.

Sara Butler, *The Catholic Priesthood and Women* (Liturgy Training Publications, 2007) explains and defends the teaching that the church has not been authorized by Christ to ordain women.

Ordination of Women—Theological and Pastoral Dimensions

Paul Jewett, *The Ordination of Women* (William B. Eerdmans, 1980) analyzes and responds to the major arguments against the possibility of ordaining women.

Phyllis Zagano, *Holy Saturday* (Crossroad, 2000) argues that women should be ordained to the deaconate rather than to the priesthood. *Women in Ministry* (Paulist Press, 2012) looks at the possibility of ordaining women to the diaconate based on precedents in history and in other churches.

Kelley Raab, *When Women Become Priests* (Columbia University Press, 2000) asks how the Catholic Church will be different when the title of the book becomes a reality.

Miriam Therese Winter, *Out of the Depths* (Crossroad, 2001) is a biography of Ludmila Javorova, who was ordained a Roman Catholic priest to bring the sacraments to women in communist Czechoslovakia.

Mary Jeremy Daigler, *Incompatible with God's Design* (Rowman and Littlefield, 2012) is a comprehensive history of the Roman Catholic women's ordination movement in the United States.

Gary Macy, William Ditewig, and Phyllis Zagano, *Women Deacons* (Paulist Press, 2012) is a very readable account of how women served as deacons in the past, and what the service of women deacons might look like in the future.

Ordination of Women—Ecumenical Dimensions

Thomas Hopko, ed., *Women and the Priesthood* (St. Vladimir's Seminary Press, 1999) presents articles that support the traditional view and some that question the exclusion of women.

Elisabeth Behr-Sigel, *The Ministry of Women in the Church* (Oakwood Publications, 1987) examines the place and privileges of women within the Orthodox tradition.

Kyriaki Kardoyanes FitzGerald, *Women Deacons in the Orthodox Church* (Holy Cross Orthodox Press, 1998) shows how this office arose and declined in the East, and argues for its restoration.

Stanley Grenz, *Women in the Church* (InterVarsity Press, 1995) sheds light on Catholic issues from a Protestant perspective.

Jacqueline Field-Bibb, *Women Towards Priesthood* (Cambridge University Press, 1991) documents and interprets movements toward women's ordination in the Methodist, Anglican, and Catholic churches.

Mark Chaves, *Ordaining Women* (Harvard University Press, 1997) looks at institutional changes taking place in churches that allow women to have pastoral roles.

A. M. Allchin and others, *A Fearful Symmetry?* (SPCK, 1992) presents arguments against the ordination of women, written by an ecumenical group of women and men.

Paul Avis, ed., *Seeking the Truth of Change in the Church* (T&T Clark, 2004) contains Anglican reflection on the ordination of women and its impact on this worldwide communion.

Ian Jones, Janet Wootten, and Kirsty Thorpe, eds., *Women and Ordination in the Christian Churches* (Continuum, 2008) examines the issue from an interdenominational and international perspective.

Expanded and Non-Ordained Ministry

Yves Congar, *Lay People in the Church* (Newman Press, 1957) is the ground-breaking classic on the importance of the vast majority of church members.

Leonard Doohan, *The Lay-Centered Church* (Winston Press, 1984) assesses the situation today in terms of ministry and spirituality.

Robert Kinast, *Caring for Society* (Thomas More Press, 1985) describes the emergence of lay ministry in the Catholic Church and develops a biblical and sociological theology of this new reality.

Peter Gilmour, *The Emerging Pastor* (Sheed and Ward, 1986) looks at what happens when sisters replace priests as administrators of rural parishes.

Kenan Osborne, *Ministry: Lay Ministry in the Roman Catholic Church* (Paulist Press, 1993) is an exhaustive study of the history and theology of ministry, lay and otherwise.

James and Evelyn Whitehead, *The Emerging Laity* (Doubleday, 1986) discusses the problems of leadership and collaboration in a church with both clerical and lay ministers.

Dean Hoge, *The Future of Catholic Leadership* (Sheed and Ward, 1987) analyzes the priest shortage with statistical research and discusses options for dealing with it.

Michael Cowan, ed., *Alternative Futures for Worship, Volume 6: Leadership Ministry in Community* (Liturgical Press, 1987) contains articles that explore the nature and function of Christian leadership and suggest new rites for a variety of church ministries.

Jay Dolan and others, *Transforming Parish Ministry* (Crossroad, 1990) closely examines the history of Catholic ministry—clerical, religious, and lay—in America from 1930 to the present.

Norman Cooper, *Collaborative Ministry* (Paulist Press, 1993) proposes a model of ministry based on a universal call to holiness and discipleship.

Greg Dues and Barbara Walkley, *Called to Parish Ministry* (Twenty-Third Publications, 1995) invites lay people who feel called to ministry to reflect on their identity, attitude, and spirituality.

Zeni Fox, *New Ecclesial Ministry* (Sheed and Ward, 1997) is a comprehensive overview of professional lay ministry as it is emerging in the United States.

Together in God's Service (NCCB, 1998) presents papers from a colloquium on ecclesial lay ministry sponsored by the National Conference of Catholic Bishops.

Loughlan Sofield and Carroll Juliano, *Collaboration* (Ave Maria Press, 2000) offers practical advice for developing and maintaining collaborative relationships in ministry.

Michael Christensen, ed., *Equipping the Saints* (Abingdon Press, 2000) gathers contributions about ministry based on the priesthood of all believers and ignoring differences between clergy and laity.

Graham Buxton, *Dancing in the Dark* (Paternoster Press, 2001) professes to be an exercise in practical theology treating theological and pastoral aspects of ministry.

Virginia Stillwell, *Priestless Parishes* (Thomas More, 2002) looks at the phenomenon and the theology of Catholic parishes without clergy in residence.

Susan Wood, ed., *Ordering the Baptismal Priesthood* (Liturgical Press, 2003) collects papers from a conference on the theology of lay and ordained ministry.

Ruth Wallace, *They Call Him Pastor* (Paulist Press, 2003) examines the phenomenon of priestless parishes with statistics, sociology, canon law, and anecdotes.

Edward Hahnenberg, *Ministries: A Relational Approach* (Crossroad, 2003) makes the case for erasing the line between clergy and laity in a re-visioning of Catholic ministry.

Co-Workers in the Vineyard of the Lord (USCCB, 2005) outlines the current understanding and practice of lay ecclesial ministry in the Catholic Church.

Paul Lakeland, *Catholicism at the Crossroads* (Continuum, 2009) argues that the laity can save the church from clericalism and irrelevance by demanding transparency in governance and by engaging in dialogue.

Matthew Clark, *Forward in Hope* (Ave Maria Press, 2009) is written by a bishop who progressed from hesitation to enthusiasm about lay ecclesial ministry.

Kathy Hendricks, *Parish Life Coordinators* (Loyola Press, 2009) is a short and clear introduction to the ministry of administering parishes that do not have priest pastors.

Zeni Fox, ed., *Lay Ecclesial Ministry* (Rowman and Littlefield, 2010) assembles articles on lay leadership from the perspectives of scripture, history, spirituality, and pastoral practice.

Donna Eschenauer and Harold Daly Horrell, eds., *Reflections on Renewal* (Liturgical Press, 2011) offers reflections on the USCCB document, *Co-Workers in the Vineyard of the Lord*, from a variety of practical and theoretical perspectives.

William Cahoy, ed., *In the Name of the Church* (Liturgical Press, 2012) collects articles on the vocation of lay ecclesial ministry and its authorization, both canonically and ritually.

Contemporary Issues

Jason Berry, *Lead Us Not Into Temptation* (Doubleday, 1992) was one of the first books to thoroughly investigate reports of pedophilia by Catholic priests.

A. W. Richard Sipe, *Sex, Priests, and Power* (Brunner/Mazel, 1995) analyzes the emerging pedophilia crisis using research data and anecdotal information.

Philip Jenkins, *Pedophiles and Priests* (Oxford University Press, 1996) reports on the clergy pedophilia crisis as it appeared in the early 1990s.

Stephen Rossetti, *A Tragic Grace* (Liturgical Press, 1996) is a short, balanced discussion of child abuse scandals and their effects on attitudes toward the priesthood.

Thomas Plante, ed., *Bless Me Father for I Have Sinned* (Praeger, 1999) presents articles by psychologists and other professionals involved in treating clergy sex abusers. *Sin Against the Innocents* (Praeger, 2004) contains articles that are critical of the church's failure to prevent clerical sex abuse, and of its institutional response to the problem.

Ron O'Grady, *The Hidden Shame of the Church* (WCC Publications, 2001) looks at the problem of child sex abuse by ministers in many churches and many countries.

Donald Cozzens, *Sacred Silence* (Liturgical Press, 2002) treats sexual issues in the context of institutional behavior, social change, and moral principles.

Ben Bradlee and others, *Betrayal: The Crisis in the Catholic Church* (Little, Brown and Company, 2002) documents the abuse of children by priests and the abuse of power by bishops, leading to scandals in Boston and other dioceses

Len Sperry, *Sex, Priestly Ministry, and the Church* (Liturgical Press, 2003) briefly but professionally reviews the major factors involved in sexual misconduct by priests.

Kathryn Flynn, *The Sexual Abuse of Women by Members of the Clergy* (McFarland and Company, 2003) is an interdenominational approach to the problem, which is as prevalent in Protestant churches as in the Catholic Church.

Promise to Protect, Pledge to Heal (USCCB, 2003) is a statement of episcopal commitment that also includes norms for dealing with allegations of sexual abuse by priests or deacons.

Donald Boisvert and Robert Goss, eds., *Gay Catholic Priests and Clerical Sexual Misconduct* (Haworth Press, 2005) attacks the premise that homosexuals commit pedophilia and therefore should not be ordained as priests.

R. Karl Hanson, Friedemann Pfäfflin, and Manfred Lütz, eds., *Sexual Abuse in the Catholic Church* (Libreria Editrice Vaticana, 2004) prints proceedings from a Vatican conference on the abuse of children and young people by Catholic clergy.

Mary Gail Frawley-Odea, *Perversion of Power* (Vanderbilt University Press, 2007) analyzes the psychological dynamics of clerical sex abuse, showing how it was enabled by bishops, laypeople and other priests.

George Wilson, *Clericalism* (Liturgical Press, 2008) looks at how clergy and laity adopt attitudes that lead to the abuse of power and betrayal of trust.

Russell Shaw, *Nothing to Hide* (Ignatius Press, 2008) discusses the clerical culture of secrecy in relation to clergy sex abuse.

Nicolas Cafardi, *Before Dallas* (Paulist Press, 2008) traces the American bishops' response to reports of clergy sex abuse before they adopted strict norms for the protection of children in 2002.

Thomas Plante and Kathleen McChesney, eds., *Sexual Abuse in the Catholic Church* (Praeger, 2012) examines the decade following the U.S. bishops' 2002 charter for protecting children against sexual abuse by church workers.

SACRAMENTS
AND THE FUTURE

In some places and circumstances, however, an even more radical adapta-
tion of the liturgy is needed, and entails greater difficulties....
There is scarcely any proper use of material things which cannot thus be
directed toward people's sanctification and the praise of God.
                                        —SECOND VATICAN COUNCIL

Sacramentality in the strict and narrow sense is gradually weakening in much of the Roman Catholic Church. It is still strong in some eastern European countries where traditional Catholicism is bound up with traditional values and lifestyles. There are pockets of strength in parts of western Europe and North America, especially among conservatives who have resisted liturgical and theological developments following the Second Vatican Council, and among traditionalists who have sought a return to pre-Vatican II modes of worship and thought. It is also strong in those parts of Latin America, Asia, and Africa where traditional practices and piety continue much as they have in the past, and it is weaker in those places where cultural adaptation has occurred and indigenous theologians are finding a voice.

The official Catholic view of the sacraments is still, of course, the traditional one. The hierarchy and most Catholics continue to think of sacraments as specifically Catholic rituals, seven in number, which cause certain spiritual and metaphysical effects. The eucharist in particular is still thought of as being the body and blood of Christ, made present on the altar by the words of consecration pronounced by a priest. Yet the scholastic theology that surrounded and supported this doctrine (the conception of the priest having supernatural powers, the theory of transubstantiation, and so forth) is being replaced by other modes of thought. Today most Catholic theologians stress the presence of Christ in the eucharistic celebration rather than in the eucharistic elements, and many ordinary Catholics no longer experience Christ's presence in communion the way their parents did. So even here a shift is occurring.

This shift in experience and concomitant theology is even more evident in the other sacraments. Ecumenically minded Catholics no longer regard baptism and membership in the Catholic Church as indispensable for getting into heaven. It is hard to specify exactly what difference confirmation makes in a Catholic's life. The anointing of the sick is no longer performed with the assurance of hidden effects, and many Catholics no longer depend on sacramental reconciliation to have all their sins forgiven. There seems to be little difference between the sacramental effects of a Catholic wedding and other religious wedding ceremonies, and even the ordination ceremony now speaks of receiving a priestly office in the church rather than receiving priestly powers, even though the *Catechism* speaks in more traditional terms.

By and large, Catholics are losing the sense that their sacraments are terribly effective, and the majority of contemporary Catholic theologians shy away from speaking about their having metaphysical effects. Without denying the traditional doctrine that the sacraments are causes of grace, theologians now emphasize that they are signs of grace, symbols of the church, and expressions of what the Christian life is all about. Thus, experientially and theologically, the Catholic sacraments are becoming more like sacraments in other religions and are being perceived as less unique than they once were.

It seems unlikely, therefore, that the official sacraments will continue to hold the central place that they once held in Catholic life and theology. Particularly during the Middle Ages, when most Christians were illiterate, the sacraments were a ritual means of preserving and teaching the central beliefs of Catholicism. And during the modern period the sacramental system was one of the primary ways that Catholics distinguished themselves from Protestants and maintained their self-identity. But today educated Catholics have other means of learning about their religion, and both ecumenism and intermarriage make it more attractive to stress the similarities rather than the differences between Christian denominations. So Catholics are no longer as dependent on the official sacraments as they once were, and even Catholic theologians put less emphasis on them than they once did.

On the other hand it is unlikely that the seven sacraments themselves will disappear from Catholicism. Besides reaffirming the connection between the church of today and the church of the past, these rituals continue to sacramentalize significant moments in the lives of Catholics and allow them to keep in touch with the sacred realities that lie at the heart of their faith. So even though the outward appearance of these sacraments may change drastically in the cultural diversity of global Catholicism during the next decades, they will continue to function as ritual religious symbols and doors to the sacred in the Catholic Church.

Perhaps the greatest change will be an increasing proliferation of unofficial sacraments as alternative ways of discovering and entering into the meaning of Christian life. It is a change that is already occurring in western Catholicism, especially as the availability of priests declines and Catholics increasingly participate in worship led by non-ordained ministers. Moreover, as Catholics in nonwestern cultures develop a greater sense of their cultural identity, they are developing their own culturally unique sacraments. Catholic worship does not have to be tied to the eucharist; there are many forms of prayer and celebration. Christian initiation does not have to be restricted to baptism and confirmation; there are other ways of entering, or entering more deeply into, the experience of salvation and community. Ordination does not have to be limited to the priesthood; there are many modes of ministry in the church.

For sacraments are, sociologically speaking, celebrations and transition rituals. They symbolize what people believe and move them into new phases of living what they believe. Psychologically speaking, they are intensification rituals. They express what people are already living and deepen their commitment to it. Historically speaking, they are therefore human creations, as human as works of art, types of education, or styles of recreation. But they are also very unique human creations, for they function as doors to sacred realities, not by chance as art and education and other experiences do, but deliberately. That is, they are specifically designed to be doors to the sacred. That is their main function, and when they fail to fulfill that function they are revised or rejected. That is why the Christian sacraments evolved over many centuries, why Protestants abandoned some of them, and why Catholics in the twentieth century reshaped their official sacraments.

But once sacraments are understood for what they are—human creations which function as doors to the sacred—there is no intrinsic reason why new sacramental forms could not be invented to reach the same sacred realities that the old forms once revealed. For sacraments are not ends in themselves but means to an end. They are doors to the sacred, and so what really counts is not the doors themselves but what lies beyond them.

GLOSSARY OF PHILOSOPHICAL AND THEOLOGICAL TERMS

[with Pronunciation Guide to Selected Words]

abbott: the head of a monastery of men; from the Aramaic word for "father" or "daddy." The head of a female monastery is called an abbess.

absolution: originally, a release from the obligation to perform additional works of public penance; later, a release from the eternal punishment of hell, hence another way to speak about forgiveness of sins.

abstinence: the penitential practice of refraining from sexual activity or from certain foods such as meat, wine, and other items regarded as luxuries. Compare with fasting, which is abstaining from all solid and/or liquid nourishment for a certain period of time.

accident: in Aristotelian-scholastic metaphysics, a quality of an individual substance, giving it a certain appearance, for example, color, size, shape, smell, or movement; from a Latin word meaning to happen.

act: in Aristotelian-scholastic metaphysics, the activation of a potency, or in plainer English, the doing of something that can be done.

alb [AWLB]: a clerical vestment; a plain, long, white garment worn under other vestments during a liturgical service.

annulment: a judgment by a civil or religious court that an apparent marriage contract is null and void because of some serious defect that was present from the beginning, for example, one of the partners was already married.

anoint: to pour or smear oil on some part of the body during a religious ritual.

apostate [uh·PAW·stayt or uh·PAW·stet]: someone who renounces their faith; from Greek words meaning to stand apart.

archbishop: the head of an archdiocese.

archdiocese: the major diocese in a given region, usually centered around a large city.

Aristotle: ancient Greek philosopher whose works influenced the medieval schoolmen.

barbarian: uncivilized; used in reference to northern and eastern peoples that invaded Europe and hastened the fall of the Roman Empire.

bishop: from the Greek word for supervisor or overseer, originally a leader and spokesperson for the local church who normally presided at eucharistic worship; eventually, a member of an upper ecclesiastical order and the ruler of a diocese.

Blessed Sacrament [BLES·sed SAC·ruh·ment]: a traditional name for the consecrated bread when it is reserved in the tabernacle or exposed for adoration, although technically both the bread and wine can be called by this name. See also eucharist.

body and blood of Christ: what the eucharistic bread and wine are called after they are consecrated by a priest. See real presence.

canon law: ecclesiastical or church law, which consists of rules and regulations; from a Greek word meaning a ruler or measure.

cardinal: from the Latin word for hinge, originally a pastor in the city of Rome who helped elect the bishop of that city; later, an honorary position given to those who are authorized to elect the pope.

cardinalate [CARD·nih·lit]: the order of cardinals.

cause: in Aristotelian-scholastic metaphysics, a partial explanation for something that exists or occurs, for example, matter (what it is made of), form (what it essentially is), agency (who or what brought it about), instrumentality (tools or other intermediary factors), and finality (the end or purpose).

celebration: See intensification ritual.

character: literally, a mark or stamp; analogously, a change in the soul caused by the rite of baptism, confirmation, or ordination; explained in scholastic theology as a set of spiritual powers received through participation in a sacramental rite.

charism [KAYR·ism]: an ability or talent, regarded as a gift. In the New Testament, abilities such as healing the sick and speaking in tongues are called charisms or gifts of the Holy Spirit.

chasuble [CHAZ·uh·bl]: a clerical vestment; a colored outer garment, usually decorated with religious symbols, worn during a liturgical service.

clandestine marriage: See secret marriage.

communion: the body and blood of Christ, when spoken of in the context of being distributed to and received by the faithful; also called holy communion.

confessor: someone who listens to a confession of sins and offers God's forgiveness.

Consubstantiation [kon·sub·stan·shee·AY·shun]: in scholastic theology, an explanation of how bread and wine become the body and blood of Christ: the reality or substance of Christ's body and blood are added to and coexist with the reality of bread and wine.

contract: a legal agreement, for example, a marriage contract.

council: an assembly of bishops for conducting church business, either disciplinary or doctrinal, convened as necessary. A local council is a meeting of bishops from a region covering a number of dioceses; an ecumenical or general council is a meeting of bishops from the whole church.

covenant: a solemn legal agreement, for example, a sacramental marriage contract.

crosier [CROW·zher]: a bishop's ceremonial staff, topped by a cross or a shepherd's hook.

cult: from the Latin word meaning to cultivate, religious veneration of a particular person or object, for example, the cult of the Virgin or the cult of the Blessed Sacrament.

curia [COO·ree·uh or CYOO·ree·uh]: the center of the ecclesiastical bureaucracy in the Catholic Church, composed of the heads of the various departments in the Vatican.

deacon: from the Greek word for minister, originally a member of the church who was designated to perform service within the community; in the patristic era, a member of the ecclesiastical order authorized to assist the bishop or to perform some type of community service; in the medieval and modern church, a man in training to become a priest; in the contemporary church, a man ordained to perform various pastoral and liturgical duties other than those reserved to priests and bishops.

diaconate [dee·A·kun·it]: the order of deacons.

diocese [DIE·uh·seez]: originally, an administrative region in the Roman Empire; eventually, an administrative region in the Catholic Church.

doctrine: an official teaching of a church or an important teaching of a theologian, for example, St. Thomas' doctrine of grace.

dogma: a central doctrine of a church and essential to its faith; denying a dogma is heresy.

ecclesial [eh·KLEE·zee·ul]: pertaining to the church as a spiritual community; from the Latin word for church.

ecclesiastical [eh·klee·zee·A·stick·ul]: pertaining to the church as an institution or organization; from the Latin word for church.

effect: the product of a cause; in scholastic theology, something that results from participating in a sacramental rite.

elder: See presbyter.

encyclical [en·SIH·klih·kuhl]: a letter, usually rather lengthy, written by a pope and meant to be circulated in the church.

episcopate [ih·PISS·kuh·pet]: the order of bishops.

eucharist [yoo·kah·rist]: literally, the giving of thanks; the name applied to early Christian meal rituals and later public worship involving the consecration and receiving of holy communion; eventually the name was applied to the consecrated elements themselves, and the word was often capitalized. See Blessed Sacrament.

ex opere operato: literally, "from the work worked," from the doing of the deed, or from the performance of the action. Contrasts with *ex opere operantis*, meaning from the work of the worker or from the activity of the minister, when asking how a sacramental ritual is effective.

excommunication: exclusion from the church; a penalty incurred by heretics, apostates and schismatics.

faithful: collective name for members of the church in good standing.

fasting: the penitential practice of not eating food or drink for a certain period of time. Compare with abstinence, which is refraining from certain forms of nourishment such as meat or wine.

form: in Aristotelian-scholastic metaphysics, the intelligible aspect of a something, or what it essentially is; in canon law, the words used in a sacramental ritual that convey the meaning of what is happening.

fruits: a name given to the good results, both spiritual and material, of having received a sacrament; for example, children are one of the fruits of marriage.

grace: literally, a gift; theologically, any gift from God; from the Latin, *gratia*. Schoolmen in the middle ages and afterward distinguished between different kinds of graces, which were regarded as different kinds of supernatural gifts bestowed by God through the sacraments.

heretic: member of a religion who rejects important doctrines and/or believes unacceptable doctrines; from the Greek word meaning to choose.

hierophany [higher·AH·funny]: an intense experience of a sacred reality; from Greek words meaning an appearance of the sacred.

illicit: See licit.

indissoluble: not able to be dissolved or broken; since the twelfth century, ascribed to sacramental marriage.

indulgence: originally, the granting of clemency to a penitent by cancelling the obligation to perform additional works of penance; later, the granting of clemency to a soul in purgatory by cancelling a certain amount of punishment due for committing sins.

intensification ritual: a ceremony designed to increase awareness of a sacred reality; also called a celebration or rite of celebration.

jurisdiction: the area over which one has legal authority; for example, a bishop has jurisdiction in his own diocese but not outside it.

justification: in biblical times, becoming just or morally upright; in later centuries, becoming a good person who can hope to go to heaven; in Lutheran theology, being made worthy of salvation in the eyes of God.

legalism: excessive reverence for law; mechanical or slavish obedience to rules.

licit: done in full accordance with canon law; therefore, proper or appropriate. Accordingly, illicit should not be thought of as illegal (since there are no penalties for violating sacramental rubrics, unless the violation also makes the sacrament invalid) but rather as improper, inappropriate, irregular, or even imperfect.

liturgy: a form of worship in which the words and actions are, for the most part, standard and prescribed by tradition or authority; commonly, eucharistic worship or the mass is referred to as "the liturgy," even though the other sacraments are also, technically speaking, liturgical.

logic: a branch of philosophy devoted to the study of correct reasoning.

magic: performing a physical or visible action in order to produce a spiritual or invisible effect, usually with no evidence that the effect actually occurred.

marriage bond: a permanent obligation between married people, regarded in scholastic theology and canon law as a metaphysical connection that can be severed only by the death of one of the spouses.

Mass: since the Middle Ages, a common name for the eucharistic liturgy; from the Latin, *missa*; hence, a missal is a mass book.

matter: in Aristotelian-scholastic metaphysics, the experienceable aspect of a physical thing, or its physical appearance; in canon law, something material used in a sacramental ritual, such as water or oil.

metaphysics: a philosophical explanation of general aspects of reality; from Greek words meaning beyond the physical.

miter: a clerical vestment; a double-pointed ceremonial headgear worn by bishops, cardinals, and the pope, usually when in processions or when performing other official functions.

monk: a man who devotes himself to God through a life of prayer and asceticism, either alone or in a monastic community; from the Greek word meaning solitary. Women who lead this type of life are called nuns, and they live almost always in community.

mortal sin: one that is so serious that it causes death to all grace in the soul and merits eternal punishment in hell.

mystery: originally, something that is experienced and not fully understood, such as a spiritual reality; later, something that is believed and not fully understood, such as the doctrine of the incarnation.

neoscholasticism: a revival of scholastic philosophy and theology that lasted from the late nineteenth century to the middle of the twentieth century.

New Law: the testament or covenant established by God through the coming of Christ and the sending of the Holy Spirit.

nuptial mass: a eucharistic liturgy that celebrates a wedding.

Old Law: the testament or covenant established by God through Abraham and Moses.

order: from the Latin *ordo*, meaning a rank or degree; since the patristic period, a way of referring to higher and lower levels of ministry in the church; hence, holy orders are grades of ecclesiastical service.

original sin: the name given by Augustine and later theologians to the sin committed by Adam and Eve in paradise, the consequences of which are inherited by all human beings.

paschal mystery: the mystery of dying and rising, usually applied to the death and resurrection of Christ.

penance: an older name for the sacrament of reconciliation; also, something that is done to change a sinful habit or to make up for having sinned.

penitent: someone who confesses sins to a priest; also, someone who is sorry for having sinned.

penitential: as an adjective, pertaining to penitence or repentance; as a noun, a medieval book for use by confessors, listing sins and appropriate penances to assign for them.

philosophy: a system of thought that explains the natural world; from Greek words meaning the love of wisdom.

Plato: ancient Greek philosopher whose ideas influenced the fathers of the church.

pope: from the Latin word for daddy or papa; originally a title of affection given to any bishop; later, the title of the bishop of Rome in his capacity as head of the universal church.

potency: in Aristotelian-scholastic metaphysics, a general term for ability, capability, power, or potential.

power: in Aristotelian-scholastic metaphysics, the ability to do something, regarded as something inherent in the soul, such as the ability to see (the power of sight), the ability to move (the power of locomotion), or the ability to reason (the power of rationality). See also supernatural power.

predestination: a teaching of John Calvin and of some churches in the Reformed tradition, based on a literal reading of some New Testament texts, that select individuals are destined by God for heaven while most people are not.

presbyter: from the Greek word for elder, originally a member of the community who is older and more experienced; later, a member of the ecclesiastical order authorized to preside at eucharistic worship or offer the sacrifice of the mass. In this context, the word became synonymous with priest.

presbyterate [prez·BIT·ur·it]: the order of presbyters.

priest: someone who presides at religious services, especially sacrifices; an intermediary between human beings and God. See presbyter.

priestly character: in scholastic theology, the sacramental reality received in ordination, conveying the ability to confect the eucharist, absolve from sins, and exercise other priestly powers.

psalter [SALT·ur]: a prayer book containing the book of Psalms, often arranged for communal singing.

real presence: a phrase used to emphasize that the presence of Christ in the eucharist is real and not just imagined or simply believed in. See body and blood of Christ.

redemption: being saved from a bad situation or condition because of what another has done, rather than through one's own efforts.

religion: a social institution for connecting people with sacred realities through myths and rituals.

religious experience: an experience of a spiritual reality that is sacred, whether divine or not, usually mediated by religious writings or practices. See also spiritual experience.

remission of sins: originally, getting rid of sinful habits; later, another way of talking about the forgiveness of sins.

res tantum: literally, a thing only, or only a reality; a spiritual reality that is received through participating in a sacramental ritual; a technical term for grace. See *sacramentum tantum* and *sacramentum et res.*

reviviscence [rev·i·VISS·ens]: in scholastic theology, the idea that a sacramental reality can become reinvigorated after having lain dormant in the soul for a period of time; used to explain why a sacrament received earlier in life can produce effects some time later.

rite: a ritual, especially in its written form, for example, the rite of baptism for children; by extension, a distinctive type of ritual, for example, eastern rite churches.

rite of passage: See transition ritual.

sacrament: a sign of the sacred; a religious symbol; can be a physical object or an enacted ritual. In scholastic theology, the term is also used to refer to the sacramental reality or *sacramentum et res.*

sacramental reality: the English equivalent of *sacramentum et res*, found in traditional sacramental theology books; sometimes rendered as symbolic reality.

sacramentary: a book of sacramental rites to be used by priests.

sacramentum et res: literally, sacrament and thing, or symbol and reality; that which is received when someone is said to receive a sacrament. See *sacramentum tantum* and *res tantum.*

sacramentum tantum: literally, only a sacrament; a sacramental ritual or religious ceremony. See *res tantum* and *sacramentum et res.*

sacred: precious, important, or significant, whether religious or not.

sacred reality: something that is immaterial but felt to be real, and also precious, important, or significant; for example, God's presence and love, but also community, love, forgiveness, fidelity, and other spiritual realities that can be experienced.

salvation: in biblical times, being saved from leading a sinful life, or from some other evil; in later centuries, being saved from hell and going to heaven.

sanctification: becoming holy, achieving sanctity.

schismatic [sihz·MA·tik or skihz·MA·tik]: someone who breaks ties with a religious authority without renouncing their faith or falling into heresy; from the Greek word meaning to cut or sever.

scholasticism: a type of philosophy and theology developed in medieval schools and universities.

scholastics: See schoolmen.

schoolmen: professors in medieval schools and universities; also called scholastics.

seal: in the ancient world, a stamp or sign impressed on an object to show ownership; could also refer to the brand on an animal or a military tattoo on a soldier; analogously, a spiritual mark or sign on a soul.

seal of the Spirit: in patristic and scholastic theology, a spiritual stamp that is impressed on the soul through baptism and confirmation, marking it as belonging to Christ. See character.

secret marriage: a marriage entered into without a priest or witnesses, but simply through a private exchange of vows, as was possible during the Middle Ages.

spiritual: not material or physical; real, but not accessible through the five senses.

spiritual experience: an experience of a spiritual reality that is sacred, whether divine or not, not necessarily mediated by religion. See also religious experience.

stole: a clerical vestment; a long ceremonial scarf that is worn over the shoulders during a liturgical service.

substance: in Aristotelian-scholastic metaphysics, a real thing or an individual reality that cannot be divided and is more than the sum of its parts; can be material or spiritual. Any individual living thing was regarded as a substance.

supernatural: beyond what is natural; from Latin words meaning above nature.

supernatural power: an ability to do something that is beyond natural human ability, such as the power to forgive sins in God's name or the power to love as God loves. Also called a supernatural virtue.

symbol: a sign representing or signifying an important spiritual reality. Since there was no word for symbol in Latin, sacraments were called sacred signs or signs of the sacred.

theology: a system of thought that explains the spiritual world; from Greek words meaning an understanding of the divine.

transcendent: beyond the realm of human experience and understanding; hence, a transcendent reality is one that cannot be known but can only be believed in.

transition ritual: a ceremony designed to change social or religious status; also called a rite of passage.

transfinalization: a contemporary explanation of how bread and wine become the body and blood of Christ: it happens because this is the end or purpose (the final cause) for which Christ instituted the eucharist.

transignification: a contemporary explanation of how bread and wine become the body and blood of Christ: by changing the meaning or significance of the bread and wine, Jesus at the last supper changed what they are in reality, as does any priest who consecrates the eucharist intending to do what Christ did.

transubstantiation: in scholastic theology, an explanation of how bread and wine become the body and blood of Christ: there is a change in reality or substance but no change in appearance or accidents.

Tridentine [try·DEN·teen]: pertaining to the Council of Trent and the style of Catholicism that lasted from the reformation until Vatican II; from the Latin word for the city of Trent.

valid: essentially correct, when said of a sacramental ritual; true and real, when said of a received sacrament or sacramental reality. Hence, a baptismal ceremony can be valid if the minimally required matter and form are used, and the baptism that is received is a valid baptism, even if the ritual was irregular or illicit in some respects.

virtue: basically, a good habit or strength of character; theologically, a spiritual strength bestowed by God through a sacrament, for example, supernatural faith, hope, and love given in baptism.

Yahweh: the name of God in Hebrew, which was written without vowels as YHWH in the Old Testament. Since Jews, out of reverence, do not speak the name of God, scholars have had to reconstruct how the name was pronounced.

INDEX OF NAMES AND TOPICS

ABOUT THE AUTHOR

Dr. Joseph Martos is a retired professor of philosophy, theology and religious studies who currently resides in Louisville, Kentucky. He taught primarily in smaller Catholic colleges and universities, and the original edition of this book was written with his students in mind. He has also been a visiting professor in many seminaries, colleges, and universities in the United States, Canada, and Australia.

In addition to *Doors to the Sacred*, Martos has written *The Sacraments: An Interdisciplinary and Interactive Study*, he has contributed scholarly articles to theological dictionaries and journals, and he has written and coauthored numerous popular books and articles on the sacraments and other subjects. At various times in his career, he has been active in the American Philosophical Association, the American Catholic Philosophical Association, the American Academy of Religion, the Religious Education Association, the Catholic Theological Society of America, and the College Theology Society.

His work is interdisciplinary, accessible, and takes a balanced approach. His website, www.TheSacraments.org, contains biographical and contact information, as well as significant material on these and related topics.